AF870372

AI '93

Also published by World Scientific:

AI '90 – Proceedings of the 4th Australian Joint Conference on Artificial Intelligence

Ed. C. P. Tsang

AI '92 – Proceedings of the 5th Australian Joint Conference on Artificial Intelligence

Eds. A. Adams & L. Stirling

Proceedings of the 6th Australian Joint Conference on Artificial Intelligence

AI '93

Melbourne, Australia **16 – 19 November 1993**

Editors

Chris Rowles
Telecom Research Laboratories
Melbourne, Victoria
Australia

Huan Liu
Telecom Research Laboratories
Melbourne, Victoria
Australia

Norman Foo
University of Sydney
Sydney, New South Wales
Australia

World Scientific
Singapore • New Jersey • London • Hong Kong

Published by

World Scientific Publishing Co Pte Ltd
5 Toh Tuck Link, Singapore 596224
USA office: 27 Warren Street, Suite 401-402, Hackensack, NJ 07601
UK office: 57 Shelton Street, Covent Garden, London WC2H 9HE

British Library Cataloguing-in-Publication Data
A catalogue record for this book is available from the British Library.

AI '93
Proceedings of the 6th Australian Joint Conference on Artificial Intelligence

Copyright © 1993 by World Scientific Publishing Co Pte Ltd

All rights reserved. This book, or parts thereof, may not be reproduced in any form or by any means, electronic or mechanical, including photocopying, recording or any information storage and retrieval system now known or to be invented, without written permission from the publisher.

For photocopying of material in this volume, please pay a copying fee through the Copyright Clearance Center, Inc., 222 Rosewood Drive, Danvers, MA 01923, USA. In this case permission to photocopy is not required from the publisher.

ISBN-13 978-981-02-1526-2
ISBN-10 981-02-1526-6

PREFACE

AI'93 is the Sixth Australian Joint Conference on Artificial Intelligence. It was held in Melbourne, Australia from November 16 to 19, 1993, with a day of tutorials and workshops, and three days of papers and poster presentations. The Conference was a mix of theoretical and application-oriented aspects of artificial intelligence. These Proceedings are a record of that conference, but also a useful indication of the current state of the art in Artificial Intelligence.

This year the conference attracted 134 paper submissions from a total of 15 countries. Of these, 61 papers came from overseas. Each paper was reviewed by at least two Australian reviewers. After a particularly strong effort by the Program Committee and the reviewers, some 62 papers were accepted for presentation, with a further 20 accepted for poster presentation.

Papers were accepted according to quality and relevance to AI, and covered the broad range of machine learning, neural networks, knowledge-based systems, automated reasoning, natural language understanding, robotics, vision, genetic algorithms, knowledge representation and knowledge acquisition.

AI'93 featured three invited speakers: Dr Earl Sacerdoti; Prof. Chris Wallace, Monash University, Melbourne, Australia: and, Prof. Mary O'Kane, University of Canberra, Australia. The focus of these speakers has been to review the contributions of AI to date and suggest some important directions for the future. Prof. O'Kane's paper is included in these proceedings.

The success of AI'93 is partly the result of the efforts of the poster and paper authors, but is also due to the members of the Organising and Technical Program Committees and the voluntary reviewers. Without the significant efforts and valuable expertise of these people, this conference would not have been possible. In particular, thanks are due to the Program Committee and reviewers for taking on, and successfully completing, such a mammoth task in the short time available for reviewing.

Chris Rowles

Technical Program Co- Chair, AI'93
Melbourne, Australia,
August 10th, 1993.

Organising Committee

Conference Co-Chairs	Dr Huan Liu, Telecom Research Laboratories
	A/Prof. Andrew Jennings, RMIT
Treasurer	Dr Ingrid Zukerman, Monash University
Committee	Dr Vic Cieselski, RMIT
	Dr Simon Goss, DSTO

Technical Program Committee

Committee Co-Chairs	Mr Chris Rowles, Telecom Research Laboratories
	A/Prof. Norman Foo, Sydney University
Committee	Dr Janet Aisbett, DSTO
	Prof. Mike Brooks, University of Adelaide
	Prof. Terry Caelli, University of Melbourne
	Dr Adam Kowalczyk, Telecom Research Laboratories
	Prof. John Gero, University of Sydney
	Prof. Rod Girle, Griffith University
	Dr Huan Liu, Telecom Research Laboratories
	Dr Anand Rao, Australian Artificial Intelligence Institute
	Dr Claude Sammut, University of New South Wales
	Dr Ingrid Zukerman, Monash University
Tutorial Co-ordinator	Dr Wilson Wen, Telecom Research Laboratories
Workshop Co-ordinator	Dr Chris Leckie, Telecom Research Laboratories

ACKNOWLEDGEMENTS

We gratefully acknowledge the support of the following organisations:

Telecom Australia
Defence Science and Technology Organisation
Faculty of Computing and Information Technology, Monash University
Centre for Intelligent Decision Systems
SUN Microsystems Australia
Australian Computer Society
AISIG ACS (Victorian Branch)
Ansett Airlines

Cover design by Carol Konheim.

LIST OF REVIEWERS

Abramson, D.
Aisbett, J.
Balachandran, B.
Baxter, R.
Bloesch, A.
Bognor, R.
Brooks, M.
Buse, R.
Butler, J.
Caelli, T.
Cameron-Jones, M.
Campbell, P.
Cheng, T-K.
Colomb, R.
Coyne, R.
Dai, W.
Dale, M.
Dance, S.
Davis, R.
de Beler, M.
Debenham, J.
Dillon, C.
Dowe, D.
Eklund, P.
Ellis, G.
Evertz, R.
Ferra, H.
Foo, N.
Ghose, A.
Gibbon, G.
Girle, R.
Guy, J.
Hagen, R.
Hood, S.
Huang, D.
Jennings, A.
Kewley, D.
Korb, K.
Kowalczyk, A
Leckie, C.
Lee, M.
Lewins, N.
Lindley, C. A.
Lister, R.
Liu, H.
Liu, Z-Q.
Ljungberg, M.
MacKay, R.
Marriot, K.
Mason, K.
McConachy, R.
Morley, D.
Nelson, M.
Newmarch, J.
Newsam, G.
Nichol, D.
Pham, B.
Pose, R.
Quinlan, R.
Ramer, A.
Rao, A.
Raskutti, B.
Redding, N.
Rist, R.
Robinson, T.
Rosenman, M.
Rowles, C.
Sammut, C.
Sattar, A.
Schulz, M.
Sember, P.
Senjen, R.
Sestito, S.
Sharma, N.
Simmons, S.
Slaney, J.
Sonenberg, L.
Sussex, R.
Tidhar, G.
Tsui, E.
Verbyla, J.
Wen, W.
Williams, M.
Wobcke, W.
Wrightson, G.
Yao, X.
Zukerman, I.

CONTENTS

KNOWLEDGE REPRESENTATION

MACHINE LEARNING

Invited Presentation

LISTENING INTELLIGENTLY AND GIVING A SENSIBLE ANSWER

M J O'KANE
Faculty of Information Sciences and Engineering
University of Canberra
PO Box 1
Belconnen ACT 2616, Australia

ABSTRACT

This paper gives a short overview of the research problems that need to be solved in order to give machines a general, useful and easy-to-construct listening and response capability. We do this by first examining what is meant by "intelligent listening" and "sensible answering" in human-human communication terms, using this as a guide to performance criteria for automatic systems. We then examine the current state of machine speech and language technologies and from that basis we identify the critical scientific problems that need to be solved in order to produce systems fully capable of listening intelligently and giving a sensible answer.

1. Listening Intelligently

When we listen to someone we are doing several things - we are trying to work out if the speaker is telling, commanding or asking us something and what it is they are telling, commanding or asking us. We are also forming an impression (model) of the speaker. We generally can tell, for example, if the person is cross, relaxed or anxious; old or young; male or female. When the speaker has finished speaking we can do something - give an answer, perform an action, say we can't follow what they are saying or that we do indeed follow what they are saying and we want to hear more (the "yes, and then ?" response).

To listen effectively we need to be adequately familiar with the vocabulary, syntax and structure of the natural language the speaker is using. We need to be able to comprehend the speaker's pronunciation. We need to be able to hear what the person is saying. We cannot hear through excessive noise or, more specifically, when the signal-to-noise ratio becomes too low. We need to be able to give the speaker adequate attention. (Try listening to someone while simultaneously watching the climax of a horror movie!)

To listen intelligently we have to have an appropriately deep knowledge of the concepts evoked by the speaker and the relationship of these concepts one to the other. In other words we have to know something of the subjects under discussion if we are listening for the purpose of providing information. (My French is adequate for listening to details of accommodation prices. I cannot listen at all intelligently to a rapid discourse in French on, say, existentialism.) We must be able to resolve the references used in the context of the discourse. We should also note that what constitutes intelligent listening is somewhat determined by the purpose of the listening. If we are listening for the purpose of transcription, then it is not crucially important that we know the subject matter but it is important that we can produce a transcript not only of the words but also of the punctuation of what was said so that the sense is captured.

The human listening mechanism is not fully understood. What is known suggests a mechanism with fabulous efficiencies and special-purpose sub-mechanisms. This is no place for a full review of these but let me mention some. There is the capacity for predicting what the person speaking is going to say next, a useful and efficient mechanism in that it converts much of the listening process into the computationally easier task of verification. Evidence for this comes from a variety of psycholinguistic experiments, including "shadowing" in which subjects are given passages to read and are asked to repeat what they hear as soon as they hear it[1]. If certain words, particularly small words, are replaced by noise the shadower often seems not to hear the noise but instead "hears" the word that makes sense in the context. If the shadower does perceive the noise, the speed of the shadowing slows considerably, suggesting a change in cognitive process.

Other human listening efficiency mechanisms are found in the perception sub-systems. The mechanism of so-called "categorical perception"[2] is one which suggests that the hearing mechanism "hardwires" through early training to a limited set of states along certain consonant continua, the states being determined by the particular consonants occurring the hearer's native language. Thus while I can quite clearly hear the three voiceless stop consonants, /p/, /t/ and /k/, that occur in my native language, Australian English, I have great difficulty hearing the dental stop consonant that occurs in Telagu. To me it sounds indistinguishable from a /t/.

Not all human hearing is done by ear. In his book on "visible speech", Massaro[3] shows how considerable amounts of speech are primarily seen rather than heard even by people with normal hearing. Demonstrations of the McGurk effect[4], in which one sees someone making a sound and simultaneously is fed another sound through the auditory channel with the resulting effect that one hears what one sees and not what one hears, are an entertaining example of this issue.

Effects such as the ones described here are useful in making the human listening mechanism efficient but they seem to serve another role as well which is that they improve the human listening system effectiveness when listening to a noisy signal.

2. Giving a Sensible Answer

Responding in a sensible way to what one hears involves at the very least giving an answer that will be considered appropriate by the listener. Thus if asked the time it would not be seen as appropriate if one responded by saying something such as "You have a funny hat". If responding to a request for information, the sensible response is either the provision of the requested information, a request for further clarification of the question, a statement that you do not know the answer or maybe a polite expression indicating that you did not hear the question properly. Dialogue shorthands abound. A simple example of one such shorthand is the habit of saying "Sorry" with the appropriate intonation to indicate that one did not hear the question and would like it repeated.

Just as it is easier to listen intelligently if one knows appropriate amounts about the subject under discussion, so to it is to give what is perceived as a sensible answer if one knows the subject under discussion. A constant response of "I don't know what you mean" might be a sensible answer in a local context but is irritating to the questioner if it is the only response the questioner gets to any question he or she asks.

We will now consider machine capabilities for handling these tasks.

3. The Current State of Spoken Languge Processing Technologies

3.1 Who Builds Machine Listening and Response Systems?

The investigation and construction of technologies to enable machines to listen intelligently and respond sensibly has been the province of two sub-fields of artificial intelligence - automatic speech recognition/understanding (ASR) (augmented, for response, with speech synthesis systems) and natural language understanding (NLU). Until relatively recently these fields have remained surprisingly separate with NLU concentrating on text-based systems while ASR concentrates on the problem of constructing systems that take speech as input and produce the equivalent (text) string of words as output. NLU has always been seen as a solid part of AI while ASR is often seen, both by those working in it and by the rest of the AI community, as somehow separate and, at various times, more akin to signal processing and applied statistics than AI. It will be evident from what I say below that I believe that for automatic systems to have a full listening and response capability, both ASR and NLU technologies are needed. Maybe a new sub-field - Machine Listening and Response - should emerge.

3.2 Developments in Automatic Speech Recognition

A necessary prerequisite to listening is the ability to perceive a sound pressure wave as human speech and translate this speech into an appropriate set of linguistic entities (phones, words, sentences, intonational structures, etc.). Speech is a highly complex and redundant code. There is no simple mapping between the sound pressure wave and useful linguistic entities. The development of adequate mapping has been the business of the ASR community for over twenty-five years.

The ARPA Speech Understanding Project in the early to mid-seventies ended in a surprising way. Of the four finalist systems carrying out the deliberately restricted task involved, only one system, Harpy, met the Project goals of over 95% correct understanding of semantically- and syntactically-restritcted utterances in a limited domain of discourse, spoken by one of the speakers for whom the system had been trained[5]. What made Harpy such a surprising winner was the simplicity of its architecture. The incoming speech was signal-processed using a single processing technique, then the transformed speech was fed into a simple phonetic decoder which assigned each successive small section of speech to one of 98 possible quasi-phonetic labels. The label string was then fed to a weighted network, paths through which represented all possible legal utterances in the restricted domain. The best-path for the input label string was declared the utterance. Other finalist systems had used much more sophisticated architectures with relatively independent sub-systems taking care variously of semantic, syntactic, pragmatic and phonetic knowledge and analysis. Somehow the concept of "compiling" most of the system knowledge into a single network seemed messy and certainly was a difficulty when new knowledge (semantic extensions, for example) was to be incorporated in the system. And this indeed was the problem! The Harpy network had been handcrafted. The handcrafting of more general systems clearly was not feasible. Until someone worked out how to generate such networks automatically, this approach seemed stuck.

After the end of the ARPA Speech Understanding Project other approaches were tried, most notably the notion of rule-based systems which had the advantage of a simple but easily modifiable architecture but which, like Harpy, did very well in restricted situations but failed increasingly as the problem was generalised. Automatic rule generation was needed here in much the same way that automatic network construction was needed to generalise Harpy. Clearly, in both cases some form of machine learning was needed.

An important step was the realisation that if machine learning was to be used, then large systematically collected and labelled speech data collections were needed to learn over. (Before this a remarkably large amount of recognition work was done on a remarkably small set of somewhat odd data.) Initiatives were started around the world to collect and label large speech databases[6].

A major breakthrough came in 1988 when Kai-Fu Lee[7] at Carnegie-Mellon University demonstrated a speaker-independent, continuous speech recognition system recognising utterances with greater than 94% accuracy from a restricted-domain, 1000-word vocabulary. The key to its success was the use of a Hidden Markov Model (HMM) as the basic architecture which recognised the speech as a series of overlapping trigrams and which in turn reasonably easily yielded word strings. The system, called SPHINX, was trained on a hand-labelled database of 4200 utterances from 105 speakers. Here was the generalised Harpy, not "understanding" much perhaps, but recognising words well - far better in fact than humans can do on certain tasks such as the recognition of digit strings.

It seemed that the recognition task (speech to string of words) was solved provided one had an appropriate training database covering all possible words in the utterance. And of course this is where one of the main problems with generalising this technology lies - understanding what constitutes, let alone collecting, an appropriate database. We will return to this issue later.

Before proceeding it is worth briefly considering the commercial spinoffs of both Harpy and then HMM technologies. The spinoff from Harpy has been the speaker-dependent, isolated-word systems marketed by firms such as Dragon, Kurzweil and Verbex. These systems have extremely large vocabularies, do not take long to train for a new speaker and are easy to use (in terms of leaving a short gap between the words) after very little practice. The early spinoffs from the HMM technology will most likely be seen in systems where the vocabulary is naturally fairly limited. Systems of this sort currently in advanced trial stages are various telephone systems such as bill-paying systems where the system is required to recognise digit strings and simple commands spoken by the caller. These systems are feasible because large databases of digit strings collected over the telephone currently exist.

3.3 Natural Language Understanding

Over the period that the ASR community has been wrestling with its attempt to achieve speaker-independent continuous speech recognition, the NLU community has been involved in various tasks less individually heroic than the ASR task perhaps but wide-ranging in effect. The breadth of the achievements in NLU make anything but the most superficial summary impractical here so all I will do is note some important trends.

A great deal of what might be called basic work has been done on such hard problems as extragrammaticality and anaphora resolution. Studies of large bodies of text corpora have led to smart text analysis and summary tools. A significant commercial spinoff from NLU research has been the relatively natural languages used to query databases.

3.4 Recent Developments and Preoccupations - The Fields Come Together

Over the last ten years, but more particularly over the last five, spoken language systems (SLS) have been identified as important goals within several national and international projects. The system specifications for these SLS require high levels of understanding and the production of suitable responses often to spoken database queries. The massive industry-government Japanese Automatic Telephony Research (ATR) Project goes even further and aims at machine translation systems although several specialist groups within the Project examine particular hard problems within the general SLS framework (see ATR annual reports which contain all papers - several hundred in 1992 - published from ATR within the year covered by the report). In the United States a major SLS effort is coordinated through DARPA. This work is notable for the regular system comparisons and evaluations that are held two to three times each year. The results of these are published by Morgan Kaufmann under the title "Proceedings of the Speech and Natural Language Workshop". In Europe large-scale, multi-language SLS work has been funded through various European Community initiatives, most notably ESPRIT. This work is published in a variety of EC-sponsored publications.

Communication between the big projects and between them and researchers in other countries not involved directly in major SLS initiatives (e.g. Australia) has been facilitated by the emergence of new and now major conferences such as Eurospeech and ICSLP (International Conference on Spoken Language Processing) and by the introduction of new topic areas into existing major conferences such as the session on Wordspotting that has been a feature of recent ICASSP (IEEE International Conference on Acoustics Speech and Signal Processing). By any measure - the capabilities of the systems demonstrated, the amount of money invested in the projects, the number and quality of the researchers working in the field, the level of industry money being spent in the area - the modern activity in SLS is impressive. The breadth of topics covered and integrated within SLS is another indication of the scope of this activity. To give some feel for this we give, in Table 1, a list of the session titles for the DARPA Speech and Natural Language Workshop held in February 1992.

Evaluating Spoken Language Systems (3 sessions)
Statistical Language Modeling
Acoustic Modeling (2 sessions)
Information Retrieval
Lexicon and Lexical Semantics
Demonstrations and Videos
Machine Translation
Robust Speech Processing
Natural Language Processing
Core NL Lexicon and Grammar
Continuous Speech Recognition and Evaluation (2 sessions)
Prosody
Government Panel

Table 1: Session Titles for the DARPA Speech and Natural Language Workshop held in February 1992.

4. Does This Mean Machines Can Listen?

Work in the big projects referred to above has progressed spoken language processing capability to the point where machine listening and response systems can be built if the complete vocabulary, syntax, semantics and pragmatics of the intended application can be modelled, if the system users are co-operative and have a good understanding of the allowable queries, and if a large speech database for training the speech recogniser part of the system is available. Spoken language systems of this type will become increasingly available particularly through large service firms such as telephone companies which can afford the high total system construction cost. These construction costs are high because of the high cost of acquiring the recognition training database, the degree of handcrafting involved in integrating the various system components and the cost of testing and embedding the system in a human-computer interaction sense.

The cost of building a system for a new application indicates some of the areas that need to be addressed if spoken language technologies are to become widely available in a range of natural languages. Tools are needed to help the system builder infer as efficiently as possible, and preferably automatically, the vocabulary, syntax, semantics and pragmatics of a new application. Do these knowledge sources have to be inferred separately and then re-integrated in the final system architecture? Can they be inferred in an already "compiled" form using statistical NLP techniques? Work carried out by the IBM SLS group[8] indicates that the number of possible words that can follow any given legal natural language string extract is remarkably small. This work can be extended to show that even across word boundaries the number of possible phonemes that can can follow a given legal phoneme string is also very small.

One obvious but unsolved question is whether systems can be built incrementally or not. How much of what has been constructed for a previous application domain can be ported, automatically adapted incrementally or generalised for some intended new application? Can a machine learning procedure be invoked so an existing system can learn a new application domain? If so, what data should be fed to such a learning algorithm?

One particularly expensive area in creating a new system is the collection of the recogniser training database. Again the question arises, can a database collected for a previous application be generalised in various ways? Can, say, a database collected in quiet conditions still be used in suitable combination with a telephone noise database to generalise the application to queries over the telephone? Can a database be extended or modified to handle speakers speaking the same native language but with a distinctively different accent?

The matter of precisely how much speech is needed to achieve a pre-set recognition level over a given test database is quite unknown. So is the question of whether or not it is possible to find an algorithm to generalise from a single speaker database or a database collected from only a very small number of speakers. High-quality, speaker-dependent continuous speech recognisers can be built from quite small amounts of training data but their performance drops considerably when speech from another speaker is used as input. The performance drop varies from speaker to speaker however, raising the question of how to construct a possible mapping from one speaker's acoustic space to another's - an important issue for automatic system adaptation to new classes of speakers. All of these matters can be summarised as coming under two headings - the question of optimum methods for database construction and the question of automatic system adaptation to new classes of speakers.

Automatic annotation of databases has been a pre-occupation of the speech community for some time. Hand-labelling, particularly at the phonetic level, is a skilled and time-consuming task and consequently expensive. Partially automated tools to assist in this task are becoming better. Recently we began an investigation of an issue to take this idea further. Is it possible to align automatically large audio data collections for which human transcription exists (e.g. court recordings and their transcriptions) and thereby derive speech recogniser training databases automatically[9] ?

Current systems are most fragile when they encounter an unknown word. They are fragile at several levels of system performance when this happens. And yet if systems are to be truly robust in performance this is a critical issue. For this reason a lot of effort recently has gone into wordspotters (at the recogniser/lexical levels) and partial parsers (at the syntactic level). The integration of wordspotters with current recognisers is still not fully understood. Nor, at a more general level, is the matter of the appropriate architecture for systems that can recognise their expected vocabulary and not fail when an unexpected or unknown section of speech is encountered. The system should handle such encounters gracefully, maybe attempting a phonetic transcription followed by dictionary lookup along the lines of Klatt's hypothesised LAFS and Scriber system[10].

Another unexplored matter is related to system architecture. In real-world use systems must be able to handle unexpected words gracefully and equally they should recognise very common words very well. Some of the issues here can be seen by reference to Figures 1 and 2. In Figure 1 we give the percentage of total text covered as a function of number of words in the vocabulary for three different large corpora - transcripts of information-seeking telephone dialogues (1,746 word vocabulary; 52,983 total words), 18 days of court transcripts from one jurisdiction (9,644 word vocabulary; 445,404 total words) and an extract from the novel 'Dracula' by Bram Stoker (9,298 word vocabulary; 159,145 total words). What is consistent for all cases is the extremely large amount of the total text that is covered by such a small number of words. Less than 10% of the vocabulary in all cases accounts for over 80% of all the words spoken. Figure 2 shows the related effect for word pairs, triples, quadruples and quintuples for five days of the court transcripts. These figures suggest that all spoken language systems can (within the limits of environmental noise) use a "common word recogniser" augmented with appropriate other systems such as wordspotters and application-specific recognisers. The construction of such a system seems obvious yet such a construction has yet to be attempted.

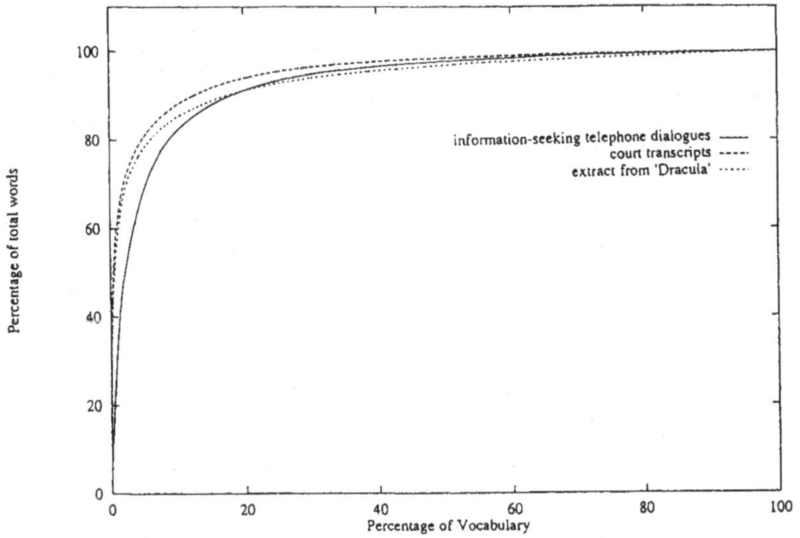

Figure1: Total number of words in text accounted for as a function of percentage of total vocabulary represented by these words for three different corpora.

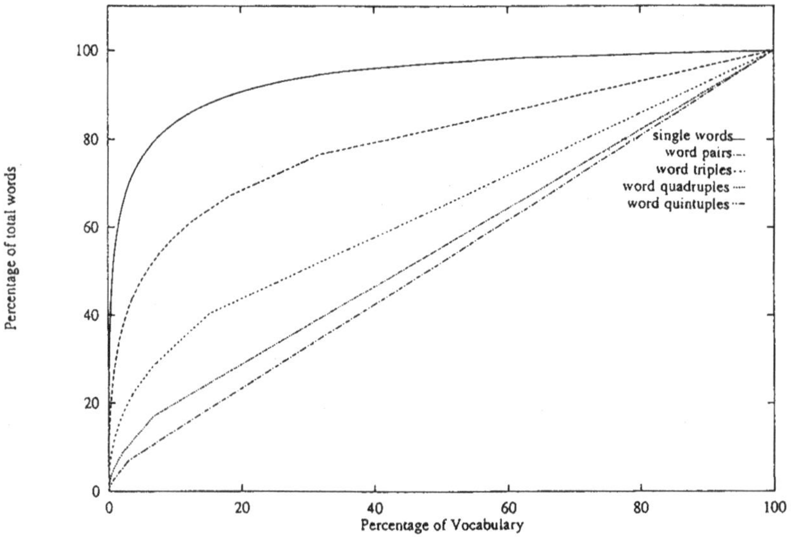

Figure 2: Total number of words, word pairs, triples, quadruples and quintuples in text accounted for as a function of percentage of distinct words word pairs, etc., these words, word pairs, etc., represent for five days of court transcrpts.

Perhaps the most difficult necessary deficiency in current systems occurs in the area of prosodics which give us so much information particularly at the syntactic level and also information about the speaker (see below). The problem here is not that prosodics has been seen as unimportant but rather that it has been hard to see how to incorporate this information into the overall SLS. To some extent this is just a more extreme case of the old problem in building SLS dating back to Harpy, of how to find a suitably simple internal data representation onto which all the knowledge can be mapped while maintaining a generalisable system architecture which can be modified easily when needed.

If a system is to be seen as listening intelligently and responding sensibly it most construct some model of the human partner in a dialogue so that it can tune its responses in such a way as to be sensitive to the user's needs (both explicit and implicit). This is very unexplored territory. Also the system must be able to decide when it does not know some requested fact and declare this, if necessary seeking information from the human partner.

And if the system is to have a fraction of the robustness and versatility of human listening and response many more back-up strategies will need to operate so that the system has grater capability to detect and deal with dialogue breakdown or change of topic. One obvious strategy (which is currently getting some attention) is the incorporation of visible speech. But, above all, systems will have to be much better at predicting, at all levels, what the speaker is going to say next and using this information effectively.

Intelligent listening and sensible response from machines is here in a very restricted way only. There is still a lot of work to be done.

5. References

1. W.D. Marslen-Wilson and A. Welsh, 'Processing interactions and lexical access during word recognition in continuous speech', *Cognitive Psychology* 10 (1978) 29-63.
2. A.M. Liberman, K.S. Harris, J.A. Kinney and H. Lane, 'The discrimination of relative onset time of the components of certain speech and non-speech patterns', *J. Exp. Psych.* 10 (1961) 379-388.
3. D.W. Massaro, *Speech perception by ear and eye: A paradigm for psychological inquiry* (Lawrence Erlbaum Associates, Hillsdale, NJ, 1987).
4. H. McGurk and J. MacDonald, 'Hearing lips and seeing voices', *Nature* 264 (1976) 746-748.
5. D.H. Klatt, 'Review of the ARPA Speech Understanding Project', *J. Acoust. Soc. Amer.* 62 (1977) 1345-1366.
6. D.S. Pallett, 'Speech Corpora and Performance Assessment in the DARPA SLS Program', presented at *ICSLP 90* Kobe (1990).
7. K.-F. Lee, *Automatic speech recognition: The development of the SPHINX system* (Kluwer Academic Publishers, Boston, 1989).
8. P. Brown, V. della Pietra, R.L. Mercer, S.A. della Pietra and J.C. Lai, 'An estimate of an upper bound for the entropy of English', *Comp. Ling.* 18 (1992) 31-40.
9. M. O'Kane and P.Kenne, 'On the feasibility of using application-specific speech to derive a general-purpose speech recogniser training database', *Proc. SST'92* Brisbane (1992) 712-717.
10. D.H. Klatt, 'Speech perception: A model of acoustic-phonetic analysis and lexical access', *J. Phonet.* 7 (1979) 279-312.

Automated Reasoning

A CONSTRAINT-BASED FRAMEWORK FOR PLAN RECOGNITION

JUN HONG RON J. THOMAS
Department of Computing, University of Bradford, West Yorkshire BD7 1DP, UK

ABSTRACT This paper presents a constraint–based framework for plan recognition, in which relations over actions in a plan are viewed as constraints and a model of plan recognition is developed on the basis of constraint satisfaction. Relations over actions are classified into generation, enablement and decomposition relations and plans are defined on the basis of these relations. An action hierarchy is used to represent relations between action types, which is then completed by using Kautz's circumscriptive approach. Using the completed action hierarchy as knowledge, constraints on actions can be propagated in both top–down and bottom–up directions. Constraints are divided into two types—structural and temporal constraints. Structural constraints are first used to infer structural plans consisting of structural actions. Then enablement actions are incorporated into structural plans by taking into account temporal constraints so that structural plans can be further completed. This framework can solve a few problems with Kautz's model of plan recognition and at the same time keep the advantages of his model.

1 Introduction

Plan recognition is a process in which an agent's plans and goals are inferred from his observed actions. To implement this process, knowledge about relations between actions needs to be represented in some formalism and a corresponding reasoning mechanism needs to be developed for the application of such knowledge. Researchers have so far tackled these two tasks and developed several models of plan recognition in which relations between actions are formalised in different ways and corresponding reasoning techniques are used. There are abductive models[8], deductive models[5], heuristic models[2, 4, 7], and parsing–based models[3].

Kautz's work[5] provides an expressive formalism to represent plans at different levels in an event hierarchy which is then circumscribed in support of deductive inferences. However, there are still a few problems with his model. First of all, an event hierarchy is actually a hierarchy of plans. It does not provide sufficient information about relations between actions. Such information is, however, important since it tells us more about the relations between actions, and will put more constraints on actions in the process of plan recognition. The second problem with Kautz's model is that although a minimum set of possible plans can be inferred, it is not certain which particular plan is really the one executed by the agent if only a single plan was executed. The third problem is that Kautz's model can not fully explain and justify its decisions on the inferred plans to the agent if there is a disagreement between them since it does not have explicit knowledge about the relations between actions.

This paper presents a constraint–based framework for plan recognition which can solve these problems with Kautz's model and at the same time keep the advantages of his model. In this framework, the knowledge about different relations between actions is explicitly represented. It uses an action hierarchy to represent enablement, generation and decomposition relations between action types. It defines plans on the basis of these relations. In a plan, generation and decomposition relations over actions in the plan are viewed as structural constraints and enablement relations over actions in the plan are viewed as temporal constraints. Because structural constraints on the actions in a plan determine the types and structures of plans, the structural plans can be inferred on the basis of structural constraints. These structural plans are considered as candidate plans. Then the details of these structural plans can be filled with other actions under appropriate temporal constraints. Our action hierarchy is circumscribed in a similar way to Kautz's event hierarchy. Such a circumscribed action hierarchy can be used to propagate constraints in both top–down and bottom–up directions.

There are several advantages in this framework over Kautz's. First of all, an action hierarchy represents different relations between action types so that plans do not need to be constructed in advance and relations between action types are more easy to be established. Secondly, our model of plan recognition makes less disjunctive inferences and turns out to have less complexity of computation than Kautz's model. Thirdly, it can distinguish a single plan from a minimum set of possible plans since temporal constraints are explored. Finally, an action hierarchy provides a good basis for the explanation and justification of the decisions on the inferred plan.

2 Actions, Relations over Actions and Plans

This section classifies actions and relations over actions. It also defines plans on the basis of relations over actions. Then the action hierarchy is defined to represent relations between action types. The relations over actions are classified into three categories—generation, enablement and decomposition.

Definition 1 Generation Relations[1]: *There is a generation relation over any two actions if by performing the first, the second is also done. The first is called a generation action and the second is called a generated action.*

Definition 2. Enablement Relations: *There is an enablement relation over any two actions if doing the first enables the second to occur. The first is called an enablement action and the second is called an enabled action.*

Definition 3. Sufficient Enablement Relations: *There is a sufficient enablement relation between a set of enablement actions and an enabled action if performing this set of enablement actions satisfies the preconditions of the enabled action. A sequence of actions are sufficient to enable another action to occur if the action is sufficiently enabled by a corresponding set of enablement actions in the sequence and each of the actions in the sequence is also sufficiently enabled by a corresponding set of enablement actions in the sequence if it needs to to enabled.*

Definition 4. Decomposition Relations: *There is a decomposition relation over an action and another set of actions if this set of actions comprise a composite action which generates the action. The action is called the decomposition action. All the actions in that set are referred to as subactions.*

Actions are classified into three types—basic, simple and complex actions. A *basic action* is one which can not be generated by another action or decomposed into another set of actions. Therefore, a basic action is an essential action which can be performed at will. A *simple action* is one which can be generated by another action. A *complex action* is one which can be decomposed into another set of actions.

Plans need to be constructed for the performance of simple or complex actions. Therefore, plans are classified into two types—*simple* and *complex plans*.

Definition 5. Simple Plans: *A simple plan for a simple action α is a sequence of actions $\alpha_1, \ldots, \alpha_n$, where α_n generates α, and $\alpha_1, \ldots, \alpha_{n-1}$ are sufficient to enable α_n to occur.*

Definition 6. Complex Plans: *A Complex plan for a complex action* α is a set of action sequences

$$\{\alpha_{11}, \ldots, \alpha_{1(m-1)}, \alpha_{1m}\}, \ldots, \{\alpha_{l1}, \ldots, \alpha_{l(n-1)}, \alpha_{ln}\}$$

where α can be decomposed into $\alpha_{1m}, \ldots, \alpha_{ln}$, and $\alpha_{11}, \ldots, \alpha_{1(m-1)}$ are sufficient to enable α_{1m} to occur, ..., and $\alpha_{l1}, \ldots, \alpha_{l(n-1)}$ are sufficient to enable α_{ln} to occur.

To further analyse the structures of simple and complex plans, we can divide the actions in a plan into two categories. In a simple plan, a *structural action* is one which generates the simple action. The other actions are *enablement actions* which only enable the structural action to occur. In a complex plan, *structural actions* are subactions which are decomposed from the complex action. A subaction generates a part of the complex action. The other actions in the same action sequence are *enablement actions* which only enable the subaction to occur.

The relations over structural actions in a plan and the planned action determine the type and structure of the plan. As long as the type and structure of a plan has been determined, the enablement actions can be linked to the structural actions in the plan by satisfying temporal constraints on rel-

1. This definition is similar to Pollack's[6].

evant actions in the plan. In this way, a complete plan may be inferred if all its constraints on actions in the plan have been satisfied.

3. Acquiring Plan Inference Knowledge

In this section, we will first show that action types and relations between action types can be represented in an action hierarchy. Then we will show how to complete the action hierarchy in a circumscriptive approach in support of propagating constraints in both top–down and bottom–up directions. Allen's interval–based temporal logic[1] is used to represent different sorts of axioms.

An action hierarchy is a collection of restricted–form first–order axioms (wffs) representing generation, enablement and decomposition relations between action types. An action hierarchy consists of H_A, H_G, H_{AB}, H_E and H_D as follows:

- H_A is the set of action type predicates. H_A contains the distinguished predicates *Any_Action* and *End_Action*.
- H_G is the set of generation axioms, each of the form:
  $\forall x, t.\ \text{Occurs}(A_1(x), t) \Rightarrow \text{Occurs}(A_2(f(x), t)$
  where $A_1, A_2 \in H_A$, and f is a mapping from A_1 to A_2.
- H_{AB} is the set of basic action type predicates, those members of H_A the actions of which are not generated by or decomposed into the actions of any other action type.
- H_D is the set of decomposition axioms, each of the form:
  $\forall x, t.\ \text{Occurs}(A_0(x), t) \Rightarrow (\exists t_1, \ldots, t_n.\ \text{During}(t_i, t), \text{for } i=1, \ldots, n$
  $\Rightarrow \text{Occurs}(A_1(s_1(x)), t_1) \wedge \ldots \wedge \text{Occurs}(A_n(s_n(x)), t_n))$
  where $A_0, \ldots, A_n \in H_A$, and $s_1, \ldots, s_n$ are role functions. A_1 through A_n are called direct components of A_0.
- H_E is the set of enablement axioms, each of the form:
  $\forall x, t.\ \text{Occurs}(A_1(x), t) \Rightarrow (\exists t_1.\ \text{Before}(t, t_1) \Rightarrow$
  $\text{Effects}(A_1(x), t) \cap \text{Preconditions}(A_2(f(x)), t_1) \neq \emptyset$
  where $A_1, A_2 \in H_A$, and f is a mapping from A_1 to A_2.

Figure 1 illustrates an action hierarchy in a simplified cooking domain. Arrows denote generation relations, arrows with component labels denote decomposition relations, arrows with enablement labels denote enablement relations.

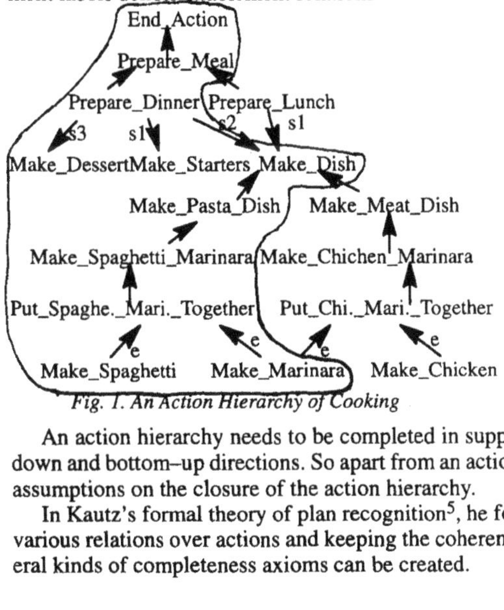

Fig. 1. An Action Hierarchy of Cooking

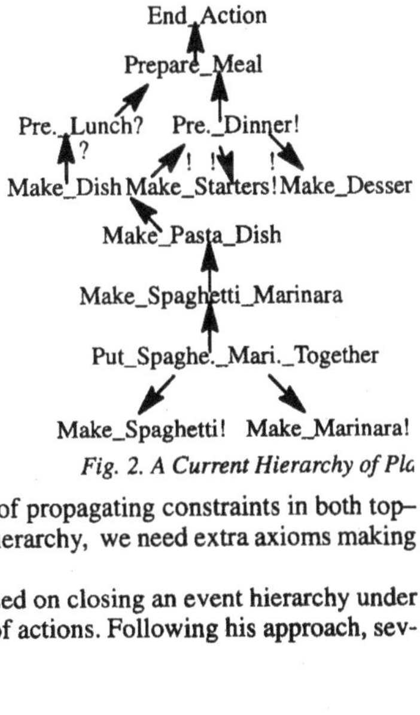

Fig. 2. A Current Hierarchy of Pla

An action hierarchy needs to be completed in support of propagating constraints in both top–down and bottom–up directions. So apart from an action hierarchy, we need extra axioms making assumptions on the closure of the action hierarchy.

In Kautz's formal theory of plan recognition[5], he focused on closing an event hierarchy under various relations over actions and keeping the coherence of actions. Following his approach, several kinds of completeness axioms can be created.

Definition 7. Generation Exhaustiveness Axioms: *Assuming $A_1, A_2, .., A_n$ are all the action types which generate A_0, then an exhaustiveness axiom, which states that the given generations of action type A_0 are exhaustive, is as follows.*

$$\forall x, t.\ \mathrm{Occurs}(A_0(x), t) \Rightarrow \exists x_1.\ \mathrm{Occurs}(A_1(x_1), t) \vee \exists x_2.\ \mathrm{Occurs}(A_2(x_2), t) \vee \ldots \vee \exists x_n.\ \mathrm{Occurs}(A_n(x_n), t)$$

Definition 8. Enablement Exhaustiveness Axioms: *Assuming $A_1, A_2,..., A_n$ are all the action types which enable A_0, then an exhaustiveness axiom, which states that the given enablements of action type A_0 are exhaustive, is as follows.*

$$\begin{aligned}\forall x, t.\ \mathrm{Occurs}(A_0(x), t) \Rightarrow\ & \exists x_1, t_1.\ \mathrm{Occurs}(A_1(x_1), t_1) \wedge \mathrm{Before}(t_1, t) \vee \\ & \exists x_2, t_2.\ \mathrm{Occurs}(A_2(x_2), t_2) \wedge \mathrm{Before}(t_2, t) \vee \\ & \ldots \vee \\ & \exists x_n, t_n.\ \mathrm{Occurs}(A_n(x_n), t_n) \wedge \mathrm{Before}(t_n, t)\end{aligned}$$

Definition 9. Component/use Axioms: *Assuming $A_1, A_2,..., A_n$ are all the action types of which A_0 is a component action type, then a component/use axiom, which states that at any time there occurs an action of A_0, there will also occur an action of action type $A_1, A_2,..., or\ A_n$, is as follows.*

$$\begin{aligned}\forall x, t.\ \mathrm{Occurs}(A_0(x), t) \Rightarrow\ & \exists y_1, t_1.\ \mathrm{Occurs}(A_1(y_1), t_1) \wedge f_1(y_1) = x \wedge \mathrm{During}(t, t_1) \vee \\ & \exists y_2, t_2.\ \mathrm{Occurs}(A_2(y_2), t_2) \wedge f_2(y_2) = x \wedge \mathrm{During}(t, t_2) \vee \\ & \ldots \vee \\ & \exists y_n, t_n.\ \mathrm{Occurs}(A_n(y_n), t_n) \wedge f_n(y_n) = x \wedge \mathrm{During}(t, t_n)\end{aligned}$$

4. Inferring Plans on the Basis of Constraint Satisfaction

In order to recognize both simple and complex plans, we need to give two axioms according to the definitions of simple and complex plans given in *Section 2*.

Simple Plan Axiom:

$$\begin{aligned}\text{S–Plan}\{(\alpha, t), [(\alpha_1, t_1), ..., (\alpha_n, t_n)]\} \Leftrightarrow\ & \mathrm{During}(t_i, t) \text{ for } i = 1, ..., n \wedge \mathrm{Generate}(\alpha_n, \alpha, t_n) \wedge \\ & \text{S–Enable}([(\alpha_1, t_1), ..., (\alpha_{n-1}, t_{n-1})], (\alpha_n, t_n))\end{aligned}$$

where S–Plan$\{(\alpha, t), [(\alpha_1, t_1), ..., (\alpha_n, t_n)]\}$ states that a simple plan for doing α at t consists of doing α_1, ..., and α_n at t_1, ..., and t_n respectively; Generate(α_n, α, t_n) states a generation relation over α_n and α; S–Enable$([(\alpha_1, t_1), ..., (\alpha_{n-1}, t_{n-1})], (\alpha_n, t_n))$ states a sufficient enablement relation over a sequence of actions $\{\alpha_1, ..., \alpha_{n-1}\}$ and α_n.

Complex Plan Axiom:

$$\begin{aligned}&\text{C–Plan}\{(\alpha, t), [(\alpha_{11}, t_{11}), ..., (\alpha_{1m}, t_{1m}), ..., (\alpha_{l1}, t_{l1}), ..., (\alpha_{ln}, t_{ln})]\} \Leftrightarrow \\ &\quad \mathrm{Decompose}\{(\alpha, t), [(\alpha_{1m}, t_{1m}), ...,(\alpha_{ln}, t_{ln})]\} \wedge \\ &\quad \text{S–Enable}\{[(\alpha_{11}, t_{11}), ..., (\alpha_{1(m-1)}, t_{1(m-1)})], (\alpha_{1m}, t_{1m})\} \wedge \\ &\quad \ldots \\ &\quad \text{S–Enable}\{[(\alpha_{l1}, t_{l1}), ..., (\alpha_{l(n-1)}, t_{l(n-1)})], (\alpha_{ln}, t_{ln})\} \wedge \\ &\quad \mathrm{During}((t_i, t) \text{ for } i = 11, ..., 1m, ..., l1, ..., ln\end{aligned}$$

where C–Plan$\{(\alpha, t), [(\alpha_{11}, t_{11}), ..., (\alpha_{1m}, t_{1m}), ..., (\alpha_{l1}, t_{l1}), ..., (\alpha_{ln}, t_{ln})]\}$ states that a complete plan for doing a complex action at α consists of doing a set of action sequences α_{11}, ..., α_{1m}, ..., and α_{l1}, ..., α_{ln} at t_{11}, ..., t_{1m}, ..., and t_{l1}, ..., t_{ln} respectively; Decompose$\{(\alpha, t), [(\alpha_{1m}, t_{1m}), ...,(\alpha_{ln}, t_{ln})]\}$ states that doing a complex action α at t can be decomposed into doing a set of α_{1m}, ..., α_{ln} at t_{1m}, ..., t_{ln} respectively.

We have developed a model of constraint–based plan recognition. This model first infers the types and structures of plans to create a hierarchy of possible structural plans on the basis of structural constraints on the structural actions in the plans. The structural constraints are propagated from the observed actions by using generation and decomposition axioms as well as their completeness axioms. These structural plans are considered as candidate plans, which are further completed on the basis of temporal constraints on both enablement and structural actions in the plans. The temporal constraints are propagated from the observed actions by using enablement axioms and their completeness axioms.

The plan recognition process is carried out by several procedures. The *constraint propagator* propagates structural constraints. The *constraint checker* checks whether expected actions have been justified. The *structural plan completer* completes structural plans. The *temporal constraint checker* checks whether the expected enablement actions have been justified by appropriate observed, generated or justified actions on the current hierarchy of plans. Finally, the *plan checker* checks plan completion.

A hierarchy of plans is maintained in the process, which is a directed graph with nodes representing actions in different states and links representing different sorts of connection between two actions. This hierarchy is changed whenever different constraints are propagated between actions at different levels. There are four kinds of actions and three sorts of links in a hierarchy of plans:

- *Observed actions*—basic actions performed by an agent and observed by the system.
- *Generated actions*—generated from observed, generated or justified actions.
- *Expected actions*—expected by observed, generated, subactions or other expected actions, labelled with question marks.
- *Justified actions*—expected by other actions but justified by one or more observed, generated or justified actions.
- *Generation links*—from generation actions to their generated actions.
- *Expectation links*—from actions to their expected actions, labelled with question marks.
- *Justification links*—changed from expectation links when the expected actions justified, labelled with exclamation marks.

A mechanism based on Allen's algorithm for propagating temporal constraints is developed to maintain temporal relations between intervals in the process of plan recognition.

5 An Example

We now show an example in a simplified cooking domain. An action hierarchy has been illustrated in Fig.1. The problem focuses on recognizing a plan for *preparing meal.* Suppose we observe that somebody has done the following actions which occurred one after another:

$\text{Occurs}(\textit{Make\_Starters}(\textit{Obs}_1), T_1)$, $\text{Occurs}(\textit{Make\_Spaghetti}(\textit{Obs}_2), T_2)$,
$\text{Occurs}(\textit{Make\_Marinara}(\textit{Obs}_3), T_3)$, $\text{Occurs}(\textit{Put\_Spaghetti\_Marinara\_Together}(\textit{Obs}_4), T_4)$,
$\text{Occurs}(\textit{Make\_Dessert}(\textit{Obs}_5), T_5)$,

Given the action hierarchy illustrated in Fig.1, we have a set of completeness axioms, some of which are as follows:

$$\forall x, t.\ \text{Occurs}(\textit{End\_Action}(x), t) \Rightarrow \exists x_1.\ \text{Occurs}(\textit{Prepare\_Meal}(x_1), t)$$

$$\forall x, t.\ \text{Occurs}(\textit{Prepare\_Meal}(x), t) \Rightarrow \exists x_1.\ \text{Occurs}(\textit{Prepare\_Lunch}(x_1), t) \vee \exists x_2.\ \text{Occurs}(\textit{Prepare\_Dinner}(x_2), t)$$

$$\forall x, t.\ \text{Occurs}(\textit{Make\_Dish}(x), t) \Rightarrow \exists y_1, t_1.\ \text{Occurs}(\textit{Prepare\_Lunch}(y_1), t_1) \wedge s_1(y_1) = x \wedge \text{During}(t, t_1) \vee \exists y_2, t_2.\ \text{Occurs}(\textit{Prepare\_Dinner}(y_2), t_2) \wedge s_2(y_2) = x \wedge \text{During}(t, t_2)$$

$$\forall x, t.\ \text{Occurs}(\textit{Make\_Starters}(x), t) \Rightarrow \exists y_1, t_1.\ \text{Occurs}(\textit{Prepare\_Dinner}(y_1), t_1) \wedge s_1(y_1) = x \wedge \text{During}(t, t_1)$$

$$\forall x, t.\ \text{Occurs}(\textit{Make\_Dessert}(x), t) \Rightarrow \exists y_1, t_1.\ \text{Occurs}(\textit{Prepare\_Dinner}(y_1), t_1) \wedge s_3(y_1) = x \wedge \text{During}(t, t_1)$$

$$\forall x, t.\ \text{Occurs}(\textit{Make\_Pasta\_Dish}(x), t) \Rightarrow \exists x_1.\ \text{Occurs}(\textit{Make\_Spaghetti\_Marinara}(x_1), \text{t})$$

$$\forall x, t.\ \text{Occurs}(\textit{Make\_Spaghetti\_Marinara}(x), t) \Rightarrow \exists x_1.\ \text{Occurs}(\textit{Put\_Spaghetti\_Marinara\_Together}(x_1), t)$$

$$\forall x, t.\ \text{Occurs}(\textit{Put\_Spaghetti\_Marinara\_Together}(x), t) \Rightarrow \exists x_1, t_1.\ \text{Occurs}(\textit{Make\_Spaghetti}(x_1), t_1) \wedge \text{Before}(t_1, t) \vee \exists x_2, t_2.\ \text{Occurs}(\text{Make\_Marinara}(x_2), t_2) \wedge \text{Before}(t_2, t)$$

Now the process of plan recognition starts. It calls the *constraint propagator,* which first applies appropriate generation axioms to generation actions on the initial hierarchy of plans and creates generated actions and generation links. It then applies a component/use axiom to a subaction *Make_Dish* and creates two expected decomposition actions *Prepare_Lunch* and *Prepare_Dinner.*

A decomposition axiom is applied to an expected decomposition action *Prepare_Dinner*[2] and a conjunctive set of expected actions *Make_Starters* and *Make_Dinner* are created. It then calls the *constraint checker* and tries to justify expected actions. This results in the expected actions *Make_Starters* and *Make_Dessert* to be justified. It further justifies the expected action *Prepare_Dinner* since *Make_Starters* and *Make_Dessert* have been justified. Afterwards, it applies again appropriate generation axioms to the generation actions and creates two generated actions. So far the first stage of plan recognition is finished.

The *structural plan completer* is called in the second stage of plan recognition, which applies enablement exhaustiveness axioms to a structural action *Put_Spaghetti–Marinara_Together* and creates two expected enablement actions *Make_Spaghetti* and *Make_Marinara* to form a new hierarchy of plans. The *temporal constraint checker* is called to justify expected enablement actions. Two expected enablement actions *Make_Spaghetti* and *Make_Marinara* are justified by two observed actions *Make_Spaghetti* and *Make_Marinara* respectively. A currently maintained hierarchy of plans is shown in Fig. 2.

Finally, the *plan checker* is called to check the completed structural plans and to determine whether they are complete by using either the simple plan axiom or the complex plan axiom respectively. All plans are represented in the completed hierarchy of plans as shown in the circled part of Fig. 1.

6 Conclusions

This paper has presented a model of constraint–based plan recognition, in which there are several distinguished features. It classifies relations over actions and defines plans on the basis of the classified relations. It recognizes plans by satisfying both structural and temporal constraints on the actions in the plans. It uses the established relations between action types as an essential knowledge source and completes it in a circumscriptive approach. The relations between action types can be easily established on the basis of action operators. This model is more tractable than Kautz's. It can distinguish an individual plan from a set of possible plans when the observed actions are complete. Since it reasons about plans on the basis of relations over actions in the plans, its decisions on the inferred plans can be explained and justified. This is a general model of plan recognition which can be applied to a wide range of application domains if an action hierarchy can be created to represent relations between actions types in any of such domains.

References

1. J.F. Allen, Maintaining Knowledge about Temporal Intervals, *Communications of the ACM* 26(11), 1983, p. 833–843.

2. S. Carberry, Incorporating Default Inferences into Plan Recognition, *Proceedings of AAAI*, 1990, p. 471–478.

3. N.F. Carver, V.S. Lesser and D.L. McCue, Focussing in Plan Recognition, *Proceedings of* AAAI, 1984, p. 42–48.

4. E. Charniak and R. Goldman, A Probabilistic Model of Plan Recognition, *Proceedings of AAAI,* 1991, p. 160–165.

5. H.A. Kautz, A Formal Theory of Plan Recognition, *Ph.D. Dissertation*, (Dept. of Computer Science, University of Rochester, 1987).

6. M.E. Pollack, Inferring Domain Plans in Question–Answering. *Ph.D. Dissertation*, (University of Pennsylvania, 1986).

7. B. Raskutti and I. Zukerman, Handling Uncertainty during Plan Recognition in Task–Oriented Consultation Systems, *UAI*, 1991, p. 308–315.

8. R. Wilensky, *Planning and Understanding: A Computational Approach to Human Reasoning*. (Addison–Wesley Publishing Company, 1983).

2. *Prepare_Dinner* is chosen in preference to *Prepare_Lunch* since it also explains two observed actions *Make_Starters* and *Make_Dessert*.

Decision Procedures for Propositional BDI Logics [1]

Anand S. Rao
Australian Artificial Intelligence Institute
1 Grattan Street, Carlton
Victoria 3053, Australia
Email: anand@aaii.oz.au

Abstract

The study of mental attitudes, such as beliefs, desires, and intentions (BDI), is important for the specification and design of artificial agents. This study has led to the development of expressive but computationally intractable logics for describing or specifying the behaviours of agents. In this paper, we formalize a restricted family of such logics and provide constructive tableau decision procedures for determining the satisfiability of formulas in these logics.

1 Introduction

The study of systems that are situated in a changing environment has received considerable attention within Artificial Intelligence. A number of different architectures have emerged as a possible basis for such systems. Some of the most interesting are *agent-oriented* architectures, in which the system is viewed as a rational agent having certain *mental attitudes* that influence its decision making and determine its behaviour. The simplest of these architectures, called a BDI architecture, is based on attitudes of *belief*, *desire*, and *intention*. The first two attitudes represent, respectively, the information and evaluative states of the agent. The last represents decisions the agent has made at a previous time, and is critical for achieving adequate or optimal performance when deliberation is subject to resource bounds [1].

Recently, a number of attempts have been made to formalize these mental attitudes and to show how these attitudes determine the actions of an agent [2,6]. Most of these studies concentrate on the specification or characterization of rational agents and their behaviours under different environmental conditions. They introduce logics that use linear or branching temporal structures, are often first-order, and tend to have a rich repertoire of modal operators to model beliefs, desires, goals, intentions, commitment, ability, actions, and plans.

However, the design of agent-oriented systems has so far had little connection with these specifications. Although the specification logics have been very powerful, no attempt has been made to devise constructive decision procedures to test for satisfiability of formulas in such logics.

This paper takes the first step in this direction by providing a family of propositional, multi-modal BDI logics that are sound, complete, and have constructive tableau-based decision procedures. Although the results are presented for BDI logics, the results are generalizable to multi-modal logics with inter-relationships between the modal operators.

[1] The research reported in this paper was funded partly by the Generic Industry Research and Development Grant on *Distributed Real-Time Artificial Intelligence* and partly by the *Cooperative Research Centre for Intelligent Decision Systems*.

	Axiom		Semantic Condition
(A7)	$\mathsf{M}_1(\phi) \supset \mathsf{M}_2(\phi)$	(SC7)	if $(x, y) \in \mathcal{R}_2$ then $(x, y) \in \mathcal{R}_1$
(A8)	$\mathsf{M}_1(\phi) \supset \mathsf{M}_2(\mathsf{M}_1(\phi))$	(SC8)	if $(x, y) \in \mathcal{R}_2$ and $(y, z) \in \mathcal{R}_1$ then $(x, z) \in \mathcal{R}_1$
(A9)	$\neg\mathsf{M}_1(\phi) \supset \mathsf{M}_2(\neg\mathsf{M}_1(\phi))$	(SC9)	if $(x, y) \in \mathcal{R}_2$ and $(x, z) \in \mathcal{R}_1$ then $(y, z) \in \mathcal{R}_1$
(A10)	$\mathsf{M}_1(\phi) \supset \neg\mathsf{M}_2(\neg\phi)$	(SC10)	if $\forall y, (x, y) \in \mathcal{R}_2$ there $\exists z, (y, z) \in \mathcal{R}_1$.

Table 1: Basic Axioms

2 Propositional BDI Logics

We first define a language $\mathcal{L}_0$ which has a non-empty set Φ of *temporal propositions*, propositional *connectives* $\wedge$, $\vee$, $\supset$, and $\neg$, and *modal operators* BEL (belief), DES (desire), and INT (intention). *Well-formed* formulas of $\mathcal{L}_0$ are defined in the usual manner. We require that the underlying temporal logic be sound and complete, but make no commitment to the underlying temporal structure — it can be a linear- or branching-time structure. This allows us to study the interactions between the different mental attitudes without worrying about the choice or expressive power of the underlying temporal logic. Of course, for a complete theory of an agent's mental state, one would have to choose an appropriate temporal model.

Elsewhere [6,7], we have investigated various branching-time logics, described a possible-worlds semantics, and analyzed the dynamic interaction of the mental attitudes with one another. In this paper, the primary focus is to adapt existing decision procedures for BDI-logics and extend them for multi-modal axioms.

We first consider some basic axiom systems for beliefs, desires, and intentions. These axiom systems are straightforward adaptations of classical modal logic axiom systems and do not capture the inter-relationships among the three different modal operators.

As we will be introducing a number of different logics we need a uniform nomenclature for these logics. As far as possible we will use the classical nomenclatures. We abbreviate beliefs, desires, and intentions by B, D, and I. The axiom system for each one of these operators is written as a superscript.

The minimal axiom system for a modal logic is the axiom system called K. For example, adopting the K-axiom system for beliefs, desires, and intentions, we have the $B^K D^K I^K$ (abbreviated as $(BDI)^K$) modal system. Following the standard modal logics [4] T, S4, S5, and KD45, we can define the axiom systems $(BDI)^T$, $(BDI)^{S4}$, $(BDI)^{S5}$, and $(BDI)^{KD45}$. Also, beliefs, desires, and intentions can adopt different axioms leading to more axiom systems, e.g., $B^{KD45} D^K I^T$, $B^{KD45} D^{S4} I^{S5}$, etc.

The axiom systems of beliefs, desires, and intentions considered so far are relatively minor extensions of current logics. In particular, they do not capture any inter-relationships between beliefs, desires, and intentions. Now we introduce various multi-modal axioms to describe these relationships and also determine corresponding multi-modal semantic conditions.

Extending the standard mono-modal relations like reflexivity, transitivity, etc. together with the corresponding axioms to the multi-modal cases, we have the multi-modal semantic conditions SC7-SC10 and multi-modal axioms A7-A10, given in Table 1 (Axiom numbers A1-A6 refer to the standard modal axioms for K, T, S4, S5, and KD45 modal systems). One

	Tableau Rule
(TC1)	if $\mathsf{M}(\phi) \in L(w)$ and $(w, w') \in \mathcal{R}$, then $\phi \in L(w')$
(TC2)	if $\neg\mathsf{M}(\phi) \in L(w)$, then there exists w' with $(w, w') \in \mathcal{R}$, and $\neg\phi \in L(w')$
(TC3)	if $\mathsf{M}(\phi) \in L(w)$, then $\phi \in L(w)$
(TC4)	if $\mathsf{M}(\phi) \in L(w)$ and $(w, w') \in \mathcal{R}$, then $\mathsf{M}(\phi) \in L(w')$
(TC5)	if $(w, w') \in \mathcal{R}$ then $\mathsf{M}(\phi) \in L(w)$ iff $\mathsf{M}(\phi) \in L(w')$
(TC5′)	if $(w, w'), (w, w'') \in \mathcal{R}$, and $\mathsf{M}(\phi) \in L(w')$, then $\mathsf{M}(\phi) \in L(w'')$ and $\phi \in L(w'')$
(TC6)	if $\mathsf{M}(\phi) \in L(w)$, then either $\phi \in L(w)$ or there exists w' with $(w, w') \in \mathcal{R}$
(TC7)	if $\mathsf{M}_1(\phi) \in L(x)$, then $\mathsf{M}_2(\phi) \in L(x)$
(TC8)	if $\mathsf{M}_1(\phi) \in L(x)$ and $(x, y) \in \mathcal{R}_2$, then $\mathsf{M}_1(\phi) \in L(y)$
(TC9)	if $(x, y) \in \mathcal{R}_2$, $(x, z) \in \mathcal{R}_1$, and $\mathsf{M}_1(\phi) \in L(y)$, then $\mathsf{M}_1(\phi) \in L(z)$ and $\phi \in L(z)$
(TC10)	if $\mathsf{M}_1(\phi) \in L(x)$ then either $\mathsf{M}_2(\phi) \in L(x)$ or there exists y such that $(x, y) \in \mathcal{R}_2$

Table 2: Tableau Rules

can substitute the modal operators BEL, DES, and INT for the modal operators M_1 and M_2 and similarly substitute the relations, $\mathcal{B}$, $\mathcal{D}$, and $\mathcal{I}$ for the relations $\mathcal{R}_1$ and $\mathcal{R}_2$. Rather than investigating all possible combinations, we assume that intentions are stronger than desires and desires are stronger than beliefs. The philosophical justification for such an assumption is that as one moves from beliefs, to desires, to intentions, the *commitment* of an agent increases [6]. In Table 1, we will therefore require that the modal operator M_1 is stronger than M_2.

Any basic axiom system as defined above, together with the axiom A7, will be called the multi-modal T system or mT system. Similarly, mT + A8 is the mS4 system and mS4 + A9 is the mS5 system. Any basic axiom system together with A10, A8, and A9 will be called the mD45 system.

We indicate the multi-modal axioms as subscripts of the basic axiom system. As a result the mT version of the basic axiom system $(BDI)^K$ is written as $(BDI)^K_{mT}$, the mD45 version of the basic axiom system $B^{KD45}D^K I^T$ is written as $(B^{KD45}D^K I^T)_{mD45}$, and so on. The soundness and completeness of all the modal systems are described elsewhere [5].

3 Tableau Decision Procedures

In this section we present constructive decision procedures for the axiom systems discussed so far using the *tableau* method. The results and proofs are extensions of those given by Halpern and Moses [3].

We first present the tableau construction for the basic axiom systems. A *propositional tableau* is a set T of formulas such that: (1) if $\neg\neg\phi \in T$, then $\phi \in T$; (2) if $\phi_1 \wedge \phi_2 \in T$, then both $\phi_1, \phi_2 \in T$; (3) if $\neg(\phi_1 \wedge \phi_2) \in T$, then either $\neg\phi_1 \in T$ or $\neg\phi_2 \in T$; and (4) it is not the case that both ϕ and $\neg\phi$ are in T for some formula ϕ. If T is a propositional tableau and $\phi \in T$, then T is a *propositional tableau for* ϕ. A propositional formula ϕ is satisfiable if and only if there is a propositional tableau for ϕ.

The above propositional tableau can be extended to tableaus for various modal logics. Starting with the simplest of all systems K, a *K tableau* is given by a tuple $T = \langle W, L, \mathcal{R}\rangle$, where W is a set of worlds, $\mathcal{R}$ is a binary relation on W, and L is a *labeling function* that associates with each world $w \in$ W a set $L(w)$ of formulas. A K tableau is a propositional tableau (i.e., it satisfies 1-4 above) that also satisfies the two conditions TC1 and TC2 given in Table 2. The set T is a *K tableau for* ϕ if T is a K tableau and $\phi \in L(w)$ for some world $w \in$ W.

Similarly, one can define T, S4, S5, and KD45 tableaus using the tableau conditions TC1-TC6. Replacing M by BEL, DES, or INT and $\mathcal{R}$ by $\mathcal{B}$, $\mathcal{D}$, or $\mathcal{I}$, we can obtain concrete tableau conditions for beliefs, desires, and intentions based on the particular basic modal system. The tableaus corresponding to the different basic axiom systems will commonly be referred to as *basic tableaus*.

Proposition 1 (Halpern and Moses [3]): *The formula ϕ is K (respectively, T, S4, S5, KD45) satisfiable if and only if there is a K (respectively, T, S4, S5, KD45) tableau for ϕ.*

From Proposition 1 it is straightforward to show that a formula is satisfiable in a basic modal system if and only if there is a corresponding basic tableau for it.

We now consider tableaus for multi-modal axiom systems. Corresponding to the multi-modal axioms A7-A10 we have the tableau conditions TC7-TC10. As before, we restrict M_1 to be stronger than M_2 and consider the situation where intentions are stronger than desires, which are in turn stronger than beliefs.

Now we can define various multi-modal tableaus as follows: A basic tableau together with the tableau condition TC7 will be called a *multi-modal T (mT) tableau.* Similarly, with tableau conditions TC8-TC10 one can define multi-modal tableaus – mS4, mS5, and mD45.

Proposition 2 : *The formula ϕ is $(BDI)^K_{mT}$ (respectively, $(BDI)^K_{mS4}$, $(BDI)^K_{mS5}$, $(BDI)^K_{mD45}$ satisfiable if and only if there is $(BDI)^K_{mT}$ (respectively, $(BDI)^K_{mS4}$, $(BDI)^K_{mS5}$, $(BDI)^K_{mD45}$ tableau for ϕ.*

One can prove similar results for all the other multi-modal systems obtained by substituting the underlying basic axiom system $(BDI)^K$ with one of the other basic axiom systems.

4 Tableau Algorithms

All tableau construction algorithms consist of four procedures. The first procedure constructs a propositional tableau. The second constructs a fully expanded propositional tableau. A set T of formulas is *fully expanded* if for every formula $\phi \in T$ and subformula ψ of ϕ either $\psi \in T$ or $\neg\psi \in T$. The third procedure creates successors to a node whose label is a fully expanded propositional tableau. The fourth procedure checks for satisfiable labels. The third and fourth procedures are dependent on the axiom system, while the first and second procedures are independent of any axiom system chosen.

Now we reproduce the standard notions of *witness* and *blatantly inconsistent* [3]. If a set of formulas T is not a propositional tableau, a formula ψ is a *witness* if (a) $\psi \in T$, T is not a propositional tableau, and one of the clauses in the definition of propositional tableau does not apply to ψ or (b) ψ is a subformula of some formula $\phi \in T$, T is not fully expanded, and neither ψ nor $\neg\psi$ is in T. A set T is *blatantly inconsistent* if for some formula ψ, both ψ and $\neg\psi$ are in T.

The construction of a $(BDI)^K_{mT}$ tableau, given below, is an extension of the K tableau given by Halpern and Moses [3].

Algorithm for Constructing a $(BDI)^K_{mT}$ Tableau
Step 1: Construct a tree consisting of a single node w_0, with $L(w_0) = \{\phi_0\}$.
Step 2: Repeat until none of (a) – (d) below applies:

(a) *Forming a propositional tableau:* A propositional tableau is generated in the standard manner [3].

(b) *Forming a fully expanded propositional tableau:* Similarly, expanding a propositional tableau is also straightforward [3].

(c) *Creating $\mathcal{R}$-successor nodes:* If w is a leaf of the tree, $L(w)$ is not blatantly inconsistent, and $L(w)$ is a fully expanded propositional tableau, then for each formula of the form $\neg\mathsf{M}(\psi) \in L(w)$ create a $\mathcal{R}$-successor node w' and let $L(w') = L(w)/\mathcal{R} \cup \{\neg\psi\}$, where M is BEL, DES, and INT, and $\mathcal{R}$ is $\mathcal{B}$, $\mathcal{D}$, and $\mathcal{I}$, respectively.

(d) *Marking nodes 'satisfiable':* If w is not marked 'satisfiable' then mark w satisfiable if condition (4) is satisfied and either one of (1)-(3) is satisfied. The conditions are as follows: (1) $L(w)$ is not a fully expanded propositional tableau and w' is marked satisfiable for some successor w' of w; (2) $L(w)$ is a fully expanded propositional tableau, w has successors and all of them are marked 'satisfiable'; (3) $L(w)$ is a fully expanded propositional tableau, there are no formulas of the form $\neg\mathsf{M}(\psi) \in L(w)$ (where M is BEL, DES, INT), and $L(w)$ is not blatantly inconsistent; (4) It is not the case that $\mathsf{M}_1(\psi) \in L(w)$ and $\neg\mathsf{M}_2(\psi) \in L(w)$ for some formula ψ; (where M_1 and M_2 can be BEL, DES, INT, with the restriction that M_1 is stronger than M_2).

Step 3: If the root of the tree is marked 'satisfiable' , then return "ϕ_0 is satisfiable"; otherwise return "ϕ_0 is unsatisfiable".

The above tableau construction can be modified to construct tableaus for other modal systems, such as $(BDI)^K$, $(BDI)^K_{mS4}$, $(BDI)^K_{mS5}$, $(B^{KD45}D^D I^T)^K_{mT}$, etc. We can show that these tableau constructions terminate. Details can be found in the full paper [5]. Here we state the theorem for the above tableau construction.

Theorem 1 : *A formula ϕ is $(BDI)^K_{mT}$ satisfiable iff the $(BDI)^K_{mT}$ tableau construction for ϕ returns "ϕ is satisfiable". The algorithm for tableau construction runs in polynomial space.*

4.1 Example

In this example we construct a $(BDI)^K_{mT}$ tableau for the formula, $\phi_0 = (\mathrm{p} \wedge \neg\mathsf{BEL}(\mathrm{p}) \wedge \neg\mathsf{DES}(\mathrm{p}) \wedge \mathsf{INT}(\mathrm{p}))$ and determine if it is $(BDI)^K_{mT}$-satisfiable or not. For example, p could be some proposition about a future that the agent intends to bring about, but neither believes it will come about nor desires it.

The construction, given in Figure 1, starts with the world w_0 being labeled with the set $\{\phi_0\}$. Applying Step 2-a-2 three times we arrive at world w_3 which is labeled with all the conjuncts of ϕ_0. The labeling for w_3 is a fully expanded propositional tableau. Applying Step 2-c we create a $\mathcal{B}$-successor node w_{41} and a $\mathcal{D}$-successor node w_{42}. The labelings for both these nodes contain only $\neg$p. Applying Step 2-d we mark both the nodes w_{41} and w_{42} as 'satisfiable' because conditions 3 and 4 of Step 2-d are true. The node w_3 cannot be marked 'satisfiable' because even though condition 2 of Step 2-d is true condition 4 is not. For similar reasons nodes w_2, w_1 and w_0 cannot be marked as being 'satisfiable'. Therefore the formula

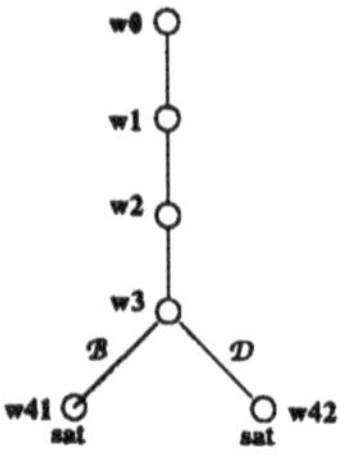

$$
\begin{array}{l}
L(w_0) = \{(p \wedge \wedge \neg \mathsf{BEL}(p) \wedge \neg \mathsf{DES}(p) \wedge \mathsf{INT}(p))\} \\
L(w_1) = L(w_0) \cup \{p, (\neg \mathsf{BEL}(p) \wedge \neg \mathsf{DES}(p) \wedge \mathsf{INT}(p))\} \\
L(w_2) = L(w_1) \cup \{\neg \mathsf{BEL}(p), (\neg \mathsf{DES}(p) \wedge \mathsf{INT}(p))\} \\
L(w_3) = L(w_2) \cup \{\neg \mathsf{DES}(p), \mathsf{INT}(p)\} \\
L(w_{41}) = \{\neg p\} \\
L(w_{42}) = \{\neg p\}
\end{array}
$$

Figure 1: $(BDI)^K_{mT}$ Tableau

$(p \wedge \neg \mathsf{BEL}(p) \wedge \neg \mathsf{DES}(p) \wedge \mathsf{INT}(p))$ is not $(BDI)^K_{mT}$-satisfiable. However, since condition 4 of Step 2-d is not required for a $(BDI)^K$ tableau, we can show that the formula ϕ_0 is indeed $(BDI)^K$-satisfiable.

5 Conclusions

The contributions of this paper are two-fold. From the viewpoint of designing agent-oriented systems it provides a sound and complete family of BDI-logics that have constructive decision procedures. So far, such decision procedures have not been available for BDI-logics.

From the viewpoint of multi-modal logics, the paper presents a principled way of classifying inter-relationships between various modal operators, introduces multi-modal versions of the reflexive, transitive, euclidean, and serial relations, and provides constructive decision procedures for satisfiability in these multi-modal logics.

Acknowledgements

I would like to thank Michael Georgeff for valuable discussions and comments on this paper.

References

[1] M. E. Bratman, D. Israel, and M. E. Pollack. Plans and resource-bounded practical reasoning. *Computational Intelligence*, 4:349–355, 1988.

[2] P. R. Cohen and H. J. Levesque. Intention is choice with commitment. *Artificial Intelligence*, 42(3), 1990.

[3] J. Y. Halpern and Y. Moses. A guide to completeness and complexity for modal logics of knowledge and belief. *Artificial Intelligence*, 54:319–379, 1992.

[4] G. E. Hughes and M. J. Cresswell. *A Companion to Modal Logic*. Methuen & Co. Ltd., London, England, 1984.

[5] A. S. Rao. Decision procedures for propositional BDI logics. Technical Report 44, Australian Artificial Intelligence Institute, Carlton, Australia, 1993.

[6] A. S. Rao and M. P. Georgeff. Modeling rational agents within a BDI-architecture. In *Proceedings of KR&R*. Morgan Kaufmann Publishers, San Mateo, CA, 1991.

[7] A. S. Rao and M. P. Georgeff. A model-theoretic approach to the verification of situated reasoning systems. In *Proceedings of IJCAI-93*, Chamberey, France, 1993.

Double Defined Logic Programs

Faye Liu, Douglas Huntington Moore
Department of Computer Science & Computer Engineering
La Trobe University Bundoora Vic 3083 Australia

Abstract Implementing negation in logic programming has long been an outstanding question. This paper provides a new solution to the question based on double defined logic programs. Double defined logic programs are logic programs defined on both positive and negative sides. In such a program, negative subgoals are no longer derived from positive subgoals by "Negation as Failure", but independent from positive subgoals. Double defined logic programs are actually Horn clause logic programs and so the reasoning on a double defined logic program is monotonic, sound and complete.

Keywords Logic programming, Double defined logic programs, Soundness and completeness, Constructive negation.

1. Introduction

An apparent limitation of Horn clause logic, as the theoretical foundation of logic programming, is that it does not support negation and hence appears to be lacking in expressive power. Two natural approaches for overcoming this problem are as follows: (a) to remove the Horn clause paradigm on which the theory of logic programming is based so that negation can be contained in the programs; (b) to retain the simplicity of the Horn clause paradigm and modify the programming system. The first case involves re-establishing the whole theorem of logic programming. The second involves directly building negation into the programming system.

One branch, going along the lines of the second approach, is to base negation on the "Negation as Failure" rule. However, applying "Negation as Failure" to general logic programs leads to the following problems: (a) It can only be applied to the completion of a general logic programs[1]; (b) Incompleteness may be caused even in the completion of a logic programs[2]; (c) The implementation of constructive negation is difficult.

An alternative approach is to define a logic program from both positive and negative sides, and that is the direction taken in this paper.

We double define facts and rules - define facts and rules not only in the positive sense, but also the negative sense. In a double defined logic program, negative and positive subgoals are both of equal status. Consequently, to prove not(p(a)), we don't need to show whether or not p(a) is provable. We define neg-predicate, neg-atom, neg-clause, neg-fact, neg-rule, double defined facts set, and double defined rules set to build up double defined logic programs. We show that logic programs can be converted to double defined logic programs, resulting in programs where the incompleteness caused by "Negation as Failure" can be avoided.

2. Complete and Incomplete Logic Programs

In this section, we consider logic programs from a set theoretical point of view.

Definition 1 (P-domain)

q(X) is a predicate defined in a general logic program P_g. We call set $D_q = \{ x \mid x \in U_l$, q(x) is a clause or a logic consequence of P_g } the P-domain of q(X). (U_l is the Herbrand universe[1][3] of P_g).

Assume that q(X) :- p(X) is the only rule of a general logic program P_g, then $D_p \subseteq U_l$ and $D_q \subseteq U_l$ and

$$D_q \supseteq D_p \qquad (1)$$

Let set $ND_p = U_l - D_p$ and set $ND_q = U_l - D_q$, then

$$ND_q \subseteq ND_p \qquad (2)$$

$\forall s \in U_l$, suppose not(p(s)) (ie. the system fails to prove p(s)). From not(p(s)), the system fails to prove q(s). According to "Negation as Failure", not(q(s)) is derived. That is $\forall s \in U_l$, if not(p(s)), then not(q(s)) (ie. not(p(s)) infers not(q(s))). Therefore, we have

$$ND_q \supseteq ND_p \qquad (3)$$

Comparing (2) and (3), we find that applying "Negation as Failure" to program P_g need the condition $ND_q = ND_p$. When the definition of the program is incomplete (ie. $D_p \subset D_q$ and $D_p \neq D_q$), using "Negation as Failure" may cause incomplete reasoning.

Definition 2 (Complete and Incomplete Logic Programs)

General logic program P_g is complete iff for every predicate q(X) defined in P_g, if R_i $q(X):-p_{i1}(X), p_{i2}(X), \ldots, p_{ik_i}(X)$ (i = 1, 2, ..., m) are all the definition rules[2][3] of q, then $D_q = \bigcup_{i=1}^{m} \bigcap_{j=1}^{k_i} D_{p_{ij}}$. Variable X may be a multi-ary variables. It is not necessary that q and p_{ij} have the same variables. The general logic program which is not complete is an incomplete logic program.

The definitions above indicate that a general logic program P_g is complete, if and only if the P-domain of each its predicate equals the union of the P-domains of the premise of its definition. For example, if *{ r(a,c). s(b). p(c). q(X) :- p(X). q(X) :- r(X,Y), not(s(Y)). }* is a complete logic program, then $D_q = D_p \cup (D_r \cap ND_s)$.

3. The Definition of Double Defined Logic Programs

Double defined logic programs will be defined in this section.

Definition 3 (Neg-predicate)

Let p(X) be a predicate with domain D. The neg-predicate of p(X) is the predicate np(X) which has the same variables and domain as predicate p(X) has. np(X) is defined

---

[1] A set of ground terms which can be formed out of constants and functions in a logic program.

[2] The rules with q in their conclusions.

as the negation of p(X). That is np(X)∧p(X) is unsatisfiable in D.

Definition 4 (Neg-atom)

Atom np(x) is defined as the neg-atom of atom p(x).

Definition 5 (Neg-clause)

Let L: p(X) ← q_1(X), ..., q_n(X) be a program clause. Any program clause with np(X) in its conclusion is called the neg-program-clause(neg-clause) of L.

Neg-clauses are Horn-clauses. Therefore if neg-clauses are added to a logic program, the newly created logic program is still a Horn clause logic program.

Definition 6 (Neg-fact, neg-rule, double defined fact set and double defined rule set)

A neg-clause without premise is defined as a neg-fact. A neg-clause with a non-empty premise is defined as a neg-rule. Let P_g be a general logic program. F and R are its fact set and rule set. The double defined fact set F_d is created by adding all possible neg-facts into the fact set without changing the P-domain of any predicate defined in p_g; the double defined rule set R_d is created by adding all possible neg-rules into the fact set without changing the P-domain of any predicate defined in P_g.

It is obvious from Definition 6 that the double defined fact set and rule set contain both positive and negative information. That is the meaning of "double defined".

Definition 7 (Double defined logic program)

Let P_g be a general logic program. The double defined logic program P_d converted from p_g is created by (a) Changing all the negations of atoms to their neg-atoms; (b) Converting the fact set to a double defined fact set; (c) Converting the rule set to a double defined rule set. The double defined logic program converted from P_g is a logic program contains all the clauses and possible neg-clauses of P_g without changing the P-domain of any its predicate.

The neg-predicate of a predicate is actually the negation of the predicate. It is in this way, negation exists independently in a double defined logic program. A negative subgoal is no longer derived from the positive subgoal.

Since neg-clauses are Horn-clauses, a double defined logic program is a Horn-clause logic program, model theory and proof theory can be applied to the program. That means interpretations can be defined for a double defined program. A double defined program may have models. A double defined program has a Herbrand universe U_l, a Herbrand base B_l, a Herbrand interpretations I_l and may have a Herbrand model M_l. The inference on a double defined program can be done with SLD-Resolution and the computation rule which is used in standard PROLOG. Double defined logic programming can be implemented in PROLOG.

4. Soundness and Completeness

In this section, we will discuss the relationship between rules and neg-rules, and the soundness and completeness of the reasoning in a double defined logic program.

Lemma 1

Let P_g be a complete logic program and F be its fact set. q(X) is a predicate defined in P_g. If q(X) does not have definition rules, then $D_q = \{ x \mid q(x) \in F \}$ and $D_{nq} = U_l - D_q$

Proof

$\forall a \in U_l$, if $q(a) \in F$ (ie. q(a) is a clause of P_g), then $a \in D_q$.

$\therefore \{ x \mid q(x) \in F \} \subseteq D_q$ (4)

$\forall a \in U_l$ and $a \notin \{ x \mid q(x) \in F \}$, since q does not have definition rules

$\therefore$ q(a) cannot be derived from the program. Therefore q(a) is not a logic consequence of P_g

$\therefore a \notin D_q$

$\therefore \{ x \mid q(x) \in F \} \supseteq D_q$ (5)

From (4) and (5), we have $\{ x \mid q(x) \in F \} = D_q$

Since P_g is a complete logic program

$\therefore D_{nq} = ND_q = U_l - D_q$ //

Lemma 2

p(X) and q(X) are two predicates defined in general logic program P_g. p(X) and q(X) are equivalent(ie. p(X) :- q(X) and q(X) :- p(X)) iff $D_p = D_q$.

The proof of the lemma is trivial.

Theorem

Let P_g be a complete logic program. q(X) is a predicate defined in P_g. If R_i $q(X):-p_{i1}(X), p_{i2}(X), \ldots, p_{ik_i}(X)$ (i = 1, 2, ..., m) are all the definition rules of q(X), then P_g has and only has $k_1 * k_2 * \ldots * k_m$ neg-rules with nq(X) as the conclusions. These neg-rules are $nq(X):-np_{1l_1}(X), np_{2l_2}(X), \ldots, np_{ml_m}(X)$ (l_1, l_2, ..., l_m are all of the combinations of 1, ..., k_1; 1, ..., k_2; ...; 1, ..., k_m).

Proof:

Since R_i $q(X):-p_{i1}(X), p_{i2}(X), \ldots, p_{ik_i}(X)$ (i = 1, 2, ..., m) are all the definition rules of q(X) and P_g is a complete logic program.

$\therefore D_q = \bigcup_{i=1}^{m} \bigcap_{j=1}^{k_i} D_{p_{ij}}$ and $D_{nq} = ND_q = U_l - D_q$

$$\therefore D_{nq} = U_l - \left(\bigcup_{i=1}^{m} \bigcap_{j=1}^{k_i} D_{p_{ij}}\right) = \bigcap_{i=1}^{m} \bigcup_{j=1}^{k_i} (U_l - D_{p_{ij}})$$

$$= \bigcap_{i=1}^{m} \left(\bigcup_{j_1=1}^{k_1} \cdots \bigcup_{j_m=1}^{k_m}\right) D_{np_{ij_i}} = \left(\bigcup_{j_1=1}^{k_1} \cdots \bigcup_{j_m=1}^{k_m}\right)\left(\bigcap_{i=1}^{m} D_{np_{ij_i}}\right)$$

$\therefore$ The neg-rules can be written as

$nq(X):-np_{1l_1}(X), np_{2l_2}(X), \ldots, np_{ml_m}(X)$ (Where l_1, l_2, ..., l_m are all the combinations of 1, ..., k_1; ...; 1, ..., k_m) //

The theorem will be used to convert a complete logic program to a double defined logic program. One of the problems in converting a complete logic program to a double defined logic program is that the converted program may not satisfy weak covering[3]. To overcome the problem, a one-ary predicate var_retor(X) has to be defined as a variable restrictor. var_retor(X) is defined as $\forall x \in U_l$, var_retor(x) is a clause of the converted program. Whenever a converted rule does not satisfy the condition of weak covering, var_retor(X) can be added to the premise part of the rule to restrict the variables without changing the P-domains of each predicates in the rule.

The following example illustrates how to derive neg-facts and neg-rules from a complete logic program, to create a variable restrictor, and to convert a complete logic program to a double defined logic program.

Example We will convert a complete logic program P_g to a double defined logic program. Program P_g:

Fact set: *r(a). r(b). s(b). s(c). t(d,b).*

Rule set: R_1 *t(X,Y) :- not(r(X)),s(Y).* R_2 *q(X,Y) :- not(t(Y,X)), r(Y).*

R_3 *p(X,Y,Z) :- t(X,Y),not(q(X,X)),s(Z).* R_4 *p(X,Y,Z) :- t(X,Z),r(Y).*

First, define all the neg-predicates and a variable restrictor var_retor(X). The neg-predicates are nr(X), ns(X), nt(X,Y), nq(X,Y), and np(X,Y,Z).

Second, convert the fact set to a double defined fact set. The Herbrand universe U_l = { a, b, c, d }. Since r(X) and s(X) have no definition rules, according to Lemma 1, D_r = { a, b }, D_s = { b, c }, D_{nr} = { c, d }, and D_{ns} = { a, d }. Therefore neg-fact *nr(c), nr(d), ns(a), ns(d)* can be added to the fact set.

The double defined fact set F_d : *r(a). r(b). s(b). s(c). t(d,b). nr(c). nr(d). ns(a). ns(d). var_retor(a). var_retor(b). var_retor(c). var_retor(d).*

Third, convert the rule set to a double defined rule set. According to theorem 1, the neg-rules derived from R_1 are *nt(X,Y) :- r(X)* and *nt(X,Y) :- ns(Y)*. After adding variable restrictors, they become *nt(X,Y) :- r(X),var_retor(Y).* and *nt(X,Y) :- ns(Y),var_retor(X).* In the same way, neg-rules *nq(X,Y) :- t(Y,X).* and *nq(X,Y) :- nr(Y),var_retor(X).* can be derived from rule R_2. neg-rules *np(X,Y,Z) :- nt(X,Y),nt(X,Z). np(X,Y,Z) :- nt(X,Y), nr(Y),var_retor(Z). np(X,Y,Z) :- q(X,X),nt(X,Z),var-retor(Y). np(X,Y,Z) :- q(X,X), nr(Y),var_retor(Z). np(X,Y,Z) :- ns(Z),nt(X,Z),var_retor(Y). and np(X,Y,Z) :- ns(Z), nr(Y),var_retor(X).* are derived from rules R_3 and R_4.

The double defined rule set R_d : *t(X,Y) :- not(r(X)),s(Y). q(X,Y) :- not(t(Y,X)), r(Y). p(X,Y,Z) :- t(X,Y),not(q(X,X)),s(Z). p(X,Y,Z) :- t(X,Z),r(Y). nt(X,Y) :- r(X), var_retor(Y). nt(X,Y) :- ns(Y),var_retor(X). nq(X,Y) :- t(Y,X). nq(X,Y) :- nr(Y), var_retor(X). np(X,Y,Z) :- nt(X,Y),nt(X,Z). np(X,Y,Z) :- nt(X,Y),nr(Y),var_retor(Z). np(X,Y,Z) :- q(X,X),nt(X,Z),var-retor(Y). np(X,Y,Z) :- q(X,X),nr(Y),var_retor(Z). np(X,Y,Z) :- ns(Z), nt(X,Z), var_retor(Y). np(X,Y,Z) :- ns(Z), nr(Y), var_retor(X).*

The converted double defined logic program $P_d = F_d + R_d$ //

Double defined logic programs are Horn clause logic programs (ie. there is no negation in the program), therefore (a) the reasoning on a double defined logic program is monotonic; (b) the reasoning on a double defined logic program is sound and

[3] A weak covering program is defined as having no variable which occurs in the conclusion part of a rule but not in the premise part of the rule.

complete. Further more, constructive negation is actually implemented in a double defined logic program.

5. Related Works

Building constructive negation through Deduced Relevant Types[4] was introduced by Foo et al. in 1988. Concepts type, deduced relevant type and typed logic programs were defined. Types are actually the domains of the variables; Relevant types are the complete and unified minimal types. Relevant types can be derived automatically in the form of a set of atoms, and added to logic programs. The logic program is, therefore, typed and transformed. The original logic program and the transformed logic program are equivalent(have the same least model) on the condition that the original logic program satisfies weak covering. The reasoning on the transformed program is domain restricted. The constructive negation can be built on it.

Constructive negation based on the completed database[5] provide another constructive negation. The definition of complete logic programs in this method is stranger than ours.

The "Constructive Negation Rule" which is formalised in SLD-CNF Resolution, is defined to handle non-ground negative subgoals as handling positive ones. When a negative subgoal, say not(q(X)), is met, the system will first search the answer for query q(X) (assume D_q is the answer), then it will answer U_l - D_q. That is the reason that the negation in this method is constructive. "Constructive Negation Rule" is based on "Negation as Failure".

6. Conclusion

Double defined logic programming has been introduced as a means of eliminating negation based on "Negation as Failure". In so doing, the resulting logic programming system returns to its historic root - Horn clause logic programming. As such, it is not surprising that the reasoning on the system is rigorously monotonic, sound and complete. The double defined logic approach retains the advantages of Horn clause logic by constructing the negation mechanism into the denotational structure of the system.

Reference

[1] K.L. Clark, *Negation as Failure*, Symposium on Logic & Databases 1977, pp. 293 - 322.
[2] L. Naish, *Negation and Control in PROLOG*, Springer-Verlag 1986, Part I.
[3] J.W. Lloyd, *Foundations of Logic Programming*, Springer-Verlag 1987.
[4] N. Foo, A. Rao, A. Taylor and A. Walker, *Deduced Relevant Types And Constructive Negation*, Proceedings of The Fifth International Conference and Symposium 1988, Vol. 1, pp. 126 - 139.
[5] D. Chan, *Constructive Negation Based On The Complete Database*, Proceedings of The Fifth International Conference and Symposium 1988, Vol. 1, pp. 111 - 125.

Epistemic Processes and Default Reasoning

Wei Li
Department of Computer Science
Beijing University of Aeronautics and Astronautics
100083 Beijing, P.R. China

Abstract

A comparative study between default reasoning and epistemic processes is given. An extension of a default theory is proved to be the limit of a δ-partial increasing epistemic process of that theory. It is also proved that there are two distinct extensions of a default theory iff a non-monotonic epistemic process can be constructed.

1 Introduction

Default reasoning [Reit 80] and epistemic processes [Li 92-1, 92-2, 93] are different approaches to describe the aspects of incompleteness of information, fallibility of knowledge, and non-monotonicity of reasoning. The difference can be seen from the following example: Consider Galileo's principle of the addition of velocity. Assume that K, K' are co-ordinate systems and that K' is moving with a uniform velocity w without rotation w.r.t. to K. We use $B(x)$ to denote "x is a body", and use $A(x)$ to denote "the velocity of x w.r.t K' depends on the velocity w of K' w.r.t K and the velocity v of the body w.r.t K, and is $w + v$". Thus, Galileo's principle is represented as: $\mathbf{V}: \quad \forall x.(B(x) \supset A(x))$.

The view of Reiter's default logic:

The principle **V** can be represented as a default: $\frac{B(x):M\ A(x)}{A(x)}$. It means that if x is a body and $A(x)$ does not conflict with the knowledge of mechanics which we know, then we accept $A(x)$.

For example, let Γ be the knowledge in Galileo's time. Then, since $A(x)$ does not conflict with Γ, the default $A(x)$ is acceptable w.r.t Γ.

Let us consider another case, we assume light c to be of particulate nature, i.e. $B(c)$ holds. We accept the following statement: *" At all events we know with great exactness that ... the velocity of propagation of light cannot depend on the velocity of motion of the body emitting the light"* ([Eins 15]), i.e. $\neg A(c)$ holds. Let $\Gamma'' = \{\Gamma, B(c), \neg A(c)\}$. For light c, $A(c)$ does contradict Γ''. Thus, the default $A(x)$ is not accepted w.r.t Γ''.

The view point of epistemic processes:

Assume that Γ denote the mechanics in the stage before Galileo's time. Since **V** does not conflict with Γ, Galileo added it into his mechanics as a new law. In this paper, we call **V** a new premise for Γ.

Thus, $\Gamma' = \{\Gamma, \mathbf{V}, B(c)\}$ is obtained to represent the mechanics in the second stage (the mechanics after Galileo but before Eistain). It is obvious that $A(c)$ can be deduced from $B(c)$ and $\mathbf{V}$. Using a Gentzen style notation, this can be represented as: $\Gamma' \vdash A(c)$ or more detailed $\Gamma, B(c), \forall x.B(x) \supset A(x) \vdash A(c)$.

It means that Γ' predicts that the velocity of propagation of light depends on the velocity of the body emitting the light. As we have seen, scientists discovered that some experiments and astronomic observations reject this prediction. We call it a **rejection** of $A(c)$ by facts. Clearly, Γ' must be revised to match the experiments and observations while maintaining consistency between laws. A simple solution is to accept $\neg A(c)$ as a new law. Since $B(c)$ and $\neg A(c)$ are not consistent with $\forall x.B(x) \supset A(x)$. We have to reject Galileo's principle. Thus we accept $\Gamma'' = \{\Gamma, B(c), \neg A(c)\}$. Γ'' represents the mechanics in the third stage (Einstein's special relativity theory).

Each Γ denotes an epistemic stage. The sequence of hypothesis: $\Gamma, \Gamma', \Gamma'', \cdots$ describes the evolution of mechanics. $\Gamma \subseteq \Gamma'$ and $\Gamma' \not\subseteq \Gamma''$ indicate that non-monotonicity is a characteristic of the sequence, when rejections by facts arise.

The purpose of this paper is to give a comparative study between default logic and epistemic processes. Since the latter has a sound model theory, the study leads to a model theoretic interpretation of the former. In this short paper, we omit all proofs which can be found in [Li 93].

2 Sequences of Formal theories

We assume that the formal language which we use is a first order language L defined in [Gal 87]. We use A, Γ and $Th(\Gamma)$ to denote a formula, a sequence of formulas and the set of all theorems deduced from Γ respectively. A sequent is a form of $\Gamma \vdash A$. We use $\mathbf{M}_{\wp}$ to denote a model of a specific problem $\wp$, and use $\mathcal{T}_{\mathbf{M}_{\wp}}$ to denote the set of all true sentences of $\mathbf{M}_{\wp}$. It is obvious that $\mathcal{T}_{\mathbf{M}_{\wp}}$ is countable. We use $\mathbf{M} \models \Gamma$ to denote $\mathbf{M} \models A$ for all A contained in Γ.

Definition 2.1 Sequence of hypotheses

A (finite or infinite) sequence (set) Γ of closed formulas is called a *hypothesis*, if Γ is consistent. The sentences contained in Γ are called premises.

$\Gamma_1, \Gamma_2, \cdots \Gamma_n, \cdots$ is called a *sequence of hypotheses*, or sequence for short, if for any n, Γ_n is a hypothesis.

A sequence is increasing (or decreasing) if $\Gamma_n \subseteq \Gamma_{n+1}$ (or $\Gamma_n \supseteq \Gamma_{n+1}$) for all n; otherwise it is non-monotonic.

Definition 2.2 Limit of sequence

Let $\{\Gamma_n\}$ be a sequence of hypotheses . The set of closed formulas:

$$\Gamma^* \equiv \bigcap_{n=1}^{\infty} \bigcup_{m=n}^{\infty} \Gamma_m$$

is called the *upper limit* of the sequence $\{\Gamma_n\}$. The set of closed formulas:

$\Gamma_* \equiv \bigcup_{n=1}^{\infty} \bigcap_{m=n}^{\infty} \Gamma_m$

is called the *lower limit* of the sequence $\{\Gamma_n\}$. A sequence of hypothesis is *convergent* iff $\Gamma_* = \Gamma^*$. The limit of a convergent sequence denoted by $\lim_n \Gamma_n$ is its lower limit (and also the upper limit).

The meaning of the definition can be seen from the following theorem:

Lemma 2.1 $A \in \Gamma^*$ iff there exist infinite many $\{k_n\}$ such that $A \in \Gamma_{k_n}$. $A \in \Gamma_*$ iff there exists an N such that $A \in \Gamma_m$ for $m > N$.

The main result about limit is that there exists a procedure that given any model and any hypothesis, all sequences generated by the procedure will start from the hypothesis and will converge to the same limit which is the truth of the model. To prove this result, we need the following concepts which are close to the concepts given in [AGM 85].

Definition 2.3 New premise.

A is called a new premise for Γ iff there exist two models $\mathbf{M}$ and $\mathbf{M}'$ such that

$$\mathbf{M} \models \Gamma \quad \mathbf{M} \models A \qquad \text{and} \qquad \mathbf{M}' \models \Gamma \quad \mathbf{M}' \models \neg A.$$

Theorem 2.1 A is a new premise for Γ iff A is logically independent of Γ, that is neither $\Gamma \vdash A$ nor $\Gamma \vdash \neg A$ is provable.

We use $\Gamma \models A$ to denote that A is a semantic consequence of Γ. It means that for any model $\mathbf{M}$, if $\mathbf{M} \models \Gamma$ then $\mathbf{M} \models A$.

Definition 2.4 Rejection by facts

Let $\Gamma \models A$. A model $\mathbf{M}$ is a rejection of A by facts iff $\mathbf{M} \models \neg A$. Let $\Gamma_{M(A)} \equiv \{A_i \mid A_i \in \Gamma,\ \ \mathbf{M} \models A_i,\ \ \mathbf{M} \models \neg A\}$. $\mathbf{M}$ is called an *ideal* rejection of A by facts iff $\Gamma_{M(A)}$ is *maximal* in the sense that there is no another rejection of A by facts $\mathbf{M}'$ such that $\Gamma_{M(A)} \subset \Gamma_{M'(A)}$. An ideal rejection of A by facts is denoted by $\overline{\mathbf{M}}(A)$. Since there may exist many ideal rejection of A by facts, we define

$$\mathcal{R}(\Gamma, A) \equiv \{\Gamma_{\overline{M}(A)} \mid \overline{\mathbf{M}} \text{ is an ideal rejection of } A \text{ by facts}\}$$

Definition 2.5 Acceptable modification

Let $\Gamma \vdash A$. An acceptable modification Λ of $\neg A$ is a maximal subset of Γ with the property that Λ is consistent with $\neg A$.

Let $\mathcal{A}(\Gamma, A)$ be the set of all acceptable modification of $\neg A$.

Theorem 2.2 $\mathcal{A}(\Gamma, A) = \mathcal{R}(\Gamma, A)$.

To reconstruct a hypothesis for a new premise or a rejection by facts, we need:

Definition 2.6 Reconstruction

Let A be a theorem of Γ. An E-reconstruction of Γ for the theorem A is Γ itself. Let A be a new premise for Γ. An N-reconstruction of Γ for the new premise A is the sequence $\{\Gamma, A\}$. Let $\Gamma \models A$ and A be rejected by some facts. An R-reconstruction of Γ for the rejection of A by facts is Δ, where $\Delta \in \mathcal{R}(\Gamma, A)$.

A hypothesis Γ' is a reconstruction of Γ iff Γ' is an E- or an N- or an R-reconstruction.

It is obvious that R-reconstruction is not unique, and that if Δ is an R-reconstruction of Γ for the rejection of A by facts then Δ is a maximal consistent subset of Γ, which is consistent with $\neg A$.

3 The limit of epistemic processes

The evolution of knowledge can be described by:

Definition 3.1 Epistemic process

A hypothesis sequence $\Gamma_1, \Gamma_2, \cdots, \Gamma_n, \cdots$ is an epistemic process, if Γ_{i+1} is a reconstruction of Γ_i for $i \geq 1$.

The evolution of a hypothesis should be represented by a tree, each branch of which is an epistemic processes.

Let $\mathbf{M}_p$ be a given model and Γ be a given hypothesis which is used to be the starting point of epistemic process. Let $\mathcal{T}_{M_p}$ be denoted by $\{A_m\}$.

Definition 3.2 The sequence $\{\Gamma_n\}$ is called an $\mathbf{M}_p$ epistemic process of Γ if it is generated by the following procedure:

Let $\{\Delta_n\}$ and $\{\Theta_n\}$ be two sequences of hypotheses. Let $\Delta_1 = \Theta_1 = \emptyset$.

1. $\Gamma_1 = \Gamma$.
2. Γ_{n+1} is defined as below:
   Do the loop for n and i from $n := 2$ and $i := 1$ properly:
   (a) If $\Gamma_n \vdash A_i$ is provable, then $\Gamma_{n+1} := \Gamma_n$ and $\Theta_{n+1} := \{\Theta_n, A_n\}$ and $\Delta_{n+1} := \Delta_n$; $i := i + 1$; $n := n + 1$.
   (b) If neither $\Gamma_n \vdash A_i$ nor $\Gamma_n \vdash \neg A_i$ is provable, then $\Gamma_{n+1} = \{A_i, \Gamma_n\}$, $\Theta_{n+1} := \Theta_n$ and $\Delta_{n+1} := \{A_i, \Delta_n\}$, and $i := i + 1$; $n := n + 1$.
   (c) If $\Gamma_n \vdash \neg A_i$ is provable, then do the following two steps consecutively:
      i. $\Gamma_{n+1} = \{\Lambda\}$ where $\Lambda \in \mathcal{A}(\Gamma_n, \neg A_i)$ and $\Delta_n \in \Lambda$. $\Delta_{n+1} := \Delta_n$; $\Theta_{n+1} := \Theta_n = \{C_1, ..., C_l\}$.

ii. Take $\Gamma_{n+2} = \{A_i, \Gamma_{n+1}\}$. Let $j = 2$. For $m = 1$ to l do the loop: If $\Gamma_{n+j} \vdash C_m$ is provable, then do nothing. If neither $\Gamma_{n+j} \vdash C_m$ nor $\Gamma_{n+j} \vdash \neg C_m$ is provable, then delete C_m from Θ_{n+j}; let $j := j + 1$ and for the C_m construct Γ_{n+j} using the method given in 2-(b).

To see why 2-(c)-ii is necessary, we suggest the reader to study the example: $\Gamma = \{A \wedge B\}$, and assume that A has met a rejection by facts.

Theorem 3.1 Let $\mathbf{M}_p$ be a model and Γ be a hypothesis. Every $\mathbf{M}_p$ epistemic process of Γ denoted by $\{\Gamma_n\}$ is convergent, and

$$Th(\lim_n \Gamma_n) = \mathcal{T}_{M_p}.$$

The procedure shows that when we deal with a rejection of A by facts at any step n, we can **arbitrarily** choose a maximal subset of Γ_n which is consistent with $\neg A$, and contains Δ_n (the set of new premises $A_k \in \mathcal{T}_{M_p}$ accepted in the 1st to n^{th} stage). Every such process has the same limit. Therefore, the unique maximal consistent subset required in [AGM 85] seems not necessary.

4 The extensions and limit of epistemic processes

For simplicity, let us consider the closed normal defaults only. A default theory is a pair $< \Gamma, \Delta >$, where Γ is a hypothesis and Δ is a sequence of closed normal defaults. A sentence B is called a consequent of Δ iff B is a consequent of a default contained in Δ.

Definition 4.1 Applicable default

For a given Γ, a closed normal default $\frac{A:MB}{B}$ is called an applicable default w.r.t Γ iff $\Gamma \vdash A$ is provable and $\Gamma \vdash \neg B$ is not provable.

The following theorem gives a key connection between two theories. It can also be seen as a semantics of applicable default:

Theorem 4.1 Given Γ, $\frac{A:MB}{B}$ is applicable w.r.t Γ iff $\Gamma \models A$, and either $\Gamma \models B$ or B is a new premise for Γ.

The basic idea of defining the epistemic processes for a default theory is: Take Γ as the starting point of the epistemic processes, i.e. $\Gamma = \Gamma_1$; and take Γ_{n+1} to be a reconstruction of Γ_n for a consequnt of Δ.

Definition 4.2 δ-epistemic processes

$\{\Gamma_n\}$ is an δ-epistemic process of the default theory $< \Gamma, \Delta >$ iff it is constructed by the following procedure:

Take $\Gamma_1 = \Gamma$. Let Δ_1 be a given order of all the defaults contained in Δ, and let Δ_n be a sequence of defaults.

Γ_{n+1} and Δ_{n+1} is constructed recursively as follows:
EX: loop: Check every default according to the order of their occurrences in Δ_n, and do the following:

1. If $\frac{A_{k_n}:MB_{k_n}}{B_{k_n}}$ is the first default such that $\Gamma_n \vdash A_{k_n}$ is provable, then delete it from Δ_n and do the following:
   (a) If $\Gamma_n \vdash B_{k_n}$ is provable, then go back to EX.
   (b) If neither $\Gamma_n \vdash B_{k_n}$ nor $\Gamma_n \vdash \neg B_{k_n}$ is provable, then take $\Gamma_{n+1} = \{B_{k_n}, \Gamma_n\}$, and $\Delta_{n+1} = \Delta_n$.
   (c) If $\Gamma_n \vdash \neg B_{k_n}$ is provable and
      i. if $\Gamma \vdash \neg B_{k_n}$ is not provable, then take $\Gamma_{n+1} = \{B_{k_n}, \Lambda\}$, where $\Lambda \in \mathcal{A}(\neg B_{k_n}, \Gamma_n)$, and $\Gamma \subseteq \Lambda$, and $\Delta_{n+1} = \Delta_n$.
      ii. if $\Gamma \vdash \neg B_{k_n}$ is also provable, then go to EX.
2. If such $\frac{A_{k_n}:MB_{k_n}}{B_{k_n}}$ does not exist, the construction of the process is finished.

$\{\Gamma_n\}$ is δ-partial increasing, if in definition 6.2, sub-item 1-(c) is replaced by the following sub-item:

(c') If $\Gamma_n \vdash \neg B_{k_n}$ is provable, then go to EX.

The relation between the extensions and δ-epistemic processes can be represented by the following two theorems:

Theorem 4.2 If $\{\Gamma_n\}$ is an δ-partial increase epistemic process of the default theory $T =< \Gamma, \Delta >$ iff $Th(\lim_n \Gamma_n)$ is an extension of the theory.

Theorem 4.3 The theory $< \Gamma, \Delta >$ has a non-monotonic δ-epistemic process iff it has two distinct extensions $< \Gamma, \Delta >$.

References

[AGM 85] Alchourrón, C.E., Gärdenfors, R. and Makinson, D., On the logic of theory change, The Journal of Symbolic Logic, Vol.50, No.2, June, 1985.
[Eins 15] Einstein, A., Relativity, the special & the general theory, Methuen, 1915.
[Gal 87] Gallier, J.H., Logic for Computer Science, John Wiley & Sons, 1987.
[Li 92-1] Li, W., Towards a theory of epistemic processes, Automated Reasoning, Elsevier Science Publishers B.V, IFIP 1992.
[Li 92-2] Li, W., An Open Logic System, Science in China, Series A, Vol.36, Oct, 1992 in Chinese, March, 1993, in English.
[Li 93] Li, W., A comparative study on default logic and open logic, *Journal of Computer Science and Technology*, July, 1993.
[Reit 80] Reiter, R., A Logic for Default Reasoning, *Artificial Intelligence*, Vol.13, 1980.

Iterated Belief Change: A Preliminary Report

Aditya K. Ghose[1] Pablo O. Hadjinian[1] Abdul Sattar[2] Jia-H. You[1]
Randy Goebel[1]
[1]Department of Computing Science
University of Alberta, Edmonton, Alberta, Canada T6G 2H1
[2]School of Comp. and Info. Technology
Griffith University, Nathan, Brisbane, QLD. 41111, Australia

Abstract

Most existing formalizations of belief change treat it as a single step process, and ignore several problems that become important when belief revision takes place over several steps. This paper identifies these problems, and argues for the need to retain all of the multiple possible outcomes of a belief change step, and for a framework in which the effects of a belief change step persist as long as is consistently possible.

1 Introduction

Belief change, the process through which a rational agent acquires new beliefs or retracts previously held ones, is a crucial component of intelligent behaviour. Alchourrón, Gärdenfors and Makinson have undertaken a systematic study of the dynamics of belief change, resulting in what is currently popularly known as the AGM framework for belief change [1], [4]. In the AGM framework, the belief state of an agent is represented by a deductively closed, consistent set of propositional sentences. Three kinds of belief change operations are defined: *expansion*, in which the new belief being added is guaranteed to be consistent with the existing body of beliefs; *contraction*, in which an existing belief is retracted; and *revision*, in which a new belief, which may possibly be inconsistent with existing beliefs, is added. They define a set of rationality postulates for each of these operations. We do not list them here for brevity. Briefly, these postulates require that beliefs be represented in the same formalism before and after a belief change step, that belief change steps succeed, that they be independent of the syntactic form of beliefs, that the process be reversible, and that changes made to the body of beliefs be minimized. The operations of revision can be defined in terms of contraction, as shown by the *Levi identity* (here, K^*_A,K^-_A and K^+_A denote, respectively, the revision, contraction and expansion of K with A): $K^*_A = (K^-_{\neg A})^+_A$. *Partial meet contraction* [1] is a representative AGM operator which satisfies all of the rationality postulates, and which appears to be more reasonable, compared to the other AGM operators, by virtue of not discarding too many beliefs and also by not forcing commitment to a truth value for every propositional letter.. Let the *removal* of x from A, denoted by $A \downarrow x$, be defined as: $A \downarrow x = \{B \subseteq A \mid B \not\vdash x, \forall C : B \subset C \subseteq A \Rightarrow C \vdash x\}$. Let S be a *selection function* that selects a nonempty subset of $K \downarrow x$ (provided $K \downarrow x$ is nonempty, $\emptyset$ otherwise). The partial meet contraction operator $-_p$ is defined as: $K^{-_p}_x = \bigcap S(K \downarrow \neg x)$ (the contraction step fails if x is logically valid). A contraction operator which uses a special class of total orderings (called *epistemic entrenchment*), defined on the entire language, to decide which beliefs to retain (and which may therefore be viewed as determining the outcome of applying the selection function S) is shown to satisfy all eight of the AGM postulates for contraction, and to be equivalent to partial meet contraction.

Nebel [9] discusses contraction operators on *belief bases* , which are finite sets of sentences instead of infinite deductively closed belief sets. The motivations for defining belief change on belief bases is twofold. First, operators defined on belief bases are computationally viable (they do not have to operate on infinite sets). Second, belief change operations on belief bases permit reason maintenance, while those on belief sets do not. The base contraction operator $\simeq$ defined as: $B \simeq x = (\bigvee_{C \in (B \downarrow x)} C) \wedge (B \vee \neg x)$ (again, the contraction step fails if x is logically valid), satisfies most, but not all, of the AGM postulates. Note that the term $(B \vee \neg x)$ ensures that the original belief base re-appears whenever x becomes true. The corresponding revision operator can be defined, as before, via the Levi identity.

We shall motivate our discussion of the dynamics of belief change by arguing for the need for the effects of a belief change step to *persist*. Belief change operators should satisfy the following *persistence postulate*:

> The effects of belief change persist until there is new evidence to indicate otherwise.

A contracted belief should not re-appear in a belief set unless there is new evidence accumulated since the contraction that requires this. Similarly, a newly added belief should remain in the belief set until new evidence obtained since the addition warrants its removal. We use the notion of *evidence* here to denote belief inputs that an agent obtains from the world, together with their prioritization relative to other beliefs. Thus, a newly added belief will be treated as sufficient evidence to contradict a previously added belief only if it brings the previously held belief into question, and has a higher priority than the previously held belief as well.

Example: Consider the AGM framework. Let the initial belief state be $K_0 = Cn\{b \rightarrow f\}$. After contracting f, let the outcome be $K_1 = Cn\{b \rightarrow f\}$ (since f is not a consequence of the beliefs in K_0, no change needs to be made to K_0). Revising K_1 with b results in the belief state $Cn\{b, b \rightarrow f\}$. Thus, the agent starts believing f again, although the new evidence obtained since f was contracted (i.e., the belief b) does not in itself require that f be believed again. Let b denote that Tweety is a bird and f denote that Tweety flies. Then, starting with a belief in an instance of the rule "birds fly", after retracting the belief that Tweety flies and then being told that Tweety is a bird, it seems reasonable to discard $b \rightarrow f$ in favour of more recent beliefs. We argue therefore that the final belief state should be $Cn\{b\}$.□

The problem stems from a very obvious source: the lack of an explicit record of every belief change step. While revision steps are usually implicitly recorded via the beliefs that they add, contraction steps are always forgotten. Thus, in the example above, the absence of a memory of the contraction step in which the belief in Tweety's flying ability was retracted, results in it playing no part in the subsequent revision step in which the belief that Tweety is a bird is added. Nebel's framework, as the example below shows, suffers from an identical problem.

Example: Consider Nebel's belief base revision [8]. Let $B_0 = \{a \rightarrow b\}$. $B_1 = B_0 \simeq b = \{a \rightarrow b, \neg b \vee B_0\}$, where we take B_0 to denote the conjunction of its elements. Revising B_1 with a gives $B_2 = \{a, a \rightarrow b, \neg b \vee B_0\}$. The contraction of b does not persist (and the spurious belief b appears in the deductive closure of B_2) due to the lack of an explicit record of belief change steps. □

Example: Consider, again, the AGM framework. Let $K = Cn\{a \rightarrow b\}$. $K' = K^*_{\neg b} = Cn\{\neg b, a \rightarrow b\}$. Let $S(K' \downarrow \neg a) = \{Cn\{a \rightarrow b, b \rightarrow a\}\}$. Then $K'' = K'^*_a = Cn\{a, a \rightarrow b, b \rightarrow a\}$. We lose the belief $\neg b$ (and the spurious belief b appears), although the more recent information (the belief a) does not require this. □

The problem here stems from contradictory belief prioritizations being used in the AGM framework. A basic premise in the AGM framework is that every belief change step must succeed. This implies that the new belief input be accorded a higher priority than all existing beliefs. However, the epistemic entrenchment ordering is not required to respect any recency-based criterion at all. In the example above, we implicitly accord $\neg b$ a higher priority than the belief $a \rightarrow b$ when we add it to the belief set. However, by returning $Cn\{a \rightarrow b, b \rightarrow a\}$ instead of $Cn\{\neg b\}$, the selection function S implicitly assigns $a \rightarrow b$ a higher priority than $\neg b$.

2 An Alternative Framework for Belief Revision

Our formalization of belief change is motivated by the following observations:

- A belief state is best represented as a collection of theories. Given that *minimal change* is a guiding principle in belief revision, it could be argued that instead of selecting some outcomes of the belief change and discarding the others (thus losing potentially useful beliefs), all outcomes should be retained, provided that there exists a compact and elegant way of representing these multiple possible outcomes. Such representation languages exist; nonmonotonic formalisms are immediate candidates for compactly representing the possibly inconsistent and incomplete picture of the world that each belief state corresponds to. The observation that real-life agents typically have incomplete (and sometimes inconsistent) knowledge about the world is independent justification for choosing such an approach.
- The persistence postulate suggests that an explicit record of belief change steps be maintained. We achieve this by propagating a set of *belief constraints* (these may be of two kinds: constraints specifying beliefs that must necessarily be held, and constraints specifying beliefs that must necessarily not be held) which may be viewed as the integrity constraints of a belief system; every theory constituting a belief state must respect them.
- Beliefs originally held to be true can become tentative as a result of belief change if they are contradicted or brought into question (the intuition is that a belief becomes questionable if it is not in every possible outcome of the belief change step) by the new evidence. In syntactically-oriented nonmonotonic formalisms, this can be viewed as a process of demotion from a fact to a default.

We shall demonstrate that a formalization that satisfies most of the common-sense requirements for belief change, as given by the AGM postulates as well as by the persistence postulate identified in the previous section, is indeed possible. To prove our point, we shall use the language of PJ-default logic [3] to represent a belief state. PJ-default logic is a variant of default logic in which default rules are restricted to be prerequisite-free and semi-normal (i.e., a PJ-default rule is of the form $\frac{:\beta}{\gamma}$ such that $\beta \models \gamma$). PJ-default logic addresses several classes of problems with Reiter's default logic , including cases where default logic is too weak, preventing the derivation of "reasonable " conclusions (the disjunctive default problem, for instance), and cases where default logic is too strong, permitting the derivation of unwanted conclusions. Additionally, PJ-default logic has several attractive properties, such as the guaranteed existence of extensions. For brevity, we do not define PJ-default extensions here, but refer the reader to [3]. Ghose and Goebel [5] have earlier defined a belief change framework in which a belief state is represented as a potentially inconsistent set of sentences, together with a partial order on these sentences. An operator is defined that identifies consistent subsets of this set of sentences, that respect the partial order as well as some set of disbelief constraints. A translation from PJ-default theories to this framework is defined such that the process of identifying PJ-default extensions is shown to be equivalent to the process of identifying consistent subsets of sentences using the operator mentioned above, with a partial order which assigns higher priority to sentences obtained from W (given a PJ-default theory (W, D)) than sentences obtained from D and with the set of disbelief constraints consisting of the conjunction of the negations of the justifications of each PJ-default rule.

Our choice of PJ-default theories to represent belief states has the additional advantage that belief constraints do not need to be represented separately but can be incorporated as part of a PJ-default theory. The set of facts W of a PJ-default theory corresponds to the beliefs that the agent is constrained to necessarily hold, since W will be contained in every consistent belief set corresponding to that belief state (i.e., every PJ-extension). Since every PJ-default rule is of the form $\frac{:\beta\wedge\gamma}{\beta}$, $\neg\gamma$ corresponds to the theory that the agent is constrained to necessarily disbelieve. The process of demoting a belief that has been contradicted, or made questionable, as a result of a belief change step to the status of a tentative belief involves removing a formula from W and adding a new PJ-default rule containing this formula as its consequent to D. Discredited beliefs are thus never totally discarded in our framework in anticipation of future situations in which these beliefs could be consistently held again. Belief change in our framework thus involves mapping one PJ-default theory to another. The possible consistent belief sets that may be held in a given belief state corresponds to the extensions of the PJ-default theory representing that belief state.

Formally, we define a *belief state* to be a set of theories $\{Th_1, Th_2, \ldots\}$. The *necessary belief set* BC_{belief}, for a given belief state, is a set of sentences such that, for every $x \in BC_{belief}$ and for all Th_i in that state, $Th_i \models x$. The *necessary disbelief set* $BC_{disbelief}$, for a given belief state, is a set of sentences such that, for every $\neg x \in BC_{disbelief}$ and for all Th_i in that state, $Th_i \not\models x$. Notice that $BC_{disbelief}$ contains the *negations* of beliefs that may not be held. We define the *belief constraint set* $BC = BC_{belief} \cup BC_{disbelief}$. We shall see later that updating the belief constraint set requires identifying maximal parts of a constraint that is consistent with some others. We therefore require a set-theoretic representation of each constraint such that each conjunct in a constraint is clearly identifiable as a set element. Representing belief constraints in clausal form satisfies these requirements. To be able to distinguish between the elements of BC_{belief} and $BC_{disbelief}$, we adopt a syntactic convention such that every disbelief constraint x is written as $-x$. Belief change will be viewed as the process of adding a new belief constraint (in the case of revision, a necessary belief constraint, and in the case of contraction, a necessary disbelief constraint).

We require that the belief constraint set be totally ordered; we shall refer to this total order $\prec$ as the *constraint prioritization.* This is similar to the orderings used in a variety of belief change frameworks, including the AGM epistemic entrenchment ordering, but there are significant differences. Whereas epistemic entrenchment requires that all beliefs be prioritized, we require that only the current set of belief constraints be prioritized. The size of the belief constraint set can typically be expected to be much smaller than the size of the theories constituting a belief state. As well, the size of the belief constraint set does not grow with time and may shrink as belief constraints are discarded (as a result, for example, of newer constraints contradicting them). This also represents a more principled approach to prioritizing beliefs, since it does not suffer from the contradictions in belief prioritization in the AGM framework pointed out in the previous section. Notice also, that, unlike AGM epistemic entrenchment, this ordering does not uniquely determine which subset of the possible outcomes is finally selected. It only determines what the new set of belief constraints should be. Several obvious heuristics suggest themselves as candidate constraint prioritization policies in the absence of any other information on the relative reliability of the belief constraints. In the case of *revision* (in the sense of Katsuno and Mendelzon [7]), a constraint prioritization base on the recency of the belief inputs appears to be appropriate. In the case of *update* [7], one might choose to accord the highest priority to physical laws at all times, since these are never questioned or discarded.

The process of belief change involves two steps. First, the belief constraint set is updated. Based on the updated belief constraint set, the PJ-default theory representing the previous belief state is modified.

Definition 1 *A belief constraint Ω is said to be* **compatible** *with a set of belief constraints BC (we write $\Omega \cup BC$ is compatible) if and only if the following conditions hold:*

1. *For every x_i such that $x_i \in BC_{belief}$, $\bigwedge_i x_i \not\models \neg\Omega$.*

2. *For every x_i such that $x_i \in BC_{disbelief}$, $\bigwedge_i \neg x_i \not\models \neg\Omega$.*

We must be able to identify subsets of an individual belief constraint (viewing each constraint as a set of clauses) that are compatible with a set of belief constraints. The operator $\uparrow$ that identifies such subsets is defined below.

Definition 2 *Let bc be a belief constraint and BC be a set of belief constraints. Then*

$$bc \uparrow BC = \{x \subseteq bc \mid \ (x \cup BC \text{ is compatible}) \wedge (\forall x' \text{ such that } x \subset x' \subseteq bc \text{ and } x' \cup BC \text{ is incompatible}\}$$

Updating the set of belief constraints involves taking the new constraint and adding as many of the previous constraints (or parts of previous constraints) as can be compatibly added, starting with the most recent constraint and working backwards to the earlier ones. We shall assume the following notational convention for referring to individual belief constraints: $\forall bc_i \in BC, bc_j \succ bc_k \leftrightarrow k < j$. In other words, a more recent constraint will have a smaller subscript. In the following, we also assume that Θ represents the new belief constraint.

$$\begin{aligned} BC_{new} = \Theta \cup \{Y \subseteq BC_{old} \mid \ & Y = \textstyle\bigcup_{i\geq 1} Y_i, \\ & \forall i \geq 1(((Y_i = \{bc_i\}) \wedge (bc_i \cup \Theta \cup (\textstyle\bigcup_{j=1}^{i-1} Y_j) \text{ is compatible})) \\ & \vee((Y_i = \textstyle\bigcap(bc_i \uparrow (\bigcup_{j=1}^{i-1} Y_j \cup \Theta)) \wedge (bc_i \cup \Theta \cup (\bigcup_{j=1}^{i-1} Y_j) \text{ is incompatible})))\} \end{aligned}$$

The new PJ-default theory (W',D') is obtained from the previous belief state (W, D) and the new belief constraint set BC_{new} as follows:

$$\begin{aligned} W' &= BC_{Belief_{new}} \\ D' &= \{\frac{:\delta_i \wedge (\bigwedge \gamma_j)}{\delta_i} \mid \delta_i \in (W - W') \ and \ \gamma_j \in BC_{Disbelief_{new}}\} \cup \\ & \{\frac{:\beta_i \wedge (\bigwedge \gamma_j)}{\beta_i} \mid \frac{:\beta_i \wedge \phi_i}{\beta_i} \in D \ and \ \gamma_j \in BC_{Disbelief_{new}}\} \end{aligned}$$

Notice that every $d \in D'$ is of the form $\frac{:\beta_i \wedge \Gamma}{\beta_i}$. The Γ in every PJ-default rule (the "semi-normal" part of the rule) represents the necessary disbelief constraints. The necessary belief constraints are contained in W'. Elements of W which are no longer necessary beliefs are demoted the status of tentative beliefs. A necessary disbelief constraint that is not retained in the updated set of constraints is discarded entirely. However, a necessary belief constraint that is removed from the set of belief constraints is still retained in the theory as a default rule. We require that the dummy default rule $\frac{:\top}{\top}$ be an element of D for every (W, D) representing a belief state. This is to enable us to record necessary disbelief constraints even if there are no tentative beliefs. By representing each belief state as a Γ-PJ-default theory, we have factored out the question of which theory (extension) to choose as the currently operative set of beliefs from the process of belief change. The user, or agent, could thus employ a variety of techniques to actually pick the currently operative set of beliefs. Besides the traditional operations of expansion, revision and contraction, our framework permits the "undoing" of a contraction step; it simply involves the removal of the relevant necessary disbelief constraint.

Revision and contraction in our framework satisfy the relevant sets of AGM rationality postulates, reformulated to reflect the change in the belief representation formalism. The requirement for minimal change, encoded in the so-called *supplementary postulates* are satisfied in a stronger sense. A reformulated version of the Levi identity is satisfied and a formal guarantee that the problem of non-persistent beliefs never appears is obtained. For the formal results and proofs, we refer the reader to the extended version of this paper [6]. Over a single step, our framework behaves in a fashion very similar to those of AGM and Nebel (we refer the reader to the extended version of this paper [6] for the formal results). Over iterated steps, we satisfy the persistence postulate while the AGM and Nebel frameworks do not. As well, we do not discard any beliefs and are able to satisfy the requirement for minimal change in a stronger sense. Brewka's belief change framework based on the *preferred subtheories framework* [2] (which is turn based on THEORIST [10]), is similar to ours but fails to satisfy the persistence postulate. For a detailed discussion of related work, we refer the reader to the extended version of the paper [6].

3 Conclusion

This paper identifies some requirements that belief change operators should satisfy when applied in an iterative fashion, and uses these requirements to motivate a new framework. A threefold categorization of belief in a belief state is introduced: ***necessary beliefs***, ***necessary disbeliefs*** and ***tentative beliefs***. A precise characterization of belief migration across these classes is provided. The problem of non-persistent beliefs is identified, and is used to motivate the need both for maintaining multiple theories in the same belief state, as well as for propagating belief constraints. One compact representation is obtained for the multiple possible outcomes of a belief change operation. By using PJ-default logic to represent a belief state, we are able to obviate the need for recording belief constraints separately; the constraints are clearly identifiable components of a PJ-default theory. Our framework can be viewed as a formalization of the process through which a default theory evolves into a more accurate representation of the world. Belief change drives this process, and in abstract terms, this involves demoting facts known to be true to the status of defaults. By showing how a nonmonotonic formalism such as default logic can be crucial to knowledge revision, this study further explicates the close relationship between these related, yet separate, areas of inquiry.

Acknowledgements: This work has been supported by the Natural Sciences and Engineering Research Council of Canada, and by the Canadian Federal Networks of Centres of Excellence Institute for Robotics and Intelligent Systems.

References

[1] Carlos E. Alchourrón, Peter Gärdenfors, and David Makinson. On the logic of theory change: partial meet contraction and revision functions. *Journal of Symbolic Logic*, 50:510–530, 1985.

[2] Gerhard Brewka. Belief revision in a framework for default reasoning. In *Proc. of the Konstanz Workshop on Belief Revision*, pages 206–222, 1989.

[3] J. P. Delgrande and W. K. Jackson. Default logic revisited. In *Proc. of the Second International Conference on the Principles of Knowledge Representation and Reasoning*, pages 118–127, 1991.

[4] Peter Gärdenfors. *Knowledge in Flux: Modeling the Dynamics of Epistemic States*. MIT Press, Cambridge, MA, 1988.

[5] Aditya K. Ghose and Randy Goebel. Default reasoning as belief change: A rationale. In *Proc. of the 2nd Pacific Rim Int'l Conf. on AI*, 1992.

[6] Aditya K. Ghose, Pablo O. Hadjinian, Abdul Sattar, Jia-H. You, and Randy Goebel. Iterated belief change. Technical Report TR93-05, University of Alberta, Dept. of Computing Science, 1993. Also published as Griffith University, School of Computing and Information Technology Research Report No. 62.

[7] Hirofumi Katsuno and Alberto O. Mendelzon. On the difference between updating a knowledge base and revising it. In *Proc. of the Second Int'l Conf. on Principles of Knowledge Representation and Reasoning*, 1991.

[8] Bernhard Nebel. A knowledge level analysis of belief revision. In *Proc. of the First International Conference on Principles of Knowledge Representation and Reasoning*, pages 301–311, 1989.

[9] Bernhard Nebel. Belief revision and default reasoning: Syntax-based approaches. In *Proc. of the Second International Conference on Principles of Knowledge Representation and Reasoning*, pages 417–428, 1991.

[10] David Poole, Randy Goebel, and Romas Aleliunas. Theorist: a logical reasoning system for defaults and diagnosis. In N.J. Cercone and G. McCalla, editors, *The Knowledge Frontier: Essays in the Representation of Knowledge*, pages 331–352. Springer Verlag, 1987.

On Computing Preferred Explanations

Scott D. Goodwin*
Department of Computer Science
University of Regina, Regina
Saskatchewan, Canada, S4S 0A2
goodwin@cs.URegina.ca

Abdul Sattar
School of Comp. & Info. Technology
Griffith University, Brsibane
Australia, 4111
sattar@kurango.cit.gu.edu.au

Abstract

In this paper, we extend a simple hypothetical reasoning framework, THEORIST, with a meta-level for describing *theory viability* and *theory preference* knowledge. We define a very useful yet fairly unrestrictive property—*monotonicity*—that, if satisfied by theory viability and preference criteria, allows *incremental* computation of preferred theories. Two theorems indicate that applying monotonic criteria to partial theories provides useful information about complete theories. The consequence is that decisions can be safely made about whether to proceed with a partially constructed proof. Based on these results, we implement an incremental nonmonotonic theorem prover. The bottleneck in this implementation is consistency checking. To address this, we augment the system with a table of potential crucial literals which is incrementally constructed during consistency checking. The table can be used for many purposes, but here we examine its use in reducing consistency checking by recording consistent ("good") and inconsistent ("nogood") theories.

KEYWORDS: Hypothetical Reasoning, Theory Preference, Consistency Checking.

1 Introduction

Comparing and choosing among competing theories in a hypothetical reasoning system involves two kinds of knowledge: *viability* $\mathcal{V}$ and *preference* $\mathcal{P}$. Theory viability knowledge is the criteria used to determine whether a theory is acceptable or appropriate. Viability knowledge is often application dependent. For some purposes, theories whose probability exceeds a given threshold may be deemed viable. Constraints may be expressed as viability knowledge, e.g., lengths, mass, and volume must be positive, causality is forward-directed, only women can be pregnant, etc. Viability may also be domain independent, e.g., consistency, nonredundancy, specificity, and simplicity are domain independent viability criteria.

These last two criteria, specificity and simplicity, are measures relative to other theories. Such criteria may be considered viability or preference knowledge. Theory preference knowledge is the criteria used to rank viable theories (for some purposes we may wish to extend the ranking to nonviable theories, ranking these below the viable ones.). In summary, viability knowledge is any criteria that indicates when a theory may be considered, while preference knowledge is any criteria that indicates when one theory is more worthy of consideration than another. The notions of viability and preference are, of course, nothing new. They have appeared in various guises in many places ([5, 3] to name just a few.).

In this paper, we extend and implement a simple hypothetical reasoning framework, THEORIST [8], with a meta-level for describing *theory viability* and *theory preference* knowledge. The bottleneck in this implementation is consistency checking, that has been addressed by augmenting it with *consistency trees* [11]. We provide some indication of the power of this system by examining its performance on a circuit diagnosis problem. Note that many details such as proofs of theorems have been left out due to the size constraint, which will appear in the extended version of this paper.

2 META-THEORIST

The THEORIST framework views reasoning as building theories that logically imply a set of observations. Statements of the underlying representation language, first order clausal logic,

*The first author was supported by the Institute for Robotics and Intelligent Systems (IRIS) and NSERC grant OGP0122131.

are divided into two types: *facts* F and *possible hypotheses* $\mathcal{H}$. Facts are statements that we accept as true and thus constitute ordinary assertions in a logical theory. Possible hypotheses, however, are given a different epistemological status than facts. They are used as a kind of schema for axioms—possible hypotheses can be viewed as the specification for the generation of logical theories which are extensions of the facts. Instances drawn from the set of possible hypotheses can be used to construct explanations for a set of observations.[1] If the user designates a sentence schema as a possible hypothesis, the user is licencing THEORIST to use ground instances of that sentence schema in forming explanations, provided these are consistent with the facts and other assumptions.

Definition 1 (EXPLANATION) T explains G if $\forall t \in T$, t is an instance of hypothesis from $\mathcal{H}$, such that $F \cup T \models G$, and $F \cup T$ is consistent.

Theorem 2 (EXPLANATION PROOFS [6, P. 34]) If F is consistent and $T = \{t_1, \ldots, t_n\}$ is a set of ground instances of elements of $\mathcal{H}$ then $F \cup T$ is an explanation of g iff there is a ground proof of g from $F \cup T$ such that $F \cup \{t_1, \ldots, t_{i-1}\} \not\vdash \neg t_i$ for all $i = 1 \ldots n$.

This theorem allows a procedure for *incremental consistency checking*[2], i.e., consistency can be checked as each new hypothesis instance is added to the current theory.

META-THEORIST extends THEORIST with a meta-level $\mathcal{M}$ to express theory viability and preference knowledge. The user's interaction with META-THEORIST is essentially the same as with THEORIST. The main difference is that the user can specify meta-level statements which can be used to specify theory viability and preference criteria. Additionally, we might have a system designer/knowledge engineer who provides the user with a pre-packaged set of viability/preference criteria for particular domains. For instance in [4], we envision defaults to be a kind of hypothesis with an associated viability criteria provided by the system designer.

For our purposes, the theory viability criteria $\mathcal{V}$ may be any specifiable property with the restriction that only consistent theories are viable; as well, we restrict the theory preference criteria $\mathcal{P}$ to be a partial order $\geq^{\mathcal{P}}$ on sets of assumptions. We indicate that T is a viable theory by $\mathcal{V}(T)$, and that T is a maximally preferred theory by $\mathcal{P}(T)$. Further, we use $\mathcal{P}_G(T)$ to indicate T is a maximally preferred theory among all the theories T_G such that $F \cup T_G \models G$.

When we speak of explanation in the context of THEORIST, we refer to *consistent* explanation; but in the context of META-THEORIST, we refer to *viable* explanation as defined below.

Definition 3 (VIABLE EXPLANATION)
$F \cup T$ is a viable explanation of G if $\forall t \in T$, t is an instance of hypothesis from $\mathcal{H}$, such that $F \cup T \models G$, and $\mathcal{M} \models \mathcal{V}(T)$ (which implies that $F \cup T$ is consistent).

Definition 4 (PREFERRED VIABLE EXPLANATION FROM $F \cup \mathcal{H}$)
If g is a closed formula then a *preferred viable explanation* of g from $F \cup \mathcal{H}$ is a viable explanation $F \cup T$ of g from $F \cup \mathcal{H}$ such that $\mathcal{P}_g(T)$.

The starting point for the definition of a procedure for generating explanations in META-THEORIST is Theorem 2 (Explanation Proofs). Examination of this theorem reveals that incremental consistency checking relies on the monotonic nature of inconsistency, i.e., if a theory is inconsistent then so is any theory containing it. As Theorem 6 shows, META-THEORIST's (viable) explanation procedure can be implemented by replacing the incremental consistency checking with incremental theory viability provided the criterion is monotonic as defined below.

Definition 5 (MONOTONIC VIABILITY CRITERION)
A viability criterion $\mathcal{V}$ is *monotonic* iff for all theories T_1 and T_2 we have

$$T_1 \subseteq T_2 \ \& \ \neg\mathcal{V}(T_1) \ \rightarrow \ \neg\mathcal{V}(T_2).$$

Consistency, nonredundancy, subset minimality, and simplicity are monotonic viability criteria.

Theorem 6 (INCREMENTAL THEORY VIABILITY)
If $\mathcal{V}$ is a monotonic viability criterion and if $T = \{t_1, \ldots, t_n\}$ is a set of ground instances of elements of $\mathcal{H}$ then $F \cup T$ is a (viable) explanation of g iff there is a ground proof of g from $F \cup T$ such that $\mathcal{V}(\{t_1, \ldots, t_i\})$ for all $i \in (1, \ldots, n)$.

[1] The formation of instances of possible hypotheses depends on the underlying universe of discourse U. Most implementations of THEORIST take U to be the Herbrand universe of $F \cup \mathcal{H} \cup G$ (as instantiation in Prolog implementations amounts to binding variables through unification), though the introduction of Skolem functions may enlarge U [1].

[2] The procedure is, of course, not even semi-decidable in general.

```
prove(Goal,Ancestors,InTheory,[Goal|InTheory]) :-
    hypothesis(Goal),
    not( member(PreviousHypothesis,InTheory),
         Goal == PreviousHypothesis ),
    viable([Goal|InTheory]).
```

Figure 1: Explain with Incremental Viability

```
prove(Goal,Ancestors,InTheory,[Goal|InTheory]) :-
    hypothesis(Goal),
    not( member(PreviousHypothesis,InTheory),
         Goal == PreviousHypothesis ),
    preferred([Goal|InTheory]),
    viable([Goal|InTheory]).

preferred([Goal|InTheory]) :-
    currentBest(CurrentBest),
    not( member(SomeTheory,CurrentBest),
         strictly_prefer(SomeTheory,[Goal|InTheory]) ).
```

Figure 2: Explain with Incremental Viability and Preference

Based on this theorem, we can modify the implementation of explanation in THEORIST by replacing the incremental consistency check in **prove**[3] with an incremental theory viability check as indicated in Figure 1. This is *sound* in the sense that all resulting explanations are viable because viability is checked each time an assumption is introduced (in particular, the last check is of the complete theory). It is also *complete* in the sense that no viable explanations are lost when a non-viable partially constructed theory is abandoned because all theories containing a non-viable subtheory are non-viable by Theorem 6.

A similar result holds for incremental theory preference.

Definition 7 (MONOTONIC PREFERENCE CRITERION) A preference criterion $\mathcal{P}$ (which induces the partial order $\geq^{\mathcal{P}}$ on the viable theories determined by the viability criterion $\mathcal{V}$) is *monotonic* iff for all viable theories T_1 and T_2 we have $T_1 \subseteq T_2 \rightarrow T_1 \geq^{\mathcal{P}} T_2$.

Note that subset preference (i.e., when $\geq^{\mathcal{P}}$ is $\subseteq$) underlies all monotonic preference criteria.

Theorem 8 (INCREMENTAL THEORY PREFERENCE)
If $\mathcal{P}$ is a monotonic preference criterion and if $T = \{t_1, \ldots, t_n\}$ is a set of ground instances of elements of $\mathcal{H}$ then $F \cup T$ is a preferred explanation of g iff there is a ground proof of g from $F \cup T$ such that there is no explanation $F \cup T'$ of g where $T' >^{\mathcal{P}} \{t_1, \ldots, t_i\}$ for any $i \in (1, \ldots, n)$.

As with the viability criterion, we can implement incremental theory preference if the preference criterion is monotonic, but there is an important difference. In the case of viability, Theorem 6 indicates that the ground proof said to exist has the property that, at every stage of partial completion, the associated partial theory is viable. The condition refers only to the partial theories involved. In the case of preference, however, the condition in Theorem 8 involves, not only the partial theories, but all other theories—no other theory is strictly preferred over the partial theories. Having to check the partial theories against all other theories defeats the purpose of incremental computation—we might as well generate all explanations and then select the best theories.

Nevertheless, we can still make use of this result. In Figure 2, we again modify the highlighted part of **prove**. The predicate **preferred** ensures that there is no member of a *predesignated* set of theories **CurrentBest** that is strictly preferred over the partial theory. The result is that the explanation procedure will now generate only theories that are at least as preferred as the ones designated by the predicate **currentBest**.

We can now take this procedure and embed it in a depth-first iterative deepening search procedure (or even in a simple branch and bound search procedure). Each time the procedure produces

[3] See a complete Prolog program for **explain** in the extended version of this paper.

an explanation, the `CurrentBest` list is revised (some theories may be dropped). Upon termination, `CurrentBest` contains all of the maximally preferred viable theories.

As an example of the utility of this procedure, consider the following:

$F = \{ \bar{f} \,\&\, g \,\&\, h \rightarrow k,\ a \,\&\, b \rightarrow k,\ a \rightarrow f,\ b \,\&\, c \rightarrow g,\ l_n,\ l_n \rightarrow l_{n-1}, \ldots, l_2 \rightarrow l_1,\ l_1 \rightarrow h \}$

$\mathcal{H} = \{ a, b, c \}$

Suppose we take the viability criterion to be consistency and the preference criterion to be subset preference. There are two viable theories explaining *k*: $T_1 = \{ a, b, c \}$ and $T_2 = \{ a, b \}$. Theory T_2 is strictly preferred over theory T_1 because it is a proper subset. Note that computing all viable theories involves the arbitrarily expensive proof of *h*. This means that finding all preferred viable theories by first finding all viable theories is arbitrarily expensive.

Our procedure, however, finds the best theory in two iterations while visiting only 12 nodes (4 at depth 1 and 8 at depth 2). After the first iteration, a proof of *k* from the theory T_2 is found and it becomes the current best theory. On the second iteration, we encounter *c* in the sub-proof of *g* having previously assumed *a* and *b*. At this point, the sub-proof of *g* is abandoned because the current best theory is strictly preferred to the partial theory { a, b, c }. Since there were no branches cutoff by depth considerations during this iteration, the procedure halts with the current best theory T_2.

fact node(1,off) & node(2,off) & node(3,off).
fact ¬node(N,on) ← node(N,off).
fact ¬ok(G) ← faulty(G).
fact opp(on,off) & opp(off,on).
fact and(off,off,off) & and(on,off,off) & and(off,on,off) & and(on,on,on).
fact or(off,off,off) & or(on,off,on) & or(off,on,on) & or(on,on,on).
fact xor(off,off,off) & xor(on,off,on) & xor(off,on,on) & xor(on,on,off).
fact node(8,H) ← node(5,E) & node(6,F) & or(F,E,H) & ok(o1).
fact node(8,H) ← node(5,E) & node(6,F) & or(F,E,NH)
  & opp(H,NH) & faulty(o1).
fact node(7,G) ← node(4,D) & node(3,C) & xor(D,C,G) & ok(x2).
fact node(7,G) ← node(4,D) & node(3,C) & xor(D,C,NG)
  & opp(G,NG) & faulty(x2).
fact node(6,F) ← node(3,C) & node(4,D) & and(C,D,F) & ok(a2).
fact node(6,F) ← node(3,C) & node(4,D) & and(C,D,NF)
  & opp(F,NF) & faulty(a2).
fact node(5,E) ← node(1,A) & node(2,B) & and(A,B,E) & ok(a1).
fact node(5,E) ← node(1,A) & node(2,B) & and(A,B,NE)
  & opp(E,NE) & faulty(a1).
fact node(4,D) ← node(1,A) & node(2,B) & xor(A,B,D) & ok(x1).
fact node(4,D) ← node(1,A) & node(2,B) & xor(A,B,ND)
  & opp(D,ND) & faulty(x1).
hypothesis ok(G).
hypothesis faulty(G).

Figure 3: Circuit Diagnosis Knowledge Base

A more practical example is the circuit diagnosis problem for a binary full adder used by Genesereth [2] (see also [9, 7, 10]). Here we wish to determine the possible faulty gates given the inputs and observed outputs. The knowledge base for the problem (with all inputs off) is given in Figure 3.

Suppose we observe *node(8,off)* and *node(7,on)*. There are eight theories (or possible diagnoses) that explain the observations (Figure 4). Now suppose that we prefer diagnoses based on ***subset minimality***. Since all theories are of the same size, all eight theories are equally preferred. Next suppose that, subject to the subset preference, we have a further preference based on ***minimum fault cardinality***. This means that theories T_1 and T_2 are preferred. Finally, suppose that, subject to subset preference and minimum fault preference, we have a further preference based on ***gate reliability***. Let's say that due to the manufacturing process, gate *x2* tends to be the least reliable gate and so, other things being equal, we prefer a diagnosis which suggests gate *x2* is faulty over a diagnosis which blames some other gate. Therefore, of all the possible diagnoses, theory T_1 is the most preferred.

T_1 = {faulty(x2),ok(o1),ok(a2),ok(x1),ok(a1)}
T_2 = {ok(x2),ok(o1),ok(a2),faulty(x1),ok(a1)}
T_3 = {faulty(x2),faulty(o1),faulty(a2),ok(x1),ok(a1)}
T_4 = {ok(x2),faulty(o1),faulty(a2),faulty(x1),ok(a1)}
T_5 = {faulty(x2),faulty(o1),ok(a2),ok(x1),faulty(a1)}
T_6 = {ok(x2),faulty(o1),ok(a2),faulty(x1),faulty(a1)}
T_7 = {faulty(x2),faulty(o1),faulty(a2),ok(x1),faulty(a1)}
T_8 = {ok(x2),faulty(o1),faulty(a2),faulty(x1),faulty(a1)}

Figure 4: Eight Possible Diagnoses

Table 1 shows the results of comparing three methods of computing preferred explanations: generate all theories and then select the best (GSTP), iterative deepening theory preference (IDTP), and branch and bound theory preference (BBTP). Here IDTP and BBTP significantly out perform GSTP. For all these examples, BBTP outperforms IDTP and GSTP; however, in the pathological example given earlier, IDTP outperforms BBTP. In general, BBTP searches at most as many nodes as GSTP and BBTP does well if reasonable solutions lie in the left side of the search space and IDTP does well if reasonable solutions are shallow in the search space.

	GSTP	IDTP	BBTP	GSTP	IDTP	BBTP
	node(7,on) & node(8,off)			node(8,off) & node(7,on)		
proof nodes	331	310	192	401	152	108
consistency nodes	3836	2106	1250	4236	952	688
total nodes	4167	2416	1442	4637	1104	796
cpu time (secs.)	5.4	3.3	2.0	6.1	1.6	1.1
	node(7,off) & node(8,on)			node(8,on) & node(7,off)		
proof nodes	331	296	178	401	284	240
consistency nodes	3828	2462	1606	4228	2358	2094
total nodes	4159	2758	1784	4629	2642	2334
cpu time (secs.)	5.3	3.7	2.4	6.2	3.7	3.3
	node(7,on) & node(8,on)			node(8,on) & node(7,on)		
proof nodes	331	441	323	401	284	240
consistency nodes	3828	3938	3082	4228	2366	2102
total nodes	4159	4379	3405	4629	2650	2342
cpu time (secs.)	5.3	5.9	4.6	6.2	3.7	3.3

Table 1: Results

The incremental viability and preference theorems only guarantee the correctness of the given implementations when the viability and preference criteria are monotonic. Many interesting criteria are monotonic. In addition to consistency and subset preference, ***simplicity*** is a monotonic criteria. A theory T_1 is simpler than T_2 if $F \cup T_2 \models T_1$. As well, the single fault assumption, typically employed in diagnosis domains, is a monotonic criteria.

3 An incremental extension based on consistency trees

The implementation of *incremental consistency checking* attempts to establish the consistency of a hypothesis instance by failing to find a proof for its negation using facts and hypothesis instances already shown to be consistent. We extend this mechanism to consider new instances of hypotheses which may enable us to identify combinations of inconsistent hypothesis instances.

In the definition below, T refers to a "theory" or working set of hypothesis instances not necessarily established as an explanation. T' is a set of instances of hypotheses not including the elements of T. The extended proof tree is referred to as a *consistency tree* [11]:

Definition 9 (CONSISTENCY TREE)
Suppose g is an observation, F is a set of facts, T is a set of instances of possible hypotheses shown

Potential Crucial Literal	*inset*	*outset*
a	$\{\}$	$\{h1, h2\}$
b	$\{h2\}$	$\{h1\}$

Table 2: $Table_{pcl}$

to be consistent and t is an instance of hypothesis such that $F \cup T \cup t \vdash g$. The *consistency tree* for t is a *success subtree* of the AND/OR tree for $F \cup T \cup T' \cup \{\neg t\}$, where T' is a set of instances of possible hypotheses such that $T \cap T' = \phi$, and is defined as follows:

- $\neg t$, is a goal which is the root.
- Each node of a tree is a conjunction of possibly empty subgoals.
- If $\leftarrow A_1, .., A_i, ..., A_n$ is a goal and a literal A_i is selected by some computation rule, then for each input fact $A \leftarrow B_1, ..., B_k$ such that A is unifiable with A_i, the successor is

$$\leftarrow (A_1, ..., A_{i-1}, B_1, .., B_k, A_{i+1}, ..., A_n)\theta$$

  where θ is a *most general unifier* of A_i and A.
- If A is a unit goal and $\neg A$ is an ancestor of A, then A has no descendant (by *reductio ad absurdum*).
- If A is a unit goal and $A \in T$ or $A \in T'$, then A has no descendant.
- Nodes which are empty goals have no descendants.

Let us consider a simple example to illustrate the consistency tree and the information that can be derived from it.

$$F = \{g \leftarrow a \,\&\, \neg b,\ a,\ \neg a \leftarrow b \,\&\, h1,\ b \leftarrow h2\} \text{ and } \mathcal{H} = \{h1, h2\}.$$

To explain an observation g, the theorem prover has to prove the two subgoals a and $\neg b$. If $\neg b$ is selected first, then it would require an hypothesis instance $h1$. Before using $h1$ in the proof tree, the nonmonotonic theorem prover has to establish the unprovability of $\neg h1$. The consistency tree is then formed by extending the failure subtree according to Def.9.

The information gathered from each consistency tree is defined in the following terms [11]:

Definition 10 (NOGOOD)
Suppose t_i is an hypothesis instance ($t_i \in H$), F is a set of facts, and $T \subseteq H$. If there is a consistency tree for t_i such that $F \cup T \vdash \neg t_i$, then $T \cup \{t_i\}$ is a **nogood**.

For example, $\{h1, h2\}$ is a nogood in Table 2. Nogoods are maintained as sets minimal w.r.t. set inclusion.

Definition 11 (POTENTIAL CRUCIAL LITERAL)
An internal node n_i in a consistency tree (CT) is a potential crucial literal (PCL) if there is no literal, say l_i, in the subtree rooted at n_i such that $\neg l_i$ is an ancestor of n_i.

Definition 12 (INSET)
Let T be the set of hypothesis instances in a consistency tree $tree(\neg h_i)$, i.e., $F \cup T \vdash \neg h_i$. Let *pcl* be a potential crucial literal in the tree $tree(\neg h_i)$. The set T' of hypothesis instances contained in the subtree rooted at *pcl* is called an inset w.r.t. *pcl*.

Definition 13 (OUTSET)
Let T be the set of hypothesis instances in a consistency tree $tree(\neg h_i)$, i.e., $F \cup T \vdash \neg h_i$. Let *pcl* be a potential crucial literal in the tree $tree(\neg h_i)$. Let T' be the set of hypothesis instances contained in the subtree tree($\neg$*pcl*). Then the set $T \cup \{h_i\} - T'$ is called an outset w.r.t. to *pcl*.

Each potential crucial literal and two respective sets of hypotheses instances, as defined above, are recorded in the tabular form (as shown in Table 2). The truth value of the literal (*pcl*) in first column supports one of the two sets of hypothesis instances (*inset*) shown in column 2, while it refutes the other set (*outset*), shown in column 3. That is, *inset* $\rightarrow$ *pcl* and *outset* $\rightarrow \neg$*pcl*. The following theorem relates *nogoods* with *inset* and *outset*:

Theorem 14
Let *pcl* be a potential crucial literal with corresponding inset *In* and outset *Out*; the union of *In* and *Out* is a nogood, i.e., $In \cup Out \vdash false$.

	GSTP+	IDTP+	BBTP+	GSTP+	IDTP+	BBTP+
	node(7,on) & node(8,off)			node(8,off) & node(7,on)		
proof nodes	331	310	192	401	152	108
consistency nodes	2814	1060	906	3036	511	444
total nodes	3145	1370	1098	3437	663	552
cpu time (secs.)	4.0	3.1	1.5	4.6	1.0	0.8
	node(7,off) & node(8,on)			node(8,on) & node(7,off)		
proof nodes	331	296	178	401	284	240
consistency nodes	2806	1352	1145	3028	1340	1340
total nodes	3137	1648	1323	3429	1624	1580
cpu time (secs.)	4.1	2.3	1.8	4.7	2.4	2.3
	node(7,on) & node(8,on)			node(8,on) & node(7,on)		
proof nodes	331	441	323	401	284	240
consistency nodes	2806	2224	2224	3028	1348	1348
total nodes	3137	2665	2547	3429	1632	1588
cpu time (secs.)	4.2	3.8	3.6	4.8	2.4	2.3

Table 3: New Results: Initial Query

4 Using the PCL table to reduce consistency checking

While computing preferred theories in consistency-based hypothetical reasoning systems, the consistency check is unavoidable and expensive—computationally semi-decidable. We view the semi-decidability of consistency checking not as a problem, but rather as an indication of the wealth of information potentially contained in the consistency tree (see Def. 9). The *PCL* table incrementally stores the useful information (partial derivations *good* and inconsistent combinations of hypothesis instances *nogood*) extracted from consistency trees.

Tables 3 and 4 show the results when the theory preference procedures are augmented with incremental construction and use of the PCL table. We refer to the augmented procedures as GSTP+, IDTP+, and BBTP+. Table 3 shows the results for the initial query. Table 4 shows the results for a repeated query.

A comparison between Table 1 and Table 3 shows a significant improvement in the number of consistency checks and the CPU time for all three search techniques (GSTP, IDTP, and BBTP). Table 4 shows that the number of consistency checks for the subsequent computations are drastically reduced (0 for example chosen here).

5 Conclusions

We have presented an extension of THEORIST [8] by introducing meta-level control for computing preferred theories. We have defined monotonic viability and preference and given two theorems which lead to a procedure for incremental computation of preferred explanations. We have also shown that the idea of consistency tree or consistency-based reason maintenance [11] can be gracefully integrated in META-THEORIST to achieve a significant performance advantage.

Although our empirical results are based on a small but widely used circuit diagnosis problem, they indicate the usefulness of our approach. In particular, BBTP never searches more nodes than GSTP and often searches fewer nodes. Further improvements have been achieved by incrementally recording consistency trees and using them in the subsequent computations.

Currently, we are working on unification of various subjective and objective theory preference criterias, and their empirically efficient implementation using hypothetical reasoning framework.

	GSTP+	IDTP+	BBTP+	GSTP+	IDTP+	BBTP+
	node(7,on) & node(8,off)			node(8,off) & node(7,on)		
proof nodes	331	310	192	401	152	108
consistency nodes	0	0	0	0	0	0
total nodes	331	310	192	401	152	108
cpu time (secs.)	0.6	0.6	0.4	0.7	0.3	0.2
	node(7,off) & node(8,on)			node(8,on) & node(7,off)		
proof nodes	331	296	178	401	284	240
consistency nodes	0	0	0	0	0	0
total nodes	331	296	178	401	284	240
cpu time (secs.)	0.6	0.6	0.4	0.7	0.6	0.5
	node(7,on) & node(8,on)			node(8,on) & node(7,on)		
proof nodes	331	441	323	401	284	240
consistency nodes	0	0	0	0	0	0
total nodes	331	441	323	401	284	240
cpu time (secs.)	0.7	1.0	0.8	0.7	0.6	0.6

Table 4: New Results: Repeat Query

References

[1] G. Ferguson. Identity and skolem functions in resolution-based hypothetical reasoning. Master's thesis, Department of Computing Science, University of Alberta, University of Alberta, August 1989.

[2] M.R. Genesereth. The use of design descriptions in automated diagnosis. In D.G. Bobrow, editor, *Qualitative Reasoning about Physical Systems*, pages 411–436. MIT Press, Cambridge, Massachusetts, 1982.

[3] R.G. Goebel and S.D. Goodwin. Applying theory formation to the planning problem. In *Proceedings of the 1987 Workshop: The Frame Problem in Artificial Intelligence*, pages 207–232, Los Altos, California, April 1987. Morgan Kaufmann.

[4] S.D. Goodwin. *Statistically Motivated Defaults*. PhD thesis, Department of Computing Science, University of Alberta, Edmonton, Alberta, 1991. [also University of Regina Computer Science TR-91-03].

[5] S. Hanks and D.V. McDermott. Default reasoning, nonmonotonic logics, and the frame problem. In *Proceedings of the Fifth National Conference on Artificial Intelligence*, pages 328–333, Los Altos, California, August 1986. Morgan Kaufmann.

[6] D.L. Poole. Defaults and conjectures: Hypothetical reasoning for explanation and prediction. Research Report CS-87-54, Department of Computer Science, University of Waterloo, Waterloo, Ontario, October 1987.

[7] D.L. Poole. Normality and faults in logic-based diagnosis. In *Proceedings of the Eleventh International Joint Conference on Artificial Intelligence*, pages 1304–1310, Detroit, August 1989.

[8] D.L. Poole, R.G. Goebel, and R. Aleliunas. Theorist: A logical reasoning system for defaults and diagnosis. In N. Cercone and G. McCalla, editors, *The Knowledge Frontier: Essays in the Representation of Knowledge*, pages 331–352. Springer-Verlag, New York, 1987.

[9] R. Reiter. A theory of diagnosis from first principles. *Artificial Intelligence*, 32:57–95, 1987.

[10] A. Sattar and R. Goebel. On the efficiency of logic-based diagnosis. In *Proceedings of the Third International Conference on Industrial and Engineering Applications of AI/Expert Systems*, volume 1, pages 23–31, Charleston, South Carolina, USA, July 15-18 1990. ACM Press.

[11] A. Sattar and R. Goebel. Consistency-motivated Reason Maintenance in Hypothetical Reasoning. Technical Report TR-91-12, Department of Computing Science, Edmonton, Alberta, June 1991.

On Persistent Semantics for Knowledge Base Update

Yan Zhang
Basser Department of Computer Science
University of Sydney
NSW 2006, Australia

and

Norman Foo
Basser Department of Computer Science
University of Sydney
NSW 2006, Australia

Abstract

Katsuno and Mendelzon suggested eight postulates for characterizing the semantics of update where the principle of *minimal change* is embedded [2]. In this paper we propose a new method for knowledge base update based on *persistence*. We examine the relations between the two different update semantics by investigating the satisfiability of Katsuno and Mendelzon's update postulates under our persistent update semantics. We show that the persistence-based update operator satisfies most of Katsuno and Mendelzon's update postulates and *sometimes* satisfies all of them, from which we can see the essential distinction between the persistent update and the minimality-based update.

1 Propositional Knowledge Base Update: Introduction and Review

Katsuno and Mendelzon suggested eight postulates for characterizing the semantics of update where the principle of minimal change is embedded [2]. In this paper, we propose a new method for knowledge base update based on *persistence* by applying the *Persistence Set Approach* (PSA) presented in [6]. Although the basic motivations between the persistence principle and minimal change for representing update are quite different, we examine the relations between them by investigating the satisfiability of Katsuno and Mendelzon's update postulates under our persistent update semantics. We show that the persistence-based update operator satisfies their postulates (U1) – (U4), (U6) and (U8), and satisfies (U5) and (U7) *sometimes*, from which we can see the essential distinction between the persistent update and the minimality-based update.

We first briefly review Katsuno and Mendelzon's work on knowledge base update. Let $\mathcal{L}$ be a finitary propositional language. We represent a *knowledge base* by a propositional formula ψ. A propositional formula ϕ is *complete* if ϕ is consistent and for any propositional formula μ, $\phi \models \mu$ or $\phi \models \neg\mu$. $Models(\psi)$ denotes the set of all models of ψ, i.e., all interpretations of $\mathcal{L}$ in which ψ is true.

The motivation of Katsuno and Mendelzon's proposal for update postulates is an observation on the difference between revision and update. Gardenfors *et al.* proposed a theory for belief revision, i.e., the AGM logic [1], in which there are some postulates that should be satisfied by any reasonable revision operator. Formally, given a knowledge base ψ and a formula μ, $\psi \circ \mu$ denotes the *revision* of ψ by μ, that is, the new knowledge base obtained by adding new knowledge μ to the old knowledge base ψ. Katsuno and Mendelzon proved that the AGM revision postulates can be equivalently presented as follows [3]:

(R1) $\psi \circ \mu$ implies μ.
(R2) If $\psi \wedge \mu$ is satisfiable then $\psi \circ \mu \equiv \psi \wedge \mu$.
(R3) If μ is satisfiable then $\psi \circ \mu$ is also satisfiable.
(R4) If $\psi_1 \equiv \psi_2$ and $\mu_1 \equiv \mu_2$ then $\psi_1 \circ \mu_1 \equiv \psi_2 \circ \mu_2$.
(R5) $(\psi \circ \mu) \wedge \phi$ implies $\psi \circ (\mu \wedge \phi)$.
(R6) If $(\psi \circ \mu) \wedge \phi$ is satisfiable then $\psi \circ (\mu \wedge \phi)$ implies $(\psi \circ \mu) \wedge \phi$.

Katsuno and Mendelzon revealed that the above postulates for revision are inappropriate for *update*, and then proposed eight postulates for characterizing the semantics of update. Let $\psi \diamond \mu$ denote the *update* of ψ by μ. Then Katsuno-Mendelzon's update postulates can be presented as follows [2]:

(U1) $\psi \diamond \mu$ implies μ.
(U2) If ψ implies μ then $\psi \diamond \mu \equiv \psi$.
(U3) If both ψ and μ are satisfiable then $\psi \diamond \mu$ is also satisfiable.
(U4) If $\psi_1 \equiv \psi_2$ and $\mu_1 \equiv \mu_2$ then $\psi_1 \diamond \mu_1 \equiv \psi_2 \diamond \mu_2$.
(U5) $(\psi \diamond \mu) \wedge \phi$ implies $\psi \diamond (\mu \wedge \phi)$.
(U6) If $\psi \diamond \mu_1$ implies μ_2 and $\psi \diamond \mu_2$ implies μ_1 then $\psi \diamond \mu_1 \equiv \psi \diamond \mu_2$.
(U7) If ψ is complete then $(\psi \diamond \mu_1) \wedge (\psi \diamond \mu_2)$ implies $\psi \diamond (\mu_1 \vee \mu_2)$.
(U8) $(\psi_1 \vee \psi_2) \diamond \mu \equiv (\psi_1 \diamond \mu) \vee (\psi_2 \diamond \mu)$.

Update operators satisfying these postulates can be characterized in terms of the following representation theorem. An *update assignment* is a function which assigns to each interpretation I a preorder $\leq_I$ over the set of interpretations of $\mathcal{L}$. We say that this assignment is *faithful* iff for any interpretation J, if $I \neq J$ then $I \leq_I J$ and $J \not\leq_I I$.

Theorem 1 (Katsuno and Mendelzon [2]) An update operator $\diamond$ satisfies (U1) – (U8) iff there exists a faithful assignment that maps each interpretation to a partial preorder $\leq_I$ such that:

$$Models(\psi \diamond \mu) = \bigcup_{I \in Models(\psi)} Min(Models(\mu), \leq_I),$$

where $Min(Models(\mu), \leq_I)$ means the set of elements of $Models(\mu)$ that are minimal under preorder $\leq_I$. □

Katsuno-Mendelzon's update postulates characterize the update semantics for a class of update operators that are based on the principle of minimal change in knowledge base update. One of these update operators satisfying (U1) - (U8) is, for example, the *Possible Models Approach* (PMA) update operator [4].

2 A Persistent Semantics for Update

In this section, we present a persistent semantics for propositional knowledge base update. We consider the occurrence of *domain constraints* in our problem domain. Let C be a consistent set of propositional formulas that represents all domain constraints of the world. Thus, for any knowledge base ψ, we require $\psi \models C$. Let I be an interpretation of $\mathcal{L}$. We say that I is a *state* of the world if $I \models C$. A knowledge base ψ can be treated as a *description* of the world, where $Models(\psi)$ is the set of *possible states* of the world with respect to ψ.

As it will be shown next, in our formalism, updating knowledge base ψ with μ is defined by updating all possible states of the world with respect to ψ with μ, and this is achieved by the *Persistence Set Approach* (PSA) as described in [6]. We first give the definition of persistence set as follows.

Definition 1 Let I be a state of the world, i.e., $I \models C$, μ a propositional formula and consistent with C. We define the *persistence set* of I with respect to μ, denoted as $\Delta(\mu, I)$, as follows:

1. $\Delta_0 = I - \{f \mid \{\mu\} \cup C \models \neg f\}$,
2. $\Delta_1 = \Delta_0 - \{f \mid$ there exists propositional letters $f_1, \cdots, f_n$, where f_i or $\neg f_i$ in I for each $i \in N = \{1, \cdots, n\}$, such that $\{\mu\} \cup C \models [\neg]f \vee \bigvee_{i \in N}[\neg]f_i$ but $C \not\models [\neg]f \vee \bigvee_{i \in N}[\neg]f_i$ and $\{\mu\} \cup C \not\models \bigvee_{i \in N}[\neg]f_i$, and for any proper subset M of N, $\{\mu\} \cup C \not\models [\neg]f \vee \bigvee_{j \in M}[\neg]f_j\}$,
3. $\Delta_i = \Delta_{i-1} - \{f_1, \cdots, f_k \mid$ there exists some subset $F \subseteq I - \Delta_{i-1}$ such that $(F \cup \Delta_{i-1} - \{f_1, \cdots, f_k\}) \cup C \models f_1 \wedge \cdots \wedge f_k$ but $(\Delta_{i-1} - \{f_1, \cdots, f_k\}) \cup C \not\models f_l$ where $1 \leq l \leq k$ $\}$,
4. $\Delta(\mu, I) = \bigcap_{i=0}^{\infty} \Delta_i$.

The notation $[\neg]$ means that the negation sign $\neg$ may or may not appear. □

We now explain this definition in detail. We propose a *persistence principle* for updating a state with a formula, which says that a fact *persists* if it is not *logically relevant* to those facts that *must* change or *may* be subject to change because of updating the state with a formula. We formalize this principle from a viewpoint of purely logical syntax and first order semantics.

Consider a state of the world I and a formula μ where μ is consistent with C. Obviously, after updating I with μ, a fact f in I *must* change if f is inconsistent with μ with respect to C, i.e., $\{\mu\} \cup C \models \neg f$. We call such a fact *non-persistent* with respect to μ (i.e., condition 1 in the above definition). On the other hand, suppose there exists some fact f where f or its negation $\neg f$ appears in a disjunction that is entailed by μ (or together with C)[1], we say that f is *indefinitely affected* by μ. The intuitive meaning of an indefinite effect is that after updating I with μ, the satisfaction of μ (together with C) in the resulting state may or may not cause a change of the truth value of f, but we do not know which is the case (i.e., condition 2). Moreover, for a fact f, if there exists a subset F of I in which some fact is non-persistent or indefinitely affected by μ, and f is entailed by F (or together with C), then f is *implicitly affected* by μ if there is no other justification for f, because after updating I with μ, f may lose its justification. In this case, it is incautious to assume that f persists (i.e., condition 3). We call those facts that are either implicitly or indefinitely affected by μ *mutable*. Finally, for a fact f, if for its every justification there exists some mutable fact in the justification, f is *mutable* (i.e., condition 3). Thus, a fact in I *must* persist if it is neither non-persistent nor mutable. We take all such facts to form the persistence set, as presented in the above definition (condition 4).

Theorem 2 (Zhang and Foo [6]) For any state of the world I and any propositional formula μ that is consistent with C, the persistence set $\Delta(\mu, I)$ is unique. □

So far, the possible state resulting from updating I with μ is defined as follows.

Definition 2 Let I be a state of the world, i.e., $I \models C$, and μ a propositional formula that is consistent with C. An interpretation I' of $\mathcal{L}$ is a *possible state* of the world resulting from updating I with μ, iff

1. $I' \models C$,
2. $I' \models \mu$, and
3. $\Delta(\mu, I) \subseteq I'$.

Denote the set of all possible states of the world resulting from updating I with μ as $Update(\mu, I)$. □

[1] Of course, the disjunction should be non-trivial in our sense, i.e., $A \models B \vee C$, but $A \not\models B$ and $A \not\models C$.

Now we can define our persistence-based update operator for knowledge base update based on the PSA.

Definition 3 Let ψ be a knowledge base, i.e., $\psi \models C$, μ a propositional formula. $\psi \diamond_{psa} \mu$ denotes the *persistent update* of ψ with μ[2], where

1. If ψ implies μ or ψ is inconsistent then $\psi \diamond_{psa} \mu \equiv \psi$, otherwise

2. $Models(\psi \diamond_{psa} \mu) = \bigcup_{I \in Models(\psi)} Update(\mu, I)$. □

In the above definition, condition 1 says that if ψ implies μ, then nothing is changed since the knowledge μ has been represented by knowledge base ψ; or if ψ is inconsistent, then any update can not change it into a consistent knowledge base. Condition 2 says that if ψ is consistent and does not imply μ, then ψ should be changed, and this change follows the persistence principle as defined previously.

3 The Persistence-based Update and Katsuno-Mendelzon's Postulates

From the previous sections, we can see that the basic motivations of the persistence-based update and minimality-based update are quite different. However, as will be seen in this section, we can examine the relations between them by investigating the satisfiability of Katsuno-Mendelzon's update postulates under our persistent update semantics. We first give the main result of this section as follows[3].

Theorem 3 The persistence-based update operator $\diamond_{psa}$ satisfies Katsuno-Mendelzon's postulates (U1) – (U4), (U6) and (U8). □

Generally, (U5) and (U7) are not satisfied under the persistent semantics because the intuitive meaning of (U5) and (U7) is to represent a minimal change for update while the persistent update does not follow this principle generally. However, we have the following theorem, which says that under some conditions, (U5) and (U7) are still satisfied by the persistent update operator.

Theorem 4 Let C be the set of domain constraints. Then the following properties hold:

(U5') If $\psi \diamond_{psa} \mu \models [\neg]\phi$ but $\psi \not\models \phi$, then $(\psi \diamond_{psa} \mu) \wedge \phi$ implies $\psi \diamond_{psa} (\mu \wedge \phi)$.
(U7') If $\psi \diamond_{psa} \mu_1 \models [\neg]\mu_2$ (or $\psi \diamond_{psa} \mu_2 \models [\neg]\mu_1$), then $(\psi \diamond_{psa} \mu_1) \wedge (\psi \diamond_{psa} \mu_2)$ implies $\psi \diamond_{psa} (\mu_1 \vee \mu_2)$.

[2] Here we only consider the *well-defined* update, that is, μ is consistent with C.

[3] Because of the space limitation, the proofs of all theorems presented in this section are referred to our full paper [5].

Intuitively, the above theorem tells us that if there does not exist the indefinite and implicit effects of update, the persistent update operator satisfies (U5) and (U7), and then satisfy all Katsuno-Mendelzon's postulates. Furthermore, from Katsuno and Mendelzon's representation theorem (Theorem 1), it follows that the indefinite and implicit effects of persistent update is *unexpressible* by any model-based minimality principle, which is the essential distinction between the persistent update and the minimality-based update.

The fact that the AGM revision postulates are inappropriate for minimality-based update [2] is paralled by the following corollary which says that the AGM revision postulates are also inappropriate for the persistence-based update.

Corollary 1 $\diamond_{psa}$ satisfies the AGM revision postulates (R1) and (R4), but violates (R2), (R3), (R5) and (R6). □

4 Conclusion

In this paper, we proposed a persistent semantics for propositional knowledge base update. We compared our method with the minimality-based update approach by investigating the satisfiability of Katsuno-Mendelzon's update postulates under our persistent update semantics, from which we can see the essential distinction between these two different approaches for knowledge base update.

References

[1] P. Gardenfors. *Knowledge in Flux.* MIT Press, Cambridge, Massachusetts, 1988.

[2] H. Katsuno and A. O. Mendelzon. On the difference between updating a knowledge database and revising it. In *Proceedings of Second International Conference on Principles of Knowledge Representation and Reasoning*, 1991.

[3] H. Katsuno and A. O. Mendelzon. Propositional knowledge base revision and minimal change. *Artificial Intelligence*, 52:263–294, 1991.

[4] M. Winslett. Reasoning about action using a possible models approach. In *Proceedings of AAAI-88*, pages 89–93, 1988.

[5] Y. Zhang and N. Y. Foo. On persistent semantics for knowledge base update. Technical Report 469, University of Sydney, July, 1993.

[6] Y. Zhang and N. Y. Foo. Reasoning about persistence: a theory of actions. In *Proceedings of Thirteenth International Joint Conference on Artificial Intelligence*, Chambery, 1993.

POSSIBLE WORLDS SEMANTICS FOR EVENTS
(extended summary)

Norman Y. Foo and Yan Zhang
Knowledge Systems Group
Basser Department of Computer Science
University of Sydney, NSW 2006, Australia

e-mail: norman@cs.su.oz.au yan@cs.su.oz.au

ABSTRACT

Various theories of events or actions have been proposed to account for commonsense conclusions. The typical way in which this proceeds is for a scenario to be invented and a logic tried against it. Then someone else may perturb the scenario a bit and the old logic fails, while a new one may succeed. The basic difficulty with this methodology is its ad hoc character. To overcome this, recent work [LS91] has tried to delineate classes of monotonic theories that the non-monotonic ones are to be measured against. We believe a better methodology is to go the whole hog and admit model classes as the arbiter. To this end we outline some postulates about a possible worlds semantics that is suitable for evaluating non-monotonic theories of events.

1. Introduction

The theory of actions or events has occupied the attention of many researchers because it is central to the understanding of how intelligent agents can reason about changes in the world. Among the established formalisms for events are STRIPS [FN71], the situation calculus [MH69], various non-monotonic logics [GI87],[RE80],[MC96], and more recently update [KM91] and belief revision theories [GA88]. The measure of success of such proposals rest on "benchmarks" such as the infamous Yale Shooting Problem [HM87]. It is characteristic of work in this area that it progresses by the invention of scenarios that formalism A that is in vogue cannot fully solve, but a new formalism B can -- that is, until the scenario is changed. Event theory appears to confuse the roles of ontology and epistemology that the classical sciences have been careful to separate.

Giere [GI88] argues for the primacy of ontology in scientific theory formation, i.e., first decide what things and relations are to be recognized before any theory is attempted. The success or failure of the theory is relative to this ontology. Lately, a number of papers have appeared that suggest that at least some event theorists are beginning to recognise this. In [LS91,DS92] Lin, Shoham and DelVal have attempted to characterize the class of *monotonic* theories relative to which a non-monotonic theory of events is correct. But a ground complete monotonic theory is so close to being essentially a (ground) model that one wonders why the comparison is not made with a model instead. The view that we should first delimit or define the class of *systems* that is of interest is in fact propounded by Sandewall [SA93] and Peppas [PE93]. The description of this class can be done in any way that can communicate its scope and general properties.

In this extended summary we outline a possible worlds description of the kind of ontology that we believe is suitable for classifying different classes of systems relative to which different classes of event theories can be evaluated. The version that we use here is Kripke semantics as treated in many books [HC84]. The basic idea is to let each state of the system be a possible world, and to let each event label an arc of a state transition regarded as a component of the accessibility relation for that event. States may be viewed as ground-complete sets of literals, i.e., for each state s, each ground literal l either l or ¬l holds in s.

In the sections to follow we will briefly review some standard material essential to the subsequent definitions that illustrate some ways to define system classes that are candidates for recent event theories. In later papers we will address questions about the relationships between theories and this kind of semantics, including frame and qualification problems, conditions and invariants. The full version of this summary is available as [FZ93].

2. Possible Worlds

The definitions required are completely routine [HC84] but reiterated for completeness. The formal language used in association with possible worlds is first order (f.o.) logic with no function symbols, which is presumed to be familiar to the reader, augmented with a modal operator.

Definition: A model M is a quadruple (S,R,V,D) where (i) S is a set of worlds or states; (ii) R is the union of binary relations R_e on S X S, each $e \in E$ being a ground event. Intuitively, R_e are the arcs that label the state transitions due to event e; (iii) D is a domain of individuals; (iv) and V is a function that: associates with each n-ary predicate symbol P an (n+1)-ary relation consisting of tuples $(d_1,..,d_n, s)$ where $d_1,..,d_n$ are elements of D, and s is a state in S. For each given s it is convenient to denote this relation by $P_s(d_1,..,d_n)$ which is a "curried" form of V. Intuitively, V says of each interpretation of P in state s which tuples in D satisfy it. Additionally, we stipulate that each element in D is named by a constant that V associates with it. In exactly the standard way, V treats variables by associating each variable x some element in D. Denote this element by V(x).

Evaluation of formulas in M: These recursive definitions are again routine and included for completeness. In the first two, read tuples in place of x and d, and we conflate d on the left (a constant symbol) with its occurrence on the right (an element in D).

(i) $M,s \models P(d)$ if $P_s(d)$ holds; (ii) $M,s \models P(x)$ if $P_s(V(x))$ holds; (iii) $M,s \models x = y$ if $V(x)=V(y)$ holds; (iv) $M,s \models \forall(x)\alpha(x)$ if for all V' differing from V in at most its association of x with V(x), $M,s \models \alpha(x)$; (v) $M,s \models \alpha \rightarrow \beta$ if $M,s \models \alpha$ implies $M,s \models \beta$; (vi) $M,s \models \neg\alpha$ if $M,s \not\models \alpha$; (vii) $M,s \models [e]\alpha$ if for all t such that sR_et, $M,t \models \alpha$.

The usual abbreviations and are assumed. In line with most work in event theory we assume that each event e has associated with it a pre-condition pre(e) and a post-condition post(e), where each is a f.o. formula.

Definition: If $M,s \models pre(e)$, the event e is applicable to s.

Transition (Causality) Axiom: For all states s and events e, pre(e) $\rightarrow$ [e]post(e).

From the semantic evaluations above this amounts to M,s $\models$ pre(e) and sR_et implies M,t $\models$ post(e).

Definition: When sR_et, call s the source state and t a target state of e.

Application Axiom: For all states s and events e, sR_et implies M,s $\models$ pre(e) and M,t $\models$ post(e).

This is needed to prevent state pairs from being spuriously attributed to event e. The implication should not in general be reversed because state t may by happenstance satisfy the post-condition of e but may not in fact be reachable from s. All models M are required to satisfy the above two axioms. In the jargon of modal logic, we regard these axioms as defining a standard frame. Additional assumptions about the relations R_e or states s are called postulates. Unlike the axioms, postulates are introduced in an attempt to to provide models that can be used to characterize various non-monotonic and other logics.

Definition: A constraint is a f.o. formula ϕ such that ϕ is not a tautology and M,s $\models \phi$ for all s in S. Denote the set of all constraints by C. If this is finite (as we shall assume here), C will also be a formula that represents all constraints.

3. Inertia and Minimal Change

As a first application of this semantics we will consider some approaches to reasoning about state and knowledge change. These are typified by the idea of *updates* [KM91] on the one hand and by *belief revision* [GA88]on the other. The cited references show that the notion of *minimal change* is central to both state and belief change. In state change the idea seems be to one that can be described as a kind of inertia -- the components of states that do not have to change as a result of an event do not in fact change. In belief revision the idea is that in revising beliefs to accept new beliefs, we should discard as few old beliefs as we can. These ideas are easy to capture as additional postulates in our semantics. Indeed the aim of this paper is to suggest that the various approaches to event theory be validated against similar postulates about possible worlds by exhibiting some interesting examples. For convenience we will denote a clause $l_1 \quad \cdots \quad l_n$ by $<l_1, \cdots, l_n>$.

Definition: If $\Gamma \models <l_1, \cdots, l_n>$ but $\Gamma \not\models <l_{i_1}, .., l_{i_k}>$ for no proper subclause of the ground clause $<l_1, \cdots, l_n>$, say that $<l_1, \cdots, l_n>$ is Γ-minimal. When n > 1, also say that $<l_1, \cdots, l_n>$ is unsubsumed.

Definition: Ram(e) = $\{<l_1, \cdots, l_n> \mid <l_1, \cdots, l_n>$ is post(e) $\cup$ C - minimal, and C $\not\models$ $<l_1, \cdots, l_n>\}$.

Ram(e) is what is usually called the ramifications of the event e, with post(e) being the immediate effects.

Definition: If s is a state, Lit(s) = $\{l \mid l$ is a ground literal and $M,s \models l\}$. A set $\Delta \subset$ Lit(s) is a support for $l \in$ Lit(s) if (i) $l \notin \Delta$, (ii) $C \not\models l$ and (iii) $C \cup \Delta \models l$. It is a minimal support if whenever $\Delta' \subset \Delta$ is also a support for l, then $\Delta' = \Delta$.

Definition: A subset $\Gamma \subset$ Lit(s) is support stable in s if every $l \in \Gamma$ that has a support has minimal support $\Delta \subset \Gamma$.

Lemma: Unions of support stable sets are support stable. Hence, there is a unique largest support stable set in any given set.

Definition: Let $\Gamma_0, \Gamma_1, \cdots$ be a sequence of sets such that $\Gamma_0 = l$, where l is a ground literal, and $\Gamma_{i+1} = \Gamma_i \cup \{l \mid l \in \Delta, \Delta$ a minimal support of $m \in \Gamma_i\}$. A foundation for l based on this sequence is $F(l) = \bigcup_{i \in \omega} \Gamma_i$.

Lemma: Every foundation F(l) is support stable.

(Weak) Permissive State Postulate: If $<l_1,..,l_n>$ is in Ram(e), then for each literal l_i in the clause $<l_1,..,l_n>$ there is a target state t such that $M,t \models l_i$.

(Strong) Permissive State Postulate: As above, but each literal holds in a separate target state.

Lemma: Both weak and strong permissiveness are realizable.

Here are some intuitively persuasive postulates that attempt to capture system "laziness".

Coherent Inertia Postulate: For all ground literals l, events e, states s and t such that $M,s \models$ pre(e) $M,s \models l$ and Ram(e) $\not\models \neg l$ ☞ $\exists t$ (sR_et and $M,t \models l$).

Coherent Minimality Postulate: For all ground literals l, events e, states s and t such that $M,s \models$ pre(e)
$\forall t$ (sR_et ☞ $M,t \models l$) ☞ ($M,s \models l$ or Ram(e) $\models l$).

Corollary
Coherent inertia is equivalent to coherent minimality.

Definition: Given state s, denote the largest support stable subset of Lit(s) in s that is consistent with Ram(e) by $\sigma(s,e)$.

Theorem
$l \notin \sigma(s,e)$ iff either l or every F(l) is inconsistent with Ram(e).

Foundational Inertia Postulate: For all ground literals l, events e, states s and t such that $M,s \models$ pre(e) $M,s \models l$ and $l \in \sigma(s,e)$ ☞ $\exists t$ (sR_et and $M,t \models l$).

Foundational Minimality Postulate: For all ground literals l, events e, states s and t such that $M,s \models pre(e)$ $\forall t\, (sR_e t \Rightarrow M,t \models l) \Rightarrow (M,s \models l$ or $\neg l \notin \sigma(s,e)$.

Corollary: Foundational inertia is equivalent to foundational minimality.

4. Sharpening Some Properties

Much of the work on event theory assumes that Ram(e) does not suffer from unsubsumed clauses. Because this is so widespread, it deserves a name.

Definition: An event e is definite if Ram(e) does not have any unsubsumed clauses.

Definition: An event e applied to state s is deterministic if there is a unique t such that $sR_e t$. Otherwise it is nondeterministic.

Lemma: If e is deterministic then Ram(e)is definite when the strong permissiveness postulate holds.

Transition Narrowing Postulate: R_e is restricted to those relations which have minimal target sets for each given source state.

Lemma: If Ram(e) is definite, then coherent minimality and transition narrowing implies e is deterministic.

Winslett [WI88] used a Hamming-like metric on possible models of (partial) theories to select the models that survive a definite event. These models are almost those resulting from coherent minimality and transition narrowing. If we denote by Cer(s,e) the subset of Lit(s) such that $l \in$ Cer(s,e) iff $M,t \models l$ for every t such that $sR_e t$, then the persistent set of Zhang and Foo [ZF93] is very nearly Cer(s,e).

5. Conclusion and Acknowledgements

This semantics cannot be captured by f.o. logic, and its full power is only hinted at in this summary. See [FZ93] for more details. This research is supported in part by grants from the Australian Research Council. The second author is partially supported by a SOPF scholarship from the University of Sydney. Members of the Knowledge Systems Group, especially Pavlos Peppas, contributed to many discussions.

6. References

[DS92]del Val, A. and Shoham, Y., "Deriving Properties of Belief Update from Theories of Action", Proc. 10th National AI Conference, AAAI'92, Morgan Kaufmann Publishers, San Mateo, CA., 1991.

[FN71]Fikes, R. and Nilsson, N., "STRIPS: a New Approach to the Application of Theorem Proving to Problem Solving", Artificial Intelligence, 2 (3/4), pp. 189-208, 1971.

[FZ93] Foo, N. and Zhang, Y., "Possible Worlds Semantics For Events", Computer Science Technical Report, University of Sydney, July, 1993.

[GA88] Gardenfors, P., "Knowledge in Flux", Bradford Books, MIT Press 1988, Cambridge, Massachusetts.

[GI88] Giere, R.N., "Explaining Science", University of Chicago Press, Chicago 1988.

[GI87] Ginsberg, M.L., (ed) "Readings in Non-monotonic Reasoning", Morgan Kaufmann Publishers, San Mateo, CA., 1987.

[GO82] Goldblatt, R., "Axiomatising the Logic of Computer Programming", LNCS 130, Springer-Verlag, Berlin, 1982.

[HM87] Hanks, S. and McDermott, D., "Non-monotonic Logic and Temporal Projection", Artificial Intelligence, 33, pp. 379-412, 1987.

[HC84] Hughes, G.E. and Cresswell, M.J., "A Companion to Modal Logic", Methuen 1984, London.

[KM91] Katsuno, H. and Mendelzon, A.O., "On the Difference between Updating a Knowledge Base and Revising It", Proc. 2nd International Conference on Principles of Knowledge Representation and Reasoning, KR'91, Morgan Kaufmann Publishers, San Mateo, CA., 1991.

[LS91] Lin, F. and Shoham, Y., "Provably Correct Theories of Action", Proc. 9th National AI Conference, AAAI'91, Morgan Kaufmann Publishers, San Mateo, CA., 1991.

[MC86] McCarthy, J., "Applications of Circumscription to Formalizing Common-Sense Knowledge", Artificial Intelligence, 28, pp. 86-116, 1986. Also in Ginsberg [GI87].

[MH69] McCarthy, J. and Hayes, P., "Some Philosophical Problems from the Standpoint of Artificial Intelligence", in Machine Intelligence 4, ed. B. Meltzer and D. Michie, pp. 463-502, Edinburgh University Press, Edingurgh, 1969. Also in Ginsberg [GI87].

[PE93] Peppas, P., PhD Thesis in draft, University of Sydney, 1993.

[RE80] Reiter, R., "A Logic for Default Reasoning", Artificial Intelligence, 13, pp. 81-132, 1980. Also in Ginsberg [GI87].

[SE93] Sandewall, E., "Features and Fluents", forthcoming book, 1993.

[WI88] Winslett, M., "Reasoning about Actions using a Possible Models Approach", Proc 7th National AI Conference, AAAI'88, Morgan Kaufmann Publishers, San Mateo, CA., 1988.

[ZF93] Zhang, Y. and Foo, N., "Reasoning about Persistence: A Theory of Actions", (to appear), Proceedings of the 13th International Joint Conference on Artificial Intelligence, IJCAI'93, France.

Predicate Discovery in a Model Identification Framework

Greg G. Gibbon
Information Technology Divn, Defence Science and Technology Organisation
Anzac Park West, Canberra ACT 2600 ggg@itd.dsto.gov.au

and

Norman Y. Foo
Basser Dept of Computer Science, University of Sydney NSW 2006
norman@cs.su.oz.au

ABSTRACT

We address a problem related to the long standing question of predicate invention. We develop an algorithm in the Model Identification framework that extends to predicate discovery, thus performing at an intermediate level between Model Identification and predicate invention. A major open problem is that of *predicate invention* of theoretical terms, where a theoretical term is a predicate that a learner needs to hypothesize in order to explain observations about the world model, Muggleton and Buntine [3]. A task intermediate in difficulty between this and the problem addressed by Shapiro is that of *predicate discovery* where the algorithm starts without knowledge of the predicates that may be presented by the 'oracle', but as the algorithm executes the discovered predicates are integrated into the conjectures. We demonstrate a predicate discovery algorithm that converges to a finite axiomatisation without requiring the a priori knowledge of the predicates it will see.

1. Introduction

This paper addresses a problem that is related to the long standing question of predicate invention. We develop an algorithm in the Model Identification framework that extends to predicate discovery, thus performing at an intermediate level between Model Identification and predicate invention. The work of Shapiro[1] in Model Identification followed developments in the previous decade by Blum & Blum[4], Gold[5], Reynolds[6], Plotkin[2], and others. Shapiro's main innovation was the Contradiction Backtracing Algorithm, which allowed the algorithm to proceed in an efficient way after finding false hypotheses.

The general idea behind Shapiro's method is that of discovery of knowledge through Popper's methodology of conjectures and refutations Popper[9], the essence of which is the observation that the only way to explain the world around us is to start with a conjecture and compare it with our observations. If our observations indicate that the conjecture is too strong then we weaken it and vice versa.

Specifically, Shapiro modelled the learning situation as though the algorithm is experiencing the real world passively through an oracle who tells it random observations about the real world and their truth values. More formally, the oracle is the sequence of formulae in the *observational language* and their truth values, as defined later. However, the experiments ceased to be passive whenever the current conjecture was found to be too strong. At such a point, directed questions are asked of the oracle in order to identify the axiom that is causing the conjecture to be too strong. At any stage of the execution of the algorithm which derives the theory, the set of rules developed so far is called the conjecture, so that the theory is the conjecture on termination. Much of the work done in the area of machine learning involves techniques for choosing the "correct" generalisations that should follow from the data, Quinlan[7]. Shapiro uses a *hypothesis language*, the language used by the algorithm to develop conjectures, which contains the observational language. In some other learning approaches, the hypothesis and observational languages are strictly the same.

A major open problem is that of *predicate invention* of theoretical terms, where a theoretical term is a predicate that a learner needs to hypothesize in order to explain observations about the world model. This predicate is not interpreted in the model -- in other words, the oracle would not understand a question about it and will never report a fact containing that predicate. A real-world analog is a theoretical term like *kinetic energy* . Temperature is the observational language predicate, yet the hypothesis language needs to know about the concept of kinetic energy to predict which of two bodies at the same temperature will cool faster. Theoretical terms are prolific in real life, as we create abstractions to explain observable events around us.

Considerable progress has been made in cases where predicates that are invented by inverting the Resolution Principle agree with facts reported by the oracle, in the sense that their truth values are consistent with those of the predicates they are inverted from, see Muggleton and Buntine[3], Muggleton and Feng[10].

Predicate invention in the Model Identification framework would involve the 'oracle' presenting random facts while the algorithm produces conjectures which may include some invented predicates or theoretical terms.

A task intermediate in difficulty between this and the problem addressed by Shapiro is that of *predicate discovery*: the algorithm starts without knowledge of the predicates that may be presented by the 'oracle', but as the algorithm executes the discovered predicates are integrated into the conjectures. The task is stronger than the algorithm presented by Shapiro since it does not require the hypothesis language to be a superset of the observational language at the start of execution, nor does it require that the algorithm is precompiled with every predicate that the oracle may present. Thus the task of learning the set of predicates is performed by the algorithm as it learns the theory of the model.

Section 2 presents notation and definitions based on Shapiro's but with some crucial differences fto accommodate the fact that the language grows as the algorithm executes. **Section 3** relates the Admissibility Requirement and the Contradiction Backtracing Algorithm. **Section 4** presents the Predicate Discovery algorithm. **Section 5** contains the main result of the paper. The proof technique depends on a way of loosening the restriction for convergence so as to allow operation with an incomplete hypothesis language, while still ensuring convergence. We show that the algorithm outputs a complete finite axiomitisation of the model in the sense that it proves all the true statements in the observational language.

2. Setting up the problem

Popper's methodology of strengthening and weakening conjectures requires an ordering on conjectures if it is to be automated. Popper's order corresponded to the natural ordering on formulae in First Order Logic (FOL) induced by material implication in proof theory. We require certain restrictions on the ordering so as to ensure conservation of the derivation process in the sense of resource bounded computation. Thus, the ordering is induced by a specifically defined *strict subsumption* relation, and the derivation procedure is required to be resolution. There are two languages which must be distinguished. These languages are subsets of a FOL **L**, of which the logical connectives and variables are known beforehand to the algorithm. However, the constants and predicates may initially be unknown to the algorithm. The real world model, call it **M**, is an interpretation of the language **L**.

Notation Denote the observational language by $\mathbf{L_o}$, a subset of the FOL **L**. All predicates in $\mathbf{L_o}$ are known to the oracle. Denote the hypothesis language by $\mathbf{L_h}$, which may contain predicates unknown to the algorithm at the start. Any newly discovered predicates are added to $\mathbf{L_h}$ as the algorithm proceeds. Note that in previous work, $\mathbf{L_o} \subset \mathbf{L_h}$. We require only that

$$\text{false} \subset \mathbf{L_o} \subset \mathbf{L}, \ \text{false} \subset \mathbf{L_h} \subset \mathbf{L}.$$

Thus our definitions of $\mathbf{L_h}$ differ.

Definition. Shapiro[1] The *model inference problem* is to find a finite $\mathbf{L_o}$-complete axiomatisation of **M** ie. a subset of $\mathbf{L_h}$ that proves all of the true observational formula that the oracle can report on. $\mathbf{L_o}^{\mathbf{M}}$ will denote this set of true observational formulae in the model **M**.

The Model Inference Algorithm in Shapiro's work was fed facts from the oracle in the form $<\alpha, V>$ where the formula α was from an effective enumeration of the language $\mathbf{L_o}$ and the output was a theory in $\mathbf{L_h}$. Our situation is new in that the algorithm is being fed facts from $\mathbf{L_o}$ as before, but $\mathbf{L_h}$ is no longer a superset of $\mathbf{L_o}$ so allowing occasional cases where the algorithm is presented with new predicates. Intuitively, it's similar to the situation where the algoritm knows that Nixon is a Quaker and a Republican, and knows that the predicate pacifist is undecidable for Nixon, and then is presented with a fact that relates the predicate pacifist with the (previously unheard of) predicate support_war. The process of determining whether a conjecture is too strong or to weak may in general be undecidable. The class of model inference algorithms is based on the principle of *resource bounded computation*, in which the strategy is to limit the proof of the formulae at hand to a predetermined number of steps, and to abandon the proof if this limit is reached. Previous work provides a computable way of predetermining the abandonment point.

Let $\alpha_1, \alpha_2, \ldots$ be a fixed effective enumeration of the formulae of $\mathbf{L_o}$ and define a proof-step counting function Φ by $\Phi(i) = \min \{ n ; \mathbf{T} \vdash_n \alpha_i \}$. Given a total recursive function h on the non-negative integers, then a set of sentences $\mathbf{T}$ is said to be *h-easy* if for almost every $i > 0$ (that is, all but a finite number), if $\mathbf{T} \vdash \alpha_i$ then $\Phi(i) \leq h(i)$.
A model $\mathbf{M}$ is *h-easy* if it has a finite *h-easy* $\mathbf{L_o}$-complete axiomatization. Following Shapiro, we first define a finiteness condition that ensures that at each stage we are dealing with a finite subset of formulae.

<u>Definition</u> Reynolds[6] *Size* is a complexity measure on formulae in $\mathbf{L}$ that assigns a positive integer to each formula such that for each $n > 0$, the set of formulae of size n is finite.
<u>Definition</u> Reynolds[6] Given two formulae p and $q \in \mathbf{L}$, q is a *refinement* of p if p *implies* q and size(p) < size(q), where implies means syntactically stronger as shown by one application of the logical axioms.

<u>Definition</u> Shapiro[1] A *refinement operator* ρ maps each formula to a subset of its refinements, such that for any $p \in \mathbf{L}$ and any $n > 0$ the set $\rho(p)(n)$, that is, the set $\rho(p)$ restricted to sentences of size $\leq n$, is computable.

Shapiro shows how to construct a computable example of this refinement operator which is a most general complete refinement operator over $\mathbf{L}$. We depart from Shapiro's work by fixing on this special case for the remainder of this paper. It will be clear that most of the following definitions apply to any refinement operators.

<u>Definition</u> Shapiro[1] A refinement operator ρ induces a strict partial order $<_\rho$ on the formulae of $\mathbf{L}$ (with the empty formula as the minimal element): say $p <_\rho q$ if there is a finite sequence of formulae $p_0, p_1, \ldots, p_n$ such that each $p_{i+1} \in \rho(p_i)$ and $p = p_0$ and $q = p_n$.
Say $p \leq_\rho q$ if $(p <_\rho q) \wedge (p \text{ implies } q) \wedge (q \text{ implies } p)$.
These generalise to sets of formulae. For any two sets of formulae $\mathbf{T}, \mathbf{S} \subseteq \mathbf{L}$, say $\mathbf{T} \leq_\rho \mathbf{S}$ if for every $q \in \mathbf{S}$ there is a $p \in \mathbf{T}$ such that $p \leq_\rho q$.

<u>Notation</u> Shapiro[1] For any formula p, the set $\{ q \in \mathbf{L} : p \leq_\rho q \}$ is denoted by $\rho^*(p)$. Thus completeness of an operator ρ can be expressed by saying that $\rho^*(p) = \mathbf{L}$.

For the given model, the set of strongest formula in $\mathbf{L_h}$ which are true in $\mathbf{M}$ constitutes an axiomisation of model $\mathbf{M}$, but of course is rarely finite. The conjectures of the algorithm at each stage will form a finite approximation to this axiomatisation. The following definition introduces notation for this axiomatisation, which we call the source set of the model.

<u>Definition</u>
A *source formula of the model* $\mathbf{M}$ is a member p of $\mathbf{L}$ with the property that p is true in $\mathbf{M}$ and every formula q for which $q <_\rho p$ is false in $\mathbf{M}$.
The set of source formulae is called the *source set of the model* $\mathbf{M}$, denoted by $\mathbf{L_\rho}^{\mathbf{M}}$.

The method of interactively strengthening or weakening conjectures according to the facts received from the oracle can be thought of as starting with an impossibly strong conjecture consisting of the empty formula which is always false and then weakening that conjecture. At the start point, everything but the empty formulae could be true. At any step, we need to label all the strongest formulae which have not yet been falsified. Now the set axiomatisation of the model **M** for which we are searching is a set of formula which are true in **M** and can prove every true formula in **M**. The conjectured axiomatisation at any step is just this set of strongest formulae which have not yet been falsified. First a label is needed for all the formulaewhich have been proved false during execution of the algorithm.

Definition Shapiro[1] A *marking* m is a set of formulae in L_h. A marking m is a *consistent marking* if it is "closed below",

$$\text{ie, if } p \in m \text{ then } \{ q \in L_h : q <_\rho p \} \subseteq m .$$

A marking m is *consistent with* **M** if it is a consistent marking and every member of m is false in **M**.
Definition A *source formula of the consistent marking* m is a member p of L_h such that $p \in \rho^* \wedge \{ q \in L_h : q <_\rho p \} \subseteq m \wedge p \notin m$.
The set of source formula of the consistent marking m is denoted by $L_\rho{}^m$.

3. The Admissibility Requirement and the Contradiction Backtracing Algorithm

As also discussed in the Introduction, there are two languages which must be distinguished. These are subsets of a first order clausal language **L**, the *observational* language L_o and the *hypothesis* language L_h. The observational language is used by the oracle to report facts about the model to the algorithm, while the hypothesis language is used by the algorithm to reason about the relative strength or weakness of the current Conjecture with respect to the reported facts. Clearly, there needs to be some conditions on these two languages so the algorithm may reconcile their respective statements. That condition is the *admissibility* requirement on the pair $< L_o, L_h >$. The only circumstance where the algorithm requires such constraints is when the current Conjecture has been demonstrated to be too strong as shown by the fact that it is capable of proving true an observational formula that is false in the model. We want to guarantee that any theory that proves precisely the true observational formulae is itself true in the model. Although there is little danger that we have produced a logically inconsistent conjecture (zero danger if not for the computation boundedness) we are wishing to avoid the possibility that our output might be a theory that is false in the model but accidentally proves the correct subset of the observational formulae. This is basically the statement of the admissibility requirement: that any false theory has a witness for its falsity in the observational language.

Definition
The pair $< L_o, L_h >$ are said to be *admissible* in **L** if for every model **M** of **L** and every false theory $T \subseteq L_h$ there is a formula $\alpha \in L_o$ such that $T \vdash \alpha$ and α is false in **M**.

It follows from this definition that any theory $T \subseteq L_h$ that proves precisely the true observational formulae is itself true in the model. For if not, there would be a false formula $\alpha \in L_o$ such that $T \vdash \alpha$. If the Conjecture is able to prove a false observational formula, then it is false in the model, by Soundness. The admissibility requirement ensures that the difference between the languages L_o and L_h is not so great that the converse can be false, that is, a conjecture could be false but never discovered to be so by the observational language. This paper fixes on the clausal form of language where the unknown language **L** is the usual clausal form of first order logic, the hypothesis language L_h is some growing subset of this, and the observational language L_o is a subset of **L** consisting only of ground unit sentences of **L**. We reproduce Theorem 2.4 of Shapiro[1] that proves the admissibility of $<L_o, L_h>$ when L_h is fixed and equal to **L**.

Theorem 3.1
Let **L** be a first order language, $L_o = \{\text{ground unit sentences of } L\}$ and $L_h = L$. Then the pair $<L_o, L_h>$ is admissible.

We observe here that this theorem applies to our PD algorithm (see Section 5) even though the observational language $\mathbf{L_o}$ is not a subset of the hypothesis language $\mathbf{L_h}$, because the algorithm is always dealing with a subset of $\mathbf{L_o}$ that is itself a subset of $\mathbf{L_h}$, so the witness found in the proof of Theorem 3.1 is in $\mathbf{L_h}$.

4. The Predicate Discovery Algorithm

In this section we present the predicate discovery algorithm (PD algorithm). Our important departure from Shapiro's MIS algorithm is to allow the hypothesis language to be minimal at the start of the algorithm, sharing only the logical connectives and normal forms where applicable. The algorithm we present discovers the predicates required to describe the model or real world. The MIS algorithm requires every predicate that would be observable by the oracle to be available to the algorithm at start-up, whereas our algorithm learns the predicates. The practical effect is to modify the MIS algorithm to enable it to incorporate new predicates reported by the oracle, and to recalculate the source formulae on receiving new predicates.

The PD Algorithm

Set k to 0, S_{false} to {false} and S_{true} to $\varnothing$.
Set m = {false}, and calculate $\mathbf{L}_\rho{}^{m}$.

repeat
    read the next fact $F_n = <\alpha, V>$ and add α to S_V.
    while the formula $\alpha \notin \mathbf{L_h}$ *do*
        add any new predicate, function and constant symbols to $\mathbf{L_h}$
        and recalculate m and $\mathbf{L}_\rho{}^{m}(k)$ and $<_\rho$ (with respect to new L_h but not wrt new α)
    repeat
        while $\mathbf{L}_\rho{}^{m}(k) \vdash_n \alpha_i$ for some $\alpha_i \in S_{false}$ *do*
            apply the Contradiction Backtracing Algorithm,
            and add the refuted hypothesis to m.
        while $\mathbf{L}_\rho{}^{m}(k) \not\vdash_{h(i)} \alpha_i$ for some $\alpha_i \in S_{true}$ *do*
            increase k by 1.
    until neither of the inner *while* loops is entered
            (that is, the conjecture is neither too strong nor too weak with respect to the facts so far).
    output $\mathbf{L}_\rho{}^{m}(k)$.
forever.

5. The output of PD is a finite axiomatization

This section contains our main result, that the conjecture output by PD is a finite axiomatisation.

Theorem

If the model **M** is *h-easy* then the PD algorithm will eventually output a finite $\mathbf{L_o}$-complete axiomatization of the form $\mathbf{L}_\rho{}^{m}(k_0)$ for some k_0, and L_h will have grown such that $\mathbf{L_o} \subset \mathbf{L_h} \subset \mathbf{L}$.

[This is often called *identifying* **M** *in the limit*, meaning that there is an n > 0 such that after fact F_n is read in, the algorithm outputs an $\mathbf{L_o}$-complete axiomatization and never again outputs a different conjecture]. Notice that the source set of the model $\mathbf{L}_\rho{}^{M}$ is defined to be a subset of the whole language **L** and not just $\mathbf{L_h}$ but this makes no difference because $\mathbf{L}_\rho{}^{M}$ contains only formulae in **L** that are true in **M** and so $\mathbf{L_h}$ must grow to include all the predicates in $\mathbf{L}_\rho{}^{M}$. That is, $\mathbf{L}_\rho{}^{M}$ is a subset of the final version of $\mathbf{L_h}$ that the algorithm outputs. To prove the theorem we need to show that if k_0 is the minimal size of a finite $\mathbf{L_o}$-complete axiomatization, then the algorithm will increase **k** up to k_0 and will increase it no further, and that $\mathbf{L}_\rho{}^{m}(k_0)$ converges point-wise to an $\mathbf{L_o}$-complete axiomatization. Further, it will converge in a finite number of steps.

Conclusion

Our paper is about predicate discovery in the framework of Shapiro, where the oracle presents facts in the observational language at random. However, the learner may start with the null hypothesis language. The output is a form of model identification where the predicates are learned as the theory is being learned. The requirement that the model **M** is h-easy is necessary in order to exclude pathological cases that would thwart a learning process. The fact that such conditions are necessary in a formal setting was demonstrated by Blum & Blum[4] and Gold[5]. These conditions are shown to be necessary in a mathematical setting, but it is obvious in any setting, commonsense or otherwise, that some constraints are required to ensure that learning as we know it is conceivable. If our real world of experience weren't constrained by physical laws that guaranteed some sort of uniformity, we would never know from one moment to the next whether a footstep would have the same effect as previously or whether a familiar object could be lifted easily by our left hand in the same way it was only recently.

Our framework is more realistic in not assuming an a priori knowledge of the world in the form of prior access to the entire language that describes the model. It is clear that the learning performance may well be compromised when the constraints on the model are not enhanced to reflect the greater learning load. In particular, we are faced with the situation where there is greater complexity due to the unknown nature of the predicates. The refinement operator is necessarily less efficient than in the case where all the prdeicates are known a priori. Future work is needed to narrow these operators for specific domains without having to dictate the actual predicates. Future work is also needed to characterise various strengthenings of the h-easy condition to improve the performance of the predicate discovery algorithm without the learning framework that we are modelling losing a sense of realism in that it resembles what is actually performed by learning agents around us. Further, there is more to be achieved in the area of developing learning theory for more expressive languages.

References

[1] E. Y. Shapiro, Inductive Inference of theories from facts. TR 192. Dept. Comp. Sc., Yale University, Connecticut, 1981.

[2] G. D. Plotkin. *Automatic Methods of Inductive Inference*. PhD Thesis. Edinburgh University. August 1971.

[3] S. Muggleton and W. Buntine. Machine invention of first order predicates by inverting resolution. In *Fifth International Conference on Machine Learning*, pp 339-352, Ann Arbor, Michigan, 1988. Morgan Kaufmann.

[4] L. Blum and M. Blum. Towards a mathematical theory of inductive inference. *Information and Control*, 28: 125-155, 1975.

[5] E. M. Gold. Language identification in the limit. *Information and Control*, 10: 447-474, 1967.

[6] J. C. Reynolds. Transformational systems and the algebraic structure of atomic formulas. In B. Meltzer and D. Michie, eds., *Machine Intelligence 5*, pp 135-153. Edinburgh University Press, Edinburgh, 1970.

[7] J. R. Quinlan. Induction of decision trees. *Machine Learning*. 1(1): 81-106, 1986.

[8] M. Machtey and P. Young. *An Introduction to the General Theory of Algorithms*. Elsevier North Holland. 1978.

[9] K. Popper. *The Logic of Scientific Discovery*. Basic Books, New York. 1959.

[10] S. Muggleton and C. Feng. Efficient Induction of Logic Programs. *First Conf. on Algorithmic Learning Theory* Ohmsha, Tokyo. 1990.

Reasoning about Action from the Perspective of Situation Semantics

Wayne Wobcke
Knowledge Systems Group, Basser Dept of Computer Science
University of Sydney, Sydney NSW 2006, Australia

Abstract

The frame, ramification and qualification problems are three well known epistemological problems facing any agent reasoning about action. Many approaches to addressing these problems suppose certain semantic principles, e.g. the frame problem is addressed by a principle of minimal change, stating that as little as necessary changes in the world as the result of performing an action. However, an agent does not reason directly with such a principle: agents are supposed to use an epistemic principle of minimal change, stating that as little as necessary changes in an agent's description of the world as the result of performing an action. We claim that much current research does not bridge the gap between the agent's epistemic principles and the theorist's intended semantic principles, and that part of the problem is the conception of actions as functions over complete world states. We propose an alternative conception of actions as primitive semantic objects occurring in the situations of situation semantics. We also argue that constraints as captured in a hierarchy of types of situations can form the basis of an agent's reasoning about action, and that the necessary constraints can be represented using a standard hierarchy of planning schemas. We claim that our approach to formalizing action models the practice of existing planning systems more closely than alternative approaches.

1. Introduction

The problem of planning is that of generating a sequence (or possibly partially-ordered set) of actions which when executed successfully in a state which satisfies some given initial facts results in a state which satisfies some given desired goals. The problem of plan recognition is to infer from a set of observations of an agent performing some actions, a coherent plan that the agent is executing. Thus in some sense, plan recognition is the inverse problem of planning. Central to both problems is the semantics of action: in planning, an agent must be able to determine the effects of performing an action in some state, and in plan recognition the observer must be able to identify conditions of some state as resulting from an agent's performing some action.

In much work in reasoning about action, an action is taken as specified by a function which maps states of the world to states of the world. Such states are sometimes called 'situations'. For McCarthy and Hayes (1969) where the term is introduced, a *situation* is 'a complete state of the universe at an instant of time'. Thus a situation is analogous to a possible world in the sense of Lewis (1986). As McCarthy and Hayes insist, a situation is too large for complete description, so an agent must reason with facts about situations rather than with situations themselves. This means that an agent cannot specify actions directly as sets of pairs of situations, but must reason about actions of which it might have only specifications that are incomplete.

Thus at least three epistemological problems face any agent reasoning about action. The *frame problem*, McCarthy and Hayes (1969), is that of the agent's knowing which fluents (facts about the world) do not change when an action is performed. The *ramification problem*, Ginsberg and Smith (1988a), is that of the agent's knowing all the (possibly unexpected) side-effects of performing an action. The *qualification problem*, McCarthy (1977), is that of specifying the conditions under which an action can be executed successfully. These epistemological problems highlight a deficiency in the formulation of the semantics of action: actions are functions from situations to situations, but it may be the case that not every such function corresponds to an instantiation of an action. If stronger constraints on the dynamics of the world could be formulated, an agent might be able to use such information to overcome the problems.

The frame problem is usually tackled by adopting a principle of *minimal change*: as little as necessary changes in the world when an action is performed. This presupposes that the possible situations can be compared to each other with respect to the degree of change made as the result of performing an action.

This is closely related to Lewis' (1973) use of a comparative similarity relation as the basis of his semantics of conditionals: the worlds that result from minimal changes to an initial world are just those that are maximally similar to that world. The principle of minimal change so stated is clearly a semantic principle. To solve the frame problem, it must be shown how an agent 'captures' the principle of minimal change, i.e. how the principle of minimal change (a semantic principle) is used by an agent to solve an epistemological problem.

This problem of linking the semantic to the epistemological is largely ignored by workers in reasoning about action, many of whom seem to adopt an epistemic version of the principle of minimal change. Indeed even in McCarthy and Hayes (1969), it is proposed to address the frame problem by a principle that as little as necessary changes in the agent's description of a situation as a frame (a state vector of fluents) as the result of performing an action. Similarly, any approach based on the situation calculus, e.g. Lifschitz (1990), uses a principle of minimizing the changes in value of some specified collection of fluents in a frame and is thus sensitive to the particular fluents taken into account. Ginsberg and Smith (1988a) adopt a principle of minimal change of world *descriptions*, despite their name 'possible worlds planning'. Winslett (1988) proposes that the degree of change be measured by the number of atomic propositions in a Tarski interpretation whose truth values change from situation to situation, which is again sensitive to the particular model of the world used. Morgenstern and Stein (1988) propose a measurement of change in a theory which is sensitive to the syntactic form of the theory.

What is the justification for an epistemic principle of minimal change? What semantic principles are captured by such epistemic principles? This question is of particular importance given McCarthy and Hayes' insistence that an agent never has a complete description of the world and can never have a complete description of an action as a state transition function. It seems that the semantic principle of minimal change in the world can be captured only by adopting a 'simplifying assumption' that only one action occurs at one time: then anything the agent does not know about can be assumed not to change. But although this assumption may be reasonable for some domains of inquiry, it is surely inadequate for the semantics of action in general. On the contrary, in reality many actions are occurring simultaneously, and the situation resulting from an agent's performing some action at some time depends crucially on all the actions performed at that time.

Thus we are left with adopting a semantic principle of minimal change, then proving or otherwise justifying that some or other reasoning method employed by an agent correctly captures that principle. Some researchers have adopted semantic principles of minimal change. For example, Shoham (1988) defines a preferential ordering on world histories intended to capture the principle of chronological ignorance (although it is questionable whether the 'ignorance' here is not really epistemic, see Galton (1991)), and similarly Kautz (1986) uses circumscription to define a class of first-order interpretations that capture the principle of delaying change for as long as possible. Recently, some researchers have tried to prove the correctness of formal theories of reasoning about action. Katsuno and Mendelzon (1991) define an update operation that is sound and complete with respect to a certain class of changes in finite propositional interpretations, Lin and Shoham (1991) show the correctness of certain nonmonotonic theories with respect to supposed correct monotonic theories of action (which could be regarded as playing the role of a semantics of action), Peppas, Foo and Wobcke (1991) show that state transition functions satisfying the belief revision postulates of Gardenfors (1988) correspond to a class of complete theories satisfying the principle of minimal change, and Sandewall (1992) advocates proving the correctness of a class of reasoning methods for chronicle completion with respect to a class of Herbrand interpretations of state vectors of fluents. However, each of these approaches suffers from the problem that the 'semantics' is based on finite interpretations, monotonic theories, complete theories or Herbrand interpretations respectively, and thus has not bridged the gap between the epistemic and the semantic.

Part of the problem lies is the conception of an action as a function from possible worlds to possible worlds, for this places heavy requirements on the proof of correctness of any reasoning method. Although it is undeniable that a simple sort of atomic, deterministic action of the sort usually considered can be executed in some world state and that after this execution, the world is in some or other state, it does not follow that an action is best modelled in this way. In this paper, we propose a modelling of action based on situation semantics and propose formulations of the frame, ramification and qualification problems based on our perspective. We argue that planning systems are best seen as reasoning with subjunctive conditionals and that their operation presupposes a semantics for action based on situations rather than possible worlds.

2. Modelling Action using Situation Semantics

An action is executed by an agent in the world, but clearly the effects of an agent's action do not extend to the whole world but only within a limited sphere of influence. Similarly, whether an action is executable or not depends only on conditions holding in the immediate environment of the agent. Thus it seems intuitive that an action be modelled as some event which occurs in a situation. Here a *situation*, Barwise and Perry (1983), is a portion of space-time consisting of individuals, objects, properties, relations, events and space-time locations. Actions and events are primitive: they are not further reduced to state transition functions.

An agent always considers itself 'in' a situation; it always views itself as acting 'on' a situation to influence the future. Which situations are appropriate for modelling an agent's actions are dependent on the goals that agent wants to achieve. Thus, as in situation semantics in general, situations arise from the interaction of an organism with its environment. There is no given 'right' set of situations (as there are supposed to be given possible worlds) and so there is no single 'right' way to model an action: two agents may use the same action in different situations to achieve different goals. Thus there is a fundamental tradeoff between the richness and variety of situations an agent can apprehend and the complexity of its actions and plans. This fundamental problem must be resolved by any agent, from the simplest cell to the most complex animal.

In planning systems too, this tradeoff must be resolved. Any computer planning system must contain a model of some aspects of the world (representing the situations that the planner can be in) and a specification of each of its possible actions (representing how the actions affect the facts holding in those situations). Modelling the world necessarily involves some abstraction, but as soon as this abstraction is made the agent gives up on the possibility of complete knowledge of the effects of its actions. Some effects of an action are of interest to the agent – hopefully these are captured in the agent's model; some are not – hopefully these can be ignored by the agent with no loss of power to achieve its goals.

It is our contention that it is this very abstraction process that results in the frame, ramification and qualification problems. The fact that this abstraction is necessary for a planning agent underlines the seriousness of these epistemological problems. They are not mere artifacts of some formalism, but inherent in any representational approach to planning. These problems are but one aspect of one epistemological problem: that of an agent's knowing that the abstraction it has made for planning purposes is in fact a useful one for achieving its goals while not being destroyed. An agent may never know all the effects of what it does, but it must learn to live with this fact and try to plan around it whenever appropriate.

Moreover, a planning system operates with representations of *types* of actions rather than action instances. Once an agent must deal with types of actions, efficiency considerations motivate the 'situatedness' of reasoning about action. For example, consider the simple Unix command *cat <file>*, which denotes a type of action. The argument of the type of action is a file name determined by the context of execution of the command: the current directory. If the agent reasons with actions as complete states of the world, it must 'resolve' the argument of the action to its actual file name. A situated agent can reason about instances of the *cat* action relative to a background context which may change with different executions of the action: thus a situated agent may gain efficiency by using context dependent descriptions of its actions.

A planner must have knowledge of the preconditions of each type of action it can execute, i.e. what facts must hold in a situation if an instance of the type of action is performed, and their effects, i.e. what facts hold at a situation after the performance of an instance of a type of action. The frame problem is that of knowing the facts that do not change through performing an action; the ramification problem that of knowing the effects of performing an action; the qualification problem that of knowing the preconditions of performing an action. These problems first arise for an agent after it has selected an abstraction of the world in which to model its actions. For example, an agent operating in a simple blocks world needs to know that if a block is picked up, the one underneath it is now clear (a ramification) and that this can be done provided the first block is clear (a qualification). The fact that an agent is situated does not change the essence of these problems, but their solution may be simpler for the situated agent *if* the knowledge can be represented using appropriate context dependent descriptions. In this form, the problems may be solvable: that is, if the variety of situations is limited and the plans the agent produces not too complex.

However, the severity of the frame, ramification and qualification problems is that the domain of action may not be limited. A general solution to these problems requires that the agent know that facts about the world which do not figure in its model of the world do not adversely affect the results of its actions. That is, the agent must be assured of the appropriateness of its world model for its purposes while working only within that model and not knowing or even being able to express the potentially disastrous facts. In this form, the problems seem unsolvable, especially when the agent must establish the correctness of its world model for every possible state and not only those states it may actually encounter.

What of epistemic principles of minimal change? Such principles can address the simplified frame problem of an agent's knowing what facts in the situations it models do not change when an action is performed. The justification for this, however, relies on prior acceptance of the appropriateness of the agent's abstraction of the world for its planning purposes: the agent models its world with the epistemic principle of minimal change in mind, so it is no surprise when such principles 'work'. The trouble is that in the case of computer systems, it is the programmer and not the system that performs this abstraction. Similarly, a principle of limited change, Peppas and Wobcke (1992), which is used to address the qualification problem in conjunction with a collection of domain constraints as originally proposed by Ginsberg and Smith (1988b), applies only in those domains where the constraints can actually be formulated. It seems highly unlikely that the laws of physics for the real world can be easily expressed in one or other formal language.

Furthermore, a computer planning system may be limited by having just one world model. Perhaps this is why some linear planners can get bogged down in complexity while solving seemingly very simple planning problems. As a system is extended so that it works in more complex and varied situations, the complexity of its world model increases so that simple problems can become more difficult to solve. The system loses ground in the tradeoff between the complexity of the model and the simplicity of planning. What a planner needs is a way of dynamically adjusting its world views as necessary: simple models for simple problems, complex models for complex problems. This seems to be precisely what motivates hierarchical planning. A hierarchical planning system uses a collection of planning schemas arranged in a hierarchy such that specific schemas are subsumed by more general schemas. A specific type of situation subsumed by a more general type of situation may include not only more facts about situations of that type, but these facts may be made up of more objects, predicates, events, etc., so the specific type of situation may represent a more finely grained abstraction of the world than the general type.

3. Constraints and Reasoning about Action

From the situation semantics perspective, it is the fact that agents are attuned to constraints that explains their success in acting to achieve their goals. A *constraint* $A \Rightarrow B$, or A *involves* B, is an informational relation, Dretske (1981), between two types of facts A and B of the form 'A carries the information that B'. An informational relation is different from a causal relation, although an informational relation is underpinned by a causal relation. A favourite example of Barwise and Perry (1983) illustrates this point. Suppose a coin is tossed and lands heads. Then there is a causal relation between the tossing of this coin and its landing heads. However, for an informational relation to hold, there must be a generally applicable lawlike constraint to the effect that a coin's being tossed carries the information that it lands heads. Clearly, there is no such general constraint: sometimes a coin lands tails, and when it does so, its landing tails is caused by its being tossed. The correct constraint is that a coin's being tossed carries the information that it lands heads or tails. That is, the general constraint $toss\,(coin) \Rightarrow land(heads) \vee land(tails)$ is obtained by abstracting the two causal relations $toss\,(coin) \rightarrow land(heads)$ and $toss\,(coin) \rightarrow land(tails)$.

According to situation theory, observations carry information about situations. In general, a proposition that some type of fact A holds at situation σ might carry the information that some type of fact B holds at situation σ'. We say information 'flows' from σ to σ'. Constraints were modelled in Barwise and Perry (1983) as relations between two types of fact A and B: the constraint $A \Rightarrow B$ holds if whenever A holds at a situation σ, B holds at some related situation σ'. The particular situation σ' is said to be a *meaningful option* of σ with respect to the constraint $A \Rightarrow B$ (provided the constraint holds). An agent 'attuned' to a constraint $A \Rightarrow B$ can, when given the information that A holds at a situation σ, infer that B holds at some related situation σ'. Such an agent may or may not use logic to make this inference: being attuned to a constraint just means having the ability to make the inference.

Following Dretske (1981), a constraint is a lawlike regularity: that is, it does not depend on the particular situation σ being observed. This lawlike quality of constraints is what accounts for the reliability of information flow. It also has the consequence that information once gained is never lost. However, information is not always conveyed: the flow of information is subject to various 'channel conditions' on the means of information flow. Barwise (1985) models the flow of information using constraints which do not hold universally, but only relative to background conditions (corresponding to channel conditions) which it may not be possible to make explicit. Consider one of Dretske's simple examples: the constraint that a doorbell ringing means that someone is at the door. This constraint holds only under certain conditions: e.g. that the wiring is not faulty. The need to admit such background assumptions, which implies a 'situatedness' to information flow, seems at first sight to conflict with the requirement that constraints be lawlike. However, constraints are still underwritten by causal laws: it is just that the whole scheme of such laws is thought of as set against an implicit background. The constraint's applicability depends on the particular situation being observed only insofar as the background conditions are satisfied.

A formalization of constraints is exactly what a planning agent needs for reasoning about actions and plans. Suppose an agent in some situation σ conceives of itself as being in a type of situation σ'. The agent needs to know what facts would hold about σ if it were to perform action A. The agent should take A as the antecedent of a constraint $A \Rightarrow B$ and ask what constraints hold with respect to σ': since constraints represent informational relations, such a B holds at the situation σ becomes if it is extended to include A. Now B may be either a precondition or an effect of A: if it is a precondition, the agent should ensure that it holds before attempting to execute A; if it is an effect, the agent should predict that B would hold after it executes A. Thus a logic of constraints such as that developed in Wobcke (1989, 1993) is essential to formalize reasoning about action based on situation semantics.

It is the fact that constraints hold only with respect to background or channel conditions that illustrates the force of the qualification problem, and explains why nonmonotonicity is essential in reasoning about action. For example, there is a constraint $charge(battery) \Rightarrow start(car)$ which captures physical laws about the electrics and mechanics of car engines. However, this constraint does not hold absolutely: it holds only with respect to a set of background facts, such as the battery being correctly connected to the engine, the engine being in good condition, and so on. Moreover, the background facts need not be known explicitly by a planning agent: the conditions are necessary for the validity of the constraint but may not be needed by an agent if it can be assumed that the 'normal' background conditions hold at the current situation. That is, because constraints hold only with respect to a number of background conditions, the epistemological problem corresponding to the qualification problem is that of the agent's knowing that the background conditions on which the constraint depends actually hold.

A planner can capture part of the implicit background by using a standard hierarchy of planning schemas to represent the meaningful options of a type of situation. However, the meaningful options of a situation depend on which type of situation is used to classify it: these change if the situation is reclassified after more information about it is discovered. So this notion of 'meaningful option of a situation' is epistemic and agent-relative. For example, suppose we have a type of situation σ_1 representing the constraint $charged(battery) \Rightarrow start(car)$ which subsumes σ_2 representing $charged(battery) \wedge \sim connect(battery) \Rightarrow \sim start(car)$. If a particular situation σ is classified as of type σ_1, any instance of σ_1 (including any instance of σ_2) is a meaningful option of σ (the battery might not be connected and the car might not start). However, if it is discovered that in σ the battery is not charged and σ is reclassified as of type σ_2, then the car does not start in any meaningful option of σ. This implies an unavoidable 'situatedness' to planning which underlines the seriousness of the qualification problem: an agent is rarely, if ever, in possession of all the potentially relevant background facts.

4. Conclusion

For a planning system to be correct, the reasoning principles used must agree with reality. We argued that an approach to the semantics of events based on possible worlds coupled with reasoning about action in formalisms such as the situation calculus is unlikely to yield the desired correspondence because of unrealistic simplifying assumptions. We proposed an alternative view of the semantics of action based on situation semantics. The frame, ramification and qualification problems are addressed not by a planning agent, but within a general theory of constraints. An agent need not reason explicitly about the persistence of arbitrary facts, nor about *all* the possible ramifications or qualifications of an action, but only with those facts that are relevant to its current plan. We argue that a plan is correct if it is based on epistemologically reasonable assumptions made by an agent. We do not see it as possible to *prove* the correctness of a planner: there are no logical grounds on which such assumptions can be made. Rather we see a planner's correctness as based on its use of reasonable epistemological principles, and its operation only as reliable as those same principles.

Acknowledgements

I would like to acknowledge discussions with Pavlos Peppas and Norman Foo of the Knowledge Systems Group at the University of Sydney which helped to clarify the ideas in this paper.

References

Barwise, J. & Perry, J. (1983) *Situations and Attitudes.* MIT Press, Cambridge, MA.

Barwise, J. (1985) 'The Situation in Logic-II: Conditionals and Conditional Information.' Technical Report CSLI-85-21, Center for the Study of Language and Information, Stanford University.

Dretske, F.I. (1981) *Knowledge and the Flow of Information.* Blackwell, Oxford.

Galton, A.P. (1991) 'A Critique of Yoav Shoham's Theory of Causal Reasoning.' *Proceedings AAAI-91,* 355-359.

Gärdenfors, P. (1988) *Knowledge in Flux.* MIT Press, Cambridge, MA.

Ginsberg, M.L. & Smith, D.E. (1988a) 'Reasoning about Action I: A Possible Worlds Approach.' *Artificial Intelligence,* **35**, 165-195.

Ginsberg, M.L. & Smith, D.E. (1988b) 'Reasoning about Action II: The Qualification Problem.' *Artificial Intelligence,* **35**, 311-342.

Katsuno, H. & Mendelzon, A.O. (1991) 'On the Difference between Updating a Knowledge Base and Revising It.' *Proceedings KR'91,* 387-394.

Kautz, H.A. (1986) 'The Logic of Persistence.' *Proceedings AAAI-86,* 401-405.

Lewis, D.K. (1973) *Counterfactuals.* Blackwell, Oxford.

Lewis, D.K. (1986) *On the Plurality of Worlds.* Blackwell, Oxford.

Lifschitz, V. (1990) 'Frames in the Space of Situations.' *Artificial Intelligence,* **46**, 365-376.

Lin, F. & Shoham, Y. (1991) 'Provably Correct Theories of Action (preliminary report).' *Proceedings AAAI-91,* 349-354.

McCarthy, J.M. (1977) 'Epistemological Problems of Artificial Intelligence.' *Proceedings IJCAI-5,* 1038-1044.

McCarthy, J.M. & Hayes, P.J. (1969) 'Some Philosophical Problems from the Standpoint of Artificial Intelligence.' in Meltzer, B. & Michie, D. (Eds) *Machine Intelligence, Volume 4.* Edinburgh University Press, Edinburgh.

Morgenstern, L. & Stein, L.A. (1988) 'Why Things Go Wrong: A Formal Theory of Causal Reasoning.' *Proceedings AAAI-88,* 518-523.

Peppas, P., Foo, N.Y. & Wobcke, W.R. (1991) 'Events as Theory Operators.' *Proceedings WOCFAI-91,* 413-426.

Peppas, P. & Wobcke, W.R. (1992) 'On the Use of Epistemic Entrenchment in Reasoning about Action.' *Proceedings ECAI-92,* 403-407.

Sandewall, E. (1992) 'Features and Fluents.' Research Report LiTH-IDA-R-92-30, Dept of Computer and Information Science, Linköping University.

Schank, R.C. & Abelson, R.P. (1977) *Scripts, Plans, Goals and Understanding.* Lawrence Erlbaum Associates, Hillsdale, NJ.

Shoham, Y. (1988) *Reasoning about Change.* MIT Press, Cambridge, MA.

Winslett, M. (1988) 'Reasoning about Action Using a Possible Models Approach.' *Proceedings AAAI-88,* 89-93.

Wobcke, W.R. (1989) 'A Schema-Based Approach to Understanding Subjunctive Conditionals.' *Proceedings IJCAI-11,* 1461-1466.

Wobcke, W.R. (1993) 'A Theory of Conditionals Based on Hierarchies of Situations.' Submitted to *Cognitive Science.*

The Alternating Semantics for Default Theories and Logic Programs *

Li Yan Yuan and Jia-Huai You
Department of Computing Science
The University of Alberta
Edmonton, CANADA T6G 2H1
{yuan, you}@cs.ualberta.ca

Abstract

In this paper we propose a semantics for default theories, based on van Gelder's alternating fixpoint theory. The distinct feature of this semantics is its preservation of Reiter's semantics when a default theory is not considered "problematic" under Reiter's semantics. Differences arise only when a default theory has no extensions, or has only "biased extensions" under Reiter's semantics. This feature allows skeptical reasoning in Reiter's logic to be properly preserved in the new semantics. By the familiar, natural translation from logic programs to default theories, the semantics proposed for default theories provides a natural extension to the stable model semantics of normal logic programs.

1 Introduction

Default logic, introduced by Reiter [7], forms one of the most important formalisms for nonmonotonic reasoning. One of the problems with this default logic is that a reasonable default theory may not always have extensions. In such a case, the semantics of the default theory is not defined. There are also default theories for which there seem to be reasonable (partial) extensions that could not be captured in Reiter's extension semantics (from now on, the extension semantics).

The aim of this paper is to define a semantics for default theories that is faithful to the extension semantics for those default theories whose extension semantics yields (arguably) perfect extensions. Arguably, if a default theory is not considered problematic under the extension semantics, one expects to get the same conclusions from any semantics that "corrects" its problem. This semantic preservation is important for preserving both choice reasoning and skeptical reasoning, as advocated originally by Reiter on the use of default logic.

Various semantics have been proposed in an attempt to resolve this problem. Marek and Truszczynski [5] introduced the concept of *weak extensions* of default theories and showed that weak extensions of a default theory correspond to expansions of suitably translated

*This research is partially supported by two NSERC operating grants

formulas in autoepistemic logic. A default theory however is not guaranteed to possess a weak extension. The well-founded semantics for logic programs has been extended to default theories (see, for example, [6]). Although the well-founded approach is computationally more attractive, it nevertheless pays the price for being unable to draw skeptical conclusions that are implied under Reiter's extensions semantics. Based on the concept of *stable class* for logic programs, Baral and Subrahmanian [2, 1] proposed the extension class semantics for default theories. This semantics is still considered weak in that there exist default theories with (arguably) perfect extensions; but its extension class semantics could not draw any useful conclusion. This phenomenon has a significant impact on identifying intended stable classes for logic programs. As a matter of fact, as we will show, some obvious unintuitive conclusions can be implied by the stable class semantics for logic programs.

Van Gelder, on the other hand, has shown that the well-founded semantics of logic programs can be defined by the alternating fixpoint theory [3]. The basic idea is that if an operator T is anti-monotonic, i.e., for E_1 and E_2, from $E_1 \subseteq E_2$ we have $T(E_2) \subseteq T(E_1)$, then T^2, the function that applies T twice, is monotonic, and thus has at least one alternating fixpoint.

The main result of this paper is to show that the alternating fixpoint theory can be used to define a semantics that corrects the problem of the extension semantics without affecting those default theories whose extension semantics have been considered appropriate.

2 Default Logic and its Semantics

We assume a propositional language L consisting of the usual well formed formulas over an alphabet $\mathcal{B}$. A *default* is a triple $d = \{p(d), j(d), c(d)\}$, where $p(d)$ and $c(d)$ are formulas of L, and $j(d)$ is a finite subset of L. $p(d)$ is called the *prerequisite* of d, $j(d)$ the *justification* of d, and $c(d)$ the *consequent*, or *conclusion* of d. Default d is usually denoted by $\frac{p(d):j(d)}{c(d)}$. A default theory is a pair (D, W), where $W \subseteq L$, and D is a collection of defaults.

The Extension Semantics of Reiter Given a default theory (D, W) and a set E of formulas (called *context*), we first define an operator $R_{E,D}$ which maps sets of formulas to sets of formulas in the following way:

$$R_{E,D}(S) = Cn(S \cup \{c(d) | d \in D, p(d) \in S, \neg j(d) \cap E = \emptyset\})$$

where Cn denotes the familiar Tarskian consequence operator and $\neg j(d) = \{\neg\alpha | \alpha \in j(d)\}$. We now define an operator T that transforms a given set E of formulas into a set $T(E)$ of formulas as follows.

Definition 2.1 ([7, 1]) Suppose (D, W) is a default theory, and E is a set of formulas, called the context. Assume

$$R^0_{E,D} = Cn(W); \qquad R^{n+1}_{E,D} = R_{E,D}(R^n_{E,D}(W)); \qquad R^\infty_{E,D} = \bigcup_{i=0}^\infty R^i_{E,D}(W);$$

Then an operator $T_{D,W}(E)$ is defined as

$$T_{D,W}(E) = R^\infty_{E,D}(W).$$

When there is no confusion, we also use $T(E)$ to denote $T_{D,W}(E)$. □

Lemma 2.1 ([2]) T is anti-monotonic, that is $T(E_1) \subseteq T(E_2)$ if $E_2 \subseteq E_1$. □

Given a default theory (D, W) and a set of formula $E = Cn(E)$, E is said to be a *fixpoint* of (D, W) if and only if $E = T(E)$. E is said to be an *alternating fixpoint* of (D, W) if and only if $E = T(T(E))$. Since T is anti-monotonic, T^2 is monotonic and therefore, (D, W) has at least one alternating fixpoint.

The extension semantics of a default theory is determined by its extensions.

Definition 2.2 ([7, 1]) E is an extension of default theory (D, W) if and only if E is a fixpoint of $T_{E,D}$. □

According to Reiter, there are two reasoning modes in using default logic: each arbitrarily chosen extension can be seen as an acceptable set of beliefs, or the truth of a formula is determined by whether it is contained in all extensions. The former is called *choice reasoning* and latter *skeptical reasoning*.

However, a default theory may have no extensions at all.

The Extension Class Semantics Baral and Subrahmanian have proposed the structure of *extension class* to represent the meaning of default theories [2, 1]. The basic idea behind the concept of extension class is that T may not always have fixpoints; however, there may exist a collection of points so that T circles around this collection of points.

Example 2.1 Consider the default theory (D, W), where $W = \{p\}$, and $D = \{\frac{:\neg q}{q}\}$. Although the default theory has no extensions at all, it has exactly one extension class

$$\{Cn(\{p\}), Cn(\{p, q\})\}$$

Thus, based on the extension class semantics, p is *true* and q is *unknown*. □

The Well-Founded Semantics Recently, Baral and Subrahmanian extend the well-founded semantics, introduced by Van Gelder, Ross, and Schlipf [4], to default theories in terms of alternating fixpoints [3, 1]. Since T is anti-monotonic, T^2, the function that applies T twice, is monotonic. Let $lpf(T^2)$ be the least fixpoint of T^2 and $gfp(T^2)$ be the greatest fixpoint of (T^2). Then the well-founded semantics is defined as follows.

Definition 2.3 ([1]) Let (D, W) be a default theory and F be a formula. Then F is true in the well-founded semantics of the theory if F is true in $lfp(T^2)$. F is false in the well-founded semantics of the theory if F is false in $gfp(T^2)$. □

3 Recent Semantics Considered Too Weak

The original extension semantics for default theories suffers from the no-extension problem, that is, some default theories may not have extensions at all, as demonstrated by Example 2.1. However, the recently proposed semantics to address this problem do not preserve Reiter's semantics for "non-problematic" default theories.

Example 3.1 Let (D, W) be the default theory, where

$$W = \{c \leftarrow a, c \leftarrow b\} \qquad D = \{\frac{: \neg b}{a}, \frac{: \neg a}{b}\}$$

There are two extensions $E_1 = Cn(\{a, c\} \cup W)$ and $E_2 = Cn(\{b, c\} \cup W)$, which seem to capture exactly the intuitive meaning of the theory.

However, under both the well-founded semantics by Baral and Subrahmanian and the three-valued approach by Przymusinski, all the atoms have the unknown value. This yields a weaker semantics, and the arguably intuitive meaning under Reiter's semantics is not preserved.

It then seems desirable for a new semantics that intends to "correct" the no-extension problem to preserve the semantics of Reiter for "non-problematic" default theories. □

The following example shows that the approach used in the stable class semantics may yield unreanonable semantics for logic programs.

Example 3.2 Let $\mathcal{P}$ be given by

$$a \leftarrow \neg a; \qquad b \leftarrow \neg b; \qquad c \leftarrow a, \neg a; \qquad c \leftarrow b, \neg b.$$

$\mathcal{P}$ has two strict stable classes, viz. $C_1 = \{\{a, b, c\}, \emptyset\}$, and $C_2 = \{\{a, c\}, \{b, c\}\}$, but only C_2 is minimal by Smyth ordering. Therefore, the stable class semantics of $\mathcal{P}$ is determined by C_2, which implies c is true.

Since the premises for deriving c can never be satisfied in any circumstance, c shall not be true in any reasonable semantics. □

4 The Alternating Semantics for Default Theories

In this section, we define the alternating semantics for default theories and demonstrate that the alternating semantics provides a satisfactory solution to the problems discussed in the previous section.

The basic idea behind the alternating semantics is that given a default theory (D, W), $T_{D,W}$ may not always have fixpoints, which is the source of the no-extension problem for the extension semantics of default logic. However, since T is anti-monotonic, T^2 is monotonic and therefore, the least fixpoint of T^2 does exist. By considering fixpoints of T^2, that is the alternating fixpoints, instead of extension classes, we are able to define a desired semantics.

Definition 4.1 Let (D, W) be a default theory, and E be a set of formulas. E is said to be an alternating point of (D, W) if and only if $E = T(T(E))$. □

Example 4.1 Consider the default theory in Example 3.1 again. The theory has four alternating fixpoints, viz. $I_1 = Cn(\{a, c\} \cup W)$, $I_2 = Cn(\{b, c\} \cup W)$, $I_3 = Cn(\{a, b, c\} \cup W)$, and $I_4 = Cn(W)$. □

It is easy to show that the well-founded semantics is characterized by the set of all alternating fixpoints of a default theory. However, not every alternating fixpoint makes positive contribution to the semantics. Consider the theory in Example 4.1 again. (D, W) has four alternating fixpoints, viz I_1, I_2, I_3, and I_4. But the intuitive meaning of the theory is characterized by the first two alternating fixpoints. The challenge here is how to eliminate those undesirable alternating fixpoints.

Let (D, W) be a default theory and I be an alternating fixpoint of the theory. Then $J = T(I)$ is also an alternating fixpoint, $\{I, J\}$ is an extension class, and I is a fixpoint if and only if $I = J$. This simple fact tells us that each fixpoint is closely attached to another alternating fixpoint. Let I and J be such two alternating fixpoints. Then $\{I, J\}$ can be used to represent the meaning of the theory without conflict only if one is a subset of another, i.e., either $I \subseteq J$ or $J \subseteq I$. This observation leads to the following definition.

Definition 4.2 Let (D, W) be a default theory, and I be an alternating fixpoint of the theory. Then I is said to be

1. a *max-alternating fixpoint* of the theory if and only if $T(I) \subseteq I$,

2. a *minimal max-alternating fixpoint* of the theory if I is a max-alternating fixpoint of the theory and there exists no man-alternating fixpoint J such that $J \subset I$, and

3. a *normal* alternating fixpoint of the theory if either I is a minimal max-alternating fixpoint or $T(I)$ is a minimal max-alternating fixpoint of the theory.

The alternating semantics of the default theory is then defined by the set of all normal alternating fixpoints of the theory. □

Example 4.2 Consider the default theory in Example 3.1 and 4.1 again. I_1, I_2 and I_3 are max-alternating fixpoints, but I_4 is not. Furthermore, only I_1 and I_2 are minimal max-alternating fixpoints, and therefore, I_1 and I_2 are the only normal alternating fixpoints of the theory. □

Theorem 4.1 Every default theory has at least one normal alternating fixpoint.

Example 4.3 Consider the default theory corresponding to the logic program in Example 3.2 as follows.

$$W = \emptyset, \qquad D = \{\frac{:\neg a}{a}, \frac{:\neg b}{b}, \frac{a:\neg a}{c}, \frac{b:\neg b}{c}\}$$

The theory has four alternating fixpoints, viz. $I_1 = Cn(\{a, b, c\})$, $I_2 = Cn(\emptyset)$, $I_3 = Cn(\{a, c\})$, and $I_4 = Cn(\{b, c\})$.

Of four alternating fixpoints, only I_1 is a max-alternating fixpoint, and therefore, I_1 and I_2 are the only normal alternating fixpoints of the theory. Hence the alternating semantics of the theory is the same as its well-founded semantics. □

There are also default theories for which there seem to be reasonable (partial) extensions that could not be captured in Reiter's extension semantics.

Example 4.4 Consider the default theory (D, W) given by

$$W = \emptyset, \qquad D = \{\frac{:\neg a}{b}, \frac{:\neg b}{a}, \frac{:\neg a}{p}, \frac{:\neg p}{p}\}$$

The default theory has three normal alternating fixpoints: $I_1 = Cn(\{b, p\}), I_2 = Cn(\{a, p\})$, and $I_3 = Cn(\{a\})$. I_1 corresponds to one extension class and the other extension class consists of I_2 and I_3. Thus, The alternating semantics of (D, W) coincides with the stable class semantics of $\mathcal{P}$. However, under the extension semantics we have exactly one extension I_1, which seems biased. □

It is straightfoward to demonstrate that the alternating semantics is not a proper extension of the stable class semantics, since a stable class may not correspond to any alternating fixpoints.

By the familiar, natural translation from logic programs to default theories [5], the alternating semantics we propose here for default theories automatically provides a natural semantics for normal logic programs.

References

[1] C.R. Baral and V.S. Subrahmanian. Dualities between alternative semantics for logic programming and nonmonotonic reasoning. *Journal of Automated Reasoning*, (to appear).

[2] C.R. Baral and V.S. Subrahmanian. Stable and extension class theory for logic programs and default logics. *Journal of Automated Reasoning*, 8:345 - 366, 1992.

[3] A. Van Gelder. The alternating fixpoints of logic programs with negation. In *Proceedings of the 8th ACM PODS*, pages 1 - 10, 1989.

[4] A. Van Gelder, K. Ross, and J.S. Schlipf. The well-founded semantics for general logic programs. *JACM*, 38:620 - 650, 1991.

[5] W. Marek and M. Truszczunski. Relating autoepistemic and default logic. In *Proc. of KR'89*, pages 276 - 288, 1989.

[6] T.C. Przymusinski. Three-valued formalizations of non-monotonic reasoning and logic programming. In *Proceedings of KR'89*, 1989.

[7] R. Reiter. A logic for default reasoning. *Artificial Intelligence*, 13:81–132, 1980.

Transmutations for Theory Bases

M.A. Williams

Information Systems Group
Department of Management
University of Newcastle, NSW 2308
Australia

Knowledge Systems Group
Department of Computer Science
University of Sydney, NSW 2006
Australia

maryanne@frey.newcastle.edu.au
Telephone: +61 49 215996

Abstract

Knowledge systems are generally not endowed with complete information about the world with which they interact, consequently they require a mechanism for modifying their knowledge as more information is acquired. The AGM paradigm is a formal approach to theory change, its principal constructions for theory change operators rely on some form of underlying preference relation. An *ensconcement* can be used to construct theory base change operators within AGM paradigm. A transmutation is the process of changing the underlying preference relation in response to new information. In this article we explore transmutations of theory bases where the underlying preference relation is similiar to an ensconcement ordering.

1 Introduction

The AGM paradigm [1,2,3] provides a formal approach to theory change, it consists of sets of postulates and various contructions for its theory change operators. These constructions rely on some form of underlying preference relation which is predetermined or given at the outset. Although this property provides desirable theoretical freedom, it leads to difficulties in designing computer-based knowledge revision systems. Therefore, in order to accommodate subsequent informational changes such a system will require guidance in revising its preference relation. We refer to the process of changing the underlying preference relation for a knowledge system as a *transmutation*. We described transmutations of preference relations on theories in [13] by generalizing Spohn's approach [9], in particular we formalized a transmutation to be a transformation of a preference relation that preserves the behaviour of theory change operators within the AGM paradigm.

In [10, 11] we introduced an ensconcement ordering of a theory base, and provided conditions under which an ensconcement can be used to construct change operators for both theories and theory bases.

In this article we explore transmutations for theory bases where the underlying preference relation is related to an ensconcement ordering. In Section 2 we outline the technical preliminaries, in Section 3 we review theory base operators and their construction using an ensconcement. In Section 4 we introduce transmutations of partial epistemic entrenchment ordinal functions, and describe the relationship between such a function and an ensconcement in constructing change operators. A discussion of related work [5, 6, 8] can be found in [12].

2 Preliminaries

Let $\mathbf{L}$ denote a language which contains a complete set of Boolean connectives. We will denote formulae in $\mathbf{L}$ by lower case Greek letters. We assume $\mathbf{L}$ is governed by a logic that is identified with its consequence relation $\vdash$. The relation $\vdash$ is assumed to satisfy the following conditions:

(a) If α is a truth-functional tautology, then $\vdash \alpha$.
(b) If $\alpha \vdash \beta$ and $\vdash \alpha$, then $\vdash \beta$ (*modus ponens*).
(c) $\vdash$ is consistent, that is, $\not\vdash \bot$, where $\bot$ denotes the inconsistent theory.
(d) $\vdash$ satisfies the deduction theorem.
(e) $\vdash$ is compact.

The set of all logical consequences of a set $\Gamma \subseteq \mathbf{L}$, that is $\{\alpha : \Gamma \vdash \alpha\}$, is denoted by $\mathrm{Cn}(\Gamma)$. The set of tautologies, $\{\alpha : \vdash \alpha\}$, is denoted by $\top$, and those formulae not in $\top$ are referred to as *nontautological*. A *theory* of $\mathbf{L}$ is any subset of $\mathbf{L}$, closed under $\vdash$. A *consistent* theory of $\mathbf{L}$ is any theory of $\mathbf{L}$ that does not contain both α and $\neg\alpha$, for any formula α of $\mathbf{L}$. Whenever a theory $T = \mathrm{Cn}(\Gamma)$, Γ is referred to as a *theory base for* T. A theory is *finite* if the consequence relation $\vdash$ partitions the elements of T into a finite number of equivalence classes. The *dual atoms* for a finite theory T are those nontautological elements $\alpha \in T$ such that for all $\beta \in \mathrm{Cn}(\{\alpha\}) \cap T$, either $\vdash \beta$ or $\vdash \alpha \equiv \beta$ [6].

3 Theory Base Change

In this section we review definitions and results from [11], in particular we describe postulates for theory base change operators, and ensconcements as a construction for them.

There are three principal operators; expansion, contraction and revision. Expansion can be defined in logical and set theoretical terms, in particular, the expansion of a theory base Γ with respect to a formula α, is defined to be $\Gamma^{\oplus}_{\alpha} = \Gamma \cup \{\alpha\}$. However due to the nonuniqueness of both contraction and revision operators, they are described using a set of rationality postulates. The postulates given below have been taken from [11], where their justification can be found.

Consider the following postulates for the contraction of a theory base Γ with respect to α, denoted by $\Gamma^{\ominus}_{\alpha}$.

($^{\ominus}1$) $\Gamma^{\ominus}_{\alpha} \subseteq \Gamma$
($^{\ominus}2$) If $\Gamma \not\vdash \alpha$ or $\vdash \alpha$, then $\Gamma \subseteq \Gamma^{\ominus}_{\alpha}$
($^{\ominus}3$) If $\not\vdash \alpha$, then $\Gamma^{\ominus}_{\alpha} \not\vdash \alpha$
($^{\ominus}4$) If $\vdash \alpha \equiv \beta$, then $\Gamma^{\ominus}_{\alpha} = \Gamma^{\ominus}_{\beta}$
($^{\ominus}5$) $\Gamma^{\ominus}_{\alpha} \cap \Gamma^{\ominus}_{\beta} \subseteq \Gamma^{\ominus}_{\alpha\wedge\beta}$
($^{\ominus}6$) If $\Gamma^{\ominus}_{\alpha\wedge\beta} \not\vdash \alpha$, then $\Gamma^{\ominus}_{\alpha\wedge\beta} \subseteq \Gamma^{\ominus}_{\alpha}$
($^{\ominus}7$) For every nonempty set Λ of nontautological formulae, there exists a formula $\alpha \in \Lambda$ such that $\alpha \notin \Gamma^{\ominus}_{\alpha\wedge\beta}$ for every $\beta \in \Lambda$.
($^{\ominus}8$) For every nonempty set Λ of nontautological formulae, there exists a formula $\alpha \in \Lambda$ such that $\beta \notin \Gamma^{\ominus}_{\alpha\wedge\beta}$ for every $\beta \in \Lambda$.

Definition: A *theory base contraction operator*, $^{\ominus}$, satisfies ($^{\ominus}1$) – ($^{\ominus}6$).

A *very well-behaved theory base contraction operator*, $^\ominus$, satisfies ($^\ominus$1) – ($^\ominus$8).

Consider the following postulates for the revision of a theory base Γ with respect to α, denoted by $\Gamma^\otimes_\alpha$.

($^\otimes$1) $\alpha \in \Gamma^\otimes_\alpha$

($^\otimes$2) $\Gamma^\oplus_\alpha \vdash \Gamma^\otimes_\alpha$

($^\otimes$3) If $\Gamma \nvdash \neg\alpha$, then $\Gamma^\oplus_\alpha \subseteq \Gamma^\otimes_\alpha$

($^\otimes$4) $\Gamma^\otimes_\alpha \vdash \perp$ if and only if $\vdash \neg\alpha$

($^\otimes$5) If $\vdash \alpha \equiv \beta$, then $\mathrm{Cn}(\Gamma^\otimes_\alpha) = \mathrm{Cn}(\Gamma^\otimes_\beta)$

($^\otimes$6) $\Gamma^\otimes_{\alpha\wedge\beta} \subseteq (\Gamma^\otimes_\alpha)^\oplus_{\alpha\wedge\beta}$

($^\otimes$7) If $\Gamma^\otimes_\alpha \nvdash \neg\beta$, then $\Gamma^\otimes_{\alpha\wedge\beta} \vdash (\Gamma^\otimes_\alpha)^\oplus_\beta$

($^\otimes$8) For every nonempty set Λ of nontautological formulae, there exists a formula $\alpha \in \Lambda$ such that $\alpha \notin \Gamma^\otimes_{\neg\alpha\vee\neg\beta}$ for every $\beta \in \Lambda$.

($^\otimes$9) For every nonempty set Λ of nontautological formulae, there exists a formula $\alpha \in \Lambda$ such that $\beta \notin \Gamma^\otimes_{\neg\alpha\vee\neg\beta}$ for every $\beta \in \Lambda$.

`Definition`: A *theory base revision operator*, $^\otimes$, satisfies ($^\otimes$1) – ($^\otimes$7).
A *very well-behaved theory base revision operator*, $^\otimes$, satisfies ($^\otimes$1) – ($^\otimes$9).

These postulates circumscribe the class of theory change operators, however they do not provide a mechanism for constructing such operators. Indeed the construction of these operators requires extralogical information. We show in [11] that an ensconcement ordering, defined below, is capable of uniquely determining a theory base change operator, and a theory change operator [1, 2, 3] for both contraction and revision.

`Definition`: Define an *ensconcement* to be a set of formulae Γ together with a total preorder $\preceq$ of Γ satisfying the following condition:

($\preceq$1) For all nontautological $\beta \in \Gamma$, $\{\alpha \in \Gamma : \beta \prec \alpha\} \nvdash \beta$

($\preceq$2) For all α, $\beta \in \Gamma$, $\beta \preceq \alpha$ whenever $\vdash \alpha$

If $\preceq$ is well-ordered, then we say that the ensconcement is well-ordered, and similarly if $\preceq$ is inversely well-ordered, then we say that the ensconcement is inversely well-ordered. If $\preceq$ is both well-ordered and inversely well-ordered, then $\preceq$ has a finite number of natural partitions. In which case we refer to the ensconcement as finite. In particular, if Γ doesn't contain any tautologies and possesses n natural partitions, or does contain a tautology and possesses $n+1$ natural partitions, then we refer to it as an *n-ensconcement*.

`Definition`: Let α be a formula in L. Let $(\Gamma, \preceq)$ be an n-ensconcement. Let $\Gamma_1, \Gamma_2 \ldots, \Gamma_{n+1}$ be the natural partitions of $\preceq$, indexed so that $\alpha \in \Gamma_i$, $\beta \in \Gamma_{i+1}$ implies $\alpha \prec \beta$ for $1 \leq i \leq n$, we define,

$$\mathrm{rank}(\alpha) = \begin{cases} \text{largest } j \text{ such that } \bigcup_{i=j}^{n} \Gamma_i \vdash \alpha & \text{if } \Gamma \vdash \alpha \\ 0 & \text{otherwise.} \end{cases}$$

`Definition`: Let $(\Gamma, \preceq)$ be an n-ensconcement. Define, $\Gamma^\ominus_\alpha$, by the following condition:

$$(E^\ominus) \qquad \Gamma^\ominus_\alpha = \begin{cases} \{\beta \in \Gamma : \bigcup_{i=\mathrm{rank}(\alpha)+1}^{n} \Gamma_i \cup \{\neg\alpha\} \vdash \beta\} & \text{if } \nvdash \alpha \\ \Gamma & \text{otherwise.} \end{cases}$$

In [11] we show that for an n-ensconcement $(E^\ominus)$ provides an explicit determination of a very well-behaved theory base contraction operator, that is, it satisfies ($^\ominus$1) – ($^\ominus$8).

Moreover, we show how to generate an epistemic entrenchment from an ensconcement, denoted by $\leq_{\preceq}$, such that the theory base contraction operator for Γ uniquely determined by $(E^{\ominus})$ and $\preceq$, is equivalent to Γ intersected with the theory contraction for $Cn(\Gamma)$, determined by the epistemic entrenchment $\leq_{\preceq}$.

Definition: Let $(\Gamma, \preceq)$ be an n-ensconcement. Define, $\Gamma^{\circledast}_{\alpha}$, by the following condition:

$$(E^{\circledast}) \qquad \Gamma^{\circledast}_{\alpha} = \begin{cases} \bigcup_{i=\text{rank}(\neg\alpha)+1}^{n} \Gamma_i \cup \{\alpha\} & \text{if } \nvdash \neg\alpha \\ \Gamma^{\oplus}_{\alpha} & \text{otherwise.} \end{cases}$$

In [11] we show $(E^{\circledast})$ provides an explicit determination of a very well-behaved theory base revision operator, that is, it satisfies $(^{\circledast}1)$ – $(^{\circledast}8)$. Furthermore, in [11] we show that $Cn(\Gamma^{\circledast}_{\alpha})$ is equivalent to the theory revision operator for $Cn(\Gamma)$ determined by $\leq_{\preceq}$.

In [11] we also show there exists a counterpart to the Levi Identity involving theory base operations, that is, $Cn(\Gamma^{\circledast}_{\alpha}) = Cn((\Gamma^{\ominus}_{\neg\alpha})^{\oplus}_{\alpha})$. Similiarly, there is a counterpart to the Harper Identity, namely $\Gamma^{\ominus}_{\alpha} = Cn(\Gamma^{\circledast}_{\neg\alpha}) \cap \Gamma$. Therefore, a theory base revision may be constructed from a theory base contraction, and vice versa. Moreover, $\Gamma^{\ominus}_{\neg\alpha} \cup \alpha$ is a theory base for $\Gamma^{\circledast}_{\alpha}$.

4 Transmutations

Intuitively, the problem of iterated revision is determining how the underlying preference relation should change in response to new information. According to Schlecta [8] "...iterated revision ...is a very common phenomenon for cognitive systems". In [12] we discuss iterated revisions, and refer to the process of changing the underlying preference relation of a theory as a *transmutation*.

We use a partial epistemic entrenchment ordinal function as the underlying preference relation, which maps a subset of formulae in **L** to the ordinals, and is formally defined below.

Definition: A *partial epistemic entrenchment ordinal function*, a PE, is a function **PE** from a subset of nontautological formulae in **L** into the class of ordinals such that the following conditions are satisfied:

(PE1) For all $\beta \in \text{Dom}(\mathbf{PE})$, $\{\alpha \in \text{Dom}(\mathbf{PE}) : \mathbf{PE}(\beta) < \mathbf{PE}(\alpha)\} \nvdash \beta$, where $\text{Dom}(\mathbf{PE})$ is the domain of **PE**.

(PE2) If $\vdash \neg\alpha$, then $\mathbf{PE}(\alpha) = 0$.

We refer to a PE with a finite range as a *finite* PE, and we denote the family of all partial epistemic entrenchment ordinal functions by $\mathcal{E}$.

Definition: Define the *explicit knowledge set* represented by $\mathbf{PE} \in \mathcal{E}$ to be $\text{Dom}(\mathbf{PE})$, and denote it by $\text{eks}(\mathbf{PE})$. Similiarly, define the *implicit knowledge set* represented by $\mathbf{PE} \in \mathcal{E}$ to be $Cn(\text{Dom}(\mathbf{PE}))$, and denote it by $\text{iks}(\mathbf{PE})$.

Definition: Let α be a formula in **L**. Let **PE** be in $\mathcal{E}$. We define, the *degree of acceptance* of a formula α to be:

$$\deg(\alpha) = \begin{cases} \text{largest } j \text{ such that } \{\beta \in \mathbf{L} : \mathbf{PE}(\beta) = j\} \vdash \alpha & \text{if eks}(\mathbf{PE}) \vdash \alpha \\ 0 & \text{otherwise.} \end{cases}$$

A formula α is *explicitly accepted* if and only if $\alpha \in \text{eks}(\mathbf{PE})$. A formula α is *implicitly accepted* if and only if $\alpha \in \text{iks}(\mathbf{PE})$. We say α is more *firmly accepted* than β if and only if $\deg(\alpha) > \deg(\beta)$.

Theorem 1: Let $\Gamma \subseteq \mathbf{L}$ be a set of nontautological formulae. For every very well-behaved theory base contraction operator $\ominus$ for Γ, there exists a $\mathbf{PE} \in \mathcal{E}$ such that $\text{eks}(\mathbf{PE}) = \Gamma$, and the $(\mathbf{PE}^{\ominus})$ condition, below, is true for every $\alpha \in \mathbf{L}$. Conversely, for every finite $\mathbf{PE} \in \mathcal{E}$, there exists a very well-behaved theory base contraction operator $\ominus$ for eks($\mathbf{PE}$) such that $(\mathbf{PE}^{\ominus})$ is true for every $\alpha \in \mathbf{L}$.

$$(\mathbf{PE}^{\ominus})\ (\text{eks}(\mathbf{PE}))^{\ominus}_{\alpha} = \begin{cases} \{\beta \in \text{eks}(\mathbf{PE}) : \{\gamma \in \text{eks}(\mathbf{PE}) : \deg(\alpha) < \mathbf{PE}(\gamma)\} \cup \{\neg\alpha\} \vdash \beta\} & \text{if } \nvdash \alpha \\ \text{eks}(\mathbf{PE}) & \text{otherwise.} \end{cases}$$

Theorem 2: Let $\Gamma \subseteq \mathbf{L}$ be a set of nontautological formulae. For every very well-behaved theory base revision operator $\circledast$ for Γ, there exists a $\mathbf{PE} \in \mathcal{E}$ such that $\text{eks}(\mathbf{PE}) = \Gamma$, and the $(\mathbf{PE}^{\circledast})$ condition, below, is true for every $\alpha \in \mathbf{L}$. Conversely, for every finite $\mathbf{PE} \in \mathcal{E}$, there exists a very well-behaved theory base revision operator $\circledast$ for eks($\mathbf{PE}$) such that $(\mathbf{PE}^{\circledast})$ is true for every $\alpha \in \mathbf{L}$.

$$(\mathbf{PE}^{\circledast}) \quad (\text{eks}(\mathbf{PE}))^{\circledast}_{\alpha} = \begin{cases} \{\beta \in \mathbf{L} : \deg(\neg\alpha) < \mathbf{PE}(\beta)\} \cup \{\alpha\} & \text{if } \nvdash \neg\alpha \\ (\text{eks}(\mathbf{PE}))^{\oplus}_{\alpha} & \text{otherwise.} \end{cases}$$

Theorem 3: Let $\Gamma \subseteq \mathbf{L}$ be a set of nontautological formulae. If $(\Gamma, \preceq)$ is a finite ensconcement, and $\mathbf{PE} \in \mathcal{E}$ is a finite PE, then $\preceq$ and $\mathbf{PE}$ represent the *same* revision operator for Γ by means of $(E^{\ominus})$ and $(\mathbf{PE}^{\circledast})$ conditions, respectively, if and only if the following condition is satisfied:

For every consistent $\alpha, \beta \in \Gamma$, $\alpha \preceq \beta$ if and only if $\mathbf{PE}(\alpha) \leq \mathbf{PE}(\beta)$.

For a given $\mathbf{PE} \in \mathcal{E}$ the conditions $(\mathbf{PE}^{\circledast})$ and $(\mathbf{PE}^{\ominus})$ determine a knowledge set after a formula α is incorporated or removed, respectively, however these conditions do not determine another PE, upon which a subsequent revision, or contraction could be specified. According to Rott [6] it is not knowledge sets that need to be revised but the underlying preference orderings. The definition below describes a transmutation of a PE to another PE, such that a nontautological, consistent formula α has the degree of acceptance i.

Definition: We define a transmutation schema for PE's, $\star$, to be a operator from $\mathcal{E} \times \{\mathbf{L} \backslash \{\bot, \top\}\} \times \mathcal{O}$ to $\mathcal{E}$, where $\mathcal{O}$ is an ordinal, such that $(\mathbf{PE}, \alpha, i) \mapsto \mathbf{PE}^{\star}(\alpha, i)$ which satisfies:

(a) $\mathbf{PE}^{\star}(\alpha, i)(\alpha) = i$, and

(b) $$\text{eks}(\mathbf{PE}^{\star}(\alpha, i)) = \begin{cases} \{\beta \in \mathbf{L} : \deg(\neg\alpha) < \mathbf{PE}(\beta)\} \cup \{\alpha\} & \text{if } i > 0 \\ \{\beta \in \text{eks}(\mathbf{PE}) : \{\gamma \in \text{eks}(\mathbf{PE}) : \deg(\alpha) < \mathbf{PE}(\gamma)\} \cup \{\neg\alpha\} \vdash \beta\} & \text{otherwise.} \end{cases}$$

We say $\mathbf{PE}^{\star}(\alpha, i)$ is an (α, i)–transmutation of $\mathbf{PE}$, and we note that it is not defined for inconsistent, or tautological α. Intuitively, a transmutation $\mathbf{PE}^{\star}(\alpha, i)$, is a PE where $\text{eks}(\mathbf{PE}^{\star}(\alpha, i))$ represents a 'minimal change' of eks($\mathbf{PE}$) such that α is assigned the degree of acceptance i.

We describe a restructuring of a PE, as a reorganization of accepted information. More precisely, we refer to a (α, i)–transmutation of an $\mathbf{PE}$ where α is implicitly accepted as a *restructuring* [7] of $\mathbf{PE}$.

Spohn has argued that *conditionalization* [10] is a desirable process for iterated revision, for instance it is reversible, and commutative. In the theorem below we define a conditionalization, and show that for $\mathbf{PE} \in \mathcal{E}$, if eks($\mathbf{PE}$) is a theory, then a conditionalization of $\mathbf{PE}$ is a transmutation.

Theorem 4: Let $\mathbf{L}$ be a finite language. Let $\mathbf{PE} \in \mathcal{E}$ such that eks($\mathbf{PE}$) = iks($\mathbf{PE}$), and i be an ordinal. Let $\alpha \in \mathbf{L}$ be such that $\nvdash \neg\alpha$, and $\nvdash \alpha$. Then $\mathbf{PE}^{\star}(\alpha, i)$, where $\star$ is defined by (Cond–$\mathbf{PE}$) below, is an (α, i)–transmutation of $\mathbf{PE}$. We refer to such a transmutation as the (α, i)–conditionalization of $\mathbf{PE}$.

(Cond–$\mathbf{PE}$)
$$\mathbf{PE}^{\star}(\alpha, i)(\beta) = \begin{cases} \mathbf{PE}(\beta) - \mathbf{PE}(\neg\alpha) & \text{if } \alpha \wedge \neg\beta \nvdash \bot \\ \mathbf{PE}(\beta) - \mathbf{PE}(\neg\alpha) + i & \text{otherwise,} \end{cases}$$
where $\beta \in \mathbf{L}$ is a dual atom.

By the definition of a PE, it is not hard to see that the degree of acceptance of the dual atoms will uniquely determine the degree of acceptance of all other formulae in eks($\mathbf{PE}$). It was shown in [12] that any transmutation of $\mathbf{PE}$, where eks($\mathbf{PE}$) is a theory in a finite language, can be achieved by a finite sequence of conditionalizations.

In the theorem below we give another condition which defines a transmutation for theories, as well as theory bases.

Theorem 5: Let $\mathbf{PE} \in \mathcal{E}$, and i be an ordinal. Let $\alpha \in \mathbf{L}$ be such that $\nvdash \neg\alpha$, and $\nvdash \alpha$. Then $\mathbf{PE}^{\star}(\alpha, i)$, where $\star$ is defined by (Adjust–$\mathbf{PE}$) below, is an (α, i)–transmutation of $\mathbf{PE}$. We refer to such a transmutation as the (α, i)–adjustment of $\mathbf{PE}$.

(Adjust–$\mathbf{PE}$)
$$\mathbf{PE}^{\star}(\alpha, i) = \begin{cases} \mathbf{PE}^{-}(\alpha) & \text{if } i = 0 \\ (\mathbf{PE}^{-}(\alpha))^{\times}(\alpha, i) & \text{if } 0 < i < \mathbf{PE}(\alpha) \\ \mathbf{PE}^{\times}(\alpha, i) & \text{otherwise.} \end{cases}$$

where,
$$\mathbf{PE}^{-}(\alpha)(\beta) = \begin{cases} 0 & \text{if } \mathbf{PE}(\alpha) = \mathbf{PE}(\alpha \vee \beta) \\ \mathbf{PE}(\beta) & \text{otherwise.} \end{cases}$$

$$\mathbf{PE}^{\times}(\alpha, i)(\beta) = \begin{cases} 0 & \text{if } \mathbf{PE}(\neg\alpha) = \mathbf{PE}(\neg\alpha \vee \beta) \\ \mathbf{PE}(\beta) & \text{if } \mathbf{PE}(\neg\alpha) < \mathbf{PE}(\neg\alpha \vee \beta) \text{ and } \mathbf{PE}(\beta) \geq i \\ \mathbf{PE}(\neg\alpha \vee \beta) & \text{otherwise.} \end{cases}$$

Intuitively, an (α, i)–adjustment of $\mathbf{PE}$ is a transmutation that minimizes the changes to $\mathbf{PE}$ so that a formula α is accepted with degree i. In general, eks($\mathbf{PE}$) will not be a theory, therefore, an adjustment is a more computationally expedient procedure than conditionalization. However, adjustments are not as expressive as conditionalizations, by this we mean that in contrast to conditionalization, a series of adjustments can not always be used to obtain any transmuted knowledge system. A shortcoming of adjustments is that all formulae β such that $\mathbf{PE}(\beta) \leq i$, are assigned $\mathbf{PE}(\neg\alpha \vee \beta)$, which may not be desirable. If formulae are being accepted and contracted on the *fringe*, that is, when i is close to zero, then this is not likely to be problem, especially if the content of most formulae are 'independent' of one another. Perhaps adjustment could be applied until it becomes necessary for the knowledge system to reorganize its knowledge, that is, undergo a restructuring, in which case a more sophisticated mechanism would be required. In the finite case a series of conditionalizations could be applied.

6 Discussion

We have described transmutations for theory bases, or explicit knowledge sets, by considering not only how the theory base itself is revised, but how its underlying preference relation is revised.

The theory bases represented by transmuted finite partial epistemic entrenchment

ordinal functions satisfy the postulates for very well-behaved theory base contraction and revision within the AGM paradigm.
Finally, we described an adjustment, a simple transmutation for theory bases, and contrast it with a transmutation for theories, namely a conditionalization. We noted that any transmutation for a finite theory can be achieved via a sequence of conditionalizations. In a future work [14] we use the model checking approach of Halpern and Vardi [4] as a basis for an implementation of transmutations for knowledge systems.

References

[1] Alchouron, C., Gärdenfors, P., Makinson, D., *On the Logic of Theory Change: Partial Meet Functions for Contraction and Revision*, Journal of Symbolic Logic, 50: 510-530, 1985.

[2] Gärdenfors, P., *Knowledge in Flux: Modeling the Dynamics of Epistemic States*, A Bradford Book, MIT Press, Cambridge Massachusetts, 1988.

[3] Gärdenfors, P., and Makinson, D., *Revisions of Knowledge Systems using Epistemic Entrenchment*, Theoretical Aspects of Reasoning about Knowledge, 1988.

[4] Halpern, J.Y. and Vardi, M.Y., *Model Checking v.'s Theorem Proving: A manifesto*, Proceedings of the International Conference on Principles of Knowledge Representation and Reasoning, Morgan Kaufmann, 325 - 334, 1991.

[5] Hansson, S.O., *A Dyadic Representation of Belief*, in Belief Revision, Gärdenfors, P. (ed), Cambridge Press, Cambridge, 1992.

[6] Rott, H., *Preferential Belief Change Using Generalized Epistemic Entrenchment*, Journal of Logic, Language and Information 1: 45-78, 1992.

[7] Rumelhart, D.E., and Norman, D.A. *Accretion, Tuning and Restructuring: three modes of learning*, in Cotton, J.W., and Klatzky (eds), *Semantic Factors in Cognition*, Lawrence Erbaum Associates, New Jersey, p37 - 54, 1978.

[8] Schlechta, K., *Theory Revision and Probability*, Notre Dame Journal of Formal Logic, 32, 2:45-78, 1991.

[9] Spohn, W., *Ordinal Conditional Functions: A Dynamic Theory of Epistemic States*, In Harper, W.L., and Skyrms, B. (eds), Causation in decision, belief change, and statistics, II, Kluwer Academic Publishers, 105 - 134, 1988.

[10] Williams, M.A., *Two Contraction Operators for Theory Base Change*, in Proceedings of the Joint Australian Conference on Artificial Intelligence, 1992.

[11] Williams, M.A., *Theory Base Change*, Research Report in Information Systems, University of Newcastle, 1993.

[12] Williams, M.A., *Transmutations of Knowledge Systems*, Research Report in Information Systems, University of Newcastle, 1993.

[13] Williams, M.A., *Implementing Transmutations of Knowledge Systems*, Technical Report, University of Sydney, in preparation.

Acknowledgements

The author gratefully acknowledges, Peter Gärdenfors for drawing attention to the work of Spohn, and suggesting how it might be used, David Makinson for pointing out other relevant results, namely those of Schlechta and Rott, and finally Norman Foo, Pavlos Peppas and Brailey Sims for their support and helpful discussions.

Using Logic to Represent Graphical Shapes

José Damski and **John Gero**
Key Centre of Design Computing
Department of Architectural and Design Science
The University of Sydney, NSW 2006, Australia
email : jose, john@archsci.arch.su.edu.au

Abstract

We present a logic representation for graphical shapes based on the concept of halfplanes. This allows for a symbolically-based representation and manipulation in contrast with numerically-based representations. Definitions and examples are shown in order to demonstrate the theory. Finally some extensions of halfplanes are proposed to represent other geometrical entities.

1 Introduction

Design, one of the complex intellectual activities practised by humans, has as its goal the changing of the world around us in order to produce a different world more convivial to our lives. The vast majority of the sense input from the world is visual. Representing this visual world in such a way that it can be usefully reasoned about is still a major research task. Design in the visual domain includes architectural design, industrial design, graphic design, textile design and to a lesser extent engineering design. In addition to such design domains visual reasoning is often used in many decision making processes, particularly in the formulation and conceptual phases. As humans we use shapes as guiding references for much of our activity. Shapes play a role not just in design domains but also in scientific discovery. Perhaps the best known example of this is Kekulé's discovery of the molecular structure of benzene.

Regularities in the visual world allow us to categorise the world into shapes with defining characteristics. Geometry (both Euclidean and Cartesian) has been developed as one means of reasoning about shapes. However, geometry does not deal with the fundamental issue of representing shapes, this is left to geometric modeling. Geometric modeling deals with representing the geometric characteristics of shapes and objects. A number of basic directions have been followed to represent geometric objects. These all follow the mathematical approach to modeling which may be described by distinguishing three separate levels of modeling:

physical objects in the world;
mathematical objects which are idealizations of physical objects; and
representations of mathematical objects suitable for computational purposes.

Shapes are recognisable images of objects often with a semantic content, however, we wish to be able to model shapes in such a complete manner that the representations are adequate for answering any arbitrary shape question without the assistance of or interaction with a human user. In the remaining sections of this paper we will quickly review the issues in shape representation and describe some alternate approaches to geometric and shape reasoning in the next section prior to developing a logic-based representation for graphical shapes utilising the concept of halfplanes. The potential of such a representation will be discussed in the Conclusion.

2 Shape Representation

Any representation should ideally have the following properties [1]: **expressive power** what can be represented amongst all possible shapes in the domain to be described; **uniqueness** do all valid representations model one shape only; **unambiguity** do all shapes have only one representation; **validity** do all representations describe some shape in the domain; **conciseness** how large do the representations become for interesting shapes; **description languages** what kind of description languages can be based on the representation and **computational ease** what kinds of algorithms can be written for the representation and what is their computational complexity.

There are four standard models of shape representation: point-set models; boundary models; space filling models and constructive solid geometry models. These are all based on mathematical models.

In addition to these four standard representations there are many others, most of which are related to them. There are however at least two which are different. The first is shape grammars [2] which are grammatically-based production rules where the atoms are shapes rather than words. The second is based on infinite maximal lines with symbolic rules for the definition and manipulation of shapes [3]. Since both these representations allow for characteristics of shapes to be represented and manipulated which could not be represented in the standard kinds of shape representation approaches, the question is raised is there a more general representation which has the capacity to extend the representation yet still have strong formal properties. This is the question which has motivated the research reported here.

What we suggest and then describe in the remainder of the paper is a logic-based approach to the representation of shapes, a representation which may be described analogously to the mathematics-based approach as:

physical objects in the world;

logic objects which are idealizations of physical objects; and

representations of logic objects suitable for computational purposes

3 Representing Shapes using Logic

3.1 Background

The concept of the halfplane [4] orginated in our basic question about how to represent a line symbolically without any reference to a particular coordinate system or any other numerical reference. An important characteristics for a given line in space is that it divides a plane into exactly two halfplanes. From this characteristic we developed a theory of halfplanes which aims to represent and manipulate shapes symbolically. We define a plane $\mathcal{U}$ (universe of elements x) divided into two halfplanes, H_i^0 and H_i^1 which are bounded by a line l_i. A formal definition for H_i^*

in $\mathcal{U}$ is $\{ H_i^0$ as a set of $x \mid x \in H_i^0\}$ and $\{ H_i^1$ as a set of $x \mid x \notin H_i^0\}$, therefore $H_i^0 \cup H_i^1 = \mathcal{U}$. This is the *Principle of Excluded Middle.* Since the halfplanes satisfy the Principle of Excluded Middle, we can evaluate them to the truth value T or False. A literal (halfplane) H_i^0 is true iff $\exists\ x \mid x \in H_i^0$ and False otherwise. We use the symbols $\neg H_i^0$ and H_i^1 interchangeably. If a halfplane H_i^0 is in H_j^0, it is equivalent to the formula $H_i^0 \rightarrow H_j^0$, iff $\forall x \mid x \in H_i^0$ and $x \in H_j^0$.

According to these principles, all shapes expressed by halfplanes can be rewritten as a Wff (Well Formed Formula) in propositional logic.

3.2 *Definitions*

Topology A *definition* $\mathcal{D}$ is the set of formulas which defines a topology.
Region Given n halfplanes, a *region* is a conjunctive formula of n H_i^*. An example of a region is **R** in Figure 1a.
Visibility A region R is said to be *visible* iff R has the truth value T under $\mathcal{D}$. The concept of visibility is important because we can distinguish what region can be "seen" in a geometrical topology (if drawn) from all possible regions.
Minimal Description A region defined by an Wff F has a *minimal description* F_{min} iff F_{min} is in a conjunctive normal form and contains only H_i^* which bounds a region F. For example in Figure 1b, **R** has the formula $F = H_1^1 \wedge H_2^0 \wedge H_3^0$ but has a minimal description $F_{min} = H_2^0 \wedge H_3^0$.
Shape A shape is any combination of adjacent regions. Shape, as well as region, also has the concepts of visibility and minimal description.

3.3 *Representation*

Here we describe how to represent geometrical topologies using propositional logic, hereafter called *logic* for short. One advantage of using logic is its capacity to express additional knowledge about geometry in the same formalism. In addition to that, once we have all facts and production rules we can apply an inference process to determine desired results as theorem proving [5]. This will enable us to process any other knowledge about geometrical contraints using production rules. Initially it is

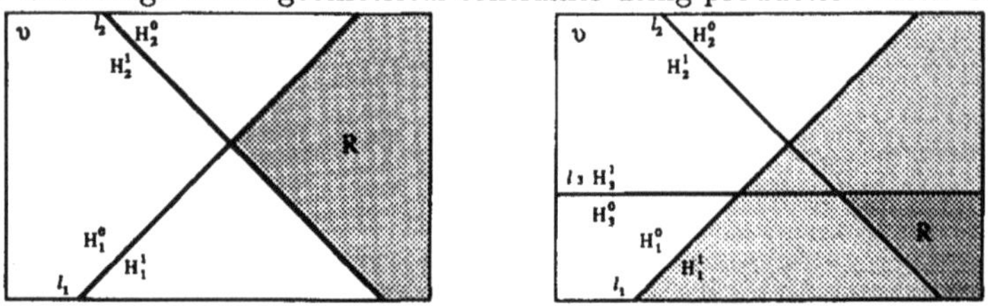

(a) Lines l_1 and l_2 in $\mathcal{U}$ (b) One possible topology for l_1, l_2 and l_3

Figure 1: Lines l_i as boundaries of halfplanes in $\mathcal{U}$

necessary to represent a topology. For example, given two non-parallel lines l_1 and l_2 in $\mathcal{U}$ (as a plane in 2D), we describe a topology $l_1 \times l_2$ between them as in Figure 1a.

The region R is formed by the intersection of H_1^1 and H_2^0, which is written in logic as: $H_1^1 \wedge H_2^0$. In Figure 1a all 4 regions can be written using a simple formula $H_1^* \wedge H_2^\#$. Adding a third line l_3 in Figure 1a, we can generate a new possible topology as in Figure 1b. In order to describe logically this topology it is necessary to describe the relation of only one line l_i to all the others. If we choose l_1 in Figure 1b, the Formula $F_1 = H_2^0 \wedge H_3^0 \rightarrow H_1^1$ is true, because region **R** $(H_2^0 \wedge H_3^0)$ is completely inside the halfplane H_1^1, $\mathbf{R} \subset H_1^1$. This enables a logical conditional to be a logical implication [6]. As no other restrictions were applied, the truth table for F_1 is given in Table T_1 in Figure 2b.

From the truth Table T_1 we can infer that, given H_i as non-empty halfplanes and F_1, all the following regions are non-empty: $H_1^0 \wedge H_2^0 \wedge H_3^1$; $H_1^0 \wedge H_2^1 \wedge H_3^0$; $H_1^0 \wedge H_2^1 \wedge H_3^1$; $H_1^1 \wedge H_2^0 \wedge H_3^0$; $H_1^1 \wedge H_2^0 \wedge H_3^1$; $H_1^1 \wedge H_2^1 \wedge H_3^0$; $H_1^1 \wedge H_2^1 \wedge H_3^1$. As more restrictions are added to a description, the fewer non-empty regions we get. For example, in Figure 1b if we move l_1 down until it reaches where l_2 meets l_3, the region $H_1^1 \wedge H_2^1 \wedge H_3^1$ will be empty as shown in Figure 2a. As we already had F_1 as $H_2^0 \wedge H_3^0 \rightarrow H_1^1$, now we have a new restriction F_2 as $H_2^1 \wedge H_3^1 \rightarrow H_1^0$. Since F_1 and F_2 have to be true together, we have F_3 as $F_1 \wedge F_2$. The truth table for F_3 is given in Table T_1 in Figure 2b. Now we can verify that the formula $H_1^1 \wedge H_2^1 \wedge H_3^1$

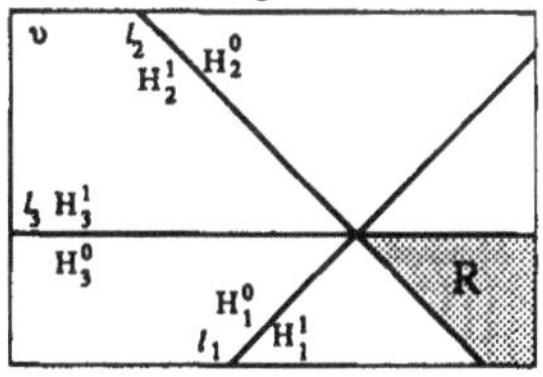

(a)

H_1^0	H_2^0	H_3^0	F_1	F_3	F_5
T	T	T	False	False	False
T	T	F	T	T	False
T	F	T	T	T	T
T	F	F	T	T	T
F	T	T	T	T	T
F	T	F	T	T	T
F	F	T	T	T	T
F	F	F	T	False	T

(b)

Figure 2: (a) Line l_1 cross where $l_2 \times l_3$ (b) Table T_1

has the truth value False, which means it is an empty or non-visible region.

Finally, another constraint can be added, when a line is parallel to another. Suppose in Figure 1b line l_1 is parallel to l_2 as represented in Figure 3a. In this case the formula $F_1 = H_2^0 \wedge H_3^0 \rightarrow H_1^1$ is still valid. The parallelism is represented by the formula F_4 as $H_2^0 \rightarrow H_1^1$ which states that the halfplane H_2^0 is entirely inside H_1^1. A new formula $F_5 = F_1 \wedge F_4$ describing the whole topology, is shown in Table T_1 in Figure 2b. We can verify from Table T_1 that the region $H_1^0 \wedge H_2^0 \wedge H_3^1$ is empty now.

3.4 Region Adjacency

The region adjacent to any visible region (or shape) R is defined as any region R' which graphically bounds R. There are two types of adjacency: border adjacency and corner adjacency.

3.4.1 Border Adjacency

Given a minimal description of a region R expressed by $F_1 \wedge F_2 \wedge ... \wedge F_n$, a region R_{adj} is **border adjacent** to R iff the difference between R_{adj} and R is in only one F_i, such as F_i in R and $\overline{F}_i$ in R_{adj} ($\overline{F}_i$ is the complement of F_i), for any i in

$1 \leq i \leq n$. For example, in Figure 1b, the region R has the minimal description $H_2^0 \wedge H_3^0$, therefore it has two border adjacent regions:
R'_{adj} is $\neg H_2^0 \wedge H_3^0$ and R''_{adj} is $H_2^0 \wedge \neg H_3^0$, as shown in Figure 3b.

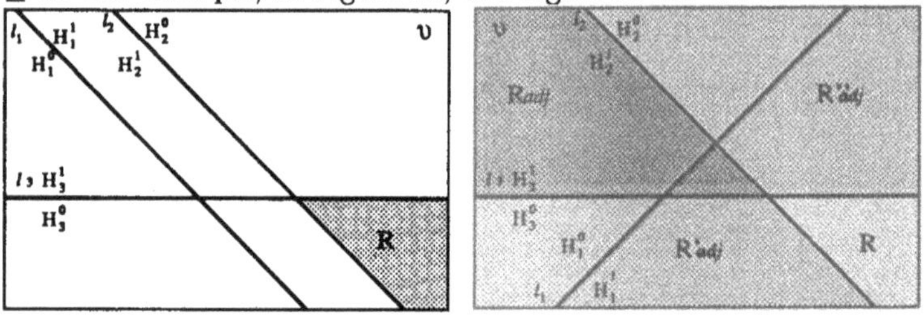

(a) (b)

Figure 3: (a) Constraint $l_1 \parallel l_2$ (b) Regions R_{adj} corner adjacent and R'_{adj} and R''_{adj} border adjacent to R

3.4.2 Corner Adjacency

Given a minimal description of a region R expressed by $F_1 \wedge F_2 \wedge \ldots \wedge F_n$. A region R_{adj} is **corner adjacent** to R iff R_{adj} differs from R only in exactly two formulas F_j and F_k in R and $\overline{F}_j$ and $\overline{F}_k$ in R_{adj} for a given j and k.

For the example in Figure 1b the region R has the minimal description $H_2^0 \wedge H_3^0$, therefore it has one corner adjacent region R_{adj} is $\neg H_2^0 \wedge \neg H_3^0$ as shown in Figure 3b.

3.5 Closed Region

For a given definition $\mathcal{D}$, a region R expressed by $F_1 \wedge F_2 \wedge \ldots F_n$ is said to be **closed** iff:
1)R is visible,
2)for all formulas F_i in the region R there exists a border adjacent region R_{adj} which is *visible* under $\mathcal{D}$,
3) all corner adjacent regions R_{adj} are visible under $\mathcal{D}$ for any two F_i and F_j in R,
4)R must have, at least, 3 different halfplanes H_i^*, H_j^* and H_k^*.

For example, in Figure 3b the region defined by $H_1^1 \wedge H_2^1 \wedge H_3^1$ is closed since it satisfies the definitions. This concept can be extended to shapes.

4 Conclusion

In this paper we have developed a logic based representation for shapes using halfplanes as the basic unit. This approach aims to represent a unique topology for a given set of halfplanes. Even though our examples used straight lines as boundaries, the same concept is valid for other geometrical entities, such as circles, closed polygons, and more generally, any path that divides the universe $\mathcal{U}$ into two parts. In addition, our representation can also be extended to shapes in 3D that divide the space into two different subspaces.

The three examples in Figure 4 have different geometric descriptions, but the relation $A \wedge B \rightarrow C$ is the same for all. This means that our representation enables us to manipulate the relations among geometrical entities regardless of their nature. This property can be useful when we are interested in how they can be combined or how we can obtain new shapes from a given one, such as in visual emergence [3]. One advantage of this representation is, as in any system based on logic, that we

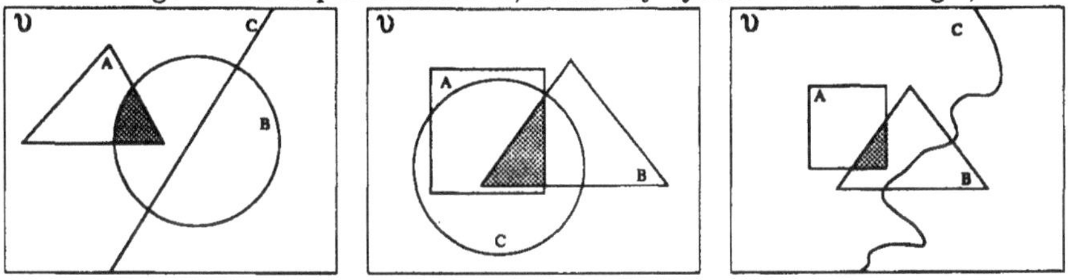

Figure 4: Different geometrical entities

use the same formalism throughout. We can express specific knowledge to operate with domain knowledge, such as heuristics about emergence, in the same formalism.

In our representation we have used propositional logic because its expressiviness was sufficient for the type of problem we were tackling. We intend to extend the representation to first order logic. The extension is necessary to process region convexity, to link our description to a numerical graphics system and finally to link it with other projects which use first order logic.

Acknowledgements

We would like to thank Prof. Norman Foo (Sydney University), Prof. John Debenham and John Potter (University of Technology of Sydney) for their valuable contributions. José C.B. Damski thanks CNPQ - Conselho Nacional de Desenvolvimento Científico e Tecnológico , Brazil, grant number 201314/90-8.

References

1. M. Mantyla, *An Introduction to Solid Modeling*, (Computer Science Press, Rockville, Maryland, USA, 1988).
2. G. Stiny, Introduction to shape and shape grammar, *Environment and Planning B*, 7 (1980), pages 343–351.
3. J. S. Gero and M. Yan, Shape emergence by symbolic reasoning, Technical report, (Key Centre of Design Computing, The University of Sydney, 1993).
4. C. Giraud, Presque half-planes: towards a general representation scheme, *Computer-aided Design*, 16(1) (January 1984), pages 17–24.
5. C. Chang and R.C. Lee, *Symbolic Logic and Mechanical Theorem Proving*, (Academic Press, 1973).
6. H. Ehlers, *Logic by Way of Set Theory*, (Holt, Rinehart and Winston, 1968).

Genetic Algorithms

A GENETIC ALGORITHM FOR OPTIMISING PROBLEMS WITH EMBEDDED DESIGN DECISIONS

Gary M. Gibson, *magmg@lv.levels.unisa.edu.au*,
School of Computer and Information Science, University of South Australia, The Levels, Pooraka, S.A. 5095, AUSTRALIA.

Keywords: Genetic Algorithms, optimisation, simulation.

ABSTRACT

A Genetic Algorithm (GA) has been developed to optimise problems which have both simple parameters (quantitative and qualitative) and embedded design decisions. Design decisions can cause complication in the optimisation process since any other parameter whose effect is limited to a particular alternative of a decision in a given string becomes redundant if that alternative is not selected. This may lead to a decline in optimisation efficiency due to the GA wasting effort manipulating non-existent parameters, particularly when employing non-traditional operators. The solution developed was to employ a 'compound string' data-structure which stored the string information in such a way that it could provide the illusion of being a variable-length 'virtual string' containing only those parameters embodied in currently selected alternatives - effectively removing irrelevant parameters. In this paper the implementation of compound strings will be discussed and associated experiment results presented.

1. Introduction

Genetic Algorithms (GAs) have been used in a wide variety of optimisation and machine learning applications*. Another area is that of design where GAs are used to design some physical or logical structure (e.g. [7]).

Although the task of designing a complete complex structure can be extremely time-consuming, even for a GA**, there are many applications where this degree of completeness is not needed. Often there are many known qualitative choices in the design of some structure (which will hereafter be referred to as structural choices) with the problem being to find the best combination of them. This problem would then become similar to a gene-selection problem (e.g. [6]) except that in many real-world domains, such as industrial simulation, it can be exacerbated by the presence of other, often quantitative, parameters to the problem which also need to be optimised. Many of these are dependent on the structural choices, i.e. they only have meaningful values if a particular structure is chosen. For example, a parameter to choose the best default boost

---

* For many examples of these see [4], p 125-129.

** The design of human beings is a very good example that problems of this nature are not intractable.

setting on a car turbo-charger will only have an effect if the turbo-charger option has actually been selected in the design.

2. The Optimisation Problem

Decision selecting GAs which have parameters dependent on structural choices are *not* the same as numeric optimising GAs or gene-selection-like GAs because when a choice is made from a number of competing structural options all the other options cease to exist for that string. Therefore, all sub-decisions and parameters to be optimised embedded in those now defunct options will also cease to exist. This is not to say that they can never be chosen again in succeeding generations but they will have *no effect whatsoever* on the current string's fitness.

Consider a complex Discrete Event Simulation (DES) model representing a computer manufacturing plant. In this problem there are traditional scalar parameters to be optimised, such as buffer sizes and conveyor speeds, as well as some structural choices.

One such choice might be deciding between the options of continued use of the existing power-supply assembly section; replacing the section with a new automated line; or closing the section and purchasing the power-supplies from another manufacturer. In the case of the first two options, there will most likely be parameters that will need to be adjusted to tune the section to the rest of the plant. In the case of the third option, the buffering and reorder volume/ frequency will have to be determined so that plant needs can be met with minimal inventories. All these scalar parameters only exist if their associated option also exists.

The optimisation objective would typically be to increase the production level of the plant, possibly with the introduction of new technology, to a required amount at a minimum cost per unit. Any change in a structural choice will more than likely require a number of other changes throughout the plant in order for the plant to perform most efficiently. Therefore, in order for different combinations of structural choices to be shown at their most efficient, and hence compete fairly, the structural choices need to be made at the same time as the optimisation of other parameters. Consequently, in these kinds of problems, there will often be parameters which exist only for certain options of a structural choice.

2.1 Effects

What does this mean to the operation of a GA working on one of these problems? First some terms need to be defined:

- An *option* is the set of all the parameters encoded in a string whose effects are limited to a particular alternative of a structural choice. It may include sub-options, and hence could be recursive in nature. It can be, and often is, empty since not all structural choices will have parameters.

- A *selection parameter* is a parameter encoded in the string which makes a structural choice in the problem. It is associated with a set of mutually exclusive options, one for each value it can take.
- An *active option* is the option that corresponds to the setting of its associated selection parameter. It is the option which will be able to influence the objective function.
- *Inactive options* are all the other options, i.e. options that do not correspond to their selection parameter.

The presence of inactive options alters the complexion of optimising these kinds of design problems. There are a number of detrimental effects to the optimisation process which can be postulated :

1. Crossover operators when acting on quantitative parameters in order to combine good high-order bits with different low-order bits will be "diluted" since they would often be acting on non-existent parameters* . The same effect can be noted in other non-traditional operators which are guaranteed to produce a change in string when called (which will hereafter be referred to as targeted operators) e.g. a creep** operator which phenotypically adjusts a randomly chosen eligible parameter by some small amount.
2. The opportunity to exploit an instance of a known good short length building block in the form of a selection parameter and its active option is lost. Crossovers in any inactive options positioned between the selection parameter and the active option will break them apart. This also introduces a positional bias in that active options encoded close to their selection parameter in the string will not feel this effect to the same extent as those further away, and thus will be advantaged.
3. Operators such as crossover and creep acting on inactive options would effectively randomise them as the generations progressed, since there is no feedback on how good or bad the changes are.
4. When a pair of strings are mated that have different active options it is likely that the child string's active option will be at least partially taken from a parent where it is inactive.
5. Phenotypic operators with a certain probability of operating on each parameter encoded in the string (usually tuned to produce a single change on average), such as Davis's creep operators, will not perform at optimum in problems where competing options are of different lengths. This is because the average number of changes that will have an effect per string will vary depending on which options are active at the time.

---

* In certain problems this may be an advantage (see [6]) but this seems to be restricted to qualitative variables. The particular GA used for testing later in this paper has its own mechanism to protect qualitative variables from unnecessary crossover disruption.

** The creep operator is a hill climbing operator which was originally defined by Davis [2]. He defined two operators - "little creep" and "big creep". Each is an operator which randomly selects parameters in a string to be altered phenotypically through a random adjustment up or down by a random amount in a given range. Big creep uses a larger range than little creep. Creep is particularly effective when employed towards the end of a run in a domain containing quantitative variables.

3. Virtual Strings

Suppose we had a way of looking at strings such that inactive options simply disappeared? The strings would then appear to be variable length *virtual strings* containing only the normal non-option problem parameters, the selection parameters and their *active* options. They would be virtual because they would appear to represent much less than they actually do. Such a structure would eliminate all of the above problems in the following ways:

1. Crossover would no longer be diluted since all the parameters it operated on would exist. Operators which apply themselves to a certain number of parameters (e.g. one in the case of a targeted creep operator) could not be diluted either since they would count the number of relevant parameters in the string being operated on and then randomly select one of them to alter.
2. The short length building blocks of selection parameters and their active options would be present since they would appear adjacent. There would be no positional bias for the same reason.
3. Operators such as crossover and creep would be unable to accidentally destroy inactive options since they would not exist in the virtual string.
4. An active option in one string could not be crossed with its corresponding option in another string if that option is inactive there since the inactive option would not exist. Under these circumstances the active option is simply copied.
5. Phenotypic operators that apply themselves to a specific proportion of eligible parameters in the string would operate exactly as required since only active options could exist (the operators would have to count the number of relevant parameters first). Any length sensitive operators, such as a crossover operator which varies the number of crosses it makes based on the length of the string, would perform properly as long as they checked the length of the virtual string before applying themselves.

3.1 Maintaining the Illusion - Compound Strings

How can we implement this virtual string abstraction? One way is to create a data-structure called a *compound string.* It contains all the information found in the traditional string including inactive options. When necessary it can create the illusion of being a variable-length virtual string and will behave appropriately when operators are applied to it.

A compound string is constructed as follows. Each problem parameter is mapped to an appropriate *segment.* Segments are of three types* ; *quantitative segments* for normal numeric parameters, *qualitative segments* for non-numeric parameters and *option switch segments* to hold selection parameters. The segments are linked together in a chain to form the string.

---

* There may be others but they are not relevant to this paper. See [3] for another example (schedule segments).

If there are option switch segments, then for each one a list of *sub-strings* is formed inside the segment, each sub-string representing a different option. The sub-strings are built up in exactly the same way as the main string, and may contain option switch segments with their own sub-strings etc. Note that many sub-strings may be empty since they will only contain data if there are parameters which exist only for that option (for other work in non-traditional string structures see [9]).

Note that this approach is not the same as that of Genetic Programming (GP) [5] in its manipulation of tree structures. Unlike GP, the tree structures here are used purely to preserve information not used in the present string for future generations, in a similar manner to recessive genes. The structures do NOT represent something which can be usefully manipulated by operators or interpreted by the objective function. This is because the information not present in the virtual string abstraction is *guaranteed* to have no impact on the problem in the context of the rest of the string, i.e. the settings of the selection parameters in the string.

See Figures 1 and 2 below for an example of a traditional string representation and its corresponding compound string representation. Note that the number of segments in either case is the same - they are simply arranged into different structures. Segments labelled with a "P" are segments corresponding to simple parameters (quantitative and qualitative) while those labelled with an "S" are option switch segments. They are labelled numerically from left to right. Two extra digits are added to the right-most end of a segment's label if it is in a sub-string (the first digit for the number of the sub-string it is in and the second for its position in that sub-string).

Figure 1: Example of traditional string representation.

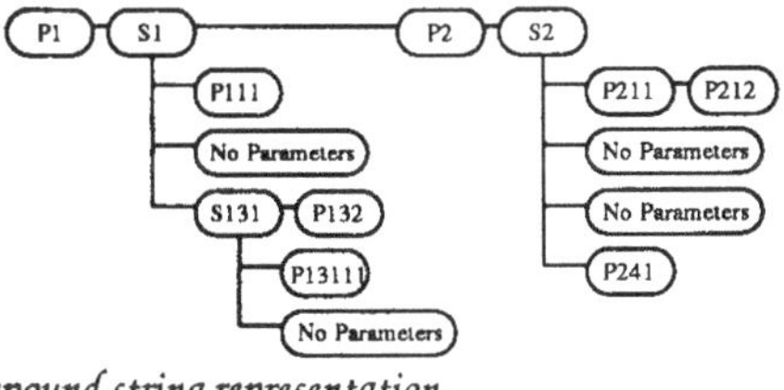

Figure 2: Example of compound string representation.

The structure of the compound string enables it to retain all the information of the traditional string and, at the same time, maintain the illusion of being a virtual string - it consults the option switch segment to determine which of the accompanying sub-strings to use in the current operation. For example, if S1 and S2 of the compound string in Figure 2 were both set to their first option, then the resultant virtual string would be as shown in Figure 3 below (The setting of S131 is ignored since the option it is embedded in has not been selected by S1).

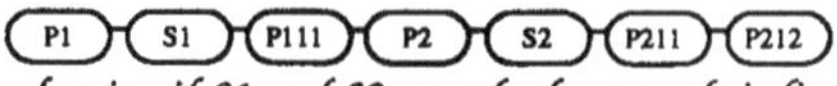

Figure 3: Example of virtual string if S1 and S2 were both set to their first option.

4. Experiments

It has been argued that there are theoretical reasons why the traditional strings will often not perform as well as they could in a domain with design choices that have other associated parameters. Below are details of experiments run to test the validity of this position.

4.1 Experiments 1a and 1b: Effective Use of Targeted Operators

An area in which any improvement in the performance of compound strings over traditional strings should be strongly apparent is in the application of phenotypic targeted operators. To test for this, two experiments were conducted.

First, for experiment 1a, a simple Discrete Event Simulation (DES) model was set up consisting of a group of servers (4 in this case), arranged in a production line as shown in the diagram below. There were 5 identical alternative lines. Items move from the source on the left, through the switch and then to the first server of the group that the switch has selected. They wait there for a period of time depending on the speed of the server, then move onto the second server, wait, then the third, etc. until finally leaving the simulation via the sink on the right.

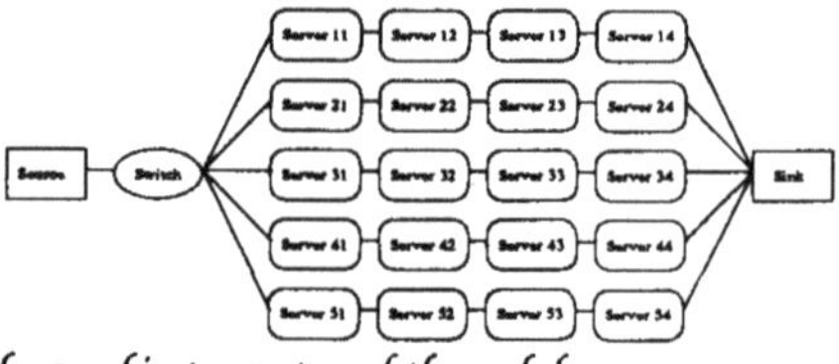

Figure 4: The possible paths an object may travel through between source and sink.

The GA controlled 21 variables; the selection parameter, which chose the group to use, and the average processing time of each server (ranging from 100 to 10000 in steps of 1). The problem to be solved was to determine the parameter values which would give the model the highest throughput. To a human being this problem is trivial since the best string must be one of the server groups, any one since they are all identical, with the processing time of all servers in that group set to their lowest possible value. However, this problem is more difficult for the GA, since it does not share our knowledge about the structure of the problem. In order to improve a string at any generation the GA must improve the *correct* server - the one with the largest delay, otherwise there will be no change in fitness.

The GA used in the experiment was of a standard, fixed-population, non-overlapping generation type. It was run 100 times using compound strings and another 100 times using traditional strings with a population size of 20 and number of generations of

2000. All factors other than the string type were identical. The mutation rate was fixed at a 1% chance of changing each bit. Operator probabilities were as follows: 50% chance of the targeted creep operator being selected; 30% chance of crossover being selected; and 20% chance of a simple copy being selected* . Traditional two point crossover was used. Note that the hypothesised positional bias did not affect this test since all options have an identical optimum fitness. Moreover the hypothesised improvement in protection of good inactive options had no effect since, in this simple test, a fitter option is better under all circumstances. There were no length variation effects since all options were the same length.

Mutation was performed on all strings, regardless of which operator was used. It affected both active and inactive options. The selection method used was stochastic remainder selection without replacement** . Elitist preservation was used with the single best string of a generation being copied to the next with no mutation. Gray-coding [1] was used to reduce Hamming-cliff problems [8]. No fitness scaling was performed.

The second problem (Experiment 1b) tested was set up and run identically to the first problem only the model to be optimised was changed. In this experiment the simulation to be optimised was a manufacturing plant set up as shown in the diagram below.

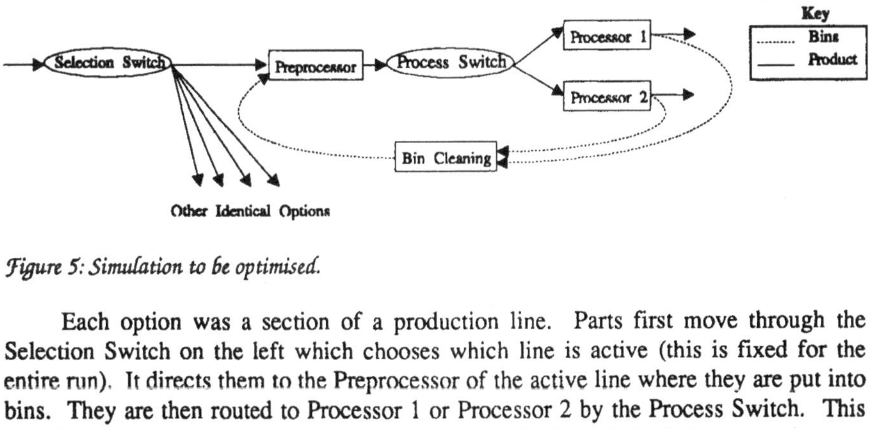

Figure 5: Simulation to be optimised.

Each option was a section of a production line. Parts first move through the Selection Switch on the left which chooses which line is active (this is fixed for the entire run). It directs them to the Preprocessor of the active line where they are put into bins. They are then routed to Processor 1 or Processor 2 by the Process Switch. This switch operates on a continuous loop switching back and forth between the two processors. Finally the parts leave the line and the bins they were in are freed. The bins are then available again after a small cleaning delay. Variables that the GA can alter are the selection parameter controlling the Selection Switch for what line to use,

---

* Normally the algorithm uses an adaptive operator weighting strategy which adjusts operator probability based on the number and type of segments currently in the virtual string abstraction.

** Goldberg D.E., *Genetic Algorithms in Search, Optimisation & Machine Learning*, Addison-Wesley, New York, 1989, p 121.

the time the Process Switch is to spend directing parts to Processor 1; the time it spends directing parts to Processor 2; and the number of bins in the system. The fitness function is the total throughput of parts less a penalty for the number of bins used.

4.2 Experiment 2 - General Effectiveness without Targeted Operators

This experiment was performed to investigate more subtle problems with the traditional representation such as crossover dilution and splitting selection parameters from their active option. This experiment was identical to Experiment 1b except that the operator probabilities were changed to 60% for crossover, 40% for copy (proportionate to the settings in Experiment 1) and 0% for creep. The GA was again run 100 for each string type. The algorithm was run for 5000 generations.

5. Discussion

It was found that the GA performed significantly better when using compound strings than when using traditional strings when employing targeted operators. A comparison of the rate at which different fitness levels were reached in Experiment 1a is shown in Table 1 below. The left column is the fitness level. The next two are the generation at which the GA reached, with its fittest string, that level of fitness using compound strings and traditional strings respectively. In the last column is column 3 over column 2 which shows the relative performance of the two approaches.

Fitness	Gen No.Comp	Gen No.Trad	Gen No.Trad / Gen No.Comp
10	44	89	2.02
20	69	159	2.30
30	86	219	2.55
40	103	272	2.64
50	121	332	2.74
60	144	396	2.75
70	169	486	2.87
80	228	669	2.93
90	401	1513	3.77

Table 1: Comparative average fitness improvements of Experiment 1a.

As can be seen in the final column, the difference between the algorithms increases continually in terms of improving fitness. The traditional version takes 102% longer to reach fitness 10, 174% longer to reach fitness 50 and 277% longer to reach fitness 90. Not shown on the table is the time taken for the GA using compound strings to reach the performance of the traditional string GA at generation 2000 (fitness 91). The GA using compound strings achieved this in 497 generations, i.e. in under one quarter of the time.

Next are the results for Experiment 1b which are shown in the table below. The columns are the same as in Table 1.

Fitness	Gen No.Comp	Gen No.Trad	Gen No.Trad / Gen No.Comp
90	10	15	1.5
95	16	26	1.63
100	26	36	1.38
105	39	53	1.36
110	55	76	1.38
115	90	129	1.43
120	153	296	1.93
125	311	969	3.11

Table 2: Comparative average fitness improvements of Experiment 1b.

As can be seen in the table, the GA using compound strings does not gain as much early in the run as it did in Experiment 1a. However towards the end it starts pulling away until, at fitness level 125, it is over three times better. At the very end of the run it performs even better still. It took only 456 generations to reach a fitness level of 127 which was the fitness level that the GA using traditional strings reached in 2000 generations. This is significantly less than one quarter of the time and slightly better than its performance against traditional strings in Experiment 1a.

There was a smaller, but still significant, improvement for the GA without targeted operators in Experiment 2 as shown in Table 3 below. Columns are the same as for Tables 1 and 2.

Fitness	Gen No.Comp	Gen No.Trad	Gen No.Trad / Gen No.Comp
90	31	14	0.45
95	41	28	0.68
100	58	45	0.78
105	86	68	0.79
110	126	112	0.89
115	185	208	1.12
120	370	436	1.18
125	1217	2527	2.08

Table 3: Comparative average fitness improvements of Experiment 2.

As can be seen, the compound string GA actually performed worse at first but then pulled away to lead substantially at the end. The compound string GA reached the best that the traditional string GA had reached at generation 5000 (just under 127) by generation 2007 which is nearly 2.5 times faster.

6. Conclusion

It has been postulated that GAs using traditional strings may have difficulty in dealing with design problems where there is a choice among competing alternative structures if some of them at least contain parameters to be optimised in conjunction with the rest of the problem. These difficulties would be primarily in the form of a decline in efficiency. One way these difficulties could be avoided is to have the GA manipulate variable length virtual strings, which do not contain inactive options, rather than traditional strings. A data-structure called a compound string has been developed which holds all the data of the traditional string but presents the illusion of being a virtual string.

Experiments were run to test the more easily isolated degradations from optimal performance that the traditional strings were expected to experience. These were in the areas of targeted operator employment and general crossover effectiveness. The results of these experiments show that the compound string representation performs substantially better than the traditional string representation where extra non-traditional operators are employed and significantly better with traditional operators alone. These results suggest that the compound string approach is a good candidate for real-world optimisation of design problems using non-traditional operators and, to a more limited extent, those employing only the traditional operators of crossover and mutation.

7. References

1. Caruana R.A. and Schaffer J.D., Representation and Hidden Bias: Gray vs. Binary Coding for Genetic Algorithms, *Proceedings of the Fifth International Conference on Machine Learning*, (1988), pp 153-161.
2. Davis L., Adapting Operator Probabilities in Genetic Algorithms, *Proceedings of the Third International Conference on Genetic Algorithms*, (1989), pp 61-69.
3. Gibson G.M., Application of Genetic Algorithms to Mixed Schedule and Parameter Optimisation for a Visual Interactive Modeller, *Proceedings of the 1993 International Simulation Technology Conference*, San Francisco, CA, Nov. 9-11 (1993).
4. Goldberg D.E., *Genetic Algorithms in Search, Optimisation & Machine Learning*, Addison-Wesley, New York, (1989).
5. Koza J.R., *Genetic Programming: On the Programming of Computers by Means of Natural Selection*, MIT Press, (1992).
6. Levenick J.R., Inserting Introns Improves Genetic Algorithm Success Rate: Taking a Cue from Biology, *Proceedings of Fourth International Conference on Genetic Algorithms*, (1991), pp 123-127.
7. Louis S.J. and Rawlins G.J.E., Designer Genetic Algorithms: Genetic Algorithms in Structure Design, *Proceedings of the Fourth International Conference on Genetic Algorithms*, (1991), pp 53-60.
8. Schaffer J.D., Caruana R.A. Eshelman L.J. and Das R., A Study of Control Parameters Affecting Online Performance of Genetic Algorithms for Function Optimisation, *Proceeding of the Third International Conference on Genetic Algorithms*, (1989), pp 51-60.
9. Varsek A., Qualitative Model Evolution, *Proceedings of the 12th International Joint Conference on Artificial Intelligence*, 24-30 August 1991, Vol. 2 (1991), pp 1311-1316.

Structural Shape Optimization by Multi-Species Genetic Algorithm

Hirokazu Watabe and Norio Okino
Division of Applied Systems Science
Faculty of Engineering, Kyoto University
Kyoto, 606-01, Japan
e-mail : watabe@kuamp.kyoto-u.ac.jp

ABSTRACT

In this paper, we propose multi-species genetic algorithm applying to structural shape optimization problem. By this algorithm, structural shape is started from a simple topological structure (a single species), and differentiated to several types of topological structures (multi-species) by T-mutation operators. It is shown that proposed algorithm can effectively solve not only the size problem of optimization but also the topological problem of optimization.

1 Introduction

In the field of Artificial Intelligence, metaphoric approaches from bionical mechanisms are exciting topics. In those approaches, GA(Genetic Algorithm)[1] is one of the optimization techniques based on concepts from population genetics.

This paper treats an application of a GA in the domain of plane truss weight optimization similar to that of Goldgerg[1] p.137. We have extended the problem, so that the number of members, their locations and connectivity are also optimized. Goldberg only optimized the cross-sectional area of a fixed number of members. The method employed is to introduce operators that change the length of the genotype/chromosomes. We call genotypes of different sizes 'multi-species'.

2 Structural Optimization Problem

2.1 Plane truss optimization problem

In this paper, one of the structural optimization problem, optimization of a plane truss structure is treated. Structures composed of bar elements are classified as truss structures. By definition, bars can only carry axial loads and deform axially. All members of a truss are subjected to only axial loads, and no transverse sharing forces and bending moments are experienced by any member. All members are connected to each other through pins that allow free rotation about the pin axis.

Truss structural optimization problems have basically two steps.

1. topological problem of optimization : decision of the total number of bar elements and layout of each member of the truss structure.
2. size problem of optimization : decision of the length and cross-sectional area of each bar element of the truss structure.

It is apparent that the topological problem is much more difficult than the size problem.

However, by applying GA to this type of problem, the topological problem can be treated relatively easy. The reasons of that can be picked up as follows.

- On GA, to generate new individual(candidate of solution), few knowledge about structural mechanics are necessary.
- Knowledge about structural mechanics is necessary only to evaluate the structure, and the evaluation does not depend on the topological form of the structure.
- GA is strong for multimodal problem.

2.2 Minimum weight design problem

In structural optimization problems, besides the classification by form of structures, there are classification by objective functions and conditions of constraints. This paper treats a minimum weight design problem with conditions of constraints to stress of each bar element. The minimum weight design problem on truss structures is the problem to minimize the weight of total structure on condition that stress of each bar element is inside between allowable compression and tension stresses.

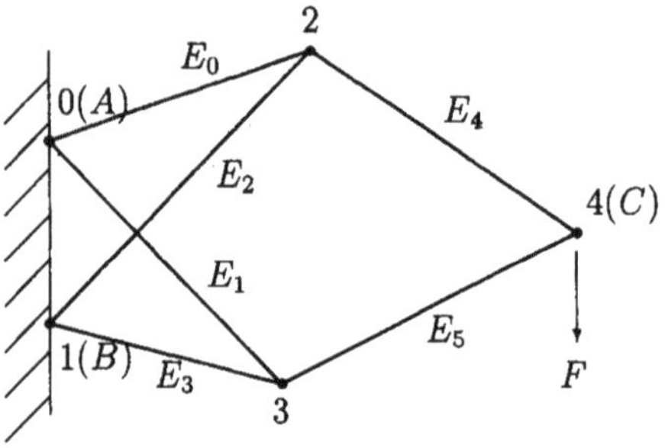

Figure 1: Coat hanger problem

node no.	node coordinate x	y
0	0.00	0.167
1	0.00	-0.167
2	0.500	0.333
3	0.445	-0.276
4	1.00	0.00

element no.	topological structure connected node no.	
E_0	0	2
E_1	0	3
E_2	1	2
E_3	1	3
E_4	2	4
E_5	3	4

Figure 2: Genotype of truss structure

As one of the examples of minimum weight design problem on truss structures, we treats the "coat hanger problem" shown in figure 1. It is a problem to realize the structure that support a vertical load F by the wall which has a distance l from the load point C. And it is specialized in this figure that support points on the wall are A and B.

3 Genetic Structural Shape Optimization

3.1 Coding of structural shape

To apply GA to structural shape optimization problem, arbitrary structural shapes, truss structures in this case, must be coded as a genotype and genetic operators should be defined for that genotype.

To solve the size problem of optimization, fixed length 1/0 bit strings can be used as a genotype because the number of bar elements is fixed and design variables are only the cross-sectional area of bar elements. A study for that type of problem is reported with good results by Goldberg[1].

But, in this paper, we must treat both the topological problem of optimization and the size problem of optimization. Design variables of our problem are as follows.

- the number of bar elements
- layout of each bar element (topological structure)
- length and cross-sectional area of each bar element

Hence, it is difficult to use fixed length 1/0 bit strings for our problem.

To realize the representations of the genotype for our problem, we can not use conventional representations of the genotype, which consists of single chromosome of character strings, but we employ directly the size of each bar element and the topological structure of bar elements as the representations of the genotype. That is, the genotype of truss structure is described by three types of chromosomes, 1) coordinates of nodes, 2) cross-sectional area of each bar element, 3) topological structure.

By the way, it is known that optimum solution of truss structure is a statically determinate structure and has the condition that stress of each bar element is equal to the allowable compression stress or the allowable tension stress.[2] Therefore, in this paper, all individuals to produce are limited to the statically determinate truss structures. By the assumption that all structures are statically determinate truss structures, axial force on each bar element can be derived without reference to the cross-sectional area of bar element. So, the cross-sectional area chromosomes can be removed from our genotype. The cross-sectional area A_i of bar element i are obtained from axial-force T_i as follows.

$$A_i = \frac{T_i}{\sigma_t} \quad \text{(in the case of tension)} \tag{1}$$

$$A_i = \frac{T_i}{\sigma_c} \quad \text{(in the case of compression)} \tag{2}$$

Where, σ_t and σ_c are the allowable tension stress and the allowable compression stress, respectively. The axial-force T_i is derived from rest of the genotype by finite element method[3].

Figure 2 expresses an example of the genotype for the truss structure shown in figure 1. There are two chromosomes, node coordinates and topological structures. Each chromosome has the flexible size depending on complexity of the truss structure. Each gene of the chromosome represents one feature of the truss structure. A gene in the node coorinate chromosome is a coordinate point (x, y).

3.2 Deformation of structural shape

Structural shape deformation by GA is realized by genetic operations to the genotype of the structural shape. Genetic operations follow from the very nature of the coding methods.

Structural shape deformation for the genotype described in previous subsection is done as the following. At first, in the aspect on size problem, to the node coordinate chromosomes, crossover operator is defined that it exchange part of chromosomes between two individuals, and mutation operator is defined that it changes one gene in the chromosome at random. By these operators, many individuals which have various node coordinates are arisen, and the search for optimum size is done.

But by those operators, since only the individuals which have the same topological structures are reproduced, the topological structures which are not included in the first generation are out of search. To treat the topological problem of optimization, topological structures must be deformed, that is, new genetic operator is necessary which operates the layout of truss structures. In this paper, we propose this new type of operator, named T-mutation, which is the mutation for the topological structure.

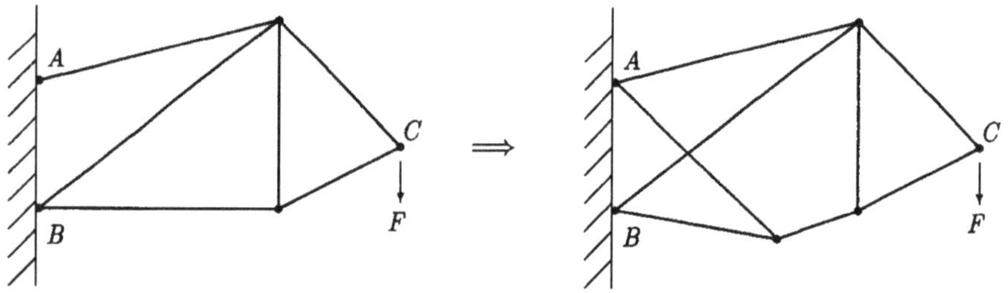

Figure 3: T1-mutation

3.3 Mutation for the topological structure : T-mutation

Because treated structure is limited in statically determinate truss structures, mutation for the topological structure (T-mutation) must translate from statically determinate truss structures to statically determinate truss structures. In this paper, two types of T-mutation are introduced, those are T1-mutation and T2-mutation.

T1-mutation is the operator which adds one new node(figure 3). Select one bar element at random and divide the selected bar element with a new node, and connect the new node to some old node, which is chosen at random, with a new bar element. The new node is moved around it at random. By this operator, numbers of node increase by 1 and numbers of bar elements increase by 2, hence the structure is kept in statically determinate truss structures.

T2-mutation is the operator which changes the topological structure without changing the number of nodes(figure 4). The operation of T2-mutation is as follows.

1. Determine the number of connected bar elements on each node, and select the node which is in the state of the minimum number of bar elements.
   The minimum number of bar elements means the necessary number of bar elements to keep the node stable in the structure. Normal node needs three bar elements to be stable, excepting that on the load node C it is two because of load F and that on the support point nodes A, B on the wall it is one because of the force from the wall.
2. Select one bar element connected to the node which is not in the state of the minimum number of bar elements.
   In the case of left side of figure 4, since the marked nodes are in the state of the minimum number of bar elements, any bar element must not be removed from these nodes.
3. Reconnect the unmarked side of the selected bar element to another node so as to keep statically determinate truss structures.

By applying those two types of T-mutation, it is expected that topological structure become more complex, and kinds of topological structures increase and differentiate.

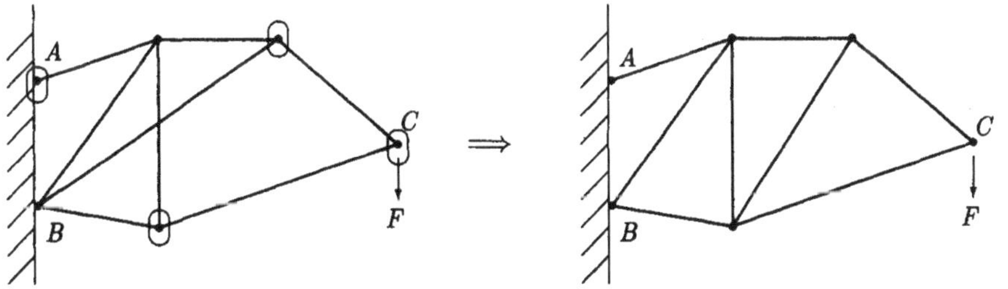

Figure 4: T2-mutation

3.4 Multi-species genetic algorithm

Since individuals which have new topological structures are produced, individuals which have the different number of nodes and different layouts of bar element are in the same generation. In the simple GA, all individuals are treated equally, but in our case it is almost impossible. Therefore, crossover operator may apply in the group of individuals which have the same topological structures. In this paper, this group of individuals is called a species. Therefore, beside that crossover is a operator only inside of the species, T-mutation is a operator to generate new species. Since all individuals are evaluated by common fitness function at the time of reproduction, all species affect each other. Hence, in the better species than the others, which have many better individuals, the number of individuals relatively increases. On the contrary, in the worse species than the others, worse individuals selected and the number of individuals relatively decreases.

4 Experimental Result

In this section, an experimental result on minimum weight design problem of the "coat hanger problem" by truss structures is shown.

At first, the first generation consists of 20 individuals which have the topological structures shown in figure 1. Locations of two nodes, excepting for fixed nodes A, B and C, are chosen at random inside of the $l \times l$ domain between loading point and the wall. To evaluate each individual, axial-force of each bar element is derived by FEM method[3] and cross-sectional area is decided from the axial-force as described before. And total volume of the structure is calculated from cross-sectional area and length of each bar element. The individual whose volume is less is better one. Then, fitness function is,

$$fitness = 1/(total\ volume). \tag{3}$$

In reproduction operator, 5% of lower rank individuals are eliminated and 5% of higher rank individuals are increased. In crossover operator, crossover rate is 50%, part of the nodes are exchanged only between individuals in common species, and exchanged nodes are moved at random in some range(mutation).

T-mutation rate is 1.0 times par a generation when the number of species is less than 12, 0.5 times par a generation when the number of species is 16, 0.0 times par generation when it is 20. And between them, T-Mutation rate is linearly decreased. In the T-mutation, T1-mutation gets 25% and T2-mutation gets 75%. By one T-mutation, ten new individuals are generated.

In a species, maximum limit of the number of individuals is 20 and minimum limit is 5.

The result of experiment on those conditions is the following. Figure 5 is a plot of volume of the best individual on each generation. And figure 6 shows graphical outputs of best individuals on some generations. The final optimum solution on generation 2000 is,

$$V_{\text{opt}} = 4.51\frac{Fl}{\sigma} \qquad \text{(20 bar elements)} \tag{4}$$

Where, $\sigma = \sigma_t$(allowable tension stress) $= \sigma_c$(allowable compression stress).

From the result of the experiment, we can conclude the following things.

- GA is successfully applied to the truss structural optimization problem since volume of the structure decreases along with the generations.
- T-mutation operator and multi-species GA is effectively working since the topological structure become more complex, and in the more complex structures there are more suitable solutions.
- Relatively good result is obtained comparing with Hemp's method[2] on the condition that the number of bar elements is as the same.

  By the Hemp's method, following result of optimum volume is reported[2].

$$V_{\text{opt}} = 4.83\frac{Fl}{\sigma} \quad \text{(12 bar elements)} \tag{5}$$

$$V_{\text{opt}} = 4.61\frac{Fl}{\sigma} \quad \text{(26 bar elements)} \tag{6}$$

$$V_{\text{opt}} = 4.42\frac{Fl}{\sigma} \quad \text{(32 bar elements)} \tag{7}$$

5 Conclusion

In this paper, we proposed multi-species genetic algorithm applying to structural shape optimization problem. By introducing multi-species GA, not only the size problem of optimization but also the topological problem of optimization was solved, and relatively good results were obtained comparing with Hemp's method.

References

1. D. E. Goldberg : *Genetic Algorithms in Search, Optimization, and Machine learning*, (Addison Wesley, 1989).
2. W. S. Hemp : *Optimum Structures*, (Clarendon Press, Oxford 1973).
3. J. N. Reddy : *An Introduction to The Finite Element Method*, (McGraw-Hill, 1993).

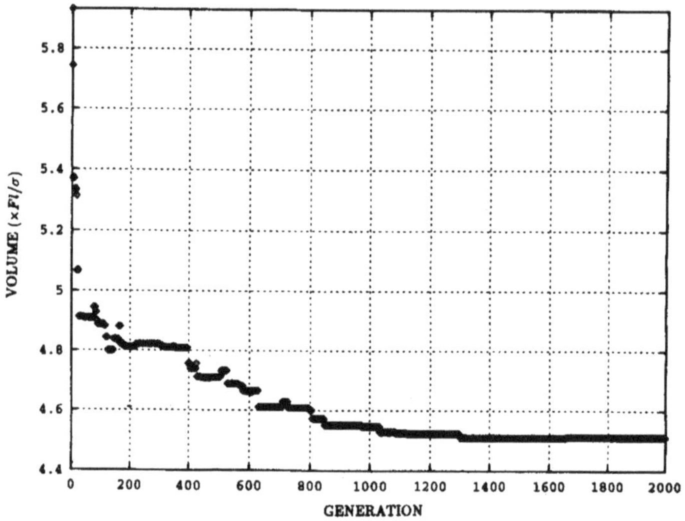

Figure 5: Plot of volume on each generation

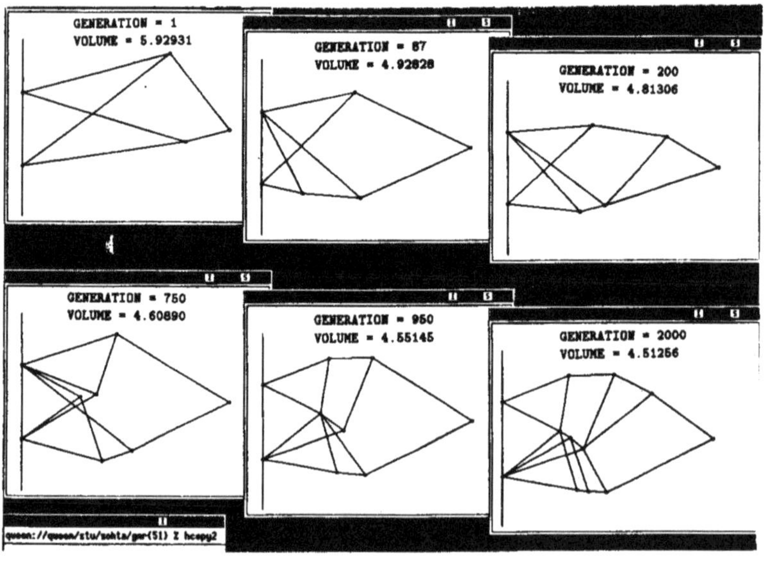

Figure 6: graphical output of truss structures on some generations

Hybrid Systems

A Fuzzy Learning Expert System and Its Applications

T. Li, D. Guo, R. Jayakumar, Y. Y. Tang and *S. Klasa*
Department of Computer Science, Concordia University
1455 de Maisonneuve Blvd. West, Montreal, P.Q. H3G 1M8, Canada
E-mail: taoli@cs.concordia.ca

Abstract. We investigate a fuzzy learning system for time series analysis in this paper. Our system combines expert knowledge and machine learning to achieve competent performance in time series analysis. Learning plays an important role in the success of forecasting. Expert knowledge is used to set up the initial system. Learning is then applied to improve the performance of the system.

1. Introduction

The outcome of fuzzy reasoning is typically some assignments of fuzzy subsets to linguistic variables. For some applications such as automatic control, the input and outputs must be real-values. In this case, some fuzzification and defuzzification operations must be performed. This corresponds to function approximation and some degree of optimization is normally needed. For applications to control systems and time series analysis, the accuracy of the results is crucial. On the other hand, the initial set up of a fuzzy knowledge based system is typically inaccurate. Therefore, such systems must be fine-tuned. Such tuning process is often inaccurate and time-consuming. In this paper, we propose a learning approach to generate fuzzy systems. We also study the application of such systems to time series analysis. Our learning fuzzy system resembles all subsymbolic connectionist systems. It is different from other symbolic learning paradigms. In this paper, we study the subsymbolic learning aspect of systems. The symbolic learning aspect such as rule extraction is beyond the scope of this paper. However, we are presently studying a fuzzy recurrent network of fuzzy rules and a scheme for rule structuring. Further result will be reported. In section 2, we outline the basic form of our fuzzy reasoning system and its advantages. Then we develop our fuzzy learning algorithm in section 3 and compare our approach with other related work. In section 4, we present some results of simulation for function approximation. In section 5, the results of time series analysis with our fuzzy learning system are discussed. A summary is given in section 6.

2. A Fuzzy Reasoning Expert System

Fuzzy reasoning systems contain knowledge bases that consist of many rules. These rules typically use linguistic variables to incorporate imprecise knowledge. Most fuzzy reasoning systems use the inference schema of the following form, as in the seminal work of Zadeh [6]. In this paper, we adopt the fuzzy inference schema of Cao and Kandel [1]. This inference schema has the following form.

$$\begin{aligned}
&\textbf{IF } X \textbf{ is } U_1 \textbf{ THEN } Y \textbf{ is } w_{11}/V_1+w_{12}/V_2+\ldots+w_{1k}/V_k\\
&\textbf{IF } X \textbf{ is } U_2 \textbf{ THEN } Y \textbf{ is } w_{21}/V_1+w_{22}/V_2+\ldots+w_{2k}/V_k\\
&\qquad\cdot\quad\cdot\quad\cdot\quad\cdot\quad\cdot\quad\cdot\quad\cdot\\
&\textbf{IF } X \textbf{ is } U_n \textbf{ THEN } Y \textbf{ is } w_{n1}/V_1+w_{n2}/V_2+\ldots+w_{nk}/V_k
\end{aligned} \qquad (1)$$

$$\frac{X \text{ is a}}{Y \text{ is b}}$$

where a and b can be real vectors. $w_{i1}/V_1+w_{i2}/V_2+ \ldots + w_{ik}/V_k$ is interpreted as V_1 with degree of confidence w_{i1}, V_2 with degree of confidence $w_{i2}, \ldots$, and V_k with degree of confidence w_{ik}.

In a system employing the above inference schema, an input value a is first mapped into a vector $<\mu_1(a),\mu_2(a), \ldots ,\mu_n(a)>$, where μ_i is the fuzzy membership function of U_i. This vector is then multiplied to the weight matrix **W**,

$$\mathbf{W} = \{ w_{ij} \}, \; i = 1, 2, \ldots, n, \text{ and } j = 1, 2, \ldots, k \tag{2}$$

The resulting vector $<y_1,y_2, \ldots ,y_k>$ is then defuzzified by the moment method to produce

$$y = \frac{h_1 y_1 + h_2 y_2 + \ldots + h_k y_k}{y_1 + y_2 + \ldots + y_k} \tag{3}$$

where $0 \le h_i \le 1$ are typically the central values of the fuzzy subsets $V_1, V_2, \ldots, V_k$. The above method makes sense for symmetric output fuzzy label subsets. The relational mapping from the input fuzzy concepts to the output fuzzy concepts is accomplished through the matrix vector product $\mu(a) \bullet \mathbf{W}$.

This system has a number of advantages. From the definition it is obvious that this system is applicable to both *discrete* universe of discourse and *continuous* universe of discourse. In addition, it can embed more elaborate features of human expert knowledge through the weight associated with each input fuzzy concept and each output fuzzy concept. Lastly, by adjusting the weights one can easily modify the input/output functional mapping. This last characteristic is particularly useful for a learning fuzzy control system since only one layer of linear units needs be adjusted during the learning process. Hence the learning process can be significantly sped up. Although simplistic, this mechanism has demonstrated its power and robustness in learning many functions.

3. The Fuzzy Learning Algorithm

The fuzzy membership functions are chosen such that they can form the basis of universal approximators. The defuzzification method requires symmetric fuzzy membership functions. In addition, smooth fuzzy membership functions can better approximate continuous functions. Based on these observations, we have used a number of fuzzy membership functions in our experimental study. These include the following fuzzy membership functions:

1. the positive half of the sine function

$$f_i(x) = \begin{cases} \sin(x\omega_i - \theta_i), & \text{if } 0 \le x - \theta_i \le \pi \\ 0, & \text{otherwise} \end{cases} \tag{4}$$

2. the Gaussian function

$$g_i(x) = \exp\left[-\frac{\|x-c_i\|^2}{\sigma_i^2}\right], \text{ where } \sigma_i = 1/\omega_i, \tag{5}$$

3. the quadratic function

$$y_i(x) = -(x\omega_i - d_i)^2 + 1, \text{ for } d_i - 1 \le x \le d_i + 1. \tag{6}$$

The shape of the last function is similar to that of the first and it is much simpler in computation. We can form a piece-wise smooth function by combining $-(x-d_i)^2+1$ with $(x-(d_i+2))^2-1$ in the internal $d_i-1 \le x \le d_i+3$. It is interesting to notice that this piece-wise function is similar in shape to the sine function. Its computational simplicity is very attractive to a fuzzy learning system. Furthermore the function is first order continuous at the connecting point $x=d_i+1$ since

$$\left[\frac{d\left(-(x-d_i)^2+1\right)}{dx}\right]_{x=d_i+1} = \left[\frac{d\left((x-(d_i+2))^2-1\right)}{dx}\right]_{x=d_i+1} = -2.$$

Our inference schema is different from the system of Takagi and Sugeno [4,5]. Hence our fuzzy learning system is different from that of Jang and Sun [2]. Jang and Sun identified the equivalence between Radial Basis Functions (RBFN) and fuzzy inference systems [2,3]. However, their adaptive network representation contains too many free variables and is difficult to optimize the weights during learning. No experimental results were reported in [2]. For the RBFN, unsupervised learning is used to identify the centers and variances of the Gaussian functions and supervised learning is used to adjust the weights. The learning process is quite complex.

Although a scaling factor ω_i is given in each of our membership functions, it is not used in our experimental study. By simply adjusting the weight matrix **W**, we have been able to approximate very complex functions. The shift factors θ_i, c_i, and d_i are also fixed during learning. Hence, we are able to eliminate many free variables without sacrificing the accuracy of function approximation. This is the major advantage of our fuzzy learning system. In our approach, the weight matrix itself can generate quite complex patterns. Only supervised learning is necessary in our system. Hence the learning process is simple.

In constructing our fuzzy learning systems, we rely on expert knowledge in selecting the number of fuzzy concepts (labels), the width of the membership functions, and the initial weight matrix **W**. Typically, the widths of the membership functions are fixed and the same. The centers of the fuzzy concepts are distributed in equal distance in the universe of discourse. A typical arrangements of the fuzzy labels is shown in Figure 1.

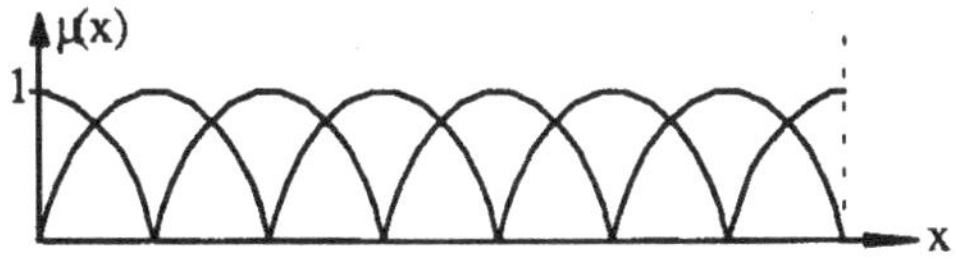

Figure 1. Typical arrangement of fuzzy subsets.

The columns of the weight matrix **W** must satisfy the condition $\sum_{j=1}^{n}\left|w_{ij}\right|=1$, for $1 \le i \le k$, which naturally arises because each summation represents the degree of contribution from every input fuzzy subset to an output fuzzy subset. Let the central values of the output fuzzy label subsets be $<h_1,h_2,\ldots,h_k>$. Using the initial configuration of a system and the initial weight matrix, the learning algorithm is described as follows.

Algorithm *Fuzzy Learning*:

1. (Forward propagation) Select an input x; $\xi=<\mu_1(x),\mu_2(x),\ldots,\mu_n(x)>$; $<\gamma_1,\gamma_2,\ldots,\gamma_k>\leftarrow\xi\times\mathbf{W}$; $y\leftarrow<h_1,h_2,\ldots,h_k>\bullet<\gamma_1,\gamma_2,\ldots,\gamma_k>$;
2. (Backward error propagation) $e\leftarrow d-y$; $<\varepsilon_1,\varepsilon_2,\ldots,\varepsilon_k>\leftarrow<F(h_1,e),F(h_2,e),\ldots,F(h_k,e)>$;
3. (Adjust weight matrix) $w_{ij}(t+1)\leftarrow w_{ij}(t)+\alpha\mu_i(x)\varepsilon_i$, for $1\le i\le n$, $1\le j\le k$; $m_i\leftarrow\sum_{j=1}^{n}\left|w_{ij}(t+1)\right|$, for $1\le i\le n$; $w_{ij}(t+1)\leftarrow w_{ij}(t+1)/m_i$, for $1\le i\le n$, $1\le j\le k$;
4. IF stopping condition is satisfied THEN halt ELSE go to step 1.

In the above algorithm, α is the learning rate. The membership functions μ_i can be f_i, g_i, or y_i. We have a choice of two functions to compute the back propagation error in step 2. The first function is $\varepsilon_i=F(h_i,e)=1/(|h_i-e|+1)$. With this function, only those nodes whose central values are close to the output error value will be affected. Since the central values are evenly distributed in the output universe of discourse, this back propagation has the effects of minimizing the loss of previous learned patterns and stabilizing the learning. The second function is $F(h_i,e)=h_ie$. It treats every output fuzzy subsets equally. In step 3, the Hebbian rule is employed to adjust the weights. The weights are then normalized to satisfy the constraint condition.

This algorithm can be easily extended to this multiple input schema. Since the conjunction of fuzzy variables can be considered as the product of their values, we only need to modify the computation of the ξ vector in step 1. Specifically, we let

$$\xi\leftarrow<\prod_{i=1}^{m}\mu_{1i}(x_i),\prod_{i=1}^{m}\mu_{2i}(x_i),\ \ldots\ ,\prod_{i=1}^{m}\mu_{ni}(x_i)>.$$

The effects of all the input values are accounted for in this formula. It is also not difficult to extend the above inference schema to allow multiple output variables.

4. Simulation Results for Function Approximation

We have simulated the fuzzy learning system to approximate a number of real-valued functions. The fuzzy learning system succeeded on learning every one of the functions with high accuracy. The learning algorithm is very fast. With only a small number of fuzzy label subsets used for the input variable, we have achieved very good performance. For brevity, we only show a simple examples here. We use a fuzzy learning system with 11 rules (input fuzzy labels) and 19 output labels. In these 11 rules, the input linguistic variable X takes on the linguistic labels *es* (extra small) , *vs* (very small), *s* (small), *ls* (a little small), *ms* (medium small), *m* (medium), *ml* (medium large), *ll* (a little large), *l* (large), *vl* (very large), and *el* (extra large), respectively. Nine of the 11 input label fuzzy sets have the half sine function described by equation (4). Two label sets are on two sides and each is a quarter sine. This arrangement is similar to that in Figure 1. Seventeen of the 19 output label fuzzy sets have the membership function described by equation (4). Two label fuzzy sets are on two sides and each is a quarter sine. Again, this arrangement has the appearance of Figure 1. The function to be approximated is $y = C[1-(x/D)^2]$ in the interval [0.8,10]. C=8 and D=10 are constants. In Figure 2, the mathematical curve is shown by the line of small diamonds (the **dy** legend) and the output of the learned fuzzy system is shown by the line of small squares (the **ay** legend).

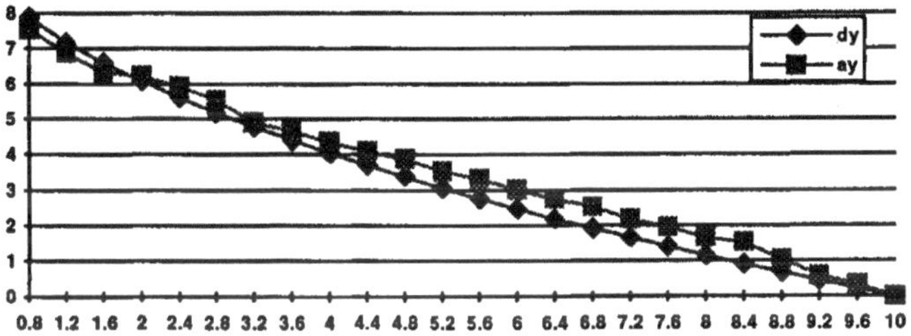

Figure 2. Approximating the function $y = C[1-(x/D)^2]$.

As demonstrated in Figure 2, the fuzzy expert system is able to approximate the desired mathematical function very well. The accuracy is very high with only a small number of rules and output label fuzzy sets.

5. Application to Time Series Prediction

We have used our learning fuzzy system in time series analysis. Both artificial and real world data have been used to test our system. A large number of the experiments have been conducted. For present purpose, we only demonstrate the result for artificial time series data in this section. In this section, we demonstrate the feasibility of our fuzzy learning approach to time series analysis. In the above example, the time series is repeatedly generated by the function $y = C(1-|\omega|)$ with minor noise added, where $\omega = \sin(x \pi/D-0.5\pi)$ and C and D are constants. There are a few sharp peaks in this series of points. We use three values in the past to predict the next value. In other words, we use x(t-2), x(t-1), and x(t) as three input values and x(t+1) as the output value. Nine rules are used in the system. Each rule contains three fuzzy propositions in the condition and nine fuzzy labels for one output variable. The result is shown in Figure 3. The **dy** line indicates the desired time series and the **ay** line indicates the prediction by the learned fuzzy system. The performance of the system is clearly satisfactory. The prediction is very accurate. Since multiple input values are used to predict a single output value, the system is not out of balance at the sharp peak points and is able to learn to predict accurately.

6. Summary

A new learning fuzzy expert system is presented in this paper. This system adopts an interesting inference schema and a fast and reliable learning algorithm. In our fuzzy learning approach, expert knowledge and machine learning are combined to form a basis for constructing and tuning expert systems.

We have applied our fuzzy learning approach to function approximation and time series analysis. Good results have been achieved in both applications. The performance of our fuzzy learning expert system is very good for such difficulty tasks as time series analysis and automatic control. Our system can be used in both classification and function approximation while traditional feedforward neural networks tend to be used only in classification. Due the limited output range of squashing function, neural networks have difficulty producing output values in arbitrary intervals. Our system does not have such problems. Simulation results on artificial and real world data demonstrate the advantages of our fuzzy learning system. We are currently studying the application of our system to scientific forecasting and corporate planning. We are also developing a feedback learning model of fuzzy expert systems. We intend to use this model to study the temporal behavior of many phenomena.

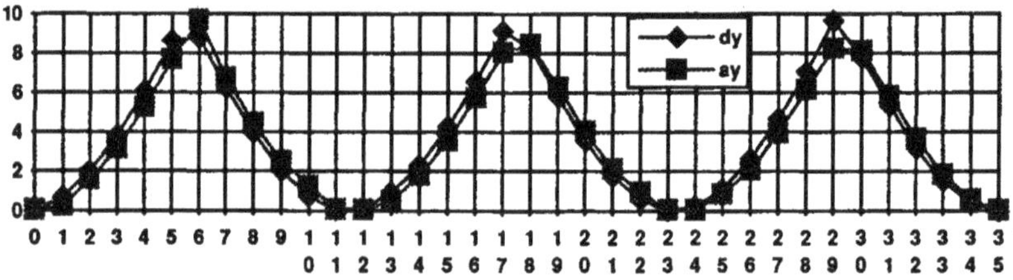

Figure 3. Time series generated by $y = C(1-|\omega|)$ and $\omega = \sin(x\pi/D-0.5\pi)$.

Acknowledgments

This research was supported in part by a FRDP grant from Concordia University and in part by a grant from the National Science and Engineering Research Council of Canada. The first author wishes to thank Dr. Z.Q. Cao for introducing him to the world of fuzzy reasoning and for many stimulating discussions. The author gained much knowledge of fuzzy reasoning from the deep and insightful views of Dr. Cao.

References

[1] Cao, A. Kandel and L-H. Li, "A new model of fuzzy reasoning", *Fuzzy Sets and Systems*, Vol.36, pp311-325, 1990.

[2] J-S. R. Jang and C-T. Sun, "Functional equivalence between radial basis function networks and fuzzy inference systems", *IEEE Trans. Neural Networks,* Vol.4, No.1, pp156-159, 1993.

[3] J. Moody and C. Darken, "Fast learning in networks of locally-tuned processing units", *Neural Computation*, Vol.1, pp281-294, 1989.

[4] T. Takagi and M. Sugeno, "Derivation of fuzzy control rules from human operator's control actions", *Proc. IFAC Symp. Fuzzy Information, Knowledge Representation and Decision Analysis*, pp55-60, 1983.

[5] T. Takagi and M. Sugeno, "Fuzzy identification of systems and its applications to modeling and control", *IEEE Trans. Systems, Man, and Cybernetics*, Vol. SMC-15, pp116-132, 1985.

[6] L.A. Zadeh, "Outline of a new approach to the analysis of complex systems and decision processes", *IEEE Trans. Systems, Man, and Cybernetics*, Vol.SMC-3, No.1, pp28-44, 1973.

A NEURAL NETWORK EXPERT SYSTEM FOR INTERNATIONAL CURRENCY OPTION TRADING*

T.S. Quah,† C.L. Tan
Department of Information Systems and Computer Science

B. Srinivasan
Department of Decision Sciences

H.H. Teh
Institute of Systems Science

National University of Singapore
10, Kent Ridge Crescent, Singapore 0511
Republic of Singapore

ABSTRACT Everyday, the international currency market weathers all forms of world-wide current affairs and governmental economics statistics releases. Such news may cause slight ripples on the exchange rate, or they may blow up extensive fluctuations in demands and supplies for major currencies. In the past, foreign exchange traders depend heavily on their experience and gut feelings when they transact. The emergence of neural-network based expert systems has overcome much of the brittleness problems faced by rule-based technology, and has become a viable tool for supporting such strategic decision makings. Besides being more flexible, such as having learning capability, these systems can also handle the fuzziness and biasness of human decision processes. Furthermore, through making the edge weights on the neural network a function of user-id, personalized logic system can be realized with ease. This paper presents a neural network expert system for supporting the forex trader in their decision processes. The system possesses the abovementioned properties.

1 Introduction

In recent years, neural network technology has demonstrated its strengths in the area of decision support systems. Neural networks, with their self-organization features, lend themselves very well to learning and parallelism. In particular, their ability to adapt to changing circumstances and environment factors, as well as being able to handle the fuzziness and biasness aspect of human decision makings, shows good promise to overcome the brittleness problems faced by many rule-based systems.[9]

The objective of this research is to develop an expert system shell with a neural network inference engine. The network model used in this research is the Neural Logic Network *(NEULONET)* studied at the National University of Singapore.[3,4] The prototype shell stores each expert system rule by a rudimentary Neural Logic Network, which we called *network element (netel)*. These small Neural Logic Networks are dynamically chained up during consultation process to derive at the conclusions.

*This project is sponsored by National University of Singapore research grant RP900628

†Please address all correspondence on this paper to Tong-Seng Quah, Email: quahts@iscs.nus.sg

Through using of netels, the shell shields users from the complexity of connectionist architecture by providing them with a much familar rule-based expert system environment. The inferencing engine of the prototype system is sensitive to different users, and can adjust its inference strategy based on previous trainings or interactions with those users. A expert system for currency option trading is built on the shell to demonstrate the feasibility of netel-based expert system.

2 Neural Logic Network - NEULONET

In this section, we will give a brief summary description of Neural Logic Network and some references for readers who are interested to know more about this particular neural network model.

Neural Logic Networks *(NEULONET)*, can incorporate both the pattern processing capability of Multi-layer Perceptions and the logical inference capability of Boolean Logic Inference Networks within a single frame of neural network environment.[3,4]

A typical NEULONET contains a set of input nodes and output nodes. Every node can take one of the three order pair activation values, (1,0) for true, (0,1) for false, and (0,0) for don't know. Every edge in the NEULONET is also associated with an ordered pair weight (x,y), where x and y are real numbers of positive, negative or zero value. The choice of weights associated with NEULONET edges offers a great variety of different logic operations for the NEULONET. In theory, for a network with 2 inputs, a total of 3^8 distinct meaningful binary logical operations are possible.[4] Many of the logical operations other than the standard ones can be used to mimic human reasoning process which is often guided by subjective opinions or biases, such as biased AND and biased OR networks. This is made possible by allowing favored inputs to carry larger arc weights in order to assert greater influence than in the usual AND and OR operations, respectively.

A further strength of NEULONET lies in its ability to incorporate probabilistic logic or fuzzy logic into its operations. In addition to the usual activation values and weights, each node will carry another ordered pair (a_1,b_1), denoting either probability or fuzziness associated with the nodal value. After the usual propagation and activation, the probability or the fuzziness associated with the output value is then computed based on some set of rules. A separate set of activation rules has been designed for both types of logic.[8]

3 Netel-based Expert System Shell

Using NEULONET as the inference mechanism, we have developed a netel-based expert system shell. It is constructed as a general purpose shell, so that different domain specific expert systems may be built upon it.[7]

On the surface, the user is presented with an environment that looks much like a familiar rule base system. Underlying the user interface, however, is a knowledge base of small Neural Logic Networks and an NEULONET inference engine to drive those rules. The shell provides users with the functions that are considered "standard" features in a general rule-based system.

3.1 *Rule Editor*

The rule editor is initiated from the user interface shell. It is a visual editing environment with split screens, one for a graphic editor and the other runs a text editor. The graphic editor displays netels in pictorial form whereas the text editor displays details of the netels in form-filling screen and pop-up subscreens. This is possible as every netel is basically a small Neural Logic Network that represents a heuristic rule from the domain expert. Editing can be performed on either editor.

3.2 *Knowledge Base*

The knowledge base consists of heuristics rules (represented as netels) as well as knowledge learnt through training examples and past inference history. Semantic meanings of the logical operator (such as AND, OR, NOT etc.) may be represented in NEULONET weights through using the *construction algorithm* for determining the correct values of those weights.[4] User-defined operators, which can fully exploit the strength of NEULONET for representing human decision making, may be used in netels too. An example is shown in figure 1, where condition-s may overrule effects bring about by condition-1 to condition-n. Using currency trading as a domain to illustrate: suppose the economic conditions and statistical figures point towards a downward movement of a currency exchange rate, the central bank may interfere by taking corrective actions, such as buying or selling in the open market, or changing the reserve requirements. These actions will ease the downward pressure on the currency exchange rate.

Every netel may also have an auxiliary weight file pointer, which serves as a function that is sensitive to user-id. With different set of weights on the edge links for different users, *user-sensitive inferencing* may thus be achieved without needing to duplicate the same rules in the knowledge base. The shell can thus handle with ease any cases where the domain experts differ in opinions. With learning capability, the system may thus be trained to behave like individual experts in the domain. This is particularly useful for applications involving subjective knowledge, such as option trading or future trading of currency.

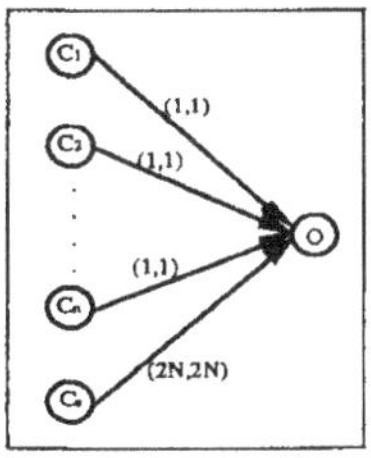

Figure 1: Overriding condition

3.3 *Inference Mechanism*

The inference engine may run in consultation or training mode. In either case it chains active rules together into a Neural Logic Network. NEULONET propagation and activation rules[4,8] are applied in the process.

With netels, the system's rules are essentially fragments of neural logic networks to be fitted together dynamically during the inferencing process, similar to the chaining of rules in the working memory of a conventional rule-based system. Two ways of chaining, i.e. forward and backward chaining, are possible. A combination of both ways are utilized during any inferencing. The chaining process continues until some goal nodes are activated, the conclusion will be presented to the user. The inference engine back-tracks when no fruitful conclusion can be reached. In such situations, the system traces those inference tree branches that carry nodes yet to be activated. More inputs may be solicited from the user. As and when new activations are obtained for some nodes, forward inference will resume.

In training mode, examples are presented to the inference engine. An inference network tree is constructed just like the case of consultation. NEULONET propagation and activation rules are applied from the first layer of the inference tree towards the final conclusion nodes of the tree. If the system is not able to derive at the expected conclusion, the error will be back propagated. Netels with modifiable edge weights are adjusted to accommodate the new examples. Furthermore, the expert system may be trained with heuristic knowledge supply by different experts, thus achieving different edge weights for the knowledge base netels. During future consultations, the inference engine will intelligently switch the weights of the netels based on user identification. This results in the expert system behaving like different experts, hence achieving the concept of personalized expert system.

3.4 *User Interface Shell*

The various components of the netel-based shell are integrated into a *"total"* environment for netel rules maintenance, training and consultation inferences.

The *query formulizer* and *explanation mechanism* serve as messengers between the user and the inference engine. During any inferencing process, when more inputs are required from the user, the inference engine calls on the *query formulizer* and passes it the request. The query formulizer is able to access the necessary data structure at the common memory pool to formulate a user friendly query. This is then passed to the *dialogue handler*, which pops up a window with the query. Users can then provide the necessary inputs, plus stating his confidence of those inputs. The dialogue handler will then update relevant data structures in the system memory, and flag the inference engine to continue its inferencing.

The *explanation mechanism* accesses the same shared memory for information on the activities of the inference engine. It may trace the inference tree of the current consultation to satisfy questions posed by the user, such as the *"why"*s and the *"how"*s.

An on-line guide is also provided by the shell.

4 Netel-based Expert System for Currency Option Trading

An advisory expert system for currency option trading has been built using the above-mentioned shell.

4.1 *The International Currency Market*

International currency trading is a volatile and risky business. The exchange rate changes continuously as the market weathers all forms of shocks ranging from governmental economic performance statistics releases, to news about worldwide events. Particularly sensitive to these current affairs is the spot rate of a currency. To reduce the effect of mistakes, risk averting traders generally involve themselves with multiple buying and selling of *calls* and *puts* options.

Interest rate, which is a major determinant of the spot rate of a currency, is tied strongly to the economic performance of a country. Influencing the interest rate movements is a set of statistics releases periodically by the government. The statistics reflects the performance of the economy, which strongly affects the demand and supply in the money market and causes the interest rate to float up or down. As interest rate changes are anticipated, forex traders will transact according to the anticipated capital movements. Past experiences and gut feelings play an important part in the decision process.

4.2 *Human Judgments*

The domain of currency option trading is appropriate for testing the netel-based shell because the trading rules for buying and selling of options carry heavy flavors of human decision makings, and can be well handled by the semantic riched NEULONET. In fact, the final decision for buying or selling is also strongly influenced by the experience and the risk profile of individual experts (such as capital in hand and financial obligations) - some traders are more aggressive, others may be more conservative. As discussed in section 3.3, the netel-based shell allows training according to different user identifications, thus realizing the idea of *personalized* expert decision support system. This is illustrated in training session 2 in the next section.

5 Implementation Results

In this section we will discuss the experimental results.

5.1 *Netel Knowledge Base*

The netel knowledge base consists of heuristic rules and customized weights. At present, the prototype system has about thirty netels. These netels represent the knowledge of domain expert in currency option trading. They formed the basic knowledge of the expert system. With the flexibility provided by *weight file pointers* of NEULONET,[6] some netels carry several set of weights for the personalized expert system knowledge base. As different weights are loaded into the working memory according to user identifications, semantically it is equivalent to having different set of rules for each user.

5.2 *Refinement Learning*

Using the basic knowledge base as a start, the system is subjected to testing with historical cases taken from The Asian Wall Street Journal. Economic performance statistics announced by the governments, and the currencies exchange rate movements that resulted were noted. With these test cases (test set A), we subjected the expert system to the reported economic conditions, and observed whether it is able to suggest the correct trading decisions.

The result is as follow:

	Simple statistic	Multiple statistic	Total
No. of cases	27	6	33
Successful	22	3	25
Successful(%)	81%	50%	76%

It is clear that the expert rules are quite good in cases of single statistic releases over the day (i.e. quite days). The few cases where the system was unable to make correct judgment were mainly due to weak signals given by the statistical figures. These weak cases were not able to activate the netel nodes sufficiently to trigger the firing of the goal nodes.

For complex cases (i.e. several pieces of statistics influencing the interest rate movements are being released on the same day), the system is much less competent to give correct advises.

We subject the netel rules to refinement training by using additional historical cases collected from the same journal (test set B). The coverage of the cases range from January 1992 to December 1992. The distribution of the cases are as followed:

	Simple statistic	Multi statistic	Total
No. of cases	45	15	60
Percentage	75%	25%	100%

Using test set B, two refinement training sessions, each with different setup conditions, were conducted.

Session 1: Training with unmodified test cases from test set B. As the training cases are presented to the expert system, NEULONET learning algorithm[5] are utilized to modify the weights of the netels. After which, the trained netel knowledge base is subjected to testing using test set A again. The results is as followed:

	Simple statistic	Multi statistic	Total
No. of cases	27	6	33
Successful	25	5	30
Successful(%)	93%	83%	91%

It is obvious that the netels perform better after refinement trainings.

Session 2: Training with hypothetical expert decisions to experiment the effects of user-sensitive inferencing.

In this session, we hypothesize a conservative trader with low risk profile, by modifying some of the training cases. The netels in the knowledge base are then subjected to training using these modified cases.

After trainings, we subject the expert systems to the some trial consultations. It is found that the system now has the tendency to make decisions of lower risk profile, as is reflected in cases where it suggests taking low risk strategies such as *buying bear spread*, instead of *buying straddles*, as it did previously.

Upon analysis, the weights of the netels were found to have shifted towards higher values on paths that lead to lower risk strategies and lower value on paths that lead to higher risk decisions.

6 Future Works

The netel-based expert system shell has demonstrated its strengths for use as decision support tool. We intend to use the shell for exploring other domains of strategic decision makings, especially areas which are rich in human logic.

In addition, we will also compare our results with other connectionist expert systems, such as FuzzyARTMAP,[2] as well as statistical methods, such as Beckman's works,[1] and enhanced the netel-based shell base on the findings.

References

[1] Thomas J. Beckman. *Stock market forecasting using technical analysis.* In Jay Liebowitz, editor, *Proceedings of the First World Congress on Expert Systems*, pages 2512–2519. Pergamon Press, December 1991.

[2] Gail A. Carpenter, Stephen Grossberg, et al. *Fuzzy ARTMAP: A neural network architecture for incremental supervised learning of analog multidimensional maps.* Technical Report CAS/CNS-TR-91-016, Department of Cognitive and Neural Systems, Boston University, August 1991.

[3] S.C. Chan, L.S. Hsu, and K.F. Loe. *Fuzzy Neural-Logic Networks.* In P.Z. Wang and K.F. Loe, editors, *Advanced In Fuzzy Systems: Applications & Theory (Vol. I)*, chapter 2. World Scientific Publication, May 1993.

[4] S.C. Chan, L.S. Hsu, K.F. Loe, and H.H. Teh. *Neural Logic Networks.* In Omid M. Omidvar, editor, *Progress In Neural Networks (Vol. II)*. Albex Publication, 1993.

[5] Pan Qiang. *Design and control strategies for connectionist expert systems.* Master's thesis, National University of Singapore, Kent Ridge Crescent, S(0511), 1992.

[6] Tong-Seng Quah, Chew-Lim Tan, Hoon-Heng Teh, and Zuliang Shen. *An enhanced NEULONET for rule-based reasoning.* In *Proceedings of the World Congress on Neural Networks*, page (accepted for publication). International Neural Network Society, July 1993.

[7] Tong-Seng Quah, Chew-Lim Tan, Hoon-Heng Teh, and Zuliang Shen. *An integrated shell for developing connectionist expert systems.* In *Proceedings of the International Joint Conference on Neural Networks*, page (accepted for publication). International Neural Network Society, October 1993.

[8] H.H. Teh and Wellington C.P. Yu. *A controlled learning environment of enhanced perception.* In *IEEE Proceedings, Future Trend in Distributed Computing Systems.* IEEE, 1988.

[9] Robert Trippi and Efraim Turban. *The impact of parallel and neural computing on managerial decision making. Journal of Management Information Systems*, 6(3):85–98, 1989.

THE SYNERGISTIC COMBINATION OF NEURAL AND SYMBOLIC COMPUTATION IN THE RECOGNITION OF WORDS DEGRADED BY NOISE

Tak Ho
Attorney General's Department
471 Little Bourke St.
Melbourne Vic 3000

Victor B. Ciesielski
Department of Computer Science
RMIT, GPO Box 2476V
Melbourne Vic 3001
vc@goanna.cs.rmit.oz.au

Abstract

Neural and symbolic systems can be regarded as complementary in the sense that neural systems work well in areas where symbolic systems are weak and vice versa. This gives the possibility of enhanced performance using a hybrid system rather than a neural or symbolic system alone on some problems. We have investigated the performance of a neural network alone and a hybrid neural/symbolic system on a character/word recognition problem — the problem of recognizing words which have been systematically degraded by noise. We found that, at all noise levels, the character recognition capabilities of the network were enhanced by the use of symbolic knowledge of how characters are assembled into legal words.

1 Introduction

Artificial neural networks are characterized by the use of computational units, called artificial neurons, used in different connectivity patterns and with different computational strategies. Each unit computes a weighted sum of its inputs, applies a transfer function to this sum and sends the result to the inputs of other neurons. Generally the weights for a network are found using a training algorithm. Many training algorithms have been developed. The use of different connectivity patterns, computation schedules and training algorithms results in an amazingly rich variety of network types. Types of networks developed so far include Madaline, Multi Layer Perceptrons, ART and Koheonen style networks[3, 5].

Symbolic computation is generally associated with knowledge representations of different kinds. In contrast to the neural networks which involve calculating with numbers, symbolic computation is concerned with symbol manipulation. This involves creating, modifying and matching complex symbolic structures. Many different knowledge representation formalisms have been developed, including semantic nets, frame systems, conceptual dependency and scripts, conceptual graphs and predicate calculus[1]. Perhaps the most common form of symbolic computation is forward or backward chaining in production rule systems[1].

Symbolic systems have excellent explanation capabilities, but are very brittle and do not deal well with noisy and erroneous data. Neural network systems have limited explanation capabilities, but generally exhibit graceful degradation gven noisy and/or erroneous data. Building a symbolic system generally requires knowledge engineering, while neural network systems are built from examples of the desired behaviour. The strengths and weaknesses of neural nets and symbolic systems give rise to two interesting questions.

1. What kinds of architectures are possible in combining neural and symbolic computation?

2. What kinds of problems are particularly well suited to these architectures?

While these questions have not yet been systematically explored a number of hybrid systems have been developed. These include a system for monitoring power-plant performance[12], for predicting stock markets/business risks[4, 13], knowledge acquisition for fault diagnosis[8] and in the control of a robot welder[6].

In the work reported in this paper we have investigated one architecture on a class of character/word recognition problems.

2 The Problem of Recognizing Words Degraded by Noise

Character recognition has been a much studied area and there have been may systems based both on image processing and neural network techniques [7, 10, 11]. Some systems are mature enough to be commercial products.

The kinds of inputs we expect our system to deal with are shown in figure 1. Each character is represented as an 8x8 matrix of pixels. As the noise[1] level increases the words become harder to read. This kind of problem could arise in practice, for example when part of an address on an envelope becomes smudged or a document is partially damaged (spilled coffee for example). Our hypothesis is that as the noise levels increase a neural network for character recognition will fail to detect some characters correctly, but that its performance can be improved by the use of knowledge about letter combinations in words. At very high levels of noise, however, no recognition will be possible.

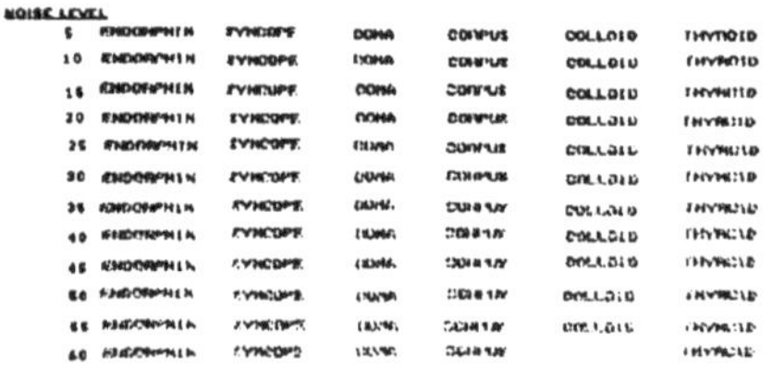

Figure 1: Words Gradually Degraded by Noise

Our goal is not character recognition per se, it is to look at possible improvements in performance by using both neural and symbolic computation.

3 Architecture of the Neural/Symbolic System

The architecture of the recognition system is shown in figure 2.

In broad terms the recognition process works as follows: Pixel maps of each character in the word to be recognized are passed into a noise generator which induces noise of a given level into the character. These characters are then

[1]For our purposes 50% noise means select 50% of the black pixels in a character at random and make them white

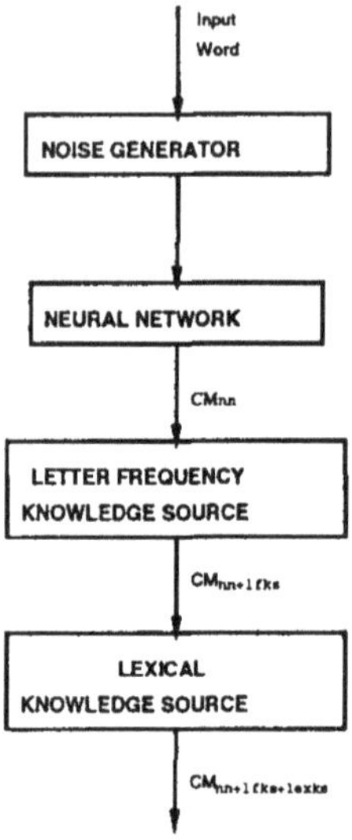

Figure 2: Architecture of the word recognition system

passed to a previously trained three layer feed forward neural network. For each character position in the input word the network delivers a list of candidate letters with associated activations. These activations are treated as 'certainty measures[2]'. Character positions which have low certainty are then examined first with a knowledge source of expected letter combinations and then by a lexical knowledge source.

The neural network topology, as determined empirically by preliminary experiments, consisted of 64 input nodes 10 hidden nodes and 27 output nodes. The 64 input nodes correspond to the number of pixels used to represent an 8x8 letter. Only white(0) and black(1) pixels were used, there were no grey levels in the images. The 27 output nodes correspond to the 26 let-

[2]We use the term 'certainty measures' since our treatment of uncertainty in this application is somewhat ad-hoc and does not correspond directly to any of the current formal methods of dealing with uncertainty. However, the goal of this work is to show a synergy of neural and symbolic computation for the word recognition problem and these certainty measures have proved to be quite adequate for this purpose.

Preceding-Current (CM_{pp})				Current-Succeeding (CM_{sp})			
YA	5	YB	3	AC	6	CC	5
YC	5	YD	6	EC	7	FC	4
YE	3	YG	2	IC	8	LC	1
YI	2	YL	11	NC	19	OC	4
YM	14	YN	11	RC	5	SC	8
YO	3	YP	12	TC	1	UC	10
YR	6	YS	12	XC	14	YC	7
YT	10						

Figure 3: Part of the Occurrence Frequency Table for Letter Pairs

ters of the alphabet and the 'blank' character. We performed a number of experiments to determine the best size for the hidden layer. The neural network software available with [9] was used. Twenty seven patterns, corresponding to the non noise degraded upper case letters and and the blank character, were used. Using training patterns with 5% noise degradation did not change accuracy of recognition.

For each character position in the word the network delivers a list of 27 candidates with associated activation levels. This activation is then used as a confidence measure (CM_{nn}) for that letter. Subsequent analysis uses a method very similar to the Mycin[2] certainty factor method to determine the most likely letter for that character position. A letter in the word is considered to be definitely determined if the following, empirically determined, condition is true: the largest $CM_{nn} > 70$ or the largest CM_{nn} is more than 7 times the next largest CM_{nn}

3.1 The Letter Frequency Knowledge Source

Character positions which do not have the above level of certainty are further examined by the knowledge source of letter frequencies. This knowledge source contains 'rules' such as those shown in figure 3.

The preceding-current 'rules' are interpreted as follows: If a letter is unknown and the previous letter is known to be a Y then 5% of the time the unknown letter will be an A, 3% of the time it will be a B and so on. The current-succeeding 'rules' are interpreted as follows: If a letter is unknown and the next letter is known to be a C then 6% of the time the unknown letter will be an A, 5% of the time it will be a C and so on. These certainty measures were derived from an analysis of of about 5000 words from a dictionary.

For those positions where the letter is not definitely known new certainty measures are computed for the candidates by 'intersecting' the sets of preceding-current and current- succeeding letters. The new confidence measure of a candidate letter CM_{pc+cs} is given by

$$CM_{pc+cs} = CM_{pc} + CM_{cs}(100 - CM_{pc})/100 \quad (1)$$

where

CM_{pc} is the confidence measure of what the letter is given its preceding letters

CM_{cs} the confidence measure of what the letter is given its succeeding letter.

The improved confidence (CM_{lfks}) measure after analysis by the combination of the neural network and the letter frequency knowledge source is

$$CM_{lfks} = CM_{nn} + CM_{pc+cs}(100 - CM_{nn})/100 \quad (2)$$

3.2 The Lexical Knowledge Source

'Rules' in the lexical knowledge source include:

1. All common groups of prefixes, suffixes; eg 'anti', 'un', 'tion', 'ing' etc.
2. The letter 'i' must come before 'e' except after 'c', with the word 'species' being the only exception.
3. The letter 'u' must come after 'q'.
4. The letter 'e' cannot precede a suffix that starts with a vowel, as in the word 'moving'.
5. The letter 'e' can precede a suffix that begins with a consonant, as in the word 'movement'.

The new confidence measure CM_{la} after analysis by the neural network, frequency knowledge source and the lexical knowledge source is

$$CM_{nn+lfks+lexks} = CM_{nn+lfks} + CM_{lexks}(100 - CM_{nn+lfks})/100 \quad (3)$$

where CM_{lexks} is the confidence measure obtained from the lexical knowledge source.

3.3 Example

The above algorithm is best illustrated with an example. Suppose that the letters 'N' and 'C' of the word 'SYNCOPE' have been degraded with 30% random noise before analysis by the neural network. The results from the network are given in the table below:

Position	1	2	3	4	5	6	7
Actual letter	S	Y	N	C	O	P	E
Candidate(s)	S	Y		C O	O	P	E
Activation(s	98	98	6	60 20	98	98	98

Figure 4: Output from the Neural Network

Since the letters 'S' 'Y' 'O' 'P' 'E' have CM_{nn} greater than 70, these letters are assumed to be definite and the symbolic knowledge sources are not used. However, the certainty measures of the letters in positions 3 and 4 can be improved by the letter frequency knowledge source through intersection of preceding-current and current-succeeding letter sets.

From figure 3 and equation 1, the list of possibilities for the uncertain letter in position 3 can be determined as 'N', 'S', 'A', 'C' or 'E' with the respective CM_{pp+sp} of 28, 19, 20, 10, 10; resulting in a $CM_{nn+lfks}$ of 57 for letter N. The lexical knowledge source gives 4 common prefixes with starting letters 'SY' (they are 'SYM, SYN, SYR, SYD); giving a CM_{lexks} of 25 (ie a possibility of 1 in 4 occurrence) for SYN. Thus the confidence measure obtained after the entire combination of symbolic and connectionist methods ($CM_{nn+lfks+lexks}$) is 71.

4 The Experiments

We have performed a number of experiments where we have have degraded all or some letters of a set of test words. The results of these experiments are shown in the figures below. Figure 1 shows a subset of these words where all of the characters are gradually degraded by noise. In figure 5 random noise ranging from 0 to 80% was introduced to every letter of the word. A total of 50 different words were used in this experiment. Words were chosen from a number of widely different disciplines (encompassing terms from medical, legal, management, computing fields). Each point on this graph is an average of 500 observations (made up of 10 noise samples for each word with a total of 50 different words).

It can be seen that, the neural net, when supplemented with the letter frequency knowledge source, generally outperforms the neural net alone. The exception at the 10% noise level appears to be an anomaly perhaps due to the set of words used in the experiments. Otherwise, the recognition improvement is very pronounced at medium noise levels (i.e. between 15 - 40%) where the word recognition performance can be improved by up to 10%.

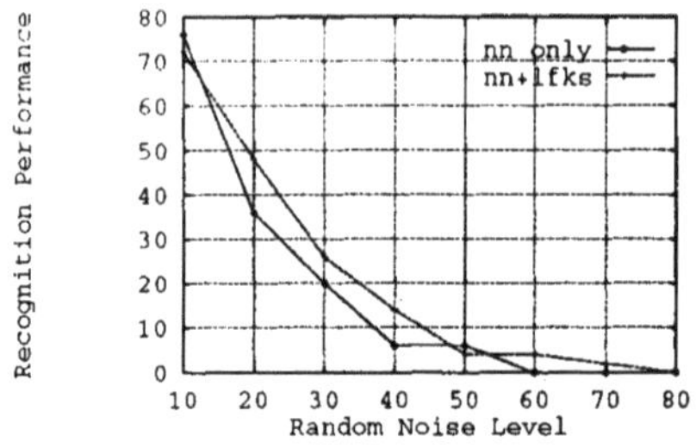

Figure 5: Word Recognition Performance for nn only only and nn+lfks: Noise Introduced to Every Letter of the Word

Figure 6 gives the performance if three consecutive letters are degraded. In this experiment a set of 20 words, each of 5 letters or more were used. At each noise level, 10 observations per word were taken. Each point on the graph is the average of 200 samples (10 samples from each word for 20 different words). Figure 7 shows results for the same data as figure 6, but with only two letters degraded. In both cases the combined neural/symbolic system out-performs the neural net alone.

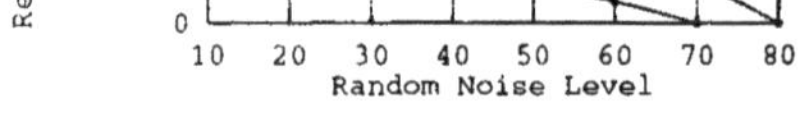

Figure 6: Word Recognition Performance nn only and nn+lfks: Noise Introduced to 3 Consecutive Letters

Figure 8 shows the results of introducing noise to a single letter only. Each experiment was conducted by introducing random noise to a single letter of the word. This was repeated until all letters of the word were noise-degraded in turn. At each noise level, 10 sam-

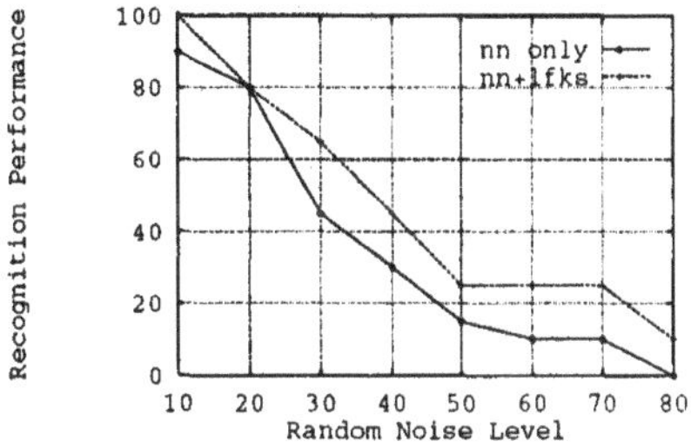

Figure 7: Word Recognition Performance by nn only and nn+lfks: Noise Introduced to 2 Consecutive Letters

ples were taken. Each point on the graph represents an average of 200 samples. (That is, 10 random samples for each letter at each noise level. There are 20 letters in the 3 chosen words totalling 200 samples per point). Again it is clear that the combined neural/symbolic system out-performs the neural net alone.

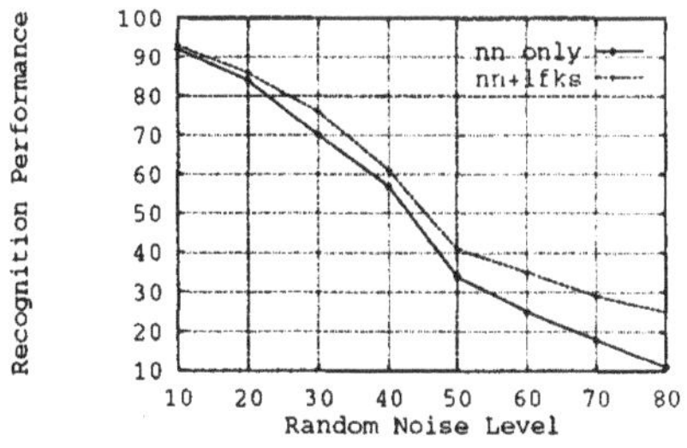

Figure 8: Word Recognition Performance by nn only and nn+lfks: Noise Introduced to a Single Letter

Figure 9 gives a summary of the performance of the combined neural/symbolic approach over all of the experiments. As expected, the more letters degraded the lower the recognition performance.

Figure 10 shows the certainty of recognition for the case where all letters are degraded. It can be seen that the certainty of recognition using the lexical knowledge source degrades only slightly with noise. This reflects the algorithm

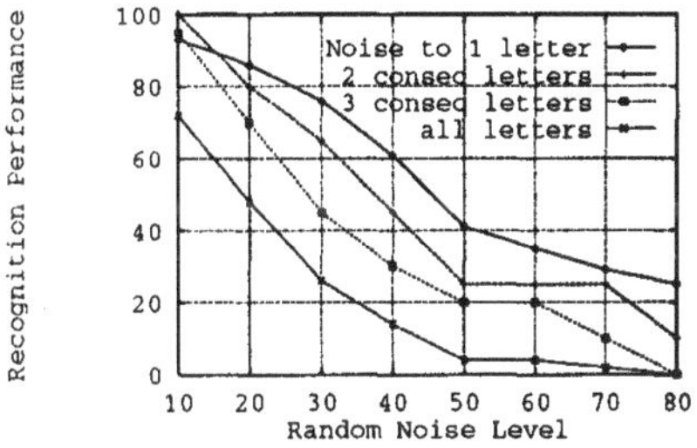

Figure 9: Summary of Word Recognition Performance by nn+lfks

used by the knowledge source. If an input letter is not recognized with absolute certainty (i.e. $CM < 70$) any prior knowledge about the letter is discarded and the letter is treated as unknown. The entire word is pattern matched with any valid letter combination encoded in the lexicon so as to derive any possible letters that satisfy the criteria. This aspect of the algorithm also accounts for the fact that, at a noise level of less than 30%, the combined method of the neural net + letter frequency knowledge source, and even the neural network alone outperform the combined method of neural net + letter frequency + lexical knowledge. The lexical knowledge source does not currently contain a complete list of rules for English words and thus the the occasional poor performance results.

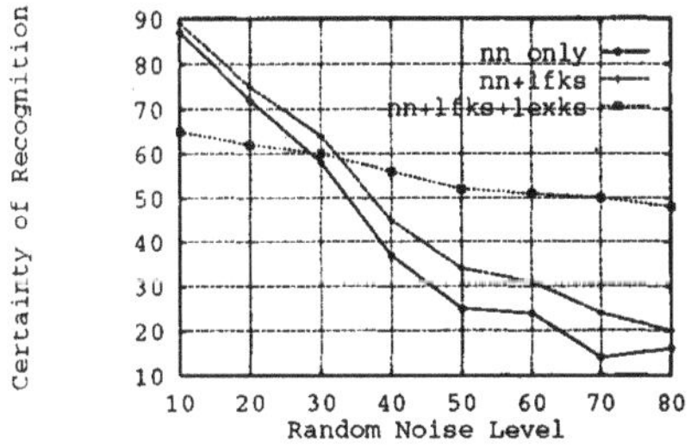

Figure 10: Certainty Measures for nn only only and nn+lfks: Noise Introduced to Every Letter of the Word

5 Conclusions

Three experiments were carried out to test the hypothesis that neural net and symbolic processing can be combined synergistically to improve the performance of recognition of noisy words. The results show that neural and symbolic processing can indeed be combined synergistically for this domain. The recognition performance of the combined neural/symbolic system is superior to that achieved by either the neural network or symbolic system alone.

Except for the anomaly in one experiment, methods incorporating symbolic knowledge always improved the character recognition ability of the neural network alone. The recognition improvement is very pronounced at medium noise levels (i.e. between 15 - 40%) where the word recognition performance can be improved by up to 10%.

This work could be extended in a number of ways. More words could be used, particularly to investigate the anomaly at the 10% noise level. A blackboard approach could be used so that the knowledge sources could be invoked in any order rather than the fixed order used above.

The kind of problem we have investigated could be characterized as 'perception' followed by 'reasoning'. There is no feedback from the symbolic component to the neural component. The architecture described in this paper should work well for problems of this kind. Architectures where there is a more complex relationship between the two components are still to be investigated.

References

[1] Avron Barr and Edward Feigenbaum [Editors]. *The Handbook of Artificial Intelligence.* William Kaufman, Los Altos, California, 1982.

[2] Bruce G. Buchanan and Edward H. Shortliffe. A model of inexact reasoning in medicine. In Bruce G. Buchanan and Edward H. Shortliffe, editors, *Rule-based expert systems: the MYCIN experiments of the Stanford Heuristic Programming Project.* Addison-Wesley, Reading, Massachusetts, 1984.

[3] James A. Freeman and David M. Skapura. *Neural Networks: Algorithms, Applications and Programming Techniques.* Addison-Wesley, Reading, Massachusetts, 1991.

[4] P.E. Hart. Syntel: An architecture for financial application. In H. Schorr and A. Rappaport, editors, *Innovative Applications of Artificial Intelligence.* MIT Press, Cambridge, Massachusetts, 1989.

[5] Robert Hecht-Neilsen. *Neurocomputing.* Addison-Wesley, Reading, Massachusetts, 1991.

[6] J. Hendler. Marker-passing over microfeatures: Towards a hybrid symbolic/connectionist model. *Cognitive Science,* 13(1), March 1989.

[7] S. Impedovo, L. Ottaviano, and Occhinegro. Optical character recognition - a survey. *International Journal of Pattern Recognition and Artificial Intelligence,* 5(1):1–24, 1991.

[8] Joo-Hwee Lim, Ho-Chung Lui, and Pei-Zhuang Wang. A framework for integrating diagnosis and incremental knowledge acquisition in connectionsis expert systems. In *Proc. 10th National Conference on Artificail Intelligence,* San Jose, California, July 12-16, 1992.

[9] James L McClelland and David E. Rumelhart. *Explorations in Parallel Distributed Processing.* MIT Press, Campridge, Massachusetts, 1989.

[10] T. F. Pawlicki, D. Lee, J. J Hull, and S. N. Srihari. Neural network models and their application to handwritten digit recognition. In *Proceedings of the IEEE First International Conference on Neural Networks,* pages 63–70, San Diego, Ca, June 1987.

[11] A. Rajavelu, M. T. Musavi, and M. V. Shirvaikar. A neural network appraoch to character recognition. *Neural Networks,* 2(3):378–393, 1989.

[12] D. J. Sobajic, Y. H. Pao, and J. Dolce. On-line monitoring and diagnosis of power system operating conditions using artificial neural networks. In *Proc. IEEE - International Symposium on Circuits and Systems,* number Vol 3, 1989.

[13] A. H. Tan and L. K. Chee. A connectionist expert system for intelligence advisory application. In *Proc. Expert Syst. Econom. Banking Management,* Singapore, Janurary 11-13, 1989.

Knowledge Acquisition

A hypertext-based knowledge organization tool

Elisabeth Ann Kendall and Rye Senjen
AI Systems Section, Telecom Research Laboratories
P.O. Box 249, Clayton, Vic., 3168.

Abstract
An electronic notebook, called the Electronic Knowledge Notebook (EKN), has been developed for knowledge acquisition and organization. Two versions have been implemented: one for design, planning, and decision making, and another for fault diagnosis. The Electronic Knowledge Notebook provides a semi- structured language for organizing concepts and relationships. It also incorporates a graphical user interface, hypermedia, multimedia, and retrieval and sorting. Written in Visual Basic 2.0, the notebook's extensible design facilitates additional capabilities in processing, parsing, and intelligent retrieval. It can be readily integrated to other Microsoft Windows applications and is available on laptop computers.

1. Introduction

Knowledge acquisition is costly and time consuming. Some researchers have suggested that to overcome this problem, the expert should author the system themselves or that an automatic knowledge acquisition tool be used. For instance, Tuhrim et. al (1988) proposed a high-level knowledge representation language, while Shaw and Gaines (1987) described a knowledge acquisition tool suitable for novices and experts alike. However both approaches suffer from similar problems: experts rarely have the time or inclination to learn these languages or use these tools. Consequently most knowledge acquisition is still carried out manually.

This paper evolved out of personal experience in several large scale expert systems projects, involving several knowledge engineers and often multiple experts. During these projects typically large amounts of disparate types of information and knowledge is acquired: books, transcripts, drawings, questionnaire replies, notes etc. This material can become quickly disorganized, bulky and outdated. In response to this problem we have designed and built a knowledge organization tool, that can organize different types of media into the one system and that fits conveniently on a laptop computer.

2. Problems with the process of knowledge acquisition

Gutekunst et. al (1991) divide the task of knowledge acquisition into knowledge elicitation, knowledge organization and knowledge representation. We are proposing to extend this model by subdividing knowledge representation into *knowledge modelling* and *knowledge conversion*. Knowledge modelling refers to choosing an abstract representation of the knowledge (rules, formal logic, objects etc.), while knowledge conversion refers to the actual encoding of the model into a computer representation, e.g., expert systems shell or programming language (figure 1).This model describes the process more accurately and helps us pinpoint those areas where a knowledge organization tool is most useful.During knowledge elicitation relevant domain knowledge is extracted from various domain sources. The knowledge engineer may collect this knowledge on various type of media such as paper, computer files, audio or video tape, etc. If the project is large, several knowledge engineers may collect information independently and in many cases duplicate information collected by other team members. When multiple experts are involved information collected may conflict.

Knowledge organization involves consolidating the information collected during

Figure 1: Task analysis of the knowledge acquisition process

knowledge elicitation into a coherent whole, linking it with previous knowledge and uncovering gaps and discrepancies in the knowledge collected sofar. If the knowledge collected is sufficient the knowledge engineer may attempt to choose a suitable knowledge representation and finally convert the knowledge model into source code. The nature and problems of various knowledge elicitation techniques have been reviewed widely (e.g.,Gaines 1988). However little has been said about how to organize the acquired knowledge before converting it into a working expert system (Gutekunst et al. 1991). Disorganized knowledge may lead to various problems such as lack of traceability, redundancy of knowledge, increased development time and lack of appropriate documentation (McGraw and Harbison-Briggs 1989).

3. Related work

A number of electronic media for knowledge capture and organization have been developed. For instance, the graphical Issue- based Information System (gIBIS) (Conklin 1988) provides a semi- structured language for communicating about decision making. It features a graphical user interface and was one of the first hypertext applications. gIBIS was adapted for acquiring and explaining design rationale and decision knowledge at Lockheed (Kellogg et al, 1989). Electronic circuit design knowledge was captured in hypertext design issue nets to facilitate redesign and knowledge acquisition and organization. gIBIS has also been used in policy decision making and strategic planning. The Electronic Design Notebook (EDN) (Lakin et al. 1989) allows for free- wheeling conceptual design, yet it also incorporates powerful processing capabilities. It centers on an editor and parser for visual languages called VMACS. VMACS and the EDN demonstrate that a performance medium and a processing medium can be brought together to go beyond pencil and paper for both freedom and interpretation.EDN has been primarily developed for conceptual designers. It is able to parse or interpret design equations, free body diagrams, tables of data, sketches of bar charts, comparison plots and circuit diagramsThe EDN has been interfaced to several systems that employ traditional artificial intelligence techniques including Dedal, the Design Reuse Assistant (Baudin 1992). Dedal is built on top of the EDN and provides knowledge- based retrieval of design information. In Dedal, design or domain concepts and terminology are used to index and later retrieve notebook entries. Heuristic knowledge from the artifact or device model guides the generation of new indices and the search for relevant information. This approach allows for looser matches between queries and the indexing patterns when no exact match is found.The Knowledge Organization Tool (KOT) (Gutekunst et al, 1991) is a domain independent hypertext- based tool for organizing and managing the knowledge acquisition cycle in expert system development. Written in SuperCard for MacIntosh computers, KOT provides general purpose facilities for knowledge engineers to record, learn about, and structure information that has been acquired about any given problem domain.

The Electronic Knowledge Notebook (EKN) discussed in this paper builds upon the ideas presented in gIBIS and EDN, yielding a more powerful software system than KOT. Whereas KOT provides tools for developing conceptualizations, EKN has well established templates for distinct generic tasks (design, planning and diagnosis). The EKN adds graphics and multimedia capabilities to gIBIS, and extends the gIBIS semi-structured language to fault diagnosis.

4. Design specifications and description of a knowledge organization tool

An electronic notebook must provide minimal interference and maximum payoff (Lakin et al, 1989). That is, it must be a performing medium and allow individuals or groups to improvise, brainstorm, and conceptualize freely. However, it must also be a processing medium that offers the strengths found in databases, CAD (computer aided-design), word and graphics processing, and other software systems. The notebook must be able to support a full spectrum of types of information (Baudin, 1992), from unstructured to formalized. This should include 1. unstructured, informal notes, sound recordings, or sketches, 2. semi- structured entries regarding concepts and relationships, and 3. formal, structured diagrams, databases, or documents. Semi- structured notebook entries can be of particular use for knowledge capture and organization because they provide a mapping for talking about a given problem domain. Examples of mappings or metaphors are truth tables, spreadsheets, and decision trees (Senjen et. al 1993), the gIBIS issue- based representation (Kellogg et al, 1989), and an artifact- based or device-based approach, commonly used in CAD, are further examples. Semi- structured templates address the knowledge modelling aspect of knowledge acquisition.Hypertext or hypermedia is a powerful facility for knowledge organization (Conklin 1987, Gutekunst et al, 1991) in that it supports linking together related information in accurate, realistic ways. Non-hierarchical, complex relationships can be indicated using hypermedia, and this also addresses the knowledge modelling phase of knowledge acquisition.As a notebook on a given topic grows, maps of the notebook become very important, along with enhanced search technology. Browsers, snapshots, and zoom facilities are required for visual navigation. Knowledge- based indexing and retrieval are needed. The notebook should support collaborative work, such as consolidation and conflict resolution.In summary, the following are desirable features for an electronic notebook:

- **Record keeping** - documentation of reasoning and decision processes.
- **Search technology** - rapid indexing and retrieval of information.
- **Agility and freedom** - a medium for performance and improvisation.
- **Parsing and interpretation** - a medium for processing and analysis.
- **Multimedia** - text, graphics, audio, video, spreadsheets, CAD drawings, tables, equations, etc.
- **Semi- structured/ semi- formalized language** - metaphors and templates for modelling concepts and relationships.
- **Hypermedia** - direct access to interrelated pieces of information. Tools for indicating non-hierarchical, complex relationships.
- **Graphical user interface** - visual navigation facilities.
- **Knowledge- based indexing and retrieval** - enhanced indexing and retrieval.
- **Support for collaboration** - tools for consolidating information and for uncovering and dealing with conflicts.
- **Convenient platform** - laptop computers and other PC's.

5.0 The Electronic Knowledge Notebook

5.1 Overview

The Electronic Knowledge Notebook (EKN) is written in Visual Basic 2.0. Developed primarily for knowledge capture and organization activities, it builds upon the ideas presented in gIBIS and the Electronic Design Notebook. EKN has the semi-structured language approach featured in gIBIS. The EKN also incorporates the multimedia, "do the right thing" versatility of EDN, and it is available on any platform that supports Microsoft Windows.

Two versions of EKN have been developed: one for fault diagnosis and one for design, decision making and planning. These can be viewed as specialized versions of the KOT with built-in mappings or conceptualizations for the generic tasks. The conceptualizations provided are well established: the gIBIS issue- based model for design, decision making or planning, and the symptom- and fault- based representation for fault diagnosis. Additionally, EKN provides templates for artifact- or device- based representations of design or fault diagnosis. These templates are intended to provide built- in models for knowledge as it is acquired, to guide the knowledge capture process, and to support collaboration.

Both versions of EKN feature the following capabilities:

- Semi- structured language for capturing and organizing information and for supporting collaboration
- Capabilities for indexing and retrieval
- Hypermedia facilities for indicating and accessing related information
- Multimedia support and integration
- Graphical user interface
- Various interactive maps of the knowledge

The Electronic Knowledge Notebook's semi- structured language centers on a selection of basic card or form types and a given set of links or relationships between the cards. This reflects the influence of gIBIS. Based upon Visual Basic's OLE (Object Linking and Embedding) Client capability, cards can contain and process data in various media, including sound, video, spreadsheets, text, and graphics. Any Microsoft Windows application can be incorporated, and this is analogous to the VMACS/ EDN architecture. Searching, sorting, browsers, and maps of the notebook entries have also been provided. Artifact or device indices are provided for both the design and the fault diagnosis notebooks. With this, the design and diagnosis information can be linked to the relevant physical component or device. Card links are set up manually by menu commands. Additionally, linking can be done automatically on the basis of keywords, and link weighting is provided in the Diagnosis Knowledge Notebook. Card link browsers are available with various features for easily viewing the relationships between cards.Because of space constraint we will only discuss the Diagnosis Knowledge Notebook in detail.

5.2 The Diagnosis Knowledge Notebook

The Diagnosis Knowledge Notebook is a multimedia environment for storing, retrieving, and organizing information about fault diagnosis. It is intended to be used by individuals or teams who are either actively carrying out these tasks or involved in knowledge acquisition about these tasks.The Diagnosis Knowledge Notebook provides a semi- structured language for communicating about fault diagnosis. The language consists of several types of concepts, represented as cards or forms of information. The following card types are provided in the Diagnosis Knowledge Notebook:

Fault - a flaw or problem in a physical device or system
Symptom - a detectable sign or indication of a problem
Recommendation - the recommended course of action to relieve or overcome a fault
Backup Data - information that supports a symptom or a recommendation
Component - a physical unit or part of the device or system being discussed

Once instances of these card types have been created, they can be linked together in the ways shown in Figure 2. Each fault is related to one or more symptoms, and one or more recommendations. Backup data can be linked to symptoms, faults or recommendations, and components can be related to faults. Additionally, faults may lead to other faults. Links in the Diagnosis Knowledge Notebook can be weighted and combinations of symptoms, either present or absent, can be indicative of certain faults. The backup data card in the Diagnosis Knowledge Notebook supports multimedia such as text files, graphics, sketches, diagrams, sound or video recordings, spreadsheets, databases, documents, any Microsoft Windows application. Each application has a distinct view with full editing and processing support. Backup data cards can be used to store knowledge elicitation text or audio files. They can also be used to store spreadsheets or databases about symptom- fault correlations.

The Diagnosis Knowledge Notebook can be used in a fault- based metaphor or an artifact- or device- based mapping. That is, component cards may be included to provide an artifact- based index to the knowledge. In the artifact- based approach, component cards play the central role.

6. Summary and Future Work

In this paper we have introduced the electronic knowledge notebook for knowledge acquisition and organization. Two task-specific versions have been implemented: one for design and planning and another for fault diagnosis. We believe these two generic tasks to be sufficiently different to warrant two separate implementations. We are at present considering the implementation of a Meta EKN, which will allow users to customize the notebook to the task they are currently interested in.Knowledge acquisition and capture are often multi-disciplinary and team efforts, hence a major impetus for this project was to provide a tool that was portable (e.g., works on a laptop). This was achieved by using Visual Basic as an implementation language. Visual Basic is a new and powerful language for hypermedia and multimedia applications. At present the EKN allows the user to store various sources of knowledge, helps structure the knowledge collected, and assists in maintaining the knowledge. The Electronic Knowledge Notebook is presently being used at Telecom Research Labs in a fault diagnosis knowledge acquisition activity. It is anticipated that this work will provide very valuable feedback on the system.

Several areas for additional capabilities are being explored, including knowledge base generation from notebook entries. For example, rule cards could be added to the Diagnosis Knowledge Notebook and once the correct combination of symptoms has been ascertained, the fault- symptom information could be encoded in a rule.

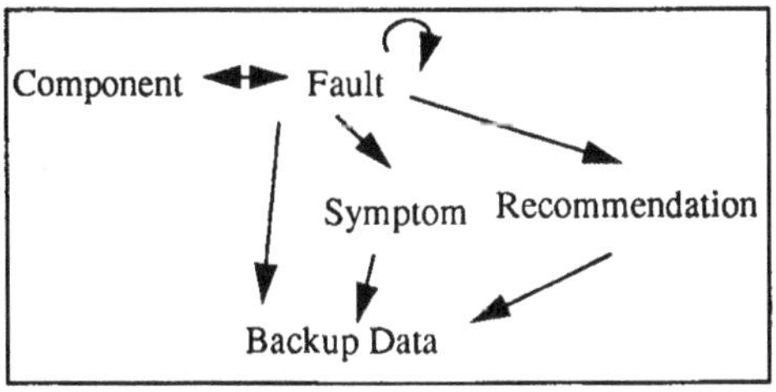

FIGURE 2: Rhetorical Moves in Diagnosis Knowledge Notebook

Knowledge-based indexing, retrieval and linking facilities need expanding. Presently only keyword indexing, retrieval and linking is supported, but the kind of capability found in Dedal could be incorporated. While the Diagnosis Knowledge Notebook can be used by several knowledge engineers, no formal facilities for collaborative work exist. These could initially be added by providing file/knowledge base comparison and file locking capabilities. Additional types of browsers, such as lattice browsers and zoom capability could enhance visual navigation and knowledge organization.

7. Acknowledgments

The permission of the Director, Telecom Research Laboratories, to publish this material is hereby acknowledged. We gratefully acknowledge the contributions of Andrew Jennings, Chris Rowles, and Chris Leckie to this research.

8. References

Baudin, C., Gevins, J., Baya, V., and Maborunje, A. (1992). Dedal: An Intelligent Assistant for the Retrieval of Multimedia Design Information. In: M. Maybury (Edt). Intelligent Multimedia Interfaces. (In press).

Conklin, J., (1987). Hypertext: A Survey and Introduction. IEEE Computer 20 (9):17-41.

Gaines, B.R. (1988). An overview of knowledge-acquisition and transfer. p.3-21 In: Gaines, B.R and J. Boose, Knowledge-based Systems Vol.1., Academic Press, London.

Gutekunst, K., Van Buijtenen, C., Ellis, N., and Simmons, D. (1991). A Hypertext-based Knowledge Organization Tool. Proceedings of the International Symposium on Artificial Intelligence: 471 - 477.

Kellogg, C., Mark, W., and Sullivan, J. W. (1989). Interactive Acquisition and Explanation of Design Knowledge. Lockheed AI Center Report and Presentation.

Lakin, F., Wambaugh J., Leifer, L., Cannon D., and Sivard C., (1989). The Electronic Design Notebook: Performing Medium and ProcessingMedium. The Visual Computer (5:) 214- 226.

McGraw,K.L. and Harbison-Briggs, K. (1989). Knowledge Acquisition. Prentice Hall,England.

Senjen, R., Rowles, C., and Sember, P., A User Interface for Interactive Knowledge Base Construction. Australian AI Conference1992: 323-328.

Shaw, M.L.G. and B.R. Gaines (1987). KITTEN: Knowledge initiation and transfer tools for expert and novices. International Journal of Man-Machine Studies 27: 251-280.

Tuhrim, S.; Reggia, J.A.; Floor, M. (1988). Expert system development: letting the domain specialist directly author knowledge bases. In: Hendler, J.A. (edt.) Expert Systems: The User Interface. Ablex Publishing Corporation, New Jersey. p.37-56.

A KADS refinement for explanatory knowledge extraction and modelling

Philippe MARTIN
INRIA Sophia Antipolis - Project ACACIA
2004, Route des Lucioles - B.P. 93 - 06902 Sophia-Antipolis Cedex - France

ABSTRACT

In order to help the knowledge engineer to extract and organize explanatory and cooperation knowledge when building an Explainable Knowledge Based System, we propose : 1) an extension of the KADS Conceptual model;
2) an explanatory knowledge extraction method which relies on KADS interpretation models.

1 Introduction

This article proposes somes *methodological* specifications on extraction and modelling of knowledge for a Knowledge Based System (KBS) which should provide user suited explanations, i.e. at a sufficient abstraction level and related to the user goals and habits.

In KADS, the analysis phase leads to a «Conceptual Model» consisting of a *model of (problem solving) expertise* and a *model of cooperation.* The first one models the necessary problem solving knowledge at a «knowledge level» [10]. Then in the design phase, these models are implemented but their high level structure are preserved. Thus, the KBS explanatory tasks may explain at a high level the KBS results or reasonings by retrieving original abstract knowledge from the used code.
In the ***first part*** of this article we will focus on the structure and types of knowledge that the Conceptual Model should have, if the KBS has to provide «good» explanations. In this way we guide the extraction and modelling of knowledge needed for explanations. The ***second part*** supplements this help in acquisition, by giving a questionnaire which enables to collect much information for instantiating an interpretation model. Both problem solving and explanatory information are collected with this method.

2 An Extended Conceptual Model

2.1 Weakness Of The KADS Standard Analysis Of Cooperation

In KADS-I, the *model of (problem solving) expertise* is modelled with a four level language : KCML (KADS Conceptual Modelling language). In KADS-II, a more formal language is used. But the *model of cooperation* is not structured as a model of expertise since it only lists and roughly defines the *transfer tasks*, i.e. tasks managing exchanges of information between the system and the user. In order to specify the interaction functions used by these transfer tasks, in [3] de Greef and Breuker propose to build another model, the «communication model» which would have two great parts : a *presentation* manager that takes care of interpreting or generating expressions, taking into account the intended effects, and a *dialogue* manager that controls topics and turn taking (possibly taking into account the fact that a same communication intention may concern multiple interactions with the user).
Despite the complexity of these tasks and the amount of knowledge they could imply, de Greef and Breuker *do not propose* to structure the communication model like a model of expertise. Moreover this model could directly include details of the interface with the user and then would be implementation-dependent like design phase models.

We think that if the communication expertise is sufficient, the model of communication should be structured like a model of expertise, for example with KCML. Then, during the design phase, this model can be refined in order to include the design constraints. Hence we suggest to include to the Conceptual model, a «model of communication expertise» which we abbreviate by **Communication-ME**.

KADS proposes to specify the alternation between system problem solving tasks and transfer tasks, by an ***algorithm***. This algorithm is then inserted to the model of (problem solving) expertise at its task (and strategy) levels. This method is simple when the expected system-user cooperation is rigid and hence may be statically defined, but in *other cases* we think that an *additional model* of expertise is needed for modelling the concepts, rules, tasks and strategies of cooperation management.

- Actually, a «real cooperation» management, e.g. an interactive work distribution between the system and the user, implies ***complex*** reasonings depending on numerous ***factors*** : knowledge and capacity of the user, his goals, the various tasks the system should accomplish or should lead the user to accomplish in order to get data or to teach him something. Furthermore, since the user progresses and since the priorities between the different goals may change, the cooperation should be dynamically managed according to these various parameters or factors.
  If cooperation is dynamically managed, it means that tasks are negotiated and planned with the user as it is already done in some KBS or tutoring systems.
- The cooperation knowledge constitutes an expertise distinct from the problem solving expertise, which therefore needs to be ***modelled in a distinct model of expertise***. As a matter of fact, it would not be much easy or modular to mix in a single model of expertise, knowledge with such different roles : problem solving vs cooperation. We call this new model, which may be structured with KCML, **Control-ME** since it calls and controls both problem solving tasks and communication tasks, in order to reach a fixed cooperation goal (see figure 2).

Cooperation is an important aspect of explanations since it controls at a high level the system-user interactions. For example, the system may introduce new topics in the dialogue. To sum up, for better specifying expertises related to explanations, i.e. the communication (and the cooperation) expertises, ***we propose to build a* Control-ME *and a* Communication-ME, *instead of the (so called) «model of cooperation»***. Similarly, we will note **Solving-ME** the «model of (problem solving) expertise».

Our extension is intended to enable the knowledge engineer to model other expertise than the problem solving one. Therefore :
1) this extension is not useful if the intended communication or cooperation with the user can be easily defined. If a good communication is expected but not a real cooperation management, the Control-ME can simply be not built;
2) this extension is not dependent on the language used to model the expertise, and hence can be applied on KADS-II Conceptual Model (moreover cooperation modelling in KADS-II is still the same as in KADS-I [3]).
3) our specifications are ***at the same abstraction level as KADS***, hence they are ***methodological*** and independent of any implementation.

Before elaborating our two new models, the next section shows some relations which they have with each other, and the data on which their tasks work on.

2.2 A New Architecture For The Conceptual Model

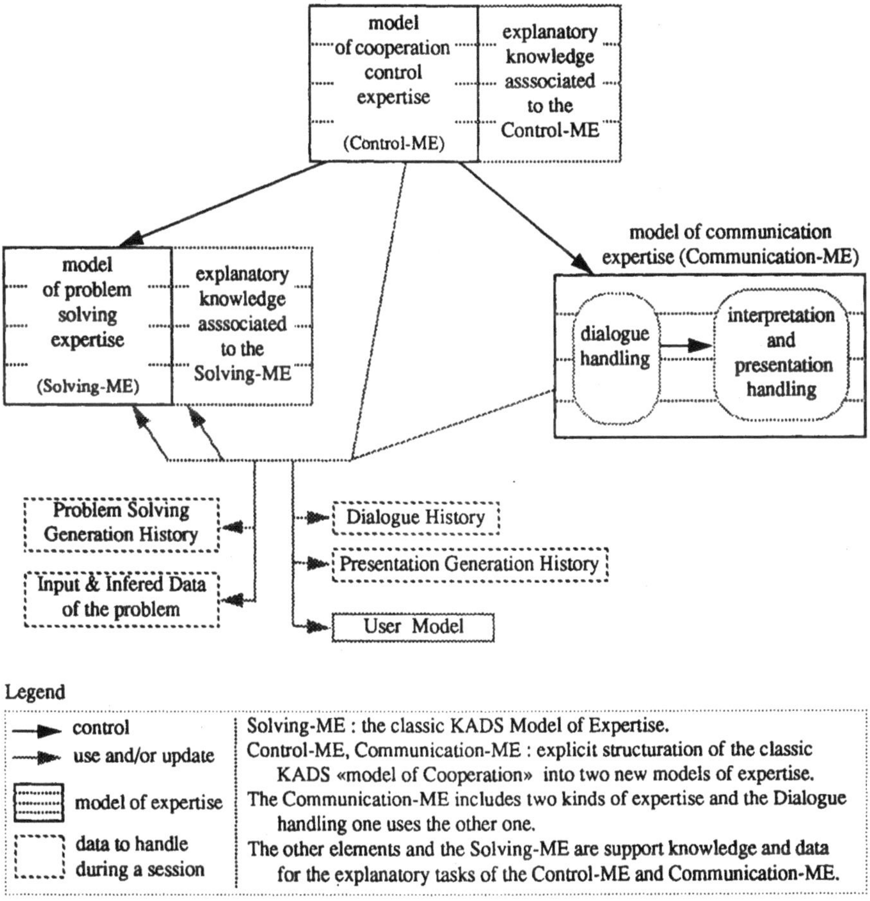

Figure 1: Architecture of submodels of expertise for the Conceptual model

This figure 1 ***shows*** that the Control-ME triggers the solving and communication tasks for managing the cooperation with the user, and ***lists*** data on which tasks of the Control-ME and of the Communication-ME may work. This list is not exhaustive but all its elements are ***necessary*** ([8][9][11]) for generating high level and user suited explanations, and each one should be *exploited* as much as possible. Hence mechanisms for this ***exploitation*** must be ***acquired or defined*** according to the explanation needs. (But during the design phase, the run time dedicated to exploit the support knowledge must be minimized and hence all its resources may not be exploited). Here are these ***«explanation (and cooperation) support» knowledge and data.***

- ***Solving-ME*** : we saw that KADS enables to link ***«Input & Infered Data»*** and elements of *traces of reasonings* with the high level elements of the Solving-ME - concept, relation, meta-classes, goal, task, etc. In [1], the authors show how to exploit each element of a «model of expertise» for interpreting user requests and answer them adequately. Sprenger [12] follows up this work and gives several algorithms for exploiting the various levels of the model *depending on* the aimed explanatory goal.
- ***Problem Solving Generation History*** : the abstracted and structured *problem solving traces* needed for explanation and cooperation reasonings. It includes : tasks, goals, methods, choices done by the system with their justifications and consequences, etc.
- ***Explanatory knowledge associated to the Solving-ME*** : for good explanations, descriptions of the Solving-ME need to be commented or completed by meta-knowledge, which may be structured as a model of expertise. With KCML, its *domain level* essentially includes the deep and/or explanatory knowledge *associated* with the domain level knowledge of the Solving-ME but which is not necessary for problem solving, e.g. causal justificative networks, definitions, explanatory schemas, figures, etc. This *domain level* may also include «explanatory interpretations or schemas» of elements of other levels of the Solving-ME. Thus, inferences, tasks and strategies may be explained in the expertise domain language. The *other levels* of this model of expertise are by definition independent of the expertise domain and hence may include explanatory schemas [4] on the interpretation models used in the Solving-ME.
  These descriptions are also valuable for the explanatory knowledge associated to the Control-ME if it is collected.
- The **«User Model»** (UM) : it may be developped by the designer and/or updated after each interaction or session with the user. A UM consists of (approximate) knowledge on the user : goals, centers of interest, habits, methods, types of questions, knowledge on the domain, types of difficulties and/or aptitudes for understanding or learning, preferences, etc. (a part of this knowledge may be acquired automatically) [8].
- The **«Dialogue History»** : it is a structured record of the system-user exchanges, e.g. data, requests, information or explanations. It enables the *interpretation* of implicit elements in requests. Furthermore, the *cooperation* and *dialogue* handling tasks rely on this history for determining subjects being discussed or to be discussed.
- The **«Presentation Generation History»** : it associates given explanations to goals sought and choices made for their generation. Such an history is essential for handling a dialogue or answering follow-up questions (i.e. questions on previous explanations) [9][1]. A similar structured trace could perhaps be useful for dialogue handling tasks.

KADS does not forbid to build several «models of (problem solving) expertise» if different kinds of problem solving expertise are needed in an application. If he wishes such a modularity, the knowledge engineer can easily adapt our architecture by building as many «Solving-ME and explanatory knowledge associated to it» as he wants. The other models of expertise have not to be modified since their tasks exploit the knowledge of a Solving-ME as data (and the tasks of the Control-ME will manage the various problem solving tasks according to the type of the given problems).
The *modularity* of this architecture and the KADS language for modelling an expertise, enable to extract and to structure adequately the various needed expertises. Moreover, most techniques which apply to the Solving-ME, are also usable for the other models of

expertise, for example : a) techniques exploiting a model of expertise for explanations ([1][12]); b) extraction, design and implementation techniques.
The acquisition of cooperation and communication expertise is therefore guided.

2.3 The model of cooperation Control expertise

For large cooperative systems, the Control-ME should include concepts, rules, methods, tasks and strategies for *distributing tasks*, for *negotiating this distribution* with the user, and for *controlling at a high level other interactions* with the user such as information exchanges and explanations. The Control-ME ***uses and directs*** tasks of the Communication-ME by the following ways : 1) it ***determines*** the ***«messages»*** to communicate to the user by ***setting*** more or less *subjects or concepts* of the discourse; 2) it ***determines*** «when to modify» or «when is modified» the *main goal of a current transaction* with the user; for Cawsey [1], these two tasks must be done by a module separate from the dialogue manager module; therefore we naturally assigned them to the Control-ME.

The *actual* explanation generation is hence mostly handled by the Communication-ME. This is due to the actual working ways and possibilities of what the Communication-ME has to model : present techniques in dialogue managing and discourse generation (these techniques look alike and work on discourse goals).

2.4 The model of Communication expertise

The Communication-ME includes a Dialogue expertise and an Interpretation/Presentation expertise. This last one models the *complex and implementation-independent* functions of the two main classes of transfer tasks : data reception and transmission.

- Interpretation consists of translating data (including request) expressed in a «language» understandable by the user (e.g. menus, keywords, request language, natural language), into a data structure the format of which is recognized by the system. Hence the ***domain and inference levels*** of the Communication-ME must include the different *concepts and methods* related to : 1) the user «language» and the system «language» (the domain level must include the lexicon, the syntax, the semantics and the pragmatics of each language); 2) the translation from a language to another and the use of the «explanation support knowledge» for this translation;
  At the task level, the knowledge engineer defines the sequencing of these methods - more precisely, of the KS (Knowledge Sources) which model the methods - according to the expected flexibility in the transformation, the interactivity with the user, etc.
- Presentation consists of providing information on some objects of the system, in a language understandable by the user. Hence this language must be defined and knowledge for discourse generation with this language must be added.
  In [7] we gave general inference structures for interpretation and presentation. For presentation, we also proposed a more detailed inference structure and we advocate modelling of *discourse generation* «operators» ([9][11]) at the domain level or as methods of KS. Then we discussed various possible controls on these operators.

Dialogue expertise is less easy to define than presentation expertise since it is even more dependent on the application : expected type of cooperation, chosen type of dialogue, etc. Moreover, the present state of the art on cooperative dialogues does not enable us to give inference structures such as for presentation. But some discourse generation control techniques may also apply for dialogues [1] and we show in [7] how to model them within KADS. For dialogue, the Communication-ME should include the following elements (more or less developed in accordance with explanation needs) :

- ***at the domain*** level : a dialogue model (conventions, design and cooperation rules) and all the other concepts and relations necessary to the inference and task levels;
- ***at the inference, task, and strategy*** levels : all the mechanisms which will manage topics, turn taking, User Model exploitation and goal application (the goal comes from the Control-ME or from a user request interpretation) which include : 1) *spontaneous explanations* (given to anticipate foreseeable user questions); 2) *adaptation* to new user aims or knowledge; 3) *updating and exploiting* the dialogue context (earlier subjects, requests, explanations, etc.).

We see that dialogue tasks use presentation tasks by giving them topics to explain. Hence in order to be useful for dialogues, presentation tasks should support interruptions and be able to continue or improve an explanation [1].

During the analysis phase, modelling is more or less accurate. For example, interruption handling may be modelled by a simple knowledge source, the methods of which can be specified later in the design phase. Therefore during the analysis phase, the Communication-ME is quite independent from the final user interface.

To sum up, this first section showed which elements are necessary for explanations, the relations that link them and where they can be modelled within KADS. In the next section, we supplement this help by giving a method for extracting complete explanatory knowledge, especially explanation support knowledge and data.

3 Knowledge To Extract For Instantiating KADS Interpretation Models

Extracting and modelling knowledge for a Model of Expertise will also generally provide constraints and knowledge for other models of expertise. The method we propose is not oriented for eliciting a particular expertise : it relies on interpretation models used by the knowledge engineer in order to be guided when extracting and modelling the expert knowledge, and hence ***can be used on any interpretation model.*** For each element of this model, our method lists via a set of questions, *the knowledge needed to instantiate it and also the explanatory meta-knowledge which comments this knowledge.* Actually, instead of questions, any elicitation technique may be used : interviews, observations, Wizard of Oz, etc. Furthermore, the pointed knowledge may be extracted ***in many steps***, for example by successive refinements.
Even when no appropriate interpretation model can be found for modelling expertise, this method gives good ideas on what shoud be obtained.

The proposed questions are very general. Hence they must be adapted by the knowledge engineer to the ***domain*** of the expertise, and some will not be appropriate. Furhermore, they include common terms in order to help the knowledge engineer to adapt his language to the expert's one. Then, words such as «concept», «relation» or «role» have common meanings. But remarks on modelling are expressed in KADS terms.

FOR each interpretation model IM (in order to model an actual task, the chosen IM must be filled and adjusted; the following questions are intended for that and also for collecting explanatory meta-knowledge)

ask goals, interest and principles of the actual task or strategy

Instantiate or adjust each KS (Knowledge Source) and meta-class of IM (see «A:», «B:» and «C:» below; thus the inference level of ME is updated, its domain level

filled, and the «explanatory knowledge associated to it» supplemented)
ask about when to use the task inferences and their sequencing (update ME's task level)
ask about when to use this task and in which context (update ME's strategy level)
(the «A:» questions are easily adaptable for asking about strategy or task control).

A: Instantiate or adjust a KS (i.e. an elementary inference or *function*)

Taking into account the context of this KS (e.g. its position in IM inference structure)
ask whether there actually exists such a function : if yes, what is it used for, what are its principles, when is it needed and when are other functions needed ?
if not, update this KS or add a new KS to IM
instantiate or adjust the KS input and output meta-classes (see «B:»)
what are the actual methods that realize this function ? (the answers will enable to model the «inference methods» or «domain view» of the KS)
what are their common features, what are the criteria for choosing a method or another ?
for each method, ask about its description and its triggering context, for example :
- which domain relation (functional, spatial, ...) does it use and could it possibly uses ?
- what are its steps, its submethods; is it used in other KS ?
- what are its triggering context : events, links with concepts, etc ?
- what are the criteria for assessing its results ?
- what is its limits, can it be improved, how to recover from a failure ?
- for which other goals may it be used, may its principles be generalized ?

with this collected information, instantiate the KS and supplement the explanatory knowledge associated to ME.; other levels of ME may also be updated.

B: instantiate or adjust a meta-class (its name underlines the role of the concepts it refers to)

Taking into account the context of this meta-class (e.g. its position in the IM inference structure)
ask whether concepts or objects have a similar role before, during or after the solving process : if yes, ask their common features, else update the meta-class or add a new one to IM
ask specifications on the actual role of the refered concepts or objects
for each concept or object, ask about its description and its triggering context (hence of course, some concepts will already be described), for example :
- with which concepts or concept classes is it related ?
- which other roles does it play during the process described by IM and in other ones ?
- how is it handled by this process or by others ?
- what are its properties and how to update or preserve them during the process ?
- what are its ranges and default values ?

with this collected information, instantiate this meta-class, supplement the domain level of ME and supplement the explanatory knowledge associated to ME.

C: extract explanatory meta-knowledge on an information (during or after «A:» and «B:»)

For each information given by the expert (concept, criterion, role, task, goal, etc.) :
- which kinds of user know this information and how do they use it ?
- is it important in the expertise domain or during the solving process ?
- from which viewpoints may it be seen ?
- in order to explain it, which knowledge must be used, in which order, in which context and for which kinds of user ?
- are there usual schemas for explaining it, and how to choose among them ?
- for which explanation types, will this information be useful and in which context ?
- if the information is a choice, is it good or just acceptable ? What alternative choices ?

For KS, we found [6] additional some question types which perhaps could not be easily infered from the generic questions that we proposed. Here is an example.

- `generalize (set of instances -> concept)` (find a concept which covers features of instances) :
  - is the concept already known, always known ?
  - what are the criteria for generalization, what must be done if more than one concept is a good candidate for the generalization ?
  - which object or object features are more important for generalisation than the others ?
  - what are the criteria for handling exceptions in values or object features ?
  - what must be done if some values or object features cannot be acquired ?

Information collected with this method will enable the explanatory tasks to give several viewpoints [5] on each element of the Solving-ME : *categorical* (how a concept fits a hierarchy), *functional* (role of an object in a process), *structural* (parts of object, steps of process), *modulatory* (how an object or a process affects another object or process), etc.

4 Conclusion

We listed «explanation support knowledge and data» necessary for really cooperative or user friendly systems, and showed how to extract and structure them using KADS techniques and framework. Then we gave a typology of questions which seems more accurate for knowledge acquisition than classic ones.

5 Acknowledgments

We are grateful to Olivier Corby, Rose Dieng, Alain Giboin and Sofiane Labidi for their comments on earlier versions of this paper.

6 References

-> AAAI-W 91: *Proceedings of the AAAI'91 Workshop on Comparative Analysis of Explanation Planning Architectures*, Anaheim, California, July 1991.

[1] A. Baumewerd-Ahlmann, P. Jaschek, J. Kalinski and H. Lehmkuhl, *Embedding Explanations into Model-Based Knowledge Engineering - Improved Decision Support in Environmental Impact Assessment*, Proc. of KMET'91 IOS Press, Sophia-Antipolis, France, April 1991.

[2] A. Cawsey, *Generating Interactive Explanations*, AAAI-W 91, pp. 6-14.

[3] P. de Greef and J. Breuker, *Analysing system-user cooperation in KADS*, Knowledge Acquisition (1992) 4, pp 89-108.

[4] B. Lemaire and B. Safar, *An architecture for representing explanatory reasoning*, Proc. of KMET'91, Sophia Antipolis, France, April 1991.

[5] J. C. Lester, B. W. Porter, *An Architecture for Planning Multi-Paragraph Pedagogical Explanation.* AAAI-W 91, pp. 27-41.

[6] Ph. Martin, *La méthodologie d'acquisition des connaissances KADS et les explications*, to appear in INRIA research report, rapport de stage de D.E.A. informatique, INRIA Sophia Antipolis, 1993.

[7] Ph. Martin, *Adaptation de KADS pour la construction de Systèmes à Base de Connaissances explicatifs*, IAC-93, Saint-Raphael, March-April 1993.

[8] M. T. Maybury, *Customs Explanations: Exploiting User Models to Plan Multisentential Text*, Proc. of the Second Int. Workshop on User Models, University of Honolulu, Hawaii, march 1990.

[9] J. D. Moore and C. L. Paris, *The EES Explanation facility: its tasks and its architecture*, AAAI-W 91, pp. 65-79.

[10] A. Newell, *The knowledge level*, Artificial intelligence, Vol 19, Nº 2, 1982, pp. 87-127.

[11] D. D. Suthers, *Task-Appropriate Hybrid Architecture for Explanation*, AAAI-W 91 pp. 80-94.

[12] M. Sprenger, *Explanations Strategies for KADS-based Expert Systems*, Technical Report 10, Universitat Bielefeld, GMD, Sankt Augustin, Germany, July 1992.

Automated Classification of Misconceptions in Physics

R.A. Hagen
C.I.T.
Griffith University
richard@cit.gu.edu.au

E.A. Sonenberg
Department of Computer Science
University of Melbourne
eas@cs.mu.oz.au

Abstract

This paper presents a system intended to aid in the classification of misconceptions held by physics students. The classification is based on predetermined misconception categories developed from student interviews by Melbourne University's Centre for the Study of Higher Education.

From our analysis of the student interviews, we developed an automated system which conducts a dialogue with a student and places that student's understanding within the provided misconception categories.

Traditionally in Intelligent Tutoring Systems [7], the evaluation of a student's knowledge and skills is carried out through close observation of problem solving activity. Our system differs in that it works with explicit data provided by the student in an automated interview, rather than relying on information inferred from the student's performance.

We discuss our approach to system design, which emphasises simplicity and extensibility, while attempting to remain faithful to the flexible and adaptable approach of the human interviewers.

1 Introduction

In this paper we present the design and implementation of a system that partially automates the diagnosis of misconceptions held by students in a simple area of physics. We were provided with a problem in physics (Figure 1), transcripts of eleven interviews conducted between teachers and high school students (see Figure 2), and a set of six misconception categories associated with the problem (Figure 3 shows two categories)[1].

The objective was to build a system which could conduct a flexible dialogue with a student, leading to a categorisation of that student's understanding within the provided misconception categories. The design approach emphasised simplicity and extensibility. The overriding design aim was to keep the system small, with feasible short-term implementation goals, providing a test-bed for further work while allowing for future extensions.

We wanted to mimic the flavour of the teacher–student interviews. From our analysis of the interviews, it appeared that the important features were: the capacity to change the topic in response to the student's inputs; the ability to detect when a given topic had been discussed exhaustively; the power to recall facts related to a particular topic (a *recap*); and the capacity to manage conflicts in the student's inputs.

These features were partially reproduced in the implemented system. It follows a student's topic shifts under certain circumstances, but ignores or only partially follows them under others. The system detects when a topic has been largely exhausted, by comparing the current knowledge-base with a central topic hierarchy. It responds immediately to a request for a recap of the whole knowledge-base or of a particular topic. It asks broad questions until a specific question is available. The issue of conflicts is handled by having the system identify when a conflict has occurred, and passing control to the student to resolve the conflict.

Traditionally, ITS systems have been pitched in the direction of the analysis of incorrect behaviour by observing the student's performance of some tutorial exercise. The domains of simple arithmetic, programming and circuit analysis have been tackled with this approach and it is clear that research adopting such a stance is by far the most common in the ITS field. The unifying element is that the task of modelling students' misconceptions is performed *as a side-effect of the teaching process.*

Our approach runs counter to this tradition in that it attempts to model a student's knowledge by appealing directly to the student's introspections

[1] The interviews and the analysis leading to the misconception categories had previously been carried out by the Centre for the Study of Higher Education (CSHE) at The University of Melbourne. The full analysis for this and another physics problem (the "boat and river" problem) is available [1]).

A small steel ball, thrown up into the air follows the trajectory shown below. Air resistance is negligible.

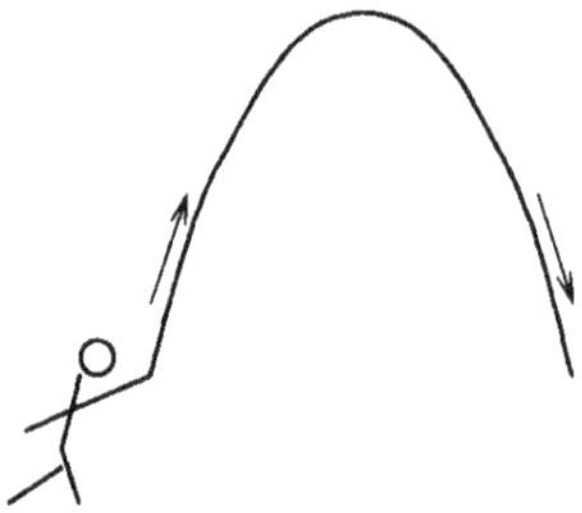

Discuss the acceleration of the ball from the time it leaves the hand until the time it approaches the ground.

Figure 1: Problem description.

S: As the ball leaves the hand, it decelerates until it reaches the peak where the acceleration is zero and then it accelerates uniformly until it hits the ground.

I: What else can you tell me about the acceleration?

S: The acceleration, that is, the vertical perspective ... from memory, I think the horizontal perspective of the acceleration is zero, it is travelling at a constant velocity, I think it is, either it initially accelerated, I think it travels constantly across unless there is air resistance. The acceleration due to gravity is $9.8m/s$ downwards and that is what produces the deceleration and the acceleration as the ball flies through the air, up and down.

I: What did you say about the acceleration, 9.8 what?

S: 9.8 m/s^2.

I: What does it mean?

S: It means that the object accelerates towards the ground increasing the speed at 9.8 per second per second, as it falls, in the first second as it falls it would be 9.8 m/s, that is the velocity it would be travelling, in the second second it would double that, it increases each second by 9.8 m/s until it reaches its terminal velocity, that is, when the ball drops from a certain height.

I: What can you tell me about the velocity?

Figure 2: Interview excerpt.

about her own knowledge. Of course, in building models from data provided by introspection, one must be cautious, c.f., [3]. This project is not intended to form the basis for an individual tutoring environment – its aim is to produce broad diagnoses of common faults in knowledge or reasoning that can be used in the future to address suspected shortcomings in particular curriculum elements.

2 Analysis

We reanalysed all of the eleven supplied interview transcripts to determine which student statements supported or undermined the diagnosis produced by the CSHE. Additionally, five of the transcripts were examined in a much more intensive way, with a view to revealing features such as recurrent interview behaviours, domain information and so forth.

Our objective was to produce a system capable of modelling a student's misconceptions by a standalone evaluation. Thus, the student model is not a collection of facts about the student's solution of the problem, but is a classification of the student's misconceptions with respect to a broad, predetermined misconception hierarchy.

This reflects the intention of the CSHE interview process – details of students' problem solving processes were not as important to the analysis as underlying misconceptions that could produce incorrect or partially correct solutions. Interviews were conducted so as to harvest as much explicit information about students' misconceptions as possible.

It could be argued that in a simplified system it would be possible to reduce the task of classifi-

Category R Acceleration is rate of change of velocity and it has constant magnitude throughout the path of the ball. It is caused by forces but there is an incomplete understanding of the relationship between gravity and acceleration. For example, on the way up acceleration is seen to be caused by the force of the throw, on the way down , by the force of gravity.

Category Fgb Acceleration of the ball is distinguished from the acceleration due to gravity; they are treated as two forces or vectors. Throughout the path of the ball the acceleration due to gravity remains constant and downwards. On the way up, acceleration due to gravity opposes the acceleration of the ball, causing it to continually decrease and the ball slows down. At the top of the path the acceleration of the ball is overcome by the acceleration due to gravity. On the way down, acceleration due to gravity contributes to the acceleration of the ball, causing it to move more quickly.

Figure 3: Two of the six misconception categories for the problem in Figure 1

cation to the presentation and analysis of a series of multiple choice (or similar) questions. Such an approach does away with many of the difficulties of conducting an interview-style dialogue, but overlooks many possibilities that a less constrained interaction might open up. For example, the student may wish to discuss topics in some particular order incompatible with that of a multiple choice system.

While our system does not try to provide all the features of a teacher–student interview, we aimed to build a system that provides flexibility and extensibility in the interface and in the underlying interview mechanism. In particular, we attempted to incorporate features to emulate the natural flow of topic focus exhibited by the teacher–student interviews.

Additionally we decided to place most of the responsibility for maintaining a consistent student model with the student. By providing a mechanism that gives feedback about potential conflicts between student inputs and student model states and the ability to explicitly assert or retract information to deal with such situations, we try to avoid the complexities of full-blown truth maintenance systems [2]. That is, students are required to resolve conflicts themselves as they arise.

2.1 Top-level Interview Features

Each interview is treated as a series of *exchanges*. An exchange represents a single step of the dialogue and is made up of the events that occur from the receipt of a student input to the output of a system response. The exchange is directed by the need to navigate navigate through a hierarchy of *topics* (Section 2.2). The processing for an exchange updates the state of the student model and the interview history and calculates the next system output using ***interviewer rules*** (**I-RULEs**, see Section 2.3). During the processing, the student's input is used to modify or query the internal ***knowledge-base*** (Section 2.4) which is maintained by a set of ***knowledge-base rules*** (**K-RULEs**, Section 2.5).

An interview ends when the student explicitly requests it or when an **I-RULE** determines that no further interviewer actions are possible. When this happens, the student model that has been built up in the knowledge-base is ***classified*** with respect to the supplied ***classification models*** (Section 2.6).

2.2 Topics

A *topic* is a name for a set of objects that share a common parent concept in a domain. In the problem of Figure 1, for instance, "acceleration" is a topic that contains all the ***sub-topics*** of the acceleration concept – its value and the value of its change, together with all their sub-topics. The topic "change in acceleration" is a sub-topic of "acceleration" and is the the topic covering the direction and the magnitude of the change of the acceleration. On the other hand, "the direction of the change of the acceleration" is a sub-topic of "the change of the acceleration" but is not a topic, since it has no internal structure.

A small section of the topic hierarchy is shown in Figure 4.

Interviews are essentially a traversal of the topic hierarchy, discussing topics until all the lowest level topics have been assigned values or the topic is changed.

2.3 Interviewer Rules (I-RULEs)

Interviewer rules are based on the transition rules of [8]. They guide the interview process and have access to the knowledge-base and the topics most recently introduced by the student and the interviewer. Five interviewer rules were found by the analysis and used in the system. The interviewer rule for dealing with continuing the interview is shown in Figure 5.

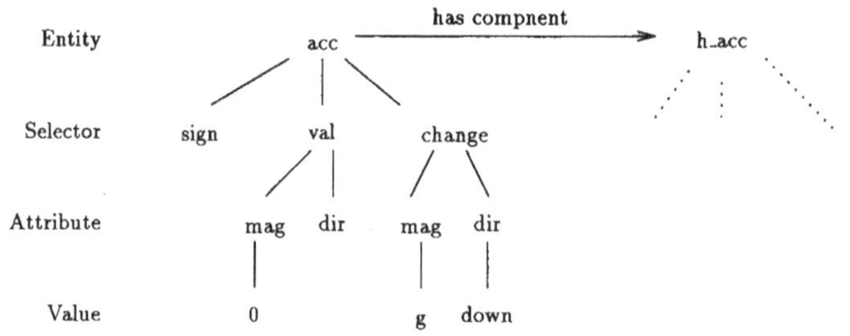

Figure 4: A small section of the topic hierarchy.

I-1: Keep Going.

Rule:

if student topic is t_1
and interview topic is t_2
and either of the topics or their generalisation is open to further exploration
then ask for an expansion of the open topic

Notes: An *open topic* is one that has not been completely discussed. A *generalisation* of a pair of topics is an ancestor topic that they have in common.

Figure 5: An **I-RULE**.

2.4 Knowledge-base Structure

The knowledge-base contains the inputs of the student and other facts that have been inferred from them. It is not intended to be a reflection of the student's thought processes, but it contains an approximation of the student's idea of her factual knowledge relating to a given problem.

From examination of the interviews, it was evident that the two most common sorts of factual utterances by students are descriptions of *values* and descriptions of *relationships* between values. Thus, the knowledge-base employs a representation that is tailored for representing these two types of facts within the interview framework. This possibly limits the expressiveness of the knowledge-base. For instance, "is a" relationships do not easily fit in this framework, since they detail a relationship between an object and a type. Extensions to the representable terms would also be required to represent terms describing some relationships between three or more objects.

Value facts are quite straightforward – they simply associate a value with a particular object – but relationships can be much more complex. Relationships that were mentioned in the interviews included, "causes", "identical to" and "equal to". While it is a simple matter to check that two values are equal, the concepts underlying the "causes" and "identical to" relationships are deeper. In the case of an "identical to" relationship we are required to check that all values added in future adhere to this constraint, and, if they do not, to note the inconsistency. Most of the knowledge-base rules are aimed at providing integrity checking mechanisms for such deep relationships.

The knowledge-base comprises four lists of facts.

Value List A collection of all the value facts input by the student, with the exception of the ones that the students has explicitly retracted.

Relationship List A list of all the relationship facts that the student has entered, excluding the ones that have been subsequently retracted.

Conflict List Possible conflicts detected by the system. For instance, two distinct value facts that suggest different values for a single object would be be on this list.

Verification List Facts that require verification. Such facts may come about through the operation of knowledge-base rules that make inferences based on inputs.

2.5 Knowledge-base Rules (K-RULEs)

Knowledge-base rules attempt to ensure that the student inputs are fully *intended*. This doesn't mean that the knowledge-base is complete or free of contradictions, but that what it contains is an accurate description of what the student said, even if this means that conflicting values have to be handled. It is very important to understand that the knowledge-base rules do not attempt to *modify* the knowledge-base in order to circumvent inconsistency. They act to bring the inconsistencies to the attention of the interview machinery so that the problem may be dealt with through consultation with the student. This is why the extra conflict and verification lists have been included in the knowledge-base.

In the same way that intensive analysis of the interviews suggested a set of interview conducting rules, a set of knowledge-base rules was also inferred. **K-RULEs** look very much like **I-RULEs** but deal with the facts contained in student inputs. Seven **K-RULEs** were identified and used in the implementation. An example is shown in Figure 6.

2.6 Classification

After the interview, the system classifies the student model in the knowledge-base. This is done by comparing its state with each of the predetermined classification models.

Classification models are internally represented in the same way as the facts of the knowledge-base. They consist of values and relationships but, in contrast to the student model, they are static and always fully defined. They were hand coded from the supplied misconception categories.

Generally, classification models are distinguished from each other by idiosyncratic relationships, and occasionally may be differentiated on the basis of "non-standard" objects.

To illustrate, Category Fgb makes a clear distinction (a strict "non-identical" relationship) between the acceleration of the ball and the acceleration due to gravity while Category R has a mysterious entity called "the force of the throw" acting on the ball during upward part of its flight. Occasionally, classification models have distinctive values for a particular object.

Classification looks for these features and orders the classification models on the basis of matches on relationship facts, non-standard objects and value facts. Presently, this ordering is based on a weighted sum of the raw number of matches with each model. When an interview is over, the output consists of a list of models and corresponding weights.

3 Implementation

From the above ideas and analyses, a Prolog system was designed and implemented[5] using LPA MacProlog running on an Apple Macintosh II.

Ideally, such a system for interviewing students would provide a sophisticated interface. However, the problems involved with the provision of such an interface go way beyond the scope of this project. In lieu of a such an interface, input is supplied in the form of simple ground terms. This is not an unreasonable restriction, as many natural language parsing systems produce output similar to this [4, 6]. This allows for potentially simpler interfacing of the input of the system to the back end of some suitable parser.

Input is specified by way of a template mechanism that is just powerful enough to encompass the domains of the facts and relationships, but allows no other inputs. The input template is shown in Figure 7. Note that it was not intended that anyone but the experimenters would use the supplied input mechanism in the development phase.

The inputs not only convey the facts expressed by the student, but also the way in which the system should act upon them. Student inputs fall into two types, those that request a modification of the knowledge-base and those that seek information about its current state. Modifications involve the assertion or retraction of some fact. Asking for information about state of the knowledge-base models the phenomenon of recapitulation which appears to be an important feature of the teacher–student interviews.

Output from the system is simplified in much the same way as the input. Outputs are also simple, ground terms, representing queries, requests, etc. Most outputs are simple requests for expansion on a particular topic. Sometimes, outputs will be queries arising from a knowledge-base conflict that requires student input to resolve. Much effort is made to keep the topic of the output relevant to the topic that the student wishes to discuss.

4 Results

So far, two of the supplied interviews have been simulated using the system. Performance of the system during the interviewing phase of the simulations suggests that the analysis of the **I-RULEs** and **K-RULEs** was worthwhile and effective. Outputs produced by the system adhered a similar topic ordering to those of the supplied interviews, but

K-2: Check newly "identical" objects for consistency.

Rule:

if the current input is an "identical to" relationship of two objects
then find all conflicting values for the two objects
and add them together with the new relationship to the conflicts list

Note: Assertion of the new relationship in the relationship list is carried out regardless of whether a conflict occurs or not.

Figure 6: A **K-RULE**.

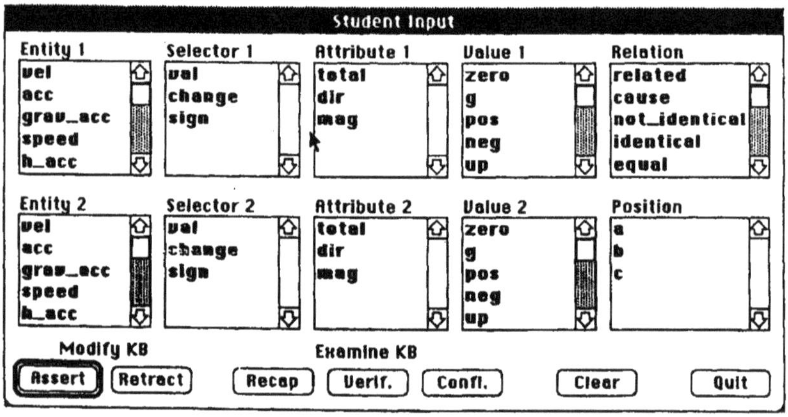

Figure 7: Input template.

tended to be more conservative in topic shifts, a feature arising from the ordering of the selection of the **I-RULE**s designed to encourage coherent stretches of interaction.

In these test runs, the classification produced by the system agreed with the human determined classification for the same inputs. While such results may look promising, several factors, most notably the lack of a deeply principled classification mechanism and the restrictions imposed by the internal representation could also undermine their credibility. Clearly, further testing is required.

5 Discussion

Currently, it is probably not feasible to produce a system that lives up to the requirements of a full-blown interview and classification system. Even the restricted classification process used in this task is complex and ultimately rests on psychological rather than analytical principles. To hope for these to be encoded in a small system is unreasonable.

Ideally, the effectiveness or utility of this sort of system would be proved in larger scale real world trials. However, some small amount of work could be done with the system in its current state. As it stands, the system is merely the prototypic core that has "hooks" allowing extension in various ways. The current lack of a sophisticated interface would rule out hands-on tests, but would not necessarily exclude parallel runs, where the same information is given to human experts and the system to check for correlation, and to fine tune the implementation. Certainly, only little effort would need to be invested to add extra entities or relationships to the existing repertoire.

Further, with a modest amount of work on the input and representation mechanism to extend its coverage of valid forms and the addition of a natural language generator for output, we expect that the system could at least be used for stand-alone data collection, with classification being carried out off-line with human supervision.

While it was not intended that anyone but the experimenters would use the supplied input mechanism, we believe that its style is an interesting alternative to other paradigms, particularly those employing natural language. The major advantage of the approach is the reduction in complexity allowed by the removal of some sources of potential error (misspellings in particular). However, it has the drawback that menus are necessarily public - their vocabulary and interrelationships are openly available. This might not be desirable in an evaluation situation as there is the chance that students could be prompted or misled by this information.

We should also consider the viability of transferring the ideas from this work to other, related, problems. As an example, suppose that we wished to encode further questions from simple physics. As possible candidates, the CSHE has 14 questions as part of their misconception studies. Our work investigated one of them which targeted the topic of the acceleration of a body in free fall. In encoding this problem, we looked at the properties of the body (its acceleration, velocity, etc.) and their relationships. We would probably not have to repeat the full domain analysis for other CSHE questions dealing with projectile motion or Newton's Third Law applied to a falling box which both involve the properties of a body moving freely through space. On the other hand, the question investigating instantaneous and average speed of two runners would need extensive recoding of the domain, since the entities involved have entirely different properties. In any case, we would not expect to need substantially more work on the **I-RULEs** and **K-RULEs**. After the misconception classification analysis had been done, future interviews for a particular problem could be automated. This assumes, of course, that the misconception categories are known, which is the most time-consuming part of the analysis process.

As to the broader question of whether the approach could be applied to classification problems drawn from other domains, the answer is unclear. This system relies on the simplicity and regularity of the relationships within the selected domain. To go beyond the domain of classical physics would almost certainly require a re-examination of the entire knowledge-base mechanism.

By far the two hardest problems to be addressed in any further work in this direction concern the classification phase. Firstly, we are asking for a classification of an individual based on what is really a single example of their performance. This is an unreasonable expectation, given that interviews are not guaranteed to be exhaustive. Secondly, and perhaps most importantly, is the matter of assigning a measure for comparing possible classification models. In our system, we used a weighted sum of various classes of match between the final knowledge-base and the various classification models. This was chosen because the major differences between classification models were generally expressed in variations in one or two relationship facts. It would be unwise to expect this to hold very broadly.

6 Acknowledgements

The authors would like to thank the Centre for the Study of Higher Education for furnishing interview transcripts and misconception categories for the problems studied. The first author would also like to extend thanks to the School of Computing and Information Technology of Griffith University for supporting him during this work.

References

[1] John A. Bowden, Gloria DAll'Alba, et al. Phenomenographic studies of understanding in physics: Displacement, velocity and frames of reference. Occasional Paper 90.6, Educational Resource and Development Unit, R.M.I.T., Melbourne, 1990.

[2] J. de Kleer. An assumption-based TMS. *Artificial Intelligence*, 28:127–162, 1986.

[3] K. Anders Ericsson and Herbert A. Simon. *Protocol analysis : verbal reports as data.* MIT Press, Cambridge, Mass., 1984.

[4] Gerald Gazdar and Chris Mellish. *Natural Language Processing in Prolog An Introduction to Computational Linguistics.* Addison Wesley, Wokingham, England, 1989.

[5] Richard A. Hagen. Automated classification of misunderstandings in physics. Master's thesis, Department of Computer Science, The University of Melbourne, 1992.

[6] Fernando C. N. Pereira and Stuart M. Shieber. *Prolog and Natural Language Analysis.* Center for the Study of Language and Information, Leland Stanford Junior Univeristy, 1987.

[7] Etienne Wenger. *Artificial Intelligence and Tutoring Systems: Computational and Cognitive Approaches to the Communication of Knowledge.* Morgan Kaufmann, 95 First Street, Los Altod, California, 94022, 1987.

[8] Beverly P. Woolf and David D. McDonald. Context dependent transitions in tutoring discourse. In *Proceedings of AAAI-84*, 1984.

Epistemological implications of the use of participant observation in knowledge engineering.

Rye Senjen and Wendy Mee
AI Systems Section and Informations Flows Group,
Telecom Research Laboratories, P.O. Box 249, Clayton, Vic., 3168.

Abstract
Difficulties in eliciting and acquiring expert knowledge are still some of the major problems encountered in the development of an expert system. The use of participant observation can overcome some of these problems, specifically it can be used to obtain and interpret cultural knowledge. In this paper we discuss primarily the implications and limitations of using this methodology.

1. Introduction

A major problem in the development of many expert systems is the so-called 'knowledge acquisition' bottleneck, i.e., the difficulties encountered when converting human expertise into expert systems. Difficulties and shortcomings of various knowledge acquisition techniques have been discussed widely (e.g., [8]). We believe, that at least in part, problems associated with knowledge acquisition arise, because there is too much emphasis on expert knowledge as a set of discrete bits of information and logical instructions (for instance see [9]) and too little interest in the transfer of cultural knowledge and skills. Collins[1] calls the former the algorithmic model of knowledge and the latter the enculturational model of knowledge. The algorithmic model assumes that knowledge can be transmitted in discrete chunks, which can be written down, classified and counted. In contrast, in the enculturational model, knowledge is transferred in face-to-face interaction or through socialization. Acquisition of knowledge here becomes a process, with a period of interpersonal interaction as a prelude to the transfer of knowledge. An emphasis on knowledge as algorithmic, in our opinion makes it difficult for the knowledge engineer to access the expert's cultural knowledge.The aim of this paper is twofold: to discuss ways of overcoming some of the above difficulties through the appropriate use of participant observation (PO), and also to raise key epistemological implications of this move for knowledge engineering through a discussion of current re-examinations of this methodology within Anthropology.

2. The use of participant observation

There is a tendency within the Artificial Intelligence community to focus on higher-level issues such as classifying information collected, while glossing over detailed questions of how to gather the data in the first place[7]. Forsythe and Buchanan call for a reinvestigation of knowledge acquisition. They suggest that knowledge acquisition for systems development is fundamentally an anthropological activity, and that both share common ground in terms of face-to-face interviewing of specialist individuals, supplemented by the use of documentary evidence and observational data[7].

PO can be defined as a field method in which the ethnographer is immersed in the day-to-day activities of the community under study[10]. Crane and Agrosino[3] go further and claim that participant observation is not so much a technique, but a framework for living in the field. PO resembles on-site observation, e.g, watching the expert solve real problems on the job. However, in contrast to on-site observation, the knowledge engineer puts herself mentally and frequently physically in the experts place, thus moving from a passive to an active observer [14]. PO can serve a number of purposes in knowledge acquisition:

1. it can familiarize the knowledge engineer with the environment and context of the expert[14];
2. it can be used to obtain information not obtainable through interviewing[14], in particular uncodified common-sense knowledge and informal and unstructured knowledge[7];
3. the knowledge engineer can learn the experts' view of themselves and their actions (what in anthropology is sometimes referred to as an emic understanding);
4. it enables the knowledge engineer to investigate the social processes by which expertise is developed and supported;
5. it can aid knowledge engineers in constructing personal models of the events and objects in the domain[14]; and,
6. it is conducive to good communication and information exchange as it builds trust and rapport between the two parties.

Underlying PO are some a ssumptions that differentiate it substantially from other knowledge acquisition methods[14]. Firstly it makes no assumptions about how people process information. Rather than using retrospective or concurrent descriptions by people about their knowledge (which are often rather unreliable), using PO, one assumes that a more reliable indicator of peoples mental models can be found in their actions and interactions. PO is not suggested as a technique to be used by itself [5], but should be used in combination with other more analytical techniques. It works best in situations where the expert has to interact with others or the environment in the course of her problem-solving activity. PO may be especially suitable where multiple experts work together on a common problem, as it allows the knowledge engineer to observe how experts integrate and evaluate the contribution of others.

3. An example of the use of participant observation

We use the domain of fault finding in the cable distribution network (e.g. the network of cables that make up the physical connection between Telcom's customers and the Telecom switching network), as an example of how we used PO in conjunction with other methodologies to obtain the knowledge necessary to construct a preventative maintenance expert system[15]. In order to familiarize ourselves with the domain we spent several days with fault repair persons locating faults in the field. PO is probably the only method suited for this purpose, especially if the domain involves interacting with others (e.g., as in advice-giving situations) or physically doing something (as in this case). During this time we were able to acquaint ourselves with the domain vocabulary, not only by reading about the domain (the usual way of familiarization advocated in the knowledge acquisition literature), but by making concrete concepts such as joints, cables, pillars. This is important in reducing biases and preconceived notions on how to represent the knowledge. We were also able to see how the repair person does her or his work in the field and the basic social environment he or she functioned in. This provided us with a very basic understanding of the process of fault finding and its principal components (electrical tests, knowledge of the type of plant entity etc.). This initial phase of familiarization was followed by structured interviews to elicit heuristics. For instance, we elicited heuristics that identify particular types of faults by combining the measurements of electrical tests with the type of plant equipment used. During this phase we could have used other structured knowledge elicitation techniques such as repertory grid analysis or other psychometric methods, but chose structured interviewing because it was the method we felt was less alienating to the repair person interviewed.

Thinking-aloud protocols (asking experts to think aloud while performing a task) have sometimes been used to elicit problem-solving strategies from expert. This technique must be used with some caution [6], because this type of knowledge is viewed as being unconscious or too informal and uncodified for people to accurately report it. However another possible explanation is that people find it difficult to describe aspects of their behavior out of context. This view sees knowledge as taking place in the 'stream of experience that encases people', rather than seeing knowledge as something that occurs independently in a person's head [14]. In certain cases, participant observation can be used to elicit problem-solving strategies, e.g., it is useful in those domains where the knowledge engineer can actually observe something and/or perform the task herself. Once we had elicited some basic heuristics and strategies we generated hypothetical fault and fault location reports. We used a mixture of interviewing and participant observation to elicit from the fault repair person more detailed problem-solving strategies. Rather than just asking questions (interviewing), we prepared solutions to fault reports, asked the fault repair person to locate faults for us (presenting tasks to solve) or 'helped' the fault repair person locate the fault in the network (participant observation). Using a combination of methods we found for instance that, if a certain fault is suspected with a high degree of confidence then whole parts of the network can be discounted as a possible location for that fault. When participant observation is used like this, in combination with other methods, it tends to become more a way of thinking, a state of mind, rather than a particular method that will achieve particular results. This should however not diminish its usefulness in the eyes of knowledge engineers.

4. Epistemological implications of the use of ethnographic methods

4.1 Introduction

Within anthropology there has been a move towards a self-reflexive, re-examination of the methodology of participant observation, and a questioning of many earlier assumptions (e.g.,[2],[4]). In particular, there has been a reconceptualisation of knowledge within anthropology; a reassessment of claims of scientific authority; and a redefinition of the "subject" (or "expert"). This section discusses the relevance and usefulness of such reconceptualisation for knowledge engineering.

4.2 Reconceptualizing knowledge

Knowledge can be divided into several generic types (e.g., corresponding to the roles they can play in the reasoning processes) as well as layers of knowledge (e.g., object level and meta level knowledge)[16]. Each layer has its own organizational principle, which reflects constraints that apply to the ways in which the objects on a particular level can be combined. While such schemes can successfully model a large part of an expert's knowledge, they ignore cultural knowledge and skills. The relevance of cultural knowledge and skills to expert decision-making has until recently been underestimated. Collins[1] coined the term 'cultural skills' to refer to the abilities required by the expert for comprehension and appropriate use of facts, rules, and heuristics. Thus the expert's cultural skills are an important component to his or her scientific, intellectual and theoretical abilities.

We divide expert knowledge into four categories: 1. facts and formal rules 2. heuristics 3. manual and perceptual skills and 4. cultural knowledge and skills. Facts and formal rules and heuristics are closely related, and both categories are easily transferrable to those in the same cultural universe. Heuristics are explicable rules of thumb, standard practices etc., that are usually not written down, because scientific thinking has developed in such a way to exclude all but the most schematic information[1]. Manual and perceptual skills may sometimes (after long or continuous use) be expressed as heuristics or facts and formal rules (see [1] for an in depth discussion). Cultural knowledge and skills can be viewed as the glue that connects together the generic types and layers of knowledge.

The domain of fault finding in the cable distribution network may illustrate the different types of expert knowledge. Facts and formal rules in this domain may relate to the type of cables that will fit into a particular joint or pillar. Additionally many heuristics exist that will tell the repair person where the fault is likely to be located. For instance if the cable is made of polyethylene and the joint is an open joint No.3, then the fault is more likely to be located in the cable then in the joint. Consequently the repair person may inspect the cable segment before opening the joint. Manual and perceptual skills may also aid in locating a fault. The repair person may be able to immediately spot the source of the fault on opening a joint, e.g two wires may be crossed or a wire may be loose. It is however cultural knowledge and skills that often guides the process of fault finding and attends to the small details that can make fault finding quick and successful. The repair person may know that certain faults never occur in an area because of the physical condition associated with such a fault, e.g she would not expect termite damage to occur in an area with no recorded termites. Unfortunately, cultural skills are not always apparent and most often operate in implicit ways. To explicate the experts cultural skills the knowledge engineer must interact with the expert in ways that lead to the articulation of these skills. PO is one method which, by reducing the cultural and contextual distance between the knowledge engineer and the expert, allows the knowledge engineer to gain some access to the experts cultural knowledge.

4.2 Reassessing the claim of scientific authority

Knowledge engineers using ethnographic methods must also consider that these methods challenge claims of 'objective scientific authority'. During PO the researcher and the researched relate to each other in highly personalized terms, which violates the separation between observer and observed. The research is further 'compromised', if you like, by the fact that no observation can ever be made unless the observer has a point of view which guides his or her selection and interest. PO has been referred to as "disciplined subjectivity" [14], and for many, this is its strength. Through PO and the sharing of the same environment and experiences, the researcher gains a "connected knowing", as distinct from a "separated knowing" characteristic of the physical sciences. It is on the basis of this connected knowing that the knowledge engineer comes to understand the expert's world and to formulate hypotheses about the expert's views and reactions[14]. It is inappropriate therefore to argue for the inclusion of ethnography within knowledge acquisition in terms of scientific positivism.

4.3 Reconsidering the definition of "expert"

The definition and exploration of expert knowledge has been of prime interest to knowledge engineers as well as cognitive scientists. For instance Johnson et al.[11] defined expertise as a kind of operative knowledge, that is characterized by the ability to act in new situations or the capacity to solve problems. Experts differ quantitatively from novices in terms of the amount they know about a particular field, as well as qualitatively in terms of how they have organized their knowledge into more structurally and hierarchically meaningful patterns[12].

Expertise has largely been viewed by cognitive science and artificial intelligence as disembodied from the expert, as wholly separable from the expert. There is a great concern with expertise as a kind of knowledge and less concern with how this expertise is produced. This partly results from an overly individualistic and rationalist view of the expert. In contrast anthropology has largely abandoned the idea of a subject (or expert) as a highly individualized, rational person, able to separate himself from his emotions, personal interests and motives. On the contrary, today's subject (or expert) and his knowledge (or expertise), is now understood as embedded in his socio-economic conditions, his interpersonal relations, and the politics of his day-to-day existence. An example of this is Latour and Woolgar's influential study of the construction of scientific fact in a laboratory [13]. Having completed PO in a biological laboratory, they concluded that science and scientific facts are not based on the demonstration of superior/inferior scientific results (as is so often claimed), but rather are constructed, as the result of economic, political and interpersonal factors.Using participant observation may well lead to a shift within knowledge engineering from a disembodied to an embodied expertise. It would aid in seeing the expert in the context of his social and work environment, as well as encourage us to observe and analyze the processes by which experts acquire their expertise.

5. Summary and Conclusion

We have discussed some of the epistemological implications associated with the use of PO. The purpose of this technique is to provide the knowledge engineer with a more complete understanding of the domain/culture and expert under study. However the use of this technique requires from the knowledge engineer a reconceptualisation of the definitions of knowledge and expert and a reassessment of the claim of scientific authority. Especially the latter may not be easy in a discipline that it still largely occupied with establishing its scientific legitimacy. Finally, PO is not a complete solution to the problems associated with the knowledge acquisition 'bottleneck', but one further necessary step in the quest for the complete picture. Like many other possible knowledge acquisition techniques it brings its best results when combined with other techniques. Future work in this area must concentrate on how to represent and encode qualitative knowledge obtained through PO. We are in the process of establishing a research project looking at these issues.

6. Acknowledgments

We are indebted to Chris Rowles, Telecom Research Laboratories, for his many helpful comments on earlier versions of this paper. The permission of the Director, Telecom Research Laboratories, to publish this material is hereby acknowledged.

7. References

1.Collins, H.M (1987). Expert Systems and the science of knowledge. pp.329-350. In: Wiebe E.,. Hughes,T. and Pinch, T(Edt).The Social Construction of Technological Systems. MIT Press.

2.Clifford, J. and Marcus G.E. (1986). Writing Culture. University of California Press, Berkeley.

3.Crane, J.G and Agrosino, M.V. (1974). Field projects in anthropology. General Learning Press. New Jersey, USA.

4.Cushman,J. and Marcus, G.E(1986). Anthropology as Cultural Critique. University of Chicago Press, Chicago.

5.Ellen, R.F.(ed), (1984), Ethnographic Research, Academic Press, London.

6.Ericson, K.A. and Simon, H.A. (1980). Verbal reports as data. Psych. Review 87(3): 215-251.

7.Forsyth, D.E. and B.G. Buchanan. (1989). Knowledge acquisition for expert systems: some pitfalls and suggestions. IEEE Transactions on Systems, Man and Cybernetics 19: 435-442.

8. Gaines, B.R. (1988). An Overview of knowledge acquisition and transfer. pp.3-21.In: Gaines, B.R. and J.H.Boose (ed). Knowledge-based Systems Vol.1. Academic Press, New York.

9.Garg-Janardan C.and G. Salvendy. (1990). A structured knowledge elicitation methodology for building expert systems. pp.85-114. In: Boose, J.H. and B.R. Gaines (ed.). The Foundation of Knowledge Acquisition. Academic Press, New York.

10.Hunter D.E. and P.Whitten. (1976). Encyclopedia of Anthropology. Harper and Row, New York.

11.Johnson, P.; Zualkernan, I.; Garber, S. (1987). Specification of expertise. Int. J Man-Machine Studies 26: 161-181.

12.LaFrance, M. (1989). The quality of expertise. SIGART Newsletter 108: 6-18.

13.Latour, B.and S. Woolgar (1979). Laboratory Life Sage Publications, Beverley Hills.

14.Meyer, M.(1992). How to apply the anthropological technique of participant observation to knowledge acquisition for expert systems. IEEE Transactions on Systems, Man and Cybernetics 22(5): 983-991.

15.Senjen, R.; de Beler, M.;. Leckie, C. and Rowles, C (1993).Hybrid expert systems for monitoring and fault diagnosis. IEEE AI Application Conference 1993, Orlando, Florida.

16. Wielanga, B. and J.Breuker (1987). Use models in the interpretation of verbal data. pp.17-42. In: Kidd, A. (Edt) Knowledge Acquisition for Expert Systems. Plenum New York.

Knowledge Discovery in Intelligent Databases : An Abductive Approach[*]

Albert K.W. Wu[†] *and Lena Sham*
Computing Department
Hong Kong Polytechnic
Kowloon
Hong Kong

Huaimin Sun
Computer Department
Beijing University of Aeronautics & Astronautics
Beijing 100083
P.R. China

ABSTRACT. Many intelligent database problems are difficult to be handled with traditional approaches. In this paper a new approach towards intelligent database problems employing abductive reasoning based on a typed first order language is proposed. The approach consists of three steps : 1) Construct a second order formula with the help of heuristic schemata; 2) Derive high order boolean equations using typed tableaux method; 3) Use the boolean equation to find out the solutions of the second order predicates. Finally, an example application of the approach is presented.

Keywords: *abduction, typed first order language, second order typed tableaux.*

1. Introduction

It is well known that the theory of first order deduction gives the model-theoretic and proof-theoretic foundations of database[1] and the SLDNF resolution[2] gives a powerful technique for query evaluation. However, for many IDB (intelligent database) problems such as automatic synthesis of query programs and deductive rules, discovering knowledge in database, first order logic is inadequate and needs to be extended. As R.A. Kowalski has suggested[3], one major extension is the use of abduction. While the first order deduction has traditionally focused upon the problem of determining whether a given conclusion C is logically implied by a given set of assumptions (or theory) T. The approach of abductive reasoning is taking the inverse direction, i.e.

> Given a theory T, integrity constraints I and a possible conclusion C. We are to find an abductive explanation of C as a set of formulae Δ such that
>
> $T \bigcup \Delta$ *logically implies C and* $T \bigcup \Delta$ *satisfies I.*

This reasoning is beyond the first order scope since it must treat the predicate variables. In this paper we shall develop an approach for abductive reasoning in IDB using typed second order tableau. Underlying the development of such an approach is the typed first order language used in [2]. The domain of this language is assumed to be finite. We extend this language with the second order predicate $P_i(\varkappa_1,\ldots,\varkappa_k)$, where P_i denotes the predicate name of an unknown relation, the term tuple $(\varkappa_1,\ldots,\varkappa_k)$ means that P must have some $\varkappa_i$ (not necessary all) as its terms.

---

* This research is sponsored by the Hong Kong Polytechnic research grant No. 340.647.A3.610.

† All correspondences should be referred to the first author Albert K.W. Wu via the following address:

Department of Computing, Hong Kong Polytechnic, Kowloon, Hong Kong.
Tel. No. : (852) 7667290,
Fax No. : (852) 7740842,
Email : csalbert@hkpcc.hkp.hk

2. Typed Second Order Tableau

The typed second order tableau can be described as a set of elements, called nodes, partially ordered and classified into levels. For each such node, it is a finite set of formulae on our extended typed language. A node can be extended into lower level according to some designated rules such as the ones shown below:

(a) ∀-rule

$\forall x A(x)$

$A(t)$ $\quad \theta = <t/X>$

t is free in A

(b) ~∀-rule

$\sim\forall x A(x)$

$\sim A(c_1)$ ..... $\sim A(c_n)$

$\{c_1, \ldots, c_n\}$ is the domain of typed term x

(c) ∃-rule

$\exists x A(x)$

$A(c_1)$ ..... $A(c_n)$

$\{c_1, \ldots, c_n\}$ is the domain of typed term x

(d) ~∃-rule

$\sim\exists x A(x)$

$\sim A(t)$

t is free to x in A

(e) .
.
.

with some of the rules omitted due to space limitation.

A branch of a tableau is closed if there is an atomic formula A such that both A and $\sim A$ belong to that branch. A tableau of a set of formulae is called a confutation of this set if all its branches are closed. Let T be a set of formulae (a theory) and G be a formula. If we can construct a confutation of $T \cup \{\sim G\}$, we say G is a consequent of T (i.e. T is a theory in which the formula G can be proved) and it is expressed as

$$T \vdash G$$

3. Reasoning with Abduction

3.1 A Card Puzzle

We shall use the famous S_P card puzzle as an example to demonstrate our approach. The puzzle is as follows:

I had in mind one card in the hand of cards:

$\spadesuit$ *J,8,4,2;* $\heartsuit$ *A,Q,4;* $\diamondsuit$ *A,5;* $\clubsuit$ *K,Q,5,4*

I told the suit of the card to Mr. S and point of the card to Mr. P. Then Mr. S said to Mr. P:

"I do not know the card, but I know you do not know it too." (I)

Mr. P said: - "Now I know it." (II)

Mr. S said: - "Now I know it too." (III)

The problems are:

With what suits that Mr. S may say (I)? *(Problem 1)*
With what cards that Mr. P may say (II)? *(Problem 2)*
With what cards that Mr. S may say (III)? *(Problem 3)*

This puzzle may be taken as an example for abductive reasoning. The known ground relations of card (X, Y) can be taken as the theory T (or the database): *card(*$\spadesuit$*,J); card(*$\spadesuit$*,8); card(*$\spadesuit$*,4); etc.*

Given a correct example of problem (1) as a possible conclusion C: *query1(*$\heartsuit$*)* and a counter example as the constraint: *~query1(*$\clubsuit$*)*. How can the machine find out a set of first order formulae Δ as an abductive explanation?

In the following sections, we shall present an approach for abductive reasoning in steps.

3.2 Step 1 : Construct a Second Order Formula

A second order formula can be constructed with a meta-knowledge base which consists of some formula schemata with second order predicates such as:

$$problem \leftarrow Key\_relation \wedge P_1 \quad (S.1)$$
$$problem \leftarrow Key\_relation \wedge \forall u(P_1(u) \rightarrow P_2(u)) \quad (S.2)$$
$$problem \leftarrow Key\_relation \wedge \forall u(P_1(u) \rightarrow \exists v P_2(v,u)) \quad (S.3)$$
$$problem \leftarrow Key\_relation \wedge \forall u(\exists v P_1(u,v) \rightarrow P_2(u)) \quad (S.4)$$

....

where Key_relation means the relation in the database that the user is concerned. Thus, the number of such formula schemata may be updated and altered by the user. In essence, the high order schemata play the role of heuristic rules.

For example, for problem (1) of the card puzzle, the successful high order formula is constructed using schema (S.3):

$$query1(x) \leftarrow card(x,\_) \wedge \forall u[P_1(u,x) \rightarrow \exists v P_2(v,u,x)] \quad (F.1)$$

3.3 *Step 2 : Derive Boolean Equations by Using Second Order Tableau*

Let T be a theory (either a relational database or deductive database), G be a relation we are concerned (e.g. a goal of query or a goal of deductive rule which we want to synthesize). $G^{\theta 1},\ldots,G^{\theta i}$ be correct examples of G and $G^{\theta i+1},\ldots,G^{\theta h}$ be counter examples of G. For each correct example $G^{\theta i}$ we can get finite boolean equations as follows:

> Add the high order formula constructed in step 1 and $\sim G^{\theta i}$ to T. Then by using the rules in the typed second order tableau laid down in section 2 we can get a finite unclosed branch.

Let $L_1,\ldots,L_j$ belong to an unclosed branch (each L is a high order atomic formula or a negation of high order atomic formula), we can obtain a boolean equation:

$$L_1 \wedge,\ldots,\wedge L_j = 0.$$

It is obvious that : $T \vdash G^{\theta i}$ iff all these equations hold.

Similarly, from each counter example $G^{\theta k}$ we may get finite boolean equations as

$$L_1 \wedge,\ldots,\wedge L_j = 1$$

....

we have $T \nvdash G^{\theta k}$ iff one of these equations holds.

Using the correct example : *query1(♥)* and the high order formula (F.1) we can get

$$P_1(A,\heartsuit) \wedge \sim P_2(v_1,A,\heartsuit) = 0 \qquad \textbf{(B.1)}$$
$$P_1(K,\heartsuit) \wedge \sim P_2(v_2,K,\heartsuit) = 0 \qquad \textbf{(B.2)}$$
$$\ldots\ldots \qquad \ldots$$
$$P_1(2,\heartsuit) \wedge \sim P_2(v_8,2,\heartsuit) = 0 \qquad \textbf{(B.8)}$$

We have $T \vdash$ query1(♥) iff (B.1) - (B.8) hold and from the counter example: ~query1(♣) we can get

$$P_1(A,\clubsuit) \wedge \sim P_2(v_9,A,\clubsuit) = 1 \qquad \textbf{(B.9)}$$
$$P_1(K,\clubsuit) \wedge \sim P_2(v_{10},K,\clubsuit) = 1 \qquad \textbf{(B.10)}$$
$$\ldots\ldots \qquad \ldots$$
$$P_1(2,\clubsuit) \wedge \sim P_2(v_{16},2,\clubsuit) = 1 \qquad \textbf{(B.16)}$$

$T \nvdash$ query1(♣) iff one of these equations (B.9 - B.16) holds.

3.4 *Step 3 : Find Out Solutions of High Order Predicates*

The solutions of the high order predicates P's can be found by using an integrated technique of inverse term rewriting[4] and searching which we call PN-unification as follows:

For every fact R of the database write down a first order boolean equation: **R = 1** and for every answer A of a deductive rule (if the database is a deductive database) get a first order equation : **A = 1**.

Select by ad hoc a high order equation : $L_1 \wedge, \ldots, \wedge L_j = 1$ obtained in step 2 and split it into equations

$$L_1 = 1$$
$$\ldots\ldots$$
$$L_j = 1$$

The principle of PN-unification is as follows:

$$\text{Let } L_i = C_i \wedge 1 \qquad \textbf{(i)}$$

be a boolean equation where L_i is a high order atomic formula or a negation of high order formula, C_i is 1 or a first order conjuncture of atomic (negative of atomic) formula. And

$$\text{let } r_j = 1 \qquad \textbf{(ii)}$$

is a first order equation, then we can replace the "1" on the right hand side of (i) by r_j on the left hand side of (ii) and get a new equation

$$L_i = C_i \wedge r_j \equiv C_i \wedge r_j \wedge 1 \qquad \textbf{(iii)}$$

If the solutions of P's obtained this way satisfy all equations obtained in step 2, then take them as the final result, otherwise, try alternative solutions.

For example, from (B.1) to (B.8), the solutions for P_1 and P_2 are found out to be:

$$P_1 = card(x, u),\ P_2 = card(v,u) \wedge v = x$$

and the abductive explanation obtained is

$$query1(x) <\!- card(x,\_) \wedge \forall u[card(x,u) -> \exists v(card(v,u) \wedge v = x)]$$

For problem (2) of the card puzzle, the system got two alternative explanations

$$query2(x,y) <\!- query1(x) \wedge \forall u[card(u,y) \wedge u = x -> \sim query1(u)]$$

and $query2(x,y) <\!- query1(x) \wedge \forall u[query1(u) \wedge u = x -> \sim card(u,y)]$

The second result is rather unexpected, nevertheless it is a correct abductive explanation.

By the same token, alternative correct explanations of problem (3) of the card puzzle can be obtained similarly.

4. Conclusion

In this paper, we have shown and demonstrated an approach for abductive reasoning. The approach may have some practicable applications for IDB, such as automatic synthesis of query programs for relational database or deductive rules for deductive database. However, it may not be unsuitable for large databases due to the large number of unification. Nevertheless, this problem may be alleviated by asking the user for more heuristics.

It is envisaged that abduction is a satisfactory approach for knowledge discovery in databases and it very well supplements the deficiency of first order deduction.

ACKNOWLEDGEMENTS

The authors would like to thank Mr. Q. Liang for his programming support for this project.

References

[1] R. Reiter, "Towards a Logical Reconstruction of Relational Database Theory", *Reading in Artificial Intelligence and Database*, Morgan Kaufmann, 1989.

[2] J.W. Lloyd, *Foundations of Logic Programming*, Springer-Verlag, 1987.

[3] R.A. Kowalski, "Problems and Promises of Computational Logic", *Proc. of Computational Logic*, Brussels. 1990.

[4] H. Sun and Q. Liang, "A Theory of Automatic Logic Programming Based on Second Order Term Rewriting Technique", *Automated Reasoning*, Elsevier Science Publishers, North-Holland, 1992.

Learning Prototypical Knowledge from Cases

Kuniaki Uehara, Masayuki Tanizawa and Sadao Maekawa
Department of Computer Science and Systems Engineering
Kobe University
Nada, Kobe 657, Japan
uehara@jedi.seg.kobe-u.ac.jp

Abstract

In this paper, we will describe one of the case-based learning paradigm [1] called Prototype-Based Learning (PBL). The PBL paradigm supports relatively robust learning algorithms. PBL can tolerate noise and irrelevant attributes and can represent both probabilistic and symbolic concept descriptions. Furthermore, PBL can provide a partial ordering on candidate categories for a new case. Thus, even the attribute importance is context sensitive, it can extract the localized concept description so as to do the accurate classification.

1 Introduction

Most of the existing inductive learning algorithms mainly concentrate on the extraction of minimum discrimination rules to classify a new case into an appropriate category. Therefore, if the set of training cases involves inappropriate ones (i.e. noisy, incomplete, or exceptional cases), the approach to extract discrimination rules may generate too complex and failure rules. On the other hand, our approach is to classify a new case into nearest categories by prototype-theory [7] and information-theory based distance metric. In other words, our approach extracts a concept description, which consists of both prototypical attributes and their attribute importances, from a set of training cases.

Our approach can learn the concept description from even a small set of training cases and is tolerant of inappropriate cases. Furthermore, our approach can provide a partial ordering on candidate categories for a new case. Thus, even the attribute importance is context sensitive, our approach can extract the localized concept description from cases under consideration so as to do the accurate classification. Finally, our approach can learn indexing knowledge directly from the concept description, which is useful for a human expert to understand and verify the concept description generated by the learning algorithms.

2 Prototypicality Ratings

PBL1 is the simplest prototype-based learning algorithm. PBL1 groups the cases according to their categories and then computes prototypicality for all of the cases in each category. Prototypicality is a rating of the representativeness of a case with respect to a category. During classification, PBL1 uses prototypicality ratings to determine the category which is the most likely to match the new case. To compute prototypicality ratings, PBL1 counts the frequency of each value that the attribute can take on. Each case is assumed to be represented by a set of attribute-value pairs and its category. The j-th case I_j described with n attributes a_1, a_2, ..., a_n in the category c is represented as follows:

$$I_j = (c, a_{1j}, a_{2j}, \ldots, a_{nj})$$

If the new case I_{new} is given, the prototypicality ratings can be computed as follows:

$$prototypicality(c, I_{new}) = \sum_{i=1}^{n} \frac{\sum_{j=1}^{N} f(a_i, a_{ij})}{N}$$

$$\text{where } f(a_i, a_{ij}) = \begin{cases} 1 & \text{if } a_i = a_{ij} \\ 0 & \text{otherwise} \end{cases}$$

where i ranges over the attributes. a_i is the value of the case I_{new} on attribute i. j ranges over the cases in the category c. N is the total number of cases in c.

Figure 1 presents the experimental evidence for the performance of PBL1. In this experiment, the performance accuracy of PBL1 was compared to ID3 [6] on the "famous" soybean database which contains the diagnosis of soybean diseases.

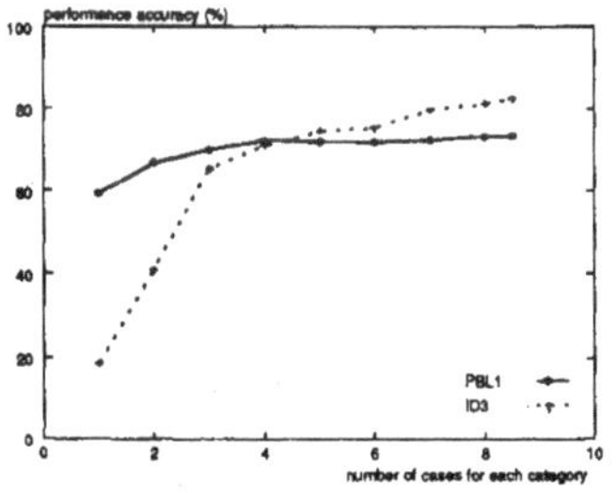

Figure 1: Performance accuracy of PBL1 and ID3.

3 Attribute Importance

PBL1 performs poorly when the database (i.e. training set) involves a large number of irrelevant attributes, since PBL1 assigns the same weight setting to each attribute, and does not pay attention to the relative importances of attributes. This leads to the development of PBL2, which learns the relative importances of attributes, represented as attribute weight settings, for the purpose of computing accurate similarity assessments.

Now we will introduce an information-theoretic approach and augment the prototypicality ratings. Intuitive basis for this augmentation is that an attribute distributed into many categories has high expected information, whereas an attribute included in only one or two categories has smaller expected information. Therefore we use the expected information as a measure of attribute importance. The attribute weight setting is defined as follows:

$$\omega(a_i) = 2^{-\left(-\sum_{c_l \in C} p(c_l|a_i) \log_2 p(c_l|a_i)\right)} = \prod p(c_l|a_i)^{p(c_l|a_i)}$$

where l ranges over the categories. $p(c_l|a_i)$ means the probability that the observed case with attribute a_i will be determined to belong to the category c_l and $\sum p(c_l|a_i) = 1$.

Now that we have defined the attribute weight setting, we will augment the definition of prototypicality rating. The definition of augmented prototypicality rating is defined as follows:

$$prototypicality(c, I_{new}) = \sum_{i=1}^{n} \frac{\sum_{j=1}^{N} f(a_i, a_{ij})}{N} \times \omega(a_i)$$

PBL2 can tolerate irrelevant attributes better than PBL1, which effectively assigns the same (static) attribute weight setting to each attribute. Figure 2 shows that PBL2 outperforms PBL1 and ID3. Furthermore, it shows that the performance accuracy of PBL2 increases as the number of cases for each category increases.

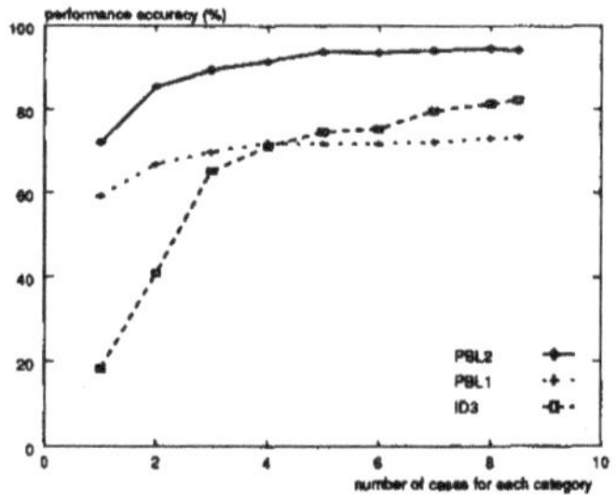

Figure 2: Performance accuracy of PBL1, PBL2 and ID3.

4 Attribute Importance in Context

Context sensitive attribute weight settings are required to derive appropriate attribute importances in applications where attribute importance differs depending on the candidate categories under consideration. Since PBL2 adopts one-shot approach which considers all training cases and computes both prototypicality ratings and attribute weight settings at one time, PBL2 cannot deal with the context sensitive problem.

Now we will propose the two-step approach to prototype-based learning algorithm named PBL3. The first stage of PBL3 is quite similar to PBL2 in that it considers all training cases at one time, but it also provides a partial ordering on categories based on prototypicality ratings. In the second stage, PBL3 selects the most promising categories (i.e. the category whose prototypicality rating is the highest and its nearest neighbors) and recomputes the attribute weight settings among them. In other words, the first stage of the classification process is to learn a prototype for each category. The second stage is to use prototypes to discriminate among the similar candidate categories.

The performance accuracies of PBL2 and PBL3 were compared to PROTO-TO [3], C4 (ID3), and Bayesian classifier [2] on eight databases. All databases except soybean data were taken from the UCI database collection [4]. The results of the comparison are shown in Table 1. Table 1 shows that PBL3 recorded higher accuracies than the others in the five domains. However, in the two of the domains, such as 'hepatitis' and 'tic-tac-toe,' PBL3 performed slightly poorly, although PBL3 is at least as accurate as Bayesian classifier. In the 'glass' domain, the performance accuracy of PBL3 was relatively poor in comparison to the other algorithms, since the 'glass' database consists of continuous attributes instead of nominal attributes. We will consider this problem in the last section.

5 Learning Indexing Knowledge

In a domain-specific system that uses case-based learning algorithm, the efficient use of cases during classification requires that they should be indexed so that they can be efficiently retrieved when they are likely to be similar to a new case. Another advantage for learning indexing knowledge is that both the prototypicality rating and attribute weight setting are difficult for a human expert

Table 1: Comparison of performance accuracy.

Name	PBL3	PBL2	PROTO-TO	C4 (ID3)	Bayesian classifier
glass	45 - 55 %	43 - 50 %	48.0 %	65.5 %	n/a
hepatitis	84.2 %	84.2 %	79.9 %	79.8 %	84.8 %
house-vote	92.1 %	92.1 %	90.4 %	95.3 %	90.5 %
soy bean data	97.1 %	96.3 %	n/a	(82.3) %	91.5 %
breast cancer	95.2 %	95.2 %	n/a	n/a	97.2 %
iris	95.4 %	95.4 %	96.0 %	94.2 %	95.3 %
zoo	92.8 %	93.0 %	n/a	n/a	93.8 %
tic-tac-toe	72.9 %	72.9 %	n/a	n/a	67.7 %

to understand, whereas indexing knowledge makes them relatively transparent. Three types of indexing knowledge can be obtained directly from the concept description generated by PBLs in the following ways:

1. If the prototypicality is equal to 1 and the attribute weight setting is also equal to 1, then extract the category c_j and the attribute a_i. These category-attribute pairs are called confirmatory indices. Confirmatory indices associate attributes with categories and they are bi-directional. That is, confirmatory index from a_i to c_j suggests that c_j is the reliable classification for cases described with a_i and that every case in c_j has the attribute a_i without uncertainty.

2. If the prototypicality rating is less than 1 and the attribute weight setting is equal to 1, then the attribute-to-category index is extracted. Attribute-to-category index also associates the attribute a_i with the category c_j, but it is uni-directional. That is, the attribute-to-category index simply enumerates a set of possible classifications for the new case described with a_i.

3. If the prototypicality is equal to 1 and the attribute weight setting is less than 1, then the category-to-attribute index is extracted. Category-to-attribute index associates a category with an attribute. This direction is opposite to that of an attribute-to-category index. In other words, category-to-attribute indices can produce what may be called "prototypical" cases by creating a case that has the most frequent value for each attribute.

The following are examples of indexing knowledge for soybean diseases. The right hand side of the index is a triple of the form:

$$[\text{attribute=value, prototypicality, attribute weight}]$$

- confirmatory index:

  powdery mildew $\leftrightarrow$ [leaf mildew growth = on upper leaf surface, 1.0, 1.0].

- attribute-to-category index:

  phytophthora $\leftarrow$ [external decay of stem = watery and soft, 0.88, 1.0].
  phytophthora $\leftarrow$ [external stem decoloration = dark brown, 0.88, 1.0].

- category-to-attribute index:

  phyllosticta $\rightarrow$ [leaf spot color = tan, 1.0, 0.50].
  phyllosticta $\rightarrow$ [leaf spot growth = from edge of leaf inward, 1.0, 0.65].

By index transformation, we extracted 2 confirmatory indices, 27 attribute-to-category indices, and 30 category-to-attribute indices. Note that, in the category-to-attribute index, the number of indices depends on the threshold of the attribute weight setting. In the above example, the threshold is set to 0.3, that is, $0.3 \leq \omega(a_i) < 1.0$. If we decrease the threshold from 0.3 to 0.2, we can extract 125 category-to-attribute indices, although some of them are 'weak' category-to-attribute indices. However, an experiment was conducted in the domain of soybean disease to determine the effect of providing 'weak' category-to-attribute indices. Table 2 shows that category-to-attribute indices provided important evidence during the classification process. Consequently, removing 'weak' category-to-attribute indices actually hurt the performance accuracy of the system.

Table 2: Contribution of category-to-attribute indices to performance accuracy.

	threshold value of $\omega(a_i)$						
	0.1	0.2	0.3	0.4	0.5	0.6	0.7
number of indices	437	125	30	13	8	4	0
performance	87 %	83 %	84 %	79 %	76 %	77 %	70 %

6 Conclusion

In this section, we will compare PBL with the related works so as to illustrate the representational issues of the PBL paradigm. Firstly, we will compare PBL2 with a neural network algorithm having both hidden units and the back propagation technique. Figure 3 depicts the experimental comparison between PBL2 and the neural network. Figure 3 shows that the probability of correctly classifying new cases is about the same for these algorithms. However, the neural network consistently takes a lot more time to learn. It takes about 18,000 times as long to learn as PBL. Another issue of neural network is the human interpretability of the acquired knowledge. PBL can produce interpretable rules while neural networks of weights are harder to interpret.

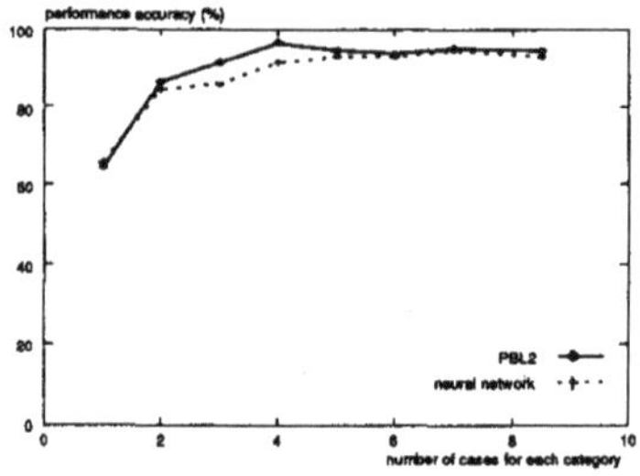

Figure 3: Comparison of performance accuracy between PBL2 and Neural Network.

Secondly, learning indexing knowledge from cases has already been proposed by Protos [5]. Protos elicits and refines domain knowledge by interacting with a human expert in the context of problem-solving failures: failures to classify cases and failures to explain its classification. Although Protos' knowledge acquisition process is rather systematic, such a process is still very time and effort consuming for the human expert. Furthermore, Protos relies heavily on the heuristic processing of explanations, which are based on a large number of underlying assumptions, although it was not believed that the appropriate heuristics could be made generally available to the system *a priori*.

Thirdly, Bayesian classifier also adopts the probabilistic approach to inductive learning. It stores a probabilistic summary for each category. The summary contains the conditional probability of each attribute value given the category as well as the probability of the category. Bayesian classifier uses an evaluation function to rank the alternative categories based on the summary and assigns the case to the highest scoring category. The definition of the evaluation function is quite different from the prototypicality rating. That is, to compute the score for the positive category description, Bayesian classifier multiplies the probabilities of attributes, whereas PBL sums the probabilities of attributes to compute the prototypicality rating. Therefore, when an attribute has never been observed in the training cases but is present in a new case, the evaluation function of Bayesian classifier turns to be 0. To avoid this deficiency, Bayesian classifier replaces the probability of the missing attribute (i.e. 0) with a small value. Figure 4 shows that the comparison of performance accuracy between them. Figure 4 involves that Bayesian classifier without this replacement cannot tolerate missing attributes and that the PBL paradigm supports relatively robust learning algorithms.

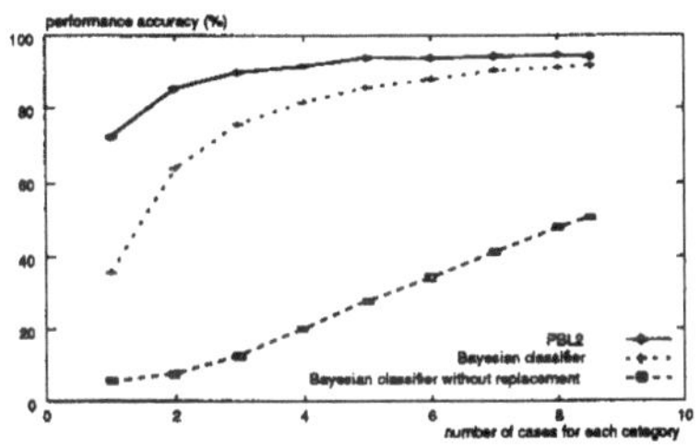

Figure 4: Comparison of performance accuracy between PBL2 and Bayesian Classifier.

Finally, we have not yet studied how the PBL approach can use continuously-valued attributes to classify a case which consists of the values of either unordered or totally-ordered attributes, whereas PROTO-TO can deal with continuously-valued attributes directly. We are now developing a labeling procedure for the continuous attributes. The labeling procedure divides all numerical data into several clusters, and labels a new nominal attribute for each cluster. The labeling procedure will be unified into the PBL algorithm so that each numerical attribute is directly translated into the nominal attribute.

References

[1] Aha, D. W.: Case-Based Learning Algorithms, Proc. of Case-Based Reasoning Workshop, pp.147–158 (1991).

[2] Langley, P., Iba, W. and Thompson, K.: An Analysis of Bayesian Classifiers, Proc. of the Tenth National Conference on Artificial Intelligence, pp.223–228 (1992).

[3] Maza, M.: A Prototype Based Symbolic Concept Learning System, Proc. of the Eighth International Workshop on Machine Learning, pp.41–45 (1991).

[4] Murphy, P. M. and Aha, D. W.: UCI Repository of machine learning databases [Machine-readable data repository]. Irvine, CA: University of California, Department of Information and Computer Science (1992).

[5] Porter, B. W., Bareiss, R. and Holte, R. C.: Knowledge Acquisition and Heuristic Classification in Weak-Theory Domains, Artificial Intelligence, Vol.45, pp.229-263 (1990).

[6] Quinlan, J. R.: Induction of Decision Trees, Machine Learning, Vol.1, pp.81–106 (1986).

[7] Rosch, E.: Principles of Categorization, in E. Rosch and B. B. Lloyd (eds.) Cognition and Categorization, Erlbaum (1978).

Knowledge-Based Systems

A Knowledge Base System Handling Incomplete Information

Hiroshi SAKAI
Department of Computer Engineering, Kyushu Institute of Technology,
Tobata, Kitakyushu 804, JAPAN, e-mail:sakai@comp.kyutech.ac.jp

Abstract

A new framework for knowledge base system is proposed. Recently, an important problem has been much discussed in the field of knowledge bases, logic programming and AI, namely how effectively we use information which may have incompleteness. In this paper, we deal with or-type information in knowledge base systems. An or-type information is a kind of disjunctive information, however they are different each other. First, we syntactically define an or-type information and a knowledge base with or-type information, which we call an or-type KB. Then, we give four interpretations to or-type information. Depending upon every interpretation, we develop every semantics for or-type KB and we discuss the realization of every theorem prover. Finally, we show a prototype system in the appendix.

1. Introduction

For the Next Generation Database Systems, it is necessary to develop the methodologies for knowledge bases with incomplete information. Usually, knowledge base systems depend upon the framework of logic programming, therefore we need a new framework for logic programming where we can deal with incomplete information. In the logic programming, a program is a set of the following definite clauses:

$\forall[p \leftarrow q_1 \wedge q_2 \wedge \cdots q_n]$, where $p, q_i (0 \leq n, 1 \leq i \leq n)$ are atoms.

We can see the above logic program as a knowledge base and a deductive database. However in this case, we can not deal with the following knowledge.

$\forall[odd(X) \vee even(X) \leftarrow natural\_number(X)]$.

Because, the head consists of a disjunction of atoms. Namely, this formula is not a definite clause. It means that it is difficult to deal with disjunctive information in knowledge bases. For this problem, Minker developed a framework of disjunctive logic programming and proposed Disjunctive Deductive DataBase(DDDB)[1,2]. In the disjunctive logic programming, a program is a set of the following clauses:

$\forall[(p_1 \vee \cdots \vee p_m) \leftarrow (q_1 \wedge \cdots \wedge q_n)]$, where p_i and q_j are atoms.

DDDB is an answer to knowledge bases with incomplete information. As for the implementation, Loveland developed a prover called near-Horn prolog[3,4].

2. Semantic Issues related to Disjunctive Information

Now in this chapter, we show semantic issues related to disjunctive information. We show three examples.

Example 1. Let's consider the following DDDB Ω.

(1) $odd(X) \vee even(X) \leftarrow natural\_number(X)$.

(2) $positive(X) \vee negative(X) \leftarrow natural\_number(X)$.

(3) $natural\_number(5)$.

(4) $natural\_number(6)$.

In the above rule (1), we can not remove every atom from the head. However in rule (2), we can remove the atom $negative(X)$ from the rule. Namely, the rule (2) is incomplete and we can replace the rule (2) by the following rule(2').

(2') $positive(X) \leftarrow natural\_number(X)$.

By applying DDDB theory, we get $even(5) \vee odd(5)$ and $even(6) \vee odd(6)$, which seem to be reasonable. However we also get $positive(5) \vee negative(5)$ and $positive(6) \vee negative(6)$, which seem strange. Because, $negative(\_)$ is not necessary in both formulas. In DDDB, it is implicitly assumed that every rule does not have the incompleteness such as rule (2). Therefore, we need another theory for DDDBs which consist of incomplete knowledge such as rule (2).

Example 2. Let's consider another DDDB Ψ.

(1) $\underline{ap([], A, A)} \vee ap(A, [], A)$.

(2) $\underline{ap([A|B], C, [A|D])} \vee ap(B, [A|C], [A|D]) \leftarrow \underline{ap(B, C, D)}$.

The fact and rule are in the form of indefinite clauses, namely we can apply the DDDB theory. Then, $ap([1], [2], [1, 2])$ is not a logical consequence of Ψ. If we select the underlined atoms, then Ψ is the append program. We can see that the Ψ comes from the incomplete knowledge for append program. If so, we should not apply the DDDB theory to Ψ. A system, which answers $ap([1], [2], [1, 2])$ is a logical consequence if the underlined atoms are selected from Ψ, is helpful for us. Such systems help us for making logic programs from incomplete knowledge, namely such systems become a tool for program synthesis.

Example 3. There are five persons $\{a, b, c, d, e\}$, five groups $\{ai, math, hard, soft, system\}$, five subjects $\{comp1, comp2, database, program, compiler\}$ and the following Ω, where lec is an abbreviation of lecture and g is an abbreviation of group.

/*** Knowledge between groups and subjects ***/

(1) $lec(X, comp1) \vee lec(X, comp2) \leftarrow g(X, ai)$.

(2) $lec(X, comp1) \vee lec(X, comp2) \leftarrow g(X, math)$.

(3) $lec(X, database) \vee lec(X, program) \leftarrow g(X, hard)$.

(4) $lec(X, program) \vee lec(X, compiler) \leftarrow g(X, soft)$.

(5) $lec(X, comp1) \leftarrow g(X, system)$.

/*** Knowledge between persons and groups ***/

(6) $g(a, ai)$.

(7) $g(b, math) \vee g(b, soft)$.

(8) $g(c, hard) \vee g(c, soft)$.

(9) $g(d, hard) \vee g(d, soft) \vee g(d, system)$.

(10) $g(e, system)$.

In this Ω, we think the following queries.

Query 1: Are there any groups where a person is decided?
Query 2: Who surely lectures on a subject?
Query 3: Are there any person who may lecture on program?
Query 4: Is it possible that every person belongs to every different group? In this case, is every subject lectured on by some person?
Query 5: Every person may belong to a same group. In this case, is every subject lectured on by some person?
Query 6: Are there any person who may lecture on database and who surely belongs to soft group?

The Queries 1, 2 and 3 are asking the assertion which surely holds or which may hold. The Queries 4 and 5 are asking the assignment problem based on Ω. The Query 6 depends upon two concepts 'surely holds' and 'may hold'. If we see the Ω a DDDB, then the above queries do not occur. Because Ω has no incompleteness, therefore two concepts 'surely holds' and 'may hold' are meaningless. However if we see the Ω a logic program with incomplete information, then the above queries naturally come to us. In order to develop the knowledge base theory, we should extend DDDB theory by adding another theorem provers which depend upon another interpretation for disjunctive information.

We showed three examples. We want to realize new question answering systems which can deal with the queries in Example 1, 2 and 3. In this paper, we apply the framework of abductive logic programming[5,6] and hypothetical reasoning[7,8,9] to DDDBs, and develop a new framework of knowledge base handling incomplete information.

3. Or-type Knowledge Bases

In the previous chapter, we showed that we need another interpretation for disjunctive information and we need another theorem prover for DDDBs.

3.1. A Definition of Or-type Knowledge Bases

First, we give the definition of or-type KBs, which is an advancement from DDDB. We are going to deal with the following formulas:

$\forall[sure([p_1, \cdots, p_m]) \leftarrow sure([q_{11}, \cdots, q_{1n_1}]) \wedge \cdots \wedge sure([q_{k1}, \cdots, q_{kn_k}])]$,

where p_i and q_{jh} are atoms, *sure* is a modal operator.

For a set of atoms $\{p_1, \cdots, p_k\}$, we call $sure([p_1, \cdots, p_k])$ an *or-type atom*. Syntactically, the above formulas are constructed by replacing every atom in definite clauses with an or-type atom. We call these formulas *modal clauses*. An or-type KB is a set of modal clauses. If a modal clause is in the form of

$\forall[sure([p_1]) \leftarrow sure([q_{11}]) \wedge \cdots \wedge sure([q_{k1}])]$,

then we call it *definite modal clause*. If every modal clause in an or-type KB is a definite modal clause, then we can see it as an usual knowledge base. Because, there is no incompleteness for every atom. Therefore, the framework of or-type KBs include that of knowledge bases. It is natural to think that we first have incomplete information and sequentially get the correct information, which is our motivation for defining or-type KBs.

Of course, the semantics and the theorem prover depend upon the interpretation of or-type atoms. We are now dealing with the following four interpretations to or-type atom.

CASE1: $sure([p_1, \cdots, p_k])$ implies $p_1 \vee \cdots \vee p_k$.

CASE2: $sure([p_1, \cdots, p_k])$ implies that only one element in $\{p_1, \cdots, p_k\}$ holds on every fact and rule.

CASE3: $sure([p_1, \cdots, p_k])$ implies that a subformula of $p_1 \vee \cdots \vee p_k$ holds on every fact and rule.

CASE4: $sure([p_1, \cdots, p_k])$ is an atom which has a disjunctive information.

Now, we give the definition for *extension* for every or-type KB.

Definition 1. We define extensions as follows.

(1) For every $P : sure([p_1, \cdots, p_k])$, a subformula of $p_1 \vee \cdots \vee p_k$ is an extension of P.

(2) For every modal clause $MC : \forall[C \leftarrow C_1 \wedge \cdots \wedge C_n]$, if C' is an extension of C and C_i' is an extension of C_i, then $\forall[C' \leftarrow C_1' \wedge \cdots \wedge C_n']$ is an extension of MC.

(3) For every or-type KB Ω, an extension of Ω is a set of every extension for every modal clause.

We denote the total set of extensions for Ω by $EX(\Omega)$. Especially, we call every extension which consist of definite clauses *complete extension*, and we denote the set of complete extensions by $COEX(\Omega)$. By using this definition, we can clarify the situation in CASE2 and CASE3. In CASE2, we want to deal with the incomplete rules as follows:

$\forall[(\underline{positive(X)} \vee negative(X)) \leftarrow \underline{natural\_number(X)}]$.

$\forall[\underline{ap([A|B], C, [A|D])} \vee ap(B, [A|C], [A|D]) \leftarrow \underline{ap(B, C, D)} \vee ap(A, B, C)]$.

The two rules are syntactically in the form of indefinite clause, however we know there is a truth complete extension. In real, the truth complete extension consists of the underlined atoms. In this case, we do not need the logical consequence of the above rules, however we need a logical consequence of the truth complete extension. In CASE3, we want to deal with the incomplete rules as follows:

$\forall[(negative(X) \vee \underline{odd(X) \vee even(X)}) \leftarrow \underline{natural\_number(X)}]$.

This rule is syntactically in the form of indefinite clause, however we know there is a truth extension. The introduction of extension for or-type KB makes the big difference from DDDB theory.

3.2. Semantics and Theorem Prover in CASE 1

In CASE 1, $sure([p_1, \cdots, p_k])$ implies $p_1 \vee \cdots \vee p_k$. Then, every modal clause can equivalently be transformed to the conjunction of the following clauses:

$\forall[p_1 \vee \cdots \vee p_m \leftarrow q_{1i_1} \wedge \cdots \wedge q_{ki_k}]$ $(1 \leq i_j \leq n_j, 1 \leq j \leq k)$.

Therefore in this case, the or-type KB can be seen as a set of clauses. Namely, the CASE1 is reduced to the framework of DDDB.

3.3. Semantics and Theorem Prover in CASE 2

In CASE 2, $sure([p_1, \cdots, p_k])$ implies that only one element in $\{p_1, \cdots, p_k\}$ holds. Therefore, there is a truth complete extension for every modal clause and there is a truth complete extension for every or-type KB. However, we can not decide which complete extension is the truth one. Therefore, we give the following definition.

Definition 2. Let Ω be an or-type KB and P be a closed formula.

(1) $\Omega \models_{CBOX} P \Leftrightarrow \Psi \models P$ for $\forall \Psi \in COEX(\Omega)$.

(2) $\Omega \models_{CDMD} P \Leftrightarrow \Psi \models P$ for $\exists \Psi \in COEX(\Omega)$.

The CBOX-system characterizes formulas which surely holds based on an unknown truth complete extension, and the CDMD-system does formulas which may hold. Every element in $COEX(\Omega)$ is a logic program, therefore we get the following proposition.

Proposition 1. Let Ω be an or-type KB, P be an element in some Herbrand base for $\Psi \in COEX(\Omega)$ and $M(\Psi)$ be the least model of Ψ.

(1) $\Omega \models_{CBOX} P \Leftrightarrow P \in \bigcap_{\Psi \in COEX(\Omega)} M(\Psi)$.

(2) $\Omega \models_{CDMD} P \Leftrightarrow P \in \bigcup_{\Psi \in COEX(\Omega)} M(\Psi)$.

Now, we discuss the proof procedure for every system. Of course, we can use SLD-resolution in every complete extension of Ω. However, we apply the hypothetical reasoning procedure to our theorem prover. We simply show the proof procedure of CDMD-system and CBOX-system.

Sketch of Proof Procedure for CDMD-system

(1) Let $\bigcup_{\Psi \in COEX(\Omega)} \{P | P$ is a clause in $\Psi\}$ be the set of all hypotheses.

(2) By using these hypotheses, solve a goal G by SLD-resolution and make a list of used hypotheses.

(3) If the set of used hypotheses is a subset of a complete extension $\Psi \in COEX(\Omega)$, then there exists a refutation of $\Omega \bigcup \{G\}$ in CDMD-system.

For example, suppose $\Omega = \{sure([a, b])\}$, then Ω has two complete extension $\{a\}$ and $\{b\}$. Therefore, $\Omega \bigcup \{\leftarrow a\}$ and $\Omega \bigcup \{\leftarrow b\}$ have a refutation on the CDMD-system. However, $\Omega \bigcup \{\leftarrow a \wedge b\}$ does not have a refutation. Because, there is no complete extension which contains a used hypotheses set $\{a, b\}$.

Sketch of Proof Procedure for CBOX-system

(1) Solve a goal G by using SLD-resolution. If there is a refutation then there exists a refutation of $\Omega \bigcup \{G\}$ in CBOX-system else goto (2).

(2) Try all refutations for a goal G by CDMD-system and assert every list of used hypotheses for every refutation.

(3) For every complete extension $\Psi \in COEX(\Omega)$, if there is a list of hypotheses which is a subset of Ψ then, there exists a refutation of $\Omega \bigcup \{G\}$ in CBOX-system.

3.4. Semantics and Theorem Prover in CASE 3

In CASE 3, $sure([p_1, \cdots, p_k])$ implies that a subformula of $p_1 \vee \cdots \vee p_k$ holds. Therefore, there is a truth extension for every modal clause and there is a truth extension for every or-type KB. However, we can not decide which extension is the truth one. We give the following definition like CASE2.

Definition 3. Let Ω be an or-type KB and P be a closed formula.

(1) $\Omega \models_{EBOX} P \Leftrightarrow \Psi \models P \quad \text{for } \forall\Psi \in EX(\Omega)$.

(2) $\Omega \models_{EDMD} P \Leftrightarrow \Psi \models P \quad \text{for } \exists\Psi \in EX(\Omega)$.

Proposition 2. Let Ω be an or-type KB and P be a closed formula.

(1) $\Omega \models_{EBOX} P \Leftrightarrow \Omega \models P$.

(2) $\Omega \models_{EDMD} P \Leftrightarrow \Omega \models_{CDMD} P$.

In CASE 3, the proof procedure of EBOX-system is realized by SLI-resolution in DDDB[1], and the proof procedure of EDMD-system is realized by the procedure of CDMD-system. From now on we identify CDMD-system and EDMD-system, and call them DMD-system.

Example 4. Let's consider an or-type KB Ω.

(1) $sure([odd(X), even(X)]) \leftarrow sure([natural\_number(X)])$.

(2) $sure([natural\_number(5)])$.

(3) $sure([natural\_number(6)])$.

In this case,

(1) $\Omega \models_{CBOX} odd(5) \vee even(5),\ odd(5) \vee even(6),\ odd(6) \vee even(5),\ odd(6) \vee even(6)$.

(2) $\Omega \models_{EBOX} odd(5) \vee even(5),\ odd(6) \vee even(6)$.

(3) $\Omega \models_{DMD} odd(5),\ odd(6),\ even(5),\ even(6)$.

For this Ω, the DMD-system is too weak and the CBOX-system is too strong. The EBOX-system is proper for Ω.

3.5. Semantics and Theorem Prover in CASE 4

In CASE 4, $sure([p_1, \cdots, p_k])$ implies an atom which expresses disjunctive information. Namely, we interpret $sure([p_1, \cdots, p_k])$ as an information such that '$(p_1 \vee \cdots \vee p_k)$ surely holds', which interpretation was introduced into relational database by Lipski[10,11]. In this case, we see *sure* not modal operator but a predicate symbol. Therefore, we can identify every modal clause and definite clause. However in this case, the following condition is necessary for the assignment f:a set of ground or-type atoms $\rightarrow \{true, false\}$.

Condition: If the value of $sure([p_1, \cdots, p_k])$ is *true*, then the value of every or-type atom which has an extension $p_1 \vee \cdots \vee p_k$ must be *true*.

According to this interpretation, we can define the logical consequence of every Ω, which we call BOX-logical consequence and we denote it by $\Omega \models_{BOX}$. As for this logical consequence, we have already shown that the following BOX-resolution is complete[12,13,14]. The BOX-logical consequence characterizes formulas which surely hold under the incomplete information.

Sketch of Proof Procedure for BOX-system

(1) Let $\leftarrow sure([p_1, \cdots, p_n])$ be a query.

(2) Find a fact $sure([q_1, \cdots, q_m])$ or a rule $sure([q_1, \cdots, q_m]) \leftarrow Q_1 \wedge \cdots \wedge Q_k$, where is a unifier θ such that $\{q_1, \cdots, q_m\}\theta \subseteq \{p_1, \cdots, p_n\}\theta$.

(3) If there is a fact then there exists a refutation else let a new resolvent be

$\leftarrow (Q_1 \wedge \cdots \wedge Q_k)\theta$ and goto (2).

Example 5. Let's consider the following or-type KB Ω.

(1) $sure([r(X)]) \leftarrow sure([p(X)])$.

(2) $sure([r(X)]) \leftarrow sure([q(X)])$.

(3) $sure([p(a), q(a)])$.

In this case, $\Omega \models_{CBOX} r(a)$ and $\Omega \models_{EBOX} r(a)$. However, $\Omega \not\models_{BOX} sure([r(a)])$. Because, we can not infer $sure([p(a)])$ nor $sure([q(a)])$ from $sure([p(a), q(a)])$. As for BOX-system, $\Omega \models_{BOX} sure([p(a), q(a), r(X)])$ holds.

Now, we clarify the difference between four cases. Let Ω be an or-type KB and $sure([p_1, \cdots, p_n])$ be a ground or-type atom. Then,

(1) $\Omega \models_{BOX} sure([p_1, \cdots, p_n])$ implies $\Omega \models_{EBOX} (p_1 \vee \cdots \vee p_n)$.

(2) $\Omega \models_{EBOX} (p_1 \vee \cdots \vee p_n)$ implies $\Omega \models_{CBOX} (p_1 \vee \cdots \vee p_n)$.

(3) $\Omega \models_{CBOX} (p_1 \vee \cdots \vee p_n)$ implies $\Omega \models_{DMD} p_i$ for every $i (1 \leq i \leq n)$.

4. A Prototype System of Or-type KB

Now, we briefly show a prototype system. We realized the following prolog programs.

(A) Converting program from an or-type KB to a set of hypotheses.

(B) Prover for DMD-system.

(C) Prover for CBOX-system.

(D) Prover for BOX-system.

Every prover is realized on apollo domain DN3500 by Ifprolog. We show an example of execution in the appendix.

(A) Converting program

First, we discuss the converting program. We realized a converting logic program 'init'. The input is an or-type KB and the outputs are hypotheses with integrity constraints and definite clauses. Every integrity constraint is in the form of $ic([p_1, \cdots, p_n])$, where the elements are hypotheses numbers. Integrity constraint, which assures the condition of CASE2, means that only one hypothesis in the list is available on a DMD-resolution. Every definite modal clause is converted to definite clause without integrity constraint. The following is an execution of converting program for Example 3.

```
| ?-stime,init,etime.  /* Initialization from or-type KB */
executing...
created 15 assumptions
Initialization Complete!!
CPUTIME = 0.16668 (sec)
yes
| ?-listing(hypo).  /* listing the created assumptions */
hypo(1,g(b,math)).
hypo(2,g(b,soft)).
hypo(3,g(c,hard)).
```

```
hypo(4,g(c,soft)).
hypo(5,(lec(X,compl):-g(X,ai))).
   .....
hypo(15,g(d,system)).
yes
| ?-listing(ic).  /* listing the integrity constraints */
ic([1,2]).
ic([3,4]).
   .....
ic([13,14,15]).
yes
```

(B) Prover for DMD-system

The following is the proof procedure for Dmd-logical consequence.

(1) Let dmd($(p_1, \cdots, p_n)$) be a query, which implies dmd(p_1) $\wedge \cdots \wedge$dmd(p_n).

(2) Solve every subgoal dmd(p_k)($1 \leq k \leq n$). In this case, the prover first uses definite clauses. If the subgoal can not be solved, then the prover uses hypotheses. Every used hypothesis number is recorded.

(2-1) If p_k is unifiable to a fact, then the subgoal is solved else go to (2-2).

(2-2) If p_k is unifiable to the head of a rule *head* $\leftarrow$ *body*, then go to (1) with dmd(*body*) else go to (2-3).

(2-3) If p_k is unifiable to a hypothesis which is a fact, then the subgoal is solved else go to (2-4). The prover records the hypothesis number, if the subgoal is solved.

(2-4) If p_k is unifiable to a head of an hypothesis *head* $\leftarrow$ *body*, then record the hypothesis number and go to (1) with dmd(*body*) else the subgoal p_k is not solvable.

(3) Check the integrity constraint. If the list of hypothesis number satisfies the condition, then there exists a DMD-refutation.

According to the above procedure, we realized predicates 'dmd' and 'dmdall' which makes exaustive search. We also realized a predicate 'dmdnounique' which omits the checking of integrity constraints. The Query 4 in Example 3 is realized by dmd predicate and the Query 5 in Example 3 is realized by dmdnounique predicate.

(C) Prover for CBOX-system

The prover for CBOX-system depends upon DMD-system. Let an or-type KB be Ω and a goal be G. In this case, we have to check $\Psi \bigcup \{G\}$ has DMD-refutation for every $\Psi \in COEX(\Omega)$. We have already showed the sketch of this procedure. In order to execute, we input the query cbox($(p_1, \cdots, p_n)$), which implies cbox(p_1) $\wedge \cdots \wedge$cbox(p_n).

(D) Prover for BOX-system

The prover for BOX-system is realized by extending the standard predicate 'clause' to 'boclause'. The condition for BOX-system is the strongest in all systems. In order to execute, we input the query box($[p_1, \cdots, p_n]$), which implies $p_1 \vee \cdots \vee p_n$ surely holds.

Let Ω be an or-type KB and $G(X)$ be a query where X is a variable. If there exists a refutation for $\Omega \bigcup \{G(X)\}$ in BOX-system, then the value of X is unique. However if there exists a refutation for $\Omega \bigcup \{G(X)\}$ in CBOX-system, then the value of X may not be unique. The prover answers that $\exists X(G(X))$ is a logical consequence of Ω in CBOX-system. Therefore, the combination of the BOX and CBOX-system will be helpful for us.

5. Concluding Remarks

We have proposed a framework for or-type KBs which deal with or-type information. We showed four interpretations for or-type information and developed every semantics depending upon every interpretation. We can use every prover to a unique or-type KB, and the usage of every prover depends upon the interpretation of or-type atom. We are going to extend this theory to logic program synthesis and learning knowledge base systems from incomplete knowledge.

This work is partially supported by the Grant-in-Aid (No.05780298), The Ministry of Education in Japan.

References

[1] J.Lobo, J.Minker and A.Rajasekar, Foundations of Disjunctive Logic Programming (MIT press, 1992), p.303.

[2] J.Minker, A.Rajasekar and j.Robo, *Theory of Disjunctive Logic Programs*, Computational Logic (MIT press, 1991).

[3] D.W.Loveland, *Near-Horn Prolog*, Proc.4th Int.Conf. on Logic Programming (1987).

[4] D.W.Loveland and D.W.Reed, *A Near-Horn Prolog for Compilation*, Computational Logic (MIT press, 1991).

[5] R.A.Kowalski, *Problems and Promises of Computational Logic*, Computational Logic (Springer-Verlag, 1990).

[6] A.C.Kakas and P.Mancarella, *Abductive Logic Programming*, Techninal Report, Department of Computing, Imperial College.

[7] S.Kunifuji, *Hypothetical Reasoning*, 2, J.Jap.Soc.for AI (1987).

[8] M.Ishizuka, *An Approach Toward Next-Generation Knowledge-Base System by Handling Incomplete Knowledge*, 3, J.Jap.Soc.for AI (1988).

[9] K.Inoue, *Principles of Abduction*, 7, J.Jap.Soc.for AI (1992).

[10] W.Lipski, *On Semantic Issues Connected with Incomplete Information Databases*, 4, ACM trans. of DBS (1979).

[11] W.Lipski, *On Databases with Incomplete Information*, 28, J.ACM (1981).

[12] H.Sakai, *Inference Methods and Semantics in Or-type Knowledge Bases*, 383, Lecture Notes in AI (1989).

[13] H.Sakai, *Completeness of Diamond-resolution in Or-type Knowledge Bases*, 24, Bulletin of Informatics and Cybernetics (1990).

[14] H.Sakai, *On a framework for Logic Programming with Incomplete Information*, 19, Fundamenta Informaticae (1993).

APPENDIX 1: Execution on Example 3

```
| ?-init. /* Initialization from Ω */
executing...
created 15 hypotheses
Initialization Complete!!
yes
| ?-boxall([g(X,Y)]). /* Query 1 */
[ 1 ] Ans = [g(a,ai)] /* Answer 1 */
[ 2 ] Ans = [g(e,system)]
no
| ?-cbox(lec(X,Y)). /* Query 2 */
X = e /* Answer 2 */
Y = comp1;
X = _27
Y = _28;
no
| ?-stime,dmdallt(lec(X,program)),
etime. /* Query 3 */
[ 1 ] Ans = lec(c,program) /* Answer 3 */
Hypothesis 3 = g(c,hard)
Hypothesis 10 = lec(_288,program):-g(_288,hard)
[ 2 ] Ans = lec(d,program)
Hypothesis 10 = lec(_208,program):-g(_208,hard)
Hypothesis 13 = g(d,hard)
[ 3 ] Ans = lec(b,program)
Hypothesis 2 = g(b,soft)
Hypothesis 11 = lec(_211,program):-g(_211,soft)
[ 4 ] Ans = lec(c,program)
Hypothesis 4 = g(c,soft)
Hypothesis 11 = lec(_211,program):-g(_211,soft)
[ 5 ] Ans = lec(d,program)
Hypothesis 11 = lec(_208,program):-g(_208,soft)
Hypothesis 14 = g(d,soft)
CPUTIME = 0.216684 (sec)
yes
| ?-dmd((g(a,X),g(b,Y),g(c,Z),g(d,M),g(e,N))),
neq([X,Y,Z,M,N]),hypotheses. /* Query 4 */
Hypothesis 1 = g(b,math) /* Answer 4 */
Hypothesis 3 = g(c,hard)
Hypothesis 14 = g(d,soft)
N = system,
M = soft,
Z = hard,
Y = math,
X = ai;
Hypothesis 1 = g(b,math)
Hypothesis 4 = g(c,soft)
Hypothesis 13 = g(d,hard)
N = system,
M = hard,
Z = soft,
Y = math,
X = ai;
no
| ?-dmd((lec(a,X),lec(b,Y),lec(c,Z),lec(d,M),
lec(e,N))),neq([X,Y,Z,M,N]). /* Query 4 */
no /* Answer 4 */
| ?-dmdnounique((lec(a,X),lec(b,Y),lec(c,Z),
lec(d,M),lec(e,N))),neq([X,Y,Z,M,N]),
hypotheses. /* Query 5 */
Hypothesis 2 = g(b,soft) /* Answer 5 */
Hypothesis 3 = g(c,hard)
Hypothesis 6 = lec(_650,comp2):-g(_650,ai)
Hypothesis 9 = lec(_661,database):-g(_661,hard)
Hypothesis 11 = lec(_672,program):-g(_672,soft)
Hypothesis 12 = lec(_683,compiler):-g(_683,soft)
Hypothesis 14 = g(d,soft)
N = comp1,
M = compiler,
Z = database,
Y = program,
X = comp2;
.......
Hypothesis 2 = g(b,soft)
Hypothesis 4 = g(c,soft)
Hypothesis 6 = lec(_654,comp2):-g(_654,ai)
Hypothesis 9 = lec(_665,database):-g(_665,hard)
Hypothesis 11 = lec(_676,program):-g(_676,soft)
Hypothesis 12 = lec(_687,compiler):-g(_687,soft)
Hypothesis 14 = g(d,hard)
N = comp1,
M = database,
Z = program,
Y = compiler,
X = comp2;
no
| ?-dmd(lec(X,database)),
cbox(g(X,soft)). /* Query 6 */
no /* Answer 6 */
```

APPENDIX 2: Execution on Example 2

```
| ?-init. /* Initialization */
executing...
created 4 hypotheses
Initialization Complete!!
yes
| ?-dmdall(ap([1],[2],[1,2])). /* Query 1 */
[ 1 ] Ans = ap([1],[2],[1,2]) /* Answer 1*/
Hypothesis 1 = ap([],_206,_206)
Hypothesis 3 = ap([_217|_218],_215,[_217|_220])
:-ap(_218,_215,_220)
no
| ?-stime,dmdallt(ap([1],[2],M)),
etime. /* Query 2 */
[ 1 ] Ans = ap([1],[2],[1,2]) /* Answer 2*/
Hypothesis 1 = ap([],_223,_233)
Hypothesis 3 = ap([_234|_235],_232,[_234|_237])
:-ap(_235,_232,_237)
[ 2 ] Ans = ap([1],[2],[2,1])
Hypothesis 2 = ap(_222,[],_222)
Hypothesis 4 = ap(_231,[_234|_235],[_234|_237])
:-ap(_231,_235,_237)
CPUTIME = 0.133344 (sec)
M = _143
yes
```

A Novel Application of Ripple Down Rules to Selecting a Method of Chemical Analysis for a Variety of Chemicals and their Sample Matrices

G.A. Delzoppo, M. Mulholland, D.B. Hibbert

Department of Analytical Chemistry, University of New South Wales, PO Box 1, Kensington, NSW 2033, Australia

KEY WORDS: Knowledge Acquisition, Ripple Down Rules, Expert System and Analytical Chemistry

ABSTRACT

This paper describes the application of a formalised knowledge acquisition and representation method known as Ripple Down Rules (RDR) to build an expert system for chemical analysis. The purpose of the expert system is to offer advice as to the best analytical method to use for a given sample and sample matrix. It is designed as a source of reference for the Centre of Chemical Analysis, UNSW, and as a teaching tool for senior chemistry undergraduates. The uses of the expert system vary from the analysis of heavy metal pollutants in water, to the analysis of vitamins in foodstuffs. Thus the attributes which define the domain include features of the compounds to be assayed and the complexity of its matrix.

INTRODUCTION

Over the past couple of decades analytical chemistry has developed rapidly from the application of wet chemical techniques, such as titrations, to the current use of sophisticated instrumentation such as mass spectroscopy and chromatography. Alongside these developments there has been an enormous growth in the application of microcomputers to these techniques. They are applied to control instruments, handle data, interpret results and there already exist several expert systems developed to aid method development and data interpretation. One of the best known examples is Dendral[1], which interprets spectra from a mass spectrometer. Other systems include ESCA expert systems, which were developed as part of an ESPRIT funded project and tackle several problems related to High Performance Liquid Chromatography (HPLC)[2-4]. Prior work by the authors applied expert systems to Ion Chromatography[5].

The aim of this project is to develop an expert system that can predict which analytical technique to use and the relevant sample preparation, when given some information on the chemical sample, its matrix and some requirements from the analysis. The expert system is being developed using a formalised knowledge acquisition and representation method known as Ripple Down Rules (RDR) developed by Paul Compton *et al* [6,7].

The School of Chemistry at the University of New South Wales (UNSW) operates a commercial consultancy known as the Centre for Chemical Analysis. The analyses performed are not of a routine nature and require specialised expertise. Consequently, many academics within the School of Chemistry and other schools (ie Material Science,

Applied Science) are employed to perform a particular analysis. The manager of the centre is employed to select which of the analytical techniques need to be performed and also assists in the many of the assays. He provides the majority of the expertise required for the expert system. Over the past four years he has built up a database of samples which have been assayed at the centre. For each client a report is prepared detailing the analyses and it is these reports that are used to help build the expert system for chemical analysis. To complete the expertise required we have referred to reference texts in analytical chemistry[8,9].

RIPPLE DOWN RULES

Background

Traditional expert systems do not arrange the rules as they are added to the system and either forward or backward chaining is used to examine the rules during a consultation. This results in an explosion in the number of potential pathways which can use a particular rule, hence if a new rule is added or an old rule modified, all these pathways need to be re-validated. In other words it becomes very difficult to maintain an expert system and predict and control the effects of additional knowledge. RDR were developed to combat these problems and they employ a rigid rule structure such that any new rule added has a predictable effect. This format not only enhances the ease of maintenance of expert system, but also provides a method for knowledge acquisition that allows the expert to easily build their own systems. For RDR the rules are formatted in a tree-like structure (a binary tree) where each rule is allowed two branches, a true branch and a false branch.

The structure is shown in Figure 1 where it is contrasted with a traditional rule-based expert system.

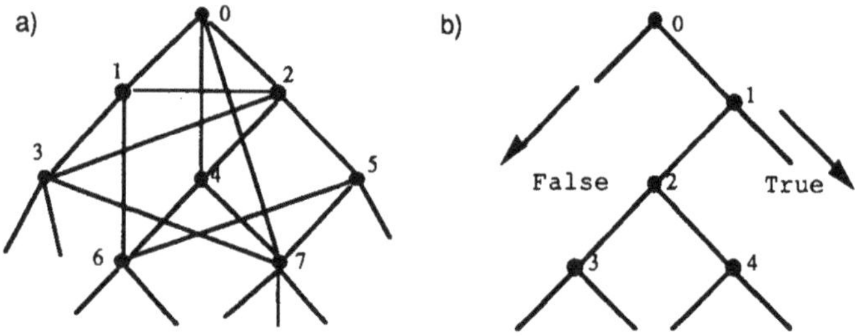

Figure 1 a) A traditional structure of rules in an expert system *b) The RDR formalised binary tree structure*

Basic Theory of Ripple Down Rules

An RDR expert system is based on a binary tree. Each node of the tree can be considered to be a rule with attached rule conditions and conclusions. There are two branches from each node, the true branch and the false branch. When a data set is presented to an RDR tree, node evaluation (either true or to false) causes the data set to be passed to the appropriate branch, and so on down to a terminal leaf. The conclusion of the last true rule is returned as the diagnosis of this data set.

If a new rule is added to the tree because of an incorrect conclusion returned by a set of data, the new rule is added as a branch of the last rule reached (whether or not it was true). It is added to the true branch if the data is evaluated to true, and to the false branch if the data is evaluated to false. In Figure 1(b) each dot in the diagram indicates a rule, and each branch a possible result of evaluating the rule - true evaluation leads to the right, while false evaluations lead to the left.

An essential part of a practical RDR system is the maintenance of cornerstone cases. These cases are data sets that caused some change to the system. For each rule in a system there is a cornerstone case. There are several reasons why these are important. Trivially, they provide a chronicle of the development of the system for documentation purposes. More fundamentally however, they provide a context within which new rules can be created.

DEVELOPMENT of the EXPERT SYSTEM

Experimental

The expert system was developed using an Apple Macintosh and using the Hypercard program. The core was written in C and then transferred to Hypercard. The database was created in Microsoft Works again on an Apple Macintosh.

Definition of the Attributes

As previously mentioned the Centre of Chemical Analysis has built up a database of samples which have been assayed at the centre, over the past four years. For each client a report was prepared detailing the nature of the problem, the materials received for analyses, the sample preparation, the particular analytical technique used and the results of the assays. This knowledge based expert system was developed using these client's report as a means of acquiring knowledge from the expert. These reports were examined and the information summarised by selecting suitable attributes to define each example. The selection of these attributes was a non-trivial task and the final design is still to be decided upon. Essentially each report contained the following information: the nature of the problem, the materials received for analyses, the sample preparation, the particular analytical technique used and the results of the assays. Table 1 contains examples of some of the attributes that were selected.

Due to the unique nature of many of the Centre's analyses, some typical or more standard methodologies have been used as examples in the database. This was done to try and overcome any abnormalities in the database's methods and try to introduce some standard techniques that more conventional laboratories may employ on a regular basis. The texts used are referenced previously and some typical examples are given in the Table 1.

These attributes were selected for several reasons, firstly and most importantly the information was available, and secondly they define properties of the sample which are relevant to the method of analysis chosen. As the work progressed it was necessary to define further attributes to illustrate other chemical and physical properties, such as volatility and required sensitivity. These attributes more specifically define a given chemical and its application and were generally required in order to select between two alternative methods of analysis.

Table 1: Some Of The Attributes Selected To Define The Domain Together With Their Values

ATTRIBUTES SELECTED					
SPECIFIC CLASS	**CHEMICAL CLASS**	**APPLICATION**	**SAMPLE MATRIX**	**SAMPLE PREPATION**	**TECHNIQUE USED**
Cations	all metals	pipe deposit	solid	acid digestion	ICPAES
Cations	heavy metals	waste disposal	solid	acid digestion	AAS
Anions	halides & oxyanions	water treatment	liquid	filtration	IC
Anions	halides	clay tiles	solid	acid digestion	ISE
Organics	polymer	cement powder	solid	solvent	IR

where

ICPAES:-	Inductively Coupled Plasma Atomic Emission Spectroscopy
AAS:-	Atomic Absorption Spectroscopy
IC:-	Ion Chromatography
ISE:-	Ion Selective Electrode
IR:-	Infrared Spectroscopy

Building the RDR Tree

In this application of RDR, part of the tree is shown in Figure 2. The cornerstone cases are those shown in Table 1. The first rule was made using case 1 and it concerns the presence of cations as the species to be analysed, and concludes that Inductively Coupled Plasma Atomic Emission Spectroscopy (ICPAES) should be used.

IF specific class is cations
THEN use ICPAES

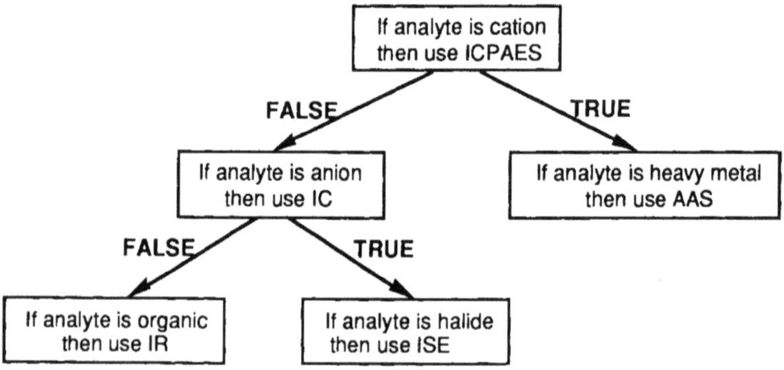

Figure 2: An Example of the RDR Tree For the Selection of Methods in Chemical Analysis

The cases were now examined until case 2 from Table 1 showed an example where the specific class is cations, however the conclusion is not ICPAES. The difference between the attribute values for case 1, the cornerstone case for rule 1, and case 2 which now becomes the cornerstone case for rule 2 is recorded. The relevant difference, in this instance the fact that the chemical class is heavy metals, now forms the basis of a new conclusion, use AAS.

This rule will be added to the true branch of rule 1 because all the conditions of rule 1 are true. The total rule for case 2 becomes:

IF specific class is cations
AND IF chemical class is heavy metals
THEN use AAS

The RDR tree continues to expand in this way as each new case is met which does not fit with the current rule conclusions. Each time a new rule is added it becomes associated with the case from which it was justified and this provides the context related information for the overall knowledge base.

RESULTS AND CONCLUSIONS

The use of RDR allows a flexible and variable approach to creating and maintaining rules. This was of a particular advantage to this expert system for it allowed more rules to be added and a means to continually update and improve the expert system when an inappropriate answer was produced. Hypercard was chosen as it allows for the developer to easily create user interfaces for explanation and help sections.

The future development of the expert system could proceed in various directions. Some of the key areas that could be addressed include: using non fixed length vector variables and the ability to produce multiple conclusions which also include the relevant sample preparation. Some work has been carried out on the use of RDR for multiple conclusions and this could be applied to this expert system[11]. The use of non fixed length variables provides some interesting problems which will need to be overcome. In chemical analysis this is essential since often more than one chemical can be assayed in a single sample matrix. There is currently no way to deal with this problem.

After the expert system completion it is important to validate it. This is done by presenting a set of typical problems to the expert system, say 50, and its conclusions are then formed. The expert, Terry Flynn, then examines the expert system's conclusions and judges them to be "workable", "good" or "ideal". Past results for the expert system on Ion Chromatography written in the same format, produced an overall result of 85% of the methods as workable and 62% as good or ideal[10].

Initially the attributes were selected manually, however as the database increases in size then a machine learning technique could be applied to the database. If this were performed then the database should be checked for any bias, such as a chronological one.

Once the system is developed further it will eventually be used as a teaching aid for second and third year analytical chemistry students within the School of Chemistry at UNSW. This could perhaps involve several explanation screens, and some user interaction with the program. Even a tutorial type of system could be implemented to test a students understanding of analytical instrumental analysis. The expert system would also find some use for Terry Flynn in the Centre of Chemical Analysis, as a means of referring to the techniques that he should employ in order to complete an analysis.

ACKNOWLEGMENTS

The authors would like to thank Paul Compton and Phil Preston from the AI laboratory at UNSW for their assistance in providing and supporting RDR software.

REFERENCES

1. M.W.Firebaugh, *Artificial Intelligence, A Knowledge-Based Approach*, PWS Kent Publishing Company, (1988) 338-342
2. M.Mulholland, "Expert systems and their implementation in chromatography", in C.Bryce (Editor), *Microcomputers and their application in Biochemistry*, Oxford University Press, Chapter 8 (1992) 243-265.
3. P.J.Schoenmakers and M.Mulholland, "An Overview of Contemporary Method Development in Liquid Chromatography', *Chromatographia*, 25, No.8,(1988), 737.
4. M.Mulholland, J.A. van Leeuwen, B.G.M. Vandeginste, "An Expert System to Design and Intelligent Spreadsheet for the Determination of the Precision of an HPLC Method", *Analytica Chemica Acta*, 223, (1989), 183
5. M. Mulholland, P. Preston, G. A. Delzoppo, D.B.Hibbert, P. Compton, "Teaching A Computer Ion Chromatography", *Chemistry in Australia*, 60 No.5 (1993) 222-225
6. P. Compton, B. Kang, P. Preston, M. Mulholland, "Knowledge Acquisition without Analysis", In Press in *Knowledge Acquisition* : Springer Lecture Notes in Computer Science 1993 (Proceedings of the European Knowledge Acquisition Workshop 1993)
7. P.Compton and R.Janson, "A Philosophical Basis for Knowledge Acquisition", *Knowledge Acquisition* 2,(1990) , 241-257.
8. D.A.Skoog, *Principles of Instrumental Analysis*, Saunders College Publishing (1985)
9. G.D Christian, *Analytical Chemistry*, Wiley (1986)
10. P.Compton, G.Edwards, B.Kang, L.Lazarus, R.Malor, P.Preston, A.Srinivasan, "Ripple down rules: Turning knowledge acquisition into knowledge maintenance", *Artificial Intelligence in Medicine* 4 (1992), 463-475.
11. M. Mulholland, P. Preston, C. Sammut, D. B. Hibbert and P. Compton. "An Expert System for Ion Chromatography Developed Using Machine Learning and Knowledge in Context", Presented at IEA/AIE- 93 Edinburgh, June 1993. Published as a long paper in the proceedings, 1993.

Federating Propositional Expert Systems*

(Extended Abstract)†

Nirad Sharma and Robert Colomb
CRC for Distributed Systems Technology
Department of Computer Science
The University of Queensland
Brisbane, QLD 4072, AUSTRALIA
email: {*nirad,colomb*}*@cs.uq.oz.au*

Abstract

Expert systems provide a rich problem-solving facility for many applications requiring domain-specific problem-solving. A federation of interacting expert systems has the potential to tackle problems of greater scope, exhibiting a collective problem-solving capability greater than the sum of its parts. We present the relationship between dependency graphs and execution autonomy for federations of propositional expert systems, taking advantage of their "nice" properties such as monotonic behaviour, fixed-point semantics and finiteness. The simplicity of propositional systems does, however, introduce some additional problems when federated, especially for inter-agent conflict resolution.

Keywords : propositional expert systems, deductive databases, federated systems

*The work reported in this paper has been funded in part by the Cooperative Research Centres Program through the Department of the Prime Minister and Cabinet of the Commonwealth Government of Australia.

†The full paper is available as University of Queensland Computer Science Technical Report 242

1 Introduction

Expert systems are commonly captured as propositional expert systems (PESs), that is rules formulated in terms of ground Horn clauses. We restrict the class of expert systems being federated to propositional systems because most expert systems are rule-based systems ([5]) that we believe are, effectively, propositional in nature. Propositional systems exhibit a number of useful properties such as :

- being a special case of deductive databases and so we may draw from many of the results known in this literature ([8, 9])
- monotonicity (by definition of being deductive databases)
- having guaranteed finiteness, i.e. will always converge to a fixed-point
- giving a well-defined result (perfect model semantics for stratified systems).
- [3] show that the rule system can be executed without searching through compile time analysis of the dependency graph. This enables a PES to be rapidly executed as a decision table or decision tree on massively parallel computers.

We wish to federate expert systems in such a way that the nice properties of the component PESs are preserved. By federating modular sub-components, we are more able to build a dynamically reconfigurable systems that can adapt to changing requirements ([6]). If there are several knowledge bases with separate ownership, we must have some means by which they can cooperate in a meaningful way.

Section 2 will define our concepts for federating PESs. The central issue of this paper is the proof presented in Section 3 that a collection of propositional expert systems agents cannot be federated in a nice way unless the dependency graph of agent interactions is acyclic. We discuss other issues relevant to federating PESs in Section 4 and present our conclusions and suggest future directions in Section 5.

2 PES Concepts

Our analysis of PESs is based on the concept of a dependency graph which arose in the study of stratified negation.

Following the conventions outlined in [1], we denote atomic formulae, or *atoms*, by a, b, c. *Ground atoms* ($ground(a)$) are atoms that contain no variables. A *literal*, denoted L, is an atom a (*positive literal*) or its negation $\neg a$ (*negative literal*). A *ground literal* ($ground(L)$) if its atoms are ground. We define a *clause* to be :

$$a \leftarrow L_1 \wedge \ldots \wedge L_n$$

The head is an atom, not a literal, hence negation is not allowed in a clause's head. The clause is a *rule* if $n > 0$. Otherwise, it is a *fact*.

A *program* P is a finite collection of clauses and is ground ($ground(P)$) if all of its literals are ground. A propositional expert system (PES) is a set a propositional Horn clauses and is equivalent to a ground program. In the context of PESs, negation as failure means that a proposition is assumed false unless proven true.

Borrowing from deductive database terminology ([8]), a set of facts is an *extensional database* (EDB) and a set of rules is the *intensional database* (IDB). We compute a *model* by repeatedly applying the rules in the IDB to the EDB until no more new symbols can be produced, reaching a *fixed point.*

2.1 Dependency Graphs And Stratification

A program P can be represented as a *dependency graph*, a directed graph that illustrates atom dependencies between clauses in P ([1]). More formally, the dependency graph for a program P is $G = (N, E)$. Each clause in P is represented by a node in $N = \{C_i\}$. $E = \{(c_j^1, c_j^2, s_j)\}$ is the set of directed edges running from node c_j^1 to c_j^2 where the consequent of clause c_j^1 appears in a literal in the antecedent of clause c_j^2. An edge is marked (s_j) with a '-' or '+' depending on whether the literal in c_j^2 is a negation or not. Figure 1 illustrates the graph for the following rules :

$$\begin{aligned} r_1 &: \; a \leftarrow b \wedge c \\ r_2 &: \; b \leftarrow d \\ r_3 &: \; c \leftarrow \neg a \end{aligned}$$

A program composed entirely of positive literals is called a *positive program* and has a fixed point independent of the order of the clauses' execution. Not all programs are positive, however, and the introduction of negation can cause model computation to becomes sensitive to execution order. Consider the

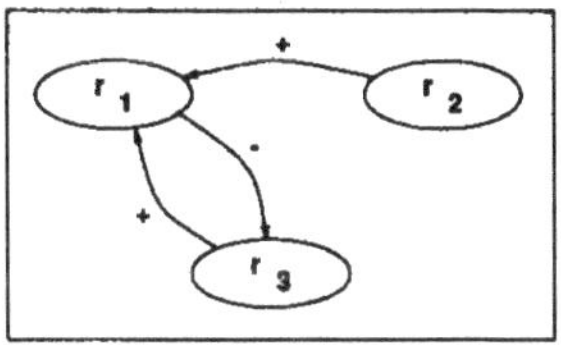

Figure 1: Dependency Graph.

EDB $\{c, d\}$ and the following program P :

$$r_1: \quad a \leftarrow \neg b$$
$$r_2: \quad b \leftarrow c \wedge d$$

If we evaluate r_1 before r_2, the model $m_{p_{12}} = \{a, b, c, d\}$. If r_2 had been evaluated before r_1, we have the model $m_{p_{21}} = \{b, c, d\}$. To cope with this problem, we evaluate all rules that produce instances of the atom before those rules that have the atom negated in their consequent. A program that can be evaluated using this rule is *stratified* ([1]), that is the dependency graph does not contain a cycle with a negative edge in it. A program P is stratified by partitioning P into a set $\{P_i\}$ such that there are no negative edges between rules in P_i and P_{i+1} in the dependency graphs. More specifically, if $i < j$, an atom defined in P_j will not appear negated in P_i. Any stratified program evaluated according to the rule has the same (perfect) model, irrespective of the order of execution within a P_i, so long as the constraint of the rule is satisfied.

Programs are not always stratified, however (cycle with negative edge in Figure 2) :

$$r_1: \quad a \leftarrow \neg b$$
$$r_2: \quad b \leftarrow a$$

This program is indeterminate, that is to compute the portion of the model for any interpretation involving a or b will result in unspecifiable behaviour. The execution a stratified program / PES is guaranteed to be determinate and finite behaviour.

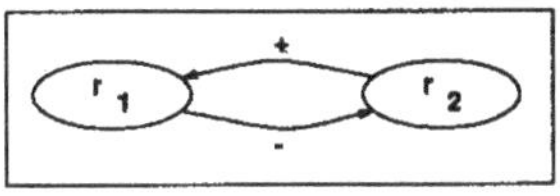

Figure 2: Not Stratified.

2.2 Resolving Inter-Agent Inconsistencies

[4] argue that the traditional federation model involving an "orchestrating" layer above the information systems (agents) to resolve inconsistencies is unrealistic, in general. Where agents' representations of semantically compatible concepts ([7]) are heterogeneous, it is likely that at least one of the agents will need be modified to facilitate interoperability. These modifications must be constrained, however, to reduce the possibility that modifications in an agent may conflict with the changes required by another. An agent should be able to interact with its original clients in the same manner as prior to its inclusion in the federation.

We assume that semantic heterogeneity has been resolved and that these issues have been dealt with accordingly. If the heterogeneity cannot be resolved, there is no point in federating the PESs in question.

2.3 Execution Autonomy

Execution autonomy exists for agents that, once provided with inputs, execute independently of other agents to produce their outputs and come together to share results or provide inputs to each other.If execution autonomy is compromised significantly, the collection of PESs ceases to be a loosely-coupled federation and becomes more of a tightly-coupled distributed expert system with little individual independence.

3 Properties of Federated PESs

A PES cannot proceed independently of other PESs if any of its inputs are dependent in some way on its outputs. If we consider PESs P_1 and P_2 in Figure 3 where the outputs a and d are connected to inputs c and b, respectively, it is apparent that there is a cycle in the dependency graph between P_1 and P_2 and that the PESs cannot execute independently. The *integrated dependency graph* (IDG) is the dependency graph of all the rules in the federation of PESs collected together. The *agent dependency graph* (ADG) reduces each PES to a node and the set of directed edges $\{(P_i^1, P_i^2)\}$ such that PES P_i^2 has a literal in its antecedents that appears in a consequent of PES P_i^1.

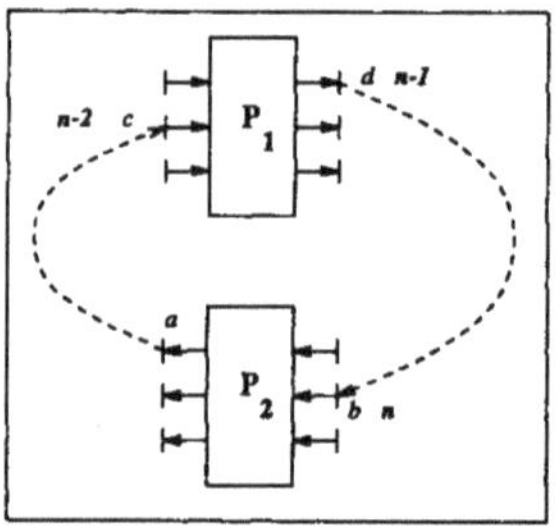

Figure 3: Cyclic PES Dependency.

Lemma 1 *The ADG has a cycle iff the IDG has a cycle (proof immediate)*

Theorem 1 *A PES P in a federation of PESs can execute autonomously (independently) iff none of its inputs are dependent directly or indirectly on its outputs, that is, the ADG is acyclic.*

Proof 1 *Proof of the forward implication (acyclic ADG $\rightarrow$ execution autonomy) from treating the choice of PES to execute as being analagous to proving graph acyclicity :*

1. *Construct the ADG $G = (N, E)$ where N is the set of PESs and E the set of directed edges $\{(n_i, n_j)\}$ where some inputs of PES n_j depends on outputs of PES n_i. ($E \subseteq \{(n_i, n_j) \mid n_i, n_i \in N\}$)*
2. *If there is a PES that depends on no other PES for its inputs ($\exists n \in N \neg \exists e \in E \cdot e = (\_, n)$), then that PES may be executed to produce outputs without any interruption. This must be possible for $N \neq \emptyset$ since the ADG is acyclic.*
3. *Let $G = (N', E')$ where $N' = N - \{n\}$ and $E' = E - \{(n, n_j) \mid (n, n_j) \in E\}$. PES n is removed from the ADG, having completed its execution and produced outputs which may now be used as inputs to the remaining PESs in G.*
4. *Iterate to step 2.*

Proof of the converse condition (acyclic ADG $\rightarrow$ execution autonomy) comes from Figure 3 which is the general case if the ADG has a cycle. If P_2 was fired first at time t_n, P_1 must have produced d at time t_{n-1}. Production of d depends on the supply of c and production of a from P_2 at time t_{n-2}. a depends on b, however. Hence, P_2 cannot retain execution autonomy and proceed independently of P_1 (and vice versa). Effectively, we have the situation where a

PES's inputs are dependent on its outputs.

Corollary A federated PES which preserves execution autonomy is stratified.

Proof The order of selection of PESs from step 2 of Proof 1 is a stratification.

We have assumed that only one PES produces an output for a proposition. In practice, the situation can occur where, even with semantic heterogeneity resolved, more than one PES supplies an output for a proposition, introducing the possibility of conflict. We show in Section 3.2 that Theorem 1 still holds if this assumption is relaxed.

3.1 Negation As Failure And Synchronisation

Negation-as-failure enables finite perfect model computation for a program. Failure unifies the concepts of *false* and *unknown* (no information available / activated, as in conventional three-valued logics), a tolerable compromise when evaluating a central rule set. A collection of expert systems introduces inter-agent *temporal* dependencies. Without a synchronisation mechanism, failure (no result) extends to include *still-computing* (computation not yet completed). Agents need to synchronise where they depend on the output propositions of others.

Consider two PESs A_1 and A_2 that both produce proposition p used in the antecedent of some rule r. If a three-valued logic (*true/false/unknown*) was being used, the presence of any output on $A_1.p$ and $A_2.p$ would indicate completion. A PES, however, can only bind *true* to the presence of an output, leaving any of the interpretations of *false*, *unknown* and *still-computing* for the absence of output for $A_1.p$ and / or $A_2.p$. To ensure consistent behaviour in the federation, inter-agent checkpoints may need to be placed in the PESs. A simple token-passing algorithm could enforce synchronisation.

3.2 Inter-Agent Conflict Resolution

An expert system resolves conflict by applying rules (of varying complexity) that may, themselves, be embodied in an expert system. For intra-expert system resolution, the conflict resolution mechanism can be incorporated into the rule structure ([2]). When integrating separate expert systems, however, the need arises for a well-defined *external* conflict resolution mechanism, perhaps in the form of a conflict resolution expert system (CRES)[1]. CRESs will be responsible for resolving multiple sources for a proposition to a single output. Therefore, the conditions for Theorem 1 still hold.

4 Conclusions and Further Work

We have shown that a federation of PESs can retain execution autonomy if and only if no input to one of its constituents is dependent directly or indirectly on one of its outputs. Consequently, any federation of PESs which retains execution autonomy is stratified if all of its members are. We have also established that a federation must have a scheduling mechanism, and that if there are

[1]Note that CRESs could be distributed throughout the network of PESs, reducing exposure to centralised CRES failures and bottlenecks. Independent partitions of the ADG (with CRESs included) represent parallelisable tasks, providing guidelines for deployment of CRESs.

conflicts, they can be resolved by introducing further expert systems to the federation.

Further work will extend the deductive database methods to more general expert systems, particularly first-order systems, and to other strategies for execution.

References

[1] K. R. Apt, H. A. Blair, and A. Walker. Towards a theory of deductive knowledge. In Jack Minker, editor, *Foundations of Deductive Databases and Logic Programming*, pages 89–148. Morgan Kauffman, 1988.

[2] R. M. Colomb, S. Srinivasan, and C. A. Sammut. Making knowledge representation independent of knowledge processing. *Integrated Computer-Aided Engineering*, 1993. *to appear.*

[3] R. M. Colomb and C. Y. Chung. Very fast decision table execution of propositional expert systems. In *AAAI-90*, pages 671–676, 1990.

[4] R. M. Colomb and M. E. Orlowska. Interoperability in information systems. Technical Report 263, Department of Computer Science, University of Queensland, March 1993.

[5] R. Irrgang, V. R. Kumar, and C. Chung. Intelligent systems in australian industry - a study of current status and future trends. Technical Report TR-LA-93-01, CSIRO-DIT, 1993.

[6] St. Kirn and G. Schlageter. Intelligent agents in federative expert systems - concepts and implementation. In S. M. Deen, editor, *Co-operating Knowledge Based Systems 1990 - University of Keele, UK*, pages 53–74. Springer-Verlag, 1990.

[7] A. Sheth and J. Larson. Federated database systems for managing distributed, heterogeneous, and autonomous databases. *ACM Computing Surveys*, 22(3):183–236, September 1990.

[8] J. D. Ullman. *Principles of Database and Knowledge-Base Systems*, volume 1. Computer Science Press, 1988.

[9] J. D. Ullman. *Principles of Database and Knowledge-Base Systems*, volume 2. Computer Science Press, 1989.

Framework For Building Intelligent Cooperative Systems

Wei Dai
Artificial Intelligence Systems, Telecom Research Laboratories
P.O. Box 249, Clayton, Victoria 3168, Australia

and

Sidney L. Wright
Computer Science Programme, Murdoch University
Murdoch, W.A. 6150, Australia

ABSTRACT This paper describes a framework for building intelligent cooperative systems within a traditional business operating environment. The framework has a multi-layer architecture ranging from the low-level domain-independent expert system development capabilities to high-level intelligent systems cooperation mechanisms. We attempt to use the framework as a generic methodology for building cooperative expert systems within traditional software environments. To demonstrate the feasibility of such an approach, we have used the framework to coordinate activities among various business divisions using multimedia technology. The aim is to integrate expert system technology with existing business applications programs in order to efficiently use the available resources and produce effective software products.

KEYWORDS : Cooperating Expert Systems, Software Environments.

1. Introduction

A corporation is usually split into multiple business divisions which are sometimes geographically dispersed requiring encoding, transmission and decoding of information (in the form of memos, telephone conversations, e-mail, tapes, disks, network links, etc). It is important to specify an efficient way to allow updated information generated by some divisions to be propagated to the others. Different divisions may encode the information in different ways, e.g. data is generated by one computer system in one format and is required by another in a different format. This will require the appropriate interpretation of information semantics among different divisions. Invalid analyses may be applied to the information by inexperienced personnel.

A substantial reduction in these problems can be achieved by formalizing descriptions of the information needs of the corporation, this involves :

1) Defining the information (entities and attributes) and processes that the corporation is dealing with. This can be done using Systems Analysis techniques.
2) Identifying which divisions generate particular pieces of information and at what times.
3) Identifying which divisions consume information and where information is transformed, together with the timing (these are the information interfaces).
4) Defining the semantics of information, i.e. the relationships between entities, how the entities and attributes are combined and transformed into other entities, etc.
5) Implementing a mechanism which will allow the cooperation of individual divisions in various ways.

With this basic understanding of information needs, it then remains to choose technical solutions for building each individual system and combining them into cooperative systems. For an individual system, issues such as what representations are to be used for the information, where it is to be stored and how it is to be processed etc need to be considered. For cooperative systems, a decision making mechanism for selecting available software tools and relevant communication and control mechanisms need to be established.

Expert System (ES) technology has proved to be a very promising problem-solving technique in many areas where sophisticated human knowledge is required. ES development tools, such as ES shells, AI languages, etc, have been available commercially for some years and have been used in many specialized computing environments. To date, system developers have been restricted to using expert system specialists to develop this software as the tools used to construct expert systems and the technical details such as knowledge representation and inference are unfamiliar to traditional software developers. This has severely limited the range of application of the technology. Many successful expert systems are still stand-alone applications for a narrow domain and are not well integrated with other application programs. Recent research[1] suggests there should be a growing trend for expert systems to be integrated with business application software. However, the knowledge based approach will not come into widespread use until the above problems are minimized.

2. Initial Design Decisions

An initial major design decision was that key ES functionalities would be integrated into traditional programming environments so that they could be combined with other software systems to produce intelligent cooperative systems. The easiest approach to this is to implement ES components using conventional languages and techniques so that all the existing tools in the environment can be used. Mechanisms for information sharing and reuse must be implemented within the framework so that effective cooperative systems can be built efficiently. This can be realized through an architecture that supports multiple knowledge bases simultaneously. The particular data used in an inference session should also be separated from the knowledge bases and put into knowledge data stores. These decisions also help support distributed and concurrent processing by allowing access to knowledge bases and knowledge data stores held on systems running on different computers, communication between which is handled by the relevant primitive routines[2]. There are many domains of interest in large corporations so the system must be able to cope with a wide range of domains and strategies for using knowledge. The solution adopted is to allow the knowledge engineer to specify all of the details of the domain information, and how it is processed, separately from the bulk of the framework, i.e. the framework is largely domain-independent. The framework should be highly modular and efficient, and only those components actually used to solve a given problem should be included in the solution code. The generated systems should also be portable as many business divisions use different computer systems for their work.

3. Cooperative Systems Framework

One of the most flexible architectures for software systems is one in which the operations to be performed are packaged into executable programs called tools. The framework has been designed and implemented using tool-oriented techniques[3], Figure 1 shows the overall architecture.

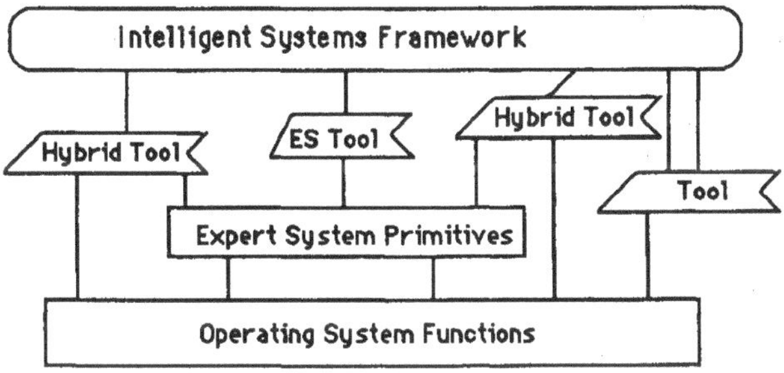

Fig 1. Tool-Oriented Architecture for Building Intelligent Systems

The control system of the framework can be as simple as the Operating System shell, but is usually an expert system which has detailed knowledge about the set of applications within the system and the best ways in which to use them. The framework also provides a set of ES Tools for performing standard operations required in an expert system and a set of facilities that can be used for building expert systems, and/or Tools which combine both ES and traditional techniques ("Hybrid" Tools). Existing application programs (shown as "Tool" in the figure) are also executed from within the Intelligent Systems Framework. The applications can communicate with each other using the normal host operating system facilities (typically the file system), or the facilities provided by the framework. The framework facilitates interactions among expert systems and conventional systems to enable the generation of intelligent cooperative systems.

ES or conventional system (CS) normally use its own data systems e.g., knowledge bases (KB) and knowledge data stores (KDS) for ES, data bases (DB) and files for CS etc. The framework supports the cooperation between CSs and ESs, and among ESs or CSs themselves. Communication among these systems can be realized using e.g., either files or i/o channels (shown by dashed lines), or the framework communication primitives (shown by dotted lines) in Figure 2.

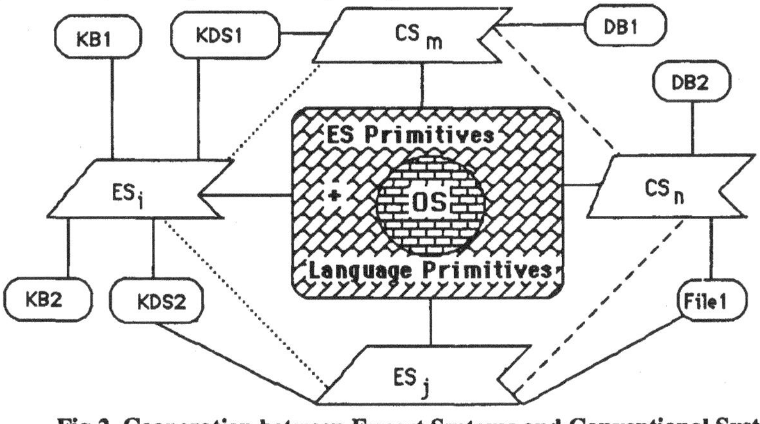

Fig 2. Cooperation between Expert Systems and Conventional Systems

If the source of the program is available then it is possible to modify it to use the framework data storage and/or communication primitives which will allow it to easily pass information to other tools within the system that also use these primitives, as illustrated by CS_m. If the existing program cannot be modified then it is necessary to write an interface tool that can create the files and other i/o data required by the program. This is normally done by generating a small ES tool that interfaces to KBs and KDSs on one side and generates the data required by the program on the other, shown as ES_j in the figure. This interfacing process is very straight-forward for batch-style programs and interactive programs that accept command-like input from their input stream. In fact it should be possible to automatically generate such an interface process given a description of the input data formats and the sequencing of the i/o as might be modeled by, for example, a petri net. However, modern interactive programs that have a GUI front-end can be difficult to integrate into such cooperative systems.

3.1 Implementation

ES primitives[2] and conventional language primitives, such as the built-in data and control structures of the implementation language, have been used to construct various capabilities required by an intelligent system.The results of those efforts are embodied in an architecture called INDEX[4]. INDEX focuses on the development of ES capabilities within conventional software environments. The components for building expert systems (or knowledge-based systems) are organized in a layered architecture ranging from the primitive, domain-independent layer to higher level capabilities that include standard inference control, domain-dependent support and expert system tools. Expert systems for a particular domain area can be built efficiently by tailoring the general capabilities offered within the INDEX architecture into specific ones. The framework provides a mechanism that will allow the intelligent systems generated from INDEX to be used cooperatively, i.e., producing various intelligent cooperative products. Figure 3 describes connections between INDEX facilities and the framework.

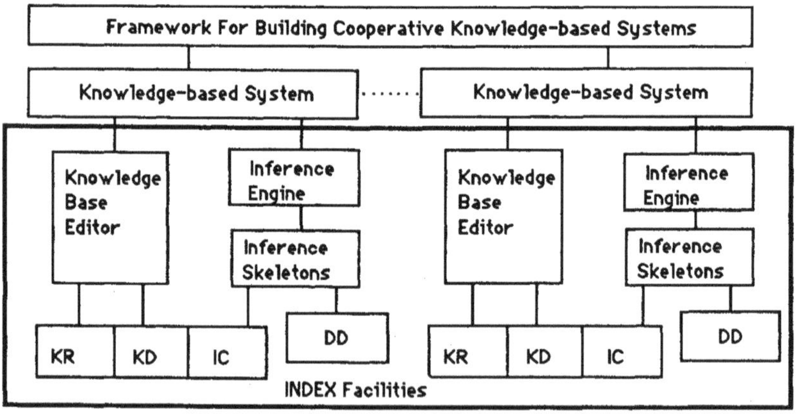

Fig 3. Building Cooperative Systems

The modules at the bottom of INDEX comprise the primitives layer: KR for knowledge representation, KD for knowledge data storage and communication, IC for inference control. These facilities can be directly called by a conventional programming language using an object library. The domain-dependent (DD) routines are skeletal routines that are fleshed out by the system builder to provide application-dependent semantics and domain knowledge interpretation for an expert system. Inference skeletons provide a higher-level of inference support that allow a variety of different styles of inference engines to be constructed easily. ES tools such as the knowledge base editor and standard inference engine are located at the tools layer. An Expert System in INDEX is formed by linking an inference engine (which may be either one of the standard engines or one produced for the application by modification of an inference skeleton) with the Domain-Dependent routines for the application and the low-level Primitive Modules, to produce an executable program. The primitives have been implemented using host environment facilities such as the file- system and inter-process communication routines of Unix.

4. An Example Application - MultiMedia Support

Modern multimedia services are another possible method for improving corporate efficiency. Facilities such as video+voice communication, multimedia documents containing video, sound, etc., can be used to improve and co-ordinate information flow between divisions. The example used here to demonstrate the capabilities of the framework is a system dealing with fault diagnosis and maintenance problems in a multimedia system. The major problem in multimedia diagnosis is that there are so many different components which have been handled traditionally by separate service divisions, e.g. audio-visual, telephone networks, etc.

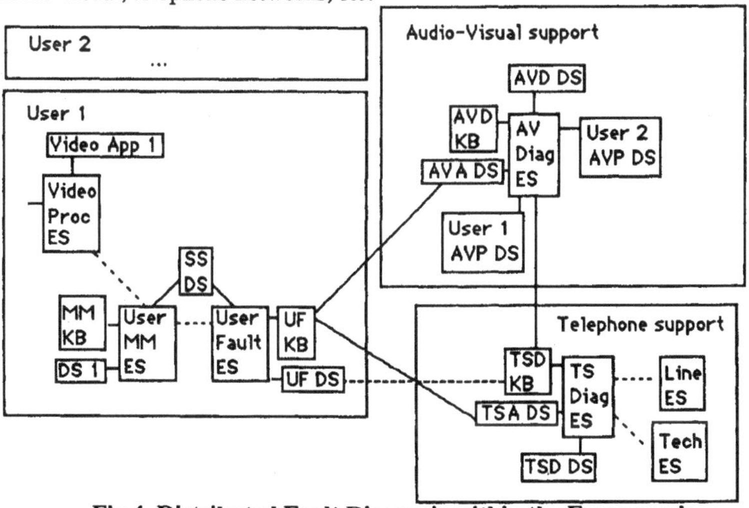

Fig 4. Distributed Fault Diagnosis within the Framework

In this example (Figure 4), the user's MultiMedia Workstation uses an expert system (User MM ES) for overall control of the facilities. This ES uses other existing application programs or expert systems for controlling individual parts of the system such as the video processing sub-system (VideoProc ES which, in turn, invokes existing traditional programs such as Video App 1 which might be an image compression program written in C, for example). Much of the domain details can not be described here because of the space limitations.

6. Related Work

ABE[5] is a new generation of software architecture which addresses the problem of combining conventional computing functions with knowledge processing capabilities to build intelligent systems. It attempts to solve the major problems of AI tools, such as information reuse, large-scaled application problems etc, by importation of existing software, including conventional and knowledge processing tools. There is a lack of interfaces with conventional programs where the software components at various levels of ABE can be directly used. It does not represent a generic solution of how intelligent cooperative systems can be built using existing software resources in conventional software environments. It ,therefore, does not provide immediate benefits to typical business operating environments. Jennings and Mamdani[6] addressed the cooperative problem solving by analyzing the intentionality (local behaviour) and responsibility (external behaviour) of each involved system. However, the algorithms (protocols) for specifying the local actions of a system and its interactions with outside systems in a cooperative problem solving process are fixed. It is unclear how the approach can be feasibly applied to solve various business tasks, e.g., cooperation of ES programs and existing conventional programs, based on the limited resources in the environment.

7.Conclusion

We attempt to use the framework as a generic methodology for building cooperative expert systems within traditional software environments. Multimedia service has been chosen as an application example to test the effectiveness of the framework capabilities. However this solution approach is only one of the many different types of systems that can be generated using the framework. The impact of the techniques briefly described in this article, will be significant on organizations that adopt them. Business divisions, previously isolated, will be able to share, distribute and process information in very effective ways, many of which currently cannot be envisaged.

Acknowledgments

Muriel De Beler provides useful feedback in improving the inference capabilities of the system. Nitin Indurkhya 's comments on an earlier version of the article are very much appreciated. The authors are also grateful to the comments given by the anonymous reviewers in shaping up this final draft. Permission of the Director of Research, Telecom Australia to publish the above article is hereby acknowledged.

References

1. R.Irrang, V.R.Kumar and C.Chung,"Intelligent Systems in Australian Industry - A Study of Current Status and Future Trends". CSIRO Technical Report, TR-LA-93-01, 1993.
2. W.Dai and S.L.Wright, "Primitives for constructing rule-based expert systems". Proceedings of 4th Australian Joint Conference on Artificial Intelligence, Perth, November, 1990, pp. 432-447.
3. D.B. Smith, P.W. Oman, "Software tools in context". IEEE Software, May, 1990, pp.15-19.
4. W.Dai and S.L.Wright, "INDEX : An Architecture That Integrates Expert System Techniques Within Conventional Software Environment". Proceedings of 5th International Joint Europe/USA Conference on Expert Systems Application and Artificial Intelligence". Paris, December, 1993. (To appear)
5. L.D.Erman,J.S.Lark and F.Hayes-Roth,"ABE: An environment for engineering intelligent systems". IEEE transactions on software engineering, vol. 14, no. 12, December 1988, pp. 1758-1770.
6. N.R.Jennings and E.H.Mamdani, "Using Joint Responsibility to Coordinate Collaborative Problem Solving in Dynamic Environments". AAAI,1992, pp. 269-275.

Polarity Analysis to Determine "Promising Operators" for Heuristic Repair Algorithms

Kerstin Voigt*
Computer Science Department, Rutgers University, New Brunswick, NJ 08903, U.S.A.

Abstract

We present a polarity analysis method called 'RAP-PA' that automatically compiles descriptions of "promising operators" for heuristic repair problem solvers that solve *resource assignment problems*. We demonstrate with empirical data that *a priori* knowledge of promising operators can reduce the effective *branching factor* of the search space at run-time. Thereby, statistically significant improvement of the problem-solving performance of heuristic repair can be achieved.

1 Introduction.

Heuristic repair algorithms typically search a space of "repaired" artifacts in a best-first, or hillclimbing fashion. Best-first search heuristic repair has been effective in solving difficult constraint satisfaction problems efficiently[1,2]. The *design* of such heuristic repair algorithms requires the derivation of an evaluation function that adequately measures the degree of constraint satisfaction exhibited by the artifact. The efficiency of the resulting algorithm not only depends on the informedness of the evaluation function, but also on the skill with which the evaluation function is put to use whenever deciding on a next modification. When evaluation functions are expensive, the ability to discriminate between repair operators that are "promising" in their ability to lead to a solution, and those that are not, can greatly reduce the branching factor, and, thus, the "cost per node" in the repair space.

This paper includes a brief presentation of the method RAP-PA, and some empirical results obtained with RAP-PA in the domains of *2D-floorplanning*, and *timetable design*. A longer, and more comprehensive version of this paper is available[3].

2 The Polarity Analysis Method RAP-PA

"Promising Operators." We introduce the notion of "promising operators" with an example problem from the domain of 2D-floorplanning. A *floorplan* is a collection

*The research reported here was supported in part by the National Science Foundation (NSF) under Grant Number IRI-9021607, and in part by the Defense Advanced Research Projects Agency (DARPA) under DARPA-funded NASA Grant NAG2-645. The opinions expressed in this paper are those of the author and do not reflect any policies, either expressed or implied, of any granting agencies. I thank Doug Smith for introducing me to polarity analysis. This paper also benefits from comments by Chris Tong and Tom Ellman.

of rectangles which we also call *rooms*. A *house* is also a rectangle. We formulate the following constraint in this domain: *"The rooms in an n-room floorplan fill the area of the house completely."* We will also refer to this constraint as the "fill house" constraint.

Each rectangular room can be defined by four parameters: an x-coordinate X, a y-coordinate Y, a length L and a width W. We assume a problem solving scenario in which an instance of an n-room floorplan has been generated, and in which all rooms are inside the house and do not overlap. The task we are interested in consists of modifying the floorplan so that the entire house area is filled by the n rooms. Thereby, rooms are to remain nonoverlapping and inside the house. When preserving these constraints, only increases in L and W can possibly lead to more filling of the house. We say that increase of L and W characterize "promising operators", and we encode these two categories by the tuples <increase, L> and <increase, W>.

Resource Assignment Problems. Resource assignment problems (RAPs) constrain the ways by which consumers in some collection of consumers, and resources in some collection of resources may be assigned to each other. In conjunction with each declarative specification of an abstract resource assignment problem, a generic *evaluation function* can be defined. An evaluation function quantifies the degree to which the corresponding resource assignment constraint is satisfied.

Evaluation functions are inputs to the method called 'RAP-PA'. RAP-PA is based on the principles of a known technique[4,5] called "polarity analysis" The style of polarity analysis reported here offers a way by which desired changes of the evaluation function value can be propagated through the definition of the evaluation function back to the artifact (the function's argument). Based on the thus determined "polarity" of the datatype of the artifact, the desired change in the evaluation function is reformulated as descriptions of promising operators.

"Utilize All Resources." One class of resource assignment problem is characterized by the requirement that consumers and resources be assigned to each other such that all resource are utilized. We call this constraint the "utilize all resources" constraint. More formally, this constraint can be written as: $\forall r[substruct(r, Resources) \Rightarrow \exists c(substruct(c, Consumers) \wedge assign(c, r))]$. The relations *substruct* and *assign* are predicate symbols of an *abstraction language* RAPL. We designed RAPL specifically to express concerns of consumer-resource assignment abstractly, that is, without reference to any specific application domain. The relation *substruct* abstractly denotes any type of substructure-superstructure relationship between its two arguments. Similarly, the relation *assign* abstractly captures the notion that both arguments are 'assigned' to each other (meaning that they relate to each other in some fashion, excluding any relationships of identity). RAPL sentences can be specialized into resource assignment constraints in specific application domains by instantiating the abstract relations *substruct* and *assign* with suitable domain specific predicates. The constraint "utilize all resources" abstractly captures, for example, the "fill house" constraint in 2D-floorplanning. The latter is formally expressed as: $\forall pt[point\_of\_rect(pt, House) \Rightarrow \exists rm(member(rm, Floorplan) \wedge point\_in\_rect(rm, pt))]$.

The specification of the abstract resource assignment problem "utilize all resources" includes an abstractly formulated *evaluation function*:

$$ef(Consumers, Resources) = \\ Count(r : substruct(r, Resources) \wedge \exists c[substruct(c, Consumers) \wedge assign(c, r)])$$

Function ef counts the number of resources that are assigned to at least one consumer. A greater count indicates a greater degree of constraint satisfaction. The evaluation function for "fill house" is derived by instantiating the abstract evaluation function with the constraint-specific details. We obtain:

$$ef(Floorplan, House) = \\ Count(pt : point\_of\_rect(pt, House) \wedge \\ \exists rm[member(rm, Floorplan) \wedge point\_in\_rect(rm, pt)])$$

Polarity Analysis. Polarity analysis applies rules ('pa-rules') which provide information about the effects qualitative changes in the values of the arguments of *monotonic functions* on the value of the function. The general form of pa-rules for a n-ary function f is given as[5]: $f(x_1, ..., x_n)^p \Rrightarrow f(x_1^{p_1}, ..., x_n^{p_n})$, where $p, p_1, ..., p_n \in \{+, -, \pm\}$. For example, the rule $f(x)^+ \Rrightarrow f(x^-)$ indicates that the value of function f monotonically increases with decreasing values of its argument x; $x' < x$ is a *sufficient condition* for $f(x') > f(x)$.

Instances of RAP evaluation functions can be *nonmonotonic*. For such functions we are not able to formulate pa-rules of the above standard form. Therefore, we propose a *weaker type of pa-rule* which can be formulated for any nonmonotonic function. One possible pa-rule for a nonmonotonic function g (here: unary) is written as $g(x)^+ \approx\!> g(x^-)$. Indicated by the new symbol '$\approx\!>$', this rules expresses the weaker statement: $g(x') > g(x)$ is a *necessary condition* for $x' < x$.

With the abstract constraint "utilize all resources" we explicitly associate the abstract weak pa-rule:

$$Count(r : substruct(r, Resources) \wedge \\ \exists c[substruct(c, Consumers) \wedge assign(c, r)])^+ \approx\!> Count(r : ...assign(c, r)^+ ...)$$

This rule states that greater numbers of $assign(c, r)$ predicates that evaluate to true have the potential of increasing the value of the evaluation function ef. For the evaluation function for "fill house", the above abstract pa-rule is instantiated to:

$$Count(pt : point\_of\_rect(pt, House) \wedge ...)^+ \approx\!> Count(...point\_in\_rect(rm, pt)^+ ...)$$

This rule states that an increase in the evaluation function ef can potentially be obtained if more instances of the predicate *point_in_rect* evaluate to *true*.

A Trace of RAP-PA. We trace an example that shows how polarity analysis derives promising operator descriptions for "fill house". The first step in the analysis instantiates the pa-rule associated with the abstract "utilize all resources" constraint with terms specific to "fill house". According to this rule, greater degrees of satisfaction can potentially be achieved if more instances of *point_in_rect* evaluate to *true*. Thus, our trace begins with (1) $point\_in\_rect(rm, pt)^+$.

Since *point_in_rect* is a nonprimitive predicate, there does not exist a pa-rule that is directly associated with it. Instead the polarities of the arguments must be derived in a bottom-up fashion from the predicates that make up the definition of *point_in_rect*. In our adopted clausal notation, *point_in_rect* is defined as: $point\_in\_rect(x, y) \leftarrow pts = rect\_points(x), member(y, pts)$. ($y$ is a point in rectangle x if it is a member in the set of points pts of x.) Suppose that the defining function *rect_points* and predicate *member* are primitive, and we can find the following weak pa-rules explicitly associated with them: (P1) $rect\_points(x)^+ \rightsquigarrow rect\_points(x^+)$, and (P2) $member(x, y)^+ \rightsquigarrow member(x, y^+)$. The annotated predicate $point\_in\_rect(rm, pt)^+$ is replaced by the similarly annotated body of the predicate's definition. This yields: (2) $pts = rect\_points(rm), member(pt, pts)^+$.

The polarity + is propagated into the body from right to left, first annotating the predicate *member*. We obtain: (3) $[pts = rect\_points(rm), member(pt, pts)^+]$.

The application of rule (P2) for the primitive predicate *member* yields: (4) $[pts = rect\_points(rm), member(pt, pts^+)]$.

The variable pts stores the value computed by the function *rect_points*. Therefore, + is transcribed from *member* to *rect_points*. We continue with (5) $rect\_points(rm)^+$. Now rule (P1) yields (6) $rect\_points(rm^+)$.

The annotated variable rm^+ is an argument in the original predicate $point\_in\_rect(rm, pt)$. It denotes a room which is a rectangle. Assume that the datatype *Rectangle* is defined in terms of parameters X, Y, L, and W. We make the datatype of rm explicit by writing (7) $Rectangle\colon\{X, Y, L, W\}^+$. Suppose that $Rectangle\colon\{X, Y, L, W\}$ is a primitive datatype and, in analogy to predicates, the following pa-rule is explicitly provided: (P3) $Rectangle\colon\{X, Y, L, W\}^+ \rightsquigarrow Rectangle\colon\{X, Y, L^+, W^+\}$. Thus, one application of (P3) to the result in step (7) yields (8) $Rectangle\colon\{X, Y, L^+, W^+\}$.

The polarity analysis process terminates after translating the obtained annotated parameters L^+ and W^+ into the characterizations of promising operators for "fill house". They are (9) {<increase,L>, <increase, W>}. The result of RAP-PA states that increases in the values of the parameters L (length) and W (width) of the rooms of *Floorplan* can achieve greater degrees of satisfaction of the "fill house" constraint.

3 Experimental Results and Discussion.

We show some of the characterizations of promising operators that our Common Lisp implementation of RAP-PA has automatically produced for constraints in two domains. Each of the below tables lists descriptions of *all* possible operators, and contrasts them with the descriptions for promising operators. 'prom:all' is the ratio of the number of promising operator classes over the total number of operator classes. Smaller ratios are more favorable because the operator selection phase of a heuristic repair problem solver can restrict the costly computation of evaluation function values to only those operators that show some *a priori* promise of improvement.

Floorplanning. When rooms are not allowed to overlap, and must be inside the house , only <increase L> and <increase W> out of eight types of operators are "promising" with respect to "fill house". These results are consistent with the outcome of the above trace.

all operators	promising operators	ratio prom:all
increase X, Y, L, W; decrease X, Y, L, W	increase L, W	2:8

Timetable design. A variety of other generic types of resource assignment problems exist. For instance, the abstract problem "assign resources uniquely" requires that each resource be assigned to at most one consumer. The constraint in the domain of NP-complete timetable design "no lecturer should be scheduled for two locations at the same day" is an instance of this problem class. The artifact to be generated and repaired is a *timetable* which consists of a collection of n entries. Each *entry* is defined in terms of five parameters: *Lect* (lecturer), *Day* (day), *Sem* (seminar), *Pay* (salary), and *Loc* (location). Each parameter addresses concerns that are relevant to one or more meaningful constraints in the domain of timetable design. However, only two out of the five possible types of repair operators – <change *Lect*> and <change *Day*> – are promising in the repair of timetables with overlapping locations and days.

all operators	promising operators	ratio prom:all
change $Lect, Day, Sem, Pay, Loc$	change $Lect, Day$	2:5

Changes of the value of the parameter *Loc* are not listed among the promising operators. This omission is intentional. When two entries overlap, there are exactly two changes to *Loc* parameters that are improving: assigning the location of the first entry to the second entry, or vice versa. The characterization of such repair operators would have to capture the *condition* that overlap be present between pairs of entries, which is beyond the representational power of our language for specifying promising operators. In addition, the run-time usage of such operator descriptions to compute the appropriate *instances* of operators would be more costly. Therefore, by omitting this category of operators, we trade some amount of problem solving completeness for the ease and efficiency of compile-time expression and run-time computation of promising operators.

Utility. Earlier we stated that the cost per node can be reduced considerably, when the computation of evaluation function values is restricted to only those operators that *a priori* show promise of improving the artifact. The table below shows some empirical measurements of CPU times of heuristic repair problem solvers that do and for those that do not take advantage of a priori knowledge of promising operators.

CPU secs to satisfy "fill house" for 3 rooms						
Heuristic Repair	House (length × width)					
	10×10	12×12	15×15	20×20	25×25	30×30
HR-prom	20.9	27.7	135.1	183.5	270.5	689.7
HR-all	27.1	72.1	1078.6	1728.4	3602.3	10981.0

The data confirm the conjectured utility of the characterizations of promising operators. Larger house dimensions imply larger branching factors which in turn lead to potentially higher costs per node when examining alternative repair moves. The first type of heuristic repair problem solver (HR-prom) utilizes the operator descriptions {<increase, L>, <increase, W>} to restrict computation of evaluation function values to only those repair operators that increase the coverage of room. The second type of problem solver (HR-all) applies the evaluation function to *all* alternative operators (increases and decreases of the parameters X, Y, L, and W for each room). The data show that HR-prom performs markedly better than HR-all. For the larger house dimensions, a paired t-test shows that the performance difference in favor of HR-prom is statistically significant at an error probability of $< 1\%$.

Constraint Incorporation. One of the goals in automatically designing efficient algorithms is to be able take advantage of constraint knowledge in early phases of the problem solving process[7]. The polarity method RAP-PA can be viewed as a knowledge compilation technique because it compiles knowledge about the constraint into descriptions of promising operators. By letting the operator selection phase of heuristic repair make use of promising operators, constraint knowledge has effectively been incorporated into the problem solver. Thus, RAP-PA is a new addition to the currently known techniques of automatic constraint incorporation.

References

1. B. Selman, HJ. Levesque, and D. Mitchell, *A New Method for Solving Hard Satisfiability Problems*, in Proceedings of AAAI-92, San Jose, July 1992.
2. S. Minton, M.D. Johnston, A.B. Philips, and P. Laird, *Minimizing Conflicts: A Heuristic Repair Method for Constraint Satisfaction and Scheduling Problems*, Artificial Intelligence, 58(1-3), December 1992.
3. K. Voigt, *Polarity Analysis to Determine "Promising Operators" for Heuristic Repair Algorithms that Solve Resource Assignment Problems*, Techreport, LCSR-TR-206, Rutgers University, 1993.
4. Z. Manna and R. Waldinger, *Special Relations in Automated Deduction.*, JACM, 33(1), January 1986.
5. D. Smith. *Constructing Specification Morphisms*, Kestrel Institute Technical Report KES.U.92.1, Kestrel Institute, April 1992.
6. W.K. Braudaway, *Knowledge Compilation for Incorporating Constraints*, Ph.D. Thesis, Rutgers University, 1991.
7. C. Tong and D. Sriram, editors, *Artificial Intelligence in Engineering Design*, Volume I, Academic Press, 1992.

TOITS a Generic Architecture for a Task Oriented Intelligent Tutoring System

Leila Alem and Maria Lee

CSIRO Division of Information Technology,
Locked Bag 17, North Ryde, NSW 2113,
Australia
[leila,lee]@syd.dit.csiro.au

ABSTRACT

The recent focus of CBT systems is to incorporate many innovative concepts in the acquisition, representation, management of expert knowledge and hypermedia technology. The advantage of combining those technologies is that all knowledge relevant to the expert system would be centralised into a hypertext knowledge base which the experts can peruse and verify before the knowledge is encoded into a representation scheme (12).The advance was realise that systems able to support a rich learning interaction. need to be built if an Intelligent Educational System (IES) was to show any glimmering of intelligence (2). Our aim is to encourage the learner to take initiative by providing assistance and explanation, rather than directive tutoring. We present our approach called "learning by doing with explanation".

Keywords: Computer-Based Training, Task Model, Intelligent Tutoring System

1. Introduction

Learning is not given, or done to a student by a tutor, but is created by the learner as the result of performing actions and experiencing their consequences in the environment (8). In fact to promote learning we should build systems that are tools for rich interactions instead of computer tutors. Focussing on learning that centres on tasks mattering to the learner suggests a constructive view of learning. This view adopts the slogan " learning by doing" (3) This phrase may suggest that a task level may be sufficient but Cumming and Self work suggests that a discussion level is also present and conclude that the phrase should be more accurately " learning by doing with reflection " (8). The learner not only does a task, but in addition monitors the attempts and assesses progress. Clancey among others suggests that a good Intelligent Educational System (IES) should be able not only to help with doing an exercise, but also to say why the exercise is helpful and how it fits with learning goals and acquires knowledge from the learner in view to improve its efficiency (7). To give more complete support for learning, a computer system must also be able to give some explanation and guidance about the task activities. Whilc thc importance of explanation is generally recognised, tutoring systems often fall short in this respect.

In this paper, we present our approach called "learning by doing with explanation", where the learning process is described in terms of the learner working at the task level while simultaneously at a higher level the system is providing explanation, guidance and control in a learning interaction. Our aim is to promote learner participation by providing effective user-task interaction.

Section two presents the task analysis approach, section three presents our task model followed by an example, section four presents the generic architecture of a Task Oriented Intelligent Tutoring System called TOITS followed by the conclusion.

2. Toward effective user-task interaction, the task analysis approach

Design of systems for effective user-task interaction depends on cognitive task analysis. Task analysis describes the knowledge that a user must have in order to carry out tasks on a device or system. It is a representation of the " how to do it ? ", knowledge that is required by a system in order to get the intended tasks accomplished. Many task models have been proposed in the literature as a conceptual entity for modelling:

a. the reasoning process (6,7),
b. the user activity being expert or non expert (11,9),
c. the problem solving (5).

Our concern is to model the user activity during the learning process in order to provide guidance and support. Adopting the task analysis approach is also a way to characterise a set of design decisions from the point of view of the user. It leads to a user-centred design that focuses on the user rather than on the system. It is also a description of what the user must learn, and so could act as a basis for training.

3. Proposed Task Model

Our concern is to model the user activity during the learning process in order to provide guidance and support. Our proposed task model is used for modelling the learner activity, it is aiming at

- monitoring student's activity and performance
- assisting the learning process
- modelling task-related knowledge
- describing what the user must learn with access to explanation.

Our task model will describe the user actions and the interface feedback. As pointed out by Boy and Falzon learning relies very much on a cooperation between the assistant system and the learner (4,10). The goal of our task model is to offer a structured way to describe the cooperative performance of a task between the user and the system.

A task contains knowledge about its :

- function, ie the goal or objective of the task ,
- structure, ie the action plan that enables the execution of the task
- behaviour, ie the status of the task
- assistance capabilities, ie its related explanations, reference to relevant part of an electronic book or appropriate tool to be used by the user.

An activity is a task. Activities are not predefined things. During an activity, a model is in a transition state between two landmark states . A task can be decomposed into sub tasks. Each task corresponds to one goal. How each goal is achieved is determined by the action-plan of the task. The concept of task is shown in Figure 1.

The notion of action plan allows direction of user activity in a collaborative way. Proving intelligent assistance to the learner means designing action plans in collaboration with the learner. Thus an action plan is dynamic, its execution is directed in collaboration with the learner (2).

Tokens and status information are associated with each task. The status of the task is represented as:

- ready - ready to perform this task,
- wait - waiting for other tasks to be finished,
- undefined - the task might or might not be performed,

• achieved - the task has been successfully preformed. At this stage the result and marking are available in the respective fields.

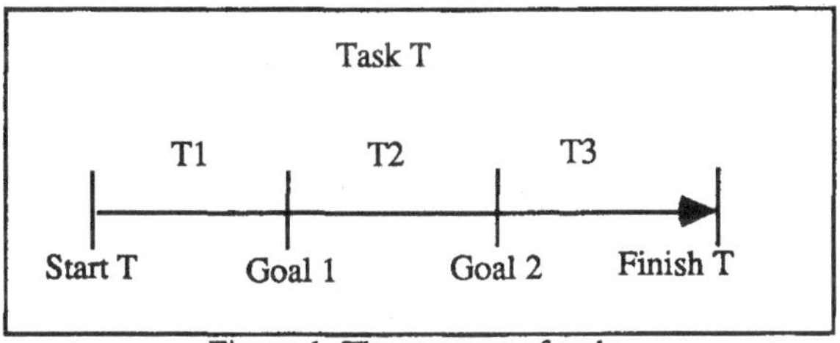

Figure 1. The concept of task.

The assistance capabilities are acquired from the expert domain knowledge and are represented in term of :

• Explanations that are context-sensitive to the learning process,
• Book References providing cross references to the relevant sections of an electronic book which contains domain knowledge, and
• Tool to indicate the recommended tools to be used while performing the task at hand.

We provide a simple example of a task model in order to illustrate the framework sketched in the previous section. The application concerns identifying vessel classes (this application is described in more detail in section four) Figure 2 shows the task-structure.

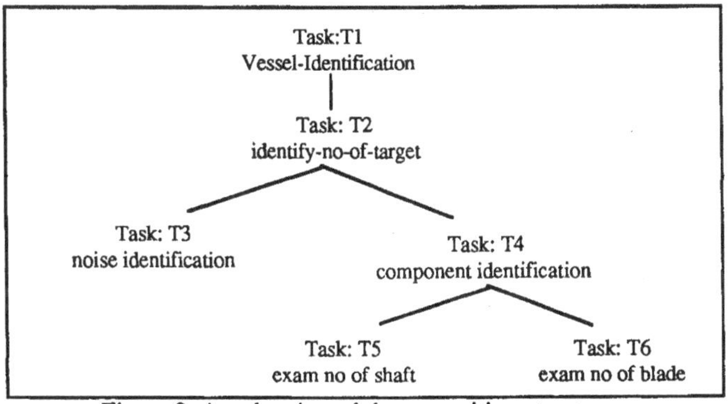

Figure 2. A task-oriented decomposition structure.

The goal of vessel-identification task is to determine the vehicle class. The vehicle identification process involves the selection of the most likely vessel class or classes from those which are known or are likely to be within the operational region. The initial tactical evaluation is to determine the number of targets to be identified. Once the target numbers are known, then the analysis will continue by attempting to identifying each target separately.
Task T1 is represented as :

Task: T1
Goal: identify the vehicle classes
Action-plan: [T2, T3, T4]

Task: T2
Goal: determine number of targets
Action-Plan: user_action [TargetNo]
Explanation: "to determine the number of vehicles represented. This is may be done by examining the Doppler shifts appearing on the lines."
Reference: chapter 1 Component Identification
Tool: use "slop tool"

The component analysis for a particular vehicle begins by attempting to determine the number of propeller shafts the vehicle has. The explanation of performing this first step is provided in the task. Once the shaft component has been identified the number of propeller blades must be determined. The result of this sub-goal returns to the top-level task.
Task: T4
Goal: determine shaft and blade components
Action-plan: [T5, T6]

The task process is controlled by the task engine, which is implemented in the M.4^{TM} expert system shell. The task engine describes the sequence of the tasks, in which order and under which conditions the task are activated and how they interact.

4. TOITS architecture

The proposed task model has been used for designing TOITS a Task Oriented Intelligent Tutoring System. Figure 3 shows TOITS' s generic architecture.

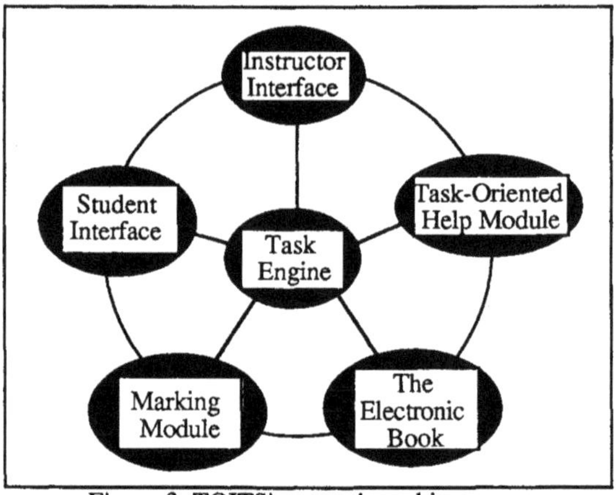

Figure 3. TOITS' s generic architecture.

TOITS offers a generic task-oriented approach for marking, supporting and explaining of the learning process. The kernel of the system is the task engine, which manages and controls the task activities. This system supports a rich learning interaction and presents learning as a more repaid and long lasting activity. TOITS is composed of :

(1). The task engine
It controls and monitors the task activities, which enables the system to provide guidance and explanation of the learning scenario. The task engine schedules the execution sequence of tasks and indicates the status of tasks.

(2). The student interface
The functions of the student interface are:

- to provide a learning scenario. The learning scenario are the management of student transaction with the goal to be achieved. The transactions are done by providing tests, assessing performance, and managing feedback.
- to provide guidance/explanation when the student is undertaking assessment and examination,
- to provide a on-line marking,
- to be able to communicate with the instructor.

(3). The task-oriented help module
We use our task model to describe the learning process including explanation, guidance and control functions. The levels of support and guidance can be catalogued as:

a. provide guidance regarding possible problem solutions
b. access to the structure database and cross-links to the tutorial
c. provide no assistance.

We provide a minimum of three levels of support and interaction during the student learning/assessing process. Level-one help provides a full help framework, which includes the above a and b type' supports; level-two help is a partial help framework, which includes above b type of support; level-three gives no help, the user will be expected to solve the problem without any support.

(4). The instructor interface
The instructor interface defines the problem specification and provides analysis methods for problem solving. Unlike "classical" CBT systems, there is no continuous dialogue between the student and the instructor. In this interface, the instructor provides on-line assistance during student performance evaluation. Hence, feedback can be managed so that instructional strategies can be individualised for the student.

(5). The marking module
The marking module controls the student's activity and scores the student's learning. The marking schema structures the students activities into hierarchical task levels corresponding with the three level help framework. The high level tasks represent the major steps during the learning process whereas the sub tasks are minor learning steps. This approach offers three types of marking: continuous marking, marking at major phases and final marking.

(6) An electronic book
The electronic book constitutes the sonar tutorial. It is composed of simulation tools used in the tutorial. It combines hypertext and multi-media techniques to present interactive domain knowledge to the user/student. It generates a relational database to support end-users during practice.

The generic architecture of TOITS provides a comprehensive framework for supporting, marking and giving guidance during learning interaction. TOITS' design promotes the learning process by providing an effective user-task interaction. The following section describes a specific application of TOITS.

An application of TOITS has been developed for a sonar tutorial. The system provides a scenario in which the student is asked to identify vessels classes. A prototype system has been built in Toolbook™ running on a PC under Windows™ using M.4™ expert system shell.

5. Conclusion

We have demonstrated that the task analysis approach provides a suitable way of structuring knowledge during the learning process. The system enables on-line control of student progress, which is used as a basis for providing assistance that is sensitive to the current student evaluation/assessment. We have presented our proposed task model that we have used for the design of TOITS a Task Oriented Intelligent Tutoring System and then we have presented a specific application of TOITS for a sonar tutorial. In TOITS, the learning process is described in terms of the learner working at the task level, by undertaking tasks while simultaneously at a higher level the system is providing explanation, guidance and control in a learning interaction. Our approach enables a student to manipulate and control his/her progress directly. Such an approach can improve the quality and cost effectiveness of the training and learning process. The ability to provide context-sensitive assistance to the learner can help promote future computer based training to devices that really teach.

References

1. L. Alem and M. Lee, " An Intelligent tutoring System for sonar application in Australia" to be publish the proceedings of The second World Congress on Expert Systems, Portugal, January 94.

2. L. Alem and M. Lee, "An intelligent Assistance in a learning interaction" to be publish in AI-ED'93 proceedings, the World Conference on Artificial Intelligence in Education, Edinburgh, August 93.

3. Anzai & H. Simon, The theory of learning by doing. Psychological review, 86, 126-140, 1979.

4. G. Boy. Intelligent Assistant Systems. Academic Press, Harcourt Brace Jovanovich Publisher, 1990.

5. J. Breuker and B. Wielinga, "Models of expertise in knowledge acquisition", Topics in Expert Systems Design: Methodologies and Tools, 1989, North Holland Publishing Co, G. Guida & C. Tasso eds., pp. 1-37.

6. B. Chandrasekaran, Toward a functional architecture for intelligence based on generic information processing tasks. IJCAI 87, August 1987, Vol. 2 pp.1183-1192.

7. W. Clancey, Knowledge based tutoring : the GUIDON program. Cambridge, MA: MIT press, 1987.

8. Cumming & Self 90, Intelligent educational systems : identifying and decoupling the conversational levels. In Instructional Science 19 : 1-17, 1990.Kluwer Academic Publishers.

9. R. Dieng and B. Trousse. 3DKAT : A dependency -driven dynamic knowledge acquisition tool. Third Symposium on knowledge engineering, Madrid 1988.

10. P. Falzon. Cognitive Ergonomics, Understanding, Learning and Design Human-Computer Interaction. Academic Press 1990.

11. Tueni Li and Fares. AMS : A knowledge-based approach to task representation, manipulation and organisation. COIS-88, Palo Alto.

12. T. L. Wells, "Hypertext As A Means for Knowledge Acquisition", J SIGART Newsletter, 108, April 1989, pp. 136-138.

Knowledge Representation

A Dynamic Model Base For Student Modelling

Mark Kuzmycz

School of Computing and Mathematics, Deakin University, Geelong, Victoria 3217, Australia

ABSTRACT

This paper examines a technique for student modelling called Focal Modelling which manipulates the problem space (model base), depending upon the student, producing a concise model of the student. This technique has the advantage of allowing models to be created that would otherwise be too large. Also it enables students to be modeled more effectively.

1. Introduction

Creating a student model for an Intelligent Tutoring system requires the system designer to decide on what level of granularity the modelling system will model. It is very difficult to correctly determine the best level of granularity considering that every student is different so that what may seem to be the ideal level of abstraction to model the student may be in fact too coarse for another. A way around this is to create a modelling system where the granularity is very fine. Unfortunately, this creates difficulties for the modelling system making it large and slow to converge on the correct model. Also, if the model is large it can be difficult to extract precise information about the student from the model as this information is hidden amongst a mass of information.

This paper presents a technique called Focal Modelling attempts to address the problem of selecting the granularity of the elements in the model base (model's building blocks) by dynamically adding and removing the elements as required.

2. Focal Modelling

Focal modelling is a tool that maintains a model base to contain only the elements needed to model the student. Focal Modelling sits on top of an existing student modelling system called the Relational Based Modelling System (RBM). RBM is a machine learning approach to student modelling similar to that of Feature Based Modelling[1]. The knowledge components of RBM consist of action relations (describes the student's response), task relations (describe the task (problem) presented to the student) and associations (mappings between an action relation and a set of task relations such that whenever a problem contains the task relations in the action relation the student will respond with a response that will contain the action relation in the association). Focal modelling adds and removes the task and action relations to obtain a concise model base. Focal modelling imitates various aspects of human cognition such as short term memory to handle concept changes and relation deletion of fruitless relations. This enables the modelling system (RBM) to only contain information which is uniquely related to the student. This system gives rise to a new type of student modelling that tailors the model's descriptive power (problem space) depending upon the student. This technique is akin to methods that select which model base to use to model the student by the observation of the student's protocol[2,3]. However, this technique differs by it's continual (dynamic) adaptation of the model base.

3. Developing The Model Base

The initial model base of the RBM system consists of no task or action relations. Therefore the modelling system is unable to (initially) model the student. As time progresses, the modelling system observes the responses made by the student and extends the model base so that it can "accurately" model the student by adding action and task relations to the model base. The development of the model base is constructed around four components (Figure 1): the current model base, model base evaluator, memory and a model constructor.

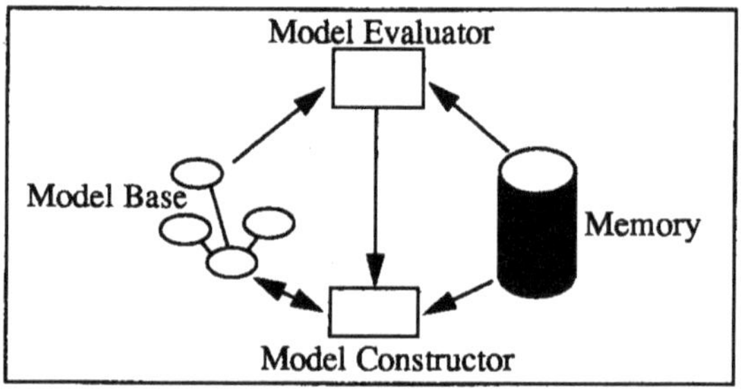

Figure 1: Model Base Development

3.1. System memory.

The modelling system stores the examples of completed tasks to use as evidence in producing new model bases. In an environment where concept changes are common (as is the case for intelligent tutoring systems) it is important to realize that storing all seen examples is not useful or practical as the information stored does not represent the student's current level of skill. The only way to closely follow the student's progression during a tutoring session is to limit the system's memory to contain a subset of all problems observed. This enables old and useless information to disappear as time progresses while still storing enough information about previous responses to make "intelligent" selections of action and task relations as they are needed. Otherwise the model base will be overly complex and largely non-representative of the student's skills. The size of the memory used is 32 problems.

3.2. Model Base evaluator/constructor

In Focal Modelling there are several hypotheses made about the model base. The model base evaluator uses these conjectures to assess the modelling system's ability to model the student. For the construction of the model, the evaluator test two hypotheses which determine whether the model base needs more task or action relations.

These hypotheses are:

The Model Base can represent the student's responses **(H1)**

This hypothesis determines whether the action relations in the model base can reproduce the results observed. If the action relations fail to recreate 90% of the observed responses then the hypothesis is considered to be invalid. The new action relation is then chosen by the model constructor. This is determined by selecting the action relation that can recreate the largest number of responses which can not be represented with the current action relations in the model base. If, by chance, there is more than one action relation that can recreate the same number of unrepresented problems then the action relation that is capable of recreating the most responses in memory is chosen. The intention of this is to select an action relation that is more general and so is more likely to be representative of the student's knowledge. If, finally, there are still some action relations that can cover the same number of problems then one such action relation is chosen at random as there is insufficient information to "intelligently" discern between the action relations. If it turns out that the action relation chosen at random is a poor choice, this will be rectified by replacing it with a better choice when more information has been acquired. Once an action relation is found the model's data is re-evaluated with regards to the new action relation leaving the rest of the model unaltered.

The model base contains all the task relations needed to separate tasks that contain a particular action relation from tasks which do not contain the action relation. **(H2)**

The purpose of a task relation is to divide problems into those that contain a specific action relation from those that do not contain the relation. Therefore, if the modelling system is unable to separate 90% of the problems (for all action relations) then one or more new task relation are required. One method for selecting the task relation that best divides the problems uses the ID3[4] algorithm to classify the action relations using task relations that are not in the model base. The resulting decision tree contains the new task relations which are then inserted into the model base. Adding the new task relations involves creating new task sets, updating the entire data for the model, based on the problems in memory, and then finding associations in the model.

4. Reducing the Model Base

As the model base evolves more and more relations are added into the model base. During the course of modelling it is possible that the student's skills will change (concept change) or as more information arrives, parts of the model become redundant. In either case the model will contain task and action relations that do not apply to the student. This excess information clutters up the model base and no longer gives concise information about what the student knows. In order to keep the model as concise as possible the modelling system needs to remove the redundant relations from the model base. Figure 2 shows the cycle for removing action/task relations from the model base.

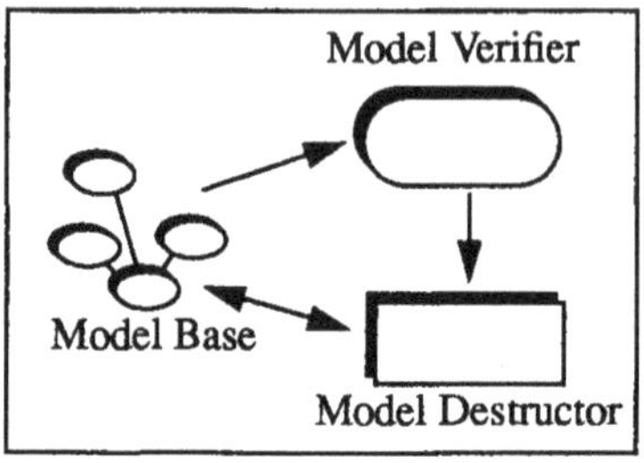

Figure 2: Model Base Redevelopment

4.1. *Model verifier/destructor*

Concept changes made by the student cause parts of the model base to become unproductive and redundant as the modelling system no longer has a need for such relationships. It is therefore unnecessary to keep such relationships in the model base as it is unlikely that the student model may need them again. Also storing redundant information inhibits tools that use information from the model to create lessons for the student especially when the tool selects the redundant information over that of a more appropriate association.

The model verifier uses several rules to determine when a task relation or an action relation should be removed from the model base. Any relation that violates a rule is deleted.

All action relations in the model base are representative of the student's responses. **(R1)**

All action relations are needed to make a model of the student. **(R2)**

Rules 1 and 2 deal specifically with action relations. To put it simply these rules express that an action relation must be in an association (R1) and that there must be a task set for which the action relation is unique (R2). In other words removing the action relation will not effect the model of the student. Removing the action relation involves removing only the information regarding the action relation. Otherwise the model is essentially untouched.

All task relations are needed to create the student model. **(R3)**

This rule deals with task relations which states that if you remove the task relation from the model base then the model remains effectively unchanged. The method used to determine that the task relations is redundant is to see if it is present in at least one association. If it is not then it is redundant. Removal of the task relation involves the rebuilding of task sets so that they no longer contain the task relation. The list of associations, however, remains untouched (as the task relations are **redundant**).

The complexity of the model base remain below a particular threshold. **(R4)**

As the model progresses it is possible that there are more appropriate action/task relations that would simplify the model base. Rule 4 simulates how a student, when the domain seems too complicated, generalizes current knowledge or induces new knowledge that is smaller and more efficient and contains a seemingly similar functionality. This is achieved by reconstructing the model base based on the problems found in the short term memory using the model constructor.

5. Implementation/Results

The modelling techniques described in this paper have been implemented and are currently undergoing extensive testing. Preliminary testing has revealed that the modelling system is able to usefully model student's misconceptions even in the face of noise and concept changes. Nonetheless, as with human counterparts, the accuracy of the model formed depends heavily on the problems presented to the student. For example if the student never errs then the modelling system/tutor cannot detect an error. However, techniques for presenting the student with a broad range of tasks structured to improve the model have been developed[5,6].

6. Summary

Focal Modelling is a technique that dynamically maintains a model base so that a modelling system can model the student. Also the system has the capability of removing redundant information in the model. Thus this technique should be a useful modelling tool for systems where there are a large number of possible misconceptions in the domain and the domain description is large or potentially infinite.

Focal modelling is also applicable for use with other modelling systems, other than RBM, such as ACT[7,8], ACM[2], BUGGY[9,10] and genetic graph[11]. This is due to the main concept of focal modelling which is to only keep the relevant knowledge that is necessary in creating an accurate cognitive model of the student. For example, in ACT many of the production rules do not apply to every student that engages in a lesson. Therefore, the addition and deletion of production rules from the problem space could improve the modelling system's accuracy and efficiency.

Finally, the larger the domain the more useful that a technique such as Focal Modelling is for modelling a student's knowledge. The ability to reduce the knowledge to only that which is needed to model the student not only improves modelling system's efficiency but also reduced the amount of spurious information that is inhibitory to teaching.

Acknowledgment

I would like to thank Geoff Webb for his input and criticisms in the creation of this paper.

References

1. Webb, G.I. *Feature Based Modelling*. To appear in Proceedings of the world conference in AI-ED93, Edinburgh, 1993.

2. Ohlsson, S. and Langley, P. *Identifying Solution Paths in Cognitive Diagnosis.*

Technical Report CMU-RI-TR-85-2, The Robotics Institute, Carnegie-Mellon University, 1985.

3. Hayes, J.R. and Simon, H. A. *Understanding written problem instructions*. In Gregg, L. W. (Ed.), Knowledge and Cognition, Potomac, Maryland: Lawrence Erlbaum Associates, 1974.

4. Quinlan, J. R. *Induction of Decision Trees*. Machine Learning, 1986, Vol 1, 81-106

5. Kuzmycz, M. A. and Webb, G.I. *Modelling Elementary Subtraction: Intelligent warfare against bugs*. In Proceedings of the Fourth Australian Society for Computers in Learning in Tertiary Education Conference, Launceston, pp. 367-376.

6. Kuzmycz, M. A. and Webb, G.I. *Evaluation of Feature Based Modelling in Subtraction*. Proceedings of the Second International Conference in ITS, ITS92, Montreal, 1992, pp. 269-276.

7. Anderson, J. R., Boyle, C. F., Corbett, A. T., Lewis, M. W. *Cognitive Modeling and Intelligent Tutoring*. Artificial Intelligence, 1990, Vol 42, pp. 7-49.

8. Anderson, J. R., Conrad, F. G., Corbett, A. T. *Skill Acquisition and the LISP Tutor*. Cognitive Science, 1989, Vol 13, pp. 467-505.

9. Brown, J. S. and Burton, R. R. *Diagnostic Models for Procedural Bugs in Basic Mathematical Skills*. Cognitive Science, 1978, Vol 2, 155-192.

10. Burton R. *Diagnosing bugs in a simple procedural skill*. In D. Sleeman and J. S. Brown (Eds.), Intelligent Tutoring Systems. Academic Press, London, 1982.

11. Goldstein, I. P. *The genetic graph: a representation for the evolution of procedural knowledge*. International J. Man-Machine Studies, 1979, Vol 11, pp. 51-77.

$\mathcal{ALC}rn$: A Decidable Terminological Language with Role Negation*

Margarida Mamede† and Luís Monteiro
Departamento de Informática
Universidade Nova de Lisboa
2825 Monte da Caparica, Portugal
{mm,lm}@fct.unl.pt

Abstract

In this paper we propose a new terminological language, $\mathcal{ALC}rn$, whose main feature is role negation, and we prove that $\mathcal{ALC}rn$ is decidable. To this end, a sound and complete algorithm for checking the satisfiability of an $\mathcal{ALC}rn$-knowledge base is presented. Since the language allows negation of arbitrary concepts, all classical decision problems for concept languages are also decidable.

1 Introduction

In recent years, several terminological languages, also called concept languages, have been proposed and studied. The kernel notion is that of "concept", which represents a set of individuals. Complex concepts are built up from primitive concepts and primitive binary relations. For example, the concept $\forall r.C$ represents the individuals whose r-sucessors belong to the concept C. These languages are interesting because concept representation is an important field of knowledge representation.

Different terminological languages are obtained by considering different concept and relation constructors. From a theoretical point of view, it is interesting to define and to analyse several terminological languages, comparing their expressive power, and studying the decidability and the complexity of the inference procedures. Satisfiability, coherence, subsumption, instantiation, realization and retrieval (see[1,5]) are the classical problems defined over concept-based knowledge bases.

Some terminological languages are very expressive but are undecidable, like $\mathcal{U}$[8] and NIKL[6], others are much less expressive but are tractable, as for example, $\mathcal{PL}_1$ and $\mathcal{PL}_2$[3], and still others are midway with respect to expressiveness and critera such as decidability and algoritmic complexity. Examples of this class are BACK[7], $\mathcal{ALC}$[9], $\mathcal{KRIS}$[1] and $\mathcal{ALCNR}$[2], which are decidable and intractable. Although these languages are quite expressive, they are somewhat asymmetric. For instance,

*This work was partially supported by JNICT and BRA 6810 COMPULOG II.
†Owns a scholarship from JNICT.

if **teach** is a binary relation (also called a role) and **GradSt** denotes the set of graduate students, we can build the set $\{a \mid (\forall b)\ \texttt{teach}(a,b) \Rightarrow b \in \texttt{GradSt}\}$, of those elements that teach only graduate students. However, we cannot represent the set $\{a \mid (\forall b)\ b \in \texttt{GradSt} \Rightarrow \texttt{teach}(a,b)\}$, of those individuals that teach all graduate students. For this reason, we propose a new terminological language whose syntax is similar to the existing ones, except that it allows negation of relations. It is called $\mathcal{ALC}rn$ because the new main feature added is "role negation". The idea is to reason by contrapositive. Since the first set is written $\forall\texttt{teach}.\texttt{GradSt}$, the second set is represented by the expression $\forall\neg\texttt{teach}.\neg\texttt{GradSt}$, which can be read $\{a \mid (\forall b)\ \neg\texttt{teach}(a,b) \Rightarrow b \notin \texttt{GradSt}\}$. Like BACK[7], $\mathcal{KRIS}$[1] and $\mathcal{ALCNR}$[2], $\mathcal{ALC}rn$ allows terminological axioms to state general relashionships between concepts.

As far as we know, and according to the overview presented in[5], the only language that accepts negation of relations is $\mathcal{U}$. Even though this language is undecidable[8], it is not true that all terminological languages with role negation and conjunction are undecidable, as one could be lead to believe by Patel-Schneider's sentence (in[6], page 264): "*A very recent result by Schild shows that subsumption is undecidable in very expressive terminological logics, ones that include conjunction and negation of roles.*" Actually, we prove in this paper that satisfiability is decidable in our language. Therefore, since $\mathcal{ALC}rn$ allows negation of arbitrary concepts, all the other classical problems are also decidable and, in particular, subsumption is decidable.

The rest of the paper is organized as follows. Section 2 describes the language $\mathcal{ALC}rn$ and Section 3 presents the algorithm that checks the satisfiability of a $\mathcal{ALC}rn$-knowledge base, informally and without getting into details due to space limitations. The complete algorithm and all the proofs can be found in[4].

2 The Language $\mathcal{ALC}rn$

The language in which the knowledge is expressed, $\mathcal{ALC}rn$= (Prim, Rel, Ind), is a tuple of pairwise disjoint sets of *primitive concepts* $P \in$ Prim, *primitive binary relations* $s \in$ Rel and *individuals* $i \in$ Ind. A *concept* C and a *relation* (or *role*) r are defined by the grammar:

$$\begin{array}{lcl} C & \longrightarrow & P \mid \top \mid \bot \mid \neg C \mid C_1 \sqcap C_2 \mid C_1 \sqcup C_2 \mid \forall r.C' \mid \exists r.C' \mid r(i) \\ r & \longrightarrow & s \mid \neg r \mid r_1 \sqcap r_2 \mid r_1 \sqcup r_2 \end{array}$$

and a *$\mathcal{ALC}rn$-assertion* is an expression of the form $i : C$ or $C_1 \sqsubseteq C_2$. (The latter is usually called a terminological axiom.) A *knowledge base* is a finite set of $\mathcal{ALC}rn$-assertions.

Intuitively, a concept C denotes: the set of individuals that belong to a primitive concept (P); the domain of discourse ($\top$); the empty set ($\bot$); the complement of a concept ($\neg C$); the intersection ($C_1 \sqcap C_2$) or the union ($C_1 \sqcup C_2$) of two concepts; the set of those individuals whose image by the relation r is contained in C' ($\forall r.C'$) or comprises at least one element that belongs to C' ($\exists r.C'$); or the image of an individual i by the relation r ($r(i)$). Complex relations are built up from complements, intersections and unions of primitive relations, which are defined also over the individuals.

Let us give the intuitive meaning of the following knowledge base, Kb_1, assuming that `MathSt` is a primitive concept, `teach` and `know` are relation names and `Tom` is an individual:

— `Tom`:$\forall$`teach.MathSt`	Tom teaches only math students.
— `Tom`:$\forall\neg$`teach.`$\neg$`MathSt`	Tom teaches all math students.
— `Tom`:$\forall$`teach`$\sqcap\neg$`know.`$\bot$	Tom knows every individual he teaches.
— `Tom`:$\forall$`teach`$\sqcap\neg$`know.`$\neg$`MathSt`	Tom knows any math student he teaches.

An *interpretation* of $\mathcal{ALC}rn$ = (Prim, Rel, Ind) is a pair $I = (\Delta^I, \cdot^I)$, where Δ^I is a nonempty set, called the *interpretation domain*, and $\cdot^I$ is the *interpretation function* which associates $P^I \subseteq \Delta^I$ with every $P \in$ Prim, $s^I \subseteq \Delta^I \times \Delta^I$ with every $s \in$ Rel, and $i^I \in \Delta^I$ with every $i \in$ Ind. We denote by $r^I(a)$, with $a \in \Delta^I$, the set $\{b \mid (a,b) \in r^I\}$. The interpretation function can be extended to arbitrary concepts and relations in the following way:

$$\begin{array}{rlrl} \top^I &= \Delta^I & \bot^I &= \emptyset \\ (\neg C)^I &= \Delta^I \setminus C^I & (\neg r)^I &= (\Delta^I \times \Delta^I) \setminus r^I \\ (C_1 \sqcap C_2)^I &= C_1^I \cap C_2^I & (r_1 \sqcap r_2)^I &= r_1^I \cap r_2^I \\ (C_1 \sqcup C_2)^I &= C_1^I \cup C_2^I & (r_1 \sqcup r_2)^I &= r_1^I \cup r_2^I \\ (\forall r.C)^I &= \{a \in \Delta^I \mid r^I(a) \subseteq C^I\} & (r(i))^I &= r^I(i^I) \\ (\exists r.C)^I &= \{a \in \Delta^I \mid r^I(a) \cap C^I \neq \emptyset\} & & \end{array}$$

An interpretation I *satisfies* $i : C$ or $C_1 \sqsubseteq C_2$ if $i^I \in C^I$ or $C_1^I \subseteq C_2^I$, respectively. A knowledge base Kb is *satisfiable* if there is an interpretation I that satisfies all of its $\mathcal{ALC}rn$-assertions. In this case, I is said to be a *model* of Kb.

In order to simplify the algorithm that checks the satisfiability of a knowledge base, it is convenient that assertions (and concepts) appearing in the knowledge base be in a special form, called "normal form". A concept C is in *normal form* if negation is applied only to primitive concepts and relations, and if disjunction of relations is not used. Concepts in normal form are generated by the grammar:

$$\begin{array}{rcl} C & \longrightarrow & P \mid \top \mid \bot \mid \neg P \mid C_1 \sqcap C_2 \mid C_1 \sqcup C_2 \mid \forall r.C' \mid \exists r.C' \mid r(i) \\ r & \longrightarrow & s \mid \neg s \mid r_1 \sqcap r_2 \end{array}$$

Note that any concept is equivalent to a concept in normal form, due to the usual boolean equalities and to equivalences such as $\forall r_1 \sqcup r_2.C \equiv (\forall r_1.C) \sqcap (\forall r_2.C)$.

An $\mathcal{ALC}rn$-assertion $i : C$ is in *normal form* if C is in normal form, and $C_1 \sqsubseteq C_2$ is in normal form if $C_1 = \neg C_1'$, and C_1' and C_2 are in normal form. As we will see later, the role of an assertion of the form $\neg C_1' \sqsubseteq C_2$, when we check the satisfiability of a knowledge base, is to generate assertions of the form $i : C_1' \sqcup C_2$, which are in normal form if C_1' and C_2 are also in normal form. The justification is that $\neg C_1' \sqsubseteq C_2$ if and only if $C_1' \sqcup C_2 \equiv \top$. From now on, we assume that all assertions of a knowledge base are in normal form.

3 Satisfiability of a Knowledge Base

We check the satisfiability of a knowledge base by generating some "propositions" that are similar to $\mathcal{ALC}rn$-assertions. For example, if $Kb_2 = \{\texttt{Tom} : \exists\texttt{teach.GradSt}\}$, every model M of Kb_2 has an element $a_M \in \Delta^M$ such that $(\texttt{Tom}^M, a_M) \in \texttt{teach}^M$ and $a_M \in \texttt{GradSt}^M$. In order to represent this element, we often make use of a variable v and generate the two "propositions" $v : \texttt{teach(Tom)}$ and $v : \texttt{GradSt}$.

Therefore, we define another language of assertions, $L = (\text{Prim}, \text{Rel}, \text{Ind}, \text{Var})$, which accepts *variables* $v \in \text{Var}$ in any place individuals may occur in $\mathcal{ALC}rn$-assertions. The set Var is also disjoint from Prim, Rel and Ind. An interpretation $I = (\Delta^I, \cdot^I)$ of L differs from an interpretatin I' of $\mathcal{ALC}rn$ only in the fact that it associates a $v^I \in \Delta^I$ with every $v \in \text{Var}$. Note that a $\mathcal{ALC}rn$-assertion is an L-assertion. When the distinction is not important or when it is clear from the context we will use only the word "assertion". Similarly, a knowledge base is either a set of $\mathcal{ALC}rn$-assertions or a set of L-assertions. A *term* t is either an individual or a variable, and Term is the set of terms, i.e., Term = Ind ∪ Var.

Our goal is to show that the process of generation of assertions gives rise to an "obvious" contradiction (formalized by the notion of "clash", see below) if and only if the knowledge base Kb is unsatisfiable. To this end, we introduce the notion of "closed" knowledge base. Intuitively, a "closed" knowledge base is a set of assertions that contains Kb and has all the assertions that have to be generated in order to conclude that Kb is satisfiable, i.e., if the "closed" knowledge base has no "obvious" contradiction, then Kb has a model. Since, in general, there are several possible alternatives to be considered, there are several "closed" knowledge bases concerning the same Kb. We prove that if one of these "closed" knowledge bases has no "obvious" contradiction, Kb has a model.

First, we need to introduce some notation. We write $\dot{s}$ to denote a primitive relation s or its negation $\neg s$, and we define $\neg\dot{s} = \neg s$ if $\dot{s} = s$, and $\neg\dot{s} = s$ if $\dot{s} = \neg s$. Since the letter r stands for a conjunction of primitive relations and negated primitive relations, we often write the expression $r = \sqcap_{j=1}^{n}\dot{s}_j$. Finally, $Kb \vdash t' : r(t)$ abbreviates $t' : \dot{s}_j(t) \in Kb$ for all $1 \leq j \leq n$, and $Kb \vdash t' : \neg r(t)$ abbreviates $t' : \neg\dot{s}_j(t) \in Kb$ for some $1 \leq j \leq n$. A knowledge base Kb has a *clash* if it contains: $t : \bot$, for some $t \in \text{Term}$; or $t : P$ and $t : \neg P$, for some $t \in \text{Term}$ and $P \in \text{Prim}$; or $t' : s(t)$ and $t' : \neg s(t)$, for some $t, t' \in \text{Term}$ and $s \in \text{Rel}$. Otherwise, we say that Kb is *clash-free*.

The assertions we have to generate, in order to conclude that a clash-free knowledge base is satisfiable, are similar to the usual ones [1,2,3,9], except in two cases that deal with universally quantified assertions, which we will explain by examples. Let us see the first one, with Kb_3 consisting of the following assertions:

(1) `Tom:∀¬teach.¬MathSt`	Tom teaches all math students.
(2) `Tom:∀teach⊓¬know.¬MathSt`	Tom knows every math student he teaches.
(3) `Joe:MathSt⊓¬know(Tom)`	Joe is a math student not known by Tom.

First, by assertion (3), we conclude that (4) `Joe:MathSt` and (5) `Joe:¬know(Tom)` are logical consequences of Kb_3. Note that if the usual rules were applied [1,2,3,9], there would be no more assertions derived from Kb_3 and the problem is that this clash-free knowledge base is unsatisfiable. So, we need a new rule for the universal quantifier.

> If we have $t : \forall r.C$, with $r = \sqcap_{j=1}^{n} \dot{s}_j$, and $t' : \dot{s}_k(t)$, for some $1 \leq k \leq n$, then **either** $Kb \vdash t' : r(t)$ **and** $t' : C$, **or** $Kb \vdash t' : \neg r(t)$.

In our example, considering assertions (2) and (5), there are two possibilities. Either (6) `Joe:teach(Tom)` and (7) `Joe:¬MathSt`; or (6') `Joe:¬teach(Tom)`, which implies, with assertion (1) and again by the same rule, (7') `Joe:¬MathSt`. Since both alternatives contain a clash — (4)/(7) and (4)/(7'), respectively — we conclude that Kb_3 is unsatisfiable.

To explain the second case, consider the following knowledge base, Kb_4:

(1) `Tom:∀teach.MathSt`	Tom teaches only math students.
(2) `Tom:∀¬teach.GradSt`	Only graduate students are not taught by Tom.
(3) `Tom:¬MathSt`	Tom is not a math student.
(4) `Tom:¬GradSt`	Tom is not a graduate student.

Although, once again, it is straightforward to see that this knowledge base is unsatisfiable, the usual rules cannot derive any assertion of Kb_4. The rule we introduce to tackle this case analyses the relations that follow the symbol "∀" in universally quantified assertions concerning the same term. For example, the relations r that occur in assertions of the form `Tom:`$\forall r.C$ are `teach` and `¬teach`. If the disjunction of these relations is a tautology, when the primitive relations are seen as atomic formulae of the propositional calculus, like `teach⊔¬teach`, we force the generation of the assertions t`:teach(Tom)⊔¬teach(Tom)`, for every term t of the knowledge base. In our example, since `Tom` is the only term that exists, only the assertion (5) `Tom:teach(Tom)⊔¬teach(Tom)` is generated. Now, either (6) `Tom:teach(Tom)` is selected from the disjunction and (7) `Tom:MathSt` will be derived, which contradicts (3), or (6') `Tom:¬teach(Tom)` is chosen, which implies (7') `Tom:GradSt` and, again, a clash is detected because of assertion (4). We conclude that Kb_4 is unsatisfiable.

Now we characterize the set of assertions we are looking for, which is formalized by the notion of "closed" knowledge base. A knowledge base is *closed* if it satisfies all the following properties:

($\sqcap_C$-pp): **If** $t : C_1 \sqcap C_2 \in Kb$ **then** $t : C_1 \in Kb$ and $t : C_2 \in Kb$.

($\sqcap_r$-pp): **If** $t' : (r_1 \sqcap r_2)(t) \in Kb$ **then** $t' : r_1(t) \in Kb$ and $t' : r_2(t) \in Kb$.

($\sqcup$-pp): **If** $t : C_1 \sqcup C_2 \in Kb$ **then** $t : C_1 \in Kb$ **or** $t : C_2 \in Kb$.

($\exists$-pp): **If** $t : \exists r.C \in Kb$
then there is some t' such that $Kb \vdash t' : r(t)$ and $t' : C \in Kb$.

($\forall$-pp): **If** $t : \forall r.C \in Kb$, $r = \sqcap_{j=1}^{n} \dot{s}_j$, and $t' : \dot{s}_k(t) \in Kb$, for some $1 \leq k \leq n$
then either $Kb \vdash t' : r(t)$ and $t' : C \in Kb$, **or** $Kb \vdash t' : \neg r(t)$.

($\top_C$-pp): **If** $\neg C_1 \sqsubseteq C_2 \in Kb$ **then** for all t, $t : C_1 \sqcup C_2 \in Kb$.

($\top_r$-pp): **If** $\sqcup_{j=1}^{n} r_j$ is a tautology and $t : \forall r_j.C_j \in Kb$ for all $1 \leq j \leq n$
then for all t', there is some $1 \leq k \leq n$ such that $Kb \vdash t' : r_k(t)$.

Proposition 1 *A knowledge base Kb is satisfiable if there is a closed and clash-free knowledge base that contains Kb.*

The algorithm that checks the satisfiability of a knowledge base Kb computes several closed knowledge bases containing Kb, each one concerning different choices made in nondeterministic rules (those respecting ($\sqcup$-pp) and ($\forall$-pp)). If at least one of those closed knowledge bases is clash-free, the algorithm concludes that Kb is satisfiable. Otherwise, Kb is said unsatisfiable.

If there is no policy to specify the order in which rules are applied, the generation process may be infinite, because of rule ($\exists$-pp), so the algorithm may not terminate. More precisely, whenever there is an assertion of the form $t : \exists r.C$ and no term t' satisfies both $Kb \vdash t' : r(t)$ and $t' : C$, a new variable v is generated and the assertions $v : r(t)$ and $v : C$ are added to the knowledge base. We call t the *creator* of v and these two assertions are the *creation* assertions.

It is easy to see that if we applied rule ($\exists$-pp) whithout restrictions to compute a closed knowledge base containing $Kb_5 = \{\neg\bot \sqsubseteq \exists s.P_1,\ i : \top,\ i : \forall s.P_2\}$, the algorithm might not terminate. Indeed, by ($\top_C$-pp), ($\exists$-pp), ($\forall$-pp) and selecting in all cases the second alternative of disjunctions in ($\sqcup$-pp), we would obtain the set:

$(a)\ \neg\bot \sqsubseteq \exists s.P_1$	$(3)\ v_1 : s(i)$			
$(b)\ i : \top$	$(4)\ v_1 : P_1$	$(8)\ v_2 : s(v_1)$	$(12)\ v_3 : s(v_2)$	$\cdots$
$(c)\ i : \forall s.P_2$	$(5)\ v_1 : P_2$	$(9)\ v_2 : P_1$	$(13)\ v_3 : P_1$	$\cdots$
$(1)\ i : \bot \sqcup \exists s.P_1$	$(6)\ v_1 : \bot \sqcup \exists s.P_1$	$(10)\ v_2 : \bot \sqcup \exists s.P_1$	$(14)\ v_3 : \bot \sqcup \exists s.P_1$	$\cdots$
$(2)\ i : \exists s.P_1$	$(7)\ v_1 : \exists s.P_1$	$(11)\ v_2 : \exists s.P_1$	$(15)\ v_3 : \exists s.P_1$	$\cdots$

The policy is now sketched. When a variable v is created by ($\exists$-pp) due to the assertion $t : \exists r.C$, we compute only the creation assertions and the "inherited" assertions. The creation assertions are $v : r(t)$ and $v : C$, as we have seen before. We call assertions *inherited* by v from its creator t those of the form $v : \dot{s}_k(t)$, $v : \neg\dot{s}_k(t)$ or $v : C'$ generated by ($\forall$-pp) because of some assertion $t : \forall r'.C'$, with $r' = \sqcap_{j=1}^{n} \dot{s}_j$ and $1 \leq k \leq n$. Together, the creation and the inherited assertions are called the *basic set* of assertions of variable v.

By *expanding* the variable v we mean computing the remaining assertions of v, which happens only if the "information" present in the basic set of v is not yet present in the set of assertions of some expanded variable w. More formally, the set of assertions of w *subsumes* the basic set of v, if replacing v by w, and the creator of v by the creator of w in every assertion in the basic set of v, we obtain an assertion of w (in fact, there is another condition which we omit for the sake of brevity). A variable v is not expanded if there is some expanded variable w that subsumes v.

Let us illustrate these ideas with Kb_5 above. First, we compute all assertions respecting the individual i ((1) by ($\top_C$-pp) and (2) by ($\sqcup$-pp)) and we also apply the rule for the existentially quantified assertion ((3) and (4)). The inherited assertions by v_1 are also derived ((5) by ($\forall$-pp)). Since there is no variable whose set of assertions subsumes the basic set of v_1, we proceed as before expanding variable

v_1 ((6) to (9)). Note that the order of the assertions may be sometimes arbitrary. The important is that the decision of expanding a variable is delayed until there are no assertions concerning individuals or already expanded variables to derive. The process terminates because variable v_2 need not to be expanded. Its basic set (from (8) to (9)) is subsumed by the set of assertions of v_1 (from (3) to (7)).

Although the knowledge base this algorithm builds is not closed, we proved in [4] the following proposition.

Proposition 2 *Let Kb be an $\mathcal{ALC}$rn-knowledge base. If an output of the algorithm is clash-free, there is a closed and clash-free knowledge base that contains Kb.*

Propositions 1 and 2 allow to state that the algorithm is sound, i.e., if the algorithm concludes that *Kb* is satisfiable, then there is a model of *Kb*. Moreover, it is easy to prove [4] that the algorithm is complete. If all knowledge bases built by the algorithm have a clash, then *Kb* is unsatisfiable. This follows from the fact that all combinations of the possible choices offered by nondeterministic rules were tried.

Finally, we also proved in [4] that the algorithm always terminates. On the one hand, the number of expanded variables is always finite, for every knowledge base and for any choices made in nondeterministic rules. On the other hand, there is only a finite number of different choices in each nondeterministic rule. Therefore, we state our main result.

Proposition 3 *The satisfiability problem in $\mathcal{ALC}$rn is decidable.*

References

1. F. Baader, B. Hollunder. A Terminological Knowledge Representation System with Complete Inference Algorithms. *Proc. PDK'91*, LNAI 567, Springer-Verlag.
2. M. Buchheit, F. Donini, A. Schaerf. Decidable Reasoning in Terminological Knowledge Representation Systems. To appear in *Proc. IJCAI'93*, Chambery.
3. F. Donini, M. Lenzerini, D. Nardi, W. Nutt. Tractable Concept Languages. *Proc. IJCAI'91*, Sidney.
4. M. Mamede, L. Monteiro. *Decidability of $\mathcal{ALC}$rn*. Technical Report RT 1/93 – DI/UNL, Universidade Nova de Lisboa, 1993.
5. B. Nebel. *Reasoning and Revision in Hybrid Representation Systems.* LNAI 422, Springer-Verlag, 1990.
6. P. Patel-Schneider. Undecidability of Subsumption in NIKL. *Artificial Intelligence*, 39(2):263–272, 1989.
7. C. Peltason. The BACK System — An Overview. *SIGART Bulletin*, 2(3):114–119, 1991.
8. K. Schild. *Undecidability of Subsumption in $\mathcal{U}$.* KIT Report 67, Technische Universität Berlin, 1988.
9. M. Schmidt-Schauß, G. Smolka. Attributive Concept Descriptions with Complements. *Artificial Intelligence*, 48(1):1–26, 1991.

Generic Memory Organisation Packets: Implementation and Evaluation

P. Williams, W.Y. Wang and J.S. Gero
Key Centre of Design Computing
Department of Architectural and Design Science
The University of Sydney, NSW 2006, Australia
Email: (peterw,wang,john)@archsci.arch.su.edu.au

Abstract

This paper discusses and evaluates some generic implementations of the memory organisation packets proposed by Schank as a model for dynamic memory. It is shown that the length of experiences is the dominating factor in determining memory requirements and that memory usage approaching optimum can be attained using relatively simple modifications that virtualise large parts of memory.

1 Introduction

The memory organisation packet (MOP) was proposed as a basic element for dynamic memory by Schank[1]. Knowledge-based generalisations of MOPs have been investigated by Kolodner[2], Hammond[3] and others. A simple tree model (similar to that used as a base case in this paper) is investigated and extended by Bardasz and Zeid[4]. Probabilistic models have been investigated by Fisher[5] and others. Lebowitz[6] has taken a pragmatic generalisation approach. Many of these implementations of dynamic memory have some reliance on domain knowledge. The generic implementations reported here are concerned with minimising memory requirements whilst maintaining functionality.

2 Memory Organisation Packet(s) – MOP(s)

When experiences are represented as sets of items an abstract representation of a MOP based on Schank's[1] proposal is given by

$$\text{MOP} \equiv (\text{C}, \text{I}, s_s, s_g) \tag{1}$$

where C is a characteristic set, I is an indexed set of MOP structures containing *all* MOPs whose characteristic sets are supersets of its own, s_s and s_g are numbers in the range 0...1 indicating the strength with which the MOP's characteristic set represents *specific* experiences and *epitome* of experiences in I respectively.

A MOP whose index set I is non-empty is known as an *epitome* and represents the characteristics are shared by its children. A MOP whose specific strength s_s is not zero represents a specific experience and is known as a *trace*. It is possible for a MOP to be both an epitome and a trace. MOPs are sometimes referred to as *nodes* and the indices in the various I as *links*.

With the representation in Equation 1, a new experience X can be said to be compatible with a MOP M if if the relation $X \supseteq M{\bullet}C$ is satisfied. The MOP whose characteristic set is the empty set is, therefore, compatible with all possible experiences and one such MOP, with no children, is used to represent an empty memory.

2.1 Queries

Two forms of primitive query together with the ability to list all traces and all epitomes contained in the structure of a particular MOP are sufficient for many higher level queries to be formulated. The first of these is *simple search*. Here the aim is, given a query set Q, to find the least general MOP that controls epitomes and traces that are supersets of Q. The second form, *maximal subset search*, handles those occasions where simple search fails and returns the set of maximal subsets of Q that are also subsets of experiences already encountered. A maximal subset is one where there are no other subsets that are proper super sets of that subset and satisfy the other requirement. These maximal subsets may then be used as query sets with simple search in order to find MOPs whose characteristic sets most closely resemble those in Q.

2.2 Analysis of Memory Requirements

The minimum number of nodes required to contain a particular sequence of experiences is given by the sum of the number of distinct pure epitomes (including the root node) required to capture the sequence and the number of distinct experiences in the sequence. If the number of possible items that may appear in experience sets is n and the maximum cardinality of an experience set is l then the maximum possible number of distinct experiences $X_{\max}$ (not counting the empty experience) and the maximum possible number of distinct epitomes $E_{\max}$ (including the most general) are given by

$$X_{\max} + 1 = \sum_{i=0}^{l} \binom{n}{i} = E_{\max} + \binom{n}{l} \tag{2}$$

When $n = l$ both of these reduce to $2^n - 1$. In the (uninteresting) case where all possible experiences are experienced there will be only one pure epitome and the minimum number of MOPs required is $X_{\max} + 1$.

For any given number of experiences the worst case, in terms of pure epitomes required, occurs when there is a maximum of overlap between experiences and no experiences match any epitome. In this case the maximum number of pure epitomes that can be generated by a sequence of length x is given by

$$E_{\max} = 1 + \sum_{i=2}^{x} \binom{x}{i} = 2^x - x \qquad \text{when } x < l \tag{3}$$

$$= \min\left(\sum_{i=0}^{l-1} \binom{n}{i}, 1 + \sum_{i=2}^{l-1} \binom{x}{i}\right) \qquad \text{when } x \geq l \tag{4}$$

These equations show that it is possible for the number of nodes required to reach that required for all possible experiences long before all possible experiences are experienced.

If the items which appear in experience sets are attribute/value pairs and any given attribute may only appear once in any experience set there are further constraints placed on the memory requirements. Let a be the number of attributes and v_i be the number of alternative values for the ith attribute. The possible numbers of distinct experiences and distinct epitomes are now restricted to

$$X_{\text{max}} + 1 = \prod_{i=1}^{a} (v_i + 1) = E_{\text{max}} + \prod_{i=1}^{a} v_i \tag{5}$$

3 Implementation

In order to reduce the storage requirements for individual MOPs, to reduce redundancy and to accelerate search algorithms the representation of Equation 1 is modified to give the implementation of a MOP as

$$\overline{\text{MOP}} \equiv (\text{C}_s, \text{I}, s_s, s_g, P, i) \tag{6}$$

where C_s is the subset of C remaining after those used to determine the address are excluded, P is a pointer to a $\overline{\text{MOP}}$ whose I directly indexes this $\overline{\text{MOP}}$, i is the item by which it is indexed in $(\star P)\bullet I$ and the other constituents are as previously described. The notation $(\star P)$ dereferences the pointer P and $\rightsquigarrow X$ is a pointer to the object X. The relation $C = \text{C}_s \cup (\star P)\bullet C \cup \{i\}$ is used when mapping this representation to a MOP. One of the effects of this implementation is that the contents of specific experiences tend to become distributed on the links of a $\overline{\text{MOP}}$ structure and this is where the term *trace* originated.

3.1 Inclusion of New Experiences into a $\overline{\text{MOP}}$

The simplest algorithm for the inclusion of a new experience represented by the set X into a $\overline{\text{MOP}}$ M is given at Figure 1. The symbol δs_s represents the specific strength allocated to new experiences. Notice that, as the new experience is passed

```
if ¬(X ⊇ M•Cs) then
  reorganize M so that (X ⊇ M•Cs)
  if X = M•Cs then
    increase M•sg
if X = M•Cs then
  increase M•ss
else
  for all j in X ∩ indices(M•I) do
    include X − M•Cs − {j} in M•I[j]
  for all j in X − (M•Cs ∪ indices(M•I)) do
    index new MOP (X − (M•Cs ∪ {j}), {}, δss, 0, ⇝M, j) in M•I under j
  increase M•sg
```

Figure 1: Inclusion of a new experience X into a $\overline{\text{MOP}}$ M

$I_c \Leftarrow$ replica of $M \bullet \mathrm{I}$
for all $\overline{\mathrm{MOP}}$ m indexed in $M \bullet \mathrm{I}$ **do**
  $m \bullet \mathrm{C}_s \Leftarrow m \bullet \mathrm{C}_s \cup (M \bullet \mathrm{C}_s - \mathrm{X})$
for all j in $M \bullet \mathrm{C}_s - \mathrm{X}$ **do**
  index new $\overline{\mathrm{MOP}}$ $(M \bullet \mathrm{C}_s - \mathrm{X} - \{j\}, \mathrm{I}_c, M \bullet s_s, M \bullet s_g, \rightsquigarrow M, j)$ in $M \bullet \mathrm{I}$ under j
$M \bullet \mathrm{C}_s \Leftarrow M \bullet \mathrm{C}_s \cap \mathrm{X}$
$M \bullet s_s \Leftarrow 0$

Figure 2: Reorganising a $\overline{\mathrm{MOP}}$ M so that $\mathrm{X} \supseteq M \bullet \mathrm{C}_s$

down the structure, its representation X is progressively reduced by removing the indices of links and reduced characteristic sets of nodes that are traversed. This allows the test for compatibility in Section 2 to be modified to use C_s rather than having to calculate the complete characteristic set. The algorithm for reorganising a $\overline{\mathrm{MOP}}$ to accept new experiences that are incompatible with its existing structure is given at Figure 2. The starting point for these algorithms is a single $\overline{\mathrm{MOP}}$ with an empty characteristic set C and no children.

3.2 Improved Inclusion of New Experiences: Method 1

Unfortunately, the numbers of $\overline{\mathrm{MOP}}$s (N) and links (L) in a memory structure constructed using the algorithms in Figures 1 and 2 that has seen all possible experiences are given by

$$L = \sum_{i=1}^{l} \mathrm{P}_i^n = N - 1 \tag{7}$$

where P_i^n is the number of permutations of n things taken i at a time. These are much larger than the number of possible distinct experiences given at Equation 2.

The $\overline{\mathrm{MOP}}$ structure generated by the sequence of experience sets $\{a, b, c\}$, $\{a, b\}$, $\{a, c\}$ and $\{b, c\}$ is shown in Figure 3(a). In this diagram $\overline{\mathrm{MOP}}$s are represented by boxes, C_s is printed in the box and indexed links between $\overline{\mathrm{MOP}}$s are represented by labelled lines. Pure epitomes have thick black borders, pure traces have no border and combined epitome/traces have a thick white border.

The $\overline{\mathrm{MOP}}$s whose addresses are $a \to b \to c$ and $a \to c \to b$ shadow one another and can be combined in order to reduce the number $\overline{\mathrm{MOP}}$s. This can be achieved by modifying the algorithms so that, whenever the creation of a new $\overline{\mathrm{MOP}}$ for indexing

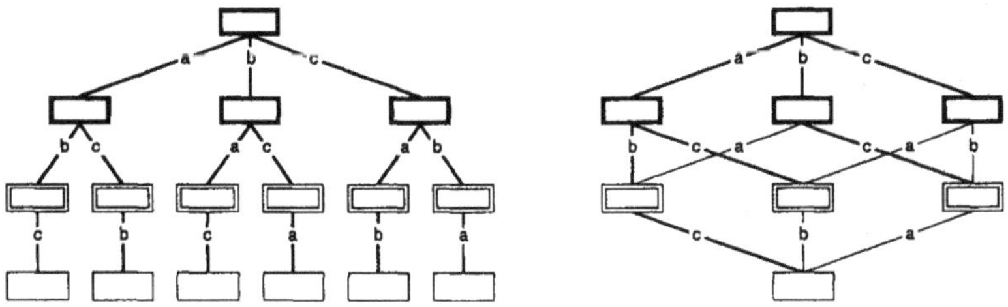

a. b.

Figure 3: $\overline{\mathrm{MOP}}$ structure created by the experience sets $\{a, b, c\}$, $\{a, b\}$, $\{a, c\}$ and $\{b, c\}$ using (a) the simple direct method and (b) improved method 1.

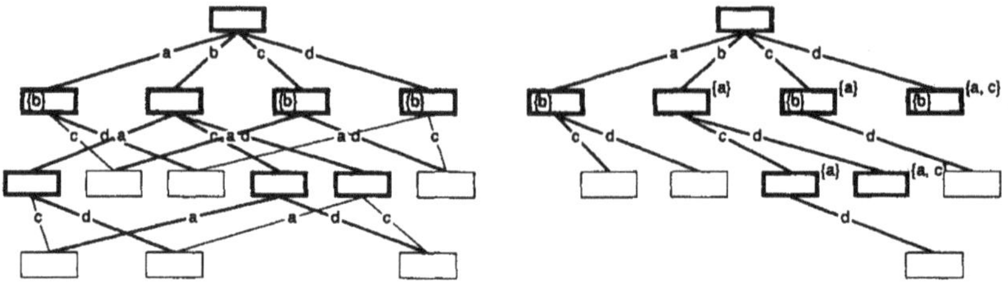

a. b.

Figure 4: $\overline{\text{MOP}}$ structure created by the experience sets $\{a, b, c\}$, $\{a, b, d\}$ and $\{b, c, d\}$ using (a) improved method 1 and (b) improved method 2.

in I is required, a check is made to determine if a shadow $\overline{\text{MOP}}$ already exists and indexing this shadow $\overline{\text{MOP}}$ in I instead. If, when updating the $\overline{\text{MOP}}$ M, we need to create a new $\overline{\text{MOP}}$ for indexing under j in $M \bullet \text{I}$ the shadow $\overline{\text{MOP}}$ if it exists will be found at $((\star(M \bullet P)) \bullet \text{I}\,[j]) \bullet \text{I}\,[M \bullet i]$. This process may be applied at all levels of the structure and when applied to the same sequence of experiences as the structure in Figure 3(a) results in the structure shown in Figure 3(b). A $\overline{\text{MOP}}$ is restricted to propagating new experiences to those children whose parent pointer points to it so that each $\overline{\text{MOP}}$ will be processed at most once for each new experience.

The maximum number of nodes required to store all possible experiences is now only one more than the number of possible experiences. In this limiting case this structure can be said to be optimal in terms of the number of nodes required. However, in the (more interesting) cases where not all possible experiences have been experienced the resulting structures are far from optimal, see Figure 4(a).

3.3 Improved Inclusion of New Experiences: Method 2

The items in query sets may be reordered according to their values in order to allow the various search algorithms to eliminate portions of the structure that will yield identical results to portions already searched from consideration. This has the effect that the children of a $\overline{\text{MOP}}$ that are indexed by a value that is less than the least value associated with the links into that $\overline{\text{MOP}}$ will never be visited. These children are unnecessary, at least as far as search is concerned, and can be eliminated from the structure without effecting search. A record of the links that should exist must, however, be retained so that lists of all traces or epitomes whose characteristic sets are supersets of a particular $\overline{\text{MOP}}$ may be constructed when required. Consequently the representation of a $\overline{\text{MOP}}$ is altered to include a new set I_g of indices that would have been included in I except for the fact that they all precede i in the sorting order. The insertion and reordering algorithms are altered so that there are no links created out of a $\overline{\text{MOP}}$ whose index is less than the least index into it and instead the index is added to I_g.

The structure that results when this modification is used to process the sequence of experiences seen by the structure in Figure 4(a) is illustrated in Figure 4(b). The contents of a $\overline{\text{MOP}}$'s I_g are printed near the top right corner of the symbol.

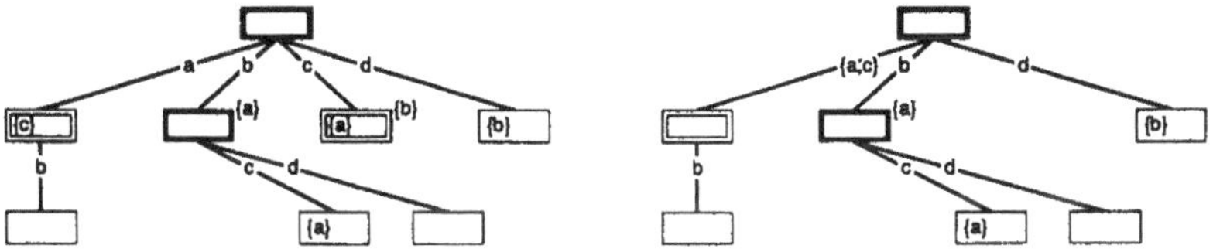

a. b.

Figure 5: $\overline{\text{MOP}}$ structure created by the experience sets $\{a, b, c\}$, $\{a, c\}$ and $\{b, d\}$ using (a) improved method 2 and (b) improved method 3.

3.4 Improved Inclusion of New Experiences: Method 3

A further opportunity to reduce the number of nodes in a structure is illustrated in Figure 5(a). The children of the root $\overline{\text{MOP}}$ indexed by a and c are clearly representing the same thing and one of them can be eliminated. This is achieved by allowing multiple links from the parent to a single child. In order to accomplish this it is necessary to modify the implementation by replacing i with I_p, the set of indices under which this $\overline{\text{MOP}}$ is indexed from its parent. The insertion and reordering algorithms must be modified so that when a requirement to add new indices to I arises a single $\overline{\text{MOP}}$ is created and indexed under all new indices rather than one per index. The resultant structure after processing the same experience set as illustrated in Figure 5(a) is illustrated in Figure 5(b). An additional modification must be made to the insertion algorithm. For instance, if the experience set $\{c, d\}$ were to be included in the structure shown at Figure 5(b) it would be necessary to change it to the structure shown in Figure 5(a) before proceeding.

4 Evaluation

The fact that the experiences $\{a, b, c\}$ and $\{b, d\}$ are each represented twice in the structure shown in Figure 5(b) demonstrates that none of the methods discussed so

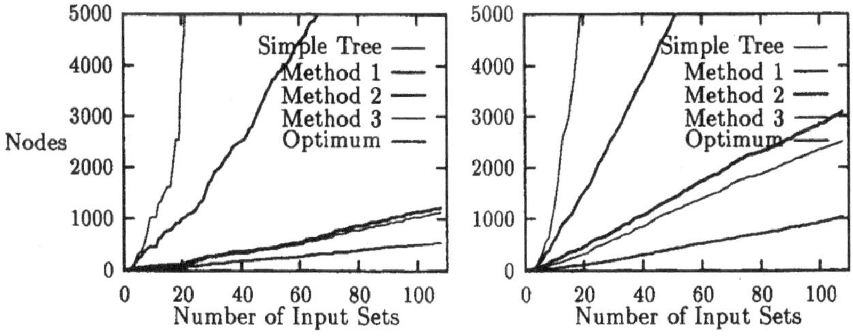

a. b.

Figure 6: Number of nodes generated by (a) the Pittsburgh bridge specification data and (b) randomly generated data far are optimal when only some of the possible experiences have been seen. However, it is interesting to evaluate their performance against this optimum on some real data.

The real data used for this evaluation are 108 specifications taken from the Pittsburgh bridge database from the UCI repository of machine learning databases. Figure 6(a) shows the number of nodes generated as a function of the number of experiences processed for each of the methods discussed. In addition, 108 random cases were generated based on the possible attributes in the bridge data and the performance of the various methods against this data is illustrated in Figure 6(b). The processing time required by the various methods indicated that there is a trade off between memory usage and processing time for Method 3.

5 Conclusions

The data in Figure 6 show that simple modifications (Methods 2 and 3) to the basic algorithms are capable of achieving memory usage comparable with the optimum. We contend that reducing memory usage to the optimum will involve more complex modifications and that there will be some trade offs involved between processing time and memory usage. This has already occurred with Method 3. These data also demonstrate that, at least in this case, real data tend to be more hierarchically structured than random data. The growth in the number of nodes required, for both the real and random data, was far less than predicted for the worst case.

The equations in Section 2.2 show that, for a finite number (n) of items that may appear in experiences, the size of memory required is dominated by the maximal cardinality (l) of the experience sets. This allows memory requirements to be controlled by limiting this factor.

References

1. R. C. Schank, *Dynamic Memory: A Theory of Reminding and Learning in Computers and People*, (Cambridge University Press, Cambridge, 1982).
2. J. Kolodner, Maintaining organization in a dynamic long-term memory, *Cognitive Science*, 7 (1983), pages 243–280.
3. K. Hammond, *Case-based Planning: Viewing Planning as a Memory Task*, (Academic Press, San Diego, California, 1989).
4. T. Bardasz and I. Zeid, Cognitive model of memory for mechanical design problems, *CAD*, 24(6) (1992), pages 327–342.
5. D. H. Fisher, Knowledge acquisition via incremental conceptual cluttering, *Machine Learning*, 2(7) (1987), pages 139–172.
6. M. Lebowitz, Experiments with incremental concept formation: UNIMEM, *Machine Learning*, 2 (1987), pages 103–138.

Knowledge Representation for Theory Construction in Qualitative Data Analysis

Hoi-Kau Yuen and Thomas J. Richards,
Department of Computer Science and Computer Engineering,
La Trobe University,
Melbourne, Victoria 3083, Australia.

Abstract: Application of knowledge-based systems to qualitative data analysis in social sciences has been recognised as an important approach to theory construction. This approach heavily depends on the availability of a suitable knowledge representation. In this paper, we introduce a knowledge representation method for grounded theory construction in qualitative data analysis, in which a hybrid approach of fuzzy set theory and semantic networks is applied.

1. Introduction

Qualitative Data Analysis (QDA) programs are software packages developed explicitly for the purpose of analysing "qualitative data" – unstructured narrative text or similar material, eg videotapes. The major achievement of most current QDA software systems has been efficient code-and-retrieve abilities. These greatly strengthen and assist the handling of qualitative data, but they do not address the crucial tasks of theory construction as traditionally understood in qualitative research.[12] The construction of theories by the computer is not only an important task in qualitative research, but it has been also a long-standing objective of AI research since the 1960s.

Among the qualitative methodologies in social sciences, Grounded Theory[5] (GT) is a very popular and frequently cited approach in theory construction.[3] GT is an approach to the handling of qualitative data and to the formulation of theoretical propositions in social sciences. The label "grounded theory", means "the discovery of theory from data". GT is not only a systematic generation of conceptual models from qualitative data; it is simultaneously a set of assumptions about the production of knowledge and a set of guidelines for approaching the empirical world.[18]

Application of knowledge-based systems to QDA has been recognised as an important approach to theory construction.[1] A knowledge-based approach depends on the availability of a suitable Knowledge Representation (KR) for such domains. Therefore, in this paper, we present a KR method for representing Grounded Theory Construction (GTC) in QDA, in which a hybrid approach includes fuzzy set theory and semantic networks.[9,15] The purpose of this method is three-fold: (i) it is able to describe the notation and operation of the knowledge bases in GTC; (ii) it is able to specify a formal way of assigning meaning to empirical data in GTC; and (iii) it is able to provide mechanisms for organising knowledge and inferencing implicit knowledge, for supporting GTC. We proceed as follows: (i) we set up a formal notation for GTC to explain concepts of categories and their relations in GTC, (ii) we describe and motivate the use of semantic networks as a KR mechanism for GTC, (iii) we demonstrate how to use fuzzy set theory to quantify relations between categories which occur as nodes in a semantic network, and (iv) we demonstrate a mechanism for transforming semantic networks into "Category-Relation Diagrams" using fuzzy set theory, and we will explain the utility of these diagrams to GTC.

2. Basic Notations for GTC

Theory construction is a mental activity. It is a process of developing ideas that can allow us to explain and understand the phenomena. Theories are built from concepts and concepts are related to each other with theoretical statements. GTC is based on a *concept-indicator model*, which directs the conceptual coding of a set of *empirical indicators*.[16] Indicators are actual data, such as behavioural actions and events, observed or described in documents and in the words of interviewees and informants. We define a set of formal notations which describes the major objects in GTC.

Definition 2.1 - Let D_i be the ith document of the data sources, and it is divided into n units. A unit is a set of words, it may be a sentence or a paragraph. A segment $S_{(i,j)}$ is the jth unit in D_i, where $D_i = S_{(i,1)} \cup S_{(i,2)} \cup \ldots \cup S_{(i,n)}$, and $\{S_{(i,1)}, S_{(i,2)}, \ldots, S_{(i,n)}\}$ forms a partition of D_i.

In QDA, most of the data sources are unstructured text documents. Therefore, it is necessary to divide the unstructured data into small segments, and a segment $S_{(i,j)}$ is the basic unit of the analysis.

Definition 2.2 - An indicator I_i is a key word or a key phrase occurred in at least one segment, for example, if an indicator I_1 occurred in $S_{(1,3)}$ and $S_{(4,8)}$, then $I_1 \in S_{(1,3)} \cap S_{(4,8)}$, and $occ(I_1) = 2$, where $occ(I_1)$ is the number of occurrences of the indicator I_1 in the data sources.

In GTC, concepts are grouped together under a higher order, more abstract concepts called categories. A category is a theoretical idea, it is a classification of concepts which is discovered to pertain to a similar phenomenon,[17] for example, in a classroom research, the indicators *teaching*, *asking questions*, and *talking* may be grouped together under the category *classroom interaction*.

Definition 2.3 - Let **C** be the set of categories, **I** be the set of indicators, and $\wp(\mathbf{I})$ be the power set of **I**, then a category is said to be coded from the indicators, which can be expressed as a partial onto functional mapping $\{ f : \wp(\mathbf{I}) \rightarrow \mathbf{C} \}$.

In GTC, the major entities are called categories. A theory is said to be built when two or more categories are conceptually related in some way. Thus, it is important to develop categories and relations from indicators. By constant comparison of indicators to indicators and their related segments, the researcher is forced into confronting similarities, differences, and degrees of consistency of meaning among indicators. This generates an underlying uniformity, which in turn results in coded categories, coded relations, definitions and properties of categories and relations, and theoretical memos. From the comparisons of additional indicators to coded categories, the categories are sharpened to achieve their best fits to data, and further properties are also generated, until yielding nothing much new.[16]

3. Semantic Network Representation

The different approaches to KR can be classified into two major groups: logical formalism (e.g. predicate logic, nonmonotonic logic) and structured representation (e.g. semantic networks, conceptual graph, scripts, and frames). Logical formalisms are often useful for representing simple facts. But the representation of theory construction is a very complex task, it cannot be just represented by formal logic. The rigidity of formal logic is not suitable for the real world description, for instance, (i) all terms used in logic are assumed completely precise and determinate in their real-world application, (ii) generalisations are completely universal, expressing no notion of meaning relationships between their terms as being relevant to their truth, or of the normal use of generalisations as heuristic guides in a language game, and (iii) epistemological and conceptual links between terms, critical to everyday discourse and social theorising is totally ignored. Thus, the power of logical formalism KR for theory construction is questionable.

Compared to logical formalism, structured representation is preferable for representing GTC. In this paper, semantic networks serve as the basis for KR in GTC, and frames are used as data structures in the implementation. Semantic networks provide powerful visual representation for GTC, which facilitates the researcher to reason, reflect and discover on the theoretical outcomes.

We may map the GTC objects categories and relations to nodes and links respectively in a semantic network. A semantic network is defined as a set of triples: $\{< m, r, n > | r \in R(A) \wedge m \in N(A) \wedge n \in N(A)\}$, where R(A) is the set of relations in the network A, and N(A) is the set of nodes in the network A.

There are advantages of using semantic network representation for GTC,[2] but semantic networks have their limits. We cannot use the binary link to represent n-place relations in a semantic network, or represent logical ideas, such as, "not", "or", "all", and "some" without losing the intuitive directness of the visual representation.[11] Some researches have been done regarding these shortcomings, for example, Harel's HiGraph and Sowa's Conceptual Graphs provide the expressive power of redicate logic in semantic networks. For GTC, the most influential shortcomings of the conventional semantic networks are rather the limited power for exploring relations and the discovery of the "core categories" (about which more later) as demanded by the GT researchers.[16] Therefore, we introduce the fuzzy set theory into semantic networks to enhance their ability in relations exploration and core categories discovery.

4. Exploration of Relations among Categories

Theories are descriptions of descriptions. A theory is simply a way of organizing our descriptions of the world, and constructing theory is to understand the relationships among the things that we study.[4] Here we define two indices, namely, inclusion index and overlap index between two categories, which enable the researcher to explore the relations among categories in theory construction.

Existing QDA software systems have been confined mainly to counting the number of occurrences of words or categories, and coding categories as if they were "hard-edged" and mutually exclusive.[14] Fuzzy set theory provides a formal foundation for handling categories to which items may belong partly, or in degree. If a category is viewed as a fuzzy set, then we may ask the degree of membership of a certain segment (S) in a certain category (C).[13]

Definition 4.1 - Let m_{ij} denote the *degree of membership* of the ith segment in the jth category (which was assigned by the researcher). Then the degree to which the ith segment is held in common by the jth and k^{th} categories is defined in standard fuzzy set theory by the minimum degree of membership in either set:

$$C(m_{ij}, m_{ik}) = \min(m_{ij}, m_{ik}) \quad (1)$$

Definition 4.2 - The extent to which the jth category *includes* the kth category is :

$$IN_{jk} = \frac{\sum_i C(m_{ij}, m_{ik})}{\sum_i m_{ij}} \quad (2)$$

Definition 4.3 - The *degree of overlap* between the two categories is then defined by the maximum extent to which each includes the other:

$$O_{jk} = \max(IN_{jk}, IN_{kj}) \quad (3)$$

In the above formulae, IN_{jk} is the inclusion index and O_{jk} is the overlap index, both of their values are from 0 to 1. From these two indices, we may know whether a pair of categories overlap and to what extent, and we may also assess the extent to which one category includes another. The overlap indices also show the "connectedness" of a category in relations to other categories.

By using the above formulae, we may obtain the following "Rank Order of Overlap Index Table". It shows the information of all indices arranged in descending order of the overlap indices. For example, from the first row of the table, the overlap index between categories C2 and C6 is 1.00, the inclusion index of C2 includes C6 is 0.54, the inclusion index of C6 includes C2 is 1.00, the degree of the segment S1 is held in common by C2 and C6 is 0.2, and so forth. That means the researcher may look at the segments S5, S4, S2, and then S1 for exploring the relation between C2 and C6. This table guides the researcher to explore the relations among categories systematically.

Rank Order of Overlap Index Table

C(j)-C(k)	O(jk)	IN(jk)	IN(kj)	S1	S2	S3	S4	S5
C2-C6	1.00	0.54	1.00	0.2	0.3	0	0.33	0.37
......	......	......	......	......	......	......	......	......
C5-C7	0.38	0.23	0.38	0	0.1	0	0.3	0

5. Discovery of the Core Categories

In GT, a core category is a category that is central to the integration of the theory, for example the concept of "force" is a core concept in the theory of mechanics. Core categories are ones with great explanatory power in the domain under analysis, which crop up in important ways in most descriptions, theories, etc in the field, which can be seen to underly what is said by subjects in the narrative data. Core categories emerge in the investigations of a researcher only when she/he has already coded the empirical indicators in the qualitative data by conceptual categories. The next task is to try to determine which of the categories are the most central in the analytic process of theorising about the data. Isolating these for study is the most direct way of articulating and refining the emerging theory, and feeding back to the earlier coding to clarify the content of the data in terms of the emerging theory. The whole process can be viewed most aptly as embodying a coherentist epistemology in a Quinean "Web of Belief", with core categories near the centre of the web.[10]

The discovery of core categories is indispensible in GTC. There are several criteria for judging which category should serve as the core category: (i) It must be central; (ii) The core category must appear frequently in the data; and (iii) The core category relates easily to other categories.[16] According to these criteria, we introduce a mechanism to transform semantic network into "Category-Relation Diagram" by using the overlap indices.

Definition 5.1 - The Category-Relation Index (CRI) is a measurement of relative "centeredness" of a category with respect to the relations in a semantic network. It is defined by the following equation:

$$CRI_i = \frac{TR_i + TC_i}{RelationTotal} \tag{4}$$

$$\text{where } RelationTotal = \sum_i TR_i = \sum_i TC_i$$

In the above equation, TR_i is the total of overlap indices in the row of Ci, and TC_i is the total of overlap indices in the column of Ci, and RelationTotal is the total of all overlap indices. The CRI_i is a number valued from 0 to 1. If the CRI_i of a category is 1, then all relations in the network are linked to this category. For example, if we have the semantic network: {<C1, R9, C3>, <C2, R5, C6>, <C3, R2, C2>, <C3, R3, C6>, <C3, R1, C7>, <C4, R10, C3>, <C4, R4, C8>, <C5, R6, C3>, <C6, R11, C5>, <C7, R7, C2>, <C8, R8, C3>}, then a "Category-Relation Index Table" can be generated based on the overlap indices:

			Category-Relation Index Table								
	C1	C2	C3	C4	C5	C6	C7	C8	TR(i)	CRI	K
C1									0	0.07	8
C2			R2(0.97)				R7(0.81)		1.78	0.28	2
C3	R9(0.73)			R10(1.00)	R6(0.86)			R8(0.90)	3.49	0.64	1
C4									0	0.20	4
C5						R11(0.81)			0.81	0.17	7
C6		R5(1.00)	R3(1.00)						2	0.28	3
C7			R1(1.00)						1	0.18	6
C8				R4(1.00)					1	0.19	5
TC(i)	0.73	1	2.97	2	0.86	0.81	0.81	0.9	[10.08]		

Definition 5.2 - A *Category-Relation Diagram* is a semantic network transformed into a polar coordinate system by the rank order (k) of CRIs. The polar coordinates of a category in the diagram are defined by the following equations: $r_k = -\log(CRI_k)$ for $0.1 \le CRI_k \le 1$ or $r_k = 1$ for $0 \le CRI_k < 0.1$, and $\theta_k = (4+n-4k)\pi/2n$, where k (rank order) $=1,2,\ldots,n$ and n is the total number of categories in the network. For example, the coordinates of C3 $(r_1, \theta_1) = (0.2, \pi/2)$.

In the following Category-Relation Diagram, the numbers in brackets are the overlap indices of the relations. From it we may discover the core categories and how they relate to the other categories. Furthermore, we are also allowed to explore the structures of the network, such as, similarities between categories and chain effects among categories.

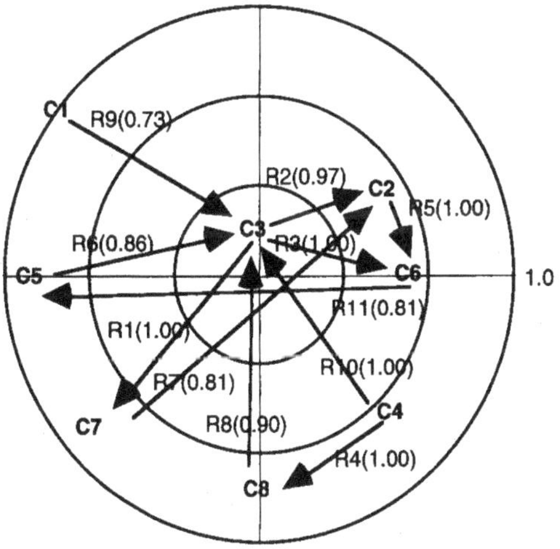

6. Conclusion

The purpose of QDA is to help us to discover theories. The task of developing concepts and contructing theories is a dynamic, creative and intuitive process. Therefore, it is really difficult to do automated analysis and theory construction, but we can make automatic and intelligent facilities to support and assist theory construction. Therefore, a salient KR method for supporting theory construction in QDA is indicated.

The KR method presented in this paper has several advantages over the existing QDA software systems[6,7,8,12] which support theory construction: (i) little attention has been paid to the fuzzinsss of the coding of categories (except for Smithson's works[13,14]), and this restricts approaches to theory construction; (ii) the rank order of overlap index table provides a systematic exploration of relations among categories; and (iii) the CRI and the Category-Relation Diagram provide a tractable way for the discovery of core categories.

References

1. R.A. Benfer, (1991) Expert Systems, London: Sage.
2. M. Bringmann, and F.E. Petry, (1992) A semantic network representation of personal construct systems, *IEEE Transactions on Systems, Man, and Cybernetics*, 23(5), 1161-1168.
3. A. Bryman, (1988) *Quantity and Quality in Social research*, London: Unwin Hyman.
4. E.M. Gerson (1990) Supplementing Grounded Theory, *Technical Report*, CA: Tremont Research Institute.
5. B. Glaser and A. Strauss, (1967) *The discovery of grounded theory*, Chicago: Aldine.
6. S. Hesse-Biber, et al., (1991) HyperRESEARCH: a computer program for the analysis of qualitative data with an emphasis on hypothesis testing and multimedia analysis, *Qualitative Sociology*, 14, 289-306.
7. G. Huber, (1990) *AQUAD 3.0,* Germany: Ingeborg Huber Publications.
8. T. Muhr, (1991) ATLAS/ti—A Prototype for the Support of Text Interpretation, *Qualitative Sociology*, 14(4), 349-371.
9. M.R. Quillian, (1968) Semantic Memory, in M. Minsky (ed.) *Semantic Information Processing*, MA: MIT Press, 216-270.
10. W. V. Quine, and J. S. Ullian, (1970) *The Web of Belief*, NY: Random House.
11. T.J. Richards, (1989) *Clausal Form Logic: the elements of computer resoning systems,* London: Addison-Wesley.
12. L. Richards, and T. Richards, (1991) Computing in Qualitative Analysis: A Healthy Development, *Qualitative Health Research*, 1(2), 234-262.
13. L.M. Scherl, and M. Smithson, (1987) A new dimension to content analysis: Exploring relationships among thematic categories, *Quality and Quantity*, 21, 199-208.
14. M. Smithson, (1982) Applications of Fuzzy set concepts to Behavioral Sciences, *Mathematical Social Sciences*, 2(3), 257-274.
15. J. F. Sowa, (1991) *Principles of Semantic Networks*, San Mateo: Morgan Kaufmann.
16. A. Strauss, (1987) *Qualitative Analysis for Social Scientists*, Cambridge: Cambridge University Press.
17. A. Strauss, and J. Corbin, (1990) *Basics of Qualitative Research*, Newbury Park: Sage.
18. S. J. Taylor, and R. Bogdan, (1984) *Introduction to Qualitative Research Methods*, 2nd ed., NY: John Wiley & Sons.

Modalities in Knowledge Representation

Ullrich Hustadt and Andreas Nonnengart
Max-Planck-Institut für Informatik,
Im Stadtwald, 66123 Saarbrücken, Germany

ABSTRACT

Standard knowledge representation systems are supposed to be able to represent either common or individual knowledge about the world.
In this paper we propose an extension to such knowledge representation systems which, in a uniform manner, allows to express beliefs of multiple agents as well as knowledge, desire, time and in fact any modality which has a first-order predicate logic possible world semantics.

1 Introduction

Since the mid-seventies a variety of knowledge representation systems in the tradition of semantic networks and terminological logics has been proposed. The most famous example is KL-ONE[3] which first appeared in 1977 in R. J. Brachman's Ph.D. thesis. Other examples are KRYPTON[2], NIKL[12], and $\mathcal{KRIS}$[1].

All these systems can be used to represent common or individual knowledge about the world. Recently, terminological logics have been extended to allow the representation of the knowledge or the beliefs of multiple agents in one knowledge base[4, 7]. In this paper, we investigate such an extension which allows not only to represent either knowledge or beliefs of multiple agents but a huge variety of modal operators for multiple agents.

2 Syntax and Semantics for Mod-$\mathcal{ALC}$

We assume four disjoint alphabets, the *primitive concepts* $\mathcal{C}$, the *primitive roles* $\mathcal{R}$, the set $\mathcal{M}$ of *modal operator names*, and the individual objects $\mathcal{O}$. In particular, there is a distinguished subset $\mathcal{A}$ of the individual objects, called the set of *agents*, containing the special agent *all* which is supposed to denote the union of all the agents in order to be able to express mutual belief. The tuple $(\mathcal{O}, \mathcal{A}, \mathcal{M}, \mathcal{C}, \mathcal{R})$ is called the *signature*, denoted by Σ.

The set of *concept terms* (or just *concepts*) and *role terms* (or just *roles*) is inductively defined as follows. Every primitive concept is a concept term and every primitive role is a role term. Now assume that C, C_1, and C_2 are concepts, R, R_1, and R_2 are roles, m is a modal operator name, a is an agent's name. Then $C_1 \sqcap C_2$, $\neg C$, $\exists\, R.C$, and $\Diamond_{(m,a)}\, C$ are concept terms, and $R_1 \sqcap R_2$, R^{-1}, $R|_C$, $\Box_{(m,a)}\, R$ and $\Diamond_{(m,a)}\, R$ are role terms.

Thus we are now able to describe the sentences of our language Mod-$\mathcal{ALC}$ which are divided into *terminological sentences* and *assertional sentences.* If C_1 and C_2 are concepts and R_1 and R_2 are roles then $C_1 \sqsubseteq C_2$, $R_1 \sqsubseteq R_2$ are terminological sentences. If C is a concept, R is a role, and O, O_1, and O_2 are individual objects then

$O \in C$ and $(O_1, O_2) \in R$ are assertional sentences. Moreover, if Φ is a terminological (respectively assertional) sentence and if m is a modal operator name and a is an agent's name then $\Box_{(m,a)} \Phi$ and $\Diamond_{(m,a)} \Phi$ are terminological (respectively assertional) sentences. A set of terminological and assertional sentences is a *knowledge base.*

So far the syntax of Mod-$\mathcal{ALC}$ has been described. Now we have to provide its semantics.

Definition 1 (Σ-Structures) As usual we define a *Σ-structure* as a pair $(\mathcal{D}, \mathcal{I})$ which consists of a domain $\mathcal{D}$ and an interpretation function $\mathcal{I}$ which maps the individual objects to elements of $\mathcal{D}$, primitive concepts to subsets of $\mathcal{D}$ and the primitive roles to subsets of $\mathcal{D} \times \mathcal{D}$.

Definition 2 (Frames and Interpretations) By a frame $\mathcal{F}$ we understand any pair $(\mathcal{W}, \Re)$ where $\mathcal{W}$ is a non-empty set (of worlds) and $\Re = \biguplus_{m \in \mathcal{M}, a \in \mathcal{A}} \Re_m^a$ where the $\Re_m^a$'s are binary relation on $\mathcal{W}$, the so-called *accessibility relations* between worlds.

By a Σ-interpretation $\Im$ based on $\mathcal{F}$ we understand any tuple $(\mathcal{D}, \mathcal{F}, \Im_{\text{loc}}, \epsilon)$ where $\mathcal{D}$ denotes the common domain of all Σ-structures in the range of $\Im_{\text{loc}}$, $\mathcal{F}$ is a frame, and $\Im_{\text{loc}}$ maps worlds to Σ-structures with common domain $\mathcal{D}$ which interpret agents' names equally.

Definition 3 (Interpretation of Terms) Let $\Im = (\mathcal{D}, \mathcal{F}, \Im_{\text{loc}}, \epsilon)$ be a Σ-interpretation and let $\Im_{\text{loc}}(\epsilon) = (\mathcal{D}, \mathcal{I})$. We define the interpretation of terms inductively over their structure:

$$\begin{array}{lcll}
\Im(C) & = & \mathcal{I}(C) & \text{if } C \text{ is a primitive concept} \\
\Im(R) & = & \mathcal{I}(R) & \text{if } R \text{ is a primitive role} \\
\Im(C_1 \sqcap C_2) & = & \Im(C_1) \cap \Im(C_2) & \\
\Im(\neg C) & = & \mathcal{D} \setminus \Im(C) & \\
\Im(\exists R.C) & = & \{d \in \mathcal{D} \mid e \in \Im(C) \text{ for some } e \text{ with } (d, e) \in \Im(R)\} & \\
\Im(\Diamond_{(m,a)} C) & = & \{d \in \mathcal{D} \mid d \in \Im[\chi](C) \text{ for some } \chi \text{ with } \Re_m^a(\epsilon, \chi)\} & \\
\Im(R_1 \sqcap R_2) & = & \Im(R_1) \cap \Im(R_2) & \\
\Im(R^{-1}) & = & \{(x, y) \in \mathcal{D} \times \mathcal{D} \mid (y, x) \in \Im(R)\} & \\
\Im(R|_C) & = & \{(x, y) \in \Im(R) \mid y \in \Im(C)\} & \\
\Im(\Box_{(m,a)} R) & = & \{(x, y) \mid (x, y) \in \Im[\chi](R) \text{ for all } \chi \text{ with } \Re_m^a(\epsilon, \chi)\} & \\
\Im(\Diamond_{(m,a)} R) & = & \{(x, y) \mid (x, y) \in \Im[\chi](R) \text{ for some } \chi \text{ with } \Re_m^a(\epsilon, \chi)\} &
\end{array}$$

where $\Im[\chi] = (\mathcal{D}, \mathcal{F}, \Im_{\text{loc}}, \chi)$.

Definition 4 (Satisfiability) Let $\Im = (\mathcal{D}, \mathcal{F}, \Im_{\text{loc}}, \epsilon)$ be a Σ-interpretation. We define the satisfiability relation $\models$ inductively over the structure of Mod-$\mathcal{ALC}$ sentences:

$$\begin{array}{lll}
\Im \models C_1 \sqsubseteq C_2 & \text{iff} & \Im(C_1) \subseteq \Im(C_2) \\
\Im \models R_1 \sqsubseteq R_2 & \text{iff} & \Im(R_1) \subseteq \Im(R_2) \\
\Im \models x \in C & \text{iff} & \mathcal{I}(x) \in \Im(C) \\
\Im \models (x, y) \in R & \text{iff} & (\mathcal{I}(x), \mathcal{I}(y)) \in \Im(R) \\
\Im \models \Box_{(m,a)} \Phi & \text{iff} & \Im[\chi] \models \Phi \text{ for every } \chi \text{ with } \Re_m^a(\epsilon, \chi) \\
\Im \models \Diamond_{(m,a)} \Phi & \text{iff} & \Im[\chi] \models \Phi \text{ for some } \chi \text{ with } \Re_m^a(\epsilon, \chi)
\end{array}$$

Definition 5 Let $\Im$ be an interpretation and let Φ be a Mod-$\mathcal{ALC}$ sentence with $\Im \models \Phi$. Then we call Φ *satisfiable* and we call $\Im$ a *model* for Φ. If all interpretations are models for Φ then we call Φ a *theorem*. Any sentence for which no model exists is called *unsatisfiable*. Thus, Φ is a theorem iff its negation is unsatisfiable.

Let T be a set of Mod-$\mathcal{ALC}$ sentences. We say T *entails* Φ, written $T \models \Phi$, iff every model of T is a model of Φ.

So far we did not consider any special properties of the given modal operators. Typical axiom schemata which reflect such potential additional properties are listed below.

Axiom Schema	Property
$\Box_{(m,a)} \Phi \Rightarrow \Diamond_{(m,a)} \Phi$	$\forall x \exists y\, \Re^a_m(x,y)$
$\Box_{(m,a)} \Phi \Rightarrow \Phi$	$\forall x\, \Re^a_m(x,x)$
$\Phi \Rightarrow \Box_{(m,a)} \Diamond_{(m,a)} \Phi$	$\forall x,y\, \Re^a_m(x,y) \Rightarrow \Re^a_m(y,x)$
$\Box_{(m,a)} \Phi \Rightarrow \Box_{(m,a)} \Box_{(m,a)} \Phi$	$\forall x,y,z\, \Re^a_m(x,y) \wedge \Re^a_m(y,z) \Rightarrow \Re^a_m(x,z)$
$\Diamond_{(m,a)} \Phi \Rightarrow \Box_{(m,a)} \Diamond_{(m,a)} \Phi$	$\forall x,y,z\, \Re^a_m(x,y) \wedge \Re^a_m(x,z) \Rightarrow \Re^a_m(y,z)$

Table 1: Properties of the accessibility relation

Historically, these properties are called D, T, B, 4, and 5 respectively.

If we consider modal operators for belief, i.e. $\Box_{(believe,a)}$ and $\Diamond_{(believe,a)}$, then 4 and 5 are axioms of introspection. Intuitively, they say that the agent a has complete insight what his own beliefs are concerned. Property T is one of the major characteristics of modal operators for knowledge, i.e. $\Box_{(knows,a)}$ and $\Diamond_{(knows,a)}$, because it enables us to deduce a fact about the real world from an agent's knowledge about the world.

Definition 6 Let $\mathcal{R}$ be a set of properties of the accessibility relation. An interpretation $\Im$ is called a *$\mathcal{R}$-interpretation* if the accessibility relation $\Re$ of the underlying frame $\mathcal{F}$ satisfies all properties in $\mathcal{R}$. We say a set of Mod-$\mathcal{ALC}$ sentences T *entails* Φ *in all $\mathcal{R}$-interpretations*, written $T \models_{\mathcal{R}} \Phi$, if all $\mathcal{R}$-interpretations which are models of T are also models of Φ.

What is remarkable for the properties from above is that they all are first-order properties. Therefore it is not too surprising that a translation of modal terminological and modal assertional axioms into first-order predicate logic can be done very easily.

3 Translating Mod-$\mathcal{ALC}$ into Classical Logic

There have been a lot of proposals for correct and complete calculi for nonclassical logics — temporal logics[11], epistemic logics[8], etc. — and terminological logics[3, 5].

Unfortunately, these calculi require implementations for their respective theorem proving system with hardly a chance to apply results and techniques of the traditional work on automated theorem proving. Therefore, we follow the approach of Ohlbach[10] to eliminate modal operators in a way that we get standard first-order predicate logic formulae that still represent the modal semantics.

However, if we take a closer look at the results of a straightforward translation of terminological and assertional sentences into first-order logic we can see quite a big problem. Already simple knowledge bases result in rather huge clause sets where many of the clauses merely express certain informations about accessibilities and role correlations. But we can exploit a property of the language Mod-$\mathcal{ALC}$ which is typical for most modal and terminological logics, namely, each accessibility relation symbol or role symbol R occurs either in the form $\exists x\ R(\ldots, x) \wedge \Phi(x)$ or in the form $\forall x\ R(\ldots, x) \Rightarrow \Phi(x)$.

First of all let us define what we mean by a *functional simulator.*

Definition 7 (Functional Simulators) Let $\Re$ be an n-ary relation. A set $\mathbf{F}_\Re$ of functions is called a *functional simulator for* $\Re$ if for any $x_1, \ldots, x_n$

$$\Re(x_1, \ldots, x_n) \text{ iff there exists a } f \in \mathbf{F}_\Re \text{ with } f(x_1, \ldots, x_{n-1}) = x_n$$

In particular, if $\Re$ is total, i.e. for any $x_1 \ldots x_{n-1}$ there is a x_n such that $\Re(x_1, \ldots, x_n)$ then each function in $\mathbf{F}_\Re$ is total, too.

I.e. a functional simulator for some relation R is a set of functions which is able to take over the responsibilities of R. What a functional simulator is on the meta-level are the simulator axioms on the object level.

Definition 8 (Simulator Axioms for Total Predicates) According to Definition 7 we call the two axioms

$$\begin{aligned} \mathrm{Sim}_1^R &= \forall u_i, v\ R(\ldots, u_i, \ldots, v) \Rightarrow \exists f{:}\mathrm{F}_R\ f(\ldots, u_i, \ldots) = v \\ \mathrm{Sim}_2^R &= \forall u_i \forall f{:}\mathrm{F}_R\ R(\ldots, u_i, \ldots, f(\ldots, u_i, \ldots)) \end{aligned}$$

the *simulator axioms* for the total predicate R. Note that in the case of non-total predicates the definition of Sim_2^R needs to be changed because in this case we have to be able to deal with partial functions instead of total functions. The collection of all axioms Sim_1^R, respectively Sim_2^R, is called Sim_1, respectively Sim_2.

Thus, for any total (serial) accessibility relation or role we can introduce functional simulators. This allows the following approach for the translation of knowledge bases into first-order predicate logic.

First, we transform all concepts and roles which occur in a given knowledge base into *negation normal form*, i.e. in a form where all negation signs occur solely in front of the primitive concepts. Now we translate the terminological and assertional sentences into first-order logic formulae using the function $[\![\ \_\ ]\!]$.

Axiom	Translation
$[\![\Box_{(m,a)} M_2 \ldots M_n \Phi]\!]_U$	$\forall V : \Re^a_m(U, V) \Rightarrow [\![M_2 \ldots M_n \Phi]\!]_V$
$[\![\Diamond_{(m,a)} M_2 \ldots M_n \Phi]\!]_U$	$\exists V{:}\mathbf{F}_{\Re^a_m}\ [\![M_2 \ldots M_n \Phi]\!]_{V(U)}$
$[\![C_1 \sqsubseteq C_2]\!]_U$	$\forall X : [\![C_1]\!]_{U,X} \Rightarrow [\![C_2]\!]_{U,X}$
$[\![R_1 \sqsubseteq R_2]\!]_U$	$\forall X, Y : [\![R_1]\!]_{U,(X,Y)} \Rightarrow [\![R_2]\!]_{U,(X,Y)}$
$[\![a \in A]\!]_U$	$[\![A]\!]_{U,a}$
$[\![(a, b) \in P]\!]_U$	$[\![P]\!]_{U,(a,b)}$

where the translation of concepts and roles is defined by:

Term	Translation
$[\![A_1]\!]_{U,X}$	$A_1(U,X)$
$[\![\neg A_1]\!]_{U,X}$	$\neg A_1(U,X)$
$[\![C_1 \sqcap \ldots \sqcap C_k]\!]_{U,X}$	$[\![C_1]\!]_{U,X} \wedge \ldots \wedge [\![C_k]\!]_{U,X}$
$[\![\exists R.C]\!]_{U,X}$	$\exists Y{:}\mathbf{F}_R\, [\![C]\!]_{U,Y(X)}$
$[\![\Diamond_{(m,a)}\, C]\!]_{U,X}$	$\exists V{:}\mathbf{F}_{\Re^a_m}\, [\![C]\!]_{V(U),X}$
$[\![P]\!]_{U,(X,Y)}$	$P(U,X,Y)$
$[\![R_1 \sqcap \ldots \sqcap R_l]\!]_{U,(X,Y)}$	$[\![R_1]\!]_{U,(X,Y)} \wedge \ldots \wedge [\![R_l]\!]_{U,(X,Y)}$
$[\![R^{-1}]\!]_{U,(X,Y)}$	$[\![R]\!]_{U,(Y,X)}$
$[\![R\vert C]\!]_{U,(X,Y)}$	$[\![R]\!]_{U,(X,Y)} \wedge [\![C]\!]_{U,Y}$
$[\![\Box_{(m,a)}\, R]\!]_{U,(X,Y)}$	$\forall V : \Re^a_m(U,V) \Rightarrow [\![R]\!]_{V,(X,Y)}$
$[\![\Diamond_{(m,a)}\, R]\!]_{U,(X,Y)}$	$\exists V{:}\mathbf{F}_{\Re^a_m} [\![R]\!]_{V(U),(X,Y)}$

Thus, given any Mod-$\mathcal{ALC}$-formula Φ, the result of the above translation, $[\![\Phi]\!]_\epsilon$ is a first-order predicate logic formula which can easily be transformed into clause normal form with the help of the well-known standard techniques.

Note that the clause form of such a translation does not contain any positive occurrence of a role or accessibility relation symbol. This fact can be exploited in a very interesting manner. Since any role or accessibility relation symbol can only occur in the additional axioms we can examine these independently from the translated formula. Nonnengart[9] presents extremely good simplifications for various modal logics. So, for instance, the whole theory for the modal logic KD45 can be simplified to the almost trivial unit clause $R(U, V(W))$.

In the following theorem we suppose that we have some simplification *Sim* which can be applied to a set $\mathcal{R}$ of formulae expressing the properties of the accessibility relation such that

$$\mathcal{R} \cup \{\mathrm{Sim}_2\} \models [\![\Phi]\!]_\epsilon \text{ iff } Sim(\mathcal{R}) \cup \{\mathrm{Sim}_2\} \models [\![\Phi]\!]_\epsilon$$

Theorem 3.1 *Let Φ be a Mod-$\mathcal{ALC}$ sentence and T a set of Mod-$\mathcal{ALC}$ sentences. Let $\mathcal{R}$ be a set of formulae which express the properties of the underlying accessibility relation. Then*

$$T \models_{\mathcal{R}} \phi$$

iff $\quad \bigcup_{\Psi \in T} [\![\Psi]\!]_\epsilon \cup Sim(\mathcal{R}) \cup \{\mathrm{Sim}_2\} \models [\![\Phi]\!]_\epsilon$

iff $[\![\Phi]\!]_\epsilon$ *is provable from* $\bigcup_{\Psi \in T} [\![\Psi]\!]_\epsilon \cup Sim(\mathcal{R}) \cup \{\mathrm{Sim}_2\}$ *using some theorem prover which is correct and complete for first-order logic with equality.*

4 Conclusion and Further Work

We presented an approach which allows to reason within modal terminological logics by utilizing an appropriate translation technique into first-order predicate logic. The main idea behind this method is the *functional simulation* of accessibility relations and roles by suitable sets of functions. This turns out to have two main advantages: it decreases the size and the number of clauses and it allows significant simplifications on the set of theory clauses.

Until now, we have only worked out the optimization for those modalities which have a simple possible world semantics. If the interaction of multiple modalities requires the more complex neighbourhood semantics, we have to rely on the straightforward translation which will result in a rather large number of clauses. Looking for optimizations for this case is part of future work.

References

1. F. Baader and B. Hollunder, *$\mathcal{KRIS}$: Knowledge Representation and Inference System — System Description —*. Technical Memo DFKI-TM-90-03 (Deutsches Forschungszentrum für Künstliche Intelligenz, Saarbrücken, 1990).

2. R. J. Brachman, V. P. Gilbert, and H. J. Levesque, *An Essential Hybrid Reasoning System: Knowledge and Symbol Level Accounts of* KRYPTON. In *Proceedings of the Ninth IJCAI*, pp. 532–539.

3. R. J. Brachman and J. G. Schmolze, *An Overview of the* KLONE *Knowledge Representation System.* Cognitive Science 9 2 (1985), pp. 171–216.

4. F. M. Donini, M. Lenzerini, D. Nardi, A. Schaerf, and W. Nutt, *Adding Epistemic Operators to Concept Languages.* In *Proceedings of the KR'92*, eds. B. Nebel, C. Rich, and W. Swartout (Morgan Kaufmann, 1992), pp. 342–353.

5. B. Hollunder and W. Nutt, *Subsumption Algorithms for Concept Languages.* Research Report DFKI-RR-90-04 (Deutsches Forschungszentrum für Künstliche Intelligenz, Saarbrücken, 1990).

6. U. Hustadt, A. Nonnengart, R. Schmidt, and J. Timm, *MOTEL User Manual.* Internal report MPI-I-92-236 (Max-Planck-Institute for Computer Science, Saarbrücken, 1992).

7. A. Kobsa, *Towards Inferences in BGP-MS: Combining Modal Logic and Partition Hierarchies for User Modeling (Preliminary Report).* In *Proceedings of the Third International Workshop on User Modeling* (1992).

8. R. C. Moore, *Autoepistemic Logic.* In *Non-Standard Logics for Automated Reasoning*, eds. Ph. Smets, E. H. Mamdani, D. Dubois, and H. Prade (Academic Press, London, 1988)

9. A. Nonnengart, *First-Order Modal Logic Theorem Proving and Standard PROLOG.* Internal report MPI-I-92-228 (Max-Planck-Institute for Computer Science, Saarbrücken, 1992).

10. H. J. Ohlbach, *A Resolution Calculus for Modal Logics.* PhD thesis (Universität Kaiserslautern, 1988).

11. N. Rescher and A. Urquhart, *Temporal Logic* (Springer, Berlin, 1971).

12. J. G. Schmolze, *The Language and Semantics of* NIKL. Technical Report 89-4 (Department of Computer Science, Tufts University, Medford, MA, 1989).

Node Subsumption in a Propositional Semantic Network with Structured Variables

SYED S. ALI
Department of Computer Science
Southwest Missouri State University
901 South National Avenue
Springfield, MO 65804-0094, USA

ABSTRACT

We present a formal description of a propositional semantic-network-based knowledge representation system. Variables in this representation are not atomic and have potentially complex structure. We start from the individual components of a semantic network system, atomics nodes and relations that connect nodes, and provide a complete specification for the structure of nodes and a subsumption procedure between nodes. We differ from other work in subsumption in that the representation language is uniform and based on a first-order predicate logic. There is no distinction between taxonomic and axiomatic knowledge. The utility of the subsumption procedure for processing natural language is illustrated.

1 Introduction

Subsumption is a partial ordering on related concepts (say, nodes in a semantic network) that relates more general concepts to more specific instances of that concept. The manner in which "more general" is determined characterizes the type of subsumption (Woods characterizes subsumption into *extensional, structural, recorded, axiomatic,* and *deduced* subsumption [9]). We present a procedure for determining *structural* and *deduced* subsumption between concept nodes in a propositional semantic network representation (one in which propositions are represented by nodes and not arcs of the network). To this end we specify the structure of the nodes of the propositional semantic network system in terms of its components, nodes and relations between nodes, and specify the subsumption procedure in terms of these components. This subsumption procedure can also do the type of subsumption inference associated with KL-ONE classification [5] and its successors (most notablely KRYPTON [4]). This subsumption procedure does this without a distinction between an assertional and terminological component. Consequently, we avoid conceptual problems associated with the sharing of information between the T-box and A-Box [3]. For a more detailed description of the semantics of nodes in a propositional semantic network (such as the one presented here) see [8, 2].

2 The Knowledge Representation Formalism

We provide a syntax and semantics of a logic whose variables are not atomic and have structure. We call these variables *structured variables.* The syntax of the logic is specified by a complete definition of a propositional semantic network representation formalism. This work augments the work of [7], who defines propositional SNePS, by specifying the extended first-order logic of a descendent of SNePS. The implemented system is called ANALOG (A NAtural LOGic) and is used here, for convenience, to refer to the logical system.

As a propositional semantic network formalism, it is necessary that nodes have some propositional meaning. Any theory of semantics that ascribes propositional meaning to nodes can be the semantics used in ANALOG. In this paper, examples are used that follow the follow the case frame semantics of [8] who provides a collection of propositional case frames and their associated semantics. Their semantics is based on an extended first-order predicate logic. We will provide semantics for nodes, in this paper, as necessary.

ANALOG nodes are terms of a formal language. The interpretation of a node is an object in the domain of interpretation, called entities. Every ANALOG node denotes an entity and if n is an ANALOG node then $[\![n]\!]$ denotes the entity represented by n. In the rest of this explication the term node will be used for ANALOG node, and relation for ANALOG relation. To help formalize this description we follow [7] in using the metapredicates *Conceive*, *Believe*, and =. If n, n_1, n_2 are metavariables ranging over nodes and p is a metavariable ranging over proposition nodes, the semantics of these metapredicates are:

Conceive(n) Means that the node is actually constructed in the network. *Conceive*(n) may be true without $[\![n]\!]$ being known to be true or false.

Believe(p) Means that the proposition is believed to be true. $[\![p]\!]$.

$n_1 = n_2$ Means that n_1 and n_2 are the same, identical, node.

Belief entails conception, as specified in Axiom one.

Axiom 1: *Believe*(p) $\Rightarrow$ *Conceive*(p)

2.1 Definition of Nodes

Informally, an node consists of a set of labeled (by relations) directed arcs to one or more nodes. Additionally, a node may be labeled by a "name" (e.g., `BILL`, `M1`, `V1`) as a useful (but extra-theoretic) way to refer to the node. This naming of a rule or proposition node is of the form `M`n, where n is some integer. A "!" is appended to the name to show that the proposition represented by the node is believed (i.e., `M1!` $\Longleftrightarrow$ `M1` $\in \Gamma$). However, the "!" does not affect the identity of the node, nor the proposition it represents. Similarly, variable nodes naming is `V`n where n is some integer, and base nodes naming is `B`n where n is some integer (additionally, base nodes may be named for the concept they represent, e.g., `man`.) More formally a node is defined as follows:

Definition 1: There is a none-empty collection of labelled atomic nodes called **base nodes**. Typically, base nodes are labelled by the entity they denote. *Example:* `bill` is a base node.

Definition 2: A **wire** is an ordered pair $<r, n>$ where r is a relation, and n is a node. Meta-variables $w, w_1, w_2, \ldots$ range over wires. *Example:* `<member, john>` is a wire.

Definition 3: A **nodeset** is a set of nodes, $\{n_1, \ldots, n_k\}$. Meta-variables $ns, ns_1, ns_2, \ldots$ range over nodesets. *Example:* `{john, bill}` is a nodeset if `john` and `bill` are nodes.

Definition 4: A **cable** is an ordered pair $\langle r, ns \rangle$, where r is a relation, and ns is a non-empty set of nodes. Meta-variables $c, c_1, c_2, \ldots$ range over cables. *Example:* <member, {john, bill}> is a cable.

Definition 5: A **cableset** is a non-empty set of cables, $\{\langle r_1, ns_1 \rangle, \ldots, \langle r_k, ns_k \rangle\}$, such that $r_i = r_j \iff i = j$. Meta-variables $cs, cs_1, cs_2, \ldots$ range over cablesets. *Example:* {<member, {john, bill}>, <class, {man}>} is a cableset.

Definition 6: Every node is either a base node or a cableset. *Examples:* bill is a base node, {<member, {john, bill}>, <class, {man}>} is a cableset.

Definition 7: We overload the **membership** relation "$\in$" so that $x \in s$ holds just under the following conditions (*Subsume* is defined in Figure 1):

1. If x is a node and s is a nodeset, $x \in s \iff \exists y\ [y \in s \land Subsume(y, x).]$
2. If x is a wire, $\langle r_1, n \rangle$ and s is a cable, $\langle r_2, ns \rangle$, then $x \in s \iff r_1 = r_2 \land n \in ns$.
3. If x is a wire and s is a cableset, then $x \in s \iff \exists c[c \in s \land x \in c]$.

Examples: M1 $\in$ {M1, M2, M3}
<member, john> $\in$ <member, {john, bill}>
<member, john> $\in$ {<member, {john, bill}>, <class, {man}>}

Definition 8: A **variable** node is a cableset of the form {<all, ns>} (**universal**) or {<some, ns_1>, <depends, ns_2>} (**existential**). A variable node is further restricted in the form it may take in the following ways:

1. If it has the form {<all, ns>}, then every $n \in ns$ *must* dominate it.
2. If it has the form {<some, ns_1>, <depends, ns_2>}, then every $n \in ns_1$ *must* dominate it *and* every $n \in ns_2$ *must* be a universal variable node.

Example: V1 = {<all, {{<member, {V1}>, <class, {man}>}}>} is the variable node corresponding to *every man*.

We define two selectors for variable nodes: $rest(\{\langle all, ns \rangle\}) = ns$ for universal variable nodes and $rest(\{\langle some, ns_1 \rangle, \langle depends, ns_2 \rangle\}) = ns_1$ and $depend(\{\langle some, ns_1 \rangle, \langle depends, ns_2 \rangle\}) = ns_2$ for existential variable nodes. Informally, $rest(v)$ is the set of restriction propositions on the types of things that may be bound to the variable node v. $Depend(v)$ is the universal variable nodes on which an existential variable node, v, is scope dependent.

Definition 9: A **molecular** node is a cableset that is *not* a variable node. *Example:* {<member, {john, bill}>, <class, {man}>} is a molecular node, since it is a cableset but not a variable node.

Definition 10: A **nrn-path** from a node n_1 to a node n_{k+1} is a sequence, $n_1, r_1, \ldots, n_k, r_k, n_{k+1}$ for $(k \geq 1)$ where the n_i are nodes, the r_i are relations, and for each i, $\langle r_i, n_{i+1} \rangle$ is a wire in n_i. *Example:* If: M1 = {<member, {john, bill}>, <class, {man}>} then M1, member, john and M1, class, man are some nrn-paths.

Definition 11: A node n_1 **dominates** a node n_2 just in case there is a nrn-path from n_1 to n_2. *Example:* If M1 = {<member, {john, bill}>, <class, {man}>} then M1 dominates john since there is an nrn-path M1, member, john from M1 to john.

Definition 12: A **rule** node is a molecular node that dominates a variable node that does not, in turn, dominate it. *Example:* Where V1 = {<all, {M1}>}, M1 = {<member, {V1}>,<class, {man}>}, and M2 = {<member, {V1}>, <class, {mortal}>}; M2 is a rule node since M2 dominates V1 which does not, in turn, dominate M2. M1 is *not* a rule node because, while it dominates V1, it is also dominated by V1. The non-rule nodes that dominate variable nodes correspond to restrictions on binders of those same variable nodes.

Definition 13: An **ANALOG model** consists of a tuple $(A, B, M, R, U, E, \Gamma)$ where A is a set of relations, B is a set of base nodes, M is a set of molecular nodes, R is a set of rule nodes, U is a set of universal variable nodes, and E is a set of existential variable nodes. B, M, R, U, and, E are disjoint. $\Gamma \subseteq M \cup R$ and consists of believed propositions.

2.1.1 Reduction

We follow [6, 7] in arguing for a form of reduction inference as being useful. Reduction inferences is peculiar to semantic network formalisms and allows a proposition to "reduce" to (logicly imply) propositions whose wires are a subset of the wires of the original proposition. However we must restrict the use of reduction inference to precisely those propositions and rules which are reducible through the use of the *IsReducible* metapredicate.

Axiom 2: $Reduce(cs_1, cs_2) \iff (\forall w[w \in cs_2 \Rightarrow w \in cs_1] \wedge IsReducible(cs_1))$.

The semantics of the metapredicate *IsReducible* will be specified in terms of the particular case frames used in a representation. This is because some propositional case frames are reducible (the brothers proposition, for example) and others are not. A proposition that is a reducible reduction of a believed proposition is also a believed proposition. Since nodes are cablesets we state this as in Axiom 3.

Axiom 3: $(Reduce(n_1, n_2) \wedge Believe(n_1)) \Rightarrow Believe(n_2)$

2.2 Subsumption

Semantic network formalisms provide "links" that relate more general concepts to more specific concepts. This is called a *taxonomy* and allows information about concepts to be associated with their most general concept, and information filters down to more specific concepts in the taxonomy via inheritance. More general concepts in such a taxonomy *subsume* more specific concepts, the subsumee inheriting information from its subsumers. For atomic concepts, subsumption relations between concepts is specified by the links of the taxonomy. The paradigmatic example of subsumption for structured concepts, is that of KL-ONE, where a description such as: *person that has children* subsumes: *person that has a son.* The intuitive idea is that more general descriptions should subsume more specific descriptions of the same sort. To define subsumption in ANALOG we require some additional definitions.

Definition 14: A binding is a pair v/u where, either u and v are both SVs of the same type (universal or existential), or u is an universal SV and v is a node. *Examples:* V1/V2 and JOHN/V1.

Definition 15: A **substitution** is a set of bindings, $\{t_1/v_1, \ldots, t_n/v_n\}$. *Examples:* {V1/V2,

JOHN/V3} and {B1/V1, M1/V2}.

Definition 16: The result of **applying** a substitution, $\theta = \{t_1/v_1, \ldots, t_n/v_n\}$, to a node n is the instance $n\theta$ of n obtained by simultaneously replacing each of the v_i dominated by n with t_i, respectively. *Example:* If M1 = {<member, {V1}>, <class, {MAN}>} then: M1{JOHN/V1} = {<member, {JOHN}>, <class, {MAN}>}

Definition 17: Let $\theta = \{s_1/u_1, \ldots, s_n/u_n\}$ and $\rho = \{t_1/v_1, \ldots, t_m/v_m\}$ be substitutions. Then the **composition** $\theta \cdot \rho$ of θ and ρ is the substitution obtained from the set $\{s_1\rho/u_1, \ldots, s_n\rho/u_n, t_1/v_1, \ldots, t_m/v_m\}$ by deleting any binding $s_i\rho/u_i$ for which $u_i = s_i\rho$. *Example:* If $\theta =$ {V1/V2, V4/V3} and $\rho =$ {V2/V1, JOHN/V4} then: $\theta \cdot \rho =$ {JOHN/V3, JOHN/V4}

Definition 18: A substitution, θ, is **consistent** iff neither of the following hold:

$$\exists u, t, s[t/u \in \theta \wedge s/u \in \theta \wedge s \neq t]$$

$$\exists u, v, t[t/u \in \theta \wedge t/v \in \theta \wedge u \neq v] \text{ (UVBR)}$$

A substitution that is not consistent is termed **inconsistent**. The motivation for the second constraint (UVBR, unique variable binding rule) is that in natural language users seldom want different variables in the same sentence to bind an identical object [6].
Examples: {JOHN/V2, BILL/V2} is inconsistent. {JOHN/V1, JOHN/V2} is inconsistent.
{JOHN/V1, BILL/V2} is consistent.

Subsume(x, y) in a model $(A,\ B,\ M,\ R,\ U,\ E,\ \Gamma)$ iff any one of:

1. $x = y$.
2. *Reduce*(x, y)
3. For $x \in U$ and $y \in B \cup M \cup R$, if there exists a substitution S such that $\forall r[r \in rest(x),\ \Gamma \vdash r\{y/x\} \cdot S]$. Logical derivation is here denoted by "$\vdash$." Substitution and substitution application with respect to a node is here denoted by "$r\{y/x\} \cdot S$."
4. For $x \in U$ and $y \in U \cup E$, if $\forall r[r \in rest(x) \Rightarrow \exists s[s \in rest(y) \wedge Subsume(r, s)]]$
5. For $x, y \in E$, if all of the following hold:
   $\forall s[s \in rest(y) \Rightarrow \exists r[r \in rest(x) \wedge Subsume(r, s)]]$
   $\forall r[r \in rest(x) \Rightarrow \exists s[s \in rest(y) \wedge Subsume(r, s)]]$
   $\forall d[d \in depends(y) \Rightarrow \exists c[c \in depends(x) \wedge Subsume(c, d)]]$

Figure 1: Subsumption Procedure

In ANALOG we specify subsumption between nodes in the network as a binary relation between arbitrary nodes in the network. We define subsumption between two nodes x and y as in Figure 1. Note that the restrictions on subsumption involving variables is stricter than *Reduce*, which only requires that the wires of one node be a subset of the other. This sort of subsumption corresponds to some traditional forms of inference. I. e., from *All x are y*, it follows *Some x are y* by universal instantiation, followed by existential introduction. For example, from *All girls love some boy*, it follows that *All girls that own a dog love some boy* directly by subsumption. As with reduction (Axiom 3) a proposition that is subsumed by a believed proposition is also a believed proposition.

Axiom 4: $(Subsume(n_1, n_2) \wedge Believe(n_1)) \Rightarrow Believe(n_2)$

For more detailed, natural language based, examples of the use of this subsumption procedure see [1, 2].

3 Summary

We have specified the structure of a propositional semantic network formalism in terms of constituent nodes and relations. We have, in these same terms specified a subsumption procedure that allows the determination of subsumption relations, without any explicit inference (although inference is possible). This subsumption procedure allows for determination of subsumption relationships between node structures corresponding to complex concepts without the need for distinguishing terminological and assertional components. All the work described, here, is currently implemented. Current work involves incorporating this subsumption procedure into a unification procedure for inference.

References

[1] Syed S. Ali. A Propositional Semantic Network with Structured Variables for Natural Language Processing. In *Proceedings of the Sixth Australian Joint Conference on Artificial Intelligence.*, November 17-19 1993.

[2] Syed S. Ali and Stuart C. Shapiro. Natural Language Processing Using a Propositional Semantic Network with Structured Variables. *Minds and Machines*, 3(4), November 1993. Special Issue on Knowledge Representation for Natural Language Processing.

[3] C. Beierle, U. Hedtstuck, U. Pletat, P. H. Schmitt, and J. Siekmann. An Order-sorted Logic for Knowledge Representation Systems. *Artificial Intelligence*, 55(2-3):149 – 191, June 1992.

[4] Ronald J. Brachman, Victoria Pigman Gilbert, and Hector J. Levesque. An Essential Hybrid Reasoning System: Knowledge and Symbol Level Accounts of KRYPTON. *Proceedings IJCAI-85*, 1:532–539, 1985.

[5] Ronald J. Brachman and J. Schmolze. An Overview of the KL-ONE Knowledge Representation System. *Cognitive Science*, 9(2):171–216, 1977.

[6] S. C. Shapiro. Symmetric relations, intensional individuals, and variable binding. *Proceedings of the IEEE*, 74(10):1354–1363, 1986.

[7] S. C. Shapiro. Cables, Paths, and "Subconscious" Reasoning in Propositional Semantic Networks. In John F. Sowa, editor, *Principles of Semantic Networks*, pages 137–156. Morgan Kaufmann, 1991.

[8] S. C. Shapiro and W. J. Rapaport. SNePS considered as a fully intensional propositional semantic network. In N. Cercone and G. McCalla, editors, *The Knowledge Frontier*, pages 263–315. Springer–Verlag, New York, 1987.

[9] William A. Woods. Understanding Subsumption and Taxonomy: A Framework for Progress. In John F. Sowa, editor, *Principles of Semantic Networks*, pages 45 – 94. Morgan Kaufmann, 1991.

The differences made by uncertainty measures

Z. An M. McLeish
Department of Computing and Information Science
University of Guelph
Guelph, Ontario, N1G 2W1, Canada

Keywords: Knowledge representation and qualitative reasoning

Abstract

In this paper, we study the preference structures which are underlying different uncertainty measures, namely, probability functions, belief functions, and possibility functions. First, we define the concept of ***differential points*** of a preference relation and show that the preference structures underlying different measures are characterized by the different layouts of differential points of a preference relation. Second, we show that the construction process of a complicated belief function can be reflected in an evidence structure in which strengths of evidential supports are represented qualitatively as a relation.

1 Introduction

It has been widely accepted that uncertainty is a comman feature in situations where intelligence is required and that proper management of uncertainty is a very important factor contributes to the success of an artificial intelligence system such as an expert system. Many methods for uncertainty management have been developed. Among those which represent uncertainty explicitly, most of them represent uncertainty using numerical degrees.

While it is important to study different measurements for uncertainty and different reasoning processes associated with those measurements, it is also important to study the preference relations which underlay those measures. Benifits of such studies is manifold. One benefit is that because there are many situations where absolute numerical degrees are not easily available, assessment of preference relations under situations like these will be much easier. Some other benifits pertain to the reason, not as obvious but more profound, that any measurement is an abstraction of comparison relationships. Because of this, studies of the underlying relations of uncertain measures will help us to clarify, explain and defend the properties of the measures; help the acquisition of these degree, which is the most difficult aspect of uncertainty management; and provide a generial base to incorporate knowledge represented in different kinds of numerical measures.

There has been much work in the literature which studies the preference structure underlying probability functions and belief functions and which tries to reveal the characteristics of these preference structures[5, 8, 12]. These studies have shown that both probability functions and belief functions can be monotonously reflected using preferences relations. It is easy to see that the same is true for possibility measures. In this paper, we show that the underlying preference relations of different kinds of measures can be characterized by the layouts of differential points of a preference relation.

On the other hand, in many uncertain situations, there is relevant information other than what is represented by uncertainty functions. For example, using Bayesian methods, information about independence is of vital importance[4]. This information on independence, however, cannot be derived from probability functions only. In practice, this information has proven to be more consistently available and should be used as guidance to assess the concrete probability values.

With belief functions, one important idea which has not been emphasized enough is that complicated beliefs are built up from simple beliefs. The information embodied in the construction process, however, is not reflected in the final belief function. In this paper, we show that if a belief function is constructed from simple beliefs, the structural information embodied in the construction process can be represented using an evidence structure in which strengths of evidential supports are represented qualitatively as a relation[1].

2 Preferences made by different uncertainty measures

In this section we inspect the relation among conclusions which are rendered by some uncertainty measures, *i.e.* the preference relations which are embodied in some kind of uncertainty functions. To make it more precise, we begin with the following definition of equivalence between two representations of evidence.

Definition 1 *Two representations of evidence are said to be* equivalent *iff they always choose the same propositions among an arbitrary set of propositions.*

It follows naturally that any numerical representation of evidence, M, is equivalent to its underlying relation defined as $p_1 \preceq p_2 \Leftrightarrow M(p_1) \leq M(p_2)$.

Obviously, the equivalence between two representations in the sense defined as above ignores information which matters in some other senses. For example, both the discount operations [10] on a belief function and the normalization of an uncertainty function do not make any changes to the underlying relation of a belief function, even though the former is practically useful and the latter is theoretically important [9]. In many other cases, such as where our purpose is to choose among a set of alternatives, the degree of difference is not important and can be safely ignored. In these cases, the definition above ignores the degree of difference and makes it possible to study belief structures relatively and qualitatively.

If the degree of difference is ignored, then what kind of relations do those eminent uncertainty functions define? Before answering this question, we need the following definitions.

First we define a preference relation simply as a partial order on propositions which is consistent with the subset relation (material implication) of propositions.

Definition 2 *A relation $\mathcal{R}$, denoted as $\preceq$, is called a* preference relation *on Θ iff*

1. *$\mathcal{R}$ is non-empty: $\Theta \not\preceq \phi$.*

2. *$\mathcal{R}$ is reflective:* $\forall p_1 \subset \Theta, p_1 \preceq p_1$.

3. *$\mathcal{R}$ is transitive:* $\forall p_1, p_2 \subset \Theta, (p_1 \preceq p_2) \wedge (p_2 \preceq p_3) \Rightarrow (p_1 \preceq p_3)$.

4. *$\mathcal{R}$ is consistent with the subset relation:* $\forall p_1, p_2 \subset \Theta, (p_1 \subset p_2) \Rightarrow (p_1 \preceq p_2)$.

We will also call a preference relation $\mathcal{R}$ *universal* iff $\forall p_1, p_2 \subset \Theta$, we have either $p_1 \preceq p_2$ or $p_2 \preceq p_1$ or both (denoted as $p_1 \simeq p_2$).

For any preference relation, it is required that any subset be no more believable than its supersets. This will allow, however, a set to be as believable as some of its subsets. Some sets are strictly more believable than ANY of their subsets and are of particular interests.

Definition **3** *Suppose $\mathcal{R}$ is a preference relation on Θ. A non-empty proposition γ in 2^Θ ($\gamma \subseteq \Theta$) is called* a differential point *of $\mathcal{R}$ if and only if* $(\forall \gamma' \subset \gamma, \ (\gamma' \preceq \gamma) \wedge (\gamma \not\preceq \gamma'))$.

Using this definition, we have the following definitions and theorems. Proofs are omitted as the proof for theorem 1 can be found in [2], the proof for theorem 2 is easily available from the literature, and the proof for theorem 3 is very straight forward.

Definition **4** *A B-relation is a universal preference relation which satisfies that for any two differential points γ_1, γ_2 of $\mathcal{R}$, $\gamma_1 \cup \gamma_2$ is also a differential point.*

Theorem 1 *For any belief function Bel on Θ, its underlying relation is a B-relation. For any B-relation, there are belief functions which are equivalent to it.*

Definition **5** *A Prob-relation is a universal preference relation such that every proposition is a differential point and $\forall p_1, p_2 \subset \Theta, p_1 \preceq p_2, p_1 \cap p_3 = \phi, (p_1 \cup p_3 \preceq p_2 \cup p_3)$.*

Theorem 2 *For any positive probability function on Θ, its underlying relation is a Prob-relation. For any Prob-relation $\mathcal{R}$, there are probability functions which are equivalent to it.*

Notice that the condition to make a preference relation to be a underlying relation for a belief function (as in definition 5) is reinforced in two ways to reach the condition to make an underlying preference relation for a probability (as in definition 6). Namely, that every non-empty subset is a differential point and that the ordering between any two propositions is retained with the adding of new elements.

Definition **6** *A Poss-relation is a universal preference relation such that every differential point is a singleton.*

Theorem 3 *For any possibility function, its underlying relation is a Poss relation. For any Poss relation, there are possibility functions which are equivalent to it.*

3 Constructive Belief

One thing one has to remember and pay particular attention to when studying a representation method of uncertainty is that there is information available which is not represented or even cannot be represented by uncertainty functions, for example, information about independence.

With belief functions, one important idea which is not emphasized is that complicated beliefs are built up from *simple beliefs*[7]. Simple beliefs are beliefs arising from pieces of *simple evidence* and an item of simple evidence is a piece of evidence which support one and only one conclusion.

There are many methods to construct complex beliefs from simple ones. Among them, the most important one is to combine two belief functions over the same frame using Dempster's combination rule. For definition of the combination rule please see [6]. Informally, the rule gives the "orthogonal sum" of the two basic probability assignments.

In this section we show, using a theorem, that the idea of evidence construction can be reflected using an evidence structure in which strengths of evidential supports are represented qualitatively as a relation.[1] In the following section, we define an evidence structure and describe very briefly the evidential reasoning with an evidence structure. In section 3.2, we present the theorem.

3.1 Evidence Structure

An evidence structure is defined as a 4-tuple as follows.

Definition 7 *A 4-tuple* $\mathcal{ES} = \langle \mathcal{L}_e, \mathcal{L}_p, \mathcal{A}, \mathcal{R} \rangle$ *is called an* evidence structure. *In the 4-tuple,*

- $\mathcal{L}_e$ *and* $\mathcal{L}_p$ *are first order logics composed of the evidence statements and conclusion statements respectively.*
- $\mathcal{A}$ *is a set of arguments. An argument is a pair* $\langle e, p \rangle$ *where* $e \in \mathcal{L}_e$ *is called the* presumption *and* $p \in \mathcal{L}_p$ *is called the conclusion. An argument should be read as "If evidence e is granted, then there is an argument supporting p."*
- $\mathcal{R}$ *is a partial order relation on* $\mathcal{A}$.

With an evidence structure, we can accumulate evidence (represented as a evidence statement) by firing all and only those arguments which have presumptions implied by the given evidence statement. The relation $\mathcal{R}$ can be projected onto the set of fired arguments. In fact, this will give us a new evidence structure which are called *the result of conditioning the original evidence structure on the given evidence.*

Then, the projected relation can be degraded to produce a preference relation among conclusions. Finally, decisions can be made with regard to this preference relation.

[1]An evidence structure can be also constructed using numerical degrees.

3.2 Construction Process

Suppose $Bel(x)$ is a belief function on the discernment frame Θ, and that it is the result of accumulating pieces of simple evidence $e_1, \ldots, e_n$. In other words, we suppose that $Bel(x)$ has mass function $m(x)$ and $m(x)$ is the orthogonal sum of *simple mass functions* $m_1(x), m_2(x), \ldots, m_n(x)$:

$$m(x) = m_1(x) \oplus m_2(x) \oplus \cdots \oplus m_n(x);$$

and

$$Bel(x) = \sum_{A \subseteq x} m(A);$$

where $m_i(x)$ are simple mass functions for simple evidence $e_i, (1 \leq i \leq n)$.

$Bel(x)$ can be viewed as the result of accumulating all these pieces of evidence. The more pieces of evidence accumulated, the more differences among the conclusions can the accumulated evidence make. We show that all the differences made in this process can be captured in an evidence structure.

Theorem 4 *Let $Bel(x)$ be a belief function with mass function*

$$m(x) = m_1(x) \oplus m_2(x) \oplus \cdots \oplus m_n(x)$$

where $m_i(x)$ are simple mass functions representing pieces of simple evidence $e_i, (1 \leq i \leq n)$. Then there is an evidence structure $\mathcal{ES}^E$ such that, for any index subset $I \subseteq \{1, 2, \ldots, n\}$, for $E_I = \wedge_{i \in I} e_i$ and with $Bel^{E_I}(x)$ being the belief function with mass function $\bigoplus_{i \in I} m_i(x)$, $\mathcal{ES}^E_{E_I}$ (the result of conditioning $\mathcal{ES}^E$ on E_I) is equivalent to $Bel^{E_I}(x)$.

That is, $\mathcal{ES}^E$ is not only equivalent to $Bel(x)$ (which is the case where $I = \{1, 2, \ldots, n\}$ in the theorem), but it also embodies the construction of $Bel(x)$ from $e_1, e_2, \ldots, e_n$ (which are the cases where $I \subset \{1, 2, \ldots, n\}$ of the theorem), *i.e.* information carried in any part (subset) of $\{e_1, e_2, \ldots, e_n\}$ is also embodied in $\mathcal{ES}^E$.[2]

∎

Apart from Dempster's combination rule, in the process of constructing complicated beliefs, other operations can be applied to convert belief functions, *e.g.* coarsening or refining frames of discernment, converting belief functions through compatibility relations and applying discount factors. How these operations can be reflected in an evidence structure is a simple matter and is omitted here.

4 Discussion

In this paper, we have shown that a lot of information which is carried by uncertainty functions can also be represented qualitatively by representing the preferences among conclusions. Namely, we have shown that the preference structure underlying uncertain functions can be characterized by the different layouts of the differential

[2] Proof removed for the length limit of the proceedings. Those who are interested can obtain a copy from the authors.

points of a preference relation. We have also shown that the construction information of building a complicated belief function can be reflected using an evidence structure in which strengths of evidential supports are represented as a relation.

It can be seen that although all differences made in the process of building up complicated beliefs can be represented in $\mathcal{RES}$, they might become too complicated to be constructed intuitively.

This shouldn't be taken as an argument against using relational methods because these complications are also embodied in numerical representations. They are implied by numerical degrees even though they are not represented explicitly. It must be realized that using numbers doesn't avoid the complications but merely makes them *implicit*, which is dangerous. Our point of view is that if any difference cannot be stated clearly, it should not be taken for granted.

This does indicate, however, that being able to only represent the preferences and the construction information is insufficient for relative method (, and numerical methods as well). Tools and theories are needed which can provide ways and help for the construction of complicated beliefs. Networks have proven to be the most promising methods[4, 3]. Our further research will then to investigate how qualitatively represented preferences can be utilized in the context of networks.

References

[1] Z. An, D. Bell, and J. Hughes. $\mathcal{RES}$—a relation based method for evidential reasoning. In *Proc. 8th Conf. on Uncertainty in AI*, pages 1–8, 1992.

[2] Z. An, D. Bell, and J. Hughes. Relation based evidential reasoning. *Int. J. on Approximate Reasoning*, accepted, in preparation.

[3] D. E. Heckerman. Probabilistic similarity networks. *Networks*, 20:607–636, 1990.

[4] J. Pearl. *Probabilistic Reasoning in Intelligent Systems: Networks for Plausible Inference.* Kaufman, 1988.

[5] L. Savage. *The Foundations of Statistics.* New York:Dover, 1972.

[6] G. Shafer. *A Mathematical Theory of Evidence.* Princeton University Press, 1976.

[7] G. Shafer. Constructive probability. *Synthesis*, 48:1–60, 1981.

[8] G. Shafer. Savage revisited. *Statistical Science*, 1(4), 1986.

[9] P. Smets. The nature of the unnormalized beliefs encountered in the transferable belief model. In *Proc. 8th Uncertainty in Artificial Intelligence*, pages 292–297, 1992.

[10] T. Strat. The generation of explanations within evidential reasoning systems. In *Proc. IJCAI'87*, pages 1097–1104, 1987.

[11] F. Voorbraak. On the justification of Dempster's rule of combination. *Artificial Intelligence*, 48:171–197, 1991.

[12] S. Wong, Y. Yao, P. Bollmann, and H. Burger. Axiomatization of qualitative belief structure. *IEEE trans. Sys. Man, and Cyb.*, 21(4):726–734, 1991.

THEORY RELATIONS AND CONTEXT DEPENDENCIES [1]

Christo Dichev
Department of Computer Science, University College Dublin
Dublin 4, Ireland
E-mail: cdichev@ccvax.ucd.ie

ABSTRACT. This paper presents a model for a logic programming oriented, knowledge representation language, based on the notion of theory relations. Instead of being restricted to one global knowledge base, this model allows segmentation into theories, which through theory relations, are connected into compound contexts. The language provides relevant expressions to specify different structuring methods, accessibility relations, various sorts of "theory interfaces" or context dependencies.

1 Introduction

In most AI applications logical propositions used for knowledge representation are supposed to be objective truth. In reality however such propositions have many contextual aspects. Representations often assume context of use. As a result there are well-developed techniques for proving propositions in a fixed context, where different types of FOPC problem solvers can be used. In this aspect it is interesting to study the problem of representing contexts and different context relations that would make context dependencies explicit. A context can be thought as a group of related assertions closed under entailment. Thus we arrive at a logical system where otherwise inaccessible objects such as theories and theory relations are made explicit and are handled as first order objects.

In the next sections we present an extension to logic programming which we call *logic programming with theory relations.* This extension provides semantics for the multiple theory knowledge representation language W-Prolog[1,2] and a conceptual basis for its further development. Each program in the multiple theory logic programming language is a collection of a finite set of named theories linked by theory relations. Some of the theories defined by a set of clauses (called *units*) are used as basic components for building the other theories. Each theory therefore is either a unit or is defined by application of theory relations to existing theories.

Our motivation is similar in many ways to *contextual logic programming*[4] and to the *general framework for structuring logic programs*[3]. A technical difference in relation to "contexts"[3,4] which might be methodologically important is that our approach is based on theory relations - a more general concept with respect to structuring logic programs. Based on our experience with W-Prolog, the notion of theory relations

[1]This work is supported by IBM under a Newman Scholarship

proved to be sufficiently general and flexible to define, build and integrate different structuring policies. Rather than viewing a program as an ordered list of units, a program is perceived in our language as a compound theory obtained by applying theory relations to a set of basic units.

2 Multiple theories and theory relations

In this section we introduce some basic concepts related to a logic programming language $\mathcal{L}_T$ with theory relations, an extension to Horn clause logic. This extension can be viewed as a computational model for describing various extensions to logic programming built upon the notion of structuring logic programs.

2.1 Basic concepts

The logic programming language with theory relations $\mathcal{L}_T$ is viewed as a system of six sets $\langle \mathbf{P}, \mathbf{F}, \mathbf{T}, \mathbf{U}, \mathbf{R}, \mathbf{Q} \rangle$, where **P** and **F** are finite disjoint sets of predicate and function symbols respectively, **T** is a finite set of theory names disjoint from **P**,**F**. The next element $\mathbf{U} \subseteq \mathbf{T}$ of 6-tuple denotes unit names, **R** is a finite set of theory relation symbols disjoint from **P**, **F**, **T** and $\mathbf{Q} \subseteq \mathbf{P}$ is a subset of predicate names denoting predicates dealing with theories. All function, predicate and theory relation symbols are equipped with arity.

In $\mathcal{L}_T$ as in contextual logic programming[4] the basic building elements forming any theory are called *units*. Each unit is a collection of clauses and is denoted by a unique atomic name. More precisely a *unit* is an expression of the form $\langle u, U \rangle$, where $u \in \mathbf{U}$ and U is a finite set of clauses. We call u the name of the unit and U its meaning. Given a denumerably infinite set of variables disjoint from **P**,**F**,**T**,**R** terms and atomic formulae are defined following the standard way. The definition of the clauses are extended to include predicates dealing with theories. A program clause is an expression of the form $A \leftarrow B_1, B_2, ..., B_n$ which contains precisely one positive literal. A goal is an expression of the form $\leftarrow B_1, B_2, ..., B_n$ which has an empty consequent. Each $B_i, i = 1, ..., n$ is an atom. Some of the atomic formulae $B_i, i = 1, 2, ..., n$ in the body of a clause are written with predicate symbols from **Q**, i.e. they have the form $q(t_1, t_2, ..., t_n), q \in \mathbf{Q}$. A program of the multiple theory logic programming language is conceived as a collection of finite set of named theories linked by theory relations. Some of the theories called *units* are defined by a finite set of clauses and are used as "basic components" for building other theories to which in turn predefined theory relations can be applied. Therefore a program can be viewed statically as a finite set of units connected via theory relations. Each theory in multiple theory logic programming language is a couple $\langle t, T \rangle$, where t is the name of the theory and T is its meaning. The theory name t is either an elementary name $t \in \mathbf{T}$ or is a theory expression of the form $R(t_1, t_2, ..., t_k), k \geq 1$, where $R \in \mathbf{R}$ and $t_i, i = 1,2,...,k$ is either a theory name or in turn a theory expression. The meaning T associated with the theory name t is defined by the expression $R(T_1, T_2, ..., T_k), k \geq 1$, where $R \in \mathbf{R}$ and $T_i, i = 1, ..., k$ is the meaning of the name t_i. By providing semantics for the set of theory relations $\mathbf{R}$ and for the set of predicates dealing with theories $\mathbf{Q}$ an instance of the multiple theory language $\mathcal{L}_\mathcal{T}$ may be created. Thus $\mathcal{L}_\mathcal{T}$ can be interpreted as a class of multiple theory languages.

3 A language with theory relations

In the next few sections we define a set of theory relations and a set of predicates dealing with theories of a particular multiple theory logic programming language $\mathcal{L}_{\mathcal{T}_w} \subseteq \mathcal{L}_\mathcal{T}$. The language $\mathcal{L}_{\mathcal{T}_w}$ is a 6-tuple $\langle$ **P**, **F**, **T**, **U**, {**acc/1**, **+/2** }, {**in/2**, **if/2** **::=/2**} $\rangle$, where **P**,**F**,**T** and **U** are finite.

3.1 Theory relations

The following set of relations is provided in the language $\mathcal{L}_{\mathcal{T}_w}$: { **acc/1**, **+/2** }.

Accessibility relation. If t is a theory then $acc(t)$ is a theory called *indirect theory*: $acc(t) = \{g | \ t \vdash g\}$. The indirect theory $acc(t)$ obtained from t can be viewed as a set of all atomic formulae derivable from t and imported into the theory named $acc(t)$. Note that if the component of an indirect theory is a unit $u \in \mathbf{U}$ then $acc(u)$ does not include the set of clauses U defined in the unit u, rather it denotes the set of atomic formulae derivable from U. Thus an indirect theory can be used for "hiding" the program clauses provided in the original theory.

Composition. If t_1 and t_2 are theories then $t_1 + t_2$ is a theory called *composition* of t_1 and t_2. The composition theory $t_1 + t_2$ can be interpreted as a new theory obtained by conceptually unifying the meaning T_1 of t_1 and the meaning T_2 of t_2. In general a goal g is provable from $t_1 + t_2$ if the goal is provable from $T_1 \cup T_2$. Note that in general $t_1 + t_2 \neq t_1 + acc(t_2)$. For instance if u_1 and u_2 are units then the composition $u_1 + acc(u_2)$ can also be interpreted as feeding the output of u_2 to u_1 as input.

3.1.1 Predicate overriding

In general, the code in two different units might overlap, i.e. they could both provide definitions for a common predicate. There are occasions when it is desirable for the most recent predicate definition to override the previous ones for the same predicate. To handle *predicate overriding* the list of the theory relations of the language $\mathcal{L}_{\mathcal{T}_w}$ can be extended with appropriate relation.

If t_1 and t_2 are two theories then $t_1 +' t_2$ is a theory called *overriding composition* of t_1 and t_2. The overriding composition $t_1 +' t_2$ can be interpreted as a new theory obtained by conceptually unifying the meaning T_1 of t_1 with the meaning of T_2 of t_2, excluding the predicates defined in any of the components of t_1.

3.1.2 Theories as first order objects

It is sometimes desirable that the propositions in one theory to be accessible to a number of other theories. This could be useful for example in situations when most of the meanings are shared by most of the objects. The language $\mathcal{L}_{T_w}$ can be extended with relations enabling us to handle quantifier over theories.

The theory relations $all(g_0(T) + t)$ and $all(g_0(T) +' t)$, where T is a variable, allow assertions in one theory to be made available for use in all theories satisfying certain conditions. Note that this relation applies a quantifier over theories. The meaning of these relations is that propositions in theory t through compositions are accessible to all theories t_i, such that $g_0(t_i)$ is true. The difference between the first and the second relation is that the second one applies a predicate overriding.

3.2 Predicates for dealing with theories

The following set of predicates dealing with theories is provided in the logic programming language with theory relations: { **in/2, if/2, / ::=/2**}.

Theory-switching. By definition each theory denotes a certain combination of theory-components. From the viewpoint of a goal evaluation each theory determines an environment (context) of proof. For switching to a new theory t proving a goal G a *theory-switching* operator G *in* t is provided. The meaning of the operator G *in* t is that the goal G is proved in the new theory t regardless of the theory in which the current theory-switching operator occurs. In general goals G and G *in* t force the evaluation of G in different theories: the first one in the current theory, the second one switches the proof to the theory t. From this aspect a composition $t_i + acc(t)$ can be seen as adding to t_i linking clauses of the form: $P \leftarrow P \ in \ t$ for all $\hat{P} \in ||t||$.

Theory-extension. The *theory-extension* operator $G \ if \ t$, where t is a theory and G is a goal, forces the proof of G in a new theory $t_i + t$ obtained by unifying t with the theory t_i, in which the theory-extension operator occurs. Note that $t_i \vdash G \ if \ t$ implies $\vdash G \ in \ (t_i + t)$. Therefore the theory extension operator can be replaced by a theory switching operator. However the opposite is not true. Note that the theory extension operator supports a form of hypothetical reasoning. A goal of the form G *if* t corresponds to assuming the set of hypotheses t to prove G.

Theory naming. The operator for naming theories has the form: *Name ::= Expression*, meaning that the name *Name* is associated with the theory defined by *Expression*. We distinguish theories denoted by expressions from those denoted by name assigned by the theory naming operator. Theories like $t_1 + t_2$ are *virtual theories* and they exists only during the execution of the corresponding goal. As a result of theory naming, once an environment for evaluating goals is created it is possible to refer to that environment by its name or to delete it.

3.3 Examples with theory relations

Let us consider the following program consisting of three units:

unit (cat)	**unit (food)**	**unit (pet)**
$eats\_catt(X) \leftarrow food(X)$	$food(meat)$	$eats\_pet(X) \leftarrow eats\_cat(X)$

The goal *eats_pet(X)* has the following top-down derivation with respect to the theory `cat+acc(food) +acc(pet)`

$\vdash$ *eats_pet(X)* `in cat+acc(food)+acc(pet)`
cat+acc(food)+acc(pet) $\vdash$ *eats_pet(X)*
pet $\vdash$ *eats_cat(X)*
$\surd$ `failure`

With respect to `cat+food` the goal *eats_pet(X)* `if pet` has the following derivation:

cat+food $\vdash$ *eats_pet(X)* `if pet`
cat+food+pet $\vdash$ *eats_pet(X)*
cat+food+pet $\vdash$ *eats_cat(X)*
cat+food+pet $\vdash$ *food(X)*
$\surd$ $X = meat$

Inheritance policies in inheritance systems can be seen as instances of theory relations. Assume that we have n objects $\mathbf{O}_j, j = 1, ..., n$, such that $\mathbf{O}_k$ ***isa*** $\mathbf{O}_i, i = 1, ..., k-1,\ k = 2, ..., n$. Assume next that the distinguishing properties of all n objects are defined by the units u_i. With each object we associate a separate theory $O_i, i = 1, ..., n$. The inheritance between related objects can be achieved by creating and naming a sequence of theories linked by the relevant theory relations: $O_1 ::= u_1$, $O_2 ::= u_2 + acc(O_1), ..., O_n ::= u_n + acc(O_{n-1})$. If we define *isa-relation* in terms of derivability i.e. X ***isa*** Y *iff* any formula derivable in Y is also derivable in X, then the relations O_k ***isa*** O_i, $i = 1, ..., k-1$, $k = 2, ..., n$ hold. Any formula derivable in O_i is also derivable in O_k. A system of two classes **cat** and **pet_cat**, where **pet_cat** inherits all properties of **cat** are illustrated by the following example in W-Prolog:

unit (u1)	**unit (u2)**
eats(meat)	*eats(canned_food)*

```
?- cat::= u1, pet_cat::= u2+acc(cat).

?- eats(X) in cat.
X = meat;
no

?- eats(X) in pet_cat.
```

```
X = canned_food;
X = meat
```

3.4 Theory abstraction

It is desirable sometimes to hide some aspects of the actual implementation of programs. Most of the module versions of Prolog are provided with facilities allowing the user to indicate which of the predicates defined within a module are to be visible and which of them are to be hidden for the outside world. The language $\mathcal{L}_{T_w}$ can be extended to a language $\mathcal{L}_{TW}$ to make it possible handle some "theory interface" aspects. Thus the list of theory relations of $\mathcal{L}_{T_w}$ is extended with new relations that would enable us to specify and "extract" from any program the intended "visible fragments" and name it as a new theory. In some occasions it might be useful before a system output an answer to other system to check it. This way it is possible to make a conceptual separation between "how to compute" and "right to know". The language $\mathcal{L}_{TW}$ includes some theory relations for specifying theories which are "intersection" or "subtraction" of their components. Thus $\mathcal{L}_{TW}$ is a 6-tuple $\langle$ **P, F, T, U, {acc/1, pj/2, +/2, +'/2, &/2, \/2 }, {in/2, if/2, ::= }** $\rangle$.

Projection. If t is a theory and $V_P \subseteq ||t||$ is a list of the "visible" predicate names then $pj(t, V_P)$ is a theory abstraction called *projection of t*: $pj(t, V_P) = \{g \mid t \vdash g \ \wedge \ \hat{g} \in V_P\}$, where $\hat{g}$ denotes the name of g.

Conjunction of theories. If t_1 and t_2 are theories then $t_1 \& t_2$ is a theory called *intersection* of t_1 and t_2: $t_1 \& t_2 = \{g \mid t_1 \vdash g \ \wedge \ t_2 \ \vdash g\}$.

Subtraction of theories. If t_1 and t_2 are theories then $t_1 \backslash t_2$ is a theory called *subtraction*: $t_1 \backslash t_2 = \{g \mid t_1 \vdash g \ \wedge \ t_2 \ \not\vdash g\}$. Note that subtraction is a *non-monotonic* theory relation.

REFERENCES

1. Dichev Ch. Knowledge representation with W-Prolog, *Proc. Eleventh Applications of Artificial Intelligence Conference, AAI-XI*, Orlando, FL, April, 1993.

2. Dichev Ch. Distributed knowledge and data processing, *Proc. Forth International Conference on Cognitive and Computer Science - ICO 93*, Montreal, Canada, pp. 272-282, 1993.

3. Lamma, E., Mello P., Natali A., An extended Warren Abstract Machine for the execution of structured logic programs, *J. Logic Programming* 14:187-222, 1992.

4. Monteiro, L., and Porto, A., Contextual logic programming, in: *Proc. of the 6th ICLP*, Lisbon, Portugal, 1989, MIT Press, pp. 284-299.

Two Level Temporal Constraints Propagation

Hany Tolba
CRIN-INRIA Lorraine
BP 239
F54506 Vandœuvre-les-Nancy cedex
France
tolba@loria.fr

Abstract

Time plays an important role in various aspects of reasoning. In this research area we study temporal information representation and how it can be exploited for reasoning purpose.

We propose a time representation based on the combination of the notions of interval algebra, to represent the different concepts of temporal information. We have extended this algebra in order to deal with symbolic temporal information as well as numerical information: numerical windows, dates and durations can be associated to symbolic intervals. The manipulation of our representation scheme is based on the notion of time map managers (TMM) [4].

1 Temporal Knowledge Representation

This representation is based on a discrete time model. It is the maximal set of discrete and adjacent temporal units **ui**. Each unit represents the smallest discrete portion of time that can be obtained over the temporal reference. Using these units another temporal entity is defined : the interval. Each interval I is identified with a lower bound and an upper bound. Events represent intervals that take place during windows, i.e. every interval is associated to one window. This model relies on the definition for each interval I of the Sets Of Possible Occurrences (SOPOs) in which I can take place. In our model a SOPO is restricted to be a temporal window; i.e. a set of intervals with a constant duration. Our SOPOs are defined by couple of units (ui, uj), where ui and uj are respectively the start and end times of the specified window. An instance of an interval taking place in a SOPO is called an occurrence. Events represent intervals that take place during windows. Thus, every event is self constrained by its duration and the window in which it takes place.This represents the quantitative constraintes of our model. The qualitative constraints are represented by any number of Allen's thirteen primitives between any two events. The 13 relations are used to define the relative position of one event with respect to others.

Since we are using a discrete model we can easily introduce the notion of time granularity to represent days, weeks, months... This notion is represented in form of *time scales*. The time scale (representing a granularity) is used as a transfer between different events of different speeds, each represented by a different granularity. That is to say, an event taking place on hours, is faster than another one taking place in years. This mechanism is a kind of focus shifting on events of a given granularity. Such a notion is feasible since most of the events share the same variable, i.e. the granularity. The different granularities are multiples of the basic unit u. This notion of shifting focus via time granularity scales is based on two notions. The first is the faster to slower one. Due to an error introduced on the time graph of faster granularity events (for example hours time scale) the propagation takes place till the time map reaches a stable point. The shifting focus is then carried out to the next slower one, etc. If we need to propagate two events of different granularity time scales, this is carried out as follows:

* discretize the interval with slower granularity with the faster one;
* propagate as we have only one granularity time scale;
* give to each event its own original granularity, eliminating the fractions due to the change from one granularity to another.

The second notion is that from slower to faster. In the case that the slower mechanism reached a stable state, we can deduce that the faster one followed it to reach an equivalent stable state. This is carried out automatically during the propagation. Using such a notion of granularity time scales we are able to:

* divide the time map (graph) into smaller sub-graphes according to the granularity; thus reducing the propagation and improving the access to events;
* allow multiple reasoning levels according to the granularity size, i.e., focusing on a class of events of certain granularity.

We have also proposed to use mathematical equations to define the window bounds and to use a real-time clock as a reference for events. This notion, called ***catching up with advancing time***, allows us to use a real time clock during the propagation and to adjust the windows of events as well as the symbolic constraints as time advances [4].

2 Temporal Constraint Propagation Tool

However, this representation of time is worthless without a powerful tool to extract useful information from it. The reasoning tasks to be achieved by the tool we have developed and the heterogeneous nature of the temporal information to be processed, both symbolic and numerical, lead us to create a new strategy of constraint propagation. Each type of temporal information is handled by a Time Map Manager, based on an algorithm of constraint propagation. The two Managers work independently and exchange their information via a communication module. Different constraint propagation algorithms from the literature were examined and GAC4 [2] was chosen as a base for the reasoning tool [3]. To improve speed and memory space occupation, we then developed an arc consistency algorithm, called ANGEL, which dynamically builds the network of constraints representing the available temporal information and deals with n-ary constraints. This allow us to overcome a problem like that of the 3-summit [1] and to obtain an order of consistency more than three, if needed, using the transitivity function as defined in [5]. The numerical propagation is carried also over n-ary constraintes, for example propagating an hyper-arc of three nodes, the propagation is carried through every couple of nodes in the hyper-arc acoording to the following:

$$\forall\ I, J, K\ \in\ N, \forall\ R_{I,J},\ R_{J,K},\ R_{i,K},$$

$$\forall\ I_i \in W_i \exists J_j \in W_j \& \exists K_k \in W_k such\ that\ I_i\ R_{i,j}\ J_j\ \wedge\ I_i\ R_{i,k}\ K_k$$

$$\forall\ J_j \in W_j \exists I_i \in W_i \& \exists K_k \in W_k such\ that\ J_j\ R_{j,k}\ K_k\ \wedge\ J_j\ R_{j,i}\ I_i$$

$$\forall\ K_k \in W_k \exists I_i \in W_i \& \exists J_j \in W_j such\ that\ K_k\ R_{k,i}\ I_i\ \wedge\ K_k\ R_{k,j}\ J_j$$

Where *I,J,K* are nodes; *R* is the relation between two nodes and *W* is the window. I_i is the occurrences of *I* in W_i.

We can thus summarize the role of each module in the following:

* The symbolic propagator's role is to delete the symbolic relations which do not participate in a consistent over all solution;

* The numerical propagator eliminates the occurrences that do not respect the symbolic constraints from every SOPO;

* The communication module's role is to update the symbolic constraints in order to carry out the numerical propagation. Then it converts the numerical constraints resulting from the numerical propagation into symbolic one. It uses a set of propagation rules defined in [4]

The result of this theoretical study is the development of the reasoning tool (TemPro). This tool was implemented as a black box to be used for different tasks like scheduling, planning or resource allocation. Modifying, updating and querying the time map are important aspects from a practical point of view. We propose an interface and a language built over our tool. This is missing in the similar representations. The syntax of this language is a Lisp-like one. As propagation of constraints over a network is time consuming, a control language has been defined to dynamically minimize the number of propagations. We extended this language so it can be easily interfaced with any inference engine.It takes the form of function calls to modify an entry or update it. This language can also be used by an inference engine to pilot the tool. Several query types are supported by the tool. For example we can ask the tool to add a new node to the graph or to use only one propagator. We can ask it to check the possible relations or to give the different forms of a temporal window of an event: SOPO or window form. Asking the tool to find a possible solution according to a given condition is also possible.

The complexity of such tool is equal to $n^3 * p * 3! * g * r^2$. Where p is the number of Allen's primitives, r is the number of elements in a SOPO, the r is raised to square and the 3! are found since we are working on hyper-arcs. g is the granularity reference.

A detailed study of the complexity and the correctness of the algorithm and the tool as well as the tool's performance can be found in [4]. Besides, a comparison with recent research works has also been presented. For example, comparing Allen's reference intervals with our granularity time scale notion, we can deduce the following. Our notion allows us to implement not only that of reference intervals but as well it is possible for us to reason at different levels. That is to say, we can focus on different events belonging to different granularity time scales. This allows us to focus on events of relative important, to the reasoning process, according to a given criteria, an example their granularity, and to control the propagation by limiting it to a group of events of a given granularity.

The first phase of coupling (loose coupling) TemPro with a real time inference engine (G2 from Gensym) has terminated with encouraging results. G2 communicates with external world through sockets via a standard interface. Since G2 does not allow one to interface lisp functions, the first step of our interface G2-Tempro (developed in lisp) was carried out through a C language interface. This interface is a producer-consumer model. G2 through its C interface produces the different requests for TemPro, which wakes up from being passive and consumes those requests and producing the results for the above requests to be consumed by G2. Afterwards, TemPro becomes passive waiting for another request to be produced by G2. An example derived from [4] for resource allocation had been implemented. We are studying now how we can totally integrate both tools. There are different possible solutions either to rewrite TemPro in C or G2 language. Another solution is to investigate RPC standard for communication.

3 Conclusion and Perspectives

We have a new temporal representation model combining qualitative and quantitative temporal information. We have also presented an original constraint propagation strategy based on two levels of propagation. The ANGEL algorithm presents the new feature of being dynamic, thus allowing to be used with an inference engine. A tool has been presented. It provides any potential user with a useful interface language allowing interfacing the tool with other modules or exploiting the advantages of the temporal model.

As for the perspectives of this research work we are working on two parallel points. The first is to improve the efficiency of the reasoning tool and to study how notions like uncertainty can be represented. The second is increasing the numerical representation expression power with disjunctive numerical constraints.

References

[1] J. F. Allen, *Maintaining Knowledge about Temporal Intervals. Communications of ACM*, 26(11):832–843,November 1983.

[2] R. Mohr and G. Masini, *Good Old Discrete Relaxation*. Proceedings of the 9th European Conference on Artificial Intelligence, pages 622–625, 1989.

[3] H. Tolba, F. Charpillet and J.P. Haton, *Representing and Propagating Constraints in Temporal Reasoning*. Proceedings of the 3rd IEEE International Conference on Tools for Artificial Intelligence, San Jose, pages 181–184, 1991.

[4] H. Tolba, *Contibution à l'étude du raisonnement temporel : integration des informations qualitatives et quantitatives et propagation de contraintes*. PhD thesis, University of Nancy 1 (in French), 1992.

[5] P. van Beek, *Approximation Algorithms for Temporal Reasoning*. In Proceedings of *IJCAI*, pages 1291–1296, 1989.

Machine Learning

A BENCHMARK FOR CLASSIFIER LEARNING

ZIJIAN ZHENG
Basser Department of Computer Science, University of Sydney, NSW 2006
Email: zijian@cs.su.oz.au

ABSTRACT: Although many algorithms for learning from examples have been developed and many comparisons have been reported, there is no generally accepted benchmark for classifier learning. The existence of a standard benchmark would greatly assist such comparisons. Sixteen dimensions are proposed to describe classification tasks. Based on these, thirteen real-world and synthetic datasets are chosen by a set covering method from the UCI Repository of machine learning databases to form such a benchmark.

1. Introduction

Many algorithms for classifier learning from examples have been developed and applied to problems from a variety of fields such as medical science, biology, and linguistics.

All of these algorithms perform differently on different domains. A great amount of literature concerning evaluating or comparing classifier learning algorithms has been published. One common problem is that only a few domains are used in each evaluation and different papers use different domains. It is very hard to judge an algorithm by seeing its performance on only a few arbitrarily selected domains.

When evaluating or comparing classifier learning algorithms the following questions are raised: how many domains are reasonable and, furthermore, what kind of domains should be used? The objective of this paper is to address this problem by proposing a benchmark for classifier learning. Section 2 gives a set of dimensions for describing classification tasks. Then, Section 3 proposes a set of datasets to form a benchmark. Finally, Section 4 briefly describes related work. Due to lack of space, we can only give a very brief description of the benchmark and its generation; further information can be found in a technical report[6].

2. A Taxonomy of Datasets

Generally speaking, the dataset of a classification problem has three aspects: the form of the attributes, the form of the classes, and the form of the instances.

The following 16 dimensions will be used to describe datasets. Four concern the attributes, five regard the instances (attribute/class values), and seven relate to the classes. One reason for adopting the 16 dimensions is that different classifier learning algorithms behave differently along each dimension. For example, some systems can deal with, but some others have difficulty with: discrete values, continuous values, missing values, noise, multiple classes, or irrelevant attributes. Some systems slow down very rapidly as the number of training examples and/or the number of attributes increases, but others do not.

To make it easier to choose the datasets for the benchmark, we first define all the dimensions using nominal values. In this paper, we use terms such as *small*, *low*, *medium*, *large*, and *high* as values of the dimensions. *Small* and *low* mean *in the first quartile* of all the candidate values. *Large* and *high* mean *in the last quartile* of all the candidate values. *Medium* means *between the small (or low) and the large (or high)*.

The dimensions and their nominal values are described briefly below, with two examples for each dimension value.

1. *Type of attributes* (4 values):
   - *Binary attributes only*, e.g. LED-24 and LED-7
   - *Nominal attributes only*, e.g. Promoter and NetTalk (Phoneme)
   - *Continuous attributes only*, e.g. Breast Cancer (W) and Diabetes
   - *Mixed attributes*, e.g. Soybean (16 binary attributes, 19 nominal attributes) and Hepatitis (13 binary attributes, 6 continuous attributes)
2. *Number of attributes* (3 values):
   - *Small*, e.g. NetTalk (Phoneme) (7) and Breast Cancer (W) (9)
   - *Medium*, e.g. Mushroom (22) and Hepatitis (19)
   - *Large*, e.g. Promoter (57) and Waveform-40 (40)
3. *Number of different nominal attribute values* (3 values):
   - *Small*, e.g. Promoter (4) and Monks-2 (4)
   - *Medium*, e.g. Soybean (7) and Lymphography (8)
   - *Large*, e.g. Mushroom (12) and NetTalk (Phoneme) (27)
4. *Number of irrelevant attributes* (2 values):
   - *With irrelevant attributes*, e.g. LED-24 and Waveform-40
   - *Without irrelevant attributes*, e.g. NetTalk (Phoneme) and LED-7
5. *Level of noise or indeterminacy*:
   This dimension is further divided into two:
   - *In attribute values* (2 values):
     - *With noise*, e.g. LED-24 and Waveform-40
     - *Without noise*, e.g. NetTalk (Phoneme) and Monks-2
   - *In class memberships* (2 values):
     - *With noise or indeterminacy*, e.g. NetTalk (Phoneme) and Breast Cancer (W)
     - *Without noise or indeterminacy*, e.g. LED-24 and Waveform-40
6. *Frequency of missing attribute values* (3 values):
   - *None*, e.g. Lymphography and NetTalk (Phoneme)

- *Few*, e.g. Mushroom (1.39%) and Breast Cancer (W) (0.25%)
- *Many*, e.g. Soybean (9.78%) and Thyroid (6.74%)

7. *Data-set size* (3 values):
   - *Small*, e.g. Promoter (106) and Lymphography (148)
   - *Medium*, e.g. Diabetes (768) and Thyroid (3163)
   - *Large*, e.g. NetTalk (Phoneme) (5438) and Mushroom (8124)
8. *Data-set density* (3 values):

$$\text{Density} = \frac{\text{Number-of-examples}}{\text{Size-of-description-space}}$$

$$\text{Size-of-description-space} = \prod_{i=1}^{n} N_i$$

where n is the number of attributes and N_i is, for the i-th attribute, the number of different values (if it is a binary or nominal attribute), or the number of different values in the dataset (if it is a continuous attribute).
   - *Low*, e.g. Promoter (5.10×10^{-33}) and Waveform-40 (8.70×10^{-92})
   - *Medium*, e.g. Soybean (5.47×10^{-13}) and Breast Cancer (W) (7.77×10^{-7})
   - *High*, e.g. LED-24 (1.19×10^{-5}) and LED-7 (1.56)
9. *Number of classes* (3 values):
   - *Binary*, e.g. Hepatitis and Promoter
   - *Small or medium*, e.g. Lymphography (4) and LED-24 (10)
   - *Large*, e.g. Soybean (19) and NetTalk (Phoneme) (52)
10. *Default accuracy* (3 values):
    - *Low*, e.g. Soybean (13.7%) and NetTalk (Phoneme) (14.7%)
    - *Medium*, e.g. Lymphography (54.7%) and Breast Cancer (W) (65.5%)
    - *High*, e.g. Hepatitis (79.4%) and Thyroid (95.0%)
11. *Entropy* (3 values):

$$Entropy = -\sum_{i}^{N} P(C_i) \times log_2 P(C_i) \text{ bits}$$

where N is the number of classes and $P(C_i)$ is the prior probability of class C_i. It is the expected amount of information for classifying an example.
    - *Low*, e.g. Hepatitis (0.73) and Thyroid (0.29)
    - *Medium*, e.g. Lymphography (1.23) and Diabetes (0.93)
    - *High*, e.g. Soybean (3.84) and NetTalk (Phoneme) (4.74)
12. *Difficulty of the domain*:
We use the following two dimensions to discuss the *difficulty of the domain*. The highest accuracy achieved by some existing algorithms, recorded in "Past Usage" in UCI ML Databases, is used as *predictive accuracy*. The corresponding *relative accuracy* is computed as

$$\text{Relative accuracy} = \frac{\text{Predictive accuracy} - \text{Default accuracy}}{100\% - \text{Default accuracy}} \times 100\%$$

- *Predictive accuracy* (3 values):
  - *Low*, e.g. Lymphography (78.4%) and LED-24 (70.0%)
  - *Medium*, e.g. Hepatitis (83.0%) and Soybean (97.1%)
  - *High*, e.g. Mushroom (99.4%) and Monks-2 (100%)
- *Relative accuracy* (3 values):
  - *Low*, e.g. Hepatitis (17.5%) and Diabetes (39.3%)
  - *Medium*, e.g. Lymphography (52.3%) and Breast Cancer (W) (84.9%)
  - *High*, e.g. Soybean (96.6%) and Mushroom (98.7%)

13. *Information score*:
To take the class prior probabilities and class distribution of a dataset into account, Kononenko and Bratko introduce the average information score and relative information score criteria[2,6]. Here, we use the well-known decision tree learning algorithm C4.5[4] as the classifier to calculate the information score, and have the following two dimensions:
    - *Average information score* (3 values):
      - *Low*, e.g. Hepatitis (0.14) and Thyroid (0.21)
      - *Medium*, e.g. Lymphography (0.61) and Mushroom (0.99)
      - *High*, e.g. Soybean (3.35) and LED-24 (2.07)
    - *Relative information score* (3 values):
      - *Low*, e.g. Hepatitis (19.1%) and Promoter (42.1%)
      - *Medium*, e.g. Lymphography (54.3%) and NetTalk (Phoneme) (78.6%)
      - *High*, e.g. Breast Cancer (W) (87.5%) and Soybean (91.4%)

3. Data Sets

It is impossible to evaluate or compare learning algorithms by using them on all possible domains. Here we use the dimensions discussed above to propose the least number of representative[I] domains as a benchmark that covers the space described by the dimensions as completely and evenly as possible. In order to cover the dimensions adequately, a requirement was imposed that every value of each dimension be represented by at least two datasets.

To minimize subjectivity when selecting domains, a two step process was followed:

- The candidates were all real-world domains and well-known synthetic domains from the UCI Repository of machine learning databases[3]. To ensure that the benchmark does not contain relatively unknown datasets, only datasets that have been referenced in the last three Proceedings of the International Workshop/Conference on Machine Learning were considered. This dual constraint guarantees that all datasets are commonly known and easily accessible. Thirty-one such datasets were identified.

[I] ***representative*** **here means that the domain has some common characters with several other domains, that is, it can be a prototype of a group of domains.**

Table 1. Datasets in the benchmark

Name	Description
Breast Cancer (W)	Medical diagnosis applied to breast cytology (Wisconsin)
Hepatitis	Hepatitis database
LED-24	LED display with 24 segments (17 irrelevant)
LED-7	LED display with 7 segments
Lymphography	Lymphography database
Monks-2	The second Monks' problem
Mushroom	Mushrooms classified as poisonous or edible
NetTalk (Phoneme)	NetTalk Corpus for the phonetic transcription of the 1000 most common English words (prediction of phoneme)
Diabetes	Pima Indians diabetes database for diagnosing diabetes
Promoter	Promoter gene sequences (DNA)
Soybean	Large soybean database
Thyroid	Hypothyroid database (thyroid disease records)
Waveform-40	Waveform database with 40 attributes (19 irrelevant)

- A set covering algorithm was used to select the smallest subset of them that satisfies the coverage requirement. The algorithm was run 50 times with different random orderings of the 31 datasets and the frequency of occurrence of each dataset in the selected subsets was noted. With the datasets sorted by this frequency, the set covering algorithm was run once more to identify the final subset.

The result was a collection of thirteen datasets described briefly in Table 1.

4. Related Work

Almost all the developers of learning algorithms use some domains to demonstrate the performance of their algorithms and to compare theirs with other methods. For example, Weiss and Kapouleas[5] use four domains to compare statistical, connectionist, and machine learning classification algorithms. To the best of our knowledge, however, there is no generally accepted benchmark for classifier learning.

Brazdil[1] uses 23 domains from the Esprit Project StatLog to compare and characterize 22 different learning algorithms using meta level learning. The test results of the algorithms on the domains together with domain descriptions are used as input data for the meta level learning and, for each algorithm, rules predicting the applicability of the algorithm are synthesized. The domains are characterized by using 3 simple measures such as the number of examples, 6 statistical measures such as SD-ratio (geometric mean ratio of standard deviations of the individual populations to the pooled standard deviation), and 11 information based measures such as Cx_class (complexity of classification scheme).

5. Conclusion

A benchmark for classifier learning is very important for evaluating or comparing algorithms for learning from examples. In this paper, sixteen dimensions are developed to describe classification tasks. Based on these, thirteen real-world and synthetic datasets are chosen from UCI Repository of machine learning databases to form a benchmark.

The benchmark provides a basis for evaluating and comparing algorithms for learning from examples. It also makes it possible to characterize any given learning algorithm. With the benchmark, we can pinpoint particular strengths and/or weaknesses of different classifier learning algorithms with respect to measures such as accuracy, theory size, and learning time.

6. Acknowledgements

This research was supported by an ARC grant (to Ross Quinlan) and by a research agreement with Digital Equipment Corporation. The author is supported by EMSS scholarship. Many thanks to Ross Quinlan for his advice and suggestions, particularly about doing this work. I'd also like to thank Mike Cameron-Jones, Alen Varšek, and Kai Ming Ting for their helpful discussions and suggestions. Finally, P.M. Murphy and D. Aha are gratefully acknowledged for creating and managing UCI Repository of machine learning databases.

7. References

1. P. Brazdil, J. Gama, and B. Henery, Comparison of ML and statistical approaches using meta level learning, *Workshop Notes on Real-World Applications of Machine Learning, ECML,* (1993).
2. I. Kononenko and I. Bratko, Information-based evaluation criterion for classifier's performance, *Machine Learning,* **6** (1991), p. 67-80.
3. P.M. Murphy and D.W. Aha, *UCI Repository of machine learning databases* [Machine-readable data repository]. Irvine, CA: University of California, Department of Information and Computer Science, (1991).
4. J.R. Quinlan, *C4.5: Programs for Machine Learning,* (Morgan Kaufman, 1993).
5. S.M. Weiss and I. Kapouleas, An empirical comparison of pattern recognition, neuralnets, and machine learning classification methods, *Proceedings of the 11th IJCAI,* (Morgan Kaufman, 1989), p. 781-787.
6. Z. Zheng, A benchmark for classifier learning, *Technical Report, Basser Department of Computer Science, The University of Sydney,* (1993).

A DECISION TREE MODEL OF BUSHFIRE ACTIVITY

David L. Dowe[1] (dld@bruce.cs.monash.edu.au)
Noreen Krusel[2] (nkrusel@arts.cc.monash.edu.au)

[1] Department of Computer Science
[2] Department of Geography and Environmental Science
Monash University, Clayton, Vic. 3168, Australia

ABSTRACT A minimum message length (MML) decision tree inference scheme is applied to the problem of predicting bushfire activity in the mallee vegetation area of north west Victoria, Australia, using over 10 years of data. Bushfire activity is a function of the local vegetation, and models such as the McArthur Forest Fire Danger Index (developed for dry sclerophyll forest) perform poorly on our Mallee data. The measure of bushfire activity is a single variable conglomerating several poorly recorded variables, such as total area burnt and number of people deployed. MML methods are resistant to learning the noise in such data.

The performance of the currently used Fire Danger Indices in predicting bushfire activity is enhanced by combining them with available meteorological data. The MML decision tree scheme inferred expert systems which performed better on average (but at worst, 1.5% worse) than linear regression models and also revealed some surprising non-monotonic and counter-intuitive dependencies.

Keywords inductive learning, decision tree, case study, expert system, decision graph, Minimum Message Length, MML, regression, fire activity, fire weather

1. Introduction

Fire danger rating and Fire Weather Warning in Victoria is currently based on the McArthur Forest Fire Danger Index (FFDI) and Grass Fire Danger Index (GFDI)[3], which were empirically developed[10] by relating known weather and fuel data to the 'fire danger', defined as "..the combined probability of fires starting, spreading and doing damage at a given time.."[10,p1]. The level of fire danger is expressed by the fire danger index (FDI) on a 1-100 scale. An FDI of 50 or greater corresponds to 'extreme' fire danger and is the level at which a Day of Total Fire Ban is usually declared. Mathematical models of the FDI were developed later[11], giving equations (1) to (3) immediately below for the FFDI and GFDI (with the variables defined in Table 1). With the drought factor, D, given by

$$D=0.191*(IU+104)*(DSR+1)^{1.5}/(3.52*(DSR+1)^{1.5}+RAIN-1), \quad (1)$$

let $$FFDI=2.0*D^{0.987}*\exp(-0.450-0.0345*RH+0.0338*T+0.0432*WSP) \quad (2)$$

and $$GFDI=2.0*C^{5.01}*\exp(-23.6+0.0281*T-0.0226\sqrt{RH}+0.633\sqrt{(1.85*WSP)}) \quad (3)$$

One purpose of such fire danger indices is to predict fire activity and provide a basis for issuing warnings. The FFDI[10], developed for dry sclerophyll forest, is the model currently used for all forest types in Victoria. Previous Australian studies analyse historical fire-weather relationships[5,6], but not the quantitative synoptic (daily) prediction of fire activity for a specific fuel type. Here we use 3833 days of meteorological data and derived FDIs to predict the fire activity in the mallee vegetation of north western Victoria. The 3225 training items correspond to the period 01/09/79 - 30/06/88, and the 608 test days to the period 01/07/88 - 28/02/90. We compare linear regression and MML decision tree models of this data.

Table 1. Description of symbols used. The calculations typically use observations taken at 1500 hours(3pm), unless stated otherwise.

SYMBOL	DESCRIPTION
RH	relative humidity (%)
T	air temperature (°C)
WSP	wind speed in the open at 10 metres (10 minute average) (knots)
IU	Keetch-Byram drought index (mm of water required to return soil to field capacity)
DSR	days since rain (measured at 9am)
RAIN	amount of precipitation to 9am (mm)
MAXT	maximum daily temperature (°C)
P	air pressure at mean seas level (hPa)
TW	wet bulb temperature (°C)
C	degree of grass curing (%), assumed to be 100% (0%=fully green grass,100%=dead grass)
D	drought factor
FFDI	forest fire danger index
GFDI	grass fire danger index

2. Data Composition

The meteorological data used are from the standard Bureau of Meteorology observing station at Ouyen (representative of the study area). The meteorological parameters used here are MAXT, DSR, IU, T, TW, WSP, RH, P, FFDI and GFDI (see Table 1). In Australia there is no consensus on the best definition of fire activity[5,6,7]. We use a definition[9] combining four noisy[8] measures of fire activity - the number of fires, area burnt, persons and units deployed on a day. The data are from the Department of Conservation and Natural Resources and the Country Fire Authority of Victoria. The newly combined variable was then given eight classes (1=no fire, 8=severe)[9], defined by the frequency distributions of the training data (01/09/79-30/06/88)(see Table 2).

Table 2. Number of days in activity classes for training data (01/09/79-30/06/88).

FIRE ACTIVITY CLASS	FREQUENCY OF DAYS Tally (%)
1	2351 (72.90)
2	334 (10.36)
3	263 (8.16)
4	153 (4.74)
5	78 (2.42)
6	31 (0.96)
7	9 (0.28)
8	6 (0.19)

3. Decision Trees, MML and Noise

MML gives an objective criterion, namely the concise encoding of model and data[22,20], for model selection. MML inference schemes are resistant to learning noise in data, and are very successful[21,22,23,19,20,15,1]. Information-theoretic decision tree methods for unordered classes include MDL trees[18], MML trees[23] and MML decision graphs[15,13,14] (and applications[4]); and are well borne out by theory[2]. We model lightning strike at best implicitly and we take human causes simply to be unmodelled random noise.

4. Results for Linear Regression and for MML Decision Trees, and Discussion

Training and test data are as described in the text next to Table 1. The models were applied to various fire activity class groupings as detailed in column 1 of Table 3.

Decision tree[23] and graph[15] methods were initially tested on the full data set of 3833 days for 'no fire'/'fire'. The MML graph was always a tree on this data-set. Subsequent analyses used the MML tree algorithm[23].

Table 3. Results of linear regression and MML decision tree analyses, with fire activity classes as defined in Table 2. (The list of explanatory variables is in Table 1.)

Fire Activity (class groupings)	**Meteorological Predictor** (Explanatory variables)	R^2 on Test Data	**Regression Prediction Rate (%)**	**Tree Message Length (bits)**	**MML Tree Prediction Rate (%)**
eight classes: 1,2,3,4,5,6,7,8	all variables	0.207	53.0	4115.2	66.9
'no fire' vs 'fire': i.e. class 1 vs classes 2-8	all variables	0.187	70.6	1873.7	80.4
	FFDI and GFDI only	0.068	68.3	2624.9	66.9
'low' vs 'high': i.e. classes 1-3 vs classes 4-8	all variables	0.117	87.2	1153.5	86.3
	FFDI and GFDI only	0.068	87.0	1272.9	86.3

The eight class fire activity prediction rate of 66.9% for the MML tree (see Table 3) compares favourably with the corresponding linear regression rate of 53.0% even though the MML decision tree method has only been developed for unordered multi-state distributions[23] and is not yet properly suited to analysis of ordered classes.

The regression predicts insignificantly better than the MML tree in the 'low'/'high' case. In the 'no fire'/'fire' case the same was true when our only explanatory variables are FFDI and GFDI but the MML tree was significantly better (80.4% to 70.6%) when using all available explanatory variables. We also note from both the message lengths and the prediction rates (see Table 3) that the MML tree obtained from using all explanatory variables is better than that obtained from just the FFDI and GFDI. We show (Figure 1) the decision trees constructed using the McArthur FFDI and GFDI, noting the sole split on FFDI.

(a) (b)

Figure 1. MML decision trees using FFDI and GFDI for (a) 'no fire'/'fire' and (b) 'low'/'high' fire activity. (Leaf probabilities here and in subsequent trees are given by[20] adding a half to the class tallies in each leaf before comparing them.)

The decision trees using all the explanatory variables for the 'no fire'/'fire' case and the 'low'/'high' fire activity cases are shown in Figures 2(a) and 2(b). Figure 2(b) demonstrates splits on MAXT and GFDI, with the highest probability[20] of 'high' fire activity $((139+0.5)/(351+139+1) \sim 28.4\%)$ occurring at max $T \geq 27.5$ and $GFDI \geq 11.855$. The GFDI has greater dependence on wind speed than the FFDI (see equations (2) and (3)) and so may be more appropriate for the mallee fuel although the GFDI does not account for the possible importance of the fuel amount or fuel continuity of mallee vegetation[12,9].

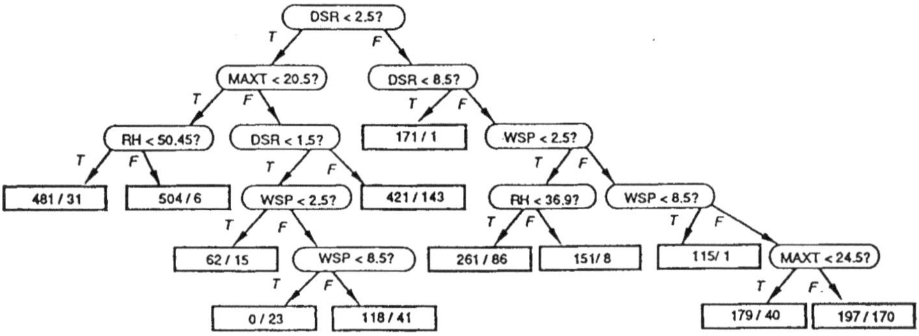

(a)

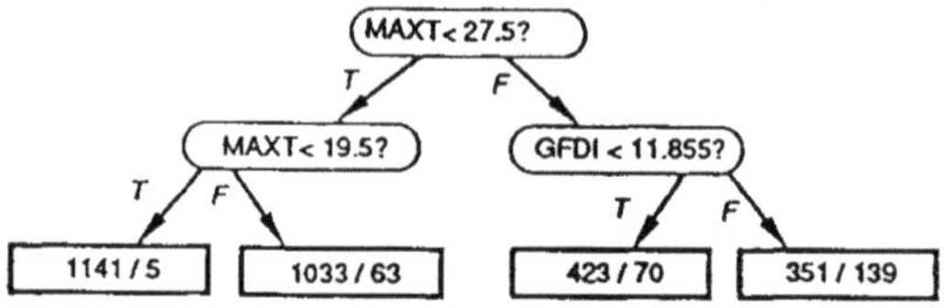

(b)

Figure 2. MML decision trees using all the explanatory variables for (a) 'no fire'/'fire', and (b) 'low'/'high' fire activity.

Partitioning into 'no fire'/'fire' (Figure 2(a)) highlighted the role of rainfall and wind speed in selecting fire days. The highest probability[20] of a fire day (98%), occurs, counter-intuitively, when $DSR < 1.5$, $MAXT \geq 20.5$, and $2.5 \leq WSP \leq 8.5$. The interesting result of high fire activity occurring so soon after rain may be explained by the association of bad fire weather with thunderstorm activity in the mallee. Figure 2(a) demonstrates more counter-intuitive findings, e.g. using only the rule $2.5 < DSR < 8.5$, then we observe 171 fire-free days and only one fire day. What is especially interesting is that if $DSR < 2.5$, or even if $DSR > 8.5$, then for no additional test made do we get as strong a tendency for fire-free days. Also, surprisingly, the next strongest tendency to fire-free days occurs with $DSR > 8.5$ and $2.5 \leq WSP \leq 8.5$, where we find 115 fire free days versus one fire day.

The tree scheme infers that a wind speed between 2.5 and 8.5 knots can give rise to high fire activity, but, if $DSR > 8.5$ then we are 98.7% fire-free, whereas if $DSR < 1.5$ and $MAXT \geq 20.5$, then we are 97.9% likely to have a fire. As well as being counter-intuitive, the results are not monotonic in the variables. More specifically, for the interior node for which ($DSR < 1.5$) and ($MAXT \geq 20.5$), let us look at the subsequent tests, which lead to leaves:

$WSP < 2.5$	gives	62 / 15	(19.9% chance of fires),
$2.5 < WSP < 8.5$	gives	0 / 23	(97.9% chance of fires),
$8.5 < WSP$	gives	118 / 41	(25.9% chance of fires).

This obvious non-monotonicity in the data shows a severe limitation in trying to model this data purely with linear regressions (without first partitioning the data space, such as by our tree means), and perhaps accounts for the comparatively poor performance on 'no fire'/'fire' using all available explanatory variables of the regression (70.6%) compared to the decision tree (80.4%).

Some data-sets (e.g. points clustering along a line) are more amenable to linear regression than to decision trees, while conversely, decision trees (and graphs) are more appropriate for modelling simple boolean functions. We have shown that an MML decision tree scheme is better suited to this data-set than linear regression. The MML decision tree scheme has an added advantage[23] of stating its confidence in a prediction. Running linear regressions in the leaf nodes of our decision trees improved our prediction rate marginally (*in preparation*). Model trees produced by M5 [17] also gave comparable prediction rates to those of our decision trees.

5. Conclusions

The MML decision tree scheme uncovered simple expert systems of no more than 15 rules which performed decidedly better or only marginally worse than (maximum likelihood) linear regression. Decision trees can be easily interpreted. Technical advancements such as MML decision trees (and graphs) with ordered multi-state (or continuous) distributions (and permitting linear or logistic regressions in the leaves) would be preferable. Quinlan[17] and others have developed such piece-wise linear models, but not using MML.

Acknowledgements

This work was supported by Australian Research Council Grant A49030439, the Country Fire Authority of Victoria and the Bureau of Meteorology. We thank J.R.

Quinlan for supplying us with results from his M5 program on this data-set and for also conveying to us results from his C4.5 and C4.5rules programs.

References

1. Allison, L., Wallace, C.S. and Yee, C.N., 'Minimum Message Length Encoding, Evolutionary Trees and Multiple-Alignment', Proceedings of the 25th Hawaii International Conference on Systems Sciences, Kauai, Hawaii, 1992.
2. Barron, A.R. and Cover, T.M., 'Minimum complexity density estimation', IEEE Transactions on Information Theory, 37, pp1034-1054, 1991.
3. Bureau of Meteorology, 'Fire Weather Directive', Melbourne, Australia, 1989.
4. Dowe, D.L., Oliver, J., Dix, T.I., Allison, L. and Wallace, C.S., 'A Decision Graph Explanation of Protein Secondary Structure Prediction', Proceedings of the 26th Hawaii International Conference on Systems Sciences (HICSS), Vol. I, pp669-678, Maui, Hawaii, January 1993.
5. Foley, J.C., 'A Study of Meteorological Conditions Associated with Bush and Grass Fires and Fire Protection Strategy in Australia', Bull. 38, Bureau of Meteorology, Melbourne, 234 pages, 1947.
6. Gill, A.M. 'Forest Fire and Drought in Eastern Australia', Paper to ASTEC Conference on Natural Hazards, CSIRO Division of Plant Industry, Canberra, 1983.
7. Gill, A.M., 'Drought, Fire Danger and Fire Occurrence', Proceedings of the Fire Weather Service Conference, Adelaide, May 1985.
8. Krusel, N., 'Error Analysis of CFA Reports Held on Computer for Seasons 1980-81 and 1984-90.', Unpublished Report Submitted to the Country Fire Authority, 5 pages, 1991.
9. Krusel, N., Packham, D.R. and Tapper, N.J., 'Wildfire Activity in the Mallee Shrubland of Victoria, Australia', accepted, to appear in International Journal of Wildland Fire.
10. McArthur, A.G., 'The Preparation and Use of Fire Danger Tables', Proceedings of the Fire Weather Conference, Bureau of Meteorology, Melbourne, 1958.
11. Noble, I.R., Bary, G.A.V. and Gill, A.M., 'McArthur's Fire Danger Meters Expressed as Equations', Journal of Ecology, pp201-203, 1980.
12. Noble, J.C. and Vines, R.G., 'Fire Studies in mallee (Eucalyptus spp.) communities of Western New South Wales: grass fuel dynamics and associated weather patterns', Rangelands Journal, In Press, 1993.
13. Oliver, J.J., 'Decision Graphs - An Extension of Decision Trees', Proceedings of the Fourth International Conf. on A.I. and Statistics, Fort Lauderdale, Miami, U.S.A., Jan. 1993.
14. Oliver, J., Dowe, D.L. and Wallace, C.S., 'Inferring Decision Graphs Using the Minimum Message Length Principle', Proc. 5th Aust. Joint Conf. on AI, Hobart, Tasmania, pp361-367, 1992.
15. Oliver, J. and Wallace, C.S., 'Inferring Decision Graphs', 12th International Joint Conf. on Artificial Intelligence (IJCAI), 1991, Workshop 8, Sydney, 1991.
16. Quinlan, J.R., C4.5: Programs for Machine Learning, Morgan Kaufmann, San Mateo, CA, 1992
17. Quinlan, J.R., 'Learning with continuous classes', Proceedings of the 5th Australian Joint Conference on Artificial Intelligence, Hobart, Tasmania, pp343-348, 1992.
18. Quinlan, J.R. and Rivest, R.L., Inferring decision trees using the minimum description length principle, Information and Computation, 80, pp227-248, 1989.
19. Wallace, C.S., 'Classification by Minimum-Message-Length Inference', S.G. Akl *et al* (eds.), Advances in Computing and Information- ICCI 1990, Niagara Falls, LNCS 468, pp72-81, 1990.
20. Wallace, C.S. and Boulton, D.M., 'An Information Measure for Classification',Computer Journal, 11, No. 2, pp185-194, 1968.
21. Wallace, C.S. and Freeman, P.R., 'Single Factor Analysis by MML Estimation', J.R.Statist. Soc. B., 54, No.1, pp195-209, 1992.
22. Wallace, C.S. and Freeman, P.R., 'Estimation and Inference by Compact Coding', The Journal of the Royal Statistical Society, Series B, Methodology, 49,3,pp223-265, 1987.
23. Wallace, C.S. and Patrick, J.D., 'Coding Decision Trees', Machine Learning, 11, pp7-22, 1993.

A Novel Approach to Matching Structured Objects

Ouarda Boudour

Department of Computer Science, University of Sheffield, Regent Court, 211 Portobello Street, Sheffield S1 4DP, United Kingdom.

P. D. Green and H. H. Lafferty

Department of Computer Science, University of Sheffield, Regent Court, 211 Portobello Street, Sheffield S1 4DP, United Kingdom.

Abstract

A mechanism is proposed here for matching structured objects. In particular, the issue of efficiency is considered. By allowing patterns to share common structures, a gain in efficiency is obtained since such structures are matched against the data only once. The results of the match can then be used in the matching of patterns comprising these structures. An 'intelligent' matcher for objects has been implemented and tested on two speech recognition applications.

Keywords: combinatorial explosion, matching, object recognition.

1.0 Introduction

The aim of the research described here is to investigate an *'intelligent'* matcher for objects. The key issue is to avoid unnecessary computation by exploiting the fact that some patterns share certain components. Using information about previous matches results in the shared parts being matched only once. We believe that by doing so, the efficiency of the matching task can be improved greatly. A matching algorithm based on these requirements is proposed and an implementation is discussed. The algorithm is intended to recognize general objects described in a relational structure; an object is described in terms of other simpler objects and relations between these objects in such a way that more complex objects can be constructed by combining simpler ones. In this way, knowledge about a particular task is represented by a hierarchy of structured objects. At the bottom of the hierarchy are primitive objects which cannot be subdivided into smaller components. This abstraction makes the system ideally suited to any domain where objects can be described as above. One potential application of this matcher - the recognition of visual objects such as formant shapes in speech spectrograms - is evaluated.

2.0 *IMAGER*: an Intelligent MAtcher for GEneral object Recognition

The work described here was aimed at devising a general methodology for finding objects in a given evidence. An object-based system has been developed that allows us to describe objects and finds instantiations of these objects in the given data (evidence). Central to the system is the matcher which, given the set of object descriptions -patterns- and the evidence, matches the patterns against the data and forms instantiations of the patterns that occur in the evidence. In particular, two aspects of the matcher are considered:

(a) generality

The matcher is kept independent of the problem domain. This ensures that it can be used in a variety of domains, provided that the objects to be recognized can be described in terms of other objects and relations between them. An advantage of doing so is that, unlike the traditional approaches to pattern recognition, such as the statistical methods, it is not tuned to a specific application, rather recognition is achieved solely by matching the object descriptions against the evidence without any aid from domain-specific information. However, generality cannot be achieved without cost; the matcher can be purchased at the expense of the power and competence of the system as power needs knowledge. Such power is no doubt essential in a system intended to accomplish object recognition. Therefore we allowed in the design of the system for domain-specific knowledge to be incorporated into the system if the need for it arises. This knowledge is offered by the descriptions of expected patterns instead of being tied to the matching process. These two key features of IMAGER ensure its generality, a property much desired in recognition systems, while preserving the power offered by domain-specific information. Thus IMAGER can combine the flexibility of a 'weak' method with the competence of an application-specific technique.

(b) efficiency

In a previous chapter, we have exposed the combinatorial problem faced in AI systems and identified the main factor that causes the problem to arise: "repeating work". One approach to alleviate the problem is to eliminate this factor. This is the approach we have followed here to tackle the combinatorial explosion problem.

A matcher has been devised that allow objects to share previously found matches, thus eliminating the need to carry out the matching task on objects that have already been encountered. Details of how this is realized are treated in a subsequent section (see section 2.3). The role of the matcher is to detect the groups of data elements that conform to the given pattern descriptions, and to form instantiations of them. These instantiations constitute the output from the matcher. The recognition task involves three stages:

1. processing the raw data in order to extract useful information and produce a description that makes such information explicit.
2. representing knowledge about the problem domain. This involves describing the patterns we are looking for.
3. matching the pattern descriptions against the data.

The three stages are discussed in the following sections. In order for a system to perform the intelligent task of object recognition, it has to 'know' about the world surrounding it. Therefore, it must be equipped with some world knowledge. This knowledge must embody information about what objects the system is likely to deal with, what properties these objects have and what relations hold between them. The task here is that of building a body of knowledge that the system needs and feeding it to it. This knowledge can be thought of as a memory of typical objects or patterns. It is encoded in terms of objects in an object-based framework.

A natural application of the system presented here is that of finding shapes or structures in an image. A shape must be described in terms of its constituent substructures and the relations between them. A straightforward example of such an application is that of finding shapes in a speech spectrogram for the purpose of speech recognition. We have chosen this particular domain for exploring our ideas and testing the system. This is discussed in section 3.0 below.

2.1 A Hierarchical Structural Model for Representing World Knowledge

We are primarily dealing with objects of arbitrary complexity, the simplest of which are the primitives; the most elementary objects that cannot be further decomposed into simpler objects. An object can be regarded as a structure made of other simpler objects or substructures which we call 'components', tied together with some relations and constraints. We are therefore led to the choice of a hierarchical structural model in which objects of arbitrary complexity can be described. The object-based paradigm lends itself to this kind of description.

Describing typical objects is a way of encoding knowledge about the world, in particular knowledge about the problem domain. The question addressed here is "How can this knowledge be represented?". After observation of the kind of information that we need to represent, it becomes clear that a natural way of describing objects is to chunk together pieces of information relating to a given object. This framework is offered by the object-based knowledge representation paradigm. The choices above culminated in an object-based representation with a hierarchical organization.

Within this framework an object is described by capturing its structure, that is its components and the relations between them. Hence the word 'structural'. We emphasize here the importance of relations because information about 'parts' is not sufficient for the recognition of an object. The same parts in different configurations make up different objects. The relations between these parts is the discriminating factor. Ullman[1] illustrates the important role of spatial relations using two pictures, one of which is immediately recognized as a human face by detecting the mouth, nose, and eyes. The second picture cannot be recognized as a human face because the parts have been displaced, thus altering the spatial relations between them.

The parts in turn may be decomposed into smaller parts and described separately in the same manner. This decomposition can be carried out to an arbitrary level of detail. Hence the word 'hierarchical'. The repeated application of this decomposition and description of all objects that may be encountered in the real world (or in the particular problem domain) results in a 'hierarchical structure' where more abstract or general descriptions lie in the higher levels of the hierarchy while more specific descriptions lie in the lower levels of the hierarchy. Primitive objects form the leaves of the hierarchy tree. The structural model described here is compatible with the way humans recognize objects. Hoffman[2] argues that the human visual system decomposes a shape into its parts for recognition:

> "We will argue that, just as syntactic analysis decomposes a sentence into its constituent structure, so the visual system decomposes a shape into a hierarchy of parts..."

We believe that modelling knowledge about familiar shapes as explained above, can facilitate the recognition task in that, simple shapes are matched first, and gradually those of increasing complexity. The complexity of the task is thus reduced by making the process as modular as possible. Perhaps it is worth noting that, in addition to the advantages offered by structural descriptions for recognition purposes, they have been advocated as a framework for representing general knowledge[3].

2.2 Organization of the Data

The input to the system is an intermediate representation of the data where primitive objects are made explicit. In the case of a visual input, this representation corresponds to the primal sketch[4] representation of the image. For the particular applications considered here, a speech sketch[5] is computed from a speech spectrogram and presented to the system for the subsequent recognition of speech objects. FIGURE 1 illustrates the computation of the speech sketch. In the simplest case, the primitives are line segments which make up object boundaries. The system is given a description of the data in terms of primitive objects. Each primitive object is referred to by its name and has a number of properties associated with it. Basically, information associated with a primitive would contain its spatial position if a visual input is considered. In the general case, such information depends on the application in hand.

Relations between objects play a central role here since our ultimate goal is the detection of objects that are tied together with certain relations. We propose that the data be organized in a structure that we call a 'relational network'. In this network nodes represent primitives and the arcs linking them denote relations between primitives. However, when dealing with visual images, we may need to express relations in more than one dimension. This can be done by building another network superposed on the first one and which contains relationships along the second dimension. Thus relations along the second dimension are expressed orthogonally to relations along the first dimension. The resultant structure can be conceived of as a superposition of two networks, each of which holds relations along one dimension. We must note here that, for economical reasons, the nodes are not duplicated, rather they are shared between the networks. This structure can be extended if some other kind of relations between objects need to be expressed. The size of the network is only constrained by the storage capacity.

FIGURE 1 Levels of description of speech data. Utterance dr1.mcpm0.sx24: "although alone, we survive", male speaker..

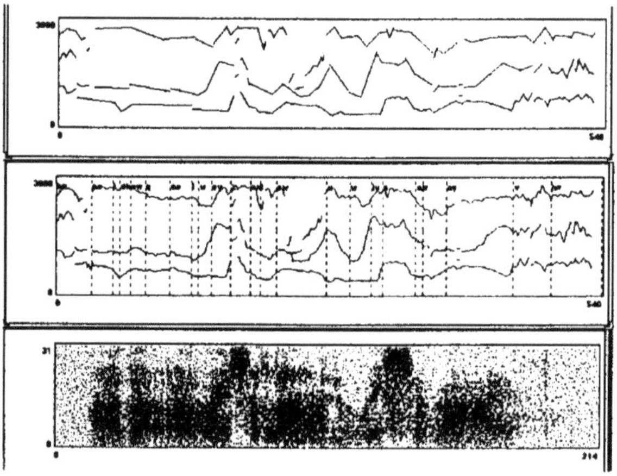

Building the network

The relational network is built in two stages:

1. A node is created for each element in the data.
2. For every data element the relations with the other elements in the data are computed and the corresponding arcs are added to the network.

Step 2 may be repeated as necessary to compute the relations between objects along a number (currently two) of dimensions.

Computing the relations

Confining the problem to that of finding shapes in a two-dimensional image, we can identify nine different relations that can occur between two objects along one dimension (the abscissa for instance). The set of these relations is adopted from Allen's[6] temporal relations (before, after, start, started-by, finish, finished-by, meet, met-by, overlap, overlapped-by, during, contain, equal). In the approach proposed here, time may be considered as one of the dimensions in which the evidence is represented. Therefore temporal relations can be thought of as relations along one dimension e.g. x axis. The two following observations can be made after examination of the relations:

(1) Every possible situation can be expressed by one of the relations.

(2) The relations are mutually exclusive which guarantee that no ambiguity will arise in computing the relation between two objects. Only one relation is true in a given situation.

Observing the set of relations more closely, we notice that this set can be reduced to a more concise set of relations without losing its expressive power. For instance, relations 'met-by' and 'overlap' can be fused into a new looser 'overlap' relation where the two objects may 'meet'. Our motivation for doing so is that the real world is not perfect, therefore deviations from the ideal often, if not always occur. A 'meet' relation for instance may not occur at all in reality, rather objects may overlap. Hence, combining some relations is beneficial because the computation of a smaller set of relations requires less computation. The tailored set of relations is given in TABLE 1. A similar set of relations can be used to express relations along the second dimension (ordinate y for instance) with a slight modification of terms for reasons of clarity. The resulting set of relations is given in TABLE 2.

2.3 Matching Patterns to the Data -finding objects in the evidence

As previously shown, the matcher is the core of the system. In this section, our prior concern is to build a matcher which, presented with some evidence, finds in it occurrences of typical objects. We propose here a mechanism for performing the matching task and highlight the main issues underlying the choice of this particular mechanism. Basically, the task is divided into two sub-tasks:

1. Compilation of a 'recognition network'.
2. Matching the patterns against the data using the compiled network. This is achieved by the bottom-up process described below {see section 2.3.2}.

The two following sections explain these two sub-tasks in more detail.

2.3.1 Compilation of the recognition network

A network is compiled from the pattern descriptions with the building elements defined as follows:

(1) The nodes may correspond to patterns or to structures that make up patterns. These structures can be as simple as the primitives and as complex as the final patterns presented for recognition.

(2) The directional links between nodes denote the relations and constraints that must be satisfied between objects corresponding to the nodes.

TABLE 1 Reduced set of spacial relations.

Relation	Illustration	Inverse Relation	Illustration
Far-Before	[---A---] <--d-->[---B---] {d > aThreshold}	Far-After	[---B---] <--d-->[---A---] {d > aThreshold}
Near-Before	[---A---] <--d-->[---B---] {d <= aThreshold}	Near-After	[---B---] <--d-->[---A---] {d <= aThreshold}
During	[----A----] [---------B----------] OR: [----A----] [---------B----------] OR: [----A----] [---------B----------]	Contain	[---------B----------] [----A----] OR: [----B----] [---------A----------] OR: [----B----] [---------A----------]
Overlap	[-------A------] [--------B-------] OR: [----A----] [----B----]	Overlapped-by	[-------B------] [--------A-------] OR: [----B----] [----A----]
Equal	[--------A-------] [--------B-------]	(itself)	

The illustrations above are read "A relation B", e.g., "A during B". A and B are the intervals occupied by the respective objects along the x axis. The first column gives the name of the relation. The second column shows the situation where the relation holds. The third and last column give the inverse relation. The 'Equal' relation is its own inverse. The value of 'aThreshold' is application-dependant. In some applications, this 'aThreshold' is specified so that if two objects are 'aThreshold' apart, then their relation is irrelevant, therefore it can be ignored.

TABLE 2 Spacial relations along the ordinate (y).

Relation	Illustration	Inverse Relation	Illustration
Below	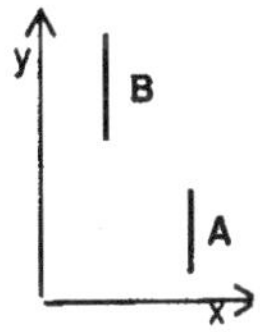	Above	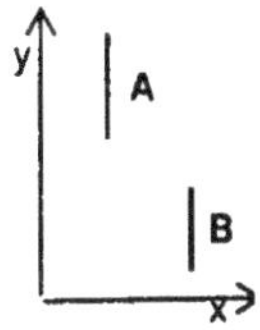
Within	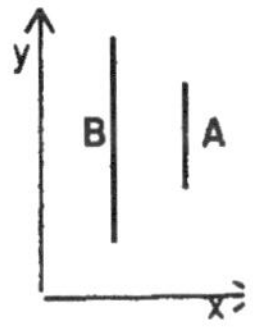	Contain	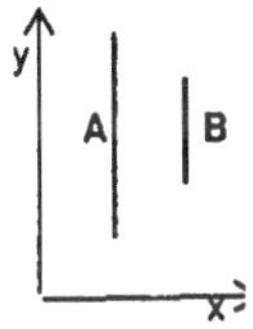
	or: 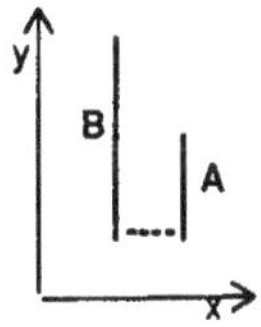		or: 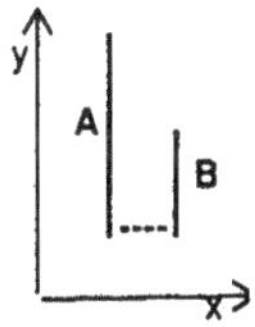
Meet	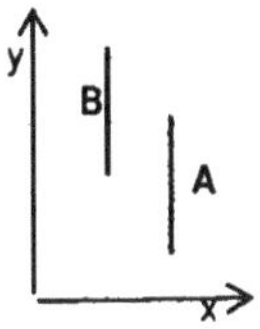	Met-by	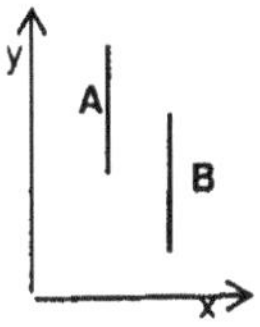
	or: 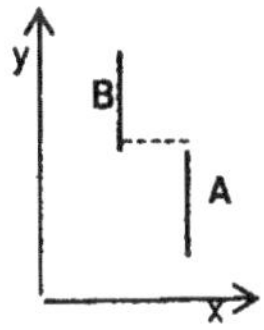		or: 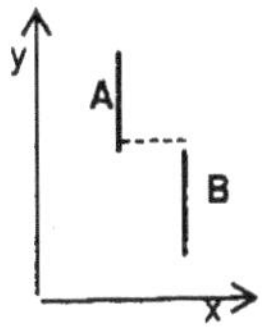
	or: 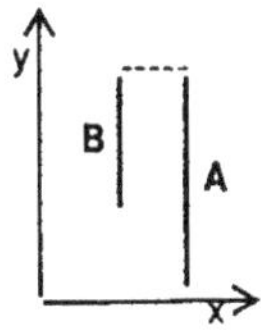		or: 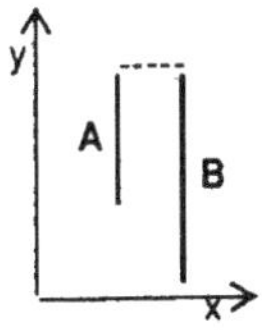

Equal 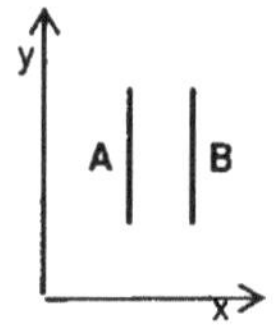 (itself)

The illustrations above are read "A relation B", e.g., "A below B". A and B are the intervals occupied by the respective objects along the y axis. The first column gives the name of the relation. The second column shows the situation where the relation holds. The third and last column give the inverse relation. The 'Equal' relation is its own inverse.

Two types of links may exist between nodes:

- Constraint-bearing links, that is links specifying the relations between objects represented by the nodes. These links act like filters, allowing only elements of data that satisfy the constraints imposed by the links to be passed on to the node's descendants.
- Non constraint-bearing links (non labelled arcs). These are simply links that connect a node with its children. Data is passed through these links without being subjected to a filtering operation.

Each path in the network starting at the root and ending at the leaves correspond to a pattern description. The structure of the pattern is made explicit by the path. Patterns may be made of iterative structures. In order to allow such patterns to be described in the framework presented here, a node can be linked to itself. Thus allowing an iterative structure whose elementary building block is the substructure represented by the node.

2.3.2 The Recognition process

The purpose of the network is to build gradually more complex objects out of elementary ones. The process involved is a bottom-up one, starting at the most elementary (bottom) level of primitives and proceeding bottom-up in an attempt to form more complex objects which are instantiations of some predefined patterns. Data is fed to the network at its root. A filtering process is activated to select among the data those elements which conform to the specifications encoded in the network. Data elements which 'survived' the filtering process accumulate at the leaves where they form instantiations of patterns represented by the leaves.

Handling different levels of complexity

The filtering process constructs complex objects out of simpler ones starting with the most elementary ones -primitives-. The process passes through a number of levels of increasing complexity and terminates when the level required is reached. This process can be broken down into simpler sub-processes responsible for increasing the level of complexity by one each time. Each of these sub-processes correspond to one stage of the recognition process. Since a sub-process consists of filtering data through a network, we are led to a concept of multiple 'filtering' networks, each of which is responsible for constructing objects of a certain degree of complexity. For instance, at the first level, 'Level1' network forms objects from primitives. The resultant objects have a 'degree 1 complexity'. Primitives have 'complexity 0' by convention. At the second level, the objects found at the first level are combined into larger objects which are one degree more complex. These new 'degree 2 complexity' objects are obtained by filtering the previously found -degree 1 complexity-objects through 'Level 2' network. To allow interactions between networks of different levels, back links are added to join nodes representing objects of 'degree n-1 complexity' in 'Level n' network with nodes representing the same objects in 'Level n-1' network. These links are not restricted to successive networks only. A 'Level n' network may have back links to any network(s) of level l where l is less than n (l<n). In this manner, objects of arbitrary degree of complexity can be constructed gradually from simpler objects.

Automatic network compilation

A mechanism is provided for compiling the networks from the given pattern descriptions in such a way to allow for common structures to be shared between objects. This sharing of structure eliminates redundant work which may be caused by common structures being matched every time the matching of the objects containing them is attempted. To avoid ambiguity, the descriptions must specify one and only one typical object (pattern).

Recognition process

With each node we associate two recipients that we refer to as 'left memory' and 'right memory'. These notions of memories were used in Rete[7], although here they play a different role to that in Rete. The right memory stores locally matched data elements, i.e., elements that conform to the specification of the object represented by the node. The left memory stores elements of data that have reached the node from the root, in other words, elements that have 'survived' the filtering process and thus form 'partial instantiations' (partially matched objects). Filtering starts by entering the data at the root, which passes it on to its successors (children). Control is then passed to these nodes in turn. The network is traversed in a 'depth-first' fashion i.e., from top to bottom and from left to right. Each node is given a type which can one of: Start, Intermediate, Terminal, Accumulator, or Abstract. When a node is activated (control is passed to it), a number of possible things can happen according to its type. An Accumulator node accumulate successfully matched data forming legal instantiations.

3.0 Application of IMAGER to Automatic Speech Recognition

The speech signal conveys information about the spoken sentence. The recovery of this information results in the recognition of the utterance. One approach to do so is spectrogram reading i.e., analysing a visual display of the speech waveform: 'spectrogram'. It has been shown that spectrograms can be read with a high degree of accuracy (80 - 97%)[8; 9; 10; 5] which lead to the belief that automatic speech recognition (ASR) can be achieved by building systems that can imitate the human phonetician. Such systems became known as 'Expert Spectrogram Readers'. A number of researchers followed this approach and a great deal of work along this line has been reported[8; 11; 12; 13; 9].

The approach here is that of analysing a FFT-derived spectrogram in order to extract significant information that will help uncover the identity of the given utterance. Among the advocators of this approach is Green et al.[5] who proposed and implemented an object-based system for acoustic phonetic processing (SPLASH2) based on this idea and which used an intermediate representation of speech data called 'Speech Sketch' -after Marr's primal sketch[4]-, a cartoon-like spectrogram. This representation is an intermediate representation of speech data which makes parameter behaviour explicit. At this level objects like 'Peak' and 'Dip' are made explicit.

The presence of some of these objects cues for the occurrence of certain sounds. This approach seems suitable for the identification of 'nonstationary' sounds like semivowels and stop consonants which are characterized by formant transitions portrayed by curved resonance bars on a spectrogram. An analysis of the resulting formant movement helps identify these sounds. The speech sketch representation computed by SPLASH2 constitutes the input to IMAGER which will perform the object recognition task. An example of input and output to and from IMAGER is shown in FIGURE 2.

In order to test the object recognition system presented here we have applied it to find shapes in a spectrogram and applied the results to the identification of semivowels and stop consonants. The result of the matcher can then be used for subsequent reasoning leading to the final recognition of the utterance. The input to the matcher is the speech sketch corresponding to the unknown utterance. The output will be instantiations of shapes found in the spectrogram. Because the matcher is meant to be general, no domain-specific knowledge is used to aid the recognition. Only general knowledge about the kind of objects that might occur is available to the matcher in the form of informal pattern descriptions. Therefore the result of the matcher must be regarded as a first guess that can be further confirmed or disproved by additional evidence, probably provided by context or domain-specific knowledge. The system has been tested on two problems, each of which is concerned with the recognition of a subset of speech sounds.

In the first application we considered the semivowels in the English language: *'r'*(read), *'w'*(we), *'y'*(you), *'l'*(let). The second application consists of recognizing combinations of stops and vowels, that is when a vowel precedes or follows a stop sound. IMAGER lends itself to this kind of problem because in both cases the sounds in question can be detected by the characteristic shapes they portray in the spectrogram. For instance, a 'Peak' shape in the second formant is a strong evidence for the occurrence of a 'y' semivowel in that part of the utterance. In this sense a 'Peak' is used as a cue for recognizing a 'y'. So the approach here is that of recognizing sounds by finding visible cue objects in the spectrogram.

4.0 Conclusion

An object-based system was developed in which objects can be described and matched against an evidence. The matcher has been devised in such a way to allow common structures among objects to be shared, thus avoiding their being matched more than once. This resulted in a considerable gain in efficiency. We believe that this is a step towards making matchers capable of matching large numbers of patterns and data in a reasonable time. The matcher was kept application-independent to ensure its generality. We hope, by doing so, we allow it to be plugged in to many applications requiring object recognition and in which objects can be described qualitatively in terms of other objects and relations between them. The system described here has been implemented on a Sparc station using the object-oriented programming language Smalltalk-80[14; 15]. To demonstrate the performance of the system we have applied it to two speech recognition problems where it was used to find objects in a speech spectrogram. The result of the matching process may be used for subsequent reasoning which will produce an interpretation or a transcription of the unknown utterance. The results obtained are quite satisfactory considering that the output of the matcher is considered as a first guess about the identity of the objects because only information about the structure of the patterns is available to the matcher. We must recall that the primary role of the matcher is to find instantiations of patterns given qualitative descriptions of them and this has been achieved. We believe that more specializing descriptions and context information backed with a measure of the quality of the instantiations will lead to better results.

FIGURE 2 Inputs and output from a sample recognition task applied to utterance *'JL02s'*, male speaker.

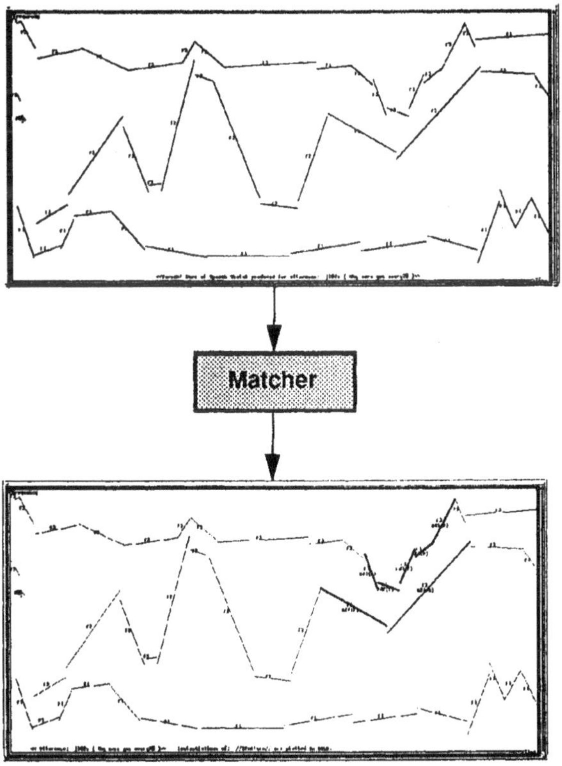

References

1. S. Ullman "*Visual Routines*" in ***Image Understanding 1985-86*** ed. S. Ullman (1987) 286-344.
2. D. D. Hoffman and W. A. Richards "*Parts of Recognition*" in ***Cognition*** Vol. 18 (1984) 65-96.
3. M. Minsky "*A Framework for Representing Knowledge*" in ***The Psychology of Computer Vision*** ed. Patrick H. Winston, (McGraw-Hill, 1975) 211-280.
4. D. Marr "*Vision*" (New York, NY : W. H. Freeman, 1982).
5. P. D. Green, G. J. Brown, M. P. Cooke, M. D. Crawford, and A. J. H. Simons "*Bridging the Gap Between Signals and Symbols in Speech Recognition*" in ***Advances in Speech, Hearing and Language Processing*** Vol. 1 (1990) 149-192.
6. J. F. Allen "*Maintaining Knowledge About Temporal Intervals*" in ***Communications of the ACM*** Vol. 26 No. 11 (1983) 832-843.
7. C. L. Forgy "*Rete: A Fast Algorithm For The Many Pattern / Many Object Pattern Match Problem*" in ***Artificial Intelligence*** 19 (1982) 17-37.
8. V. W. Zue and L. F. Lamel "*An Expert Spectrogram Reader: A Knowledge-Based Approach to Speech Recognition*" in ***Proc. ICASSP*** Vol. 4 (1986) 1197-1200.
9. F. Lonchamp "*Reading Spectrograms: The View from the Expert*" in ***Fundamentals in Computer Understanding: Speech and Vision. An advanced course*** ed. J. P. Haton (1987) 181-206.
10. W. A. Ainsworth "*Speech Recognition By Machine*" (Peter Peregrinus Ltd., London, 1988), p. 38.
11. V. W. Zue "*The Use of Speech Knowledge in Automatic Speech Recognition*" Invited Paper in ***Proc. IEEE Special Issue on Human-Machine Communication by Speech*** Vol. 73 No. 11 (1985) 1602-1615.
12. R. De Mori, L. Lam, and D. Probst "*Rule-Based Detection of Speech Features for Automatic Speech Recognition*" in ***Fundamentals in Computer Understanding: Speech and Vision. An advanced course*** ed. J. P. Haton (1987) 155-179.
13. R. DeMori, A. Giordana, P. Laface, and L. Saitta "*An Expert System for Interpreting Speech Patterns*" in ***Proceedings of the American Association for Artificial Intelligence (AAAI)*** (1982) 107-110.
14. A. Goldberg "*Smalltalk-80. An Interactive Programming Environment*" (Addison-Wesley, Reading, MA, 1984).
15. A. Goldberg and D. Robson "*Smalltalk-80. The Language and Its Implementation*" (Addison-Wesley, Reading, MA, 1983).

Being Correct is Not Enough - The Role of Domain Knowledge in the Utility Problem

Christopher Leckie
Telecom Australia Research Laboratories, P.O. Box 249, Clayton, Victoria 3168

Abstract

Many learning systems make extensive use of domain knowledge to improve the correctness of the rules that they learn. However, an important issue when learning search control knowledge to improve the speed of a problem-solving system is whether the savings of the learned knowledge outweigh its costs. This is known as the utility problem. This phenomenon raises new questions about the importance of correctness, and the effects of relying solely on domain knowledge when learning. In this paper, we describe a class of domains which can cause theory-based systems to learn correct rules of negative utility, and show the advantages of an inductive learning system, called Grasshopper, for this class of domains.

1. Introduction

An important feature of different learning techniques is their use of domain knowledge. Techniques such as *explanation-based learning* (EBL) use detailed domain knowledge to learn rules that are provably correct. In contrast, *inductive* techniques are able to learn without the assistance of domain knowledge by characterising patterns in a number of training examples. However, without a domain theory, inductive learning techniques cannot guarantee the correctness of the rules that they learn. Consequently, EBL has usually been preferred to inductive learning when a satisfactory domain theory is available.

If the only cost in problem-solving is backtracking out of incorrect choices, then the aim of learning is to reduce the number of times we make an incorrect choice. Unfortunately, there is an additional cost involved in problem-solving, namely, the time required to make a decision. When using trial and error, this cost is trivial. It is merely the time required to retrieve the next available option. But once we provide a system with additional knowledge to help make a decision, we must wait while it decides whether that knowledge is relevant to the current decision. If this knowledge is rarely applicable or expensive to apply, then this search control knowledge may have the effect of increasing the total time required for the search. This phenomenon is known as the *utility problem.*

While domain knowledge may be used to guarantee the correctness of learned knowledge, correctness does not necessarily imply utility. In this paper, we demonstrate this point by presenting a class of problem-solving domains for which EBL techniques generate correct rules of negative utility, and show the advantages of an inductive learning system, called Grasshopper, for this class of domains.

2. The Utility of Search Control Knowledge in Planning

The utility of learned knowledge is a measure of its value to the task at hand. In this paper, we focus on the task of plan generation. In this context, the aim of learning is to reduce the time required to generate plans. Let us begin by describing the search space for planning and the scope for learning in this kind of search. This will provide us with an example of the utility problem in practice.

A planning problem is defined by a goal state to be achieved, a starting state from which the goal must be achieved, and a set of operators that can be used to achieve the goal. At each successive stage in generating a plan the planner must decide which goal should be satisfied next, which operator should be used for that goal, and how that operator should be instantiated. Having made these decisions, the planner will attempt to generate a new node in the plan search tree. The opportunity for learning in plan generation lies in improving this decision-making process in order to avoid unsuccessful choices.

Before a rule is given to the planner, we need to consider its utility. The utility of a rule depends on the costs of testing its applicability, and the savings in search time that will be incurred when the rule is applicable. The cost of a rule is the time required to test its antecedent at a node in a plan search tree. The savings of a rule may be measured in terms of the time required to create nodes over which the planner would later have to backtrack had the rule not been available. If a rule is seldom needed, then savings may be outweighed by the costs of the rule on average and it will have negative utility.

3. Two Approaches to Learning

Historically, there have been two main methods for learning search control rules: *inductive* and *explanation-based learning*. In this section, we outline an example of each approach, and discuss the relative merits and limitations of each approach from the point of view of the utility problem.

3.1 Explanation-based Learning

The main advantages of explanation-based techniques are that they are capable of learning knowledge that is provably correct from a single training example. An important example of an explanation-based system for learning search control knowledge in planning is PRODIGY/EBL[1]. PRODIGY/EBL uses individual planning decisions as examples of target concepts for learning. Once an example decision has been found, PRODIGY/EBL constructs a proof explaining why the example is an instance of the target concept. This proof is then used as the basis for a new search control rule.

The only restrictions on the use of EBL is that the domain theory must be complete, consistent and tractable[2]. However, this is not normally considered to be a problem when learning about domains in the classical planning model. This is because a theory describing the domain is implicit in the planning operators, and a theory describing the planner need only be encoded once, as shown by PRODIGY/EBL for a STRIPS-type planner[1].

Although explanation-based techniques can guarantee correctness, they provide no such guarantee from the point of view of utility, since it is possible to encode the same explanation in many different ways. Systems such as PRODIGY/EBL try to compress the explanations that they produce, but this is a complex search problem in itself, and often requires additional domain-specific knowledge to be explicitly encoded in order to be effective. In addition, explanation-based techniques have certain limitations from the point of view of utility, since they cannot learn from more than one example at a time, and cannot learn about distributions of problems. For example, two decisions of the same type may be encoded as two separate rules if the explanation of the first problem was not sufficiently general to match the second problem. Finally, explanation-based techniques are not able to learn from features that are not encoded in the domain theory. In principle, an explanation may be produced without referring to such features. However, these features may be of heuristic value in avoiding incorrect choices in planning.

3.2 Inductive Learning

A technique that can address the problems of EBL is inductive learning. An example of such an approach is a system that we have developed called Grasshopper[3]. Like PRODIGY/EBL, Grasshopper learns search control rules from the decisions made by a planning system. There are five main stages in Grasshopper[4]: (1) First, the *Decision Extraction* stage extracts interesting examples of planning decisions from a new plan search tree. (2) Next, the *Decision Clustering* stage groups these decisions according to the type of search control advice they provide. (3) The *Choice Characterisation* stage then learns a unique description for each cluster of decisions, in order to recognise when the corresponding advice is applicable. The inductive learning algorithm used in this stage is based on the FOIL algorithm[5]. (4) The *Rule Generation* stage compiles the characterisation and advice from a cluster of decisions into a search control rule. (5) Finally, the *Utility Optimisation* stage estimates the utility of new rules, and decides whether they should be passed on to the planner.

An important advantage of the approach used by Grasshopper is that it does not rely on any form of domain theory to generate the search control rules that it learns. In addition, it has the potential to improve the utility of these rules since it learns from more than one example at a time. Consequently, it does not require any additional domain knowledge or heuristics to help simplify the rules that it learns.

4. Heuristically Incomplete Domains

As mentioned in the previous section, there is no guarantee that a correct explanation will result in an efficient search control rule. Although the preconditions of an operator specify the conditions under which the operator is applicable, they may provide no heuristic information that indicates whether the operator is likely to be useful in the current problem-solving context. In some domains, there may be additional contextual knowledge that has heuristic value in predicting whether an operator is likely to be useful. However, these heuristic features would not appear in the domain theory because they are not necessary conditions for making a particular choice. In these situations, we consider the domain theory to be *heuristically incomplete*. An explanation-based learner would be unable to make use of these heuristic features, because they are not mentioned in any of the operator definitions for the domain.

Let us now consider two examples of heuristically incomplete domains[4]. Although these two domains are rather restricted, they have been included to demonstrate plausible problem solving scenarios in which heuristically incomplete domain theories may occur. Our expectation is that Grasshopper would be able to learn rules of higher utility in these test domains than would PRODIGY/EBL.

4.1 The Parser Domain

This test domain implements a parser that is designed to parse sentences of a simple but ambiguous grammar (Figure 1). There are three categories of sentences in this grammar, which may be characterised by the last token that appears in each sentence. Unfortunately, the grammar requires the parser to decide which is the appropriate category at the start of the sentence, which may lead to backtracking.

In order to illustrate the use of heuristic features, we have included in the problem state description of each sentence an additional predicate that we refer to as PITCH. There are three values that may be assigned to the argument of this predicate, namely RISING, FALLING or STEADY. Each category of sentence has its own pitch value, which may be used to help the planner decide which parsing rule should be used at the start of a sentence. It is important to realise that the domain theory is formally complete for this problem, since the planning operators define how to parse any legal sentence that belongs to the grammar. However, the domain theory is heuristically incomplete in the sense that

$S \rightarrow aX$	$S \rightarrow aY$	$S \rightarrow aZ$
$X \rightarrow bX_1$	$X_1 \rightarrow cX_1$	$X_1 \rightarrow x$
$Y \rightarrow bY_1$	$Y_1 \rightarrow cY_1$	$Y_1 \rightarrow y$
$Z \rightarrow bZ_1$	$Z_1 \rightarrow cZ_1$	$Z_1 \rightarrow z$

Figure 1: Grammar Rules for Parser Domain

```
GOAL:
    (and (engineering) (applied-maths)
         (chemistry) (physics))

INITIAL-STATE:
    (free t1)          (free t2)
    (free t3)          (free t4)
    (eng-faculty)
```

Figure 2: A Timetable Domain Problem

there are additional features outside of this domain theory that have heuristic value in reducing the amount of search required to find parses for these sentences.

4.2 The Timetable Domain

This domain is designed to generate customised timetables for university students. In this domain, there is a fixed timetable that specifies which subjects are offered at which times. Each student is enrolled in four subjects out of a range of ten subjects that are available. Each subject is offered at one or more alternative times during the week. Given the subjects in which a student is enrolled, the aim is to generate a timetable for the student by allocating a class time to each subject in which the student is enrolled. Each subject taken by a student has its own goal predicate. Different operators for the same subject represent alternative times at which the subject is offered. A precondition of each operator is that the student is free at the time of that class. The planner must find a combination of operators that represent compatible class times for the subjects being taken by the student. Figure 2 contains an example of a problem in this domain.

This is a form of constraint satisfaction problem. The opportunity for learning in this domain is to recognise which operator to choose for a goal, given the other goals that appear in the problem. As with the previous domain, we have provided an additional background feature that may help the planner predict which is the correct operator for a goal. This feature specifies the faculty to which a student belongs. Some subjects are taken only by students from a particular faculty, whereas other subjects are common to students from a number of faculties. In addition, students from certain faculties take a predetermined combination of subjects. In those faculties, all of the students normally have the same standard timetable. This makes it possible to predict which class to take for a subject based on the faculty to which a student belongs.

5. Experimental Evaluation

In a previous paper, we demonstrated the advantages of Grasshopper in two standard test domains[3]. The aim of our experiments in this paper are to observe the effects of domains with heuristically incomplete theories on the utility of the search control rules generated by Grasshopper and PRODIGY/EBL. The standard procedure that we follow in these experiments is to measure how search control rules learned using each method change the total time required by the PRODIGY planner to solve a fixed set of test problems.

For the purposes of these tests we have used the two domains described in the previous section. Since the heuristic features of these domains do not appear in the domain theory, they are inaccessible to PRODIGY/EBL. Consequently, there would be a clear advantage to using an inductive approach to learn search control rules for these domains. We are interested in testing whether Grasshopper can benefit by using problem features that do not appear in the domain theory of a heuristically incomplete domain. Table 1

Domain	Training Problems	Test Problems	Time Bound	Node Bound
Parser	10	50	300 CPU sec	2500
Timetable	24	27	300 CPU sec	2500

Table 1: Experimental Conditions for Each Domain

contains the test conditions for each of these two domains. The results for the parser and timetable domains are summarised in Tables 2 and 3, respectively.

6. Discussion

In both domains, the rules learned by PRODIGY/EBL led to an increase in the total planning time, despite the fact that they reduced the number of nodes expanded by the same amount as Grasshopper's rules. The difference was that Grasshopper was able to make use of the heuristic features, whereas PRODIGY/EBL had to resort to learning a larger number of more specialised rules. The particular structure of these domains also made the antecedents of these rules more complex, and thus more expensive to match. Let us consider the structure of each of these domains in more detail.

The main source of complexity in the parser domain lay in deciding which operator should be used to achieve the top-level goal. There are three choices for this decision, each corresponding to a rule of the grammar. Due to the structure of the grammar, the planner does not find out whether it has made the correct choice until it reaches the end of the sentence. If the planner has made the wrong choice, then it is forced to backtrack to the start of the sentence.

PRODIGY/EBL is forced to explain this kind of choice by memorising a detailed description of the sentence. The antecedent of the rule that is derived from this explanation may be considered as a *macro-precondition.* This macro-precondition is compiled from the important preconditions of each operator that appears in the final plan. The recursive nature of the grammar makes it difficult to find an efficient generalisation of this precondition, and thus the utility of the rule is low. In contrast, Grasshopper merely tests the pitch of the sentence in order to recognise which operator to use at the start of the sentence. In this way, Grasshopper is able to eliminate all of the backtracking.

Similar problems arise in the timetable domain. The correct choice of a class time for a subject for any given student depends upon the other subjects that the student is taking. This means that the correct operator choice for each top-level goal depends upon what other top-level goals appear in the problem. The scope for learning lies in recognising which combinations of goals lead to a particular operator choice. Grasshopper is able to do this by testing the faculty of a student. This strategy is plausible since students in certain faculties are enrolled in a predetermined set of subjects. This information constrains the problem so that the choice of a class time for each subject is obvious. However, PRODIGY/EBL is unable to make use of this short cut, because the student's faculty is not mentioned in any of the domain operators. Therefore, it must test explicitly whether

Strategy	Nodes Expanded	Improvement over default	Total Time (CPU seconds)	Improvement over default	Problems Unsolved
Default	1736	-	307	-	0
Grasshopper	912	48%	225	37%	0
PRODIGY/EBL	936	46%	2532	-720%	3

Table 2: Summary of Test Results for the Parser Domain

Strategy	Nodes Expanded	Improvement over default	Total Time (CPU seconds)	Improvement over default	Problems Unsolved
Default	1070	-	127	-	0
Grasshopper	301	72%	93	**27%**	0
PRODIGY/EBL	299	72%	165	**-31%**	0

Table 3: Summary of Test Results for the Timetable Domain

the student is enrolled in a certain combination of subjects. This kind of memorisation forces PRODGY/EBL to learn less general rules than those learned by Grasshopper.

7. Conclusion and Further Work

The main advantages of using a domain theory are that it introduces a strong bias in the search for a characterisation of a target concept, and that it guarantees the correctness of what has been learned. In other words, it helps reduce the complexity of learning, and eliminates the risk of making incorrect generalisations. However, there are other sides to both of these arguments. In particular, a domain theory explains only those features that the author of this theory is able to formalise. However, we have shown that a problem may contain heuristic features that are helpful in making the right choice. Since the heuristic merit of these features may be uncertain, the author of the domain theory may decide to exclude these features from the formal definition of the domain. As a result, the domain theory provides too strong a bias in learning, because it excludes these features from consideration. Moreover, correctness does not guarantee utility. Although a simple rule that is almost correct may provide the wrong advice in certain circumstances, it may provide satisfactory results most of the time. So long as the advice is expressed as a preference, the planner still has a chance of finding the right choice, even when the advice is taken out of context. In contrast, a more complex rule that is always correct may turn out to have a lower utility due to the cost of matching the rule.

The relative importance of these arguments varies, depending on the particular domain, the way it is encoded, and the way in which learning is used. These are all aspects of the problem solving environment where learning occurs. An important issue for further research is to investigate these issues in more complex application domains.

8. Acknowledgements

The permission of the Director, Telecom Research Laboratories, to publish this paper is hereby acknowledged. I am extremely grateful to the PRODIGY project team at Carnegie Mellon University for providing a copy of their system. I would also like to thank Dr. Ingrid Zukerman from Monash University for her contribution to this research.

9. References

1. Minton, S. (1988), Quantitative Results Concerning the Utility of Explanation-Based Learning. In *AAAI-88 Proceedings*, pp. 564-569.
2. Mitchell, T.M., Keller, R.M. and Kedar-Cabelli, S.T. (1986), Explanation-Based Generalization: A Unifying View. In *Machine Learning* 1(1), pp. 47-80.
3. Leckie, C.A. and Zukerman, I. (1993), An Inductive Approach to Learning Search Control Rules for Planning. To appear in *IJCAI-93 Proceedings*.
4. Leckie, C.A. (1993), Inductive Learning of Search Control Rules for Planning. Ph.D. Thesis, Dept. of Computer Science, Monash University, Australia.
5. Quinlan, J.R. (1990), Learning Logical Definitions from Relations. In *Machine Learning* 5(3), pp. 239-266.

EMPIRICAL EVALUATION OF THE CFP ALGORITHM

İZZET ŞİRİN and **H. ALTAY GÜVENİR**
Computer Engineering and Information Science Department
Bilkent University, Ankara 06533 TURKEY
E-mail: {sirin, guvenir}@firat.bcc.bilkent.edu.tr

ABSTRACT

This paper presents a new methodology for concept learning from examples, called *Classification by Feature Partitioning* (CFP), which is an inductive, incremental and supervised learning method. Learning in CFP is accomplished by storing the objects separately in each feature dimension as disjoint partitions of values. A partition is expanded through generalization or specialized by dividing it into subpartitions. An empirical evaluation of the CFP on real-world data sets is presented.

1. Introduction

This paper presents a form of exemplar-based learning, called *Classification by Feature Partitioning* (CFP). In exemplar-based learning examples are stored in memory verbatim. The CFP technique makes several significant improvements over other exemplar-based learning algorithms. For example, IBL[1] algorithms learn a set of instances which is a representative subset of all training examples. Another algorithm called EACH[5] learns a set of hyperrectangles of the examples. On the other hand, the CFP method stores the instances as factored out by their feature values. The CFP partitions each feature into segments corresponding to concepts. Therefore, the concept description learned by the CFP is a collection of feature partitions.

Each feature contributes the classification process by its local knowledge. Final classification is based on a voting among the predictions of the features. The CFP algorithm significantly reduces the classification complexity, over other exemplar-based techniques. The strength of the contribution of a feature in the voting process is determined by the weight of that feature.

Most real-world data sets contain missing attribute values. Previous learning systems usually overcome this problem by either filling in missing attribute values, or looking at the probability distribution of values of attributes. Most common approaches are compared in Quinlan (1993), leading to a general conclusion that no one approach is uniformly superior to others. In contrast, CFP solves this problem very naturally. Since CFP treats each attribute value separately, in the case of an unknown attribute value, it simply leaves the partitioning of that feature intact.

In the next section the CFP algorithm is described (precise details are given Şirin (1993)). The voting process of the CFP is illustrated through an example. Section 3 presents an empirical evaluation of the CFP algorithm on various real-world data sets. The final section discusses the applicability of the CFP algorithm.

```
train(Training Set):
begin
    foreach e in Training Set
        foreach feature f
            if class of partition(f, e_f) = e_class
                then w_f = (1 + Δ)w_f
                else w_f = (1 − Δ)w_f
            update-feature-partitioning(f, e_f)
end
```

Figure 1: Training algorithm of the CFP

2. The CFP Algorithm

An example is defined as a vector of feature values plus a label that represents its class. The CFP algorithm learns partitions of the set of possible values for each feature. For each partition, lower and upper bounds of the feature values, its associated class and the number of instances it represents are maintained.

Initially, a partition is a point (lower and upper limits are equal) on the line representing the feature dimension. Suppose that the first example e_1 of class C_1 is given during the training phase. If the value of e_1 for feature f is x_1, then the set of possible values for feature f will be partitioned into three partitions: $< [-\infty, x_1], U, 0 >$, $< [x_1, x_1], C_1, 1 >$ and $< [x_1, \infty], U, 0 >$; where the elements indicate the range of the partition, its class*, and the representativeness value†, respectively. A partition can be extended through generalization with other neighboring points in the same feature dimension. If the second example e_2 is close to e_1 in feature f and also of the same class, the CFP algorithm will generalize the partition for x_1 into a range partition: $< [x_1, x_2], C_1, 2 >$, which represents two examples.

The training process of the CFP algorithm has two steps: learning feature weights and learning feature partitions (Fig. 1). For each training example, the prediction of each feature is compared with the actual class of the example. If the prediction of a feature is correct, the weight of that feature is incremented by Δ (global feature weight adjustment rate) percent; otherwise, it is decremented by the same amount.

The second step in the training process is to update the partitioning of each feature-space using the given training example. If the feature value of a training example falls in a partition with the same class, then simply its representativeness value is incremented. If the new feature value falls in a range partition with a different class than that of the example, the CFP algorithm specializes the existing partition by dividing it into two subpartitions and inserting a point partition (corresponding to the new feature value) in between them. On the other hand, if the example falls in an undetermined partition, the CFP algorithm tries to generalize a near partition with the feature value. If one of the nearest partitions to the left and the right of the new example is in D_f distance and of the same class as the example, then it is generalized to cover the new feature value. Otherwise, a new

*U represents undetermined class

†representativeness value indicates the number of examples represented by a partition.

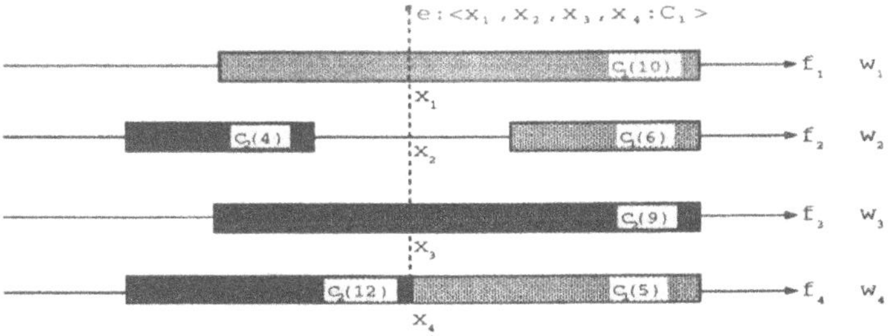

Figure 2: Classification process of the CFP

point partition that corresponds to the new feature value, is inserted.

The classification process of the CFP is based on a voting taken among the predictions made by each feature separately. For a given instance e, the prediction based on a feature f is determined by the value of e_f. If e_f falls properly within a partition with a determined class then the prediction is the class of that partition. If e_f falls into the border of more than one partitions, then among all the partitions at this point the one with the highest representativeness value is chosen. If e_f falls in a partition with no known class value, then no prediction for that feature is made. The effect of the prediction of a feature in the voting is proportional with the weight of that feature. All feature weights are initialized to one, before the training process begins. The predicted class of a given instance is the one which receives the highest amount of votes among all predictions. Figure 2 shows an example of classification process of the CFP. Consider a test example e of class C_1 with feature values x_1, x_2, x_3, and x_4. The prediction of the first feature is C_1. The second feature does not predict any class value (*undetermined*). The prediction of the third feature is C_2. The forth feature value x_4 of e falls into the border of two partitions. In this case the representativeness values are used to determine the class value. Since the partition of class C_2 has a greater representativeness value than that of C_1 partition, the prediction of the forth feature is C_2. Final prediction of the CFP depends on the values of the feature weights (w_f's). If $w_1 > (w_3 + w_4)$ then CFP will classify e as a member of C_1; otherwise the prediction would be C_2.

The *sample complexity* and *training complexity* analysis of the CFP algorithm with respect to PAC-learning theory (Probably Approximately Correct learning) shows that, it requires small number of examples and a small amount of memory to learn a given concept, compared to many other similar algorithms.[3] Another outcome of this analysis is that, the CFP has a low learning complexity.

3. Empirical Evaluation

The performance of the CFP algorithm has been tested with various widely used real-world data sets. The use of real data in these tests provide a measure of the system's accuracy on noisy and incomplete data sets, and most importantly, allowed comparisons between CFP and other systems. All results in Table 1 were averaged

Table 1: Achieved accuracy (%) by CFP with various data sets

Database	CFP	Database	CFP
Cleveland	84.5	Mushroom	98.5
Hungarian	82.3	Thyroid Disease	90.8
Ionosphere	87.6	Voting	95.5
Iris	96.7	Wine	91.6

over 50 trials, unless indicated otherwise. The training and test sets were always disjoint. The instances were drawn randomly from the data sets. 80 % of the instances are used in training and the remaining are used in testing.

Ionosphere database: The radar data was collected by a system in Goose Bay, Labrador. The targets were free electrons in the ionosphere. *Good* radar returns are those showing evidence of some type of structure in the ionosphere. *Bad* returns are those that do not; their signals pass through the ionosphere. This data set contains 351 instances. 200 of the instances are used in training, the rest are used in testing. Each instance consist of 34 continuous-valued features. It is a binary (good or bad) classification problem.

Wine: The data are the results of a chemical analysis of wines grown in the same region in Italy, but derived from three different cultures. The analysis determined the quantities of 13 constituents found in each of the three types. Data set contains 178 instances and all attributes are continuous valued. The leave-one-out technique is used in the experiment.

Thyroid Disease: Five continuous-valued laboratory tests are used to predict a patient's thyroid type. The diagnosis was based on a complete medical record. There are 215 patient records in the data set each of which has one of the three classes (normal, hyperthyroid, or hypothyroid).

Mushroom: This data set includes descriptions of hypothetical samples corresponding to 23 species of gilled mushrooms in the Agaricus and Lepiota Family. Each species is identified as edible, or poisonous. The database contains 8124 instances with 22 nominal-valued features. 1000 instances are used in training the remaining 7124 are used in testing.

Congressional Voting: It contains the voting records of the members of the United States House of Representatives during the second session of 1984. It is described by 16 boolean attributes and has 288 missing values among 435 instances. 350 of the voting records are used in training and remaining 85 are used in testing. The goal is to predict is the political party of a member given their voting record. The reported accuracies by IB1 and C4 on this data set, are 91.8 and 95.5, respectively[1].

Iris Flowers: Iris flowers data set consists of four integer-valued features and a particular species of iris out of three classes. The data set contains 150 instances. EACH[5] achieved 95.3 accuracy on this data using leave-one-out technique.

Medical Diagnosis: The Cleveland and Hungarian data sets contain heart disease diagnoses collected from the Cleveland Clinic Foundation and Hungarian Institute of Cardiology, respectively. Diagnoses are described by 13 numeric-valued features.

The objective is to determine whether a patient has a heart disease. The Cleveland data consists of 303 instances and the Hungarian data consists of 294 instances. Achieved accuracies by IB3 and C4 on Hungarian data, are 80.5 and 78.2 respectively. For Cleveland data, accuracies of IB3 and C4 are 78.0 and 75.5, respectively[1].

The feature weight adjustment rate and the generalization limits are domain dependent parameters of the CFP. In these experiments their values are determined (settings are given in Şirin (1993)) by trial and error, separately for each application domain. However, we noticed that the performance was not sensitive to the small changes in Δ and D_f settings.

4. Conclusion

The CFP algorithm is applicable to concepts, where each feature, independent of other features, can classify the concept. Usually, real-world data sets presents this behavior. Empirical results of the CFP on real-world data sets justify this claim.

This approach is a variant of algorithms that learn by projecting into one feature dimension at a time. The novelty of CFP is that it retains a feature-by-feature representation and uses voting to categorize. Algorithms that learn by projecting into one dimension at a time are limited in their ability to represent complex concepts. For domains, where concepts are nested or projection of the concepts are overlapping, performance of the CFP degrades.

One of the improvements of the CFP over other exemplar-based algorithms is its low classification complexity. Another important improvement is natural handling of unknown attribute values. Since the value of each attribute is handled separately, attributes with unknown values are simply ignored by the CFP.

The CFP uses feature weights to cope with irrelevant attributes. Determining the best values for the domain dependent parameters of the CFP is an optimization problem for a given domain. GA-CFP is a version of CFP that uses genetic algorithm to find a good setting of these parameters.[2]

References

1. D. W. Aha, D. Kibler and M. K. Albert. Instance–Based Learning Algorithms. *Machine Learning* **6** 37–66, 1991.
2. H. A. Güvenir and İ. Şirin. A Genetic Algorithm for Classification by Feature Partitioning. In *The Proceedings of ICGA'93*, (Illinois, 1993), pp. 543–548.
3. H. A. Güvenir and İ. Şirin. The Complexity of CFP: A Method for Classification Based on Feature Partitioning. (to appear) In *Lecture Notes on Artificial Intelligence*, Proceedings of the AI*IA'93, (Torino, 1993).
4. J. R. Quinlan, *C4.5: Programs for Machine Learning.* California: Morgan Kaufmann, 1993.
5. S. Salzberg, A Nearest Hyperrectangle Learning Method. *Machine Learning*, **6** 251-276, 1991.
6. İ. Şirin and H. A. Güvenir , *An Algorithm for Classification by Feature Partitioning.* Technical Report CIS-TR-9301, Bilkent University, Turkey, 1993.

FIRST ORDER LEARNING, ZEROTH ORDER DATA

R.M. CAMERON-JONES and J.R. QUINLAN
Basser Department of Computer Science
The University of Sydney, NSW 2006
Australia

ABSTRACT: The augmentation of FOIL to handle data with continuous variables and data with missing values enables it to be applied to a wider range of problems, including conventional attribute-value classification problems. This paper reports the results of comparing FOIL to C4.5rules on attribute-value problems. On the domains tried, FOIL is computationally practical and similar in resulting accuracy.

1 Introduction

First-order learning differs from the familiar attribute-value learning in two ways: data may consist of several relations rather than a single file of examples, and theories are expressed as Horn clause programs rather than zeroth-order structures such as decision trees or rulesets. First-order systems like FOIL[1] are commonly demonstrated on abstract tasks such as learning recursive definitions of relations on lists of discrete constants[2]. Such domains are markedly different from the real-world datasets successfully tackled by zeroth-order systems such as CART[3] and C4.5[4], particularly when some attributes have continuous numeric values and when some attribute values are unknown.

However, FOCL[5] demonstrates that tests on continuous-valued variables can be incorporated into first-order theories. FOIL has been similarly extended to allow continuous variables to be compared either to a threshold or to another continuous variable of the same type, and to allow for missing values of any variable. These changes are sufficient to enable FOIL to be applied to binary classification tasks studied by zeroth-order systems. Each of the n attributes becomes an argument in a single n-ary relation; a definition is learned for one class and any instance not satisfying the definition is assigned to the other class.

In "traditional" zeroth-order theories each test involves a single attribute. FOIL's comparison of two variables of the same type extends the theory language. Such "extended" theories can be barred by declaring all attributes to be of distinct types, allowing us to compare the costs and benefits associated with a richer theory language.

We now (sketchily) describe FOIL and compare its performance on commonly-studied zeroth order datasets to that of C4.5rules, a system specifically designed for such tasks. Results demonstrate that FOIL can be applied effectively to attribute-value learning tasks.

2 FOIL

FOIL learns a Horn clause definition of a target relation in terms of the target and other relations, each defined as a set of tuples of constants. For example, a relation *Father* might include a tuple ⟨*John,Mary*⟩ to indicate that *John* is the father of *Mary*. The target relation is specified extensionally by a set of (positive) tuples for which the relation holds, and by an additional set of (negative) tuples for which it is known to be false.

Each clause is developed by adding literals to the (initially empty) body, succesively specialising it until it covers no negative tuples. The process is basically a greedy search, guided by an information-based heuristic, with a limited mechanism for backing-up from dead ends. Complete clauses are simplified by removing unnecessary literals that may have been added during the search. FOIL uses the standard covering method: as each clause is completed, all positive tuples that it covers are removed before starting the next clause. When all positive tuples in the target relation have been covered by one or more clauses, redundant clauses are pruned out.

Of course, noise in the data may rule out a perfect cover. Instead, FOIL finds clauses that cover most (rather than all) of the positive tuples while excluding most (rather than all) of the negative tuples. The heuristic used to prevent over-complex theories is similar to that previously used in a decision tree context[6]. The idea is to try to minimize the cost of encoding the theory (i.e., the clauses defining the target relation), together with the cost of identifying exceptions to the theory, in accordance with Rissanen's Minimum Description Length principle[7]. In previous versions, the cost of coding literals in the theory varied from relation to relation. The new release includes an option, used in these experiments, in which the cost of encoding literals is uniform across relations.

The introduction of the continuous variables has brought with it two new built-in predicates. The first is a $>$ comparison between two continuous variables of the same type, analogous to the built-in equality for discrete variables of the same type. The second is the comparison of a variable with a threshold, implemented using a method akin to that of C4.5.

FOIL has been extended to handle missing values in a simple manner – a test on a missing value always fails. Thus a tuple with a missing value for a variable in a literal is neither an instance of the relation being true, nor of it being false.

3 Experiments

The experiments consisted of the application of FOIL to various standard attribute-value tasks, most taken from the UCI Data Repository, with some multi-class data sets reduced to two-class problems. A conversion program, included in the current FOIL release, was used to translate attribute-value data from the format used by

Domain	Instances	Discrete Attributes	Continuous Attributes	Missing Values	Class A	Class B
Monk's 1	124	6	0	No	0	1
Monk's 2	169	6	0	No	0	1
Monk's 3	122	6	0	No	0	1
KRKN	551	39	0	No	0	1
Promoters	106	57	0	No	+	–
Symptoms	44	12	0	Yes	Absent	Present
Iris	100	0	4	No	Versi.	Viginica
Othello	5022	0	16	No	sb	sw
C vs G	1509	0	16	No	C	G
Segment	660	0	17	No	Cement	Path
Labor	57	8	8	Yes	Bad	Good
Credit	690	9	6	Yes	+	–
AIDS	86	6	6	Yes	Absent	Present

Table 1: Domain descriptions

C4.5 to the relational format used by FOIL. The only extra information required for the conversion was the type of each attribute; when all such types are unique, FOIL is restricted to traditional theories.

Most results are reported for n-fold or "leave one out" cross-validations. However this was computationally impractical for the "Othello" domain, for which a 10-fold cross-validation was used, and inappropriate for the artificial "Monk's" problems[8], for which the specified training and (432 instance) test sets were used.

The domains are briefly described in Table 1 in terms of the number of instances (training set sizes in the Monk's problems), the number of discrete attributes, the number of continuous attributes, whether missing values are present, and the names of the two classes, hereafter referred to as classes "A" and "B". A further factor in the application of FOIL to two-class attribute-value problems is that the quality of definition for class "A" can be greatly different from that for class "B". Results are presented for learning a definition for each of the two classes, then for choosing the one for which the sum of the number of clauses and training errors is less (with arbitrary tie-break). This choice is made *separately* on each trial of a cross-validation.

3.1 Results

In each trial, C4.5 and C4.5rules were applied to each task using default options. FOIL was applied in several ways:

- learning the definition for class "A", restricted to a traditional theory;

Domain	C4.5		FOIL traditional			FOIL extended		
	Trees	Rules	A	B	A|B	A	B	A|B
Monk's 1	24.3	0.0	0.0	0.0	0.0	0.0	0.0	0.0
Monk's 2	35.0	34.7	25.2	25.7	**25.7**	22.7	15.7	**15.7**
Monk's 3	2.8	3.7	10.0	5.1	**10.0**	6.2	6.0	**6.2**
KRKN	8.3	8.2	7.6	5.3	**5.8**	8.3	5.3	4.5
Promoters	17.0	10.4	23.6	15.1	16.0	22.6	19.8	20.8
Symptoms	15.9	29.5	27.3	18.2	20.5	29.5	15.9	20.5
Iris	8.0	6.0	7.0	9.0	7.0	7.0	9.0	7.0
Othello	12.5	14.6	13.1	13.3	**12.6**	12.0	12.5	12.1
C vs G	4.8	4.3	2.9	3.7	4.1	3.4	3.4	3.4
Segment	12.7	13.8	12.4	12.4	11.8	12.7	13.3	12.3
Labor	15.8	15.8	7.0	29.8	7.0	7.0	29.8	7.0
Credit	15.1	15.5	17.8	17.4	17.0	18.0	16.4	16.4
AIDS	17.4	16.3	10.5	17.4	**10.5**	10.5	17.4	10.5

Table 2: Test error rates on the problem domains

- learning the definition for class "B", restricted to a traditional theory;
- learning the definition for class "A", permitted an extended theory;
- learning the definition for class "B", permitted an extended theory.

FOIL's traditional theories for the two classes are then compared and the one with the lower total of clauses and training set errors chosen as the combined result "A|B", similarly for the extended theories. The percentage error rate of each theory is determined on the test set.

Accuracy results are presented in Table 2. The FOIL "A|B" results for the traditional theory are in bold face if they are significantly different to the results from C4.5rules. The "A|B" results for the extended theory are in bold face if they are significantly different to the "A|B" results for the traditional theory. The significance test used was a paired sign test, pairing across the folds for the cross-validations and across the test instances for the Monk's problems. Results are considered significantly different if they are at least 90% significant in a two tailed test.

These results show that the definitions found by FOIL depend greatly upon the choice of class to learn and that the simple method for choosing between the two theories generally performs well. Further, the chosen traditional FOIL theories are significantly better than the results from C4.5rules more often than they are significantly worse. The chosen extended theories are also sometimes significantly better than the traditional ones, but never significantly worse. The overall results suggest that FOIL has a similar level of performance to C4.5rules.

Domain	C4.5		FOIL traditional			FOIL extended		
	Trees	Rules	A	B	A|B	A	B	A|B
Monk's 1	0.0	0.5	0.2	0.2	0.4	0.1	0.1	0.2
Monk's 2	0.0	1.3	0.9	1.5	2.4	0.9	1.2	2.1
Monk's 3	0.0	0.6	0.7	0.3	1.0	0.3	0.4	0.7
KRKN	0.6	6.4	9.0	94.9	103.9	65.5	114.6	180.1
Promoters	0.1	1.0	1.8	1.1	2.9	5.3	4.2	9.5
Symptoms	0.0	0.0	0.0	0.1	0.1	0.0	0.1	0.1
Iris	0.0	0.0	0.0	0.0	0.0	0.0	0.0	0.0
Othello	43.4	2047.0	194.5	183.2	377.7	207.6	204.2	411.8
C vs G	5.0	20.3	5.8	6.6	12.4	7.6	6.9	14.5
Segment	4.1	9.6	5.2	4.8	10.0	5.4	6.6	12.0
Labor	0.0	0.0	0.0	0.1	0.1	0.0	0.1	0.1
Credit	1.0	13.8	8.9	8.2	17.1	9.6	10.4	20.0
AIDS	0.0	0.0	0.1	0.3	0.4	0.1	0.3	0.4

Table 3: Learning times on the problem domains

Table 3 reports the comparative execution times in seconds on a DECstation 5000/240. Tabulated times for FOIL's "A|B" results are simply the sum of the corresponding table entries for "A" and "B" as the time to choose between the two definitions is negligible. Times for C4.5rules do not include execution times for C4.5. The double application of FOIL is typically slower than the use of C4.5 and C4.5rules. FOIL is much slower in the KRKN domain, due to extensive backtracking of little utility. C4.5rules is much slower in the Othello domain which has many examples and many rules from C4.5's tree.

4 Conclusions and Further Work

FOIL can now handle continuous variables and missing values and can thus be applied to two-class attribute-value problems. The system's performance is similar to that of C4.5rules, a program developed for such tasks. In short, a "first order learner" can be successfully applied to "zeroth order data". This could be done in a manner in which the system first searches for traditional theories before looking for extended theories.

FOIL hence seems reasonably capable on a diverse range of learning tasks, and (to use a suggestion of Donald Michie's) could thus be used on real world tasks that, while currently lacking the structure necessitating a first order learner, may acquire such structure in the future.

The approach of choosing between two definitions, used here to enable a comparison with C4.5rules, needs to be extended if multi-class problems are to be addressed, as is done by HYDRA[9]. As FOIL has been originally developed on a very different style of learning task, its performance in noisy attribute-value domains could well be improved in some other respects.

The version of FOIL used for these experiments is obtainable is available by anonymous ftp from ftp.cs.su.oz.au (file name `foil5.sh`, directory `pub`). A more detailed version of this paper is available as Technical Report 468, Basser Department of Computer Science.

Acknowledgements

This research has been made possible by grants from the Australian Research Council and assisted by research agreements with Digital Equipment Corporation. The use of the data sets from the UCI repository has been most valuable.

References

1. J.R. Quinlan. Learning logical definitions from relations. *Machine Learning*, 5:239–266, 1990.

2. J.R. Quinlan and R.M. Cameron-Jones. FOIL: A midterm report. In *Proceedings of the European Conference on Machine Learning*, pages 3–20. Springer Verlag, 1993.

3. L. Breiman, J.H. Friedman, R.A. Olshen, and C.J. Stone. *Classification and Regression Trees*. Belmont, CA: Wadsworth International, 1984.

4. J.R. Quinlan. *C4.5: Programs for Machine Learning*. San Mateo, CA: Morgan Kaufmann, 1993.

5. G. Silverstein and M.J. Pazzani. Relational clichés: Constraining constructive induction during relational learning. In *Proceedings of the Eighth International Workshop on Machine Learning (ML91)*, pages 203–207. Morgan Kaufmann, 1991.

6. J.R. Quinlan and R.L Rivest. Inferring decision trees using the minimum description length principle. *Information and Computation*, 80:227–248, 1989.

7. J. Rissanen. A universal prior for integers and estimation by minimum description length. *Annals of Statistics*, 11:416-431, 1983.

8. S.B. Thrun, *et al.* The monk's problems: A performance comparison of different learning algorithms. Technical Report CMU-CS-91-197, Carnegie Mellon University, 1991.

9. K.M. Ali and M. Pazzani. HYDRA: A noise-tolerant relational concept learning algorithm. In *Proceedings of the Thirteenth International Joint Conference on Artificial Intelligence*. Morgan Kaufmann, 1993.

GENERALIZATION BY CONTROLLED INTERSECTION OF EXAMPLES†

Cory Barker and Tony Martinez
Computer Science Department, Brigham Young University, Provo, Utah 84602
cory@axon.cs.byu.edu, martinez@cs.byu.edu

Abstract

SG (Specific to General) is a network for supervised inductive learning from examples that uses ideas from neural networks and symbolic inductive learning to gain benefits of both methods. The network is built of many simple nodes that learn important features in the input space and then monitor the ability of the features to predict output values. The network avoids the exponential nature of the number of features by creating specific features for each example and then expanding those features; making them more general. Expansion of a feature terminates when it encounters another feature with contradicting outputs. Empirical evaluation of the model on real-world data has shown that the network provides good generalization performance. Convergence is accomplished within a small number of training passes. The network provides these benefits while automatically allocating and deleting nodes and without requiring user adjustment of any parameters. The network learns incrementally and operates in a parallel fashion.

1. Introduction

This paper describes a network architecture for *supervised learning* that combines techniques used in neural networks[1,7,8] with symbolic machine learning[3,4,6] to gain advantages of both approaches. In supervised learning the network is given a *training set* containing *examples*. Each example gives an *input* pattern along with the corresponding *output* that the network should produce when presented with the input. The task of the network is not only to converge to a *representation* that contains the information given by the training set, but to *generalize* that information so that the network will respond well to inputs that it has not been trained on.

One approach to generalization is to look for important *features* in the input space. A feature is some subset of network inputs along with their associated values. A feature is *matched* when the values on the network inputs that are part of the feature are equal to the values for those inputs as given in the feature. Inputs that are not part of the feature can be any value. A feature that predicts an output with high probability is an important feature. The number of inputs contained in a feature is the *order* of the feature and determines the *generality* of the feature. A feature with few inputs is a *general* feature, while a feature with many inputs is a *specific* feature. It is impractical to monitor all possible input features because the number of features is exponential in the number of inputs.

This paper proposes SG (Specific to General), a network that creates specific input features and then generalizes those features. One way SG generalizes is by combining similar specific features. If two features are similar, they are close to each other in the input space. Combining the two features by dropping inputs that are not common between the features creates a new feature that encompasses both of the original features. The new feature is general; it matches points in the input space that have not been defined by any example.

This section presents an overview of the model while later sections provide detail about the system. The network is made up of many simple nodes. Each node contains the input feature that it monitors. During training, the node gathers statistics giving the discrete conditional probability of each possible output value given the input feature.

† This Research Supported in Part by the Air Force Office of Scientific Research

We use a simplified version of the problem of deciding when to use manual or automatic flight controls when landing an aircraft to illustrate learning in one version of the model. The problem has three inputs (Visibility, Wind Direction, and Wind Speed, abbreviated V, D, and S, respectively) and one output that can be set to either Manual or Automatic (abbreviated Man and Auto, respectively). Several examples are presented to an empty network.

Example 1 (V, High) (D, Head) (S, High) → Man

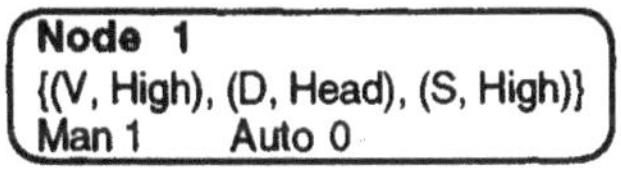

When a new example is presented a node is always created with a specific feature exactly equal to the example unless an equivalent node already exists. The first example causes the creation of Node 1. Node 1 sets its probabilities according to the input example (i.e., Man has probability 1 since the only example seen matching Node 1's feature has output manual). The network has no other nodes to combine with Node 1 so no additional nodes are created.

Example 2 (V, Low) (D, Tail) (S, Low) → Auto

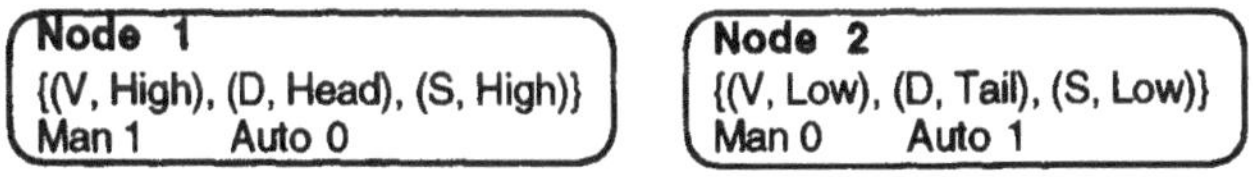

Example 2 causes the creation of Node 2 with the specific feature equal to the example. Node 2 sets its probabilities according to the input example. Node 1 does not match the input example so its probabilities remain unchanged. Node 1 has a different highest probability output than Node 2 so the two nodes cannot combine and no additional nodes are created.

Example 3 (V, High) (D, Tail) (S, High) → Auto

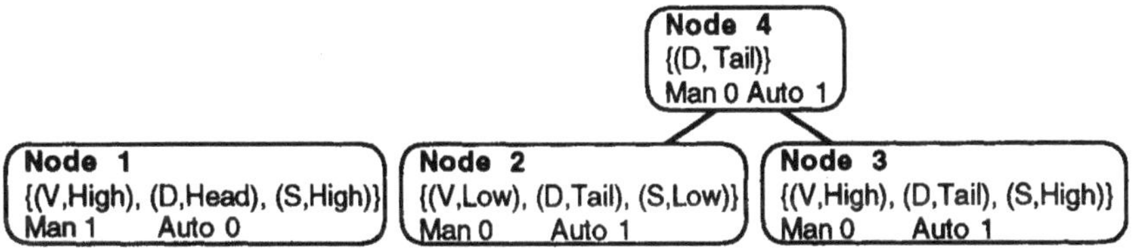

Example 3 causes the creation of the specific Node 3. Node 3 sets its probabilities according to the input example. Nodes 2 and 3 both have the same highest probability output (Automatic) so they create Node 4 with a feature that has all the inputs that are common to both Nodes 2 and 3. Node 4 has a general feature; it matches input examples that have not been presented yet (e.g., (V, Low) (D, Tail) (S, High) → Auto). Node 4 sets its probabilities by combining the probabilities from Nodes 2 and 3. Note that specific nodes can learn the training set perfectly but do not generalize. Generalization has the effect of expanding the area of the input space covered by a node until eventually the entire input space is covered.

The SG network has a number of potential advantages. Typical neural network training procedures require a large number of iterations over the training set while the SG model converges in a small number of passes. Most networks require the user to specify the number of hidden nodes as well as control many learning parameters, but the SG model automatically creates and deletes nodes and has no parameters to set. Empirical tests of SG show promising generalization performance.

2. Definitions

An SG network N has *inputs* $i_1, ..., i_n$, with domains $X_1, ..., X_n$, respectively and *outputs* $o_1, ..., o_m$, with domains $Y_1, ..., Y_m$, respectively. The *input space* of N is $I = X_1 \times ... \times X_n$ (the cross product of the input domains) and the *output space* is $O = Y_1 \times ... \times Y_m$. The network N implements a function f_N from I into O. A training *example* is a pair (i, o) from $I \times O$. A training set is a subset of $I \times O$. The SG model restricts the input and output domains, $X_1, ..., X_n$ and $Y_1, ..., Y_m$, to be finite sets of discrete values.

The aircraft landing problem introduced above has three inputs, Visibility, Wind Direction, and Wind Speed, with domains {Low, High}, {Head, Tail}, and {Low, High}, respectively. There is a single output, Flight Control, with domain {Automatic, Manual}. The input space has eight members {(Low, Head, Low), ..., (High, Tail, High)}.

3. Node Architecture

This section describes the structure of individual nodes. Each node in an SG network contains:

- A *feature* which is a set of pairs (i_j, x), where i_j is an input and x is a member of the input domain X_j.
- A vector c_j of *counters* for each output o_j, with a counter for each value of output o_j.
- A total counter T.

The SG model has several variations. In some variations the nodes contain additional information.

A typical node is shown below. The node monitors the feature {(Wind Speed, Low)}. There is a counter for each of the possible output values and a total counter.

Each pair (i_j, x) in a feature specifies that an input must equal a specific value. A node *matches* the presented input values if, for each pair (i_j, x) in its feature, the value of input i_j is equal to x. The *specificity* of a node is the number of inputs contained in the feature divided by the total number of inputs n. A node whose feature contains all n inputs is maximally specific; it matches only a single input example. A node whose feature contains no inputs is maximally general; it matches all possible input examples. If an input i_j is removed from a feature the feature covers k times the input space that it would cover with the input, where k is the size of the input domain X_j, or in other words, the number of values possible for the input.

The counters in each node allow the node to calculate the discrete probability of each output value based on the input examples that the node has seen. During training with example (i, o), all nodes that match i do the following:

- Increment the total counter T.
- For each output o_j, increment the counter in c_j associated with the value for the output o_j given in the training example.

The *probability* of value y for output o_j is $P(o_j = y \mid \text{feature match}) = c_j^y / T$ (where c_j^y is the counter in c_j for the value y). Counter update in a typical node is shown below.

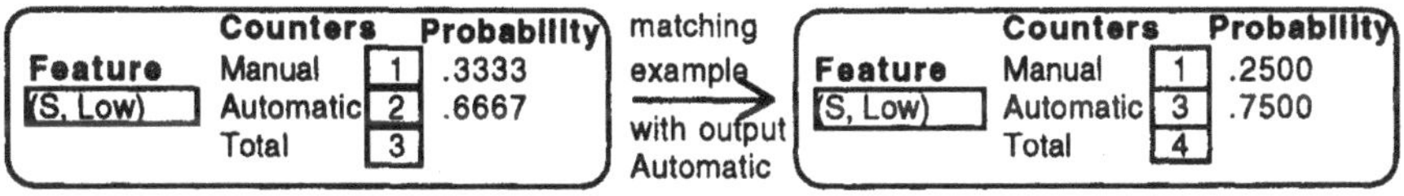

Two nodes or two examples are said to be *concordant* if they both have the same output values. They are *discordant* if they have different output values.

The *strength* of a node is the probability of its highest-probability output value.

Node *A covers* node *B* if *A* matches every example matched by *B*, nodes *A* and *B* are concordant, and node *A* is stronger than node *B*. It can be shown that *A* matches every example matched by *B* if and only if *A's* feature is a *subset* of *B's* feature.

Node *A fully contradicts* node *B* if *A* matches every example matched by *B*, nodes *A* and *B* are discordant, and node *A* is stronger than node *B*.

Node *A partially contradicts* node *B* if *A* matches at least one example matched by *B*, nodes *A* and *B* are discordant, and node *A* is stronger than node *B*.

4. Execution

When given input values, a network of nodes executes and produces an output as follows. Each node that matches the input values calculates its probability for each output value. The purpose of each node is to approximate the conditional probability of an output value given that the input values match a particular feature. The node with highest probability wins the competition and the best output value of that node is asserted as the output value of the network. This paper intentionally avoids network interconnect issues. However, note that any interconnect that supports broadcast and gather operations (e.g., tree or hypercube) is sufficient to do network execution and learning.

Network Execution

1. The input values presented to the network inputs are broadcast to all nodes in the network
2. Each node compares the input values to the feature stored at the node.
3. Nodes that match
    4. Calculate the probability of each output value
    5. Send the maximum probability output value along with its probability out to the network
6. End.
7. The network gathers the outputs from each node.
8. The output value with maximum probability is the network output.

End.

---

5. Learning Features

This section presents how an SG network learns the features that are important in the problem it is solving. The network should approximate the minimum possible set of features if it is to provide the best generalization. The SG approach to creating features is to start with specific nodes and expand around those nodes creating general nodes. Nodes are first created with features that match the input example exactly. Inputs are removed from the feature to create more general nodes until the new nodes conflict with discordant nodes.

When a new example is presented during learning the network executes using only general nodes. Nodes that are completely specific do not participate since the network output would always be correct for the training examples after the first pass. The network creates a node that matches only the new example if such a node does not already exist. If the network outputs differ from the training example, then new general nodes are added to the network. The problem of deciding what general nodes to create is solved in two different ways giving two unique learning models; *combination* and *generalization*. Combination is described in the next section. Generalization is described in elsewhere[2]. In both methods, existing nodes create new candidate features based upon their current feature and the new example.

Network Learning

1. The training example (i, o) is broadcast to all nodes in the network and the general nodes execute giving an output r.
2. Create a new feature $F = \{(i_1, x_1), ..., (i_n, x_n)\}$, where $x_1, ..., x_n$ are the values given in i.
3. If a node with feature F does not already exist, create a new node with feature F.
4. Each node that matches i increments its counters as described above.
5. If the network output is not correct ($r \neq o$) then create general nodes by either Combination or Generalization.

End.

5.1. Combination

One method for creating general features is for existing nodes that are concordant with the training example to combine their current feature with the training example. When the two features combine to create a new node, the feature for the new node is the intersection of the features of the other nodes. An example of feature combination was shown in the introduction where two nodes with features {(V, Low), (D, Tail), (S, Low)} and {(V, High), (D, Tail), (S, High)} combine to create a node with feature {(D, Tail)}.

Once a node has created a new candidate feature by intersection with the training example, the feature must be broadcast to the network to determine if the feature is covered or contradicted by another node. If the new feature is covered or contradicted there is no need to create a node with the feature since the node would not affect the network output. If the new feature is not covered or contradicted then a new node is created with the feature.

Combination

1. All nodes concordant with the training example do the following in parallel
2. Create new candidate feature G by intersection of the node's current feature and the training example
3. If G is not covered and not contradicted then create a new node N with feature G.
4. Initialize counters in N to the sum of counters in fully specific nodes covered by N.

End.

Note that in the worst case Combination requires $O(n \log n)$ steps, where n is the number of nodes. At most n nodes will broadcast a new candidate feature to check for covered and contradicted conditions. Each broadcast is a $\log n$ operation on a tree architecture.

6. Deletion

Because nodes are created incrementally, many times nodes will be created that are not essential for representing the training set. Deletion of unnecessary nodes can improve generalization. Nodes determine if they should delete themselves by monitoring their own usage. All nodes keep a flag that is set whenever the node is used. After each pass over the training set, each node checks and resets its use flag. If the flag was not set during the training iteration, the node deletes itself.

7. Results

SG was tested using four real world training sets acquired from the UC Irvine repository of machine learning databases[5]; iris plant classification, 1984 Congressional voting records, hepatitis data, and mushroom classification. Both learning models (combination and generalization) were tested on each problem. The results given here are averages over ten runs. For each run half of the examples were randomly selected for the training set. The remaining examples were used as a test set to test generalization performance. The results shown in the table below are the percent correct on the training set followed by the percent correct on the test set and finally the average number of training set iterations.

	Combination			Generalization		
Iris	98.13	90.67	2.3	100.0	94.13	2.8
Voting	99.95	94.24	5.3	99.86	91.61	5.9
Hepatitis	99.74	77.69	6.1	99.74	80.77	2.8
Mushroom	100.0	99.97	4.6	100.0	89.33	5.5

Based on these results, SG networks compare favorably to other supervised learning approaches. Combination performs better on voting and mushroom data while generalization performs better on iris and hepatitis data. Both models learn the training set well and require a small number of training iterations.

8. Conclusions

The SG network has been presented as a system capable of supervised learning with benefits of both neural networks and symbolic inductive learning. Evaluation of the model on four problems has shown that the network provides good generalization performance. Convergence is accomplished within a small number of training passes. The network provides these benefits while automatically allocating and deleting nodes and without requiring user adjustment of any parameters. The network learns incrementally and operates in a parallel fashion.

Future research will focus on improved methods for creating general nodes, the development of network architectures to support learning with better parallelism, testing on additional data sets, and extensions to real-valued inputs.

References

[1] Ackley, D. H., Hinton, D. E., & Sejnowski, T. J. (1985). A Learning Algorithm for Boltzmann Machines. *Cognitive Science, 9*, 147-169.

[2] Barker, J. C. (1993). Generalization by Controlled Expansion of Examples. *In preparation.*

[3] Michalski, R. S. (1983). A Theory and Methodology of Inductive Learning. *Artificial Intelligence, 20*, 111-161.

[4] Mitchell, T. M. (1982). Generalization as Search. *Artificial Intelligence, 18*, 203-226

[5] Murphy, P. M. & Aha, D. W. (1992). *UCI Repository of machine learning databases.* Irvine, CA: University of California, Department of Information and Computer Science.

[6] Quinlan, J. R. (1986). Induction of Decision Trees. *Machine Learning, 1*, 81-106.

[7] Rosenblatt, F. (1958). The Perceptron: A Probabilistic Model for Information Storage and Organization in the Brain. *Psychological Review, 65*, 386-408.

[8] Rumelhart, D. E., Hinton, G. E., & Williams, R. J. (1986). Learning Internal Representations by Error Propagation. In D. E. Rumelhart and J. L. McClelland (Eds.) *Parallel Distributed Processing* (Vol. 1). Cambridge, MA: MIT Press.

On Self-Learning Patterns in the 'Othello' Board Game, by the Method of Temporal Differences

Steven Walker,† Raymond Lister, and Tom Downs
Department of Electrical and Computer Engineering,
University of Queensland 4072, Australia

Abstract: We have trained a system to play a reasonably strong game of Othello, using the method of temporal differences. The most attractive feature of this approach is that the system learns by playing against itself, eliminating the tedious task of constructing and annotating training examples. The system's capacity to recognize board patterns is entirely self-learnt: there are no hand-crafted feature detectors. Whereas Tesauro's temporal difference system relied upon the stochastic nature of Backgammon, we show that deterministic board games like Othello can also be learnt, by introducing noise into the system.

1. Introduction

Research on board games has lost its way. These games were once a means to an end. That is, they were a useful vehicle for developing general purpose Artificial Intelligence (AI) techniques. But these board games have become an end in themselves. That is, the sole criterion for judging a system is its level of play. This has led to an emphasis on game-specific algorithms and hardware. Such systems may have application, and may exhibit a research content from the perspective of disciplines such as computer architecture, but in our view these systems do not generally exhibit an AI research content. If game playing is once again to become central to AI research, then the criteria for judging game playing systems must change: its not whether the system wins or loses, but how it plays the game.

1.1. Against Brute Force: Deep Search

The research emphasis has been upon fast methods of elaborating the game tree to a great depth. It is our view, however, that the most interesting aspect of human game playing is our capacity to ignore most of the game tree, and concentrate on just a small number of promising moves. This probably indicates that humans use a sophisticated pattern recognition approach. To benchmark a system's pattern recognition capabilities, it may be appropriate to limit search to just a few moves ahead.

1.2. Against Brute Force: Hand Crafting

The apparent power of many game playing learning programs comes from the use of carefully constructed feature recognizers. For example Berliner's[1] Backgammon program played a very sophisticated game - it even beat the world champion on one lucky occasion - but it was the result of a four person-year effort in devising and implementing detectors for various patterns of pieces on the board. To benchmark learning algorithms, it may be appropriate to exclude hand-crafted feature detectors.

† *Now at BHA Computer Pty Ltd, Milton, Queensland.*

1.3. Against Brute Force: Training Data

The manual generation of training data for a game playing system exhibits all the tedium and problems of a knowledge engineering project. First, there must be a human expert to assess the many board positions. It may be difficult for the expert to make estimates for some board positions, and mistakes are inevitable. Data "tuning" (i.e. the iterative process of identifying weak aspects of the system's play, and the generation of compensating training examples) is a particularly tedious and difficult process.

Tesauro and Sejnowski[2] trained a Multilayer Perceptron to play Backgammon, from a database of 3202 board positions. Their network defeated all rivals at the First Computer Olympiad, but it made blunders that were obvious to non-expert human players. Tesauro[3] concluded that improving the standard of play would require "*either an intractably large number of* [training] *examples, or a major overhaul in either the pre-computed features or the training paradigm*".

1.4. TD-Gammon

Tesauro[4] has since successfully changed his training paradigm, by using the method of temporal differences (TD). This method was formalized by Sutton[5] from techniques used in control problems. The beauty of Tesauro's system is that it *self-learns*, by playing against itself, thus eliminating the need for manual generation of training data.

Tesauro started with a simple system that did not include any special hand coded features. After learning from 200,000 games of self-play, this TD system won around half of its games against Tesauro's best network trained on the manually generated data (which also used hand-crafted pattern detectors). Tesauro has since built more elaborate TD-trained systems, that use hand-crafted feature detectors, and search. His most recent system[6] is estimated to play at the level of a strong international master.

While Tesauro's more elaborate TD systems are of undoubted interest and value, from our perspective it is the performance of his early TD system that is most surprising and impressive. It is Tesauro's early TD system that we have attempted to emulate in our work on Othello.

2. The Othello Board Game

Othello is played on a 8×8 board, with discs which have a black side and a white side. The two players alternate in placing a single disc, with their assigned colour showing. Play begins from the initial board position shown in Figure 1 (a). A player may only place a disc on an empty square and in a position that creates a line of discs from that position through a series of the opposite coloured discs and ending in a disc of the player's colour. There may be more than one line thus formed, and it may be horizontal, vertical, or diagonal. The asterisks in Figure 1 (b) indicate all the legal moves available to white. Once the disc has been placed all discs of opposite colour in the line(s) are flipped, to show the current player's colour. This is illustrated in Figure 1 (c). Play proceeds until all 64 positions are filled, or no more valid moves can be made. The winner is the player with the most discs showing his colour.

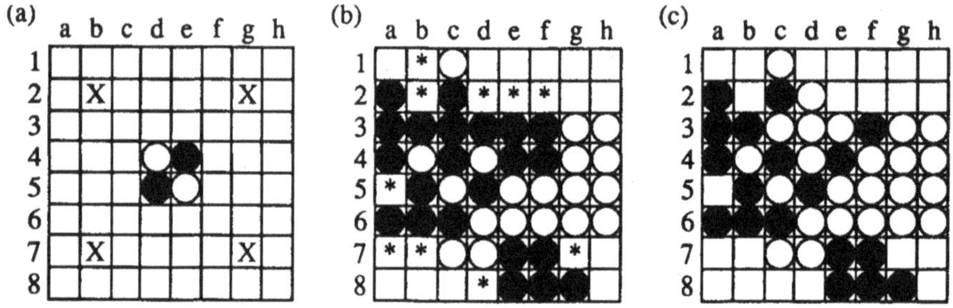

Figure 1. (a) The initial board showing the standard names of squares, including the "X" squares. In (b) the asterisks indicate white's legal moves, and (c) shows the result of white selecting to play onto d2.

2.1. Strategic Concepts

The most obvious strategy to the beginner is to maximize the number of discs gained on each move, but that is a poor strategy. The following are well known concepts and strategies for Othello:

a) *Corners*: the focal point of the game. Since a disc on a corner cannot be flipped by the opponent, corners can be used to secure large areas of the board.
b) *X Squares*: as shown in Figure 1 (a). Playing onto these squares almost always concedes the corner.
c) *Edges*: are secondary to corners, but control of edges usually helps stability.
d) *Mobility*: is generally the number of legal moves a player can make that do not directly concede a corner. If one player can reduce the other's mobility sufficiently then he/she can dictate exactly where the other has to move.

2.2. Phases of Play

Othello exhibits three phases of play: *opening*, *middle*, and *end* games. In the opening game, it is generally best to remain close to the centre of the board, so as to avoid conceding the edges. During the middle game, mobility is paramount, as player's strive to force the other to concede edges and corners. Towards the end of the game, middle game strategies break down. For example, dominating an edge is little use if the opponent wins an adjacent corner.

2.3. Existing Othello-playing Systems

IAGO[7] and BILL[8] are two programs that play a very high standard of Othello. However, both programs are largely hand-crafted. Both use look-up tables for all possible edge positions, of which there are many thousand, and both employ extensive game tree searching. BILL is capable of constructing the complete game tree for the final 18 moves.

A Microsoft product called *Windows Reversi* (version 3.0) plays Othello to several different standards: *Beginner*, *Novice*, *Expert*, *Master*. We have no direct knowledge of the internals of *Windows Reversi*, but we surmise that it has a simple hand-crafted board configuration evaluator, and its power comes primarily from the depth of search, which varys according to the level selected. The first author learnt Othello by regularly playing against *Windows Reversi*. After around 3 months, he could consistently beat it at the *Expert* level. After around 3 more months, he could consistently beat it at the *Master* level.

3. Problem Representation

Since a major aspect of this study was to develop Othello-playing systems with little hand-crafting of *a priori* knowledge, we elected to use a direct method of representing the game. We used Multilayer Perceptrons, with single hidden layers of 10 to 50 units. We settled upon an input layer of 128 units; two sets of 64 units, with each set representing an 8×8 board. The first set of input units represent the actual board configuration. Each unit in this set has one of three possible values: 0.0 for a white disc, 0.5 for a blank square, and 1.0 for a black disc. The second set of 64 units indicate the squares on which the opponent could legally place a disc. The output layer consisted of a single output unit. An extreme zero/one value was indication of a certain loss/win for white. Intermediate values were interpreted as a bias towards one or the other eventual outcome.

4. DB-Othello: Learning Othello from a Data Base

The manual construction of the data base exhibited most of the tedium and dangers described in section 1.3. Initially there was no human expert: the first author played many games over several months against *Windows Reversi* to become our "expert" annotator. The data base was being constructed while the first author's play was still improving, so there was the danger of mistakes and inconsistencies.

In fact there was three data bases, each with an associated network, for the opening, middle and end games respectively. We felt that the differing strategies at the different stages argued against a single network. (Though experience with a single TD network has since thrown this reasoning into doubt.) The system shifted from the opening game network to the middle game network after 20 moves (i.e. the placement of 10 discs by each player), and to the end game network after 40 moves.

Collecting training data was not simply a matter of playing a lot of games. The three databases had to be "tuned" to counter observed weaknesses in earlier trained systems. The final databases contained respectively 216, 300, and 150 canonical patterns. As the board representation was not invariant under transformation, these canonical patterns were expanded by the eight possible transformations to give databases of 1728, 2400, and 1200 positions.

5. TD-Othello: Self-Learning Othello by Temporal Differences

The general TD(λ) update equation devised by Sutton[5] is shown in the equation below. In our Othello application, P_t is the estimate at move t of the likelihood of white winning, w_t is the network's weights at move t, and $\nabla_w P_t$ is the gradient of the output unit with respect to the network's weights at move t. In any one TD run λ is constant, but we varied it across runs in the range $0.4 \le \lambda \le 0.7$. Self-learning did not seem sensitive to variations of λ within this range. In all experiments, $\alpha=0.1$.

$$\Delta w_t = \alpha (P_{t+1} - P_t) \sum_{k=1}^{t} \lambda^{t-k} \nabla_w P_k$$

Self-play was achieved by selecting the move for white/black that maximized/minimized P_t. This requires an extra input node to indicate the player about to move.

An important difference between Othello and Backgammon is that the latter contains a stochastic component: possible moves are defined by a dice throw. Tesauro[6] has conjectured that this stochastic element was "*critical*" in TD-Gammon, as the dice rolls "*enforce a certain minimum amount of exploration of the state space*". A stochastic component is common in applications of TD to control problems, due to errors in sensors and actuators. Our application of TD to an entirely deterministic system is unusual. We added to each P_m a small random quantity ε_m uniformly distributed in the range $[-\xi<\varepsilon_m<\xi]$, where ξ is constant. We settled upon $\xi = 0.1$, but small variations made little difference.

A TD-Othello network with 30 hidden units and trained for 30,000 games was chosen for benchmarking against DB-Othello. Such a system could be trained in 24 elapsed hours, using otherwise idle CPU time on a Sony RISC 3860 computer.

6. TD-Othello versus DB-Othello

The benchmark TD-Othello system consistently wins more than two thirds of its games against DB-Othello. The relative performance of the two approaches varied slightly, depending on variations in DB-Othello's number of hidden units, training times, and learning parameters, but the variation was only of a few percent. It bears emphasis that DB-Othello contains three equal-sized networks, one for each stage of play, whereas TD-Othello is a single network. From observing the style of play of TD-Othello and DB-Othello, the following differences emerged:

1. TD-Othello's play tends to improve towards the end of a game. This might be expected, since the final reward signal P_M is not the estimated outcome, but the actual outcome. In contrast, DB-Othello's play tends to fall away as the game proceeds. This may be due to over-generalization in the end game network: it may be memorizing training cases, rather than learning principles. Or perhaps it is because the construction of a representative set of opening game examples is easier than constructing examples for later in the game.
2. TD-Othello was more likely to seize corner-attacking opportunities. This is illustrated in Figure 1 (b), where the best move is white to a5. This will lead to the capture of the top left corner. Training DB-Othello to recognize such opportunities proved difficult, even when the training data was "tuned" to contain a large number of such examples. (Note that a search-based approach does not need to recognize these types of patterns, as the opportunity will become apparent as the search tree is constructed.)
3. TD-Othello appeared to pay more attention to mobility than DB-Othello. Mobility may be a very general concept that requires far more data than that used to train DB-Othello. We believe that this aspect of TD-Othello is most responsible for its superior performance.
4. The performance of DB-Othello tends to fall away when the outcome of a game appears to be fairly certain - even when it is winning! This probably reflects a bias in the data base for closely matched scenarios. TD-Othello plays a particularly good game in such a situation.

7. TD-Othello versus Windows Reversi

TD-Othello tends to beat *Windows Reversi* at the *Novice* (2nd) level, but tends to lose at the *Expert* (3rd) level. Given that TD-Othello does not perform any game tree search, does not include any hand-crafted feature detectors, this performance demonstrates that it has self-learnt some non-trivial pattern recognition capabilities. (In contrast, DB-Othello plays somewhere between the *Beginner* (1st) and *Novice* (2nd) levels.)

We also implemented a version of TD-Othello that could perform a single level of search. That is, the system would consider all of its possible moves, and all resultant moves of the opponent. This is how far most human Othello players would look, given the visually volatile nature of Othello. With this one level of search, TD-Othello consistently beat *Windows Reversi* at the *Expert* (3rd) level, and even had occasional wins at the *Master* (4th) level. We take this to be an indication that TD-Othello has self-learnt feature detectors that are at least the equal of those hand-crafted into *Windows Reversi*.

8. Conclusion

We set out to test whether a system trained by temporal difference (TD) could self-learn significant pattern recognition capabilities. To do so, we deliberately chose not to use lookup tables, or hand-crafted feature recognizers, and we restricted search. When run without any capacity for search, our system demonstrates that it has acquired non-trivial pattern recognition capabilities. When run with only a single level of search, it is capable of beating a commercial product that searches further.

Our primary aim was to compare TD self-learning with learning from a data base of examples. Not only did we find TD to be an attractive alternative to the tedious compilation of annotated set of comprehensive examples, but our TD-Othello system usually beats the system we trained from such a database.

References

1. Berliner, H (1979) 'Backgammon computer program beats world champion' *Artificial Intelligence* **14**.
2. Tesauro, G and Sejnowski, T (1989) 'A parallel network that learns to play backgammon' *Artificial Intelligence* **39**, pp 357-390.
3. Tesauro, G (1989) 'Neurogammon: A neural network backgammon learning program'. In *Heuristic Programming in Artificial Intelligence: The First Computer Olympiad*, ed. D. Levy and D. Beal (Ellis Horwood, Chichester, England).
4. Tesauro, G (1992) 'Practical issues in temporal difference learning' *Machine Learning* **8**, pp 257-277.
5. Sutton, R (1988) 'Learning to predict by the method of temporal differences' *Machine Learning* **3**, pp 9-44.
6. Tesauro, G (*to appear*) 'TD-Gammon, A Self-Teaching Backgammon Program, Achieves Master-level Play'. *Neural Computation*.
7. Rosenbloom, P (1982) 'A world-championship-level Othello program' *Artificial Intelligence* **19**, pp 279-320.
8. Lee, K, and Mahajan, S (1990) 'The Development of a World Class Othello Program' *Artificial Intelligence* **43**, pp 21-36.

Problems with Sample-Based Utility Analysis for EBL

Nick Lewins* and C. P. Tsang
Logic and AI Laboratory, Department of Computer Science,
The University of Western Australia, Nedlands 6009 Australia

Abstract

Explanation-based learning (EBL) systems typically aim to improve the efficiency of a problem-solver. This can be achieved by the extraction of a macro-rule from the solution trace of each problem, and the subsequent use of that macro to guide problem-solving on unseen problems. However, the use of such macros does not necessarily result in faster problem-solving. A macro's net effect on average execution time is called its "utility", and the phenomenon of EBL *degrading* the performance of a problem-solver is called the "utility problem".

Some proposed solutions to the utility problem attempt to calculate bounds on a macro's utility (this process is called "utility analysis"). A macro's utility can be estimated by sampling the macro's effect on a number of problems. Macros are stored in a "candidate set" until their utility can be estimated to a user-specified level of confidence. If the macro's utility is estimated to be (probably) positive, the macro is utilised within the problem-solver.

The first problem with this approach stems from the monotonically-increasing nature of the set of macros. It is possible for the system to become stuck in a local minimum set of macros. The second problem is more fundamental and is due to the difficulty of assessing the sign of the utility of macros, by sampling methods, when the macros have utilities near zero.

The above problems were observed in experiments with PROCACHE, an EBL system for Prolog programs which implements sample-based utility analysis. This paper includes experimental results which show the problems occurring and discusses possible solution methods.

1 Introduction

Explanation-based learning (EBL)[1,2] is a paradigm for speedup learning. EBL works by the extraction of a macro-rule from the solution trace of each problem, and the subsequent use of the macro-rule to guide problem-solving on unseen problems. The

*Current address: Information Technology Division, Defence Science and Technology Organisation, PO Box 1500, Salisbury, South Australia, 5108. Email: Nick_Lewins@itd.dsto.gov.au

well-known "utility problem"[3,4] occurs when the use of a set of such macros causes the problem solver to take *longer* (on average) to solve problems.

The utility problem comes about because the search for a relevant macro-rule may take longer than solving the query without learned macro-rules. The expense of this search may be due to the number macros present, or to the complexity of using particular macros. Many ideas have been proposed to cope with the utility problem (for an overview, see reference 5, page 431). The last couple of years have seen systems reported which effectively solve the problem.[6,7] Many of these proposed solutions build a more powerful operationality criterion, commonly called *utility analysis*, which is applied to macro-rules after they are learned. Such utility analysis typically involves the collection of information about the effect of the macro-rule on the execution of a number of queries. The average effect of the macro-rule is then deduced from this information.

The COMPOSER,[6] PALO,[7] and PROCACHE[8] systems implement similar utility analysis mechanisms. They maintain a "candidate set" of macro-rules. The first candidate showing (via a statistical sampling technique) that it has positive utility will be added to the macro-rule set. The addition of multiple candidate macro-rules in one step is not considered. Macro-rules are added one at a time, (probably) making the program more efficient with each addition. The first rule that is determined to have positive utility is added. This implements a hill-climbing search through the space of macro-rule sets. This could be called a *fastest-ascent* hillclimbing search. This is in contrast to the common *steepest-ascent* form of hillclimbing search, which evaluates all of the possible one-step modifications and adopts the best one.

Like the steepest-ascent hillclimbing algorithm, the fastest-ascent hillclimbing algorithm can become trapped in local maxima. In utility analysis terms, this means that a particular set of macro-rules may not be able to be improved upon (by adding more macro-rules to it), but there may exist other macro-rule sets which provide greater benefit. Although possible, experimental evidence of such a phenomenon has not been reported in the literature. This paper provides experimental evidence of local maxima occurring in an EBL system.

The COMPOSER,[6] PALO,[7] and PROCACHE[8] systems implement statistical methods for deducing the utility of a macro-rule from a sequence of observations*. These methods predict the sign of the macro-rule's utility. They continue to take samples until some pre-specified confidence is achieved. When the average effect is close to zero, the statistical method will require many samples to determine the sign of the macro's utility. This paper provides experimental evidence which indicates that this behaviour can cause EBL systems to learn extremely slowly. It is believed that this problem is fundamental to sample-based utility estimation.

*COMPOSER and PROCACHE use a different statistical method from PALO. In the context of this paper, they can be considered to be identical. See reference 8 for details of each method and a comparison between the two.

2 The PROCACHE System

This section presents PROCACHE, an EBL system which adapts Prolog programs to their execution environment. PROCACHE employs a few important restrictions on the way that macro-rules are used. These restrictions enable an inexpensive solution to the utility problem. The restrictions state that learned rules in PROCACHE:

can only be used to answer top-level queries: Conceptually, PROCACHE augments the program with a single cache of macro-rules, each macro-rule being capable of solving an entire top-level query. If all of these macro-rules fail, the original program is used without any modifications to its behaviour.

cannot backtrack between subgoals: Each subgoal of a macro-rule is attempted at most once. That is to say, no backtracking is allowed between the subgoals of macro-rules. Note, however, that no restriction is placed on the amount of backtracking between subgoals in the original program clauses.

These restrictions make utility analysis easier. The change in the execution time of a query due to the addition of one of the candidate macro-rules can be easily calculated. The query is firstly attempted by the program without any candidate macro-rules. Then each candidate macro-rule is invoked to see what it would have achieved. This invocation is performed to see what would have happened. If the invocation fails, then the effect of the macro-rule is to increase the time taken to solve the query (by the time taken for the macro-rule to fail). If the invocation succeeds, then the effect of the macro-rule is to alter the time taken (the new time to solve the query is the amount of time taken by the macro-rule). The effect of the rule on the execution of the query can thus be calculated without having to solve the query twice using the entire program with and without the macro-rule. Using this method to sample the effect of macro-rules on queries drawn from the execution environment, PROCACHE uses a probabilistic method to ensure[†] that the system does not transform programs into slower ones. This overcomes the utility problem, and allows PROCACHE to find macro-rules which improve performance amongst those which would degrade it.

The design of the PROCACHE system also resolves the problem of recursion-depth specificity and that of deciding which rules to compile into a macro-rule. The solution employed is to conduct a search through the various levels of generality.[9] This search must be approximate because an exhaustive search would require the evaluation of each level of generality, and the number of levels is exponential in the depth of the proof tree.[9] The PROCACHE system includes an approximate level-of-generality search which allows the EBL mechanism to extract rules at an appropriate level of generality. The novel approximation in the search allows it to be performed

[†]The system ensures that each addition of a learned rule to the program speeds the program with some user-specified probability. That is, the system gives a *probabilistic* assurance that the macro-rules it adds are worthwhile.

in a computationally efficient way‡. This efficient level-of-generality search is also made possible by the knowledge that rules are only used to answer top-level queries. This restriction makes it easier to establish the effect of a rule on problem solving efficiency. See reference 8 for more details.

The net result of PROCACHE's restrictions on the use of learned rules is that the system can afford to perform more reasoning about the rules it finds. This added reasoning means that PROCACHE is effective for Prolog programs where other systems would not be. Experiments with an implementation of the PROCACHE system[8] include cases where PROCACHE not only avoids the utility problem but also provides speedup, while other systems degrade performance. However, these experiments also provide evidence of local maxima and slow learning rate, which are the subject of the current paper.

3 Experimental Methodology

Queries are randomly drawn from a fixed distribution of queries. The process of drawing a query is defined procedurally for each program on which we evaluate PROCACHE. Before learning starts, 100 queries are randomly drawn from the distribution and placed in a "test set". The test set remains fixed for the duration of each experiment. Single queries are then randomly drawn from the distribution and analysed by PROCACHE. At regular intervals (for these experiments, every 10 queries), the learning process is suspended and the solution of the entire test set by the current program is timed. This process continues until some maximum number of queries is reached, whereupon the system halts.

No time bound is placed on the execution of individual queries from the distribution, as the Prolog program is assumed to be efficient enough to be usable in its original state. This removes one of the major methodological problems with previous evaluations of EBL systems.[10] Individual queries from the distribution may fail, and this time is taken into account (as is the effect of the cached rules on the time the query took to fail).

4 The Occurrence of Local Minima

The simplest domain on which PROCACHE is evaluated is the domain of list appending. The Prolog program for the append domain is given in Figure 1.

The performance of the PROCACHE system is examined on this domain with a query distribution of queries **append**$(l1, l2, v1)$. $l1$ and $l2$ are fully-instantiated lists of length between 0 and 999 (inclusive) whose elements are randomly chosen integers, and $v1$ is a variable. Each such query has equal frequency in the distribution.

A system consisting of EBL with utility analysis, but without generality analysis, was evaluated on this domain. The system could not find any macro-rules probably

‡In fact, linear in the number of nodes of the proof tree in the worst case.

```
append(A,B,C):-
    append_aux(A,B,C).

append_aux([],X,X).
append_aux([H|T],X,[H|R]):-
    append_aux(T,X,R).
```

Figure 1: Definition of the append domain

possessing positive utility. In other words, the initial program was judged to be locally optimal with respect to the addition of EBL macro-rules.

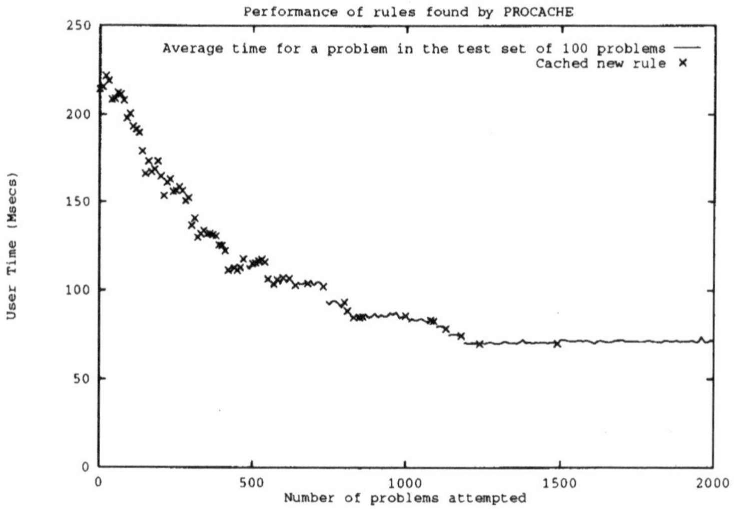

Figure 2: The effect of EBL on problem-solving time in the append domain

A graph depicting the performance of vanilla EBL (without utility analysis or generality analysis) in this domain is given in Figure 2. The graph shows that although an overall speedup is achieved by the end of learning, the first few rules made the performance of the program worse. This suggests that the lack of effectiveness of the system with utility analysis but without level-of-generality analysis is due to the existence of a local minima. The initial program cannot be improved by the addition of any single macro-rule, but can be improved by the addition of a number of macro-rules. This sort of behaviour is the unfortunate consequence of the one-positive-step-at-a-time (i.e. hill-climbing) search performed by the utility analysis mechanism used.

This problem could be overcome by making the EBL system consider adding multiple macro-rules simultaneously. Unfortunately, this is unlikely to be feasible in practice, as there is an exponential explosion in the number of candidate macro-rule sequences which could be added. It is interesting to note, however, that the full PROCACHE system does not encounter this local minima because it has more options available to it - the rules at better levels of generality supply a path downwards from the initial program. This shows that another solution to the problem is to increase the vocabulary of macro-rules so as to increase the probability of the existence of individual macro-rules with positive utility.

5 Macros With Near-Zero Utility

PROCACHE was also evaluated in the domain of token parsing for Prolog. This domain implements the syntax of Prolog tokens as strings, as given in the SICS-tus Prolog manual.[11] The grammar classifies strings as containing a name (i.e. a predicate name or constant), a natural number, a variable, a comment or one of a few other things depending on the characters which go to make up the string. The domain theory can be found in reference 8.

The performance of the PROCACHE system is examined on this domain with a query distribution of queries `token(`sl, vl`)`. sl is a list of characters and vl is a variable which becomes instantiated to the classification of sl found by the syntax. The query distribution is based on the tokens from an actual Prolog program. The Prolog program used was, in fact, the code for the PROCACHE system. The strings corresponding to tokens were stripped (by hand) from the program and stored (duplicates preserved) in a list. Queries are drawn by randomly choosing an element from this list.

Vanilla EBL performs very well on this domain, as the best strategy is to form one macro-rule for each token in the query distribution. The indexing provided by Prolog allows the applicable macro to be located quickly, saving a search through the grammar. Unfortunately, PROCACHE does not perform as well. The problem lies in the sample-based utility analysis mechanism. Macro-rules for this domain often classify exactly one token as belonging to a particular syntactic category. For most queries, such a macro-rule has a small negative effect, as it takes a small amount of time to determine that it does not match. Occasionally, there is a large positive benefit when the macro-rule does apply. Any statistical technique which is asked to predict the sign of the mean of such a measurement sequence will take a very large number of samples to reach a reliable conclusion. Unfortunately, this problem seems to be inherent in the sampling of utility from examples. Sample-based utility analysis will take a long time in such domains.

Early EBL systems incorporating utility analysis[12] attempted to evaluate utility of macro-rules during their use in problem-solving. The strategy was one of "learn now, delete later". This approach was seen to be deficient because macro-rules interact in non-trivial ways to change each others utility.[13] This observation inspired the construction of hill-climbing, sample-based utility analysis mechanisms which perform a single step at a time. In-use utility analysis may still be possible if the interactions between rules can be computed easily. This approach requires more research.

Other alternatives to sample-based utility analysis have been proposed, based on cost modelling.[14,15] These approaches claim that an approximate cost model for problem-solving can provide useful utility estimates. The cost models predict the utility of new macro-rules, based on easily-collectible statistics and timings of previous program execution. This task is made computationally feasible via the introduction of simplifications and assumptions. Thus, the accuracy of such utility estimates is due not only to sampling errors, but also to shortcomings of the cost model. While these approaches may provide heuristics which help avoid the utility problem, they do not solve the general problem. The applicability of these heuristics must be validated on a domain-by-domain basis.

6 Conclusions

This paper has presented two problems with recent solutions to the utility problem in Explanation-Based Learning systems. Solutions based on hill-climbing sample-based utility analysis (such as COMPOSER,[6] PALO,[7] and PROCACHE[8]) suffer from these problems. The hill-climbing nature of the utility analysis employed by these systems can cause EBL to become stuck in a local minimum. Experimental results were presented which indicate that this can happen in practice. Experiments with the PROCACHE system[8] indicate that this problem is lessened by generality analysis. Generality analysis allows the EBL system to find macro-rules at differing levels of generality, which appears to make local minima less likely.

The second problem involves the number of samples needed to reach a pre-set level of confidence in a utility assessment. This number of samples can become very large when a macro-rule's utility is close to zero. A domain was discussed in which all macro-rules with positive utility have only a small positive utility. However, a large collection of such macros provides a large increase in efficiency. EBL systems using sample-based utility analysis will be very slow to learn in such domains. This problem seems to be inherent in the sample-based method of utility analysis.

7 Acknowledgments

The first author was supported by a Cadetship from the Defence Science and Technology Organisation, Australia. Support for this research was also received from the British Council under the Postgraduate Bursary scheme.

References

1. T. M. Mitchell, R. M. Keller, and S. T. Kedar-Cabelli, "Explanation-based learning: A unifying view," *Machine Learning*, vol. 1, no. 1, pp. 47–80, 1986.

2. G. DeJong and R. Mooney, "Explanation-based learning: An alternative view," *Machine Learning*, vol. 1, no. 2, pp. 145–176, 1986.

3. S. Minton, *Learning Effective Search Control Knowledge: An Explanation-Based Approach*. PhD thesis, Department of Computer Science, Carnegie-Mellon University, Pittsburgh, PA, 1988.

4. S. Minton, "Quantitative results concerning the utility of explanation-based learning," in *Proceedings of the Sixth National Conference on Artificial Intelligence, AAAI-88*, (St. Paul, MN), pp. 564–569, Morgan Kaufmann, 1988.

5. J. W. Shavlik and T. G. Dietterich, eds., *Readings in Machine Learning*. Morgan Kaufmann, 1990.

6. J. M. Gratch and G. F. DeJong, "Composer: A probabilistic solution to the utility problem in speed-up learning," in *Proceedings of the Tenth National Conference on Artificial Intelligence, AAAI-92*, 1992.

7. R. Greiner and I. Jurisica, "A statistical approach to solving the EBL utility problem," in *Proceedings of the Tenth National Conference on Artificial Intelligence, AAAI-92*, 1992.

8. N. J. Lewins, *Practical Solution-Caching for Prolog: An Explanation-Based Learning Approach*. PhD thesis, Department of Computer Science, The University of Western Australia, Nedlands, Western Australia, 1993.

9. M. S. Braverman and S. J. Russell, "Imex: Overcoming intractability in explanation-based learning," in *Proceedings of the Seventh National Conference on Artificial Intelligence*, (St. Paul, MN), pp. 575–579, Morgan Kaufmann, 1988.

10. A. Segre, C. Elkan, and A. Russell, "Technical note: A critial look at experimental evaluations of EBL," *Machine Learning*, vol. 6, pp. 183–195, March 1991.

11. M. Carlsson and J. Widen, "SICStus Prolog user's manual," Tech. Rep. T91:11B, Swedish Institute of Computer Science, Kista, Sweeden, October 1991.

12. S. Minton, J. G. Carbonell, O. Etzioni, C. A. Knoblock, and D. R. Kuokka, "Acquiring effective search control rules: Explanation-based learning in the PRODIGY system," *Proceedings of the Fourth International Workshop on Machine Learning*, pp. 122–133, 1987.

13. J. M. Gratch and G. F. DeJong, "Utility generalization and composability problems in explanation-based learning," Tech. Rep. UIUUCDCS-R-91-1681, Department of Computer Science, University of Illinois, 1991.

14. T. Yamanouchi and T. Mitchell, "A statistical model for evaluating the utility of macro-rules." Unpublished manuscript, 1992.

15. D. Subramanian and S. Hunter, "Measuring utility and the design of provably good EBL algorithms," in *Proceedings of the AAAI Spring Symposium on Knowledge Assimilation*, 1992.

Systematic search for categorical attribute-value data-driven machine learning

Geoffrey I. Webb
School of Computing and Mathematics, Deakin University
Geelong, Vic., 3217, Australia.

Abstract

Optimal Pruning for Unordered Search is a search algorithm that enables complete search through the space of possible disjuncts at the inner level of a covering algorithm. This algorithm takes as inputs an evaluation function, *e*, a training set, *t*, and a set of specialisation operators, *o*. It outputs a set of operators from *o* that creates a classifier that maximises *e* with respect to *t*. While OPUS has exponential worst case time complexity, the algorithm is demonstrated to reach solutions for complex real world domains within reasonable time frames. Indeed, for some domains, the algorithm exhibits greater computational efficiency than common heuristic search algorithms.

Introduction

A *class description* (hereafter referred to as simply *description*) is an expression that describes a class of objects. Covering algorithms[1,2,3,4] use two levels of search to infer a disjunctive description. Although there is considerable minor variation, at the outer level they all operate approximately as follows:

description = false
while the training set is not empty
  form *disjunct*, the best non-disjunctive description with respect to the training set
  remove all cases covered by *disjunct* from the training set
  description ← *description* ∨ *disjunct*
end while

Some algorithms develop ordered descriptions by allowing disjuncts to be developed for any class at any stage[2]. Other algorithms[1,3,4] develop unordered descriptions by developing all non-disjunctive descriptions for a single class at one time.

Each disjunct is formed by search. Typically, the search space from which a disjunct is selected is extremely large. To enable search of such large search spaces, previous algorithms have employed heuristic search.

In recent years, there has been considerable interest in systematic search algorithms for use within the inner level of a covering algorithm. The first of these, LEI[5], was restricted to inferring classifiers that were complete and consistent with regard to the training set and used the strict AQ technique of searching only the generalisations of the most specialised description that covered a randomly selected positive case. Rymon's algorithm[6] constrains the size of the search space by exploring only conjunctions of clauses where each clause allows a single value only for an attribute. Schlimmer[7] performs systematic search through the same space as is explored in this research. To achieve this, its search is bounded by specifying a maximum depth to be considered.

This paper presents an algorithm for systematic search through the space of all possible non-disjunctive descriptions.

Optimal Pruning for Unordered Search: A systematic search algorithm

The Optimal Pruning for Unordered Search (OPUS) algorithm is applicable to any

An expanded version of this paper is available as Deakin University School of Computing and Mathematics Technical Report C93/17.

language for expressing descriptions in which:

- a non-disjunctive description can be constructed from the most general description ANYTHING by the application of a sequence of specialisation operators; and
- the order in which those specialisation operators are applied does not affect the cover of the resulting description.

Although OPUS is applicable to inferring ordered or unordered rules[8], this paper considers only the latter case.

Inductive bias is specified to the algorithm via a value function. *value*() is a function that provides a numeric evaluation of a description such that the higher the evaluation the higher the preference for the description. This research uses the Laplace function[8],

$$value(D) = \frac{\mathrm{pos\_cover}(D) + 1}{\mathrm{total\_cover}(D) + no\_of\_classes}$$

where *pos_cover(D)* is the number of cases covered by *D* that belong to the class with which *D* is associated, *total_cover(D)* is the total number of cases covered by *D* and *no_of_classes* is the number of classes in the domain.

To reduce time complexity OPUS prunes the search space through optimistic pruning and other pruning techniques. The efficiency of OPUS arises from the manner in which it ensures that the size of the region pruned by each pruning action is maximised.

Two functions complement the value function to support pruning. An optimistic estimate (value that is not lower than the actual maximum) of the maximum value of any specialisation of *description* obtained by application of any combination of operators in the set *operators* is provided by *potential_value(description, operators)*. One definition for use with the Laplace value function when developing unordered rules is

$$potential\_value(D,O) = \frac{pos\_cover(D) + 1}{pos\_cover(D) + neg\_cover(D \& O) + no\_of\_classes}$$

where *neg_cover(D & O)* is the total number of cases not belonging to the class that are covered by the description formed by applying all specialisation operators in *O* to *D*.

Another function, *cannot_improve(D, E, O)* is true only if

- no specialisation obtained by application of any combination of operators in *O* to *E* can have a higher value than the highest valued specialisation obtained by application of any combination of operators in *O* to *D* given that *O* does not contain the specialisation operator used to derive *S* from *D*; and
- if *cannot_improve* holds between a node and all of its children, then no specialisation of a child can improve upon the parent.

Within OPUS, three items are stored within the data structure associated with a description, the actual description (*x→desc*), the last specialisation operator applied in order to obtain the description (*x→most_recent_operator*) and a set of operators that remain to be applied in the search space descending from the description (*x→search_map*). The left arrow '←' denotes assignment.

```
Algorithm: OPUS
  best→desc ← ANYTHING
  best→search_map ← {operator1, operator2, ... operatorn)
  open ← { best }
  while open is not empty
    remove current, the node that maximises potential_value(current→desc,
    current→search_map), from open
    new_descs ← {}.
    for o ← each operator in current→search_map in turn
      new→desc ← current →desc & o
```

```
      new→most_recent_operator ← o
      if value(new→desc) > value(best→desc) then
         best ← new
      end if
      if potential_value(new→desc, current→search_map) > value(best→desc) and
      not cannot_improve(current→desc, new→desc, current→search_map )
         add new to new_descs
      else
         current→search_map ← current→search_map − o
      end if
   end for
   for every description d in new_descs
      if for some x in new_descs, cannot_improve(x→desc, d→desc,
      current→search_map )
         remove d from new_descs
         current→search_map ← current→search_map − d→most_recent_operator
      end if
   end for
   for every description d in new_descs ordered from lowest to highest value on
   potential_value(d→desc, current→search_map)
      current→search_map ← current→search_map − d→ most_recent_operator
      d→search_map ← current→search_map
      if potential_value(d→desc, d→search_map) > value(best→desc)
         add d to open
      end if
   end for
end while
```

OPUS maximises the effect of any pruning that can be performed. However, in the worst case, OPUS will not be able to perform any pruning resulting in the examination of all 2^n points in the search space. Thus, the worst case complexity is exponential. The important issue with regard to the algorithm's utility is to what extent is it successful in decreasing computation time on real world induction problems. This is a matter for experimental evaluation.

Experimental evaluation

OPUS has been implemented in 'C' on a Solbourne 5/602 computer. This implementation of OPUS handles categorical attribute-value data only. It uses the Laplace evaluation function and the associated *potential_value* and *cannot_improve* functions, described above. Thus, it is applicable only to develop unordered rules.

The OPUS algorithm is embodied within the following covering algorithm (Class).

```
for class ← each class in turn
   while the training set contains objects belonging to class class
      divide the training set into POS and NEG where POS contains all objects in the
      training set belonging to class and NEG contains all other objects
      disjunct ← OPUS(POS, NEG)
      remove all objects of class class covered by disjunct from the training set
      add to the ruleset the rule IF disjunct THEN class
   end while
   restore to the training set all objects removed above
end for
```

This is equivalent to the ordered rules version of the CN2 algorithm with OPUS

Table 1: Summary of experimental data sets.

Domain	Description	#Attribs	#Attrib Vals	#Objects	#Classes
Breast Cancer	Medical prognosis.	9	57	286	2
HouseVotes 84	Predict political affiliation of US Senators from voting record.	16	48	435	2
Lymphography	Medical diagnosis.	18	60	148	4
F11 Multiplexer	Artificial data.	11	22	500	2
Primary Tumor	Medical diagnosis.	17	42	339	22

employed in the place of the CN2 *find_best_complex* heuristic search function.

When the rules so developed are applied to previously unsighted objects, three classes of outcome are possible.

1. One rule fires. In this case the conclusion for the rule is applied to the object.
2. Multiple rules fire. In this case the conclusion for the rule with the highest value, as determined by the evaluation function during induction, is applied to the object.
3. No rule fires. In this case the object is deemed to belong to the class represented by the most objects in the training set.

For evaluation, Class was applied to a number of widely studied data sets from the UCI machine learning repository[9]. These data sets are described in Table 1. The number of attribute values (presented in column 5) treats missing values as distinct values. The number of class descriptions OPUS considers for each domain is 2^n, where n is the number of attribute values.

Each data set was randomly divided into training (80% of data) and evaluation (remaining 20% of data) sets. The Class, Einstein[10] and CN2[2] induction systems were applied to each training set. Each classifier so developed was evaluated against the corresponding evaluation set. This process was repeated 100 times for each data set.

Einstein employs a variant of the AQ learning algorithm that performs search from specific to general classifiers. It was used with most extreme start, most extreme ordering, multiple start rule optimisation with a beam width of 20 and conservative conjunct deletion[10,11]. CN2 is an re-implementation of the unordered rules version of the CN2 algorithm[8]. It was used with a beam width of 20 and no significance testing. Class, Einstein and CN2 all used the same covering algorithm and Laplace evaluation function, differing only in that Einstein and CN2 used different heuristic search techniques to try to maximise the evaluation function when developing each disjunct whereas Class employed systematic search. The rule sets developed by the systems were applied with the same conflict resolution strategies (resolution of multiple or no matches), those outlined above.

Table 2 presents a summary of the experimental results. For each data set it presents

- The mean accuracy obtained when applying the classifier to the evaluation set.
- The mean number of CPU seconds taken to execute the program.
- The mean value of the first rule inferred for each class.
- The mean value of all rules inferred.
- The mean number of rules developed.

All means, other than those for Class, are accompanied by the p value for a matched pairs two-tailed t-test comparing the value with the corresponding value for Class. A p of 0.05 or lower indicates that the difference is statistically significant at the 0.05 level.

For all data sets other than F11 multiplexer (for which the most extreme ordering heuristic, employed in this study, produces a poor result for Einstein[11]), and Lymphography, the accuracy of both the classifiers produced by heuristic search (Einstein and CN2) was greater than that of the classifiers produced by systematic search

Table 2: Summary of experimental results.

Data set	Algorithm	Accuracy	CPU secs	First val	All vals	#Rules
Breast Cancer	Class	70.7	553.8	0.96	0.82	29.8
	CN2	74.1 (*p* 0.00)	51.3 (*p* 0.00)	0.95 (*p* 0.00)	0.86 (*p* 0.00)	21.0 (*p* 0.00)
	Einstein	71.0 (*p* 0.58)	22.3 (*p* 0.00)	0.93 (*p* 0.00)	0.89 (*p* 0.00)	27.4 (*p* 0.00)
HouseVotes 84	Class	93.9	2.3	0.99	0.82	14.3
	CN2	94.7 (*p* 0.00)	27.0 (*p* 0.00)	0.99 (*p* 1.00)	0.84 (*p* 0.00)	12.8 (*p* 0.00)
	Einstein	94.7 (*p* 0.00)	22.9 (*p* 0.00)	0.99 (*p* 1.00)	0.97 (*p* 0.00)	11.7 (*p* 0.00)
Lymphography	Class	78.1	2.9	0.71	0.66	11.4
	CN2	76.4 (*p* 0.03)	14.7 (*p* 0.00)	0.70 (*p* 0.00)	0.63 (*p* 0.00)	12.7 (*p* 0.00)
	Einstein	83.0 (*p* 0.00)	2.2 (*p* 0.00)	0.71 (*p* 0.00)	0.80 (*p* 0.00)	9.9 (*p* 0.00)
F11 Multiplexer	Class	99.1	2.8	0.97	0.93	22.3
	CN2	99.9 (*p* 0.00)	12.6 (*p* 0.00)	0.97 (*p* 1.00)	0.93 (*p* 1.00)	21.6 (*p* 0.00)
	Einstein	96.4 (*p* 0.00)	33.1 (*p* 0.00)	0.96 (*p* 0.00)	0.96 (*p* 0.00)	21.9 (*p* 0.18)
Primary Tumor	Class	34.2	21.1	0.21	0.17	57.6
	CN2	35.4 (*p* 0.01)	141.6 (*p* 0.00)	0.20 (*p* 0.00)	0.16 (*p* 0.00)	61.1 (*p* 0.00)
	Einstein	42.6 (*p* 0.00)	7.2 (*p* 0.00)	0.20 (*p* 0.00)	0.20 (*p* 0.00)	45.7 (*p* 0.00)

(Class). In all but one of these cases, the difference in accuracy was statistically significant. This suggests that the Laplace value function is not an optimal selection criteria for a covering algorithm and that it interacts with the heuristics employed by Einstein and CN2 to create a superior, implicit, evaluation function.

Caution is required in comparing computation time, due to variation in implementation efficiency between programs. Nonetheless, it is surprising that the mean computation time of Class was only in one case (breast cancer) significantly greater than those of both heuristic search techniques. For two of the five data sets the mean computation time for Class was actually significantly less than that for either of the heuristic search covering algorithms. That is, Class, performing repeated search, each time finding a solution that maximised the evaluation function, did so in less time than the heuristic search techniques took to find a solution.

The highest computation time for Class is recorded for the breast cancer data. One possible contributing factor to this effect is that this data has the highest mean number of values per attribute. In consequence, each specialisation step will, on average, alter the proportion of objects covered by the least amount. To illustrate this effect, consider specialisation on an attribute with two values. Specialisation to exclude one value will, on average, reduce the cover of a description by half. By contrast, if an attribute has ten mutually exclusive values, then specialisation by one value will, on average, reduce the cover by only one tenth. With a smaller effect of specialisation, it is likely to be less apparent whether or not one such specialisation leads to an optimum solution.

The mean value of the first rule developed for each class provides a measure of the relative performance of the covering algorithms on the same search task. (Once the first rule has been developed, cases are deleted from the training set, altering the potential value that can be achieved.)While the values of the classifiers found by the heuristic search algorithms are in many cases significantly lower than the actual maxima (found by Class), the magnitude of these differences is small. The mean value of all rules shows that maximising the value of the first rule will often lead to the development of subsequent rules with lower value. There appears to be a correspondence between the number of rules developed and the mean value of the rules. In general, a larger number of rules co-occurs with in a lower mean value. There appears to be little correlation between the mean value of the rules and the mean accuracy.

There is no apparent pattern to the relative complexities of the rule sets produced by the three covering algorithms.

Conclusion

Class is a data driven induction algorithm that performs systematic search to find a class description that maximises a classifier evaluation function. Although the worst case complexity of the algorithm is exponential, the performance of an implementation of this algorithm on real world data exhibits quite adequate performance, and, indeed, in many cases outperforms common heuristic search algorithms.

Comparative evaluation of the classifiers developed using systematic and heuristic search with the Laplace classifier evaluation function, demonstrates that, in most cases, maximisation of Laplace actually leads to a decrease in classification performance. This strongly suggests that the Laplace classifier evaluation function interacts with heuristic search algorithms to form implicit evaluation functions that outperform the explicit Laplace function when evaluating disjuncts within a covering algorithm. Explicit representation of such implicit evaluation functions presents a challenge for future machine learning research.

Acknowledgments

This research was supported by the Australian Research Council. Fred Brkich, Doug Newlands and Ross Quinlan made many helpful comments on drafts of this paper.

References

1. Michalski, R. S. (1980) Pattern recognition as rule-guided inductive inference. IEEE Transactions on Pattern Recognition and Machine Intelligence, 2, 349-361.

2. Clark, P. & Niblett, T. (1989) The CN2 induction algorithm. Machine Learning, 3, 261-284.

3. Muggleton, S. & Feng, S. (1990). Efficient induction of logic programs In Proceedings of the First Conference on Algorithmic Learning Theory, Tokyo.

4. Quinlan, J. R. (1991) Determinate Literals in Inductive Logic Programming. Proceedings of the Twelfth International Joint Conference on Artificial Intelligence, Morgan Kauffman, Los Altos, pp. 746-750.

5. Webb, G. (1990) Techniques for efficient empirical induction. In C. J. Barter & M. J. Brooks (Eds) *AI '88*. Springer-Verlag, Berlin, pp. 225–239.

6. Rymon, R. An SE-tree based characterization of the induction problem. *Proceedings of the 1993 International Conference on Machine Learning*.

7. Schlimmer, J. C. (1983) Efficiently inducing determinations: A complete and systematic search algorithm that uses optimal pruning. *Proceedings of the 1993 International Conference on Machine Learning*.

8. Clark, P. & Boswell, R. (1991) Rule induction with CN2: some recent improvements. In *Proceedings of the Fifth European Working Session on Learning*, pp. 151-163.

9. Murphy, P. & Aha, D. (1993). *UCI Repository of machine learning databases*. [Machine-readable data repository]. University of California, Department of Information and Computer Science, Irvine, CA.

10. Webb, G. (1992) Man-machine collaboration for knowledge acquisition. In A. Adams & L. Sterling (Eds) *AI '92*. World Scientific, Singapore, pp. 329–334.

11. Webb, G. (1993) *Search strategies for induction by generalization*. Technical Report TR C93/03 Deakin University School of Computing and Mathematics, 13pp.

The BBG Rule Induction Algorithm

Kevin S. Van Horn and Tony R. Martinez
Computer Science Department, Brigham Young University
Provo, UT 84602 U.S.A.

Abstract: We present an algorithm (BBG) for inductive learning from examples that outputs a rule list. BBG uses a combination of greedy and branch-and-bound techniques, and naturally handles noisy or stochastic learning situations. We also present the results of an empirical study comparing BBG with Quinlan's C4.5 on 1050 synthetic data sets. We find that BBG greatly outperforms C4.5 on rule-oriented problems, and equals or exceeds C4.5's performance on tree-oriented problems.

1 Background

BBG is an algorithm for learning to classify vectors of binary attributes. (It is straightforward to extend it to arbitrary nominal attributes.[7]) BBG outputs a rule list, i.e. an ordered list of if-then rules which are tried in order until one is found that applies. In this section we introduce the basic concepts and vocabulary relevant to BBG.

An *example* is a pair $(\mathbf{x}, c)$, where $\mathbf{x} \in X = \{0,1\}^n$ and $c \in C$ for some fixed n and finite set of *classes* C. A *hypothesis* is a function $h : X \to C$. We say that h *misclassifies* an example $(\mathbf{x}, c)$ if $h(\mathbf{x}) \neq c$.

A *rule* is a pair $(\mathbf{t}, c)$, where $c \in C$ and $\mathbf{t} \in \{-,0,1\}^n$; $\mathbf{t}$ is called the rule's *precondition*. We say that a vector $\mathbf{x}$ (or example $(\mathbf{x}, c)$) *matches* $\mathbf{t}$ (or rule $(\mathbf{t}, c')$) if $x_i = t_i$ whenever t_i is not $-$. The *size* of a rule $(\mathbf{t}, c)$, written $\mathrm{siz}(\mathbf{t}, c)$, is one plus the number of 0's and 1's in $\mathbf{t}$.

A *rule list* is a list of rules $(\mathbf{t}_1, c_1) \cdots (\mathbf{t}_k, c_k)$, with $\mathbf{t}_k = \mathbf{true}$ (the vector of all $-$'s). It represents the hypothesis h such that $h(\mathbf{x}) = c_i$, where $(\mathbf{t}_i, c_i)$ is the first rule that $\mathbf{x}$ matches. The *size* of a rule list is the sum of the sizes of its rules, i.e. the number of rules plus the total number of literals appearing in rules.

BBG takes as input a collection of examples called the *training sample*, which are presumed to be drawn independently and randomly from some unknown probability distribution $\mathcal{D}$ over $X \times C$. Note that this implies that the relationship between a vector $\mathbf{x}$ and its class c is in general a stochastic one, and not necessarily deterministic.

The *error* of a hypothesis h is the probability that $h(\mathbf{x}) \neq c$ when $(\mathbf{x}, c)$ is drawn at random from the same distribution $\mathcal{D}$ from which the training sample was drawn. The *empirical error* of a hypothesis h is $\mathrm{err}(h, S)/|S|$, where S is the training sample and $\mathrm{err}(h, S)$ is the number of training examples misclassified by h.

2 Outline of the Algorithm

The BBG algorithm consists of two parts:

1. An algorithm G which produces a sequence of rule lists of increasing size and decreasing empirical error.
2. A method for trading off empirical error and complexity to choose one of the rule lists output by G. (There is a tendency to fit noise or statistical flukes of the data when excessively complex hypotheses are allowed.[1,8])

These two parts are entirely independent. The literature contains various methods for the second part: cross-validation,[2] hold-out sets,[3] the minimum description-length principle,[6] structural risk minimization,[8] and heuristic error estimates.[5] BBG uses a heuristic error estimate described in a separate paper.[7] This paper concentrates on algorithm G, which is outlined below:

$i := 0$
$h_0 := h :=$ the single rule $(\textbf{true}, c)$, where c is the most common class in S
while $(\text{err}(h, S) > 0)$
  $(\mathbf{t}, c, p) := \text{bestRule}(h, S)$
  insert rule $(\mathbf{t}, c)$ into h just before its p-th rule
  $i := i + 1;\ h_i := h$

S is the training sample, and $h_0, h_1, \ldots$ is the output. The procedure bestRule() tries to find a rule $(\mathbf{t}, c)$ and position p maximizing the ratio (decrease in empirical error) / (rule size). We call this the *gain-cost ratio* of $(\mathbf{t}, c, p)$.

3 Finding the Best Rule to Insert

The difficult part, of course, is implementing bestRule(). We use a branch-and-bound algorithm with memory and time limits, which cannot guarantee optimality, but usually produces optimal or near-optimal results.

Branch-and-bound algorithms explore a search tree, the nodes of which correspond to sets of possible solutions, and the leaves of which are single solutions. The children of a node comprise a partition of the set of solutions represented by the node. The goal is to find a solution y maximizing $\phi(y)$, for some given function ϕ. When a node z is reached one computes an upper bound u on the value of ϕ for leaf nodes descended from z; if u is no greater than $\phi(y^\star)$ for the best solution $y^\star$ found so far, there is no need to explore the subtree rooted at z.

3.1 Preliminaries

For our purposes a node is a tuple $(\mathbf{v}, c, p)$, where $\mathbf{v} \in \{*, -, 0, 1\}^n$, $c \in C$, and p is a position to insert a rule. If $\mathbf{v}$ has no $*$ (undetermined) entries then the node is a leaf, otherwise its children are obtained by choosing one index i for which $v_i = *$ and setting v_i to $-$, 0, or 1. We say that the node is *expanded on variable i*.

If $z = (\mathbf{v}, c, p)$ is a leaf node then $(\mathbf{v}, c)$ is a rule. If z is not a leaf node but $y = (\mathbf{t}, c, p)$ *is* a leaf node, then y is a descendant of z in the search tree if and only if $\mathbf{t}$ may be obtained from $\mathbf{v}$ by replacing each $*$ entry with $-$, 0, or 1; this holds regardless of the method for choosing the variable on which to expand a node.

We write solns(z) for the set of all leaf nodes descended from z. We define $z^\circ = (\mathbf{t}, c, p)$, where $\mathbf{t}$ is obtained from $\mathbf{v}$ by replacing each $*$ entry with $-$. We write solns$^\circ(z)$ for solns$(z) - \{z^\circ\}$. As will be seen, considering z° separately allows us to obtain a tighter upper bound on the gain-cost ratio.

Associated with bestRule() are constants μ (a memory bound) and τ (a time bound). It also uses variables Z (the collection of unexpanded nodes, with some associated information), N (the number of nodes evaluated so far), $g^\star$ (the gain-cost ratio of the best solution found so far), and $y^\star$ (the best solution found so far).

3.2 The Branch-and-bound Algorithm

Letting $\boldsymbol{*} = (*, \ldots, *)$, here is the algorithm for bestRule(h, S):

```
Z := ∅; N := 0; g* := 0
initialize information needed by eval(), using h and S
for (each class c and position p)
    z := (*, c, p)
    (u, j) := eval(z)
    insert(u, j, z, Z)
while (Z ≠ ∅ and N < τ)
    (u, j, z) := remove from Z its best element
    while (u > g*)
        let (v, c, p) = z
        (z0, z1, z2) := children of z obtained by setting v_j to -, 1, and 0
        for (i := 0 to 2) (u_i, j_i) := eval(z_i)
        if (u1 > u2) swap (u1, j1, z1) and (u2, j2, z2)
        for (i := 0 to 1) insert(u_i, j_i, z_i, Z)
        (u, j, z) := (u2, j2, z2)
return y*
```

The procedure insert(u, j, z, Z) adds (u, j, z) to the collection Z if $u > g^\star$ and either (1) $|Z| < \mu$ (the memory bound has not been reached), or (2) (u, j, z) is better than the worst element w of Z (in which case w is removed to make room for (u, j, z)). We consider (u, j, z) to be better than (u', j', z') if $u > u'$ (it has a better upper bound) or $u = u'$ and z contains fewer $*$'s than z' (z is closer to a leaf node than z').

The procedure eval(z) does the following:

1. It increments N, the number of nodes evaluated.
2. It computes an upper bound u on the gain-cost ratio for elements of solns$^\circ(z)$ (see Section 3.3). If z is a leaf node then solns$^\circ(z)$ is empty, so it sets $u = 0$.
3. As a side-effect of the upper-bound computation it produces two more values: the variable j on which the node is to be expanded, and the gain-cost ratio g of the solution z°. If $g > g^\star$, then it sets $g^\star$ to g and $y^\star$ to z°.
4. The procedure returns (u, j) as its result.

Note that bestRule() uses a combination of best-first search and depth-first search: it repeatedly removes the most promising node from Z and explores a linear path down from the node. As each node z is reached the solution z° is considered and evaluated. No leaf is ever expanded because the upper bound $u = 0$ associated with it is never more than $g^\star$.

3.3 Computing the Upper Bound

We now give the details of steps 2 and 3 of eval(). Let us define the following:

- $\Delta(y) = \text{err}(h, S) - \text{err}(h', S)$, where $y = (\mathbf{t}, c, p)$ is a leaf and h' is obtained from h by inserting the rule $(\mathbf{t}, c)$ at position p.
- $\text{msiz}(z) = \text{siz}(\mathbf{t}, c)$, where $z^\circ = (\mathbf{t}, c, p)$. Note that $\text{msiz}(z) \leq \text{msiz}(y)$ for any $y \in \text{solns}(z)$.

The gain-cost ratio of a leaf y is just $\Delta(y)/\text{msiz}(y)$. Thus if δ is an upper bound on $\Delta(y)$ for $y \in \text{solns}^\circ(z)$ then $\delta/\text{msiz}(z)$ is an upper bound on the gain-cost ratio for elements of $\text{solns}^\circ(z)$.

Let us consider the computation of $\Delta(\mathbf{t}, c, p)$. We define the following:

- S_p = those examples in S that match none of the first $p - 1$ rules of h.
- $S_p^{\mathbf{t}}$ = those examples in S_p that match $\mathbf{t}$.
- $G(\mathbf{t}, c, p)$ = those examples $(\mathbf{x}, c')$ in $S_p^{\mathbf{t}}$ for which $c' = c$ and $h(\mathbf{x}) \neq c'$; $G(z) = G(z^\circ)$ if z is a non-leaf node.
- $B(\mathbf{t}, c, p)$ = those examples $(\mathbf{x}, c')$ in $S_p^{\mathbf{t}}$ for which $c' \neq c$ and $h(\mathbf{x}) = c'$.

$G(\mathbf{t}, c, p)$ is the collection of previously *misclassified* examples which are *correctly classified* after inserting rule $(\mathbf{t}, c)$ at position p. $B(\mathbf{t}, c, p)$ is the collection of previously *correctly-classified examples* which are *misclassified* after inserting the new rule. Then $\Delta(\mathbf{t}, c, p) = |G(\mathbf{t}, c, p)| - |B(\mathbf{t}, c, p)|$, i.e. the number of old errors corrected minus the number of new errors introduced.

Let $y = (\mathbf{t}', c, p) \in \text{solns}^\circ(z)$ and $z^\circ = (\mathbf{t}, c, p)$. Then $S_p^{\mathbf{t}'} \subseteq S_p^{\mathbf{t}}$ (since $t_i' = t_i$ whenever t_i is not -), hence $G(y) \subseteq G(z^\circ) = G(z)$. Then $|G(z)| \geq |G(y)| \geq \Delta(y)$ for every $y \in \text{solns}^\circ(z)$, and we obtain $|G(z)|/\text{msiz}(z)$ as an upper bound on the gain-cost ratio for elements of $\text{solns}^\circ(z)$.

We can improve this bound without increasing the asymptotic time complexity of eval(z), at the same time computing the gain-cost ratio of z° and identifying a promising variable on which to expand z. BestRule() precomputes the various S_p by ordering the examples in S according to the first rule in h which they match, and computing for each p the index $f[p]$ of the first example matching none of the first $p - 1$ rules of h. If there are m examples then S_p is just $S[f[p]]$ through $S[m]$. BestRule() also precomputes an array K such that $K[i] = h(\mathbf{x})$, where $(\mathbf{x}, c')$ is the i-th example. Letting $z = (\mathbf{v}, c, p)$ and $z^\circ = (\mathbf{t}, c, p)$, $|G(z)|$ is computed by stepping through the examples $S[f[p]]$ through $S[m]$, checking to see if each example $S[i] = (\mathbf{x}, c')$ matches $\mathbf{t}$, and if so, comparing c' to $K[i]$ and c to determine if $S[i] \in G(z)$. This test of example i takes $\Theta(n)$ worst-case time. In $\Theta(1)$ additional time eval() determines if $S[i] \in B(z^\circ)$; summing over the examples this gives $|B(z^\circ)|$, which combined with $|G(z)| = |G(z^\circ)|$ and msiz(z°) gives the gain-cost ratio for z°.

Eval() also use counters $\kappa[i, b]$ ($1 \le i \le n$, $b \in \{0, 1\}$) initialized to 0. Once an example $(\mathbf{x}, c')$ has been identified as an element of $G(z)$, eval() uses $\Theta(n)$ time to step through the entries of $\mathbf{x}$, incrementing $\kappa[i, x_i]$ whenever $v_i = *$. This does not increase the asymptotic time complexity. Let $z[i : b]$ be the possible child of z obtained by replacing v_i with b. Then after all the examples in S_p have been processed we have $\kappa[i, b] = |G(z[i : b])|$ for all i such that $v_i = *$. Since msiz$(z[i : b]) =$ msiz$(z) + 1$, we then have $\kappa[i, b]/(\text{msiz}(z) + 1)$ as an upper bound on the gain-cost ratio for elements of solns$(z[i : b])$. Taking the maximum over $b \in \{0, 1\}$ and all i for which $v_i = *$ gives an upper bound on the gain-cost ratio for elements of solns$^\circ(z)$. Furthermore, the i which attains this maximum is an obvious choice for the variable on which to expand z in order to quickly reach a good solution in the depth-first part of our search.

Putting all of this together gives the following algorithm for steps 2 and 3 of eval():

```
let (v, c, p) = z and (t, c, p) = z°
γ := 0; β := 0; d := 0
init all κ[i, b] to 0
for (j := f[p] to m) if (S[j] matches t)
    let (x, c') = S[j]
    if (c' ≠ c and c' = K[j]) increment β          — S[j] ∈ B(z°)
    if (c' = c and c' ≠ K[j])                     — S[j] ∈ G(z°)
        increment γ
        for (i := 1 to n) if (v_i = *) increment κ[i, x_i]
g := (γ − β)/msiz(z°)                              — gain-cost ratio of z°
for (i := 1 to n and b := 0 to 1) if (κ[i, b] > d)
    d := κ[i, b]; j := i
u := d/(msiz(z) + 1)
```

4 Experimental Results

We tested BBG on 1050 synthetic data sets. We wanted to compare its performance on the same data sets with that of some well-respected and widely-known learning algorithm; for this purpose we chose Quinlan's C4.5. We compiled the code that came with his book[5] on DECstation 5000's and HP 710's. Since C4.5 can produce either decision trees (the c4.5 program) or rule lists (the c4.5rules program), we tested both alternatives. The default parameters were always used with these programs. Each data set consisted of 500 training examples and 30000 test examples for estimating the actual error of the hypothesis output by a learning algorithm.

For BBG we set the memory limit μ and time limit τ as follows. Let m be the number of examples (500) and n the number of Boolean attributes. For the 500 data

Table 1: Comparison of BBG and C4.5 on rule-oriented problems

l	r	n	k	η	BBG	c4.5	c4.5rules
29	12	38	3	0.03	4.85 ± 0.84	14.31 ± 1.65	13.15 ± 1.43
32	9	38	5	0.02	3.38 ± 0.51	15.58 ± 2.13	13.14 ± 1.70
30	11	45	5	0	0.45 ± 0.26	11.86 ± 1.64	8.75 ± 1.70
34	7	50	4	0.04	7.56 ± 0.77	20.78 ± 2.32	20.78 ± 2.14
34	7	52	2	0.05	9.05 ± 1.01	17.22 ± 1.50	16.49 ± 1.37
30	11	54	6	0	0.58 ± 0.30	13.15 ± 1.84	9.88 ± 1.57
32	9	61	4	0.02	4.19 ± 0.82	16.69 ± 1.69	15.18 ± 1.71
36	5	64	3	0.05	11.21 ± 0.93	17.96 ± 1.30	19.38 ± 1.29
31	10	67	3	0.04	6.97 ± 0.80	20.70 ± 2.06	19.07 ± 2.04
28	13	79	2	0.02	6.36 ± 1.02	12.75 ± 1.63	11.66 ± 1.52

sets summarized in Table 1 we set μ to $2mn$. For the 550 data sets summarized in Table 2 we set μ to $\max(50000, 2mn)$. In both cases we set τ to $\max(250000, 10mn)$. Typical execution times on an HP 710 workstation were around 25 minutes.

The data sets were produced using two problem generators, rgenex and tgenex. These generators take the parameters n, k (number of classes), η (noise level), m, and m'. Rgenex takes additional parameters r and l, and tgenex takes the additional parameter s. Rgenex and tgenex work as follows:

1. A *target* h is randomly generated. For rgenex h is a rule list having r non-default rules and size $r + l + 1$. In addition, each class c appears in approximately $(r + 1)/k$ rules and h has no superfluous rules (rules matched only when some preceding rule is also matched.) For tgenex h is a decision tree having s leaf nodes, with no class labeling more than twice as many leaf nodes as any other class. In both cases we have n binary attributes and k classes.
2. A probability distribution $\mathcal{D}$ over $\{0, 1\}^n$ is constructed. For rgenex each of the rules is equally often the first matched, and for tgenex the s leaf nodes are equally often reached. The distribution "within" each rule / leaf is uniform.
3. m training examples and m' testing examples $(\mathbf{x}, c)$ are generated. First, $\mathbf{x}$ is randomly selected from $\mathcal{D}$. Then with probability $1 - \eta$ we set $c = h(\mathbf{x})$, and with probability η we set $c = d$ for some class $d \neq h(\mathbf{x})$ chosen uniformly and randomly. This gives a uniform noise level of η.

Complete details on rgenex and tgenex are in another paper.[7]

For any fixed setting of the parameters to rgenex and tgenex one can investigate the expected error of a learning algorithm by generating a series of data sets using these parameters, running the algorithm on the training samples and averaging the resultant error rates on the test samples. We generated 50 data sets for each parameter setting investigated, in order to get a good estimate of the expected error rate, and also calculated 95% confidence intervals. Note that the target h has an error of η, which is the minimum possible error.

Table 2: Comparison of BBG and C4.5 on tree-oriented problems

s	n	k	η	BBG	c4.5	c4.5rules
20	38	3	0.03	5.33 ± 0.56	14.27 ± 1.93	8.58 ± 1.23
20	38	5	0.02	2.69 ± 0.28	5.56 ± 1.08	3.56 ± 0.60
20	45	5	0	0.58 ± 0.32	4.46 ± 1.28	0.67 ± 0.22
20	50	4	0.04	5.43 ± 0.49	11.76 ± 1.64	8.56 ± 1.00
20	52	2	0.05	15.69 ± 1.90	30.14 ± 2.13	28.53 ± 2.44
20	54	6	0	0.76 ± 0.43	2.39 ± 0.77	0.59 ± 0.18
20	61	4	0.02	3.77 ± 0.54	10.78 ± 2.18	5.91 ± 1.35
20	64	3	0.05	9.68 ± 0.96	22.61 ± 2.86	18.08 ± 2.58
20	67	3	0.04	8.66 ± 1.36	20.87 ± 2.49	14.90 ± 1.98
20	79	2	0.02	14.95 ± 2.63	30.74 ± 2.43	27.93 ± 3.03
20	50	2	0	3.33 ± 0.93	24.64 ± 2.34	18.04 ± 2.59

We first compared BBG and C4.5 for 10 different parameter settings of rgenex randomly chosen subject to $r + l = 41$. The results are summarized in Table 1, where the columns labeled BBG, c4.5 and c4.5rules give the average error of the three learning algorithms (in percent). For each of the ten settings of parameter values, BBG outperforms both c4.5 and c4.5rules by wide margins.

We next compared BBG and C4.5 for 11 different parameter settings of tgenex. We set $s = 20$ in all cases and, except for the eleventh parameter setting, kept the same values for n, k, and η as used for rgenex.

The results are summarized in Table 2. In each case the average performance of BBG exceeds that of c4.5 and either is very close to or exceeds that of c4.5rules. BBG's performance advantage is greater when there are few classes, and is quite striking when $k = 2$ and $\eta = 0$ (the last case).

Next we compared BBG and C4.5 on four data sets from the UC Irvine machine learning repository:[4] chess, tic-tac-toe, mushroom, and zoo. All of these have only nominal attributes. We made a minor modification to BBG to handle non-binary attributes, described elsewhere.[7] We handled unknown attribute values by having BBG treat "unknown" as just another possible attribute value.

We randomly partitioned the mushroom data set into 200 training examples and 7924 test examples (the problem is too easy if we use more training examples). Each of the other data sets was randomly partitioned into 10 nearly-equal parts and the learning algorithms run 10 times, each time choosing one part as the test sample and the remaining data as the training sample; the errors were averaged. Table 3 contains the results, with m, n and k having the same meaning as before, and error rates in percent. BBG used $\mu = 50000$ and $\tau = 250000$ in all cases.

Though not bad, these last results are a bit disappointing. This may simply be due to chance, given the small number of data sets, but there is another possibility. Our analysis of bestRule() reveals that that if there are strong correlations between

Table 3: Comparison of BBG and C4.5 on some UCI repository data sets

Data Set	m	n	k	BBG	c4.5	c4.5rules
chess	3196	36	2	0.97	0.47	0.44
tic-tac-toe	958	9	2	1.15	14.61	1.04
mushroom	200	22	2	1.72	1.49	1.11
zoo	90	16	7	6.67	10.0	10.0

attributes, *and these correlations are independent of class*, BBG's branch-and-bound search could be led down unproductive paths. While such correlations would be uncommon in our synthetic data sets, they might be much more common in real-world data sets.

5 Conclusions and Directions for Further Research

Our results indicate considerable promise for BBG, although the matter of correlated attributes needs to be addressed; this can be investigated with more sophisticated problem generators. Further research will look at other implementations of bestRule() intended to be more robust and able to handle real-valued attributes and internal disjunction for nominal attributes.

References

[1] A. Blumer et al. (1989.) Learnability and the Vapnik-Chervonenkis dimension. *Journal of the ACM* 36, 929–965.

[2] L. Breiman et al. (1984.) *Classification and Regression Trees.* Belmont, CA: Wadsworth.

[3] L. Devroye (1988.) Automatic pattern recognition: a study of the probability of error. *IEEE Transactions on Pattern Analysis and Machine Intelligence* 10, 530–543.

[4] P. M. Murphy & D. W. Aha (1992.) *UCI Repository of machine learning databases.* Irvine, CA: University of California at Irvine, Dept. of Information and Computer Sciences.

[5] J. R. Quinlan (1993.) *C4.5: Programs for Machine Learning.* San Mateo, CA: Morgan Kaufmann.

[6] J. R. Quinlan & R. L. Rivest (1989.) Inferring decision trees using the Minimum Description Length Principle. *Information and Computation* 80, 227–248.

[7] K. S. Van Horn & T. R. Martinez (1993.) The Design and Evaluation of a Rule Induction Algorithm. Technical Report BYU-CS-93-11, Computer Science Department, Brigham Young University.

[8] V. N. Vapnik (1982.) *Estimation of Dependences Based on Empirical Data.* New York: Springer-Verlag.

The Potential of Prototype Styles of Generalization†

D. Randall Wilson
Tony R. Martinez

Computer Science Department, Brigham Young University, Provo, Utah 84602
e-mail: randy@axon.cs.byu.edu, martinez@cs.byu.edu

Abstract. There are many ways for a learning system to generalize from training set data. This paper presents several generalization styles using prototypes in an attempt to provide accurate generalization on training set data for a wide variety of applications. These generalization styles are efficient in terms of time and space, and lend themselves well to massively parallel architectures. Empirical results of generalizing on several real-world applications are given, and these results indicate that the prototype styles of generalization presented have potential to provide accurate generalization for many applications.

1. Introduction

There are many ways for a learning system to generalize from training set data. This paper proposes several generalization styles using prototypes in an attempt to provide accurate generalization on training set data for a wide variety of applications. These generalization styles are efficient in terms of time and space, and lend themselves well to massively parallel architectures.

Traditional computer programming requires the programmer to explicitly define what the computer should do given any particular input. Even expert systems depend on the knowledge of experts in the field and their ability to explain how they make their decisions. When a solid knowledge of the application domain is available, this process has often worked quite well. In some applications, however, there is not enough known about the subject to derive a formula or write a program to solve the problem.

In such cases, it is often possible to collect a set of examples of what the output of the system should be in specific situations. Each such example is called an *instance*, and usually consists of a vector of input values (the *inputs*) representing certain features of the environment, as well as the value(s) that the system should output in response to these input values (the *output*). A collection of such instances is called a *training set*.

Neural networks[1,2,3] provide one way to learn by example. That is, given a training set of instances, they can often "learn" the relationship between the inputs and outputs well enough to be able to receive an input and produce the correct output with a high probability, even if that input did not appear in the training set. This ability is called *generalization*.

Some styles of neural networks which have been successful in accurately learning to generalize from a training set, such as the backpropagation network[4], have required many iterations through the learning algorithm to solve the problem, and thus have not always been able to solve problems in an acceptable amount of time. In addition, they often suffer from problems of getting stuck in a local minima, so several runs of the algorithm are often necessary.

Some machine learning techniques attempt to generalize from training set data as well, but they often suffer from the problems of exponential search times and/or exponential storage requirements.

---

† This research was supported in part by grants from Novell, Inc., and WordPerfect Corporation.

The ASOCS (Adaptive Self-Organizing Concurrent System) model[5,6,7] has the attractive feature of fast (one-shot) learning. It also lends itself to simple hierarchical architectures which can be efficiently implemented in hardware[8]. These features make it attractive for solving large problems very quickly, without hardware constraints.

The ASOCS models, however, expect rule-based instances rather than training set data. In addition, some ASOCS models do not perform much generalization by themselves.

The research presented in this paper began with the goal of extending ASOCS models to perform generalization on training set data. It makes use of several generalization styles in an attempt to provide accurate generalization which is efficient in terms of time and space, and which lends itself well to simple parallel architectures.

In section 2, the styles of generalization studied in this research are presented, along with several extensions of each. Section 3 gives empirical results of simulations run on a variety of applications using each of these generalization styles, and gives a preliminary analysis of these results. Section 4 provides conclusions and future research areas.

2. Prototype Styles of Generalization

The research presented in this paper makes use of several generalization styles which use prototypes in an attempt to provide accurate generalization in an efficient and potentially parallel manner. *Prototypes* are similar to instances in the training set, but may represent several instances with the same output, and can have additional features. When prototypes are used, they are compared with new inputs to determine the output. In such approaches, generalization styles determine both how the prototypes are created and how they are used. In this research prototypes consist of:

- A vector of input values representing features in the environment (*inputs*) and one or more output values, representing the supposedly correct response of the system to the input values (*output*).
- A *count* of how many instances the prototype represents,
- A count of how many instances with the same inputs had different outputs (the *conflict*),
- A ratio of *count* to *total*, where *total* = *count* + *conflict*. This gives a probability that the inputs of the prototype should map to its output(s), and is called the *integrity*.

Figure 1, below, illustrates an typical instance in a training set and a prototype.

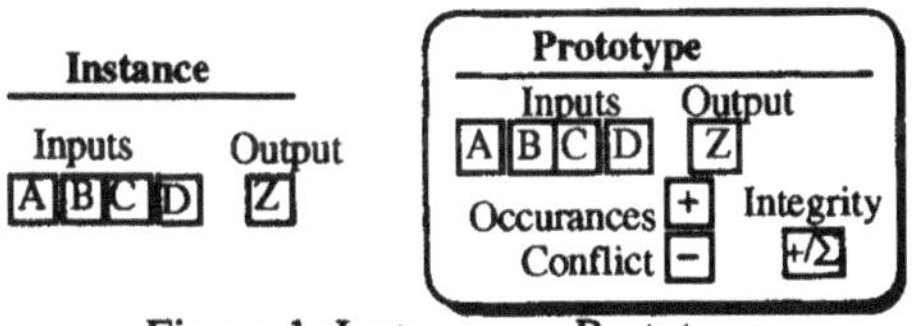

Figure 1. Instance vs. Prototype

The styles of generalization presented in this paper have several attractive features:

- They can learn a training set quickly (usually in O(n) or O($nlogn$) time),
- They are simple and intuitive,
- They lend themselves well to massively parallel architectures (e.g. a binary tree)
- They do not suffer from exponential storage or processing problems.

On the other hand, they do store most of the instances in the training set, which can be sizable for large training sets, and because they do not throw away any information, they may "overlearn" the training set instead of picking out only the most relevant attributes of an application. This can result in a susceptibility to noise and reduced generalization.

Several styles of generalization were used in this research, among which were several distance metrics, and some critical variable detection algorithms, along with voting schemes to enhance each of these. These styles are discussed in sections 2.1 and 2.2 below.

2.1. Distance Metrics

Distance metrics are used to find out which prototype or prototypes are "closest" to the new input in question. The output value of the closest prototype or group of prototypes is used for the output value in response to the new input. There are several ways of determining how "close" an input is to one of the prototypes.

Hamming distance. Hamming distance is an intuitive metric, and is simply the number of input variables which do not match the prototype. The prototype with the least number of mismatched variables wins using this metric.

State difference. In multi-state variables where the states represent a linear value, the closeness of the state number itself may help indicate the "distance" of an input variable to a variable in an instance. Thus, a sum of the (absolute) differences of the inputs of the prototype from the inputs of the new input can be used as a measure of closeness.

Dividing by number of states. An extension of the State Distance scheme is to divide the state difference for each variable by the number of states that that variable can have, in order to normalize the distance measures. This can be done for Hamming distance as well.

Euclidean distance. Euclidean distance is similar to the State Difference scheme, except that the individual distances are squared before they are summed.

As an example, consider a training set with four input variables, the first three of which are Boolean, and the last of which is a 10-state variable (with values 0 through 9). If a prototype with input values 0, 0, 1, and 5, respectively, was compared to the input 0, 1, 1, 1, the distance metrics mentioned above would be computed as shown in Figure 2.

Variable Name:	A	B	C	D		Out
Number of States:	2	2	2	10		2
Prototype:	0	0	1	5	->	1
New input to be classified:	0	1	1	1	->	?

Distance Metric		Distance
1. Hamming Distance:	0+1 +0+1	= 2
2. Hamming/No. of States:	0+1/2+0+1/10	= 0.6
3. State Difference:	0+1 +0+4	= 5
4. State Diff/Num States:	0+1/2+0+4/10	= 0.9
5. Euclidean Distance:	0+1 +0+16	= 17

Figure 2. Results of various distance metrics (from example 1).

Voting. Regardless of the distance metric used, there will often be several prototypes which are the same "distance" from the new input. Instead of arbitrarily choosing one of the several equally close prototypes to be the winner, the prototypes can vote for their output. One way to do this is to let each of these prototypes cast a number of votes equal to its *count*, since prototypes may represent several instances.

2.2. Critical Features.

One way to determine which variables are most important is to find those which tend to have a strong correlation with an output value. In order to discover critical variables, a new kind of prototype called a *first-order feature* is created for each input variable of each instance. Each feature has only the output and one input variable asserted, and the rest of the input variables are "don't care" variables (denoted by an asterisk, "*").

It is possible to use combinations of variables instead of only one variable at a time and thus create higher-order features, but such methods run into exponential factors in both storage and computation time, and are thus not pursued in this research. The term *feature* will therefore be used to mean first-order feature.

As an example, the instance "0 0 1 5 -> 1", would result in the following four first-order features: "0***->1", "*0**->1", "**1*->1", and "***5->1". If any of these features already existed in the system, the new one would be discarded, and the old one's *count* would be incremented and its *integrity* recomputed. If any features existed which had the same input but a different output (e.g., 0 * * * -> 0), then both features would increment their *conflict* and recompute their *integrity*. The first few instances in the training set will probably add quite a few features to the system, but later instances will usually find matches for most of the features they try to add.

During generalization, a feature is said to *match* the input if the variable which is asserted matches the corresponding variable in the input. The other "don't care" variables are always considered to match.

In Figure 3, a few instances from a training set are listed, along with the features that would be generated for the first and second variables. Note that the conflict field is simply the sum of the counts of all other prototypes with the same inputs.

A B C D	-> Out	A B C D	-> Out	Count	Conflict	Integrity
0 1 1 3	0	0 * * *	0	1	3	1/4=.25
0 0 0 0	1	0 * * *	1	3	1	3/4=.75
0 0 1 0	1	1 * * *	0	1	1	1/2=.50
0 1 1 5	1	1 * * *	1	1	1	1/2=.50
1 1 0 1	0	* 0 * *	1	3	0	3/3=1.0
1 0 1 0	1	* 1 * *	0	2	1	2/3=.66
⋮		* 1 * *	1	1	3	1/3=.33
		⋮				

Figure 3. Features generated from instances.

There are several ways to use these prototypes for generalization. One is to select the one very best feature that matches the input and use its output. The "best" feature can be either the one with the highest *count* (meaning it occurred most often), or the one with the highest *integrity* (meaning it was relatively undisputed). Another method is to select the best feature for each input variable, and let these vote on the output. A third method is to allow all matching features to vote for the output they want. In each case, a feature's voting power equals its *count*, which is the number of instances it represents.

	A B C D	-> Out	Count	Conflict	Integrity
1.	0 * * *	-> 0	1	3	.25
2.	**0 * * ***	**-> 1**	3	1	.75
3.	*** 1 * ***	**-> 0**	2	1	.66
4.	* 1 * *	-> 1	1	2	.33
5.	* * 1 *	-> 0	1	3	.25
6.	*** * 1 ***	**-> 1**	3	1	.75
7.	*** * * 1**	**-> 0**	1	0	1.0

Figure 4 Features matching an input of "0 1 1 1".

To continue the above example, assume that the rest of the features for the instances listed in Figure 3 were available. Given an input of 0 1 1 1, the features shown in Figure 4 would match the input.

The one with the highest *integrity* is feature 7, which was never contradicted, and it would choose an output of 1. The one with the best *count* is either #2 or #6, both of which also opt for an output of 1.

The features in bold (numbers 2, 3, 6 and 7) are the best in terms of both *integrity* and *count* for the four input variables, respectively. These would cast 2+1=3 votes for an output of 0, and 3+3=6 votes for an output of 1, so 1 would win again in this case.

Finally, if all of these matching features were allowed to vote, an output of 0 would get 1+2+1+1=5 votes, and an output of 1 would get 3+1+3=7 votes. In this example, all of the various styles chose an output of 1, but there are cases in which the styles would pick conflicting outputs.

3. Empirical Results

Each of the generalization styles described above was implemented and tested on several well-known training sets from the repository of Machine Learning Databases at University of California Irvine[9], and the generalization accuracy of each style on each application is given in Table 5. The column labeled "Max" contains the maximum generalization accuracy of any of the styles for each application. The applications are ordered from best to worst in terms of maximum generalization ability.

Table 5. Percentages of Accurate Generalization
("vt"=use voting; "/#st"=divide distance by number of states; "cnt"=count; "int"=integrity)

		Distance Metrics										First-Order Features					
		Hamming Distance				State Distance				Euclid. Dist.		Single best one		Best ones vote		All vote	
				/#st.				/#st.									
Database	**Max**	1st	vt	1st	vt	1st	vt	1st	vt	1st	vt	cnt	int	cnt	int	cnt	int
Soybean (Small)	00	00	100	100	100	100	00	100	100	98	98	36	98	36	64	36	36
Zoo	99	98	97	98	97	99	98	98	98	99	98	41	78	41	62	41	41
Vowel	98	89	91	89	91	97	97	97	97	98	98	40	40	43	34	53	65
Iris	96	91	90	91	90	96	95	96	95	96	95	87	93	92	89	85	90
Segmentation	95	89	90	89	90	94	95	94	95	94	94	28	73	56	62	63	69
House-Votes-84	93	93	93	93	93	93	93	93	93	93	93	76	92	89	83	89	89
Soybean (Large)	93	91	93	90	91	89	87	92	91	87	87	0	58	2	46	29	35
Sonar	88	84	84	84	84	88	87	87	87	88	88	70	70	68	69	70	70
Shuttle-Landing	87	87	87	40	40	87	87	53	53	87	87	53	53	53	53	53	53
Credit-Screening	86	81	81	81	81	76	76	82	82	73	73	56	86	56	66	80	80
Audiology	81	75	77	78	81	68	71	78	78	65	66	24	53	24	44	24	24
Nettalk	77	63	77	63	77	48	59	48	59	42	47	17	42	17	40	19	21
Glass	76	73	74	73	74	74	76	73	76	72	74	37	58	55	44	63	63
Indians-Diabetes	72	64	65	64	65	67	66	67	66	68	68	68	71	65	72	66	66
Hepatitis	70	58	59	61	59	59	60	63	61	60	61	55	69	55	70	58	58
Lung-Cancer	53	38	34	38	34	41	47	41	47	53	41	41	28	41	53	41	41

The results are encouraging, for they suggest that prototype styles of generalization can be effective on many applications, although there were some applications for which none of the styles was able to achieve acceptable generalization.

There are a few interesting things to note from this table. First of all, note that there was no one style which generalized most accurately on all applications. This suggests that by using a collection of simple generalization styles, and by picking the one that did the best on the test set, the best style for a given application can be found[10]. Also note that the distance metric styles of generalization that used voting did as well or better than their corresponding non-voting style in almost every case.

4. Future Research and Conclusions

The results of this research are promising, and suggest that for some applications using prototype styles of generalization can provide efficient and accurate generalization without the need for iteration, numerous "system parameters", exponential searches or storage, and without fear of getting stuck in a local minima. In addition, by using a collection of such generalization styles and picking the one that generalizes most accurately, even greater generalization accuracy can be achieved. There are a variety of simple styles of generalization which can be added to this system's repertoire. Combining styles could be beneficial as well, such as using features to weight the variables when computing distances, or to weight voting power.

Current research is also involved in answering such questions as how to best discretize analog variables, how to handle missing input values, and how to determine which style or styles to use for a given application without testing all instances on all the styles.

The ultimate goal of this research is to build up a good collection of generalization styles and then construct systems which automatically determine the generalization style or styles that work best with any given application, and thus provide fast, accurate solutions to applications for which automated solutions were previously intractable or unknown.

5. Bibliography

1. Lippmann, Richard P., "An Introduction to Computing with Neural Nets," *IEEE ASSP Magazine*, 3, no. 4, April 1987, pp. 4-22.
2. Widrow, Bernard, Rodney Winter, "Neural Nets for Adaptive Filtering and Adaptive Pattern Recognition," *IEEE Computer Magazine*, March 1988, pp. 25-39.
3. Widrow, Bernard, and Michael A. Lehr, "30 Years of Adaptive Neural Networks: Perceptron, Madaline, and Backpropagation," *Proceedings of the IEEE*, 78, no. 9, September 1990, pp. 1415-144.
4. Rumelhart, D. E., and J. L. McClelland, *Parallel Distributed Processing*, MIT Press, Ch. 8, 1986, pp. 318-362.
5. Martinez, Tony R., "Adaptive Self-Organizing Logic Networks," Ph.D. Dissertation, University of California Los Angeles Technical Report - CSD 860093, June, 1986.
6. Martinez, Tony R., Douglas M. Campbell, Brent W. Hughes, "Priority ASOCS," to appear in *Journal of Artificial Neural Networks*.
7. Martinez, Tony R., "Adaptive Self-Organizing Concurrent Systems," *Progress in Neural Networks*, 1, ch. 5, O. Omidvar (Ed), Ablex Publishing, 1990, pp. 105-126.
8. Rudolph, George L., and Tony R. Martinez, "An Efficient Static Topology For Modeling ASOCS," *International Conference on Artificial Neural Networks*, Helsinki, Finland. In *Artificial Neural Networks*, Kohonen, et. al. (Eds), Elsevier Science Publishers, North Holland, 1991, pp. 729-734.
9. Murphy, P. M., and D. W. Aha, *UCI Repository of Machine Learning Databases*. Irvine, CA: University of California Irvine, Department of Information and Computer Science, 1993.
10. Wilson, D. Randall, "The Importance of Using Multiple Styles of Generalization", to appear in *Proceedings of he First New Zealand International Conference on Artificial Neural Networks and Expert Systems—ANNES '93*.

Natural Language

A Propositional Semantic Network with Structured Variables for Natural Language Processing

SYED S. ALI
Department of Computer Science
Southwest Missouri State University
901 South National Avenue
Springfield, MO 65804-0094, USA

ABSTRACT

This paper suggests some goals for knowledge representation for natural language processing: natural form, conceptual completeness, structure sharing. To address these goals, an augmentation to the representation of variables so that variables are not atomic terms is suggested. This leads to an extended, more "natural" representation language whose use and representations are consistent with the use of variables in natural language. It is shown how this representation simplifies the representation and use of complex noun phrases and resolves some representational difficulties with sentences involving nonlinear quantifier scoping, in particular, donkey sentences.

1 Introduction

The intent of the work in this paper is to specify a knowledge representation and reasoning formalism for natural language processing. To this end, I believe the following natural-language-specific goals must be addressed. First, the mapping from natural language sentences into the representation language should be as direct as possible, and the representation should reflect the structure of the natural language (NL) sentence it purports to represent. I call this the "natural form" constraint. This is particularly well illustrated by rule-type sentences, such as *small dogs bite harder than big dogs,* where the representation takes the form of an implication whose antecedent constraints specify what kind of dog bite harder than another type. This representation, as a logical rule, contrasts with the predicate-argument structure of the original sentence, as below:

$$\forall x, y((\text{small}(x) \land \text{dog}(x) \land \text{large}(y) \land \text{dog}(y)) \Rightarrow \text{bites-harder}(x, y)) \tag{1}$$

By comparison, the representation of *Fido bites harder than Rover* is more consistent with the structure of the original sentence,

$$\text{bites-harder}(\text{Fido, Rover}) \tag{2}$$

This is so, despite the intuitive observation that the two sentences have nearly identical syntactic structure, and similar meaning.

Second, the subunits of the representation should be conceptually complete in the sense that any component of the representation of a sentence should have a meaningful interpretation independent of the interpretation of the entire sentence representation. For example, for the representation of the sentence as in (1) above, we might ask what is the meaning of x or y? Presumably, some thing in the world, or a set denoting the non-empty universe. Note that the original sentence mentions only dogs. I suggest that a better translation might be:

$$\text{bites-harder}(\forall x \text{ such that small dog}(x), \forall y \text{ such that large dog}(y))$$

where the variables, x and y, have their own internal structure that reflects their conceptualization. Note that I am suggesting something stronger than just restricted quantification (simple type constraints can certainly be felicitously represented using restricted quantifiers). Complex internalized constraints (that is, other than simple type) and internalized quantifier structures characterize this approach to the representation of variables. Thus the representation of the sentence: *Every small dog that is owned by a bad-tempered person bites harder than a large dog* should reflect the structure of the representation of (2).

Third, a high degree of structure sharing should be possible, as multi-sentence connected discourse often uses reduced forms of previously used terms in subsequent reference to those terms. This corresponds to the use of pronouns and and some forms of ellipsis in discourse. An example of this phenomena is the representation of intersentential pronominal reference to scoped terms, e.g.,

Every apartment had *a dishwasher*. In some of them *it* had just been installed.
Every chess set comes with *a spare pawn*. *It* is taped to the top of the box.

(examples from [7]). The structures that are being shared in these sentences are the variables corresponding to the italicized noun phrases. Logical representations can only model this "sharing" by combining multiple sentences of natural language into one sentence of logic. This method is unnatural for at least two reasons. First, when several sentences must be combined into one sentence the resulting logical sentence, as a conjunction of several potentially disparate sentences, is overly complex. Second, this approach is counter-intuitive in that a language user can re-articulate the original sentences that he/she represents. This argues for some form of separate representations of the original sentences. The problem with logic in this task is that logic requires the complete specification of a variable, corresponding to a noun phrase, and its constraints in the scope of some quantifier. This difficulty is not restricted to noun phrases, indeed it is frequently the case that entire subclauses of sentences are referred to using reduced forms such as "too" e.g.,

John *went to the party*. Mary did, *too*.

A language-motivated knowledge representation formalism should model this sort of reference, minimally by structure sharing.

The *donkey sentences* [6] illustrate the utility of the goals of conceptual completeness and structure sharing. These are sentences that pronominally refer to quantified variables in closed subclauses, for example *Every farmer who owns a donkey beats it* where the noun phrase *a donkey* is a variable inside the scope of a universally quantified variable (*every farmer*) and is referred to pronominally outside the scope of the existentially quantified donkey. Figure 1 has some attempts to represent the above sentence in FOPL.

Representation (a) says that *every* farmer owns a donkey that he beats, which is clearly more than the original sentence intends. Representation (b) is a better attempt, since it captures the notion that we are considering only farmers who own donkeys; however, it contains a free variable. Representation (c) fails to capture the sense of the original sentence in that it quantifies over *all* farmers and donkeys, rather than just farmers that own donkeys. To see this, consider the case of the farmers that own two donkeys and beat only one of them. Clearly, the donkey sentence can apply to this case, but interpretation (c) does not. This is the interpretation I am interested in representing.

Summarizing, I have presented some general arguments for considering the use of a more "natural" (with respect to language) formalism for the repesentation of natural

(a) $\forall x$ (farmer(x) $\Rightarrow$ $\exists y$ (donkey(y) & owns(x,y) & beats(x, y)))
(b) $\forall x$ (farmer(x) $\Rightarrow$ (($\exists y$ donkey(y) & owns(x,y)) $\Rightarrow$ beats(x, y)))
(c) $\forall x$ $\forall y$ ((farmer(x) & donkey(y) & owns(x,y)) $\Rightarrow$ beats(x, y))

Figure 1: Three FOPL Representations of the Donkey Sentence

language sentences. I have also presented some characteristics of natural language that a knowledge representation and reasoning system should support.

2 The Representation

I am attempting to represent variables as a "bundle" of constraints and a binding structure (quantifier). I term these bundles "structured variables" because variables, in this scheme, are non-atomic terms. The syntax and semantics of the associated logic is specified by an augmentation of a propositional semantic network representation formalism [9]. ANALOG (A NAtural Logic) is described in [1, 3, 2, 4]. An example of an universal structured variable (the node labelled `V1`) is given in Figure 2. In Figure 3 node `V2` is an existential structured variable node. The semantics of structured variables is largely unspecified, here, due to space limitations. It is an augmented (by the addition of arbitrary individuals) semantic theory based on [5, 10].

2.1 Natural Form

I suggest that the representation of numerous types of quantifying expressions, using structured variables, is more "natural" than typical logics. This is because the mapping of natural language sentences into representations is direct. An example is given in Figure 2.[1] Note that the shaded node, labelled `M1!`, corresponds to the asserted proposition that *all men are mortal.* `V1` is the structured variable corresponding to *all men.* The `member-class` case frame is the representation for the proposition that an object is a member of a class. This representation is more natural in that the top-level proposition is one of class membership, rather than a rule-like if-then proposition.

2.2 Conceptual Completeness and Structure Sharing

In typical logics, terms in one formula are not referenced in other formulas. In general, re-using a term involves re-writing the term in the new formula. Ideally, we would like to re-use exactly the same terms in different formulas, and we would like these terms to be closed formulas, i. e., *complete*, so that they may be meaningfully re-used and shared by multiple formulas. Variables with this property are called conceptually complete. This is also an issue in the representation of multisentential dialog, where intersentential reference to sententially scoped objects frequently occurs. For example, *All cars come with a spare tire. It is not a full-sized tire*, can only be represented by re-writing the terms

[1] a node may be labeled by a "name" (e. g., `BILL`, `M1`, `V1`) as a useful (but extra-theoretic) way to refer to the node. This naming of a rule or proposition node is of the form `M`n, where n is some integer. A "!" is appended to the name to show that the proposition represented by the node is believed to be true. However, the "!" does not affect the identity of the node, nor the proposition it represents. Similarly, variable nodes naming is `V`n and base nodes naming is `B`n where n is some integer.

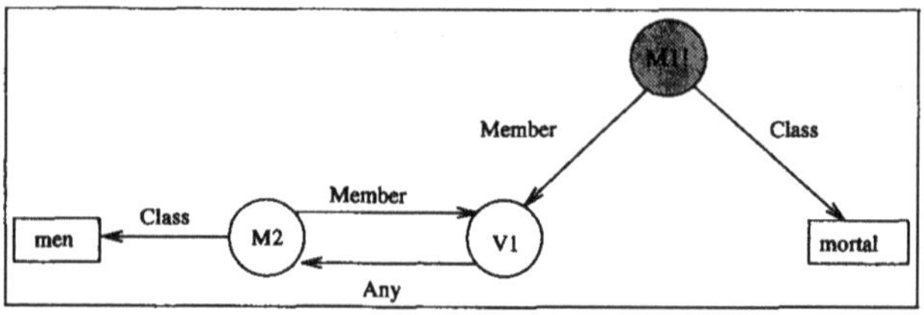

Figure 2: Structured Variable Representation of *All men are mortal.*

corresponding to the shared variables in all representations of sentences that use them or combining several sentences into one logic representation. In these cases, there is a clear advantage to a conceptually complete (closed) variable representation (since there are no scope traps) as well as the structure sharing associated with a semantic network representation. With structured variables that contain their own binding structures (quantifiers), no open sentences are possible. Further, with structure sharing, distinct formulas may share constituents which would have been open formulas in a FOPL representation.

2.3 Donkey Sentences

Since there are no open subformulas, it is possible for formulas to use constituent variables at any level, including at a level which would result in an unscoped variable in a FOPL representation. Figure 3 shows the representation for *Every farmer who owns a donkey beats it.* Note that the shaded node, labelled `M1!`, denotes the proposition *Every farmer who owns a donkey beats it* and `V1` and `V2` are *every farmer that beats a donkey he owns* and *a beaten donkey that is owned by any farmer*, respectively. This representation is also more natural because the top-level proposition is one of an act of beating, thus it is similar to any other sentence about beating such as *Fred beats a donkey.* This is the representation that is built and generated from when the donkey sentence is processed.

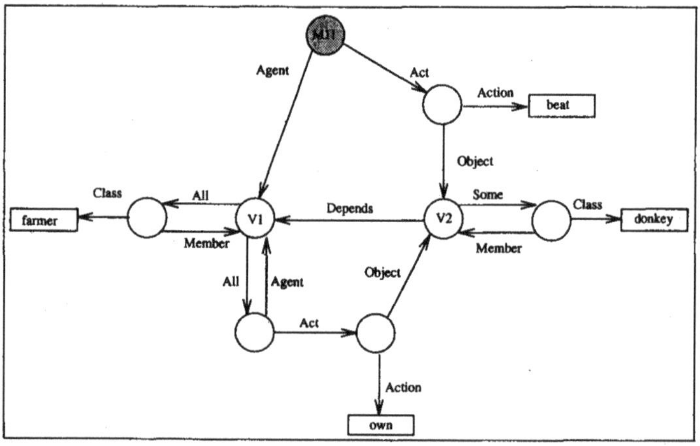

Figure 3: Donkey Sentence Representation

2.3.1 The Donkey Sentence Example

ANALOG includes a generalized augmented transition network (GATN) natural language parser and generation component linked up to the knowledge base (based on [8]). A GATN grammar specifies the translation/generation of sentences involving complex noun phrases into/from ANALOG structured variable representations.

Since this representational formalism is grounded in a nonlinear notation, the representation of tree-like quantifier scopings is straightforward. ANALOG's semantic network representation allows structure-sharing (and, indeed, may require it) to a high degree. One the initial goals was the representation of coreference and structure sharing in multisentential dialog. Because the parser/generator maintains a very simple discourse model, we do not illustrate complex examples (involving such multi-sentence connected discourse) of this structure sharing in natural language (although such representations may readily be built). A simpler example is the donkey sentence, where a scoped constituent of a noun phrase (the *donkey* in *Every farmer who owns a donkey beats it*) in used in the main clause of the sentence. Figure 4 illustrates a (slightly edited) dialog involving the donkey sentence.

: *Every farmer that owns some donkey beats it*
`I understand that every farmer that owns some donkey beats some donkey.` (1)
: *Fred is a farmer*
`I understand that Fred is a farmer.`
: *Doc is a donkey*
`I understand that Doc is a donkey.`
: *Dumbo is a donkey*
`I understand that Dumbo is a donkey.`
: *Fred owns Doc*
`I understand that Fred owns Doc.`
: *Fred owns Dumbo*
`I understand that Fred owns Dumbo.`
: *Does Fred beat Doc*
`I don't know.` (2)
: *Does any farmer beat some donkey*
`Yes, every farmer that owns some donkey beats some donkey.` (3)
: *Every farmer that owns any donkey beats it*
`I understand that every farmer that owns any donkey beats every donkey.` (4)
: *Does Fred beat Doc*
`Yes, Fred beats Doc.`
: *Does any farmer beat some donkey*
`Yes, every farmer that owns some donkey beats some donkey.`
: *Does any farmer beat any donkey*
`Yes, Fred beats Doc and every farmer that owns any donkey beats every donkey and every farmer that owns some donkey beats some donkey.`

Figure 4: Example of structure sharing in donkey sentence.

In Figure 4 the system reiterates its understanding of the donkey sentence with sentence (1). Note that the `some donkey` referred to in the subclause and main clause are the identical existential structured variable, the system cannot generate pronouns. The system's response with sentence (2) indicated that the representation of the donkey sentence is not that of Figure 1(c), since it would have answered yes had that been the case. The system's response with sentence (3) indicates that the representation of the donkey sentence is not that of Figure 1(a), since the system just reiterates the rule rather than stating that Fred beats some donkey. Note that the system is initially unable to determine whether Fred beats Doc or Dumbo. This is because the initial rule (`every farmer that owns some donkey beats it`) is satisfied in a model where only one of the donkeys is being beaten. After the system is told that *all* such donkeys are beaten (sentence (4)), it does determine that Fred beats Doc. The answers to many questions are often rules themselves (e. g., `Who beats a donkey` has as one answer `Every farmer that owns some donkey`). This is possible because the representations for rules have the same structure as ground propositions (a consequence the natural form and completeness constraints) and is illustrated in the remainder of the dialog.

3 Summary

I have presented some goals for a KRR system that would aid the process of NLP. I have described part of a KRR system that addresses these goals. ANALOG is a propositional semantic-network-based knowledge representation and reasoning system that supports many aspects of NLP, in particular, the representation and generation of complex noun phrases and sentences (natural form), the representation of various types of quantified variable scoping (conceptual completeness), and a high degree of structure sharing.

References

[1] Syed S. Ali. *A "Natural Logic" for Natural Language Processing and Knowledge Representation.* PhD thesis, State University of New York at Buffalo, Computer Science, 1993. Forthcoming.

[2] Syed S. Ali. A Structured Representation for Noun Phrases and Anaphora. In *Proceedings of the Fifteenth Annual Conference of the Cognitive Science Society*, pages 197–20, Hillsdale, NJ, June 1993. Lawrence Erlbaum.

[3] Syed S. Ali. Node Subsumption in a Propositional Semantic Network with Structured Variables. In *Proceedings of the Sixth Australian Joint Conference on Artificial Intelligence.*, November 17-19 1993.

[4] Syed S. Ali and Stuart C. Shapiro. Natural Language Processing Using a Propositional Semantic Network with Structured Variables. *Minds and Machines*, 3(4), November 1993. Special Issue on Knowledge Representation for Natural Language Processing.

[5] Kit Fine. *Reasoning with Arbitrary Objects.* Basil Blackwell, Oxford, 1985.

[6] Peter Thomas Geach. *Reference and Generality.* Cornell University Press, Ithaca, New York, 1962.

[7] Irene Heim. Discourse Representation Theory, 1990. Tutorial material from ACL-90.

[8] S. C. Shapiro. Generalized augmented transition network grammars for generation from semantic networks. *The American Journal of Computational Linguistics*, 8(1):12–25, 1982.

[9] S. C. Shapiro. Cables, Paths, and "Subconscious" Reasoning in Propositional Semantic Networks. In John F. Sowa, editor, *Principles of Semantic Networks*, pages 137–156. Morgan Kaufmann, 1991.

[10] S. C. Shapiro and W. J. Rapaport. SNePS considered as a fully intensional propositional semantic network. In N. Cercone and G. McCalla, editors, *The Knowledge Frontier*, pages 263–315. Springer–Verlag, New York, 1987.

An Interactive Model for Plan Explanation

Susan M. Haller
Department of Computer Science
State University of New York at Buffalo
Buffalo, New York 14260, USA
haller@cs.buffalo.edu

ABSTRACT I am implementing a system that plans discourse to describe and justify domain plans interactively. The model I have developed tries to account for one mode of collaboration during which the system primarily speaks, and the user primarily listens. In this mode, the system is responsible for planning text to describe and/or justify a domain plan, and the user is responsible for providing feedback that lets the system know how to extend its explanation in a way that is helpful. This has resulted in a system that can interpret vaguely articulated feedback, generate concise replies, and detect digressions. As a testbed, my system discusses driving routes as the domain plans.

1 Introduction

I am implementing a system that plans discourse to describe and justify domain plans interactively. The model I have developed tries to account for one mode of collaboration during which the system primarily speaks, and the user primarily listens. In this mode, the system is responsible for planning text to describe and/or justify a domain plan, and the user is responsible for providing feedback that lets the system know how to extend its explanation in a way that is helpful. This has resulted in a system that can interpret vaguely articulated feedback, generate concise replies, and detect digressions. As a testbed, my system discusses driving routes as the domain plans.

Plan description is a task undertaken by a speaker to enable a hearer to execute a domain plan. In contrast, plan justification is used to have a hearer adopt a domain plan that has been recommended. As the primary speaker, my system incrementally formulates and executes a text plan (TP) to try to reach a state in which the user (who primarily listens) is able to execute a domain plan (DP), or has adopted a DP that has been recommended. The system's TP is represented uniformly in the knowledge base with the DPs that are under discussion. In this way the TP and the DPs are both accessible for analyzing user feedback.

2 Related Work

Planning to discuss plans interactively relates two areas of research. The first area, plan recognition, focuses on analyzing natural language that is *about* plans to recognize the user's intent and provide helpful responses. The second area, text planning, is concerned with *using* plans for selecting and structuring text to achieve communicative goals. From the perspective of plan recognition, models have been developed where the user is in control of the conversation and the system's role is passive. Hence, researchers in plan recognition have developed analysis techniques for tracking the discourse focus to recognize the user's domain plans and goals[1,2] and his discourse plans and goals.[3,13]

In contrast, researchers in text planning have designed systems that generate explanations to achieve their own communicative goals. These systems evaluate the success of their explanations and plan additional text by accepting user feedback. This produces discussions that are tailored to the individual user's needs. The process is called *interactive generation.* Situations that call for interactive generation arise when the system is acting as an expert advisor or a tutor which must be able to explain adequately and justify what is said.

There are two strategies for planning text for interactive generation. The first is to plan text to achieve a discourse goal, and then to formulate additional TPs after analyzing the user's response. This type of reactive planning is appropriate for situations in which the principal objective is to plan explanation until the user is satisfied. The Explainable Expert System (EES) Text Planner, is the primary example of a system that implements this strategy.[16,17] The second approach calls for formulating a single TP in advance and then incrementally executing it. The Explanatory Discourse Planner (EDGE), uses this approach for planning explanations that involve teaching the user.[4] In teaching situations, the system has a prespecified set of discourse goals that have to do with concepts that the user will know as a result of the interaction. Because they are known in advance, the system can formulate and represent its TP beforehand.

3 The Problem

In highly interactive settings, people often are called upon to analyze and respond to vaguely articulated questions like *Why?* and *What?*, and ill-formed queries like *Why take Maple?* and *What about Sheridan Drive?*. The explanations that are used are themselves concise and often fragmentary. The following interaction illustrates this point:

A: Take Maple.
B: Why?
A: Maple avoids heavy traffic.
B: Why?
A: Because there are fewer businesses along it than Sheridan.

These types of interactions are coherent because both participants know how their contribution fits in. This discourse property is what Levelt refers to as *discourse deixis*.[12] However, current systems that plan in reaction to user feedback produce text that is cluttered with information from a previous exchange. This point is illustrated by the following interaction:

A: You should take Maple.
B: Why?
A: Take Maple because it avoids heavy traffic.
B: Why?
A: Taking Maple avoids heavy traffic because there are fewer businesses on it.
B: Why?
A: There are fewer businesses on it because...

Over several exchanges, this type of response can make explanations laborious, and difficult to follow. These systems tend to repeat portions of text because they formulate a new TP for each exchange. TP-operators link new information to old by having argument slots for both types of information in the statement of each TP-operator. This leads to TPs that call for repeating old (or given) information along with new information. For giving driving directions and route advice, the system does not have a preset agenda. In the role of the primary speaker, the system describes routes and/or justifies a route choice until the user's feedback indicates that he is satisfied. This calls for planning the text reactively, but it is difficult to do so in a way that links new information to old while avoiding repetition.

4 Using Plan Recognition

My solution is motivated by work in plan recognition: Carberry's theory for inferring a user's domain plans, and an alternative formulation of speech acts. Carberry's system, TRACK, analyzes fragmentary utterances using a tree structure that represents the domain plan that the system has inferred for the user so far.[2] This is the context that is used to interpret each additional utterance by trying to extend the user's DP. My system builds and executes a single, evolving TP, and uses it as the relevant context. My system analyzes user feedback for indications as to how to extend its own TP.

Text planning systems, typically treat speech acts like requesting and informing as primitive acts. However, plan recognition research has carefully considered the role of speech acts, and some researchers have noted that successful execution of a speech act may take place over several utterances, and may involve reattempts.[5,6] To build a single TP that evolves with each exchange, the system treats speech acts as complex discourse actions that can be carried out with different plans. If a chosen TP does not succeed, it can be replanned with different content.

5 The System Description

There is a one-way flow of control though three of the five components of my system: the parser, the analyzer and the planner-actor. During a complete user-system exchange, this flow starts with, and cycles back to, the parsing component. These three components have access to the knowledge base, which they consult to find, or deduce information. After the planner has selected a text structure, it sends its output to the generation component written in the Generalized Augmented Transition Network (GATN) formalism.[18] The same formalism is used for the parsing grammar. Due to space limitations, only the knowledge base and the planner are discussed here.

The several sources of information that the system needs to analyze and plan the interaction are all represented uniformly, using the Semantic Network Processing System (SNePS).[19,20] This knowledge includes the TP operators, the DPs, information about entities in the domain, the user model, and rules for reasoning about all of the above. My system exploits the SNePS Belief Revision facility (SNeBR).[15] The planner-actor is a modification of the SNePS Actor. The SNePS Actor integrates inference and acting by representing beliefs, plans, and acts as structured intensional entities in the SNePs formalism.[9,10]

6 The Text Plan Operators

The system's TP-operators are based on Rhetorical Structure Theory (RST).[14] Mann and Thompson describe a two-way division of the rhetorical relations. Each *presentational relation* relates two text spans for the purpose of increasing an inclination in the hearer. In contrast, a *subject-matter* relation is used by a speaker to inform the hearer of the rhetorical relation itself.

I use the above classification of rhetorical relations to distinguish two kinds of text plans: *discourse text plans* (DTPs), and *content-selection text plans* (CTPs). In my system, DTPs are used to attempt and reattempt the achievement the system's discourse goals. Since these goals have to do with affecting the attitudes and abilities of the user, DTPs are based on speech acts and presentational rhetorical relations. The DTPs describe how to try to achieve discourse goals by selecting some minimal text content. This minimal content can be augmented with additional content by using one or more CTPs. Figure 1(a) shows a DTP for *motivate*. This DTP includes references to two additional CTPs that may or may not be used: *circumstantiate* and *restate*. A plan for the CTP *circumstantiate* is given in Figure 1(b). Each act expands into one or more plans. While the act refers to old information, each plan for the act incorporates new information separating new information from old. Given an act, the system instantiates plans for an act by satisfying constraints on the plan.

7 An Example

In this section, I explain some of the processing behind a demonstration run produced by the system. Shown in Figure 2, the lines that start with the colon prompt (:) are user

```
ACT-PLAN(   motivate (user, DO(user, *maple-plan)),
            snsequence  ( advise (user, DO(user, *maple-plan)),
                          circumstantiate (ACT-PLAN (avoid(heavy-traffic), *maple-plan)),
                          express  ( ACT -PLAN( avoid( heavy-traffic), *maple-plan)),
                          restate  ( ACT -PLAN( avoid( heavy-traffic), *maple-plan)))))
(a)
-----------------------------------------------------------------------------------------
ACT-PLAN(   circumstantiate  ( ACT-PLAN( avoid( heavy-traffic), *maple-plan)),
            snsequence  ( express ( OBJECT-PROPERTY( *maple-plan, fewer-businesses))
                          forget ( content-goal ( know( user, OBJECT-PROPERTY( *maple-plan, ...))))))
(b)
```

Figure 1: (a) A DTP for Motivate (b) A CTP for Circumstantiate

```
: Should I take Maple or Sheridan
   to go to the Eastern Hills Mall?  (1)
take maple.                           (2)
 : Why?                               (3)
taking maple avoids heavy traffic.    (4)
 : Why?                               (5)
since taking maple there are fewer
businesses than taking sheridan.      (6)

: Why?                                     (7)
going on maple is a newer route
than taking sheridan.                      (8)
as I was expressing, taking maple is
a plan for avoiding heavy traffic.         (9)
: Ok.                                     (10)
```

Figure 2: An Example

input, and those without are generated by the system. The parser processes the user's question at line (1) to try to recognize an initial DTP that the question implicitly requests. Since the user has mentioned two plans (taking Maple and taking Sheridan) and a goal act (to go to the Eastern Hills Mall), the parser adds to the user model that the user knows both plans and the goal act. Motivated by Lambert's tripartite plan recognition strategy,[11] my system recognizes a DTP through satisfaction of its preconditions from the input. In this way, the parser recognizes the DTP *recommend* and deduces a discourse goal for it. See Haller for a more detailed explanation.[7,8]

The system has two planning modes. In this example, the system is not looking ahead at the effects of its DTP, so there are no additional content goals. In this situation, the planner prefers simple plans to complex ones, so it chooses to plan the recommendation with the speech act *advise*. Following Carberry, my model makes use of the notion of an *active path*. The active path marks that portion of the system's DTP that was most recently expanded and executed. The analyzer considers it to be the most focussed portion of the discourse, and it is analyzed first when the user responds. The active path after the system's response at line (2) is shown in Figure 3 at the dotted line labeled **1**.

At line (3), Figure 2, the user responds with the question *Why?*. The analyzer processes these types of questions using the active path of its DTP, possible expansions of it, and a set of propositions that are the reasoning closely associated with the last proposition that was expressed and that the user does not know. These propositions are called the *localized unknowns*. The analyzer proceeds by backing up the active path, trying to find a way of expanding one of the DTPs on it so that the user will know one of the localized unknowns.

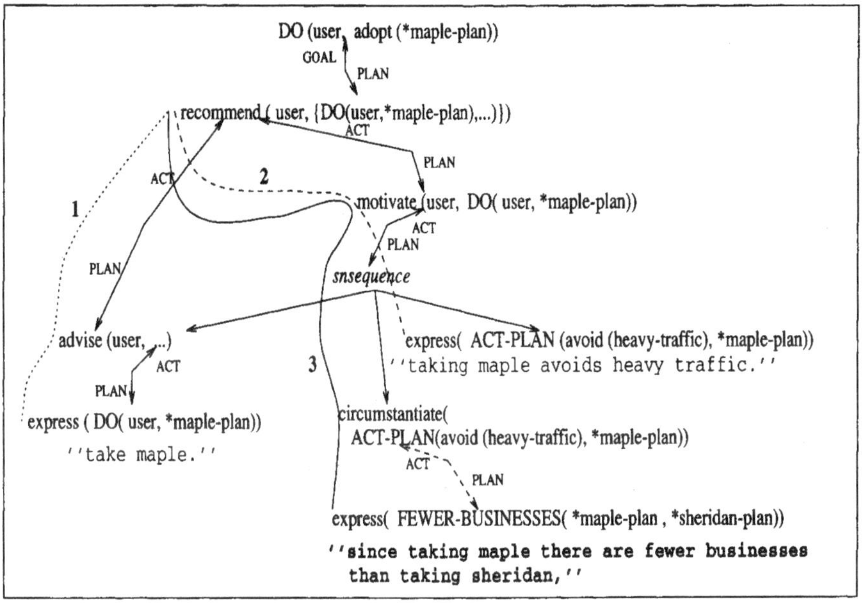

Figure 3: Three Stages of the TP

In this example, the analyzer finds another way of expanding the DTP *recommend*. The new expansion calls for using *motivate* to inform the user of a secondary goal that the Maple Road route satisfies. This expands the DTP along the active path through the dashed path labeled **2** in Figure 3, and leads to the system response at line (4). Since the system's recorded DTP indicates that it previously executed *advise*, it does not perform it again. Instead, it simply adds on the motivation.

At line (5), the user follows up with *Why?* once more. Once again the analyzer tries to find an expansion of a discourse act along the active path. When this fails, the analyzer looks at the last DTP on the active path (in this example, the expansion of *motivate*, Figure 1 (b)) to see if any augmenting content plan that has not been used lets the user know one of the localized unknowns. The analyzer discovers that *circumstantiate* does this. This leads to the production at line (6) and the active path labeled **3**, Figure 3.

The user asks *Why?* a third time at line (7). At this point, the system detects one of three types of user-initiated digressions that it can process. This happens when the analyzer fails to find an expansion of a DTP along the active path, or a CTP in the last DTP *motivate*. As a final measure, the analyzer checks to see if a used CTP can itself be expanded with another CTP to include a localized unknown. In this example, the CTP: *circumstantiate(avoid(heavy traffic, maple-plan))* can be expanded further with another CTP: *circumstantiate(now(heavy traffic))*. This leads to the system's response at line (8). The analyzer also adds to the knowledge base that a digression has occurred. This satisfies the constraints on another CTP *restate* that is used to augment the *motivate* plan when the system returns to the active path. Consistent with Zukerman's approach, the uniform representation of plans makes it possible for the system to use the previous TP as a DP thereby generating a *metacomment* at line (9).[21]

8 Current Status and Future Work

The system I have demonstrated currently uses five DTPs and four CTPs to formulate TPs for justifying DP advice and justification. In future work, I will extend the system to engage in DP descriptions and system-imposed topic shifts. Since my model calls for representing the TP uniformly with the DPs that is under discussion, another objective is to extend the system so that it can engage in full-blown, meta-level discussions of its own TP.

References

[1] J. Allen and C. R. Perrault. Analyzing intention in utterances. *Artificial Intelligence*, 15:143–178, 1980.

[2] S. Carberry. Modeling the user's plans and goals. *Computational Linguistics*, 14(3), 1988.

[3] S. Carberry. A pragmatics-based approach to ellipsis resolution. *Computational Linguistics*, 15(4), 1989.

[4] A. Cawsey. Generating explanatory discouse. In R. Dale, C. Mellish, and M. Zock, editors, *Current Research in Natural Language Generation*, chapter 4, pages 75–101. Academic Press, 1990.

[5] P. R. Cohen and H. J. Levesque. Rational interaction as the basis for communication. In P. R. Cohen, J. Morgan, and M. E. Pollack, editors, *Intentions in Communication*, pages 221–256. MIT Press, 1990.

[6] B. J. Grosz and C. L. Sidner. Attention, intentions, and the structure of discourse. *Computational Linquistics*, 12:175–204, 1986.

[7] S. M. Haller. *Interactive Generation of Plan Descriptions and Justifications.* PhD thesis, Department of Computer Science, State University of New York at Buffalo, 1993. In progress.

[8] S. M. Haller. Interactive generation of plan justifications. In *Proceedings of the Fourth European Workshop on Natural Language Generation*, pages 79–90, 1993.

[9] D. Kumar and S. C. Shapiro. Architecture of an intelligent agent in SNePS. *SIGART Bulletin*, 2(4):89–92, August 1991.

[10] D. Kumar and S. C. Shapiro. Modeling a rational cognitive agent in SNePS. In B. Barahona, L. Moniz Pereira, and A. Porto, editors, *EPIA 91: 5th Portugese Conference on Artificial Intelligence, Lecture Notes in Artificial Intelligence 541*, pages 120–134. Springer-Verlag, Heidelberg, 1991.

[11] L. Lambert. Tripartite plan-based model of dialogue. In *Proceedings of the Association for Computational Linguistics*, 1991.

[12] W. J. M. Levelt. *Speaking: From Intention to Articulation.* MIT Press, Cambridge, 1989.

[13] D. Litman and J. Allen. Discourse processing and commonsense plans. In P. R. Cohen, J. Morgan, and M. E. Pollack, editors, *Intentions in Communication*, pages 365–388. MIT Press, 1990.

[14] W. C. Mann and S. A. Thompson. Rhetorical structure theory: A theory of text organization. Technical report, Information Sciences Institute, 1987.

[15] J. P. Martins and S. C. Shapiro. A model for belief revision. *Artificial Intelligence*, 35(1):25–79, 1988.

[16] J. Moore and W. Swartout. A reactive approach to explanation. In *International Joint Conference on Artificial Intelligence*, pages 1504–1510, 1989.

[17] J. Moore and W. Swartout. A reactive approach to explanation: Taking the user's feedback into account. In C. Paris, W. Swartout, and W. Mann, editors, *Natural Language Generation in Artificial Intelligence and Computational Linguistics*, chapter 1, pages 3–48. Kluwer Academic Publishers, 1991.

[18] S. C. Shapiro. Generalized augmented transition network grammars for generation from semantic networks. *American Association of Computational Linguistics*, 8:12–25, 1982.

[19] S. C. Shapiro. Case studies of SNePS. *SIGART Bulletin*, 2(3):128–134, June 1991.

[20] S. C. Shapiro and W. J. Rapaport. SNePS considered as a fully intensional propositional semantic network. In N. Cercone and G. McCalla, editors, *The Knowledge Frontier*, pages 263–315. Springer-Verlag, New York, 1987.

[21] I. Zukerman. Using meta-comments to generate fluent text in a technical domain. *Computational Intelligence*, 7(4), 1991.

CORTEX : A Corpus-Based Teaching Expert

AKIVA QUINN
Survey of English Usage, University College London, Gower Street, London, WC1E 6BT, United Kingdom

and

DAVID QUINN
Department of Business Computing, City University, Northampton Square, London, EC1V 0HB, United Kingdom

ABSTRACT

The CORpus-based Teaching EXpert (**CORTEX**) provides a design for exploiting computerised corpora of natural language in **computer assisted language learning** (**CALL**). A linguistically annotated corpus like the International Corpus of English (ICE) provides, as the **Corpus Module** of CORTEX, an extensive range of examples of written and spoken English, overcoming the problem of CALL systems being limited to a fixed set of predefined examples. The CORTEX **Expert Module** is a model of the structure of this linguistic information. The CORTEX **Teaching/Advice Module** contains rules for using the Corpus and Expert Modules to teach students and to advise researchers. For language learning it can, as a rule-based resource, remove the limitations of predefined CALL teaching scripts, using the linguistic knowledge in the Expert Module and the examples in the Corpus Module. For researchers, the Teaching/Advice Module acts as an extra layer, or conceptual map, between the researcher and the corpus helping them formulate and refine corpus queries.

1. Introduction

This paper describes the design of a knowledge-based system to advise researchers in their use of a linguistically annotated corpus and to teach students language based on this material. The CORpus-based Teaching EXpert (CORTEX) models the linguistic domain, and draws examples from a large corpus, thus removing key shortcomings in traditional computer-based teaching - the use of predefined scripts and the use of preselected lesson material. The value of corpora in teaching is widely recognised, but intelligent tutoring systems which support discovery learning have yet to be exploited[1]. Many levels of linguistic information, such as the internal structure of words, word classes, the structure of sentences and of texts, can be represented and taught. We begin by presenting the model devised for CORTEX, after which we explore the domain knowledge and the rules needed to teach or advise on word morphology and word classes. This is followed by a brief discussion on the implementation and we conclude with the benefits of combining corpus-based and knowledge-based techniques.

2. The CORTEX Model

We identify two major limitations in the design of existing CALL systems which our knowledge-based and corpus-based approach can overcome :

> **conceptual scope**: scripts produced with an authoring tool or coded in a procedural language cover a fixed range of topics, and can only be extended by the author scripting further lesson plans.
>
> **example range**: the range of examples to illustrate or test a lesson concept must be defined exhaustively in advance. Extending the range of examples involves human selection of further relevant examples.

The conceptual scope in CORTEX is defined in terms of linguistic rules, which can easily be extended or replaced by a completely new set. CORTEX is designed to work with the International Corpus of English (ICE, spoken and written, 1990-94) but could be applied to other corpora like Brown (written US English, 1961) or LOB (UK English parallel of Brown) as the same logical formalism can be used to model each tagset. CORTEX's range of examples is limited only by the size of the corpus or corpora to which it has access - millions of words of tagged and parsed material is available, providing a rich linguistic resource that can be utilised for teaching and research.

Intelligent CALL, or ICALL, seeks to be more flexible, plus easier to modify and extend than traditional computer-assisted language learning[2]. This flexibility stems from the explicit coding of linguistic information as a knowledge base, and the separate modelling of the teaching method and of the student's progress. The framework promulgated for Intelligent Tutoring Systems[3] and Intelligent Computer Aided Instruction has been adopted for ICALL[4]. The CORTEX model includes the modules used for ICALL:

> Expert Module - the domain knowledge to be conveyed.
> Tutorial Module - what and how to teach.
> Student Module - what the student knows.
> User Interface - manage mixed-mode, mixed-initiative dialogs with the user.

CORTEX also introduces a new module, the **Corpus Module**, which forms part of the Expert Module's model of the domain, but also provides a source of examples for the Teaching Module. This can be seen as complementing the Expert Module's rules (linguistic generalisations) with a large database of facts about words, their word-classes, and their distribution patterns (linguistic specifics). This mode of access, corpus **browsing**, is similar to hypertext browsing[5] and facilitates discovery learning.

For the remainder of this paper we focus on the linguistic annotations used in the International Corpus of English (ICE) - a compilation of one million word national or regional corpora, collected along parallel lines in 17 countries where English is spoken as a first or official language[6]. Each corpus is marked up for typographic and content features, then automatically tagged for word-class (part of speech) and parsed to determine syntactic categories and functions. Each stage is post-edited to ensure accurate results. The ICE Corpus Utility Program (ICECUP) allows queries for combinations of lexical items, word-class tags, and syntactic markers[7]. The queries can get complicated and the complex of annotations is large, so CORTEX is needed to guide the user.

3. Intelligent Advice and Teaching

The following sections illustrate the linguistic knowledge needed for the Expert Module to reason about the two major areas of word morphology and word classes. Each area uses a model of the concepts and their interrelationships which is readily converted into a Prolog knowledge base. The resulting representation is one that linguists can readily understand, and hence update in accordance with their knowledge of the domain.

3.1 *Word Morphology*

In accumulating results or insights from a corpus, researchers and, particularly, students should be pointed to related forms of the word they are looking up. For instance, examining the inflections of *watch* (*watches*, *watching*, *watched*) will give a better view of the usage or distribution of this lemma. Similarly, looking at compound words derived from *black* (*blackball*, *blackboard*, *blackguard*, etc.) shows the productivity of this word.

3.1.1 *The expert module*

To allow reasoning about inflectional morphology, a dictionary of exceptions is used along with morphemic and spelling rules for nouns, verbs, adjectives, etc. The inflectional rules are used both for analysis (to get the base form) and to generate the inflected forms to be offered as alternative queries. Words can also be compounded to form new words, for example the words *ice* and *cream* can appear as an open compound *ice cream*, a hyphenated compound *ice-cream*, or a solid compound *icecream*. Compounding rules produce these alternative forms. Similarly derivation rules for clitics relate words to their contracted forms, for example *will* produces *he'll*, *we'll* and so on as alternatives. These examples just serve to illustrate the complex of morphological relationships that can be represented as rules, and utilised to guide the user.

3.1.2 *The teaching/advice module*

Given an ICECUP query, the Teaching/Advice Module applies the inflection and derivation rules to see if further queries can be suggested. In all cases the Corpus Module is consulted to see if the original and alternative word forms occur in the corpus. This determines if the inflections are to be offered as **additional** or **alternative** queries. Advice is provided along with the alternatives to explain the relationship of the alternatives to the original query.

3.2 *Lexical Tags*

3.2.1 *The expert module*

Inheritance networks[8] have often been used in computational linguistics, and have proven very useful here, to represent the domain of lexical tags in ICE[9]. Each entity in an ICE corpus has an associated **tag**. Not only words are tagged, but sometimes parts of a word are tagged separately (for example *Susan* and *'s* in *Susan's*), while entities such as punctuation and pauses also have tags. Tags assigned to words or parts of words are **lexical tags**. For example, the tag *N(prop,sing)* is assigned to all proper singular nouns, such as *Melbourne*. The tag's first symbol represents the **word class** (Noun, abbreviated as *N*), and the symbols within the parentheses represent the **features** (Proper and Singular, abbreviated as *prop* and *sing*).

In ICE there are 22 word classes, including the basic ones such as Adjective, Noun and Adverb, and also more specialised ones such as Genitive Marker. There are five different tags used for words that are **members** of the **class** of Adjectives: *ADJ*, *ADJ(comp)*, *ADJ(sup)*, *ADJ(edp)*, *ADJ(ingp)*. The class of Adjectives is divided into **subclasses**, yielding the implicit **hierarchical structure** shown in Figure 1:

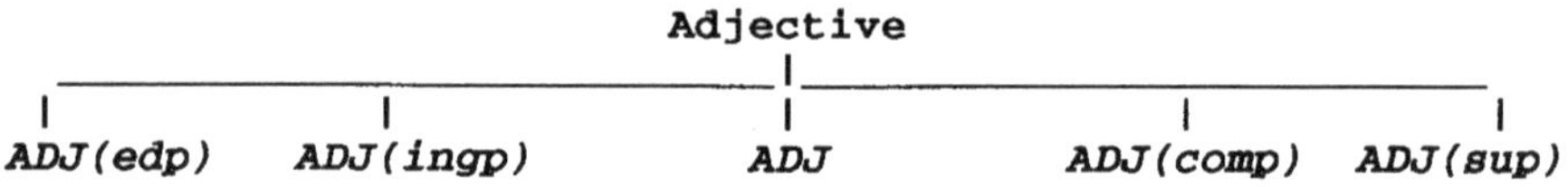

Figure 1

This structure is almost flat, and does not adequately represent the richer underlying relations between tags. Within the word class Adjective, more detailed relations are represented in the Expert Module by the hierarchy in Figure 2:

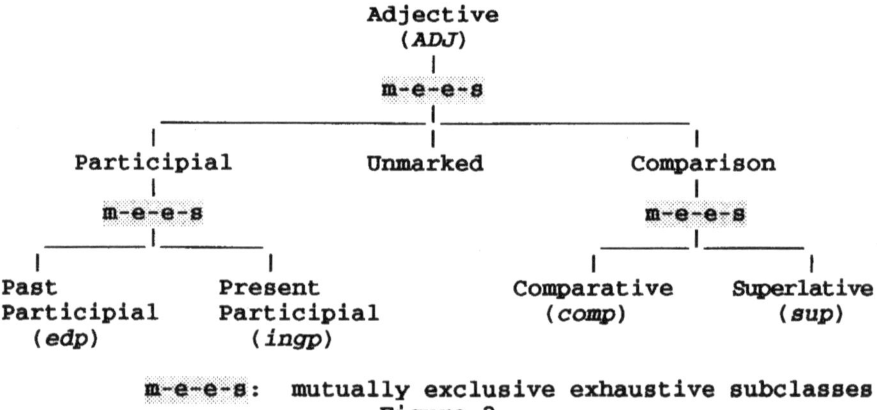

Figure 2

This hierarchy represents the subdivision of the class of Adjectives into three **mutually exclusive exhaustive** subclasses (Participial, Unmarked, and Comparison), and the further subdivision of the classes Participial (into Past Participial and Present Participial) and Comparison (into Comparative and Superlative). Mutually exclusive subclasses have no members in common. Exhaustive means that their combined membership is equal to that of the class of which they are subclasses. The links between classes are labelled, to enable the indication of different types of links.

A word of word class Adjective has *ADJ* as the first part of its tag, and this appears in parentheses below the class Adjective in the hierarchy. A word that is a member of any subclass of the class Adjective **inherits** *ADJ* as the first symbol of its tag. A class whose members have a particular feature has the feature abbreviation in parentheses below it.

Only **single inheritance** is needed in the Adjective hierarchy. Elsewhere in the system **multiple inheritance** is needed too, for instance in the Noun hierarchy. Nouns are either Common or Proper, **and also** either Singular or Plural. A word of word class Noun inherits from both branches of the hierarchy, which are labelled o-s (**orthogonal subclasses**).

3.2.2 *The teaching/advice module*

The Teaching/Advice Module utilises the linguistic model contained in the Expert Module. The user's initial query against the corpus will be mapped to one or more classes in the linguistic model, the user's current focus, and will result in the retrieval of examples from the corpus for examination. Several types of help may be offered by the system to guide the selection of succeeding sets of examples.

The user will be asked to indicate whether the size of a retrieved examples set is satisfactory. If there are too many examples a **narrowing** rule is used to suggest a more selective focusing on a part of the current class. The list of subclasses of the current class is displayed to the user for selection. For example, the class Comparison may be narrowed by selection of one of the classes Comparative or Superlative. Similarly, if there are not enough examples, a **broadening** rule is used. The larger class in which the current class is contained is displayed for selection. For example, the class Superlative may be broadened by selection of the class Comparison.

The user will also be asked to indicate whether a different, but related, examples set is required. A **supplementing** rule is used to display all the siblings of the class that is in focus (all those classes that are subclasses of the class's parent). For example, Comparison may be supplemented by selection of Participial or Unmarked. A **relating** rule is used where a feature appears in more than one word class. This occurs for instance in the word classes Adjective and Adverb which share the feature Comparison. If the user is focused on the class Comparison in the Adjective hierarchy, the retrieval of corpus entities from the corresponding class in the Adverb hierarchy is suggested.

4. Implementation

CORTEX needs to interface with ICECUP which was written in C++ to exploit object-oriented programming and for ease of access to the Windows™ Graphical User Interface. As Prolog provides a good rule-based environment for reasoning about queries and citations, a mixed language implementation would be most effective. Initially, loose coupling between environments is appropriate - all data relevant to a query is retrieved in C++, asserted in a Prolog database, and used to prove an advice goal. So far a standalone Prolog prototype has been implemented.

5. Conclusions

By using a linguistically annotated corpus as its **Corpus Module**, CORTEX provides users with a wide range of natural examples from written and spoken English. The **Expert Module** represents the structure of the linguistic domain, relating concepts to each other and to annotations in the corpus. The **Teaching/Advice Module** contains rules for using the Corpus and Expert Modules to advise researchers in their use of the corpus and to guide language learners. CORTEX demonstrates the combination of corpus-based and knowledge-based techniques in providing a Teaching and Advice Expert.

Note

ICE project funded in part by Economic & Social Research Council grant R00 23 2077.

References

1. S. Fligelstone, Some Reflections on the Question of Teaching, from a Corpus Linguistics Perspective, *ICAME Journal* 17 (1993) 97-109.
2. M. Yazdani, The LINGER Project: An Artificial Intelligence Approach to Second-Language Tutoring, *Computer Assisted Language Learning* 4 (2) (1991) 107-116.
3. E. Wenger, *Artificial Intelligence and Tutoring Systems: Computational and Cognitive Approaches to the Communication of Knowledge* (Morgan Kaufmann, Los Altos, 1987).
4. C. Matthews, Going AI: Foundations of ICALL, *Computer Assisted Language Learning* 5 (1-2) (1992) 13-31.
5. B. Ansel and A.H. Jucker, Learning Linguistics with Computers: Hypertext as a Key to Linguistic Networks, *Literary and Linguistic Computing* 7 (2) (1992) 124-131.
6. S. Greenbaum, A New Corpus of English: ICE, in *Directions in Corpus Linguistics*, ed. J. Svartvik (Mouton de Gruyter, Berlin - New York, 1992) 171-179.
7. A. Quinn, An object-oriented design for a Corpus Utility Program, in *English Language Corpora: Design, Analysis and Exploitation*, eds. J. Aarts, P. de Haan, and N. Oostdijk (Rodopi, Amsterdam, 1992) 215-225.
8. W. Daelemans, K. De Smedt, and G. Gazdar, Inheritance in Natural Language Processing, *Computational Linguistics* 18 (2) (1992) 205-218.
9. S. Greenbaum, *The ICE Tagset Manual* (University College London, 1992).

From Discourse Features to Discourse Organization[1#]

Ingrid Zukerman and **Richard McConachy**
Department of Computer Science
Monash University
Clayton, Victoria 3168, Australia

Abstract

In this paper, we consider discourse features which emerge from the relations between planned utterances and the propositions conveyed by these utterances. We then derive from these features three types of relations between utterances: inferential, enhancement and prerequisite. Inferential relations emerge as a result of opportunistic inferences from planned utterances. Enhancement relations hold between utterances that are intentionally planned to strengthen each others effect. Prerequisite relations hold when utterances are planned in order to convey information that is needed to understand other utterances. These relations in turn yield ordering relations and constraints, which are used in a discourse structuring mechanism that generates maximally connected discourse. This mechanism has been implemented as the discourse organization component of an explanation generation system called WISHFUL.

1 Introduction

Research in Natural Language Generation (NLG) has postulated two main discourse planning methods: *prescriptive* and *opportunistic*[8]. A prescriptive mechanism is used to plan utterances that achieve the communicative goal for which the discourse is initiated[1,5,6]. An opportunistic mechanism is applied to generate utterances that address an undesirable event that is not part of the given goal[2,3,9]. To illustrate these concepts, consider the following sample discourse.

```
S1. Wallabies are like kangaroos.
S2. They have a pouch and they hop.
S3. However, they are smaller than kangaroos.
```

In this discourse, S2 provides evidential support for S1, and S3 contradicts an erroneous inference from S1, namely that wallabies are the same size as kangaroos. The relation between S1 and S2 is prescriptive, while the relation between S1 and S3 is opportunistic.

In this paper, we discuss discourse relations that arise from prescriptive and opportunistic discourse planning, and present a discourse organization mechanism which structures discourse generated by both types of discourse planning processes. To this effect our mechanism takes into consideration ordering constraints and relations derived from these discourse relations. Our mechanism has been implemented as a component of WISHFUL, the content planner described in [10,11]. The output of WISHFUL is a set of *Rhetorical Devices (RDs)*, where an RD is composed of a rhetorical action, such as Assert or Instantiate, applied to a proposition.

2 Relations between Rhetorical Devices and Propositions

The following features of relations between RDs and propositions affect the organization of the discourse: *intentionality*, *support*, *soundness* and *directness*.

Intentionality indicates whether an RD conveys a proposition *intentionally* or *incidentally*. An RD conveys a proposition intentionally if it is generated with the purpose of conveying this proposition. An RD conveys a proposition incidentally if the proposition is conveyed as an unplanned side effect of the RD.

Support indicates whether an inference from an RD supports or contradicts a proposition. Inferences that support a proposition are *positive (+)*, while inferences that contradict it are *negative (−)*.

Soundness indicates the level of soundness of a positive inference from an RD. We distinguish between the following types of positive inferences based on their soundness:

[1#] This research was supported in part by grant A49030462 from the Australian Research Council.

Support of RD_j for p	Soundness of the inference	Inferential Relation	Conjunction
−		EXPECTATION-VIOLATE(RD_j,RD_i)	'however','but'
+	sound	CAUSE(RD_j,RD_i)	'therefore','hence'
+	acceptable	EXPECTATION-REALIZE(RD_j,RD_i)	'indeed'
+	unacceptable	ADD(RD_j,RD_i)	'also', 'further'

Table 1: *Inferential Relations obtained from Support and Soundness*

Sound inferences (s), which are logically sound, e.g., a sound inference from the statement "All men are mortal" is that Socrates is a mortal.

Acceptable inferences (a), which are sensible, and whose results hold often, e.g., an acceptable inference from the statement "In Bracket Simplification we first add or subtract, e.g., $2(3x + 5x) = 2 \times 8x$" is that Bracket Simplification applies to bracketed Like Terms.

Unacceptable inferences (u), which hold only occasionally, and hence should not be reinforced, e.g., an unacceptable inference from the statement "You can whip pure cream" is that one can also whip eggs.

Finally, **Directness** conveys the length of the inference chain which links an RD to a proposition. A directness of level 0 corresponds to a direct inference, level 1 corresponds to inferences drawn from one inference step, such as a generalization or a specialization, level 2 corresponds to the combination of two inference steps, etc. Direct inferences are intentional and they have a positive support for the proposition they convey, e.g., the RDs Assert(p) and Negate(p) are generated to give a positive support to p and $\neg p$, respectively.

3 Discourse Relations between Rhetorical Devices

The features discussed in the previous section yield two types of discourse relations: *inferential* and *enhancement*. These relations are defined below.

Definition 1 An RD RD_j is linked to an RD RD_i by the relation *inference*(RD_j,RD_i) if RD_i conveys a proposition by means of a direct (and therefore intentional) inference, and an incidental (and therefore indirect) inference from RD_j either corroborates or contradicts the information conveyed by RD_i.

Given a proposition p conveyed directly by RD_i and incidentally by RD_j, the inferential relation between RD_j and RD_i is obtained from the support and soundness information in the relation between RD_j and p as shown in Table 1. To illustrate the derivation of inferential relations, let us consider the following propositions:

p_1: [Bracket-Simplification ¬apply-to bracketed-Unlike-Terms]
p_2: [Bracket-Simplification ¬(always)apply-to bracketed-Algebraic-Terms]

The Negations "Bracket Simplification does not apply to bracketed Unlike Terms" (n_1) and "Bracket Simplification does not always apply to bracketed Algebraic Terms" (n_2) have a direct (and hence intentional) relation with propositions p_1 and p_2, respectively. In addition, a generalization from n_1 yields the proposition p_2. This generalization (unintentional and indirect with directness=1) is sound and has a positive support for this proposition, resulting in the inferential relation CAUSE(n_1,n_2). As indicated in Table 1, this relation is conveyed by a causal conjunction, yielding text such as "Bracket Simplification does not apply to bracketed Unlike Terms, *therefore* it does not always apply to bracketed Algebraic Terms."

Definition 2 An RD RD_j *enhances* the effect of an RD RD_i if RD_i conveys a particular proposition directly (and therefore intentionally), and RD_j conveys this proposition intentionally and indirectly.

The following enhancement relations are considered at present by our mechanism:

ILLUSTRATED(Assertion,Instantiation)	SUMMARIZED(Assertion,Simile)
GENERALIZED(Instantiation,Assertion)	EVIDENCED(Simile,Assertion)

For instance, if proposition p is conveyed by means of an Assertion A which is instantiated by Instantiation I, the relations ILLUSTRATED(A,I) and GENERALIZED(I,A) hold. These relations yield text such as "A. *For example,* I" and "I. *In general,* A," respectively. To illustrate the derivation of enhancement relations, let us reconsider sentences S1 and S2 from the sample discourse in Section 1, which are reproduced below with their corresponding RDs.

Wallabies are like kangaroos.	S: Say-Simile [Wallaby is-like Kangaroo]
They have a pouch and they hop.	A_1: Assert [Wallaby has-part pouch] A_2: Assert [Wallaby hop]

The Simile S is an intentional and indirect way of getting the hearer to transfer what s/he knows about kangaroos to wallabies. However, if the user is not sure that kangaroos have a pouch and hop, the Simile will be insufficient to convey this information about wallabies. Hence, the Assertions are necessary in addition to the Simile. Since the Assertions convey the intended information intentionally and directly, while the Simile conveys this information intentionally and indirectly, the following enhancement relations hold: SUMMARIZED($\{A_1, A_2\}$,S) and EVIDENCED(S,$\{A_1, A_2\}$).

As seen in the above examples, inferential and enhancement discourse relations connect between RDs that convey a set of propositions. However, it is possible that a concept mentioned in an RD is not sufficiently understood by the user to enable him/her to understand this RD. For instance, in order to understand the statement "Bracket Simplification applies to bracketed Like Terms" the user must understand the relevant aspects of bracketed Like Terms. This prompts the generation of a statement such as "Bracketed Like Terms are expressions such as $2(3x + 5x)$." In order to represent this situation we require an additional discourse relation which depends on domain-based relations between concepts, rather than on the features discussed in Section 2. This relation is defined as follows:

Definition 3 A set of RDs $\{RD_j\}$ is a *prerequisite* to an RD RD_i if the information conveyed by $\{RD_j\}$ is necessary for the hearer to understand RD_i.

Note that the individual RDs in the set $\{RD_j\}$ may be connected by means of inferential and enhancement relations.

4 Deriving Ordering Constraints and Relations

Ordering constraints are strict injunctions to position RDs in a particular order. They are extracted directly from prerequisite discourse relations by the following rule:

If *prerequisite*($\{RD_j\}$,RD_i) Then BEFORE($\{RD_j\}$,RD_i) or IMMEDIATE-PRECEDE(RD_i,$\{RD_j\}$).

This rule stipulates that a set of RDs which contains prerequisite information for the understanding of an RD must be presented either sometime before this RD or immediately after it. The latter case yields a subordinate clause, and therefore can only be applied when the prerequisite information is short, e.g., "Bracket Simplification applies to bracketed Like Terms, *which are expressions such as* $2(3x + 5x)$."

Ordering relations are suggestions regarding which RDs should be positioned in the vicinity of each other if possible. They are obtained directly from the inferential and enhancement discourse relations derived in the previous section.

The combined use of ordering relations and constraints supports a discourse organization process that is more flexible than a purely constraint-based process.

5 Operation of the Discourse Structuring Mechanism

Our discourse structuring mechanism generates a partial ordering of the RDs generated by the content planner, so that this ordering is optimal and satisfies the ordering constraints. Our optimality criterion is *maximum connectivity*, which stipulates that the generated discourse should include the strongest possible ordering relations between the RDs.

Our procedure receives as input an *RD-Graph* generated by the content planner, where an RD-Graph is a directed graph that contains the following components: (1) the set of propositions to be conveyed (p_1, p_2, p_3, p_4, p_5 in Figure 1); (2) the RDs generated by the content planner ($RD_1, RD_2, RD_3, RD_4, RD_5$); (3) the relations between the RDs and the propositions (labelled with intentionality, support, directness and soundness information); and (4) the relations between the RDs that contain prerequisite information (RD_5) and the RDs which convey the propositions (RD_1). The RDs $RD_1, \ldots, RD_4$ in Figure 1 are generated to convey propositions $p_1, \ldots, p_5$ about wallabies. However, since the user is not familiar with the concept pouch, RD_5 is generated as a prerequisite to RD_1. All the links between the Simile (RD_3) and the propositions it conveys are labelled *int*+1*a* (intentional, positive, directness=1 and acceptable), with the exception of the link to proposition p_5, which is labelled *inc*–1 (incidental, negative, directness=1). This is due to the fact that the Simile conveys intentionally all the propositions which are correct with respect to wallabies, but it conveys unintentionally the erroneous belief that wallabies are the same size as kangaroos. The remaining links between RDs and propositions are labelled *int*+0 (intentional, positive, direct).

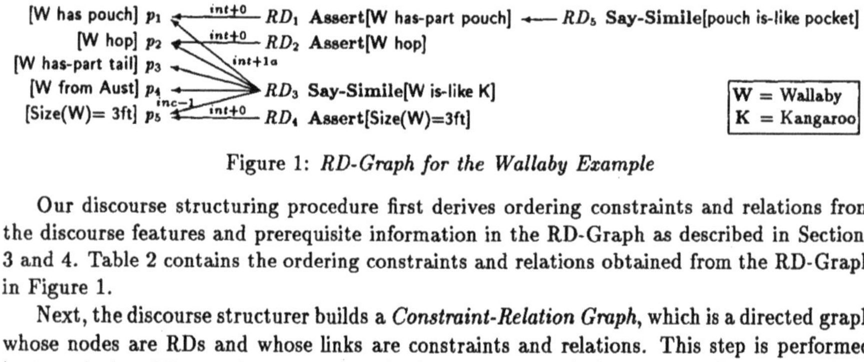

Figure 1: *RD-Graph for the Wallaby Example*

Our discourse structuring procedure first derives ordering constraints and relations from the discourse features and prerequisite information in the RD-Graph as described in Sections 3 and 4. Table 2 contains the ordering constraints and relations obtained from the RD-Graph in Figure 1.

Next, the discourse structurer builds a *Constraint-Relation Graph*, which is a directed graph whose nodes are RDs and whose links are constraints and relations. This step is performed by iteratively adding each constraint and relation to a graph that starts off empty, without disrupting the links built previously. In order to support a numerical optimization process, the ordering constraints and relations are assigned weights. The ordering constraints (BEFORE and IMMEDIATE-PRECEDE) are assigned a weight of ∞ to indicate that they should never be violated. The inferential and enhancement relations are assigned weights according to their strength. In the current implementation, the weights assigned to the inferential relations

Type	Relation/Constraint
inferential	EXPECTATION-VIOLATE(RD_3,RD_4)
enhancement	EVIDENCED(RD_3,RD_1) OR SUMMARIZED(RD_1,RD_3) EVIDENCED(RD_3,RD_2) OR SUMMARIZED(RD_2,RD_3)
prerequisite	BEFORE(RD_5,RD_1) OR IMMEDIATE-PRECEDE(RD_1,RD_5)

Table 2: *Ordering Constraints and Relations for the Wallaby Example*

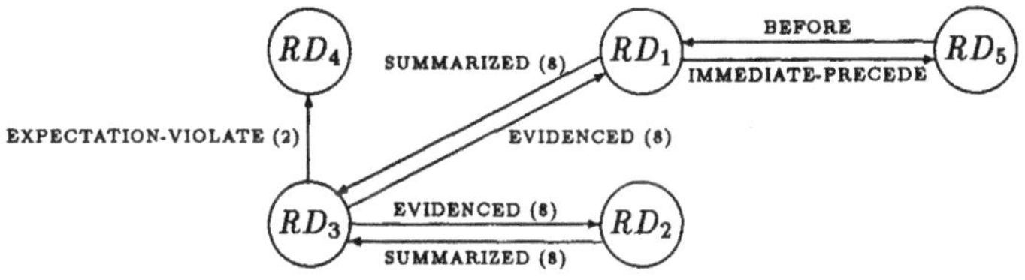

Figure 2: *The Constraint-Relation Graph for the Wallaby Example*

are: CAUSE 4, REALIZE 2, VIOLATE 2 and ADD 1. The enhancement relations (EVIDENCED, SUMMARIZED, ILLUSTRATED and GENERALIZED) are assigned a weight of 8. Figure 2 illustrates the Constraint-Relation Graph built from the constraints and relations in Table 2.

Finally, the discourse structurer finds an optimal set of paths that cover the nodes in the Constraint-Relation Graph, so that the paths in this set use the strongest links in the Constraint-Relation Graph and violate no constraints. This process has the following stages: (1) *path extraction*, (2) *filtering*, and (3) *optimization*.

The **path extraction** stage generates all the *terminal paths* starting from each node in the Constraint-Relation Graph, where a terminal path is one that continues until a dead-end is reached, e.g., RD_3 – EXPECTATION-VIOLATE – RD_4. Terminal paths may contain *Aggregate Nodes*, *Side Tracks* and *Subordinate Paths*.

An **Aggregate Node** is generated by collecting into a set the nodes that are connected to a single node by means of links of the same type. For example, since RD_1 and RD_2 are both connected to RD_3 by means of EVIDENCED/SUMMARIZED links, they may be joined into the aggregate node $\{RD_1, RD_2\}$.

A **Side Track** is a short deviation from the main path which takes place when a link of a different type to that of the rest of the path is followed. For example, the path RD_3 – EXPECTATION-VIOLATE – RD_4 may be temporarily side tracked to $\{RD_1, RD_2\}$, yielding (RD_3 – EVIDENCED – $\{RD_1, RD_2\}$) – EXPECTATION-VIOLATE – RD_4.

A **Subordinate Path** is generated when an IMMEDIATE-PRECEDE link is followed from a node to a Constraint-Relation Sub-graph which contains prerequisite information for this node. For example, any path containing RD_1 may branch into the subordinate path RD_1 – IMMEDIATE-PRECEDE – RD_5.

When the terminal paths are generated, all the options starting at each node are considered, i.e., with and without aggregate nodes, side tracks or subordinate paths. The number and length of side tracks and subordinate paths is determined empirically, so that only a few short breaks from the main path are allowed. Table 3 illustrates some of the terminal paths generated for the Constraint-Relation Graph in Figure 2.

The **filtering** stage deletes *redundant* and *irregular* paths. A path is redundant if there exists another path which subsumes it exactly (with no intervening nodes). For example, $Path_1$ in Table 3 is redundant, since it is subsumed by $Path_4$. A path from node RD_i to node RD_j is irregular if it contains consecutive EXPECTATION-VIOLATE links, and there exists

$Path_1$:$\{RD_1, RD_2\}$–SUMMARIZED–RD_3–EXPECTATION-VIOLATE–RD_4
$Path_2$:(RD_3–EVIDENCED–$\{RD_1, RD_2\}$)–EXPECTATION-VIOLATE–RD_4
$Path_3$:(RD_3–EVIDENCED–{[RD_1–IMMEDIATE-PRECEDE–RD_5],RD_2})–EXPECTATION-VIOLATE–RD_4
$Path_4$:{[RD_5–BEFORE–RD_1],RD_2}–SUMMARIZED–RD_3–EXPECTATION-VIOLATE–RD_4

Table 3: *Sample Terminal Paths for the Wallaby Example*

another path from node RD_i to node RD_j that is composed of positive links only. The deletion of redundant paths cuts down the search, and the deletion of irregular paths prevents the generation of sentences of the form "RD_i, but RD_k. However RD_j" if a sentence of the form "RD_i and RD_j. However RD_k" is possible.

Finally, the **optimization** stage selects a partially ordered set of terminal paths which cover all the nodes in the Constraint-Relation Graph, so that the sum of the weights of the links in these paths is maximal, and no constraints are violated. To this effect we apply an A*-like algorithm[7] which returns all the sets of paths that are maximally connected. In our example, two of these sets are $\{Path_3\}$ and $\{Path_4\}$ from Table 3, which have a total weight of $8\times2+2=18$. The following are possible realizations of $Path_3$ and $Path_4$[2#]:

$Path_3$	`Wallabies are like kangaroos. They have a pouch, which is like a pocket, and they hop.` *However*, `they are 3 ft tall.`
$Path_4$	`An animal's pouch is like a pocket. Wallabies have a pouch and they hop. They are like kangaroos,` *but* `they are 3 ft tall.`

6 Conclusion

In this paper, we have derived ordering relations for discourse based on the intentionality, support, soundness and directness of relations between RDs and propositions. In addition, we have obtained ordering constraints based on the domain-based prerequisite relation. These relations and constraints are used in an optimizing discourse structuring mechanism which can be applied to discourse that is planned both by opportunistic and by prescriptive mechanisms.

Additional discourse relations still remain to be incorporated into our mechanism[4]. However, preliminary tests in the domains of algebra (14 examples) and zoology (8 examples, including the one explained throughout this paper) show that the output of our mechanism is similar in structure to text found in instructional books.

References

1. A. Cawsey, Generating Explanatory Discourse. In *Current Research in Natural Language Generation*, R. Dale, C. Mellish, and M. Zock (Eds.) (Academic Press, 1990), p. 75-102.
2. H. Horacek, Exploiting Conversational Implicature for Generating Concise Explanations. In *EACL-91 Proceedings, the Meeting of the European Association of Computational Linguistics* (1991).
3. A. Joshi, B.L. Webber and R.M. Weischedel, Living Up to Expectations: Computing Expert Responses. In *AAAI-84 Proceedings, the National Conference on Artificial Intelligence* (1984), p. 169-175.
4. W.C. Mann and S.A. Thompson, Rhetorical Structure Theory: A Theory of Text Organization. Technical Report No. ISI/RS-87-190, Information Sciences Institute, Los Angeles (June 1987).
5. K. McKeown, Discourse Strategies for Generating Natural Language Text. In *Artificial Intelligence* 27(1) (1985), p. 1-41.
6. J.D. Moore and W.R. Swartout, A Reactive Approach to Explanation. In *IJCAI-11 Proceedings, International Joint Conference on Artificial Intelligence* (1989), p. 1504-1510.
7. N. Nilsson, *Principles of Artificial Intelligence* (Tioga Publishing Company, 1980).
8. D.D. Suthers, A Task-appropriate Hybrid Architecture for Explanations. In *Computational Intelligence* 7(4), Special Issue on Natural Language Generation (1991), p. 315-333.
9. I. Zukerman, A Predictive Approach for the Generation of Rhetorical Devices. In *Computational Intelligence* 6(1) (1990), p. 25-40.
10. I. Zukerman and R.S. McConachy, Generating Concise Discourse that Addresses a User's Inferences. In *IJCAI-93 Proceedings, International Joint Conference on Artificial Intelligence* (1993).
11. I. Zukerman and R.S. McConachy, Consulting A User Model to Address a User's Inferences during Content Planning. In *User Modeling and User Adaptive Interaction* (1993).

[2#] At present, our system generates RDs connected by constraints and relations. The English realization is presented for illustrative purposes.

Generating Queries during Cooperative Consultations[1#]

Bhavani Raskutti
Artificial Intelligence Section
Telecom Research Labs

Ingrid Zukerman
Department of Computer Science
Monash University

Clayton, Victoria 3168, Australia

Abstract

Analysis of naturally occurring information-seeking dialogues indicates that information providers often query a user when there is confusion regarding the user's intentions. In this paper, we present a mechanism for generating queries to disambiguate between multiple alternatives. Given a hierarchical representation of the alternatives possibly intended by the user, and the probabilities of these alternatives, our mechanism determines the hierarchy level at which a query must be directed, and the query to be posed. The determination is done by taking into account the nuisance factor associated with posing a query regarding an alternative that was not intended, and the number of additional queries that the system expects to generate after a particular query. Our mechanism for query generation has been implemented in a system called RADAR, a computerized information providing system that functions as a travel agent.

1 Introduction

Consider the following excerpt from a real-life conversation at a Melbourne travel agency (**TA** stands for the travel agent, and **USER** for the customer/user).

```
1. USER: I need to get some information about flights to Bombay.
2. TA: There are no direct flights to Bombay from Melbourne.
       The best fare I can get is via Colombo. Is that OK or ...?
```

It is apparent from the above excerpt that in order to provide appropriate assistance to a user, information providers[2#] often need to query a user in order to determine his/her plan, e.g., the query to determine which route the user has in mind (line 2 of the above excerpt). Querying is usually done when the information provider is unable to recognize the plan underlying the user's request.

The importance of recognizing plans for generating appropriate responses during an information-seeking interaction has been widely accepted in the artificial intelligence community. The incorporation of plan recognition capabilities into computerized information providers has enabled a range of cooperative behaviours, such as supplying more information than what is explicitly requested [1], responding to ill-formed queries[3], and understanding (a) indirect speech acts[6], (b) inter-sentential ellipsis[2,4], (c) queries based on invalid plans[7], and (d) sub-dialogues entered into to debug or correct plans[10,5].

However, the systems described above are not concerned with query generation to promote the cooperative process. When there is doubt regarding a speaker's intentions,

1# This research was supported in part by grant Y90/03/22 from the Australian Telecommunications and Electronics Research Board.

2# The terms *information provider* and *system* are used interchangeably in this paper. Similarly, the terms *speaker* and *user* have the same meaning.

these systems use heuristics to decide which of their inferences is the one intended by the speaker. If the heuristics do not determine a single alternative, then the speaker is expected to provide information without being requested to do so. This, however, is an unrealistic expectation since the user does not have access to the system's inferences.

Query generation for the purpose of disambiguating between multiple possible interpretations of a user's request has been considered by van Beek and Cohen[11] and by Wu[12]. Wu (1991) uses a decision-theoretic search approach to decide whether active acquisition of information is warranted. Van Beek and Cohen (1991) do not generate a disambiguating query if all the recognized plans are faultless, or if all of the plans have the same fault. In all other situations, however, there is ambiguity, and it is resolved by querying at the top-most level of a hierarchy of plans and slowly proceeding downward through the hierarchy. Note that this may not generate the most appropriate query when some of the branches in the hierarchy are much more plausible than others.

In the mechanism presented in this paper, this situation is prevented by taking into account two factors when determining the hierarchy level where a query should be directed: (1) the *nuisance factor* from generating a query that does not pertain to the user's intentions, and (2) *estimated queries*, i.e., the number of additional queries that the system expects to generate after a particular query. These factors are determined by using the probabilities of the possible alternatives and the contents of the alternatives themselves. By altering the relative weights assigned to each of these factors, the query generation process can emulate different approaches, one of which is the top-down approach exhibited by van Beek and Cohen's system[11].

2 Generating a Disambiguating Query

The query generation mechanism described in this paper is implemented as part of RADAR, a computerized information provider that **R**ecognizes **A**nd **D**iscriminates between **A**lternatives and **R**esponds. Query generation is done on the basis of the alternatives inferred by a plan recognizer in RADAR, and the probabilities of these alternatives. Each alternative is one possible *interpretation* of the user's request, and it is assigned a probability that represents the likelihood that this interpretation is indeed the one intended by the user. This probability is determined by the plan recognizer on the basis of a number of factors, such as the coherence of the dialogue, the amount of relevant information in the interpretation, and the practicality of the plan proposed in the interpretation[8,9]. The interpretations and their probabilities are represented as an *inference tree*, which is used in the process of query generation.

The inference tree consists of *leaves* and *decision nodes*. The leaves represent final interpretations. The decision nodes are the points where the plan recognizer considers a decision that generates multiple paths. For instance, when a new utterance is assimilated into the previous discourse, the plan recognizer considers a number of discourse relations as possibilities. If these possibilities lead to multiple paths, then a decision node is created.

Given an inference tree, the content of a disambiguating query depends on (1) the decision node that is selected for querying, and (2) the reason why this node was created.

2.1 Node Selection

When the inference tree consists of many decision nodes (Figure 1(a)) the system must choose the node at which a query should be directed. For the query to be helpful, it is necessary to consider the influence of two factors: (1) the **nuisance factor** from generating

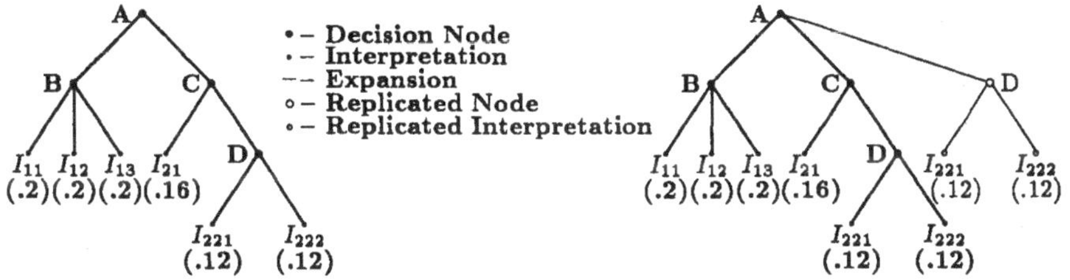

(a) Initial Inference Tree

(b) Expanded Tree for node A

Figure 1: Sample Inference Tree

a query that does not pertain to the user's intentions, and (2) **estimated queries**, i.e., the number of additional queries that the system expects to generate after this query. These two factors are then combined to yield a utility value for each decision node in the inference tree. The utilities of all the nodes are then compared, and the node with the greatest utility is chosen for querying.

Nuisance Factor: The nuisance factor represents the annoyance caused to the user when a query is directed at a decision node that does not lie in the path of the interpretation intended by the user. For instance, if the query is directed at node D in Figure 1(a), and the user did not intend any of the interpretations under node D (I_{221} or I_{222}), then the query is mis-directed, and is likely to annoy the user. Hence, nodes with a low nuisance factor are preferred for querying.

The nuisance factor of a node is proportional to the sum of the probabilities of the interpretations that are not under this node in the inference tree. Hence, NF_x, the nuisance factor for a node x of the inference tree T, is as follows:

$$NF_x = NuisanceWeight \times \left(\sum_{\{\text{leaf}_i \in T\}} Prob_{\text{leaf}_i} - \sum_{\{\text{leaf}_j \in X\}} Prob_{\text{leaf}_j} \right)$$

where X is the sub-tree under x. The value chosen for *NuisanceWeight* determines the weight allocated to the influence of the nuisance factor.

Estimated Queries: Estimated queries at a particular node is an indication of the system's expectation about the number of queries that may be needed before determining a unique interpretation under this node. For instance, in Figure 1(a), if a query is directed at node A then it is necessary to generate at least one more follow-up query. A query directed at a node which has a chain of nodes under it may require many follow-up queries to determine a user's intention, and a system that poses an endless stream of queries is clearly unhelpful. Hence, nodes with low estimated queries are preferred.

In order to determine the estimated queries at a particular decision node, the system takes into account the following: (1) estimated queries at each of the children of the node in question, (2) the relative probability that the child nodes are in the path of the intended interpretation, and (3) the possibility that an intermediate node may be bypassed when generating the next query.

As an illustration, consider the inference tree in Figure 1(a). After presenting a query about node A, the next query generated may be about B, C or D (bypassing C). In addition, if node C is queried, a query about node D may still be necessary. Therefore, in order to determine the estimated queries at node A, it is necessary to take into account the estimated queries and probabilities of its descendant nodes B, C and D. To this effect, before determining the estimated queries at a particular node x, we convert the sub-tree under x into an *expanded tree*. In this tree, all the decision nodes that are non-immediate descendants of x are replicated as children of x. This accounts for the possibility that a distant descendant of x could be chosen for querying immediately after querying x. For instance, for node A in Figure 1(a), the expanded tree is as shown in Figure 1(b), where node D is replicated as a child of A. The structure of the expanded tree and the relative probabilities of the nodes in the expanded tree are then used to determine the contribution of each branch of the expanded tree to the estimated queries at node x.

EQ_x, the estimated queries at node x in an inference tree, is determined on the basis of XE, the expanded sub-tree under x. Since the estimate is based on the fact that a query is generated at node x, EQ_x is one more than the sum of the contribution of all the child nodes xe_i of node x in the expanded tree XE. This contribution is expressed in terms of $RelProb_{xe_i}$, the relative probability of node xe_i, and EQ_{xe_i}, the estimated queries at xe_i. Hence, EQ_x is determined by the following formula:

$$EQ_x = 1 + \sum_{\{xe_i \in XE\}} (EQ_{xe_i} \times RelProb_{xe_i}) \quad (1)$$

$RelProb_{xe_i}$ is the fraction of the total probability of the expanded tree that is allocated to the cluster corresponding to node xe_i. Hence, $RelProb_{xe_i}$ is determined as follows:

$$RelProb_{xe_i} = \frac{\sum_{\{\mathrm{leaf_j} \in XE_i\}} Prob_{\mathrm{leaf_j}}}{\sum_{\{\mathrm{leaf_k} \in XE\}} Prob_{\mathrm{leaf_k}}} \quad (2)$$

where XE_i is the sub-tree under node xe_i.

According to this formula, the relative probability of node C in Figure 1(b) is $\frac{0.4}{1.24}$, where 0.4 represents the sum of the probabilities of the leaves under node C, and 1.24 is sum of the probabilities of all the leaves in the expanded tree. Note that the sum in the expanded tree is greater than 1 because the sub-tree under D is counted twice.

Substituting equation (2) in equation (1) yields the following formula for EQ_x, the estimated queries at any node x in an inference tree:

$$EQ_x = 1 + \sum_{\{xe_i \in XE\}} \left\{ EQ_{xe_i} \times \left(\frac{\sum_{\{\mathrm{leaf_j} \in XE_i\}} Prob_{\mathrm{leaf_j}}}{\sum_{\{\mathrm{leaf_k} \in XE\}} Prob_{\mathrm{leaf_k}}} \right) \right\} \quad (3)$$

Since the computation process is recursive, the computation of estimated queries at any node uses the estimated queries at lower nodes, e.g., EQ_D is necessary for determining EQ_C which in turn is needed for determining EQ_A.

Using equation (3), the estimated queries at the decisions nodes B and D in the inference tree in Figure 1(a) are 1, while the estimated queries of A and C are as follows:

$$EQ_A = 1 + EQ_B \left(\frac{0.6}{1.24}\right) + EQ_C \left(\frac{0.4}{1.24}\right) + EQ_D \left(\frac{0.24}{1.24}\right) = 2.19$$

$$EQ_C = 1 + EQ_D \left(\frac{0.24}{0.4}\right) = 1.6$$

Utility of a Node: U_x, the utility of a node x in an inference tree, is defined as the reciprocal of the sum of the nuisance factor of this node and the estimated queries at this node, i.e., $U_x = \frac{1}{NF_x + EQ_x}$. When choosing a node for querying, the utilities of all the decision nodes in the inference tree are compared, and the node with the maximum utility is chosen for generating a query. When two nodes have the same maximum utility, then the node at the higher level in the inference tree is chosen.

Table 1: **The Impact of *Nuisance Weight* on the Utility of a Node**

Node Name	Utilities for *Nuisance Weight*		
	= 0	= 2	= 4
A	0.457	0.457	<u>0.457</u>
B	<u>1.000</u>	<u>0.555</u>	0.385
C	0.625	0.357	0.250
D	1.000	0.397	0.248

Modelling Different Attitudes: Due to the explicit representation of the nuisance factor and the estimated queries when computing the utility of a node, the system is capable of modelling different attitudes of an information provider as follows:

- With a value of 0 for *Nuisance Weight*, the system disregards the nuisance factor and poses a query directed at the node with a minimum number of estimated queries, i.e., lower level nodes with a high probability are favoured. In this case, the behaviour exhibited by the system is that of a reckless information provider who will rather risk asking the wrong question than consider the annoyance caused to the user by posing an endless stream of possibly unrelated queries.
- With a high value for *Nuisance Weight*, e.g., a value of 4, the influence of the number of estimated queries is reduced. In this case, the behaviour of the system is similar to that exhibited by the system developed by van Beek and Cohen[11], where queries are directed at the top node of the tree. This setting models the attitude of a cautious information provider, who prefers the safe path of posing several orderly queries.
- An intermediate value for *Nuisance Weight*, e.g., a value of 2, takes into account both the nuisance factor and the estimated queries at a particular node, thus modelling an information provider who takes into consideration the annoyance caused to the user by directing a query at an unintended interpretation as well as that caused by asking a lot of questions. At present, the value for *Nuisance Weight* in RADAR is set at 2.

Table 1 contains the utilities of the nodes of the inference tree in Figure 1(a) for the three values of *Nuisance Weight* modelling the above described attitudes of an information provider. For each value, the utility of the chosen node is underlined. The node that is chosen by RADAR after processing the inference tree in Figure 1(a) is node *B*.

2.2 Content of a Query

The content of the generated query is determined by the reason why the interpretations diverged at the selected node. This determination is done as follows:

1. If the reason for multiple possibilities is the multiple discourse relations considered when assimilating a new utterance, then the user is queried about the intended relation. For instance, the following request results in the inference of two interpretations. "Get me a ticket to Sydney. I am going to Hawaii on the 11 am flight the day after tomorrow. I'll be flying from Adelaide." This is because the third sentence can be interpreted as elaborating on the Sydney trip or on the Hawaii trip. Hence, the reason for divergence is the different possible discourse relations, and the following query is generated: "Where are you going from Adelaide, to Sydney or to Hawaii?".
2. If the divergence is due to the different temporal sequences considered, then the user is queried about his/her preferred sequence. The query generated for the two possible orderings of the trips to Hawaii and Sydney is as follows: "I am not sure which itinerary you prefer. Is it first to Sydney then to Hawaii or first to Hawaii then to Sydney?"

3. If the reason for divergence is the different plans proposed by the plan generator, then the user is simply asked which one s/he prefers. The query lists all the plans if they are substantially different, e.g., different routing. Otherwise the query is about the difference, e.g., if the plan generator proposes two possible departure times from Sydney to Melbourne, then the generated query is as follows: "You can depart from Sydney to Melbourne at 9:00 am or 6:00 pm. Which would you prefer?"

3 Conclusion

In this paper we have presented a mechanism for generating disambiguation queries. Our mechanism takes into account both the nuisance factor and the estimated queries of a particular query, and thus is capable of emulating different attitudes of information providers. The mechanism is integrated into RADAR, a computerized information provider that operates in the domain of travel agencies. RADAR has been used to process 8 markedly different requests, each of which highlights a different capability of the system. In each case, the queries generated by RADAR (with $NuisanceWeight = 2$) were consistent with those generated by human information providers.

References

1. Allen, J.F. and Perrault, C.R. (1980), Analyzing Intention in Utterances. In *Artificial Intelligence* 15, pp. 143–178.
2. Carberry, S. (1985), A Pragmatics-based Approach to Understanding Intersentential Ellipsis. *Proceedings of the 23rd Annual Meeting of the Association of Computational Linguistics*, pp. 188–197, Chicago, Illinois.
3. Carberry, S. (1988), Modeling the User's Plans and Goals. In *Computational Linguistics* 14(3), pp. 23–37.
4. Litman, D. (1986), Understanding Plan Ellipsis. In *Proceedings of the Fifth National Conference on Artificial Intelligence*, pp. 32–37, Philadelphia, Pennsylvania.
5. Litman, D. and Allen, J.F. (1987), A Plan Recognition Model for Subdialogues in Conversation. In *Cognitive Science* 11, pp. 163–200.
6. Perrault, C.R. and Allen, J.F. (1980), A Plan-Based Analysis of Indirect Speech Acts. In *American Journal of Computational Linguistics* 6, 167–182.
7. Pollack, M.E. (1990), Plans as Complex Mental Attitudes. In Cohen, P., Morgan, J. and Pollack, M.E. (Eds.), *Intentions in Communication*, MIT Press.
8. Raskutti, B. & Zukerman, I. (1991), Generation and Selection of Likely Interpretations during Plan Recognition in Task-Oriented Consultations Systems. In *User Modeling and User Adapted Interaction* 1(2), pp. 323–353.
9. Raskutti, B. & Zukerman, I. (1992), What does a System Need to Know to Understand a User's Plans? In *Proceedings of the Fourteenth Annual Conference of the Cognitive Science Society*, pp. 1056–1061, Bloomington, Indiana.
10. Sidner, C.L. (1985), Plan Parsing for Intended Response Recognition in Discourse. In *Computational Intelligence* 1(1), pp. 1–10.
11. Van Beek, P. and Cohen, R. (1991), Resolving Plan Ambiguity for Cooperative Response Generation. In *Proceedings of the 12th International Joint Conference on Artificial Intelligence*, pp. 938–944, Sydney, Australia.
12. Wu, D. (1991), Implications of Active User Model Acquisition for Decision-Theoretic Dialog Planning and Plan Recognition. In *User Modeling and User Adapted Interaction* 1(2), pp. 149-172.

Rules and Strategies in Dialogue Logic

Larry Stewart-Zerba and Roderic Girle
School of Computing and Information Technology
Griffith University Nathan, Brisbane (Australia) 4111
{larry,rag}@cit.gu.edu.au

Abstract

The thesis of this paper is that the redeeming qualities of ELIZA when viewed properly can be utilised to develop a viable system. We propose and discuss the development of a multiautomata dialogue system that employs ELIZA's reactive nature and the most recent work in dialogue logic and dialogue game theory.

1 Introduction

What was it that offended most people about the ELIZA program [9], besides its lack of philosophical and cognitive grounding? The most offensive thing, barring these qualities, would have to be its simplistic superficial interaction with a person. Moreover there were no apparent rules or strategies to allow an interactive rational argument or discusion with a user. However, ELIZA did have the important and useful quality of treating activity as automatic and reactive. When some simple mechanisms are implemented in a system that treats activity in this way, some surprisingly complex responses emerge. The reactive robots of Rodney Brooks [2] are one example.

The thesis of this paper is that the redeeming qualities of ELIZA, when viewed properly, can be utilised to develop a viable system. This view concentrates on ELIZA's foremost ability, dialogue. We propose and discuss the development of a dialogue system that employs ELIZA's reactive nature, but overcomes its superfical interaction through the use of the most recent work in dialogue logic and dialogue game theory.

There are two main areas of research considering dialogue. One is linguistic discourse analysis and the second is dialogue logic. The first uses empirical research into natural language, its structure and processing.

The second views dialogue as having two levels, namely, a natural language level, and logical structure level, the former driving the later. The dialogicians see dialogue as an activity much like argumentation. In dialogue-logic, the interaction is explained by rules for particular kinds of responses and interactions. These rules ensure that the dialogue is a joint activity between the participants.

In the following paper, the dialogue-logic point of view is investigated in terms of implementing a dialogue logic system that enforces a joint activity. First we set out an investigation of dialogue systems, followed by a detailed account of the our DL system (Dialogue Logic). We then conclude by discussing how to extend the DL system, by using strategies so that we might replace one person with a computer.

2 Dialogue Systems

The work of dialogicians has created several dialogue systems. Examples of these dialogue systems can be found in the area of logic [3, 4, 5, 6, 7, 8],(see [1], for a more complete bibliography). Despite their differences, they share common features.

Two common features are the notion of locutions and a commitment store for each participant. There is a set of rules to govern each of these features. There are also syntactic stipulations which govern the type of locutions allowed by the logic. The syntactic list contains the sort of locutions found in a real discourse: statements, withdrawals, responses, challenges and questions.

One type of rule is *Interaction Rules*. These rules govern the sequence in which the locutions are asserted to ensure that a dialogue is sustained. For example, a question of the form *Why do you believe P?* must be followed by the reasons for the conclusion of *P*. These rules ensure that the dialogue is a joint activity.

The second type of rule is *Commitment Store Rules*. These rules govern the expansion and the contraction of each participant's commitment stores, based on the statements, withdrawals, responses challenges and questions used. The contents of the participant's commitment stores need not be logically consistent. If there is a *prima face* inconsistency in a commitment store then it is a participant's responsibility to detect and demand its resolution.

3 The DL System

The initial focus in building the DL system was to investigate the effects of adding reactive rules to a set of formal dialogue logic rules to sustain an interactive rational argument between two participants. Therefore to test DL's rules, the cannons of fallacious arguments will be used. The following section outlines the architecture of DL.

DL incorporates the basic set of rules governing formal dialogue systems. More complete dialogue systems are found in [4, 5, 6, 7]. The DL system has an ELIZA like front end, which simplifies a participant's input. The simplified input is then syntactically checked and transformed into its locution type, by a Definite Clause Grammar.

In this stage of the system there are five types of locutions allowed [4]. A more extensive set of rules are found in [4] (note at the time of this publication DL has been updated to include these rules).

- **Categorical Statements:** These are statements such as *P*, *P and Q*, *P or Q* and *If P then Q*.
- **Withdrawals:** The *withdraw* of the statement *P* is of the form *I withdrawal P* or *I do not accept P*.
- **TF-Questions:** The *tf-questions* are of the form *Is it the case that P?*
- **Challenges:** The challenges are of the form *Why is it supposed to be that P?*
- **Resolution Demands:** The resolution demands of the statement *P* are of the form *Resolve whether P*.

Each of the above locutions has commitment store rules. We now set out these rules, with a brief explanation of each. There are four types of commitment store rules [4].

(C1) Statements: After a statement *P*, unless the previous event was a challenge, *P* goes into the commitment store of both participants.

(C2) Defences: After the statement of grounds, *Because P*, when the previous event was *Why Q?*, both P and *If P then Q* are add to the commitment store of both participants.

(C3) Withdrawals: After the withdrawal of P, statement of ignorance about P, or a denial of P, the statement P is removed from the speaker's commitment store. The hearer's commitment store remains unchanged.

(C4) Challenges: After the challenge of P, the statement P is included in the hearer's commitment store, the statement P is removed from the speaker's commitment store, and the challenge $WhyP?$ is added to the speaker's commitment store.

The commitment to the challenge rule above seems strange at first glance. However, the inclusion of P into the hearer's commitment store can be removed by a withdrawal or a denial (see (v)(a) below and (C3) above). Also, if P was in the speaker's commitment store it is removed, because if the speaker had no problem with the statement, it should not have been challenged.

There are also seven rules of interaction, which for the purposes of this paper only Challenge is set out in full:

(v) Chall: After *Why P?*, the next event must be either:

(a) a withdrawal or denial of P, or

(b) the resolution demand of an immediate consequence conditional whose consequent is P and whose antecedent is a conjunction of statements to which the challenger is committed, or

(c) a statement of grounds *acceptable* to the challenger. (An acceptable statement of grounds (*Because P*) is acceptable to a participant X, iff either P is not under challenge by X, or if it is, then there is a set of statements each of which X is committed to and none of which X is committed to challenge, and P is an immediate modus ponens consequence of the set (see [7] for a complete discussion).

The remaining 6; RepStat, Imcom, LogChall, TF-Question, Resolve and Resolution, can be retrieved from [4].

The rules which structure the sequence of locutions, and regulate the content of the participant's commitment stores, can be viewed as reactive agents. They are reactive in the sense that they base their present actions on previous locutions.

4 The Referee

In the present implementation DL, the computer manages a debate, or dialogue between two people. In this arrangement the computer acts as the referee, only interceding, or reacting, when one of the participants has violated an interaction rule. For example:

Person	Locution	Commitment Store
X	P	$X + P$
		$Y + P$

(The statement P is entered into both commitment stores (C1).)

Person	Locution	Commitment Store
Y	$WhyP?$	$Y + WhyP?$
		$Y - P$
		$X + P$

(Y has challenged the statement P (C4))

Person	Locution	Commitment Store
X	Q	

This is the referee: You cannot issue a statement. The previous locution was a challenge, you can only respond with a withdrawal, challenge or a defence of the statement under challenge. eg I withdraw P, Because Q, Why ask why P?.

As this example demonstrates, when a participant violates a locution rule, or the dialogue has broken down, the referee intercedes and instructs the participant on how to respond properly.

However, there are situations where the referee does not intercede and the dialogue is no longer a joint activity. For example, if X states *I hate penguins*, to which Y states *Clyde the elephant has no trunk.* and then X states *I do not personally know any penguins.*. The referee will not intercede in this situation, even though the dialogue has clearly broken down. The reason for this is due to the issue of irrelevance, rather than the violation of an interaction rule. The question at this stage is should relevance be an issue for the referee?

Here is another example, which brings further issues to bear on the above question.

Person	Locution
X	P
Y	$WhyP?$
X	$BecauseQ?$
Y	$WhyQ?$

In this example, Y is actually performing a strategy, that is whenever an assertion is made, challenge it. X could also have a strategy of withdrawing any statement under challenge. The strategies that a participant uses sets up the way in which they will react to the other participant's locutions. What is needed is a strategic point of view to examine how strategies will effect a dialogue debate.

5 Strategy Rules

The question for the next stage of the DL system is how to replace one of the participants with the computer? What is needed is some strategy, or strategies for the computer as participant to use. One way of implementing strategies is through a set of rules. When implementing Interaction Rules we are concerned with what is allowed to follow a locution such as $WhyP?$ However, when implementing a strategy as rules we have to be concerned with asking $WhyP?$ of a participant that states P, where $\sim P$ already exists in the questioner's commitment store.

The Strategy Rules shall be implemented as meta-rules. They will contain knowledge about the Interaction Rules, and organise the order that the possible next locution events are tried. The personality implemented through the strategy rules dictates this ordering. For example:

Participant	Locution	Stores	Possible Strategy Rules
X	P	$X+P$ $Y+P$	1.If X asserts P then assert interest in P 2. ...
Y	Tell more about P	$X+Interest$ $Y+Interest$	

In this example, Y's strategy is first to show interest in P whether or not Y has any prior commitment to P. This means Y is a passive arguer, interested only in the other participant's point of view. Contrast this with an arguer who is committed to their own beliefs (we view a participant's commitment store as their beliefs).

Participant	Locution	Stores	Possible Strategy Rules
X	P	$X+P$ $Y+P$	1.If X asserts P and $\sim P$ in Y's commitment store then deny P. 2. ...
Y	I do not accept P	$Y-P$	

Here, Y's strategy is to deny P, because of their commitment to $\sim P$. In denying P, the locution P is removed from Y's commitment store, but X still retains their commitment to P. This type of strategy allows both participants to retain their beliefs, but allows Y to avoid any further argument. Contrast the previous two strategies with that of the aggressive arguer.

Participant	Locution	Stores	Possible Strategy Rules
X	P	$X+P$ $Y+P$	1.If X asserts P and $\sim P$ in Y's commitment store then challenge P. 2. ...
Y	Why P accept P	$Y+WhyP?$ $Y-P$ $X+P$	

The aggressive arguer when confronted with an opposing point of view immediately challenges it. The challenge not only removes the locution P from Y's commitment store, it also threatens the existence of P in the other participant's commitment store. Thus, the aggressive arguer is concerned with both their beliefs and the other participant's beliefs as well.

Through the use of strategies, it is possible to implement a broad spectrum of personalities, from passive to aggressive. The strategies can also be mixed. For example, participant Y strategy is: always be passive, while retaining all beliefs, unless X persists in asserting P, then become aggressive. This strategy permits a participant to retain their beliefs, while still listening to another persistent participant's view. Another complex strategy is for Y to be either passive or aggressive until X enters a locution relevant to a topic Y is interested. When this happens Y becomes completely passive and obtains as much information about the topic as possible.

The topic of relevance is thus important to both strategies and to the refereed DL system. Should the referee handle relevance, or should strategy rules address this issue? What if a strategy is to allow a participant ample time to make their point before interrupting and demanding the relevance of locutions? The problem of relevance therefore is a borderline case between rules and strategies.

6 Conclusion

The advantage of the dialogue account is that we are not worried about considering the intensions or beliefs of the participants *a priori*. Instead, we account for the rules that allow the participant to express their intensions and beliefs. This allows the DL system to react, or respond, in appropriate ways to any participant. When this advantage is used in extending the DL system through the implementation of strategies, we can use a computer to replace one of the participants.

Further work needs to be done on implementing a suite of strategies to use in different situations. These different strategies could be used in the full DL system to investigate different instruction methods and their effect on learning, and utility. Also further research is required to resolve the overlap between rules and strategies.

References

[1] E.M. Barth and Martens J.L. *Argumentation Approaches to Theory Formation.* John Benjamins B.V., Amsterdam, 1982.

[2] Rodney A. Brooks. A robust layered control system for a mobile robot. *IEEE Journal of Robotics and Automation*, RA-2(1):14–23, March 1986.

[3] R.A. Girle. Dialogue and discource. In *Proceedings of the Fourth Annual Computer Assisted Learning Tertiary Conference*, pages 123–135, Adelaide, Australia, 1986.

[4] R.A. Girle. Eliza and the automata. In *Proceedings of the Third Annual Conference of AI, Simulation and Planning in High Autonomy Systems*, pages 287–293, Perth, Australia, 1992.

[5] C.L. Hamblin. *Fallacies.* Methuen, London, 1970.

[6] J.D. Mackenzie. Question-begging in non-cumulative systems. *Journal of Philosophical Logic*, 8:117–133, 1979.

[7] J.D. Mackenzie. Begging the question in dialogue. *Australian Journal of Philosophy*, 62(2):174–181, 1984.

[8] D.N. Walton. *Logical Dialogue-Games and Fallacies.* University Press of America, Lanham, 1984.

[9] J. Weizenbaum. *Computer Power and Human Reason.* Pelican, Harmondsworth, 1976.

THE USE OF CONTEXT IN THE UNDERSTANDING OF SPOKEN ENGLISH

C. Rowles, M. de Beler [1], M. O'Donnell and P. Sefton [2]

[1] Telecom Research Laboratories P.O. Box 249 Clayton, Victoria, 3168

[2] Sydney University

Abstract

The automatic understanding of spoken English is more difficult than understanding text, in that we have the additional problems of speech recogniser errors, ungrammaticality and large shifts of focus in spontaneously generated dialogues. This paper presents a model of spoken language dialogues which integrates the contexts of exchange, task, semantics and phonology to help overcome these problems. We illustrate how this model works in an experimental system for the understanding and response to telephone-based, spoken, information-seeking queries.

Introduction

Spoken dialogues often include terse and fragmented components, and speech recognisers do not always recognise every word correctly. Word recognition errors occur, as do insertions and deletions due to incorrect segmentation. For computers to accurately understand spoken dialogues, they must use all available linguistic resources, including prosody, syntax, the semantics of words and phrases, and the context of conversational exchange, task and domain.

In this paper, we present a dialogue model that integrates prosody, semantics and dialogue and task contexts in the understanding of spoken, English, information-seeking, telephone dialogues. Our work has centred on the construction of an experimental spoken language understanding system that takes its input as an unsegmented stream of words from a speech recogniser, segments it using prosodic and syntactic information, parses the stream into discourse and propositional moves and analyses these to determine the speaker's intentions (Rowles et al 1993). A dialogue manager, managing turn-taking and generating responses to the speaker. In this paper, we concentrate on the dialogue analysis and management tasks.

A Spoken Dialogue Model

Our model of spoken dialogues integrates syntactic, semantic, pragmatic and phonological resources and is based on the systemic-functional view of language (O'Donnell 1990, Eggins et al 1991). In this view, dialogues are seen as systems of conversational moves focused on specific information exchanges, with each utterance having a specific function within the dialogue. The model represents dialogues between two agents (e.g. the caller and the system) as a set of communicative states and communicative actions that move the dialogue from one state to another. Each action is a distinct conversational move (or utterance). From any given state there are many possible actions depending on the communicative context of that state, and each action has its own activation conditions and its own effects, which are new dialogue states.

Each state in a caller-system dialogue has a generic domain context (i.e. domain pragmatics: what the call is about) and an interactional context (i.e. where we are in the dialogue, such as answering a question). Each action has an interactional context and a speech function (i.e. what an agent is trying to achieve with an individual conversational move, in other words a task context). Moves are realised within lexico-grammatical and phonological bounds. The organisation of moves into specific interactional exchanges, and exchanges into sub-dialogues achieving specific domain objectives produces the hierarchical linguistic strata of the systemic-functional model. Each stratum provides a communicative context for the strata below, and in turn provides a realisation of the strata above using the currency of that stratum (Figure 1). Each move is interpreted within the contexts defined at each stratum. Thus, a move must be understood in terms of the roles it plays within the interactional or exchange context (i.e. move vs response), the task

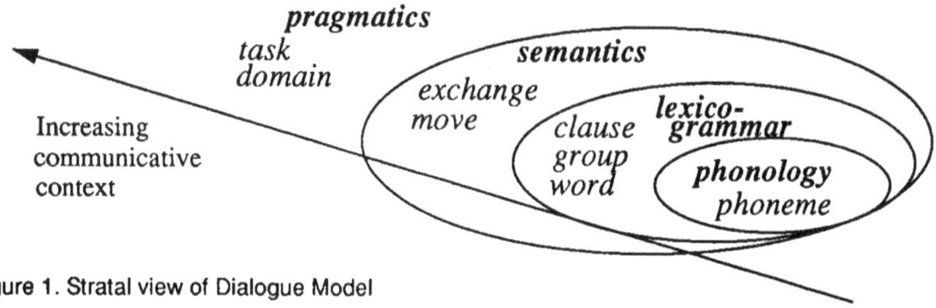

Figure 1. Stratal view of Dialogue Model

context (i.e. the dialogue function of each move within an exchange), the generic context (i.e. domain task being carried out) and the domain semantics (i.e. the task domain).

The contexts impact on the understanding in different ways. The pragmatics of domain and domain task determine the correct sense of ambiguous words or grammatical constructions, and so constrain how the propositional content of a move is interpreted. Prosody provides a context in terms of how a move was articulated and what interpretation the hearer should place on that move. The generic context constrains the sort of topics to be discussed and the potential speech functions, as it limits the types of query that can be answered. Lastly, the exchange context restricts potential speech functions, such as in a question usually being followed by an answer.

The model integrates these contexts and allows conversational moves to inherit appropriate dialogue contexts. This is done via taxonomic inheritance networks for Generic Context, Exchange Context and Speech Function. Each network provides a taxonomic classification of moves within that context, and allows the roles of a move to be understood in terms of the dialogue. Network branches provide alternative or combined choices. In the Generic Context Network, combined choices provide conjoined sub-goals that complete various stages in an information seeking dialogue. The Exchange Context Network provides a move classification in terms of its turn-taking, initiation and completion roles, while the Speech Function Network classifies moves according to their dialogue structuring or propositional roles within an exchange.

Each move from the caller is analysed and classified according to each network. At each branching point in a network, attributes of the current move and dialogue state are compared to matching conditions for the next lower classifications to select the most appropriate to describe that move. The Speech Function Network uses the move attributes mood, prosody and type (e.g. declarative), and knowledge of the current state of the dialogue, to classify the speech function of the move and hence, determine the caller's proposition or dialogue structuring intentions.

Once the speech function of a move is known, the Generic Context Network uses the propositional content of the move (i.e. a query) to classify the move according to which sub-goals have been completed and what information is still required. The Exchange Context Network then uses the speech function and tone contour to update the current state of the dialogue, such as who initiated the current exchange and who is expected to continue the dialogue. If the caller's query is complete, and the caller does not wish to change it, a database may be queried. If not complete, the Exchange and Generic Contexts indicate how the system should respond, such as asking for more information or waiting for the caller to complete the query. If the system should respond, the Exchange and Generic Contexts are used to determine the type of response required and the Speech Function Network is used to determine the attributes (i.e. mood, tone contour, etc.) of the system move to be generated.

The model can thus be used to analyse a caller's moves as well as generate appropriate responses. The sequence of actions is shown in Figure 2. Of course, dialogues do not always proceed as planned and the model is sufficiently dynamic to allow for linguistic actions such as

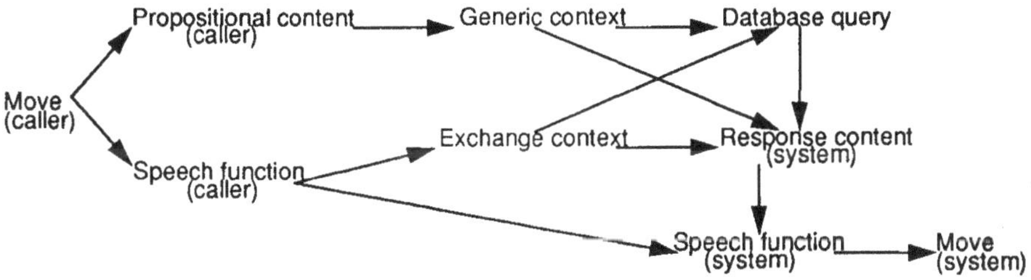

Figure 2. Information flow during analysis and generation.

confirmatory repetitions, unexpected responses resulting from misunderstandings, and so on.

Dialogue Analysis and Management

The dialogue analyser takes the parse tree with tone contour annotation from a parser that itself has used prosodic information to disambiguate structures which cannot be disambiguated syntactically/semantically, and to speed up processing (Rowles & Huang 1992). The dialogue analyser matches the mood and tone-contour of the current move, constrained by context of the previous move, against the taxonomic networks to determine the speech function and propositional content (i.e. query specification) of the move.

The dialogue manager controls the dialogue, manages turn taking and generates the machine's responses or actions (i.e. initiate a database query). The Speech Function, Exchange Context and Generic Context networks are implemented as system resources, and can be accessed and updated by both the dialogue analyser and dialogue manager. Figure 3 shows the algorithm implemented in the dialogue manager.

In our application, the first turn is always the machine's: "Hello, Information Service, can I help you?". The current features of the taxonomic networks are updated and a response generated. When the caller takes the turn, a move is created and used by the dialogue analyser to

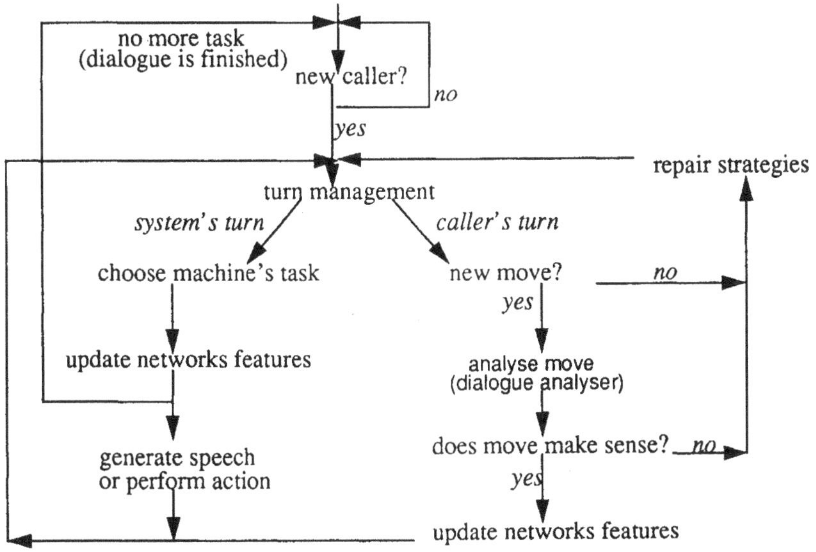

Figure 3. Turn management and dialogue analysis

match its speech-functional content against the Speech Function network and its propositional content against the proposition of the different generic tasks activated at this stage. If one of the matches is not possible, i.e. the move doesn't make sense, repair strategies are available. Once the dialogue analyser has analysed the move, the networks are updated: current features in the Speech Function Network, state of the current exchange in the Exchange Context Network, generic tasks achieved and/or activated in the Generic Context Network.

The Speech Function Network classifies moves according to their role within an exchange (Figure 4). A move is described in terms of its propositional and a speech-functional components. An exchange is a set of moves which together complete a single proposition. For analysis, this network allows us to derive a semantic analysis from a given grammatical analysis, the parse tree. A set of mapping rules are used to build up the propositional and speech-functional components of the move. For the purpose of generation, the network allows us to use the propositional plus speech-functional options as input to determine the attributes of the system move.

Figure 5 shows a fragment of the Exchange Context Network, which provides a classification for turn taking, initiation and completion within exchange moves. The exchange context is changed by each new move. Because an exchange can be suspended and returned to, we to keep a history of all exchanges in a stack, the current exchange context being on top. Each exchange context records the state of negotiation so far, who initiated the exchange, whose turn it is and the propositional content. When the caller or machine needs to resume a prior, not closed exchange, we can retrieve the relevant exchange context from the stack and resume the exchange with this context as the current exchange.

The Generic Context Network (Figure 6) classifies the different generic tasks to be achieved in order to query the database. This network is different to the previous two, as features or attributes are incrementally gathered throughout the dialogue The dialogue is modelled as a sequence of tasks, each working towards the achievement of the information retrieval goal,. Each task has a set of contextual constraints (the activation conditions) and a set of contextual effects (the change in the generic context brought by the completion of the task).

The interface between the Exchange and Generic Contexts is done through generic tasks (e.g. greeting, location specification). Tasks still to be done are indicated by the Generic Context Network, while the Exchange Context determines when a task may be done. The contextual effects of the current task give us the new Generic Context attributes. The tasks with true activation conditions are now members of the new system's or caller's do-able tasks list.

Dialogue Handling Example

At the beginning of the dialogue, the system says: "Hello, Information Service, can I help you?". The caller may return the greeting, then say: "I need to buy a new radiator for my car" . The following move is created from the parse tree:

(mood 'decl tone-contour '3 type 'system speech-function 'info-request prop (:bus-type 'radiator))

The mood, tone-contour and speech-function of the move are matched against the expected speech function in the Speech Function Network (generated from the previous move), to obtain the most likely set of speech function attributes, which are in this case:

'(initiate-new-exchange negotiatory-initiation initiating-prop continuing either-speaker-next).

The features *'continuing* and *'either-speaker-next* are derived from the tone-contour, which is flat in this case. Rules are applied to generate the exchange context attributes:

'(callers-turn caller-initiated negotiatory-exchange prop-completed speaker-may-continue)

Because the caller is initiating a new exchange, a new context object is pushed on the exchange stack and the generic domain context changes: the speech function and propositional content of the move are matched against the generic tasks that are possible for the caller at this

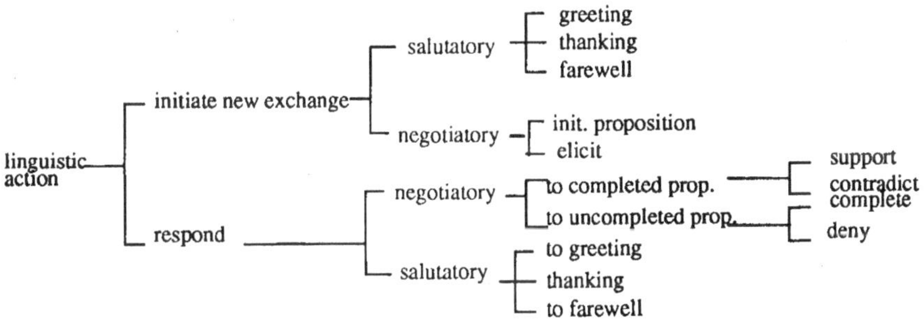

Figure 4. Fragment of Speech Function Taxonomic Network

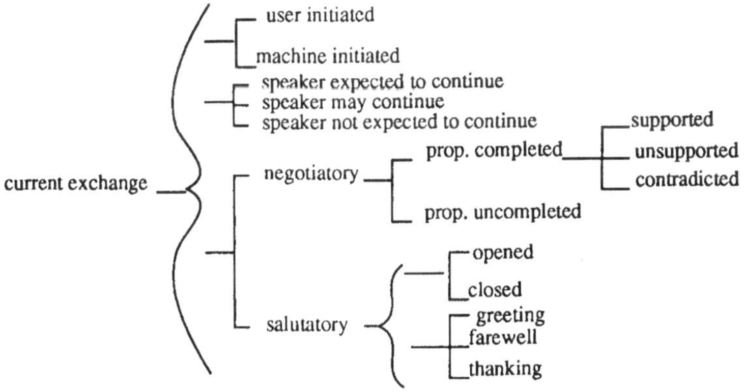

Figure 5. Fragment of Exchange Context Taxonomic Network

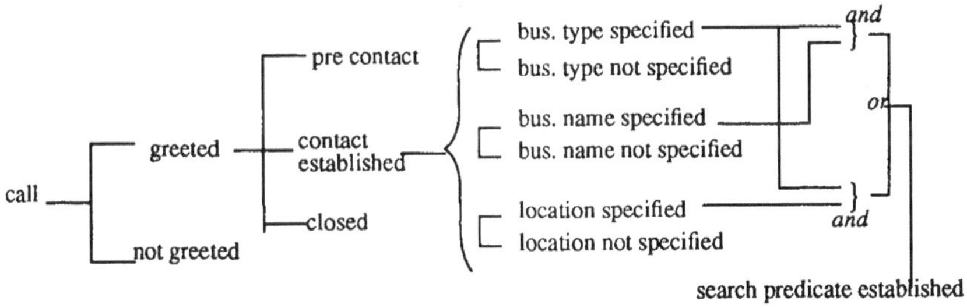

Figure 6. Fragment of Generic Context Taxonomic Network

stage (generated by the generic context attributes of the previous move). At this point, the most likely generic task is: *'specification-of-business-type*. The generic task leads us to a new set of generic context attributes:

(call-connected greeted contact-established bus-type-specified).

The turn management function works out that the system has to wait to give a chance to the caller to say something, because *'either-speaker-next* is an active attribute of the speech function. If the caller doesn't say anything, then the turn is given to the system. If the current exchange doesn't need to be continued and there is no prior closed exchange on the stack that could be resumed, the machine initiates a new exchange. The next highest priority task on the system's agenda is to get a location for the database request. The generic domain task is now *'location-specification*. The move associated with the task is the following:

(mood 'wh tone-contour '2 type 'system speech-function 'info-request :prop (:location 'Variable))

Tone-contour 2 indicates a question. The speech function attributes of this move are:

'(initiate-new-exchange negotiatory-initiation elicit elicit-content congruent-content-question terminating strong-termination).

The exchange context attributes now become:

'(machines-turn machine-initiated negotiatory-exchange prop-uncompleted content-question speaker-not-expected-to-continue)

The system uses the system's response move and speech function attributes to generate the question: "Which location would you like?". The system was not expected to continue, so the turn is given to the caller who may answer: "In Clayton". From this, the parser outputs:

(mood 'decl tone-contour '1 type 'discourse speech-function 'clarify prop (:location 'Clayton)).

This move is successfully matched against the speech function attributes expected:

'(negotiatory-response respond-to-uncompleted-prop complete-prop content-completion).

The exchange context attributes are:

'(callers-turn machine-initiated negotiatory-exch prop-completed speaker-not-expected-to-cont)

The system checks that the move is consistent with the current generic domain task, i.e. that the caller is giving a location. Because this is not a new exchange, the generic context attributes do not change. The turn management function gives the turn to the system which will find that it now has enough information to start a database request.

Conclusion

We have presented a systemic-functional model for the understanding and generation of conversational moves in an information-seeking, spoken dialogue setting. The model represents various linguistic strata and allows the integration of a wide range of linguistic resources and allows these resources to be used at various stages of analysis and generation.

Acknowledgements

The permission of the Director of Research, Telecom Australia to present this paper is gratefully acknowledged. The authors are grateful to Julie Vonwiller, Robin King and Christian Matthiesson, Sydney University, and Xiuming Huang and Bhavani Raskutti, TRL, for important contributions to this project.

References

Eggins, S., Vonwiller, J., Matthiesson, C., and Sefton, P., (1991), *Analysis and Models of Information Seeking Dialogues*, 18th International Systemic Congress, Tokyo, 1991.

O'Donnell, M. (1990), *A Dynamic Model of Exchange*, Word, Vol. 41, 3, December, 1990.

Rowles, C. & Huang, X. (1992), *Prosodic Aids to Syntactic and Semantic Analysis of Spoken English*, 30th Annual Meeting of the Association for Computational Linguistics, Delaware.

Rowles, C.D., Huang, X., M. de Beler, J. Vonwiller, R. King, C. Matthiesson, P. Sefton & M. O'Donnell, (1993),*Understanding Spoken English Using a Systemic Functional Framework.* First Pacific Association Conference on Computational Linguistics, Vancouver, Canada.

Cruttenden, A., (1986), *Intonation*, Cambridge University Press.

Neural Networks

The Classification of NOAA Images Using Multilayer Neural Network

Tao Chen Mikio Takagi

Department of Electronics Engineering
Institute of Industrial Science, University of Tokyo
7-22-1 Roppongi, Minato-ku, Tokyo 106, Japan

ABSTRACT

Analysis of satellite images often requires classification of image objects. It is widely recognized that the assumptions required by conventional classification methods (maximum likelihood estimation, etc.) are suspect for textural features based on image pixel brightness. We propose an image feature based neural network approach for the classification of NOAA images. The learning algorithm is a generalized back-propagation with gain and weight decay. The classification accuracy of 100% is reached for validation data set. The classification result is satisfied after careful visual investigation.

1 Introduction

The classification accuracy of NOAA (National Oceanic Atmospheric Administration) image has been greatly effected by existence of clouds. Clouds, especially cloud boundaries are often classified uncorrectly as cold lands, snow, fog. Meanwhile, the discrimination of high, middle and low cloud is also not an easy task. Many classes in NOAA images are overlapped by using the convenient classifiers based upon the first order statistics. Many classification methods assume that the form of class-conditional densities is known. The popular maximum likelihood estimation approach assumes multivariate normality. However, it is widely recognized that this assumption is suspect for textural features based on cloud pixel brightness.

The use of neural network in the geosciences is relatively new, and includes applications to problems such as cloud classification and sunspot predictions. Lee et al. [7] used a neural network software package by Neural Ware Inc. to distinguish between three cloud types. Koons and Gorney [5] predicted the timing and number of the sunspot maxima using a neural network software package. The backpropagation based pixel-by-pixel classification method proposed by Bischof in [1] usually

IR \ VIS	white	light gray	dark gray	black
white	thick/high	high	thin	-
light gray	middle	middle	thin	-
dark gray	low	low	low	cold front
black	sunglint	low/fog	land	forest

Table 1: Spectral Property of Image Objects

has a salt-and-pepper appearance, and the classification accuracy is remained on the same level with conventional Bayesian classifiers because of the insufficience of hidden layer and image features.

2 Spectral Properties of NOAA Images

NOAA has 5 channel data. CH-1 (0.58-0.68 um) and 2 (0.725-1.1 um) are visible channels, and CH-3 (3.55-3.93 um), 4 (10.3-11.3 um) , and 5 (11.5-12.5 um) belong to infrared channels. The high reflectance in CH3 denotes water clouds [2], the medium means ice clouds, and the low reflectance represents snow. The cloud and snow are also determined by the temperature difference of CH4 and CH5 [3]. The reflectance difference between CH1 and CH2 can be used to detect fog, sunglint(positive value) and plants(negative value).

The brightness information only is not enough to classify NOAA image correctly. Different categories may have almost the same brightness or feature, and therefore overlap with each other. For example, the cirrus scenes include cirrus, cirrostratus, cirrocumulus, and even contrails. The difference between fog (low-lying cloud) and other clouds as detected by satellite is very small.

3 Image Data Set

The role of statistical image features in high dimension data has become more and more important in classifying and segmenting the multiband images. In high dimensional remote sensing data, the amount of information is scattered in many bands, the adjacent bands are very highly correlated and most of the data are distributed only along a few major components. The classes are often overlapped with each other in traditional statistical classification methods and pixel-by-pixel method. Therefore, the high classification accuracies can not be expected by using traditional statistical classifiers. The experiment images used are at 1506LT on April 18th, 1991. The short straight line in the right middle corner is noise. The selection of a training set consists of two steps. At first, Kohonen's self organization map [4] is applied to the multiband data. Then several small homogeneous regions inside

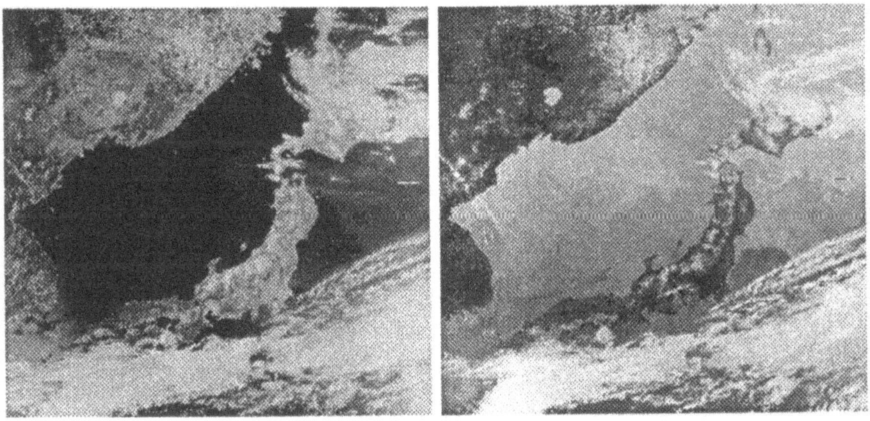

(a) (b)

Fig 1: Original Images(512×480) (a)CH-2 (b)CH-4

the clusters are selected by hand to represent each corresponding category. Half of the experimental data is determined randomly as training data set, the other half is left for validation.

4 Network Architecture

Neural networks have been recognized as one of a class of flexible non-linear regression methods due to the classification ability via regression. It has becoming clear that the nonlinear, nonparametric neural network classifiers provide the highest cloud classification accuracy of existing approaches.

For an N-input and M-output L layer feedforward network, the output error between the neural output Y_p and teacher signal O_p for pattern p can be defined: $E_p^{bp} = \frac{1}{2}\sum_{i=0}^{M-1}(O_{pi}-Y_{pi})^2$. The learning algorithm is: $\Delta w_{ij}^l(t) = -[\sum_k \delta_k w_{jk}]F_j'(\sum_k w_{kj}y_k)y(i)$ and $\Delta w_{ij}^l(t+1) = \eta\delta_j x_i' + \alpha\Delta w_{ij}^l(t)$. Where

$$\delta_j = \begin{cases} Y_j(1-Y_j)(O_j-Y_j) & \text{output nodes} \\ x_j'(1-x_j')\sum_k \delta_k w_{jk} & \text{otherwise} \end{cases} \tag{1}$$

After introducing gain and weight decay, the learning rule for weight is as follow: $\Delta w_{ij}^l = \varepsilon_w \frac{\partial E_p^{bp}}{\partial net_i^l} a_j^{l-1} - \lambda w_{ij}^l$, where a_i^l denotes the activation of ith node in layer l, $net_i^l = \sum_k w_{ik}^l a_k^{l-1}$ is the net input to the ith node of layer l, ε_w and λ are small positive constants.

Gain can be seen as modulating the stepsize of weight change, and amplifying learning in nodes that find successful directions in weight space [6]. weight decay

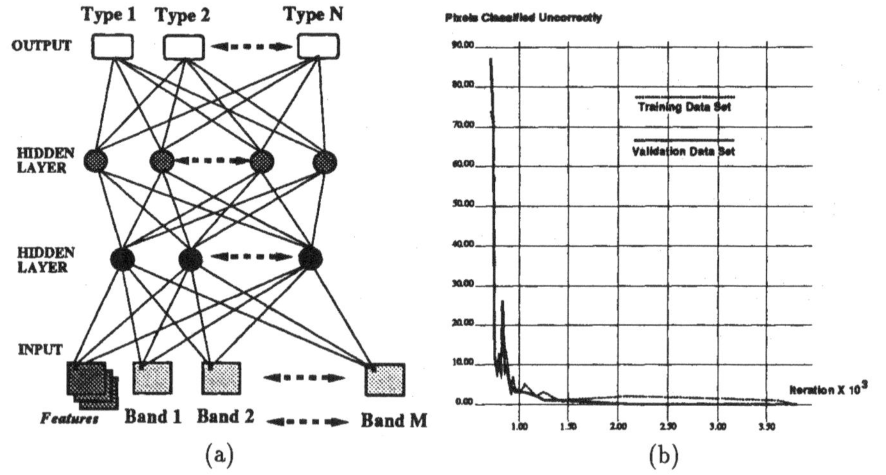

Fig 2: (a)System Structure (b)Classification Errors of Training and Validation Set

can improve the generalization performance of networks, and suppress irrelevant components of weight vectors by penalizing large weight vector.

The system structure is shown in Fig 2(a). The learning algorithm is a generalized backpropagation. The input layer has 29 units, corresponding the graylevel values, 7×7 region averages and variances of 5 channels for a given pixel, direction-oriented features and graylevel differences between channels. 10 outputs are repectively: 0: high cloud(HI-CLD), 1: greenless land(LAND), 2: water(WATER), 3: snow(SNOW), 4: ice, 5: low cloud(LO-CLD), 6: plant(PNT), 7: sunglint(SUNGLN), 8: cold water(CWT), and 9: thin cloud(TN-CLD).

The hidden layer allows the network to form its own internal representation of the data, on which the decision boundaries are formed. The network may not contain sufficient degrees of freedom to form a representation if too few middle nodes are selected. The learning algorithm, since it is based on a heuristic, may also improperly train hidden nodes.

5 Result Analysis

For validation data set, the classification accuracy is 100% for each category. The classification result corresponds with original image very well after visual interpretation. During the training, we let the offsets of each layer be changeable according to weight change. The offset changes is plotted in Fig 4(a).

The classification errors of training and validation data set is shown in Fig 2(b).

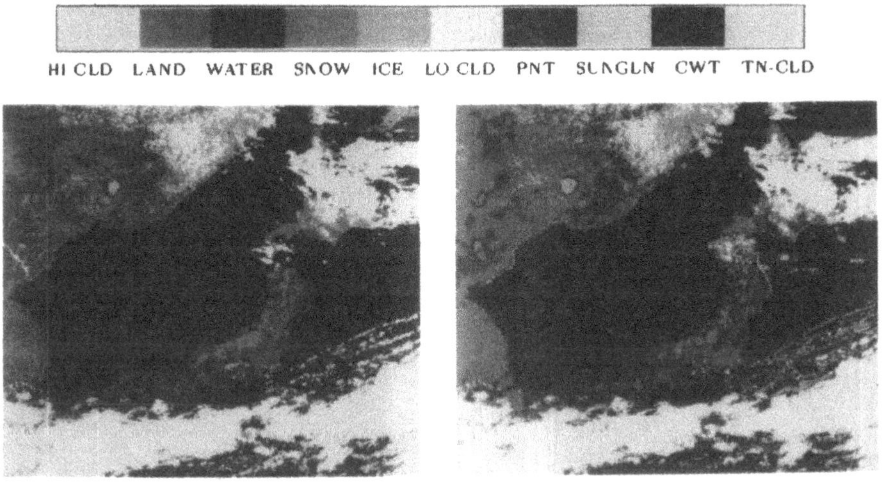

(a) (b)

Fig 3: Classification Results (a)Our Method (b)Kohonen's LVQ

After 3800 iterations of training, the classification accuracies of validation sets reached 100%. This result is very good beyond our expectation, since the accuracies of many classification methods by neural network and traditional statistical methods proposed can only reach about 85%-90%.

The training under different neural network parameters is implemented. Fig 4(b) shows the misclassified pixels of different combination of hidden units after 1000 iteration of training. The first hidden layer has 12 units, and the second hidden units range from 10 to 38.

We also experimented the same classification task using Kohonen's LVQ (Learning Vector Quantization) algorithm, since LVQ's high speech recognition rate of Finnish and Japanese phonemes comparing with parametric Bayesian classifier and the well-known k-nearest-neighbor kNN method. Kohonen's LVQ gives the accuracy of 98% for validation data. However, the classification result for the original image is not corresponding to true (visual) interpretation. For example, the cloud flow in the right middle corner was misclassified into cold water; the low cloud in left bottom and the ice and snow in the top was not detected; the water in the bottom was misclassified into plant and land; the greenless land was over-estimated all over the image; the coastal area was misclassified to water, etc.. The region near the noise were misclassified also.

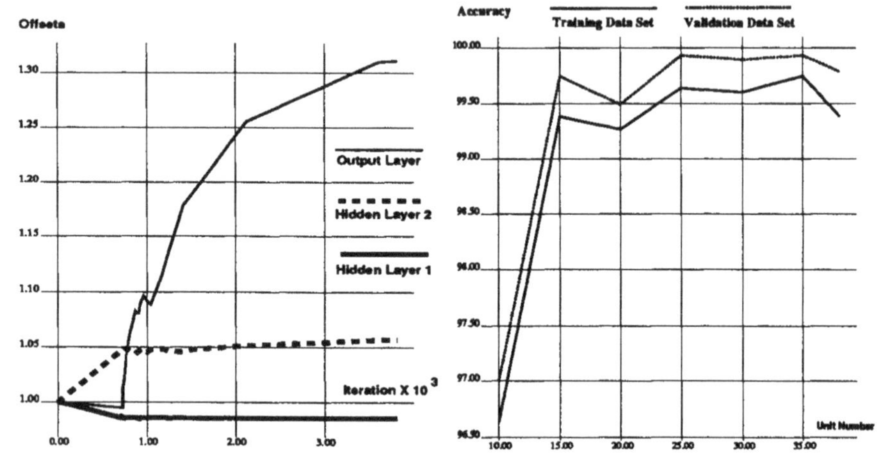

(a) (b)

Fig 4: (a)Offset Changes (b)Classification Errors for Different Unit Numbers

6 Conclusion

We proposed an second order statistics based neural network approach for the classification of NOAA images. The implementations have shown that the second order statistics method surpassed the conventional first order statistics method and other neural network methods.

References

[1] H. Bischof, W. Schneider, and A. J. Pinz. Multispectral classification of landsat-image using neural network. *IEEE Trans. Geoscience and Remote Sensing*, 30(3), 5 1992.

[2] G. Gesell. An algorithm for snow and ice detection using avhrr data-an extension to the apollo software package. *Intl. J. of Remote Sensing*, 10(4-5):897–905, 1989.

[3] Kathryn A. Kelly. Seperating clouds from ocean in infrared images. *Remote Sensing of Environment*, 17:67–83, 1985.

[4] Teuvo Kohonen. *Self-Organization and Associative Memory.* Springer-Verlag, Berlin-Heidelberg-New York-Tokyo, 1989. Third Edition.

[5] H. C. Koons and D. J. Gorney. A sunspot maximum prediction using a neural network. *EOS Trans., Am. Geophys. Union*, 71(18):677–688, 1990.

[6] J. K. Kruschke and J. R. Movellan. Benefits of gain: Speeded learning and minimal hidden layers in back-propagation networks. *IEEE Trans. Systems, Man, and Cybernetics*, 21:273–280, 1991.

[7] Jonathan Lee, Ronald C. Weger, Sailes K. Sengupta, and Ronald M. Welch. A neural network approach to cloud classification. *IEEE Trans. Geoscience and Remote Sensing*, 28(5):845–855, 1990.

Neural Network Learning in Artificial Organisms

Ross Milward[1] and Olivier de Vel

Department of Computer Science,
James Cook University,
Townsville Q4811,
Australia.
olivier@curacoa.cs.jcu.edu.au

Abstract : *In this paper we briefly describe* **Evol**, *an artificial life system, and investigate three different types of artificial neural network learning algorithms for the study of insect population behaviour and evolution. We present the back-propagation, reinforcement and evolutionary learning algorithms and give preliminary results of simulations.*

1 Introduction

Artificial life studies and simulates natural life by attempting to capture the behaviour of the constituent low-level components of a living system and simulating an aggregate of components of one or more artificial organisms with similar behaviour [1]. In an artificial life system, the low-level semi-autonomous components are subject to local simple interactions with one another. The high-level (global) structures and dynamics of the system are emergent complex properties that develop over time from all of the local interactions of the low-level components. As well as enabling researchers to simulate the processes of ecological, adaptive, and evolutionary systems, artificial life techniques can be used in a number of other fields, such as evolutionary robotics [4].

We have developed at CS-JCU an artificial life system, **Evol**, for modeling and simulating insect population behaviour and evolution [7]. This system consists of an artificial environment comprising of artificial insects, food patches and obstacles. Each insect, each gene in each insect, and each environmental effect is simulated in detail. This is sometimes referred to as *microanalytic evolutionary simulation* [2]. Insects rely on touch, sight and smell to survive in the environment, to collect food and to interact with other insects.

An artificial neural network (ANN) is the basic insect behavioural model used. A set of sensors detect the environment of the insect and is used as inputs to the neural network. The resulting outputs are used to determine the actions (behaviour) undertaken by the insects. The training of the network is undertaken by using supervised and evolutionary learning algorithms. The insects evolve in time by eating the food at their current lattice grid location, and sensing the presence or

[1]Current address : Atlas Elektronik, 6/39 Herbert Street, St Leonards NSW 2065

absence of food, obstacles and other insects in a field surrounding their current grid location. Limited proximal visual and olfactory processing is undertaken. The fields of view and smell of the insects are narrow and the field depths are fixed but programmable.

Each insect is characterised by a health attribute and an age attribute. When an insect is born, a maximum health value and minimum age value are attributed to the insect. For each move on the lattice, the health and age values are decremented and incremented respectively. Each insect that eats food increments its health attribute. Upon reaching a maturity threshold (a given age value) and exceeding an infertility time, an insect may mate with other insects of the same species using genetic algorithms to create new offspring with attributes similar to those of their parents. The number of offspring is determined by the health and amount of food collected by the parents. An insect dies when its health drops to zero or its age exceeds a threshold value.

In this paper, we describe and evaluate various neural network learning algorithms used to train the insect's behaviour.

2 Neural Network Learning Algorithms

Various types of ANN learning algorithms exist. In this paper we examine the back-propagation, reinforcement and evolutionary learning algorithms.

2.1 Back-propagation Learning

Learning of weights and thresholds in the multi-layer perceptron (MLP) is most commonly achieved by the supervised back-propagation (BP) algorithm [5]. The major problem with the back-propagation technique in relation to artificial life is that the neural network must be supplied with the training set consisting of specific input and output vectors. Therefore, the insect's behaviour is determined by the well-defined training set. For evolutionary and artificial life techniques this type of learning does not always seem to be suitable, due to the need for a teacher providing specific input-output training data. Therefore, two other learning algorithms were also examined.

2.2 Reinforcement Learning

In reinforcement learning, the environment of the ANN generates reward and punishment signals in response to an ANN's output. Compared with BP ANNs, little work has been done on reinforcement learning techniques. This method is similar to BP learning, in that weights are reinforced for properly performed actions and punished for poorly performed actions. The difference between BP and reinforcement, although both are supervised, is that BP learning utilises more specific error information by collecting error values from each output-layer processing unit, while reinforcement learning uses non-specific error information to determine the performance of the network [8]. This form of learning is ideal in situations where specific information is not available but overall performance information is, such as in prediction and control.

The technique used for the updating of the neural network is as follows:

1. Propagate an input vector forward through the neural network to calculate the output values of the network.
2. Given an output vector, determine whether this output is correct or incorrect. If the output is correct, perform the updating of the MLP using the standard BP technique. If the output is incorrect, toggle the bits of the vector, and then update the connection weights of the MLP.

2.3 Evolutionary Learning

With both the BP and reinforcement methods, input from a teacher is necessary. While the reinforcement technique seemed quite applicable to the study of evolution during the artificial organism's lifetime, it was considered appropriate to introduce another method of learning, which occurs at the reproduction stage of the organism – that of evolutionary artificial neural network (EANN) [9]. EANNs utilise the genetic algorithm (GA) in an attempt to achieve optimal neural networks. A GA performs a multi-directional search by maintaining a population of potential solutions and encourages information collection and exchange between these directions. For a more detailed description of the genetic algorithm and reproduction operators refer to [3].

To implement the EANN, a bit-string representation of the neural network connection weights was designed [6]. Using the genetic algorithm, new neural networks with modified weights can be obtained. Evolving neural network architectures, where the connectivity pattern and/or the number of nodes are subject to genetic control, are not considered here. In the implemented simulation program, the creation of new neural networks occurs when two insects mate. This process creates a number of offspring who have neural networks generated from both parents.

EANNs have no supervision, and the only performance measure obtained from the neural network is that it has survived. No feedback on which aspects of the behaviour were good or bad is provided. The learning and evolution of the insect rely totally on the genetic algorithm operations at birth. Thus, during its lifetime no modifications of the neural network are performed. A resulting network in no way is guaranteed to be a better solution. However, some networks may produce improved results and it is these solutions that will survive to the next generation with more chance of collecting food and reproducing. Thus, over many generations, the remaining networks should theoretically converge to the set of optimal network weights. A detailed implementation of the EANN is described in [7].

2.4 Hybrid Learning

Although EANNs seem to provide an unsupervised method based on natural evolution, they do not cater for learning during an insect's lifetime. Using a combination of the EANN and reinforcement technique, improvements in the neural network can occur during the life of the insect as well as in reproduction. By implementing this combination, a more realistic study of natural evolution can be achieved. Due to the excessive computation times required for the EANN, the majority of results examined in this paper detail the reinforcement learning during the insect's lifetime. However, some preliminary results of hybrid learning will be presented at the conference.

3 Simulation Experiments

We present results of experiments with the simulation environment **Evol**, with particular reference to a comparative analysis of the learning algorithms. The environment consists of a 2-dimensional biosphere grid where the grid size (default 25×25), as well as a number of other attributes, can be specified by the user. The attributes for each grid location include walls and food patches – denoted by solid bold lines and grey stippled squares, respectively.

3.1 Back-propagation Learning

Initial results were good on small, simple environments where the combination of input bits were small. However, the method quickly deteriorated when larger, more complex environments were tested. The major problem with this method was the requirement of entering the input-output relationships. With a total of 25 inputs, to have an insect which could cater for any type of input would require an entry of 2^{25} vectors. This, of course, is infeasible, and, as a result, the number was reduced significantly to a manageable 200 combinations of input numbers.

The reduction in the number of combinations of input vectors generated additional problems. For example, if an input to the neural network was not one found in the training set, an incorrect output may often be chosen. This could result in infinite loops where the insect moves back and forth between two neighbouring grid locations or run around the exterior boundary endlessly. In an effort to overcome this, refraction was included in the insect's behaviour, i.e. a one-move memory was added to the insect. This, however, still did not prevent larger loops being effected.

3.2 Reinforcement Learning

Initially an insect begins with random connection weights in the ANN. Based on these weights and the inputs received from the environment, the highest resulting output is selected, and the insect performs the corresponding move. The insect is then punished or rewarded depending on the conditions defined. Example conditions implemented include rewarding the insect when it eats food, punishing it when it runs into an obstacle, rewarding it when it smells food to the north and moves there etc...

To test the ability of the reinforcement learning paradigm, we present results in different environments [7].

3.2.1 Environment 1

The first test for determining the success of the reinforcement method involves releasing an insect in a simple environment (see Figure 1(a)). The test was performed using five insects each with different initial random neural networks. The average time taken to collect all food is calculated from the five insects. The test parameters were 50 runs for a maximum of 500 moves.

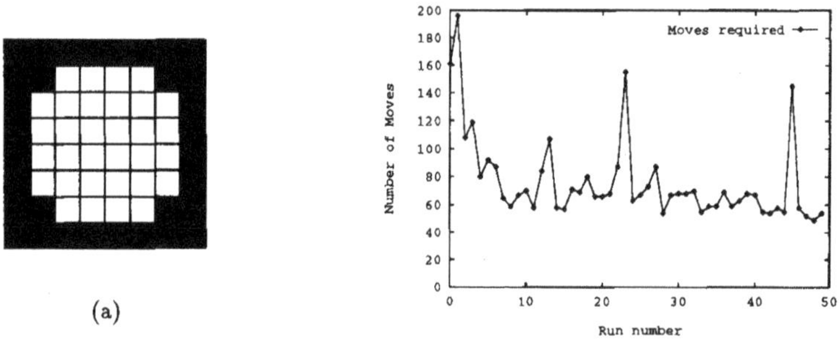

(a) (b)

Fig. 1 : a) *Environment 1*, b) *Average number of moves required to collect all food*

Figure 1(b) displays a downward trend in the number of moves as a function of the run number. In the first two runs the number of moves taken to eat all the available food was above 160, but after further runs, the insect took less time to collect all the food. Three peaks exist which indicate that for some reason the insect took longer to collect the food. These type of results are due to the insect having decided in a previous move that one direction is better than the other. As the graph only shows 50 runs it can't be expected to have constant behaviour due to the amount of time it takes to train a neural network. After a large number of runs ($\gg 100$), the number of moves required to collect all the food should stabilise. From the trend it is apparent that learning is actually occurring.

3.2.2 Environment 2

In this environment (Figure 2(a)) a small alcove was added to remove the routine nature of the square map. Five insects were used and the average number of moves required to collect the food was graphed (Figure 2(b)). This graph shows a similar trend to the previous results. In the first run the number of moves required was high at 300 but after that the trend improves with the number of moves required decreasing.

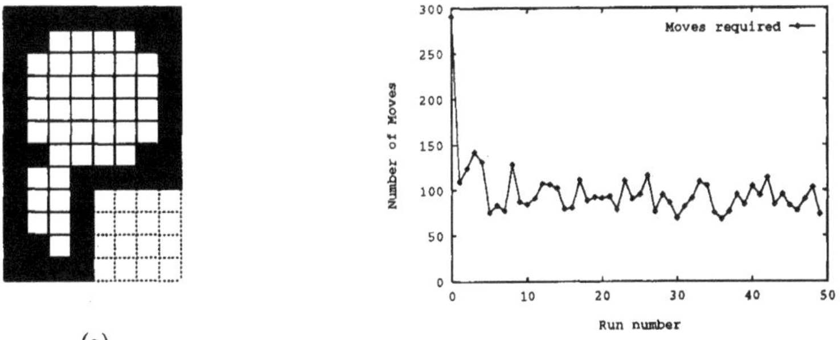

(a) (b)

Fig. 2 : a) *Environment 2*, b) *Average number of moves required to collect all food*

Tests using more complex environments (with obstacles etc...) and the testing of the adaptibility of insects in new environments have also been undertaken (to be presented) [7].

3.3 Evolutionary and Hybrid Learning

As noted, the large computing times required for obtaining results using the evolutionary learning method make it difficult to determine the effectiveness of this approach. However, even based on the limited testing performed, the initial indications are favourable in that, if two parents mated, the children often had good capabilities and managed to collect food in a shorter time than the initial population defined at the beginning of the run. Increased numbers of simulations would enable a further evaluation of the evolutionary learning method and its combination with reinforcement learning hybrid EANNs. Simulations are currently being undertaken.

4 Conclusions

In comparing the learning methods it is evident that the back-propagation technique is not suitable for artificial life due to its requirement of having a teacher and its lack of learning during an insect's lifetime. The reinforcement technique overcomes this by providing a more realistic model of evolution and learning. Although the rules governing punishment or reward are defined by a teacher, by being implemented in the program, it can be argued that these rules are a form of built-in knowledge of living animals, such as insects, and hence defining these can be considered acceptable. To further improve the realism, the genetic algorithm was applied to the evolutionary learning where the genetic code is passed onto the offspring from the parents during reproduction.

Work on **Evol** is still in progress and, although the simulations within computing constraints were unable to obtain conclusive results using the genetic algorithm, the incorporation of the construct, its hybridisation with reinforcement learning, and its implementation on a parallel architecture will be examined in the future.

References

[1] Langton C. "Artificial life". In C. Langton, editor, *Artificial Life*, Reading, Massachusetts, 1989. Addison-Wesley.

[2] R. J. Collins and D. R. Jefferson. "Antfarm: Towards simulated evolution". In S. Rasmussen J. Farmer, C. Langton and C. Taylor, editors, *Artificial Life II*, Reading, Massachusetts, 1991. Addison-Wesley.

[3] D. E. Goldberg. *Genetic Algorithms in Search, Optimization, and Machine Learning.* Addison-Wesley, United States of America, 1989.

[4] Husbands P. Harvey I. and Cliff D. "Issues in evolutionary robotics". In Roitblat H. Meyer J.-A. and Wilson S., editors, *Proc. Second Int. Conf. on Simulation of Adaptive Behaviour*, Cambridge, Massachusetts, 1993. MIT Press Bradford Books.

[5] Werbos P. *Beyond regression : New tools for prediction and analysis in the behavioural sciences.* PhD thesis, Harvard University, Massachusetts, 1974.

[6] Milward R. "A study of genetic algorithms in function optimisation and artificial life". B.Sc. honours, James Cook University, Department of Computer Science, 1992.

[7] Milward R. and de Vel O. "The simulation of the behaviour and evolution of artificial organisms". Technical Report TR-93/7, Dept of Computer Science, James Cook University, 1993.

[8] P. K. Simpson. "Foundations of neural networks". In *Artificial Neural Netorks: Paradigms, Applications, and Hardware Implementations.* IEEE Press, 1992.

[9] Xin Yao. "A review of evolutionary artificial neural networks". *International Journal of Intelligent Systems*, 1993.

Robotics & Vision

A Sensor Driven Autonomous Mobile Robot: The Whole System

Ray Jarvis
Director, Intelligent Robotics Research Centre
Monash University, Clayton, Victoria 3168, Australia
e-mail: Ray.Jarvis@eng.monash.edu.au.

Keywords: Autonomous, Robots, Sensors, Navigation

0. ABSTRACT

In order to autonomously (and reliably) carry out tasks such as optimal path finding, search, exploration and coverall (as for cleaning) in complex obstacle strewn environments, a mobile robot must be supported by a number of specialised sub-systems which have to function effectively and robustly in an integrated manner. Much of the earlier reported research has concentrated on one or several of the necessary sub-systems but has given insufficient consideration to the balanced integration of those sub-systems in supporting the total expected behaviour of an artificially intelligent entity.

The result of such narrowly focussed work has often been the creation of a fragile and inadequate system which functions somewhat eccentrically and erratically in real situations and whose behaviour is unable to gain the confidence of potential developers interested in commercially viable products for well defined markets.

This paper describes a sensor driven autonomous mobile robot system which has been built with the requirements of simplicity, adequacy, robustness, extensibility, timeliness of reaction and effective integration as the motivational core of the research effort. The current state of the project and the plans for the future are described. Paper presentation will include video sequences of operation.

1. INTRODUCTION

There are five sub-system requirements for support of autonomous mobile robot functionality in complex environments:

(i) Localisation - the position and orientation of the robot must be evaluated at sufficiently short intervals to adequately guide its movements.

(ii) Environmental Modelling - a map of the working environment of the robot must either be initially known or acquired incrementally using sensory data.

(iii) Path Finding - a navigation strategy of optimal path planning must be available to cater for known, initially unknown or time varying environments according to the operational requirements of the system.

(iv) Communications - adequate provision for transferring command and sensor information between the sub-systems must be provided. This requirement is always important but especially crucial if the system is split between on-board and home-station support without an umbilical cable in-between.

(v) Motion Control - whether locomotion is by wheels, tracks, legs or whatever adequate control must be provided. Motion start and stop operations may require special consideration. Prompt response to command is also important.

Earlier papers [1,2] have provided tutorial discussion of each of the above issues in general and these details will not be repeated here except to make particular points illuminating design choices with respect to the system to be described in subsequent sections.

The overall objective of this research project is to both demonstrate the viability of a balanced robot design based on fairly well known principals of localisation, environmental modelling, path finding, communications and motion control but where reliability, compatibility and complementarity was of special concern, and to provide a system platform for more adventurous research in which new approaches would replace existing capabilities through a process of 'graceful degradation' of the old function in favour of the new. The latter part of this dual objective will be discussed in a later section of the paper. The following task scenarios (in order of increasing complexity) were considered as defining the functional requirements of the mobile robot system:

(i) Devise and execute an optimal path from a given starting point to a given goal in a known and unchanging obstacle field environment.

(ii) Devise and execute a piece-wise optimal path from a given starting point to a given goal in an initially unknown but unchanging obstacle field environment. Incremental sensor based mapping is to be the basis of path hypothesis. Piece-wise optimality refers to the requirement that the best possible path is hypothesized at each stage of the experiment using what is known about the environment at that time. Assumptions concerning the unknown parts of the environment condition the optimality measure.

(iii) Visit every part of the free space of a known environment in a reasonable pattern of coverage (of value for cleaning and surveillance operations).

(iv) Explore and map an initially unknown but unchanging obstacle field environment.

(v) Carry out tasks defined in (i), (ii) and (iv) above for slowly changing obstacle field environments.

Extensions of capability for future development:

(vi) Carry out tasks defined in (i), (ii) and (iv) for relatively fast changing environments - essentially environments with some moving obstacles.

(vii) Find a defined object target by searching a known and unchanging obstacle field environment.

(viii) Find a defined object target whilst exploring an initially unknown but unchanging obstacle field environment.

The following sections will describe the various sub-systems in the order given (in this introduction) which support the whole autonomous robot system. Then the overall capability of the system will be dealt with in the context of the task scenarios outlined from (i) to (v) above. Extensions related to future research will be covered in the following section. The use of the developed platform for new approaches to navigation will then be touched upon. Finally, a conclusion section closes the paper.

2. FUNCTIONAL SUB-SYSTEMS

Localisation. As is documented in [3], a considerable variety of approaches to determining the position and orientation of a mobile robot during motion can be pursued with varying degrees of adequacy in relation to speed, cost, accuracy and scope of application. The need for reliable if not wholly accurate data is often insufficiently emphasised. Localisation data is needed not only for path execution control in known obstacle field environments but is crucial for determining the positions of obstacles which are detected by on-board sensors in world reference rather than robot centred terms. Inaccuracies in mapping due to inadequate localisation can render a whole experiment non-viable since mapping uncertainty can not be resolved to a sufficient degree to allow planning to be worthwhile.

The localisation system chosen for this project is based on a Denning Lasernav 2 instrument which determines the angular position and the identity of large bar code panels at known positions around the room up to 100 feet away. This bar code scanning system [shown in Figure 1] spins its rotating mirror at 10 revolutions per second; up to 10 bar code targets can be measured and reported via 9600 baud RS232 serial line protocol at this rate of scan. The raw angle/identity data must be processed to determine a 'fix' (position/orientation) of the robot. Only three targets need be detected to provide a 'fix' in ideal conditions, but ill posed geometric distributions and possibilities of obscurances strongly argue for a redundancy based evaluation to guarantee high reliability at the cost of computational effort. For this project, two simple approaches have been developed and the latter one currently adopted for normal use; further developments are also being considered. In the first approach, a simple search amongst more than three detected beacons (bar code targets) was carried out to find which three were closest to being 120° apart, this being a generally good geometry to make an accurate 'fix'; only one 'fixing' calculation was carried out. If the 'best' set is not particularly good a poor 'fix' would result; however the calculation was very quick and a number of 'fixes' per second (perhaps 5) could be made.

The second approach is fairly exhaustive but more reliable though slower. All possible triplets of observed beacons are used to determine a complete set of possible 'fixes'. These results are clustered and the largest, hopefully most consistent cluster average used for the final determination. Approximately a 1/2 second of computation is involved. This second approach has proven very reliable though a little slow. To date, dead reckoning calculations and continuity constraints have not been used. Clearly, dead reckoning (based on wheel turns perhaps) can provide an estimate of where the robot ought to be at any time instant and it certainly can't move from one place to another far off place in a short period of time. Any beacon based 'fix' which is not consistent with dead reckoning and continuity tolerance estimates could be discarded as being incorrect. It may be sensible to adopt this approach to speeding up calculations without reducing reliability.

Environmental Modelling. Earlier research [4] clearly indicated the parameters of a compromise between the quality of range data used for environmental modelling and the speed at which it could be gathered and processed. It is excruciating to have to wait, say 30 seconds, for a sensor to map its surroundings, particularly when obstacles are sparce. In this project range data is gathered quickly by a rotating time-of-flight scanner and crudely organised into straight line segments which represent floor projections of faces of obstacles. A 4.5 metre radius circle around the robot is scanned at one complete revolution per second and the scan and segment analysis completed in 5 seconds. An ESP Technologies ORS-1 infrared optical time-of-flight rangefinder was used for this purpose. The instrument [see Figure 2] has a vertical coaxial outward and return beam arrangement and uses a spinning inclined mirror to distribute and collect the radial beam from around the robot. The manufacturer claims 6 inch accuracy but experience suggests this is only under unrealistically ideal conditions. As supplied, this rangefinder's rotating mirror is fixed at 45° so that the beam scan is strictly horizontal when the instrument is mounted in its normal orientation. To enable full 3D range scanning, the mirror has been remounted and can be driven by servo motors (powered through a commutator) to any angle of orientation within a useful range to allow cone like sweeps so that, with each rotation, difference cone beams provide time-of-flight range data. The simple geometry of the scans allows 3D positions to be determined. Ordinarily, for the experiments carried out so far, the mirror is positioned to direct the beam slightly downward from a high vantage point at the top of the robot. However, the capability to collect full 3D data is available for use in very complex environments where not all obstacles may have vertical faces or where overhangs can be critical. Straight line segment analysis for a number of different scan angles can be simply combined to give a worst case floor projection map; alternatively, the raw data can be combined before segment analysis. The essential reason for carrying out the segment analysis is to summarize the data for low bandwidth transmission with the data set consisting of line end coordinate pairs. It was discovered that the rangefinder is very temperature sensitive; a temperature reading is used as an input parameter to range calibration data. A number of signal processing ideas have also been incorporated to filter out noisy readings and to incorporate automatic gain control signals in culling out unreliable readings. After a considerable effort towards understanding the behaviour of the rangefinder in typical environments, a number of special analysis procedures have lead to a reasonably reliable set of range values being available from the instrument.

Path Finding. It was in this aspect of the total system that considerable previous work [5,6,7,8,9] was considered to provide adequate methodology for incorporation into this mobile robot project. For this reason this sub-system was left till last since existing, home developed packages could be edited to provide the robust path planning capability for a variety of different task scenarios. Details can be found in the papers cited above, so only overall descriptive summaries of capability will be presented here. Considerable experience in the use of A* based optimal path finding algorithms [9], for convex polygonal obstacles was available along with a whole suite of algorithms for distance transform based path planning [7,8]. The latter approach has a number of distinct advantages over the former in terms of simplicity and ease of applicability to a variety of situations of differing complexity along the lines indicated in the introductory section. The essential idea behind distance transform based optimal path finding is that of propagating distances out from a goal point to all parts of the unoccupied space of an environment with the distance propagation 'flowing around' the obstacles (occupied spaces). A regular cellular tessellation is normally used but quad-trees and oct-trees versions can also be formulated. The methodology extends naturally to higher dimensioned spaces [10] and can be applied to partially known environments on the basis of assumptions concerning unknown space (e.g. that it is unoccupied until proven otherwise).

An optimal collision-free path to a goal is found simply by following the distance measure (in steps) downwards in a steepest descent trajectory to the goal, which is considered to be zero distance from itself. Multiple start points and multiple goal points are also easily accommodated as are exploration and coverall modes of operation. It is also fairly easy to extend the methodology to time-varying obstacle field environments [5]. The fineness of the cellular tessellation determines the resolution of the path and the computational effort required. The known obstacles can be grown to allow for the physical extent of the robot which can then be regarded as a point in space. Altogether this is an excellent methodology upon which to base a large variety of robot navigation experiments. Various examples of its application are illustrated in Figure 3.

Communications. If all the sensory acquisition apparatus, the computational support and the motor control systems are all in one place, usually on-board the robot, then communications requirements are nothing more than the provision of appropriate wired data channels between the components. However, there are often good reasons to distribute the components between on-board and home-station sites. For example, the central control of a number of robots in completing a cooperative task is more easily handled using a fixed base station. Another reason may be the need for computational resources not easily made available on-board because of size, weight, fragility or power consumption and also the flexibility of being able to enhance computational power through upgrades and connections to mainframes and even supercomputers at other sites, without having to consider the payload restrictions of the robot itself. In these circumstances communications between the mobile robot and the home-station become crucial since two way data traffic must be adequately accommodated with high reliability. If only relatively low bandwidth links are available (e.g. 9600 baud radio modem), clearly signals like real-time video cannot be handled. The detail of just 'what' is collected and processed 'where' becomes important to decide fairly early on in the project design. The use of umbilical cord connection is to be discouraged due to the snaring and entanglement possiblities.

In this project considerable thought went into just how to distribute the sub-system responsibilities between on-board and home-station sites. It was regarded as important to have full graphics and interaction capability on a home-station, along with fairly high powered computational support which could be easily upgraded and enhanced. At the same time only a 9600 baud full duplex radio modem link was available for communications purposes (high quality high bandwidth systems being very expensive) and it became clear that a certain amount on on-board processing could ease the bandwidth requirements. A master/slave approach was adopted because of its simplicity and flexibility, the home-station being in command under human supervision. The block diagram of this arrangement is shown in Figure 4. An on-board 486 PC running at 66 MHz receives two kinds of requests/commands from the home-station, a Silicon Graphics Iris.

(i) Move commands are restricted to a straight line path to a specified destination. The on-board PC determines the required orientation and distance and issues a turn and a move instruction to the robot motion control system. During the movement the position of the robot is monitored using the beacon localiser and direction corrections are made to get the robot on track to its destination. Deviations from the straight line path cause the robot to stop slightly short of its destination; a small adjustment is made to correct this. Thus the on-board PC carries out the task of getting the robot to a point specified by the home-station. Position and orientation data is relayed back to the home-station for display and monitoring purposes.

(ii) Range data collection requests from the home-station are responded to by the on-board PC which collects one complete sweep of range data from the rotating time-of-flight rangefinder and carries out a number of operations to refine the data. Unreliable data is culled out using signal processing techniques and the valid data transformed through a calibration table which also takes account of mirror angle and temperature. Corrected floor projection range data is further analysed and transformed into straight line segments which are communicated back to the home-station as line end point pairs. The robot centred range data line segments are transformed to world coordinate segments and displayed on the home-station screen along with robot track and current position orientation data.

The on-board PC screen is disconnected during navigation experiments since there is no space for it on the robot and because it consumes too much power from the battery supplies. The screen data is transmitted via a video transmitter to a colour TV receiver near the home station. Robot centred latest range data and localisation data are displayed along with diagnostic comments (See Figure 6). Thus both the activity of the on-board PC and the home-station computer can be monitored from the one site.

The world frame range data is displaced in a cellular form (See Figure 7) on a 256x256 grid in anticipation of being used for distance transform based path planning. Cells in the vicinity of the straight line approximations of the range segments are also 'filled' to indicate uncertainty in the range data.

At the beginning of a navigation experiment and at each point at the end of a straight line movement range data is gathered, refined, segmented and transferred to the home-station. A specified number of range sets can be displayed on the common world coordinate display using a colour code to identify the sets. thus, over a tour of a large part of a room, incrementally acquired range data can be integrated into an almost complete floor projection map of the room.

3. THE WHOLE SYSTEM

Working out where everything went on the Denning robot was an important part of the design strategy. The Denning robot has three wheels which rotate and steer together, enabling the robot to move in any direction without rotating its body. An instrument platform which rotates with the steering system allows sensory equipment to be oriented with respect to motion direction. Anything on the platform can only communicate with something that was not through a communicator system provided; this system had a limited number of channels of light current carrying capacity. It was decided to place the sensing equipment close to the processing unit (PC) and to make sure the localiser could have line of sight clearance to bar code targets and the rangefinder an obstructed view from a good vantage point. This meant that the PC, localiser, rangefinder, TV transmitter and battery power supplies and 12V DC to 240V AC inverter all had to be carried by the instrument platform. This platform was not designed to carry such a combined weight. Skateboard wheels were attached to the instrument platform to carry the load with two batteries and the inverter slung under the platform and the PC, localiser and rangefinder on top of it in that order upwards. The rangefinder was mounted on the perspex dome cover of the localiser so that no mounting fittings would obscure the localiser's view of its targets. With the rangefinder topmost it had a clear view of the environment through which the robot was to navigate.

To test the quality and reliability of the localisation, environmental modelling, communications and motion control sub-systems prior to the inclusion of the path planning sub-systems (for which previous research has already established the basic algorithmic tools), a simple way of entering a path using a mouse was devised. A complex path can be specified on the home-station screen as a number of connected straight line components. The robot is then commanded to execute the path. This it does with considerable reliability, faithfully relying back its tracking and environmental range data along the way. The path planning sub-system will specify this path once the task is indicated. Previous experience with path planning algorithms will mean that this aspect can be included with great confidence of correct behaviour. The manual entry option will be retained as it allows for simple checking of all the sub-systems other than path planning and can be used to specify path which, when followed, will allow a complete environmental map to be constructed for use in subsequent experiments. In automatic explore mode the path planner will itself determine the collision-free path which will allow all unknown space to be mapped. With a known environment, a coverall path can be calculated; following this path will allow every cell of free space to be visited by the robot. Using the explore mode in a slowly time varying obstacle field environment will keep the robot on the move revisiting places associated with previously known environments details of which are deliberately erased from the map. Dealing with environments with relatively fast moving obstacles will be a more difficult operation but one which has practical merit since many environments in which mobile robots are likely to be used will also contain other moving robots and moving human beings and their vehicles (e.g. forklift trucks). A somewhat simplified approach to this problem may be to estimate if and when the robot should stop on its planned path to avoid colliding with a moving obstacle.

Experiments based on manual entry of path segments have shown that the system is quite reliable and acceptably fast, though speed can certainly be improved. Typically, the robot stops for 5 to 8 seconds at each end point in its path and moves at about $^1/_2$ metre/second along each straight line trajectory. The motion speed can be increased but this would not improve the total performance to any practical extent. Thus, for a 50 metre total path with 10 straight line segments the total time for path completion is approximately $1^1/_2$ minutes, which is reasonably acceptable; of course, fewer straight line segments will result in a comparatively shorter completion time.

4. FUTURE DEVELOPMENTS

Once the basic system described in previous sections is fully operational and reliable it is intended that the system be used as an experimental platform for natural landmark based navigation in possibly (but slowly) changing environments. This is a very challenging task but one which humans accomplish with ease. The sensed environmental data must provide both localisation and mapping information simultaneously. This means that landmarks discovered in the range data must be capable of being rediscovered from other vantage points and unstable landmarks (moving or obscured) somehow not allowed to pollute the computations. Eventually the beacon localiser should not be needed; this would mean there would be no need to set out the bar code targets at known positions. This, in turn will mean that the robot system should be able to operate in new unprepared environments without prior notice. Environmental data will need to provide not only obstacle occupancy data but recognition ones for detection and re-detection of salient features of the environment, coping with ambiguity through exploiting redundancy and continually reconciling localisation and mapping as a unified process. Being able to vary the mirror angle of the rotating range scanner could play an important part in combining volumemetic modelling within landmark detection.

5. CONCLUSIONS

This paper has described the basic sub-systems of a complete autonomous mobile robot which has been constructed to carry out path finding, exploration and coverall tasks in environments which may be initially unknown and time varying. The rationale for the design choices made has been exposed and the current capabilities of the system stated. Future work to extend the capabilities of the system to enable the robot to navigate in unprepared, previously unknown environments using natural landmarks has been outlined.

6. BIBLIOGRAPHY

1. Jarvis, R.A. Mobile Robot Navigation, invited Plenary Address, Proc. Third National Conference on Robotics, Melbourne, June 3-6,1990 - pp.8-24.
2. Jarvis, R.A., Computer Vision and Robotics - Hand/Eye Co-ordination and Autonomous Navigation,Proc. Australian Computer Science Conference 15, Hobart 29-31 Jan. 1992, pp.399-410
3. Jarvis, R.A. A Selective Survey of Localisation Methodology for Autonomous Mobile Robot Navigation, accepted for presentation at the Robots for Competitive Industry Conference, July 14-16, 1993, Brisbane Australia.
4 Badcock, J.M., Dun, J.A., Ajay, K., Kleeman, L. and Jarvis, R.A. An Autonomous Robot Navigation System - Integrating Environmental Mapping, Path Planning, Localisation and Motion Control. Robotica (1993), Vol.11, pp.97-103.
5. Jarvis, R.A. Collision-Free Path Planning in Time Varying Environments, Proc. I.E.E.E./R.S.J. International Workshop on Intelligent Robots and Systems, '89, Tsukuba, Japan, Sept. 4-6 '89, pp 99-106.
6. Jarvis, R.A. and Byrne, J.C., An Automated Guided Vehicle with Map Building and Path Finding Capabilities, invited paper, Fourth International Symposium of Robotics Research, University of California at Santa Cruz, 9-14 Aug., 1987, pp. 155-162.
7. Jarvis, R.A. and Byrne, J.C., Robot Navigation : Touching, Seeing and Knowing, 1st Australian Artificial Intelligence Congress, Melbourne, 18-20 Nov., 1986, Section e.
8. Jarvis, R.A., Collision-Free Trajectory Planning Using Distance Transforms, Proc. National Conference and Exhibition on Robotics - 1984, Melbourne 20-24 August 1984.
9. Jarvis, R.A., Polyhedra Obstacle Growing for Collision-Free Path Planning, Department of Computer Science, A.N.U., Technical Report TR-CS-81-16. Also Proc. Australian Computer Science Conference, Perth, February 1982, pp.203-213.
10. Jarvis, R.A., Configuration Space Collision-Free Path Planning for Robotic Manipulators, Proc. 10th Australian Computer Science Conference, Deakin University, Victoria, 4–6 Feb., 1987, pp.193-204.

Figure 1 Denning Remote Bar-Code Reading Localiser

Figure 2. ESP Technologies' Infrared Time-of-Flight Range Scanner

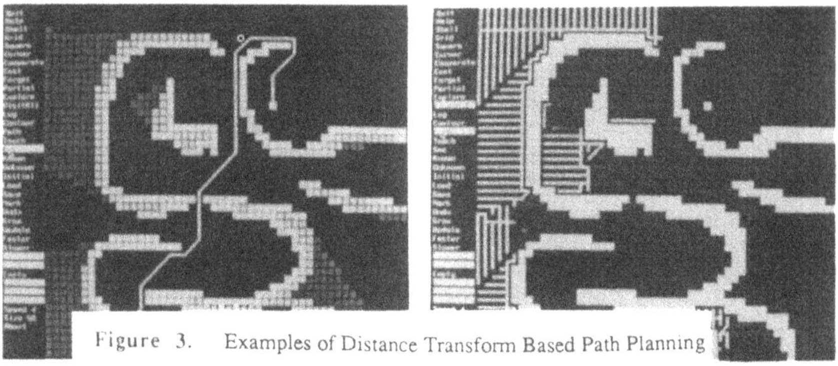

Figure 3. Examples of Distance Transform Based Path Planning

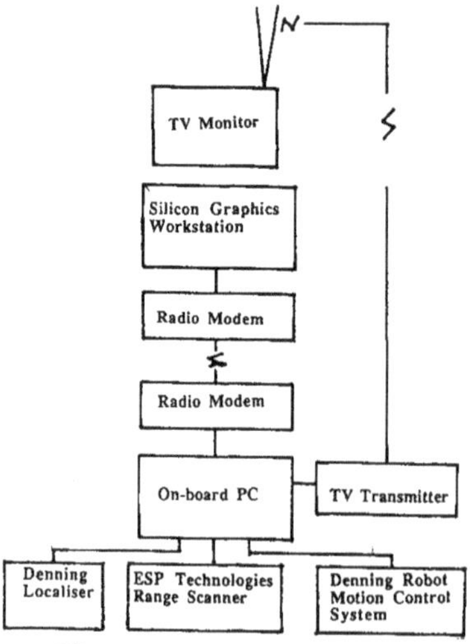

Figure 4. Block Schematic of Master/Slave Structure

Figure 5. Denning Robot Fully Instrumented

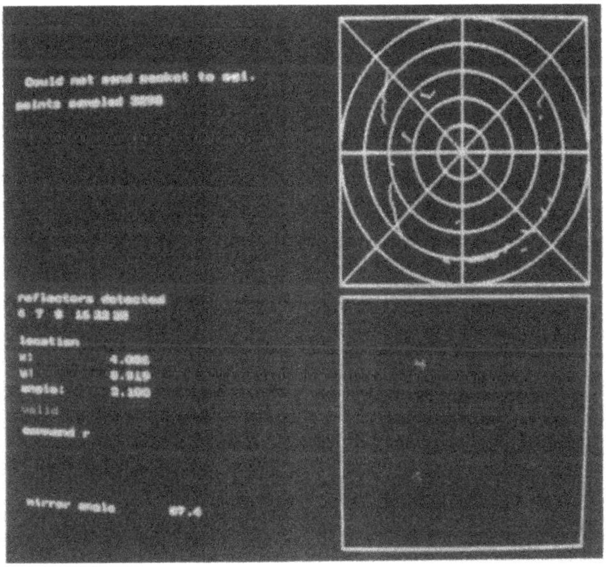

Figure 6. On-Board PC Screen

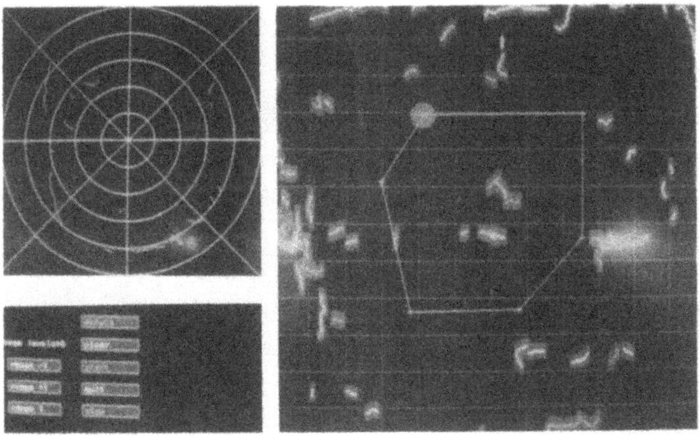

Figure 7. Home-Station Screen Showing a Path Following Experiment

FREE FORM SURFACE REGISTRATION FOR 3D ROBOT VISION

Chin Seng Chua and Ray Jarvis
Intelligent Robotics Research Centre
Monash University, Wellington Road
Clayton, Victoria 3168, Australia

ABSTRACT. *A new technique is developed to translate and rotate a free-form surface represented by a set of 3-D sensed data points, to bring it into registration with another surface, represented by (often more complete) another set of 3-D model data points, without prior knowledge of correspondence between the two point sets. The transformation to bring the sensed data set into registration with the model data set is based on discovering three points in the model data set, the search of which uses the principal directions of curvatures, which correspond to three points in the sensed data set. Invariably, many possible model 3-point sets will be found, most of which are very close to the optimal correspondence triplet of points. This optimal triplet may be identified by transforming the remaining sensed points into the model space, for each possible transformation; the transformation with the lowest registration error is associated with the optimal triplet sought. Preliminary experiments using data obtained from a rangefinder have indicated fast registration for relatively complex test cases.*

1. INTRODUCTION

Being able to efficiently discover the optimal registration transformation of a sensed 2-1/2-D data set (single viewpoint) provided by a rangefinder with an often more complete (perhaps, 3-D) data set which represents a free-form model is critical to the task of object identity and pose determination in the context of 3-D robot vision. Such a capability permits robotic selection and manipulation of 3-D objects, perhaps in support of an industrial application. The optimal registration of a sensed 2-1/2-D data set with each of a set of models representing the potential identity of the sensed object can be used as a basis of 3D object recognition and simultaneously provides pose data to guide robot manipulation and reorientation of work pieces in anticipation of subsequent processing steps. Unifying recognition and pose determination in this way is a significant step towards providing a generic solution to robotic 'hand/eye' coordination which is an essential requirement of many industrial automation tasks.

In much of the 3-D object recognition research reported to date, only polygonal plane faced objects[5] or those which can be constructed by combining geometrically simple rectangular, cylindrical and spherical solids[3] have been dealt with, severely restricting the application scope of the proposed methodology. Here, such restrictions are deliberately abandoned to preserve generality of approach and guarantee a breadth of applications.

Given a set of 2-1/2-D sensor data, $S=\{s_i|i=1,2...p\}$, and a set of 3-D model data, $M=\{m_j|j=1,2...q\}$, $p<q$, the task is to discover the transformation (translation and rotation) which optimally registers the sensed shape with the model shape. If the correspondence between the two point sets is known, then a least square estimation of rotation R and translation T such as that in [1] may be followed. But, in most cases, the correspondence between points is not known and is difficult to determine. An expedient method is required to obviate the high computational complexity of an exhaustive search approach.

This paper introduces a solution to the free-form surface registration problem without correspondence provided *a priori*. Instead of trying to register all sensed points directly, it is possible to register the whole sensor data set by using a 'key' based on a minimum of three point pairs. The method begins by choosing three reference points in the sensed data. Next, a set of three points on the model is hypothesized to correspond to the sensed reference points. If the hypothesis is acceptable, the transformation from the sensed reference set to the model set represents a possible registration solution. This solution is verified by transforming the other sensed points into the model space. If the transformed points match the points in the model space well, registration is achieved with measurable quality.

Two major issues must be addressed with this approach.

(i) If there are q (e.g. 1000) data points for the model, there will be approximately q^3 ($1000^3=10^9$) possible sets of three points. An efficient pruning method is required to reduce this set to a manageable size.

(ii) Assuming that it is possible to prune the hypothesis set to a manageable size, say t=1000, the next step is to verify every hypothesis within the set with the remainder of the sensed points. However, to search exhaustively through t transformations for each of the p sensed points would again be computationally expensive.

This paper is structured as follows : Section 2 presents the hypothesis generation phase of finding triplets of model points that correspond to the reference set. This section addresses the first issue mentioned above. The next section, Section 3, presents a solution to the second issue. In this section, the idea of a competitive search is discussed. This form of searching reduces the amount of search required to find the best transformation based on the verification of the rest of the sensed points. Implementation details of a test case are presented in Section 4. Finally, Section 5 deals with the conclusions and further work.

2. Pruning the 3-Point Transformation Set

The objective of this section is to find all the possible triplets of model points corresponding to a chosen set of three sensed points $\{s_\alpha, s_\beta, s_\gamma\}$. Each triplet, represented by the set $\{m_{\alpha(k)'}, m_{\beta(k)'}, m_{\gamma(k)'}\}$ $k=1,2\ldots t$, gives a possible transformation $\mathbf{T}_k$ from the sensed space into the model space. If there are q model points, then there would be $t=q*(q-1)*(q-2)$ possible transformations. This huge set of approximately q^3 possibilities have to be reduced before verification (Section 3). Pruning may be accomplished simply by distance checking between any two points in the 3-point set. But the very essence of checking the distance between 2 points for each of the q^3 possibilities is itself very time consuming and impractical. Other means of pruning must be incorporated such that distance checking is applied as a final check only to those points that have the likelihood of being the acceptable points.

Three reference points on the sensed data must first be chosen. To find these three points, one way is to perform a segmentation procedure on the sensed data based on techniques described in [2]. From the regions formed, the three largest regions are selected. For each region, the pixel with the best n*n surface patch fit (in terms of the smallest least square error) is selected as the representative for that region.

After finding the three reference sensed points, the next step is to find the three corresponding model points. This is accomplished in two stages by first finding the set of model points $\{m_{\alpha'}\}$corresponding to s_α and then sets of $\{m_{\beta'}\}$ and $\{m_{\gamma'}\}$ corresponding to s_β and s_γ. Models points $\{m_{\alpha'}\}$ are easily identified as those points whose principal curvatures are close to that of s_α, within a specified tolerance. It is well known in differential geometry [6] that, at any point on a surface, there exist two orthogonal vectors corresponding to the directions of principal curvatures. These two vectors, together with the normal vector, form an orthonormal frame. Given the point pair of s_α and its correspondence, $m_{\alpha'}$ and their orthonormal frames, theoretically, it is possible to orientate the sensed object to align with the model object using this point-pair[7]. Unfortunately the orthonormal frame for both points must be computed very accurately (using error free data) before the correct registration could be achieved. Instead of using the orthonormal frames of corresponding point pairs to compute the appropriate transformation for registration, they are used to direct the search to find the other two points. Based on s_α's orthonormal frame, the relative positions of s_β and s_γ, with reference to s_α, are defined. If now, a model point $m_{\alpha'}$ is hypothesized to correspond to s_α, then based on $m_{\alpha'}$'s orthonormal frame and the relative positions of s_β and s_γ with respect to s_α, approximate positions for possible $m_{\beta'}$ and $m_{\gamma'}$ can be identified. Let these positions in the 3-D model space be $\mathbf{M}_\beta$ and $\mathbf{M}_\gamma$. Searching around the neighbourhood of $\mathbf{M}_\beta$ and $\mathbf{M}_\gamma$, model points which are close to $\mathbf{M}_\beta$ would be hypothesized as possible $m_{\beta'}$ points and model points which are close to $\mathbf{M}_\gamma$ would be hypothesized as possible $m_{\gamma'}$ points. Each combination of points, represented as a set of triplet $\{m_{\alpha'}, m_{\beta'}, m_{\gamma'}\}$, establishes a possible transformation from $\{s_\alpha, s_\beta, s_\gamma\}$.

3. Competitive Search

Despite the pruning of the set of hypothesized transformations, the resultant set is still large, typically in the region of $t \approx 500$. Each transformation must now be verified with the remaining p sensed points. This requires $t*p$ point transformations in a complete search. If, a threshold could be determined such that transformations of high accumulated errors are thrown away as verification progresses, then the number of point transformations required would be drastically reduced, and a partial search is effected. Unfortunately, presetting a correct threshold is difficult, subjective and may lead to a premature rejection of an optimal transformation.

Instead, a competitive search is pursued. This search is based on the assumption that a transformation which contributes a higher error tends not to be in the final solution while that which contributes a lower error has a high probability of being the optimal transformation. In competitive searching, at each iteration, selected competing transformations are applied to one sensed point at a time and the registration error due to each point transformation recorded. The current accumulated average error with respect to each competing transformation is used as a means of directing the search in favour of more promising transformations. This is effected by testing transformations with small errors more frequently than those with higher errors.

The basic algorithm is as follows : At each iteration, the transformation with the lowest average error is determined. This lowest error is multiplied by a preset factor, f (e.g. f = 2), to give the upper bound of inclusion. All transformations that have average errors below this upper bound of inclusion will be tested within this iteration. This involves transforming the next incoming sensed point into the model space and checking for its nearest neighbour.

There is a possibility that transformations which give high errors due to noisy initial estimates may not be tested initially, but they are not rejected totally. At the start of the search, the high error transformations would not be tested frequently. Nevertheless, they are still tested but only sporadically. As more sensed points are considered at each iteration, the accumulated average error corresponding to the optimal transformation would become increasingly lower as compared to the accumulated average error due to other transformations. The optimal transformation would then progress from the back of the queue, where the testing rate is low, towards the front. As it moves forward, it will be tested more and more depending on its position within the queue.

4. Implementation Details and Experimental Results

In this section, we present the results of registering a 2-1/2-D sensed range data set with an almost full 3-D model range data set. Inputs were taken from an actual rangefinder[4] which has a maximum resolution of 64 x 64 rangels (range cells). All programs were written in C and tested on a 486 PC running at 25 MHz. The 3-D model data was obtained as follows : The model was placed on a graduated turntable with the camera looking on in the horizontal direction. As the turntable was rotated, four range data sets at 0, 90, 180 and 270 degrees were captured and integrated to represent the model data (Figure 1b, side view). To represent the 2-1/2-D sensed data, another range data set was taken with the turntable rotated at 60 degrees (Figure 1a). Figure 1c shows the result after transforming the sensed data set into the model space. Due to the difficulty of representing the shape alignment of both data sets, the transformed sensed data set was intentionally pruned (by discarding rangels belonging to the back of the head) and then displaced by a fixed distance in the horizontal direction.

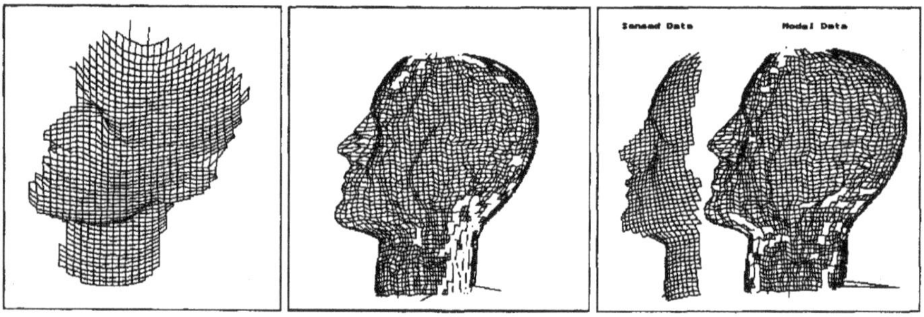

(a) (b) (c)

Figure 1. Test Case, Head. (a) 2-1/2-D Sensed Range Data (b) 3-D Model Range Data. (c) Part of sensed range data transformed into model space and displaced by a fixed distance in the horizontal direction to show the alignment of contours between the sensed data and model data.

TEST CASE : HEAD	
Number of Sensed Points	: 1244
Number of Model Points	: 3775
Number of possible First Reference Points	: 1133
Number of possible Transformations	: 879
Number of verifications	: 34415
Time taken to find :	
Possible First Reference Points	: 4 secs
Possible Transformations	: 80 secs
Verification/Solution	: 73 secs
Translation	: (-0.61, -0.14, -0.16)
Rotation axis	: (-0.99, 0.07, -0.14)
Rotation angle	: 57.8 degrees
Registration Error	: 0.418

Figure 2. Statistics For Test Case.

From the 1244 sensed points and 3775 model points, the initial pruning results in 1133 initial model points that could be matched to s_α. Pruning this set in Section 3 produces 879 possible transformations. The competitive search is executed through the 879 possible transformations against the remaining 1241 (i.e. 1244-3) sensed points. If one was to use brute force in finding the solution, then, to match 1244 points to 3775 points require 1244^{3775} tests. Even if one uses the 3-point set matching arbitrarily, there would still be $3775^3 \approx 5.38 \times 10^{10}$ sets. Instead, in our test, only 879 sets are found. With 879 sets and 1241 points, 879 x 1241 = 1,090,839 point transformations are required in a complete search. But, in our test, only 34,415 point transformations were performed to produce the same result. A savings of $\approx$ 32:1 is achieved if the comparison is made at the last stage. If the comparison is made against the arbitrary 3-point set (having 5.38×10^{10} possible transformations), then a savings of $1.56 \times 10^{6} : 1$ is achieved. The statistical results are summarized in Figure 2.

5. CONCLUSIONS AND FURTHER WORK

The algorithm presented is able to register a shape represented by a set of 2-1/2-D data points to another shape represented by another set of 3-D (or 2-1/2-D) points. The type of surface to be registered is not limited to any class of shapes and may be free-form. We have shown promising results with fast registration times on the test case of relative complexity : head. Future work would be directed towards test cases which exhibit symmetry. Possibly, if the orientation vectors, such as those of quadric objects could be extracted, they could be incorporated into the above to reduce the search time even further. Registration of many objects with occlusion would also be investigated.

Also, the procedure outlined above will be used as a basis of sensed 3D object recognition by choosing one of a number of models, against which best registration transformations are derived, as the identity of the sensed model. The comparative quality of the set of best registrations can be used as the recognition discriminant. In this way pose determination and recognition will be achieved simultaneously by a generic process of wide applicability to many robotic automation tasks. In principal, the discovery and evaluation of each best registration, one for each model, can be undertaken as an independent parallel process, with the independent quality of fit discriminants being brought together in a single final process for recognition purposes. Early evidence of very poor registrations or the evaluation of more global indicators (e.g. gross surface shape properties) may be used to cull the model set to a minimal, most likely set, over which the more rigorous computation can be applied to achieve a simultaneous recognition and pose determination result.

References

[1] K. S. Arun, T. S. Huang and S. D. Blostein, "Least-Squares Fitting of Two 3-D Point Sets," *IEEE Trans. Patt. Anal. Machine Intell.,* v9, n5, p698-700, 1987.

[2] P. J. Besl and R. C. Jain, "Invariant Surface Characteristics for 3D Object Recognition in Range Images," *CVGIP,* v33, p33-80, 1986.

[3] C. H. Chen and A. C. Kak, "Robot Vision System for Recognizing 3-D Objects in Low-Order Polynomial Time," *IEEE Trans. Syst. Man Cybernetics,* v19, n6, p1535-1563, 1989.

[4] J. Dun, "Shape Measurement Using a Puma 500," *Tech. Rep. GIRD 16011-7,* 1990.

[5] W. E. L. Grimson and T. Lozano-Perez, "Model-based Recognition and Localization from Sparse Range or Tactile Data," *Int'l J. of Robotics Res,* v3, n3, p3-35, 1984.

[6] M. M. Lipschutz, *Differential Geometry.* New York: McGraw-Hill, 1969.

[7] B. C. Vemuri and J. K. Aggarwal, "Localization of Objects from Range Data," *IEEE Conf. Comput. Vision Patt. Recog.*, pp. 893-898, 1988.

Poster Presentations

A Comprehensive Synthesis Strategy for Conflict Resolutions in Distributed Expert Systems

Minjie Zhang Chengqi Zhang

Department of Mathematics, Statistics and Computing Science
University of New England, Armidale, N.S.W. 2351, Australia
{minjie,chengqi }@neumann.une.edu.au

ABSTRACT

Nowadays, one of the central aspects of research issues in Distributed Artificial Intelligence (DAI) is the avoidance, detection and resolution of conflicts among the participants. Because conflicts are inevitable in DAI, the conflict resolution is necessary and important for any DAI system. Generally speaking, there are three kinds of conflicts in DAI systems. There are belief conflicts, resource conflicts, and goal conflicts [2]. In this paper, a comprehensive synthesis strategy to solve belief conflicts in Distributed Expert Systems (DESs) is proposed. This strategy can solve a wide range of conflicts in DESs because we combine different strategies together and improve some of them significantly. It consists of four steps:

(a) If the range of uncertainties is not in [0,1], we will use the heterogeneous transformation functions to transform the uncertainties of propositions from that range to the range of [0, 1] [1];

(b) If the conflict degree is great, the cluster strategy is used to classify the uncertainties into several subsets to reduce the conflict degree;

(c) For each subset, we will use the synthesis strategy part A to get the final uncertainty in the inconsistent case if there are more than one uncertainty value in the subset; and

(d) If there are more than one subset, we will use the synthesis strategy B to get the final uncertainty even in the contradiction case.

In each step, we have selected the values for some important parameters.

The innovations of this strategy are that

(a) it can handle quite wide range of conflicts in DESs and

(b) it is feasible because we have set the values for some important parameters reasonably.

References

[1] C. Zhang, Homomorphic Transformation of Uncertainties of Propositions among Inexact Reasoning Models. *IEEE transactions on Knowledge and Data Engineering*, Vol. **KDE-5**, 1993.

[2] M. Zhang & C. Zhang, Negotiation as a Metaphor for Conflict Resolution in Distributed Artificial Intelligence. In *Proceedings of CWC ICIA'93*, Beijing, China, 1993.

A Formal Basis for Hierarchical Planning

Maria Fox
Dept. of Comp.Sci., University College London, Gower St.,London, England.
mfox@uk.ac.ucl.cs

Since the planning problem is NP-hard the useful application of general problem solvers to non-trivial domains relies upon the development of powerful heuristic mechanisms. One heuristic mechanism that has been proposed for planning is the use of abstraction to organise the search space explored by the planner in the construction of a plan (see, for example, [1,2]). For a heuristic technique to gain acceptance it must extend the scope of application of planning techniques while preserving the formal properties of the classical planning framework. Planning research has been developed on a strong theoretical basis and the foundations of linear and non-linear planning are now well-understood. However, the use of abstraction as a heuristic in planning is less well explored and there is not yet consensus on the theoretical foundations of hierarchical planning.

In this paper the axioms that describe hierarchical planning using a particular form of abstraction are presented. The form of abstraction proposed involves the organisation of the planner's search space into distinct planning levels, culminating in correct completed abstract plans, connected together by a correctness-preserving refinement operation. Refinement expands abstract plans into finer detail, revealing goals that must be achieved to realise their effects in the finer-grained context. The progressive refinement of planning levels reduces the size of the search space likely to be explored in the construction of a plan because detailed plans must be consistent with their abstract ancestors. As refinement progresses choice is restricted by this constraint.

A modal truth criterion for hierarchical planning based on refinement is presented and proved necessary and sufficient for determining the validity of a partial plan which might be at an abstract stage of refinement. The role of the hierarchical modal truth criterion as a checking procedure is discussed and its usefulness as a basis for plan construction is considered. The role of the criterion as a basis for plan construction motivates the introduction of a third modal operator, currency, which allows properties to be inferred for plans at detailed planning levels if they are true of their ancestors at abstract levels. This captures the inheritance of plan structure through refinement. The development of a full axiomatic system together with a correct modal truth criterion is an important step towards the development of a complete formal system for hierarchical planning. Other work by the author considers the efficient implementation of the syntactic system discussed here and work is progressing on the formal semantics of the system.

1. C.A. Knoblock, *Learning hierarchies of abstraction spaces*, in Proceedings of AAAI, 1991.

2. D. Wilkins, *Practical planning: extending the classical AI paradigm*, Addison-Wesley, 1988.

A Neural Network Tuner for PI controllers

K. C. Chan and S. S. Leong
School of Mechanical and Manufacturing Engineering
University of New South Wales
G. C. I. Lin
School of Mechanical Engineering
University of South Australia

Abstract

This paper presents a technique of using artificial neural network (ANN) for tuning conventional proportional and integral (PI) feedback controllers. The tuner uses a pattern recognition technique which emulates manual tuning to adjust controller gains iteratively according to closed loop controlled step responses. The system structure is shown in Fig. 1. The ANN PI tuner is implemented on a 486 personal computer using the Borland C programming language.

The PI tuner is added on top of the PI controller for the adjustment of the proportional gain Kp, and integral time Ti. The knowledge stored in the neural network is intended to cover a wide variety of process dynamics. Similar to a human operator, the tuner will look at the shape and size of the response curve and then make adjustments accordingly. To quantify the response curve, four variables are chosen: (1) peak rise time, R, (2) peak to peak height, P, (3) overshoot, O, and (4) final error, E, Fig. 2. These four variables are normalized and used as inputs to the neural net. A number of multi-layered back-propagation networks with different structures were trained and tested. The final structure was a 4-8-8-8-2 net which gives very satisfactory result. The result of an example is given in Fig. 3 and Fig. 4. The transfer function of the plant is given as: $\frac{Y(s)}{U(s)} = \frac{0.75e^{-0.65s}}{3s+1}$. The user is required to provide initial gains. The gains for each iteration for 20 cycles are shown in Fig. 3. The closed loop responses for the first 3 and the last 2 cycles are shown in Fig. 4.

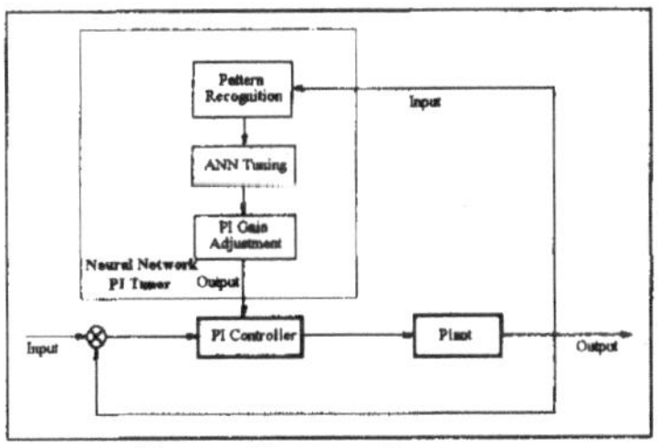

Fig. 1. System Structure

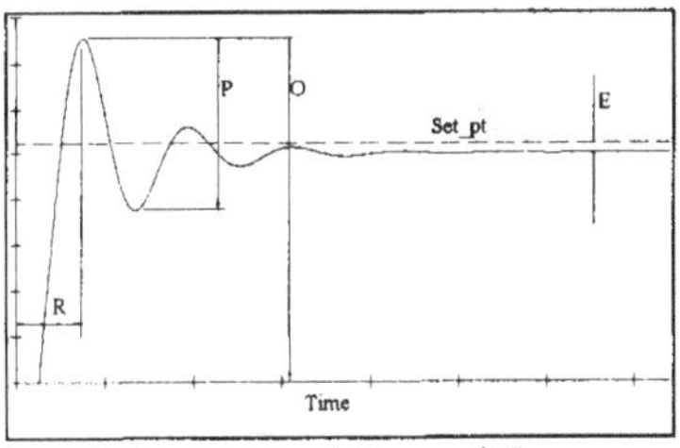

Fig. 2. Neural Network Input

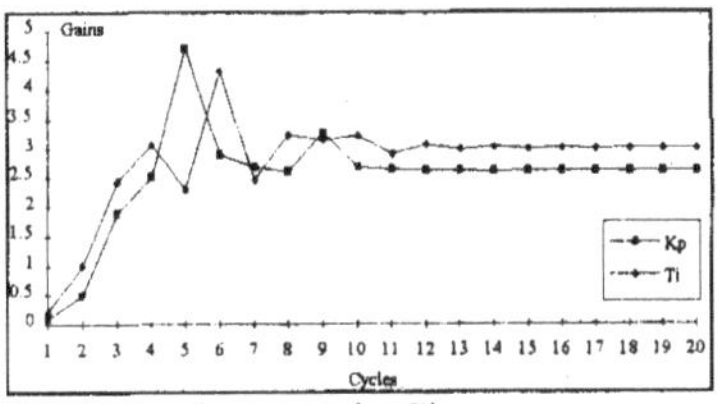

Fig. 3. Gain Changes

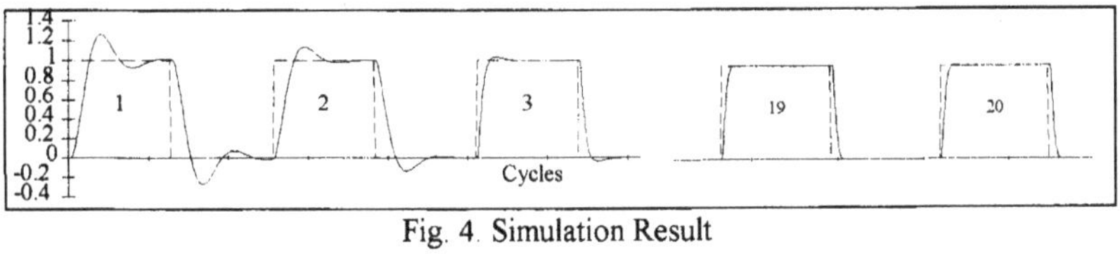

Fig. 4. Simulation Result

A technique for dealing with uncertainty in neural network classification

Tim Freeman and Anthony Adams
Department of Computer Science, University of Tasmania
PO Box 252C, Hobart 7001, Australia
email : T.W.Freeman@cs.utas.edu.au, A.Adams@cs.utas.edu.au

Introduction

The backpropagation neural network architecture is being used to solve many real world classification problems. Unfortunately, many of these problems have genuine overlap in class boundaries that gives rise to uncertainty in classification.

This paper proposes a technique for providing a backpropagation neural network with the ability to indicate when it is 'uncertain' of a classification, thus allowing the network to identify possible mis-classifications and improve its overall classification performance.

Background

In solving real world classification problems the correctness of classification is often an important issue (*eg* medical diagnosis). Unfortunately, if class regions are overlapping then the desired classification performance may not be attainable. In such situations, the only way to improve the performance of a classifier is to attempt to classify examples in overlapping regions as 'uncertain'.

Gish [2] shows (theoretically) that training a neural network using a mean square error criterion can give outputs that approximate posterior class probabilities. It is proposed [1] that if the network outputs do approximate posterior class probabilities, then a 'probability threshold' could be set such that any classification output that is below this threshold it is considered 'uncertain'.

Methods Investigated

Three output thresholding techniques for identifying 'uncertain' regions were investigated: thresholding a single network, thresholding a summing-committee of networks, and thresholding a voting-committee of networks [1]. These three techniques were applied to a number of real world data sets [1].

Results

In general, all three thresholding techniques eliminated a greater proportion of mis-classifications than correct classifications, and therefore improved the overall performance of the networks.

References

[1] T Freeman, A Adams (1993), A technique for dealing with uncertainty in neural network classification, *Technical Report R93-4*, Department of Computer Science, University of Tasmania, Australia.

[2] H Gish (1990), A probabilistic approach to the understanding and training of neural network classifiers, in *Proceedings of the 1990 IEEE Conference on Acoustics, Speech and Signal Processing*, pp. 1361–364, 1990.

[3] J Hampshire, B Pearlmutter (1990), Equivalence proof for multi-layer perceptron and the Bayesian discriminant function, in *Proceedings of the 1990 Connectionist Models Summer School*, Morgan Kaufmann, 1990.

Approximate Reasoning with Uncertainty and Imprecision in an Expert System

Richard Kowalczyk

Knowledge-Based Systems Section

CRA Advanced Technical Development

P.O. Box 347, Cannington, WA 6107, Australia

rk@perth.atd.craatd.telememo.au

Abstract

The paper presents a method of approximate reasoning for processing both uncertain and imprecise knowledge in expert systems. Extended fuzzy rules with uncertainty measures associated to rule's conclusions and uncertain fuzzy premises are used for knowledge representation. The method is based on processing of such knowledge simultaneously without interferences between spaces of uncertainty and imprecision. Extension of both generalised modus ponens and modus tollens inference schemes are presented. Control criteria used in inference process has allowed the method to be implemented in an expert system with several control strategies.

Keywords: Expert systems, approximate reasoning, extended fuzzy rules, uncertainty, imprecision.

Building and Maintaining Causal Qualitative Theories Using Inductive Logic Programing

Ashesh Mahidadia, Claude Sammut, Paul Compton

School of Computer Science & Engineering
University of NSW, PO Box 1, Kensington NSW, Australia 2033
email : {ashesh, claude, compton}@cse.unsw.edu.au

We describe tools for assisting experimental scientists in the process of theory formation and revision. The tools incorporate methods from machine learning to revise causal qualitative models and have been applied to neuroendocrinology. JUSTIN is a program that has been used by neuroendocrinologists as an aid in constructing and testing physiological models. Originally, JUSTIN could maintain the researcher's model, but was unable to devise new models. By representing models as logic programs we can now use methods from Inductive Logic Programming (ILP) [1], a branch of machine learning, to test and construct new models. Some of the problems involved in testing and modifying a theory are:

- The researcher finds an experimental result that the current theory can not explain, and the current theory must be extended such that it can also explain new experiment result.
- The researcher finds that the current theory implies some behaviours which are known to be not true, and the current theory must be altered such that it will no longer imply behaviours which are known to be not true.

For the purposes of this paper, we will use Sammut's method for generalising a logic program [2].

1. The current theory is used to generate all possible effects that can be derived from given causes. This can be done by forward-chaining on the clauses that represent the qualitative model, using the predicates that represent the causes, as inputs to the chaining process.
2. If there are any effects that cannot be generated by the current theory, the absorption operator is used to hypothesise new clauses which will allow the effects to be derived from the augmented theory.
3. There may be more than one set of clauses that can be added to the current theory to cover the effects, i.e. there may be more than one new theory constructed in step 2. We choose the *simplest* theory using a method such as Minimum Description Length (MDL) encoding [3]. As presented here, this generate-and-test approach is naive and will not scale well to large problems. However, there are a number of ways in which the basic scheme can be improved in efficiency.

References

1. Muggleton, S. (Ed.). (1992). *Inductive Logic Programming*. Academic Press.
2. Sammut, C. A., & Banerji, R. B. (1986). Learning Concepts by Asking Questions. In R. S. Michalski Carbonell, J.G. and Mitchell, T.M. (Eds.), *Machine Learning: An Artificial Intelligence Approach, Vol 2* (pp. 167-192). Los Altos, California: Morgan Kaufmann.
3. Rissanen, J. (1982). A Universal Prior for Integers and Estimation by Minimum Description Length. *Annals of Statistics*, 11, pp 416-431.

Comparison of Inductive Learning of Classification Tasks by Neural Networks

Sam Waugh and Anthony Adams
Department of Computer Science, University of Tasmania, PO Box 252C Hobart, 7001
email: waugh@cs.utas.edu.au

Aim of this study

One of the major problems with studies into inductive learning, especially using neural networks, is the lack of consistent benchmarks for techniques. The aim of this paper is to give details of a variety of benchmark data sets, taken from inductive learning, neural network and statistical literature, and to test the performance of a number of algorithms on those data sets. Furthermore, the validity of Quinlan's S and P-type classification [1] of problems is examined, to test whether such a distinction is evident.

Materials and Methods

The data sets used for the classification experiments have been chosen partly for the features that they demonstrate, but mainly because they are commonly used for testing inductive techniques and are readily available to researchers [2]. The different classes of data and how they can be presented to neural networks is also discussed in [2]. For example, the encoding of discrete unordered attributes.

The learning techniques which are examined in this paper are standard neural networks with some variations: backprop (BP), quickprop (QP), committees of BP and QP [3], and cascade correlation (Cascor) [4]; and C4.5 [5] for a decision tree approach.

For the neural network methods standard techniques were used to decide when to stop training and similar values were used for the training parameters [2]. Furthermore, standard metrics were used to measure the results of the experiments. Specific details of the network settings and results of classification percentage and training time measurements are presented in [2].

Results

The data sets that are used here, and hence in other literature, tend to be fairly simple in nature — mostly linearly separable. For these, it has been found that the S and P-type classification is valid. Selecting the relevant topology adds an extra level to the fine tuning that is required for neural networks, apart from Cascor, and was found to be the major drawback of the methods.

This study has given an indication of the power of a variety of commonly used feed-forward supervised learning algorithms. On classification ability the networks tend to produce much the same results. Cascor can out perform the other techniques due to the formation of network topology being part of the training algorithm. QP generally is the fastest learning algorithm, though this result can vary from data set to data set and from differing parameter settings. C4.5 performs well — especially on S-type problems.

References

[1] J R Quinlan (1993) Comparing connectionist and symbolic learning methods, in S Hanson, G Drastal, & R Rivest (eds.), *Computational Learning Theory and Natural Learning Systems: Constraints and Prospects.* Camb, MA: MIT Press.

[2] S Waugh & A Adams. (1993) *Comparison of Inductive Learning of Classification Tasks by Neural Networks* Department of Computer Science, University of Tasmania Tech. Report R93-5.

[3] P Vamplew & A Adams. (1991) *Real World Problems in Backpropagation.* Department of Computer Science, University of Tasmania Tech. Report R91-4.

[4] S E Fahlman (1991) The Cascade-correlation learning architecture, in D S Touretzky (ed) *Advances in Neural Information Processing Systems 2*, Morgan Kaufmann, pp524 - 532.

[5] J R Quinlan (1992) *C4.5: Programs for Machine Learning.* Morgan Kaufmann Publishers.

FPOSS: A Fuzzy Prolog-based Object-oriented Simulation System

T. Van Le
Faculty of Information Sciences & Engineering,
University of Canberra,
PO Box 1, Belconnen, ACT 2616, Australia.

FPOSS is a simulation system that combines the concept of object-oriented system modelling with the powerful mechanisms of non-deterministic programming in Prolog. Prolog's unification and backtracking mechanisms are used to implement non-deterministic object selection, multi-object accession and rendez-vous. Fuzzy objects and messages are used in the simulation models, and they can be approximately matched. This makes system simulation in FPOSS more flexible and realistic than in traditional simulation languages. In brief, simulation programming in FPOSS has the following advantages:

- The simulation program has declarative style and contains no explicit controls.
- The program style is uniform and is very close to the form of a system model.
- Objects and messages can be represented in fuzzy forms that provide high flexibility and produce more realistic results.
- Non-deterministic object selection, multi-object accession and rendez-vous are standard.
- The small number of built-in messages makes it easy to learn.

In object-oriented simulation modelling, an operational system is considered as a collection of objects that interact by sending messages to each other. Each object in the system has its own patterns of reaction to specific types of messages. When an object receives a message, it may perform some domestic work before responding to the message. Thus, in general, a simulation model in FPOSS consists of a number of object descriptions of the following form:

```
object(Time,object_set,
    [(message_type1 :-
        do(domestic_work1),
        respond([(response11),...,(response1p)])),
      .
      .
      .
     (message_typen :-
        do(domestic_workn),
        respond([(responsen1),...,(responsenq)]))]).
```

Here, `object_set` represents a class of (crisp or fuzzy) objects, and the `message_types` also contain fuzzy and non-determinate terms.

Inheritance Hierarchies—The Way Towards Commonsense Reasoning

Boon Toh LOW boontoh@cs.su.oz.au Norman Y. FOO norman@cs.su.oz.au
Knowledge Systems Group, Basser Department of Computer Science
University of Sydney, NSW, Australia 2006

ABSTRACT

Classification of concepts into hierarchies is one of the fundamental but essential functions of human belief organization. It allows us to systematically build up our knowledge and at the same time reason and communicate at appropriate contextual granularities. The importance of representing knowledge in hierarchical structure can be observed from the popularity of Object-Oriented Paradigms (e.g. [5]). The study of inheritance hierarchies has a long history in AI (e.g. [1], [4]), including the nonmonotonic reasoning community (e.g. [3]). Two main issues have to be addressed: (1) to represent knowledge in inheritance hierarchies, and (2) to intuitively resolve inconsistencies resulting from problems such as inheritance with exceptions and contradictory multiple inheritance.

We propose a new approach for hierarchically embedding inheritance knowledge in a hybrid belief representation system called Neural-Logic Belief Networks [2]. On the one hand, this formalism resembles the computations of a neural-net, on the other hand, with a fixed semantic interpretation, symbolic knowledge is explicitly represented. This symbolic network formalism represents beliefs in four truth values (believe, not-believe, unknown and contradiction) together with measures for belief certainties/strengths (degree-of-belief values), and it resolves the above problems with definite belief states.

References

[1] Scott E. Fahlman. *NETL: A System for Representing and Using Real-World Knowledge*. The MIT Press, Cambridge, Massachusetts, 1979.

[2] Boon Toh Low. Neural-logic belief networks—a tool for knowledge representation and reasoning. In *Proceedings of the 5th IEEE International Conference on Tools with Artificial Intelligence*, Boston, 1993.

[3] R. Reiter. A logic for default reasoning. *Artificial Intelligence J.*, 13:81–132, 1980.

[4] David S Touretzky. *The Mathematics of Inheritance Systems*. Pitman, London, 1986.

[5] Stanley B. Zdonik and David Maier, editors. *Readings in Object Oriented Database Systems*. Morgan Kaufmann, San Mateo, California, 1990.

Learning and Generalization with Bounded Order Critical Feature Sets

Timothy L. Andersen and Tony R. Martinez

Computer Science Department, Brigham Young University, Provo, Utah 84602 USA

A common approach used in the field of pattern recognition is to try to learn about a particular problem by analyzing an existing data set that contains pre-classified examples from the problem domain (called a training set). The goal then is to find a function which reasonably approximates the correct mapping of inputs to outputs for all possible examples in the problem domain through direct analysis of the data in the training set.

This paper utilizes a learning method which extracts critical features from an existing data set by searching through the possible input pattern space. The search space is bounded by placing an upper bound on feature order (the number of intputs which the feature considers). If the order of stored features is bounded, the main question that arises is whether or not the resultant set of features will be capable of producing a sufficient degree of generalization accuracy. This paper attempts to demonstrate how limiting the order of stored critical features affects the ability to learn and generalize correctly. The results show that pattern classification methods involving lower-order feature sets have promise and warrant further research.

Features are assigned a metric that attempts to indicate the relative strength or predictive power of that feature in relation to other features. Three different methods are used to calculate each feature's metric The first two methods are $m = P[y/x]$, and $m = P[y/x]P[xy]$, where m is the metric value, x is the feature, y is the output state associated with that feature, and $P[y/x]$ indicates the probability of y occurring given that x has occurred. The third method utilizes a simple training algorithm similar to the perceptron algorithm to calculate a metric for each feature.

On presentation of a new example, each matched feature votes for an output state according to the strength of its metric. The output state with the highest total is chosen as that examples most likely classification.

Results from two data sets are given below (m1 = metric 1, etc.). The trained metric was limited to a maximum of 200 iterations.

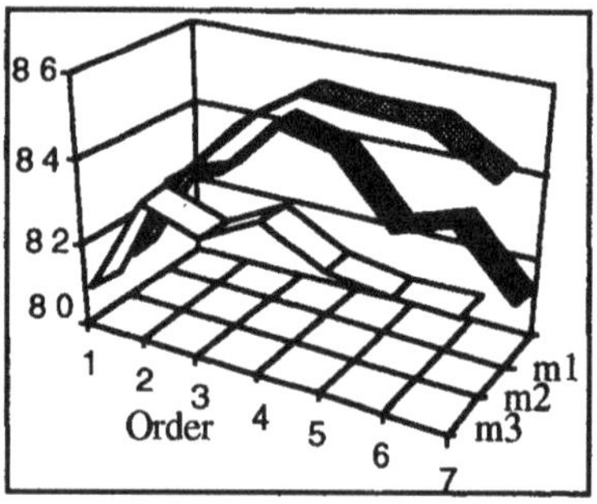

Figure 1. CPU data set

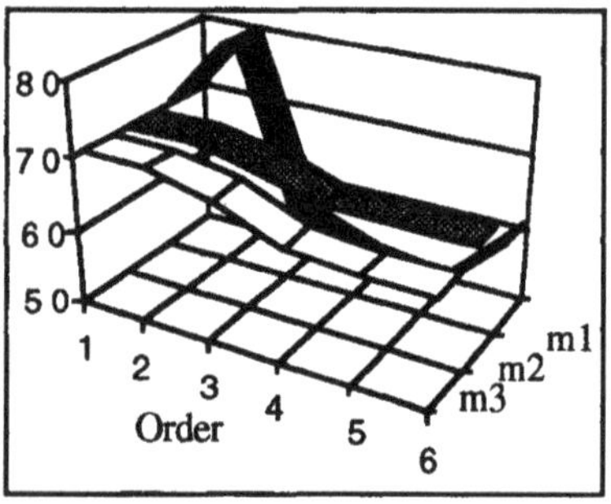

Figure 2. Monk 2 data set

These results represent a four run average of generalization accuracy on a test set. From these results, it would appear that in some cases the use of higher-order features can actually have a negative effect on generalization accuracy, due to overfitting of the data and other phenomena. Results obtained on other data sets indicate that peak generalization accuracy generally occurs well before the order of stored features is at a maximum.

Modelling Knowledge for Decision Support Using Morphological Analysis

FRADA BURSTEIN

Department of Information Systems, Monash University, Caulfield Campus, PO Box 197, Caulfield East, Victoria, 3145, Australia

HELEN SMITH

Department of Information Systems, Monash University, Caulfield Campus, PO Box 197, Caulfield East, Victoria, 3145, Australia

ABSTRACT

The problem of describing a knowledge domain and representing its underlying structure is the first of a number of steps in the process of developing a knowledge base for any application domain. This is not a trivial process and is dependent on many factors. Some of those factors are specific to the problem, while some are more general. The general part can be obtained relatively easily and its structural description can be reused for several applications within that problem domain.

When constructing information systems for decision support, general information about the problem domain helps to define the "boundaries" of the problem and to identify the entities that are involved in the decision making process. This general information includes deep causal dependencies which are useful for representing the structure and behaviour of physical systems.

One of the main aims of information systems for decision making is to increase human capacity for rational decision making. It is generally accepted that the human mind has a limited capacity for formulating and solving complex problems, particularly those in the real world. While acknowledging that these limitations are inherent in human beings, we suggest that giving decision makers a model of the problem and a structure for the task will increase their capacity for rational decision making.

One of the techniques proposed for problem area modelling is morphological analysis. This technique takes a general view of the problem in order to define classification variables (characteristics) and to produce descriptions of the various outcomes (decisions) of this problem. Each potential decision is described as a combination of values of each of the characteristics identified. This approach supports a decision maker in investigating a wide range of problem solutions.

We have investigated the role of morphological analysis as a technique for modelling the general knowledge of a problem domain. The model developed by morphological analysis can be viewed as a collection of knowledge about the domain, and thus if automated can become in some sense a knowledge base. The knowledge base developed this way gives problem oriented information that can be used for a range of situations within the problem domain.

We suggest that morphological analysis can help decision makers address a problem by providing a greater degree of structure for the identification and evaluation of alternative courses of action. The method is suitable for automating to the extent that it can prompt decision makers for stages in the problem definition process and for further details about each alternative course of action.

More Efficient Heuristic Repair through Compile-Time Reduction of "Cost per Node"

Kerstin Voigt
Computer Science Department
Rutgers University
New Brunswick, NJ 08903, U.S.A.

Abstract

Recently there have been several reports on impressive performances of heuristic local search algorithms for solving large-scale instances of difficult constraint satisfaction problems such as the propositional satisfiability problem, or the n-queens problem (e.g., (1),(2)). However, in all accounts of these problem solvers, the *cost per node* arising from the process of evaluating and selecting repair moves has not been dealt with as a factor that is potentially detrimental to the efficiency of local search.

This poster intends to contribute to the discussion of heuristic repair for solving constraint satisfaction problems by explicitly elaborating on the issue of cost per node for domains and constraints where the effects of a high cost per node can be detrimental, and that need to be handled to allow the full benefits of local search to translate to these domains. We introduce a method that allows the elimination of considerable amounts of cost per node through a *compile-time* analysis of the constraint. In a constraint-dependent fashion, our method compiles descriptions of three *operator categories*: (1) improving operators, (2) nonchanging operators, and (3) worsening operators. At *run-time*, these operator descriptions enable the heuristic repair problem solver to selectively evaluate and sort only those operators that can lead to improvement. Nonchanging and worsening operators are considered only if no applicable improving operators exist. Thereby, the potentially costly and ultimately futile examination of operators that are *a priori* known to be ineffective, or even worsening, can be suspended and possibly eliminated.

The benefits of this method are demonstrated by results in the domains of 2D-floorplanning and timetable design (an NP-complete scheduling problem).

References

1. B. Selman, HJ. Levesque, and D. Mitchell, *A New Method for Solving Hard Satisfiability Problems*, in Proceedings of AAAI-92, San Jose, July 1992.
2. S. Minton, M.D. Johnston, A.B. Philips, and P. Laird, *Minimizing Conflicts: A Heuristic Repair Method for Constraint Satisfaction and Scheduling Problems*, Artificial Intelligence, 58(1-3), December 1992.

PROSPECTS FOR A GENERAL PURPOSE ITS ARCHITECTURE BASED ON TUTORIAL CONTROL

C.A. BRIFFA
School of Communication and Information Studies
University of South Australia
Lorne Avenue, Magill 5072
Australia

P.W. EKLUND
Department of Computer Science
University of Adelaide
Adelaide 5005
Australia

ABSTRACT

The principle of *tutorial control* in ITS is supported by the the view that teaching is a process in which a pre-planned conditional sequence is delivered (Leinhardt & Greeno 1986). The principle states that the competence of an expert teacher lies in his/her ability to monitor the execution of this pre-defined sequence (strategies and examples) and attempt alternative sequences when the sequence fails. On the basis of this principle, this paper describes a general purpose architecture for a self-improving ITS.

The proposed architecture helps resolve a number of outstanding questions in ITS research and empirically test a metaphor based on Leinhardt & Greeno's theory of classroom management as well as produce a generic architecture for ITS applications. It determines: (i) whether lesson planning can be decided prior to the planning of the delivery of content; and (ii) if an appropriate next exercise can be determined independent of delivery style or whether is it optimal to consider exercise-style pairs.

Solving Space Planning Problems Using Constraint Technology

Philippe CHARMAN
SECOIA Project
CERMICS-INRIA
2004, route des Lucioles BP 93
06902 SOPHIA-ANTIPOLIS Cedex
Email: charman@snoopy.inria.fr
Tel: 93.65.77.48

Abstract

Techniques from constraint programming has proven their efficiency for solving high combinatory problems. We study the adaptation, the extension and the limits of these techniques for the space planning problem which is the problem of finding the locations and the sizes of several objects under geometric constraints in a location space. For this, we define the formalism of a Geometric Constraint Satisfaction Problem (GCSP) with multi-dimensional and continuous domains for representing the position variables of the objects. We developed in particular an intelligent and geometric backtrack based on constraint propagations and an environment dedicated to this problem for rectangles of variable sizes.

Keywords: Space planning, constraint programming, geometric constraint, GCSP, placement, space partitioning.

Systemic Design: A Methodology For Investigating Emotional Phenomena

Tim Read

Cognitive Science Research Centre, School of Computer Science
University of Birmingham, Birmingham, UK

Obtaining a theoretical understanding of emotions is not an easy task partly because researchers disagree on the definition of 'emotion'. We must therefore define the specific emotional phenomena in question before trying to postulate their genesis and functionality (1).

The design-based approach for developing a theoretical understanding of such phenomena is a powerful tool for such a task (2), but for our purposes needs refinement. Firstly a biological agent's architectural functionality may exist as a 'network of interdependencies' which can't be split into unitary phenomena to be modelled. Secondly, systems built using the design-based approach to fulfil a set of biologically detached abstract requirements will not generate any useful theoretical knowledge about human capabilities as the requirements are not under the same constraints that apply to naturally evolved intelligent systems (3). Lastly, it is suggested that as there is no clear understanding of the relation between mechanism and behaviour, it is impossible to build accurate models of the underlying mechanisms (4).

Systemic Design is a methodology which is an advance on the design-based approach, and addresses the problems outlined above. It consists of the design-based approach with four things added: organismic phylogenetic considerations, a holistic design strategy (combining 'top down' and 'bottom up' engineering design, with data taken from other research areas), and a consideration of resource limitations. Systemic Design deals with the previous three refinements as follows: The 'network of interdependencies' hypothesis can be tested by sketching out the shape of the network using data from other research areas combined with a consideration of the resource limits. Detailed design can then be carried out for specific parts, in the context of network. The second criticism is dealt with by the combination of phylogenetic considerations with a notion of resource limitations. This yields a more tractable approach to the problem than attempting to build simplistic models of neurally plausible agents. The final point is addressed by using the phylogenetic considerations to suggest relations of behaviours to mechanisms, and tested by the use of the holistic design strategy.

References

1. T. Read and A. Sloman, The Terminological Pitfalls of Studying Emotion, in prep.
2. A. Sloman, Prospects for AI as the General Science of Intelligence, in: *Prospects for Artificial Intelligence*, (1993), p1-10, IOS Press.
3. A. Clark, *Microcognition*, chapter 4, (1989).
4. R. Pfeifer, The New Age of the Fungus Eater, a shortened version to be published in: *Proceedings of ECAL93*, (1993).

Temporal Reasoning for Commonsense Beliefs

Boon Toh LOW boontoh@cs.su.oz.au
Knowledge Systems Group, Basser Department of Computer Science
University of Sydney, NSW, Australia 2006

ABSTRACT

In Temporal Reasoning, there are two major views about time. Situation calculus [6], possible world approach [3], etc., view time as a series of discrete points where situations or states are transformed from one time-point to another via actions. The other group bases their formalisms on time-intervals. This includes Allen's work on temporal intervals [1], event calculus [2], etc. To provide a better model for temporal reasoning, we believe that both time-points and time-intervals have to be included in the same formalism (e.g. [4]) and propose a new approach based on a directed graph belief representation system: Neural-Logic Belief Networks [5]. In this formalism, time is a linear and continuous dimension where successive belief states occur. With the ability to reason about relative- and/or specific- time, commonsense temporal reasoning problems such as the "Yale shooting problem" and "stolen car problem" are handled straightforwardly according to our intuition.

References

[1] James F Allen. Maintaining knowledge about temporal intervals. *Communiations of the ACM*, 26(11):832–843, 1983.

[2] Gary C. Borchardt. Event calculus. In *Proceedings of the IJCAI'85*, pages 524–527, Los Angeles, CA, 1985.

[3] Matthew L. Ginsberg and David E. Smith. Reasoning about action I : A possible worlds approach. In *Proceedings of the Frame Problem in Artificial Intelligence Workshop*, pages 233–258. Morgan Kaufmann, 1987.

[4] Robert A. Kowalski and Marek Sergot. A logic-based calculus of events. *New Generation Computing*, 4(1):202–219, 1986.

[5] Boon Toh Low and Norman Y. Foo. A network formalism for commonsense reasoning. In *Proceedings of the Sixteenth Australian Computer Science Conference*, pages 425–434, Brisbane, 1993.

[6] John McCarthy and Patrick J. Hayes. Some philosophical problems from the standpoint of artificial intelligence. In B. Meltxer and D. Mitchie, editors, *Machine Intelligence 4*, pages 463–502. Edinburgh University Press, 1969.

AUTHOR INDEX

ERRATUM

Page 287

Please see corrections in TR #93/190,
Department of Computer Science, Monash University

www.ingramcontent.com/pod-product-compliance
Lightning Source LLC
LaVergne TN
LVHW082254241026
850861LV00008B/44